The Flavians

Second Edition

T0382476

LACTOR Sourcebooks in Ancient History

For more than half a century, *LACTOR Sourcebooks in Ancient History* have been providing for the needs of students at schools and universities who are studying ancient history in English translation. Each volume focuses on a particular period or topic and offers a generous and judicious selection of primary texts in new translations. The texts selected include not only extracts from important literary sources but also numerous inscriptions, coin legends and extracts from legal and other texts, which are not otherwise easy for students to access. Many volumes include annotation as well as a glossary, maps and other relevant illustrations, and sometimes a short Introduction. The volumes are written and reviewed by experienced teachers of ancient history at both schools and universities. The series is now being published in print and digital form by Cambridge University Press, with plans for both new editions and completely new volumes.

Osborne	*The Athenian Empire*
Osborne	*The Old Oligarch*
Cooley	*Cicero's Consulship Campaign*
Grocock	*Inscriptions of Roman Britain*
Osborne	*Athenian Democracy*
Santangelo	*Late Republican Rome, 88-31 BC*
Warmington/Miller	*Inscriptions of the Roman Empire, AD 14-117*
Treggiari	*Cicero's Cilician Letters*
Rathbone/Rathbone	*Literary Sources for Roman Britain*
Sabben-Clare/Warman	*The Culture of Athens*
Stockton	*From the Gracchi to Sulla*
Edmondson	*Dio: the Julio-Claudians*
Brosius	*The Persian Empire from Cyrus II to Artaxerxes I*
Cooley/Wilson	*The Age of Augustus*
Levick	*The High Tide of Empire*
Cooley	*Tiberius to Nero*
Cooley	*The Flavians*
Cooley	*Sparta*

The Flavians

Second Edition

———

Edited by

M. G. L. COOLEY
Warwick School

With contributions by
A. E. COOLEY, M. H. CRAWFORD,
T. EDWARDS, A. HARKER, B. W. J. G. WILSON

 CAMBRIDGE
UNIVERSITY PRESS

Shaftesbury Road, Cambridge CB2 8EA, United Kingdom

One Liberty Plaza, 20th Floor, New York, NY 10006, USA

477 Williamstown Road, Port Melbourne, VIC 3207, Australia

314–321, 3rd Floor, Plot 3, Splendor Forum, Jasola District Centre, New Delhi – 110025, India

103 Penang Road, #05–06/07, Visioncrest Commercial, Singapore 238467

Cambridge University Press is part of Cambridge University Press & Assessment,
a department of the University of Cambridge.

We share the University's mission to contribute to society through the pursuit of
education, learning and research at the highest international levels of excellence.

www.cambridge.org
Information on this title: www.cambridge.org/9781009382816
DOI: 10.1017/9781009382793

First edition © The London Association of Classical Teachers 2015.

Second edition published by Cambridge University Press and Assessment, © The London Association of
Classical Teachers 2023.

First published 2023

A catalogue record for this publication is available from the British Library.

A Cataloging-in-Publication data record for this book is available from the Library of Congress.

ISBN 978-1-009-38281-6 Paperback

TABLE OF CONTENTS

4

6

Abbreviations

AE	*L'Année épigraphique*
Birley	A.R. Birley, The Roman Government of Britain (Oxford 2005)
BM	The British Museum, London
BMCRE[2]	H. Mattingly, *Coins of the Roman Empire in the British Museum,* volume II: *Vespasian to Domitian,* (2nd ed. London 1976)
CIL	*Corpus Inscriptionum Latinarum*
Claridge, *Rome*	A. Claridge, *Rome, an Oxford Archaeological Guide,* (2nd ed. Oxford 2010)
Cooley[2]	A.E. and M.G.L. Cooley, *Pompeii and Herculaneum* (London 2014)
EDCS	Epigraphik-Datenbank Clauss / Slaby http://db.edcs.eu/epigr/epi_de.php
IGRR	*Inscriptiones Graecae ad Res Romanas Pertinentes*
ILS	*Inscriptiones Latinae Selectae* (ed. Dessau) http://www.archive.org/details/inscriptionesla01dessgoog
InscrIt	*Inscriptiones Italiae* XIII – *Fasti et Elogia,* fasc. 2, *Fasti Anni Numani et Iuliani,* ed A. Degrassi (1963)
IRT	*Inscriptions of Roman Tripolitania,* by J. M. Reynolds & J. B. Ward-Perkins, electronic reissue by Bodard & Roueché (2009) http://irt.kcl.ac.uk/irt2009/
Jones	B.W. Jones, *The Emperor Domitian* (London 1992)
Jones, *Suetonius*	B.W. Jones & R. Milns, *Suetonius: The Flavian Emperors, A Historical Commentary* (Bristol 2002)
LACTOR 15	J. Edmondson, *Dio: the Julio-Claudians* (1992)
LACTOR 17	M.G.L. Cooley & B.W.J.G. Wilson, *The Age of Augustus* (2003)
LACTOR 19	M.G.L. Cooley & B.W.J.G. Wilson, *Tiberius to Nero* (2011)
Levick, *Vesp.*	B.M. Levick, *Vespasian* (London 1999)
Millar, *ERW*	F.G.B. Millar, *The Emperor in the Roman World, 31 BC – AD 337* (2nd edition London 1992)
Murison	C.L. Murison, *Rebellion and Reconstruction Galba to Domitian, An Historical Commentary on Cassius Dio's* Roman History *books 64–67 (AD 68–96)*
MW	M. McCrum & A.G. Woodhead, *Select Documents of the Principates of the Flavian Emperors* (Cambridge 1961)
OCD	S. Hornblower and A. Spawforth, edd., *The Oxford Classical Dictionary* (3rd edition, Oxford 1996)
PIR	*Prosopographia Imperii Romani* (ed. E. Klebs *et al.* Berlin 1897–8; 2nd edition 1933 and ongoing)
RIC	I.A. Carradice & T.V. Buttrey, *The Roman Imperial Coinage,* volume II – part 1 second fully revised ed. (London 2007)
RPC	A. Burnett, M. Amandry & P.P. Ripollès, *Roman Provincial Coinage I: From the Death of Caesar to the Death of Vitellius* (London/Paris, 1992)
Rüpke	J. Rüpke , *Fasti Sacerdotum* (Oxford 2008)

8

SEG	*Supplementum Epigraphicum Graecum*
Sherk	R.K. Sherk, *The Roman Empire: Augustus to Hadrian* (1988)
SIG	*Sylloge Inscriptionum Graecarum*
Syme, *RP*	R. Syme, *Roman Papers,* ed. A.R. Birley (Oxford)
Syme, *Tacitus*	R. Syme, *Tacitus* (Oxford 1958)

Select Bibliography

Commentaries and Translations of Literary Texts

Aurelius Victor, de Caesaribus, H.W. Bird (Liverpool 1994)
Eutropius, Breviarium, H.W. Bird (Liverpool 1993)
Juvenal Book 1, S. Braund (CUP 1996)
Martial, Liber Spectaculorum, K.M. Coleman (Oxford 2006)
A Commentary on Book One of the Epigrams of Martial, P. Howell, (London 1980)
Martial, Epigrams Book Two, C.A. Williams (Oxford 2004)
Martial, Epigrams V, P. Howell (Warminster 1995)
A Commentary on Martial Epigrams Book 9, C. Henriksén, (Oxford 2012)
The Epigrams of Martial, Selected and translated by James Michie (London 1972)
Martial's Epigrams – a Selection, G. Wills (London 2008)
Statius Silvae IV, K.M. Coleman, (Oxford 1988)
Cornelii Taciti de Vita Agricolae, R.M. Ogilvie & Sir I. Richmond (Oxford 1967)
A Historical Commentary on Tacitus' Histories I and II, G.E.F. Chilver (Oxford 1979)
Tacitus, Histories Book II, Ash, R. (Cambridge 2007)
Cornelius Tacitus, The Histories Book III, K. Wellesley (Sydney 1972)
A Historical Commentary on Tacitus' Histories IV and V, G.E.F. Chilver and G.B.
    Townend (Oxford 1979)

Other books and articles

Beard, M., *The Roman Triumph* (Harvard 2009)
Cooley, A.E., *Cambridge Manual of Latin Epigraphy*, (2012) Appendix 1.
Crawford, M.H., ed., *Roman Statutes* I (London 1996)
Crook, J., 'Titus and Berenice' *AJP* 72 (1951) 162–176.
Crook, J., Consilium Principis: Imperial Councils and Counsellors from Augustus to
    Diocletian (New York, 1975)
Gallivan, J. 'The Fasti for AD 70–96' *Classical Quarterly* 31 = 1981, pages 186–220
González, J. and Crawford, M.H., 'The Lex Irnitana: A New Copy of the Flavian
    Municipal Law' in *The Journal of Roman Studies,* 76 (1986), pages 147–243
Grainger, J.D., *Nerva and the Roman Succession Crisis of AD 96–99*
Maxfield, V.A., *The Military Decorations of the Roman Army* (London 1981)
Millar, F., Last Year in Jerusalem: Monuments of the Jewish War in Rome' in
    Edmondson, Mason, Rives, edd. *Flavius Josephus & Flavian Rome* (Oxford
    2005)
Murison, C.L., *Rebellion and Reconstruction, Galba to Domitian, An Historical
    Commentary on Cassius Dio's* Roman History Books 64–67 (A.D. 68–96),
    (Atlanta, Georgia, 1999)
Pollard, N. & Berry, J., *The Complete Roman Legions* (London 2012)
Rajak, T., *Josephus* (2nd edition, London 2002)
Scheid, J., Commentarii fratrum arvalium qui supersunt (Rome 1998)
Sullivan, J.P., *Martial: the unexpected classic* (Cambridge 1991)
Wellesley, K., *The Year of the Four Emperors* (3rd ed. London 2000)
Wirszubski, C., Libertas *as a Political Idea at Rome during the Late Republic and
    Early Principate,* (Cambridge 1950).

Preface

This volume aims to provide source material for students of the Roman Empire under the Flavian emperors. For fear of making a long book longer, it includes nothing of Suetonius' *Lives of the Caesars*, and only a few passages from Tacitus, *Histories*. Instead it concentrates on a much greater range of literary, epigraphic and numismatic material, which is far less readily available in translation. I hope that the resulting volume will be of use to students and teachers of the A2 level Roman History option in the UK (or whatever succeeds it), and also to students at English-speaking universities.

The material has been structured in a similar way to LACTORs 17 and 19. Part I consists of texts of various genres which make more sense presented whole than in pieces. Part II is arranged by themes most relevant to the fairly traditional approach of a political history concentrating on the emperors (as currently required by A level). Sections in part two deliberately follow the numbering of LACTORs 17 and 19, e.g. Section N is about war, P about conspiracies etc. This sourcebook is not intended as a textbook for social history and it deliberately avoid using much material from Pompeii and Herculaneum.

It is a great pleasure to thank the many people who have spent a great deal of their free time on this book. Brian Wilson translated Dio and Juvenal; Andrew Harker translated and commented on Josephus; Terence Edwards translated the letters of Pliny. I have made use of some material from previous LACTORs by Barbara Levick (LACTOR 18) and B.H. Warmington & S.J. Miller (LACTOR 8). Remaining translations are my own, with the significant exception of the Flavian Municipal Law which appears in Michael Crawford's translation for *JRS,* by kind permission of the translator and of Cambridge University Press. All the coins pictured are from the British Museum, and its marvellous website. That this volume is well-illustrated without being prohibitively expensive is entirely due to the British Museum's generous and superb non-commercial image service. All coin images remain copyright of the trustees of the British Museum.

This book will certainly contain inconsistencies, sometimes due to the ancient evidence, sometimes due to the number of contributors to the book and the oversight of the editor. For these and for other mistakes of fact, interpretation, or proof-reading, I most sincerely beg the reader's pardon.

The book has benefited greatly from being tried out on students at Warwick School over the last few years. By far my greatest debt, however, is due to my wife Alison, without whose unfailing support in so many ways, this book would never have been produced. So it is dedicated with love to her and to our children, Emma and Paul.

June 2015

M.G.L. Cooley
Head of Scholars, Warwick School

Notes on Sources

Minor authors are given brief introductions where passages from their works are given.

Censorinus: a Roman grammarian of the third century whose work preserves a great deal of accurate information on time and the Centennial Games.

Chronicle of 354: see note on **K2**.

Dio (Cassius): see introduction to Section C

Dio of Prusa (Dio Chrysostom): *c.* AD 40/50 to after 110. Popular philosopher and lecturer, born to a wealthy family in Prusa, Bithynia. Exiled from Rome by Domitian he went on lecture tours throughout the Greek East.

Epitome: a short history of the emperors from Augustus to Theodosius by an unknown author probably at the end of the fourth century. Much of the information is very similar to the histories of Aurelius Victor and Eutropius, and all three texts derive from a common source, known as the *Kaisergeschichte* (Caesar-history or *KG*), though with the Epitomator showing especial interest in the character of the emperors. The *Epitome* preserves the general tradition about the emperors, but is very weak on analysis or interpretation.

Eutropius: chief secretary of the emperor Valens (364–78), published a *Brief History from the Foundation of Rome* (to 364), described as 'well-balanced, showing good judgement and impartiality' (*OCD*). But it inevitable relies on the available sources, especially the *KG* (see on *Epitome*).

Frontinus: Sextus Julius Frontinus lived from about AD 30 to 104, and was given important positions by the emperors Vespasian, Domitian, Nerva and Trajan, including three consulships and the post of Water Commissioner for which he wrote a detailed account of Rome's aqueducts. His *Stratagems*, written after AD 84, give examples of military tactics from Greek and Roman history and a few from his own experience (see note to **N18–N22**).

Gellius: Aulus Gellius published his 'Attic Nights' around AD 180 repeating material on a great variety of topics which he read during the long nights in Attica (Athens).

Jerome: St. Jerome's *Chronicle* is a year by year compendium of world history from the birth of Abraham to AD 378. Jerome shows particular interest in Roman history, literature and scholarship, and despite an 'apparent indifference to exact dating' (J.N.D. Kelly, *Jerome* 1975) he preserves many interesting items of information and is often our only means of dating Flavian events.

Josephus: Flavius Josephus, Jewish leader and historian, AD 37/8 – *c.* 100. See introduction to Section E.

Juvenal: Decimus Junius Juvenalis, Roman satirist, active *c.* AD 120. His 16 poems satirise and exaggerate aspects of contemporary Roman life. Juvenal often uses historical examples to back up his point. These are often explained in ancient commentaries which sometimes completely misidentify figures, and occasionally provide important historical information.

Macrobius was probably praetorian prefect of Italy in AD 430. His *Saturnalia* is set as a dialogue taking place in 383 with pagan scholars discussing a variety of topics.

Martial: Marcus Valerius Martialis, AD 38/41 to 101/4, was born and died at Bilbilis in Spain. He moved to Rome *c.* AD 64, as a protégé of Seneca the Younger. He published 15 books of epigrams on a huge variety of themes, beginning in AD

12

80 with a *Book on the Shows* for the inauguration of the Flavian Amphitheatre and thereafter almost a book each year during Domitian's reign, thus proving an important source, not least because we can date his books to within a year. He received favour from the Flavians and frequently flattered Domitian and many others of wealth and power. Attempts to change sides after Domitian's fall seem to have failed and effectively ended his career.

Orosius: fifth-century historian who wrote from an explicitly Christian viewpoint and was able to use a still complete text of Tacitus, *Histories.*

Pausanias: Greek writer of mid-second century who wrote a *Guide to Greece* for Roman tourists.

Philostratos: member of the court circle of Julia Domna, wife of Septimius Severus (reigned 193–211). She commissioned his *Life of Apollonius,* presenting the philosopher as a holy man. The work 'remains suspect both in sources and details' (*OCD*).

Pliny the Elder (Gaius Plinius Secundus), *c.* AD 23/4–79, was a prominent equestrian and author, who famously died while commanding the Roman fleet at Misenum, in the eruption of Vesuvius. His 37-book *Natural History*, in his words, 'tells the story of nature, that is to say, life.' It is a priceless source about his day and what was thought and known in his day, relating 20,000 facts derived from 2,000 books (his reckoning, certainly an under-estimate). Historical works are lost. He was favourable to the Flavians and a member of Vespasian's council (see **R13, R14**).

Pliny the Younger: (Gaius Plinius Secundus), *c.* AD 61 to *c.* 112). Nephew and heir of Pliny the Elder. Originally from Comum in N. Italy, his career (**U33d**) progressed rapidly under Domitian, which explains his bitter denunciation in the nauseous *Panegyric to Trajan.* After Domitian's death he edited and published (**R28**) 9 books of letters to friends on a variety of literary, social, political and historical matters intended to portray him in a good light to other members of the upper classes. A tenth book contains letters to Trajan and his replies on questions concerning his governorship of Bithynia-Pontus where he died in office.

Plutarch c. AD 45–120 is best known for his biographies of Greek and Roman leaders, *Parallel Lives* linking the lives of Greeks and Romans, and often drawing moral conclusions. His *Moralia* includes moral and philosophical essays, literary criticism. It also includes a section on famous sayings of kings and emperors.

Quintilian: Marcus Fabius Quintilianus born *c.* AD 35 in Spain. Vespasian made him the first 'regius professor' (**R15, R16**) and Domitian made him tutor to his heirs (**J18b**). *The Orator's Education* (*Institutio Oratoria*) gives lengthy and detailed advice on writing speeches, including many famous remarks of historical figures and judgements on Roman authors.

'Regionary Catalogues' two catalogues listing (with minor differences) the buildings in each of the 14 city-districts of Rome at the time of Constantine (312–337).

Statius: (Publius Papinius Statius), Roman poet, born around AD 50 in Naples. He wrote a surviving epic poem, *Thebaid*, a poem on Domitian's German War now lost (see **G2**) and a collection of poems, *Silvae*, published in the 90s, which celebrate, in learned and encomiastic style, various occasions in the lives of a circle of upper-class acquaintances, including Domitian.

Suetonius (Gaius Suetonius Tranquillus), born *c.* AD 69, died after AD 130, author of *Lives of the Caesars*. He was an equestrian who worked as imperial secretary for Trajan and Hadrian in the AD 110s, involving him in administrative tasks such as helping to handle the emperor's correspondence. Thus Suetonius had direct access to the imperial archives, which he was able to use in his early *Lives*. However he lost this privileged access for *Lives* from *Nero* onwards after being dismissed from the imperial staff in AD 122 and had to rely on publicly-available source material. Despite Suetonius having lived in Rome for Domitian's reign, *Life of Domitian* is 18 pages, compared to the slightly shorter reigns of Nero (38 pages) and Claudius (31 pages). The inevitable impression is that Suetonius wanted to finish his project. Suetonius wrote biography, not history. So while the structure of the *Lives* is very broadly chronological, the bulk of each biography is usually thematic. Suetonius also places greater emphasis on the private lives and personalities of the emperors centre often from a very 'gossipy' perspective.

Tacitus (Publius Cornelius Tacitus) was born c. AD 56 probably in Gaul. He came to Rome by AD 75 and had a senatorial career of rapid advancement under the Flavian emperors (see **U32a, U33f**) including a consulship in 97 which may well have been already allocated by Domitian before his death. Tacitus began his literary career around AD 98, with various minor works, including a dialogue on oratory set in Vespasian's reign and a biography of his father-in-law, Agricola who felt undervalued by Domitian. His *Histories* covered the period AD 69–96: only the first five books survive, covering only a little more than the year 69. He then went back to cover the period AD 14–68 in his *Annals*.

Xiphilinus: 11th century monk whose abridgement of Dio's history survives for the Flavian period, see introduction to Section C.

Zonaras: 12th century epitomator of Dio, see introduction to Section C.

Notes on Inscriptions

The Flavian period is incredibly rich in epigraphy, with all areas of the empire and all classes of people seemingly in the grip of the 'epigraphic habit' – a desire to create a permanent written record to be seen by others. What is recorded is not just the obvious building or funerary inscriptions, but ranges from the incredibly detailed regulations on local life and government beautifully inscribed on bronze from an otherwise completely unknown small town in Spain (Section **F**) to discharge diplomas attesting Roman citizenship. Or, to give another example, around 10,000 examples of epigraphy have been found at Pompeii, a perfectly normal Roman town. Bricks were stamped with their place of origin, so too, it seems were loaves of bread. Inscriptions are therefore far more representative of Roman life than literary texts which were produced by and for the upper classes. In addition, many types of inscriptions are exactly dated by reference to the consuls of the day. Inscriptions seem to convey authority and reliability ('set in stone'), though it should be remembered that someone has chosen and paid for the inscription to be made. Many inscriptions survive broken, battered, eroded or even reused, so gaps may have to be restored with varying degrees of confidence.

Editorial Conventions for Texts

[ ]	square brackets enclose words which are missing in the original text and have been restored by the editor or translator.
[…]	dots in square brackets indicate words or letters missing in the original text.
( )	round brackets are used to expand words abbreviated in the original text.
…	dots outside brackets mark where the translator has omitted part of the text.
[5]	numbers in square brackets indicate chapter or section numbers of the text.
~~Name~~	text struck through indicates a deliberate deletion or erasure of a text in antiquity.
< >	words or letters in angled brackets were mistakenly included in antiquity.
* *	asterisks indicate a dubious or corrupt text.

Notes on Coins

Almost all Roman coins were produced at the official mint in Rome or Lugdunum (Lyons, in France). Messages that appear on coins therefore represent imperial policy. Gold coins give the best photographic images but similar images would also have appeared on coins of very low value, such as the poorest would need to use to buy their daily food. Lower value coins in widespread circulation are as close to state propaganda as anything in the ancient world, conveying a chosen image and message. The great majority of coins can be closely dated by imperial titles.

Roman Coin	HS equivalent	material	diameter	weight*	notes
aureus	100 HS	gold	18mm	8g	Augustan
denarius	4 HS	silver	18mm	4g	3rd century BC
sestertius	1 HS	brass	35mm	28g	Augustan
dupondius	½ HS	brass	28mm	14g	
as	¼ HS	copper	28mm	10g	traditional unit
semis	⅛ HS	brass	17mm	3g	
quadrans	1/16 HS	copper	17mm	3g	

* notional weights – in practice coins staying in circulation become slightly worn and lighter.

HS: the usual Roman abbreviation of *sesterius* – the basic unit of currency, anglicised to sesterce(s).
Obv: obverse, the 'heads' side of a coin: usually the head of the emperor.
Rev: reverse, the 'tails' side of a coin.
Legend: term used for any text on a coin.

A guide to monetary values	**Sesterces**
Augustus claimed to have given away, in his principate	2,400,000,000
Vibius Crispus was worth (**U4a**)	300,000,000
Pliny the Younger bought one estate (*Letter* 3.19.7) for	3,000,000
The property qualification for a Roman senator was	1,000,000
The property qualification for a Roman equestrian was	400,000
The annual salary for Vespasian's professors of rhetoric was	100,000
The annual pay of a Roman legionary was	900
Domitian increased this to	1,200
Discharge payment for Roman legionary veterans was	12,000
The town council at Pompeii occasionally allocated, for funerals of local dignitaries,	2,000
The annual corn dole of 60 *modii* (measures) was worth around	300–360
Domitian gave two cash gifts to Roman citizens in of AD 84 and 93 (**H61**), of	300
One book of Martial poems cost (*Epigram* 1.117.17)	20
A tunic (of unknown quality) at Pompeii cost	15
A cup of Falernian (high quality) wine at a bar in Pompeii cost	4
A cup of cheap wine from the same bar cost	1

16

Glossary

aedile: a junior magistrate in Rome and also in local government.

as **(pl. asses)**: the base-unit of Roman currency, a small value coin.

augur: a priest, especially responsible for predictions based on flights of birds.

Augustalis: a priest, usually a freedman, involved in emperor-worship.

Augustus: (1) the name adopted by Octavian (2) part of the title adopted by Julio-Claudian and Flavian emperors, and meaning 'emperor' (3) as a Latin adjective, meaning 'imperial'.

aureus: the highest value coin, made of gold, worth 100 sesterces.

beneficiarius: soldier or sailor given special privileges by his commanding officer.

censor: traditionally one of two senior senators, elected for eighteen months every five years, responsible for revising the roll of the senate, according to financial and moral standards.

civic crown: (*corona civica*) an honour traditionally awarded for saving the life of a citizen in battle, but usurped by the emperors.

client: a citizen who voluntarily paid his respects to a richer, more powerful patron, in return for his protection.

cognomen: the last of a Roman's names, sometimes a type of 'nickname', but often distinguishing not just an individual, but a branch of a large family.

colony: a settlement of Roman citizens (often army veterans) with its own local constitution.

consilium principis: the emperor's advisory council.

consul: the highest political office in the republic. Two consuls were elected each year to serve for one year.

cursus honorum: the 'career path' of a member of the senatorial classes.

denarius: small silver coin worth 4 sesterces.

dictator: magistrate appointed in time of emergency in the Roman republic.

Divus/Diva: 'God(dess)', especially of those officially deified

equestrian: (1) a member of this class in Rome, almost equal in status to the senatorial class (2) equestrian statue: statue of a man on horseback (compare *pedestrian*)

fasces: symbols of the authority of a magistrate carried by his attendants

fasti: publicly inscribed lists of various sorts: dates, consuls, etc.

flamen: prestigious priesthood (translated 'high priest').

Flavialis: a priest, usually a freedman, involved in emperor-worship.

freedman: a slave, formally set free by his master, automatically becoming a Roman citizen (and the client of his former master).

genius: the spirit of a person (or place).

imperator: originally a title given by Roman troops to their general after a major victory, such as would merit a triumph, adopted by Augustus as part of his name and used as part of the emperor's official title, though also to mark military victories.

imperium: the power invested in a magistrate (*e.g.* consul, praetor or governor)

laurel crown: originally worn by a general in his triumph, but adopted as a symbol of the emperor.

legate: (1) anyone to whom authority is delegated, *e.g.* a military officer (2) *legatus Augusti propraetore* (propraetorian legate of Augustus) – the official term for someone appointed to govern a (major) imperial province.

libation: liquid (usually wine) poured as an offering to gods or spirits of the dead

ludi saeculares: (Centennial Games) games held every 100/110 years, to celebrate a new age.

magistrate: an official elected for a year both at Rome and in local government.

manumission: the formal freeing of a slave, resulting in his attaining citizenship.

military tribune: one of 6 officers in a Roman legion subordinate to the legionary commander. Usually one was of senatorial class, the other five equestrians; so the post was effectively a step on the *cursus honorum*. Occasionally centurions were promoted to this post.

municipium: a city within the Roman empire whose citizens were also Roman citizens and which was allowed to govern itself on a Roman model.

optio: an adjutant or assistant to a centurion.

pater patriae: Father of the Fatherland. Title granted to Augustus in 2 BC and taken by most subsequent emperors, suggestive of absolute authority over the empire similar to that of a father over his family.

patron: a more wealthy and important citizen who looked after the interests of poorer clients in return for their support and public deference.

pedestrian: pedestrian statue: statue of a man standing up (compare *equestrian*)

plebs: the proper term for the ordinary citizen body of Rome.

pontifex maximus: chief priest, a post taken on accession by all emperors after Augustus.

portico: a colonnade around a central (open-air) area.

praetor: annually 'elected' magistrate ranking between consul and quaestor. Ex-praetors governed the less important public provinces.

Praetorian guard: elite bodyguard of the emperor. The only troops stationed in Italy.

Praetorian prefect: commander of the guard, an increasingly powerful position.

prefect: someone 'put in charge of' something: often an appointee of the *princeps*.

primipilus: chief centurion of a legion.

princeps: the word, meaning 'leader' of 'chief' was the one chosen by Augustus to designate his position.

princeps iuventutis: (leader of the younger generation) – title invented by Augustus for his grandsons to show that they would become *princeps*.

proconsul: a former consul, retaining his former official power, usually as governor of a major public province.

procurator: someone taking care of something for the *princeps*, from an estate to a minor imperial province.

propraetor: someone granted the power of a praetor, usually as governor of a minor public province.

quaestor: junior member of the senate: being quaestor of the emperor was a great privilege (**U33d**).

quindecimvir: a member of a college of fifteen priests in charge of sacrifices, chosen by the *princeps* as a permanent honour.

republican: modern usage to refer to the period when Rome was governed by elected magistrates (rather than emperors), roughly 510–50 BC

Salii: an archaic college of priests who sang a hymn on public occasions.

septemvir: a member of board of seven priests responsible for feasts put on in honour of Jupiter at Games. A signal honour, chosen by the *princeps*.

sesterces: the unit of currency in Rome.

Sodalis: member of prestigious brotherhoods relating to worship of deified emperors.

suffect: replacement magistrate, especially consul, appointed in the republic after death of an incumbent, but under the principate, pairs of suffect consuls were usually appointed as a way of sharing the honour of a consulship more widely.

tribe: all citizens were formally a member of one of 35 tribes, by this period of no discernible significance.

tribunician power: a power created by Augustus, adopted by all later emperors as the mark of imperial power which marked an emperor's regnal years but could also be shared.

19

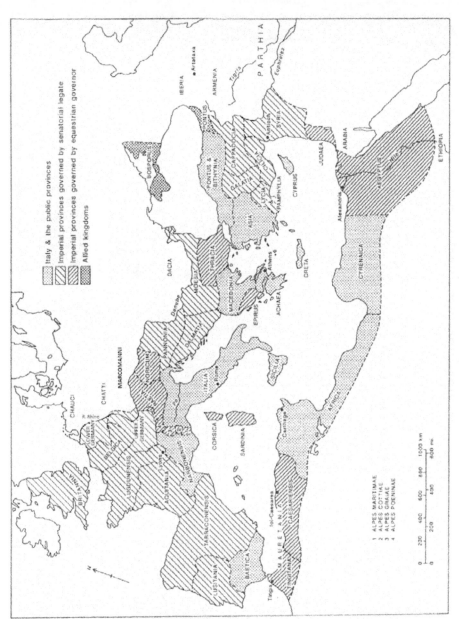

Map 1: The Roman Empire, AD 96

20

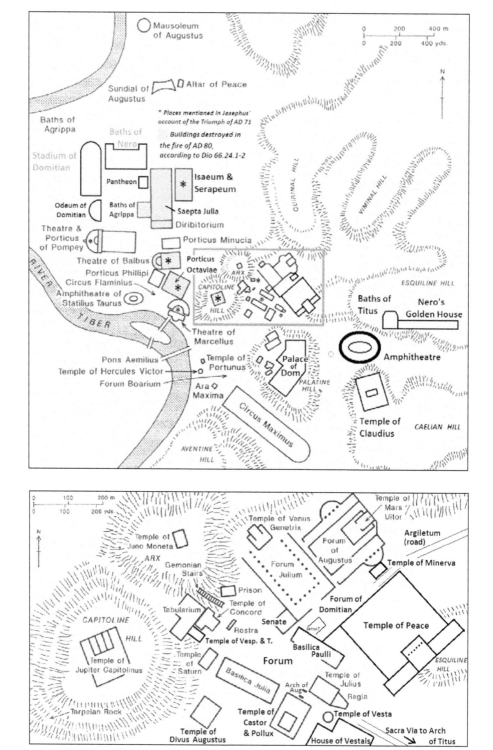

Map 2: Rome in the Flavian Period

SECTION A

THE ACTS OF THE ARVAL BROTHERS
(ACTA FRATRUM ARVALIUM)

Introduction: The Arval Brothers were an archaic priesthood revived by Augustus. They worshipped the obscure Dea Dia in a sacred grove just outside Rome, at modern Magliana, but their activities increasingly focused on honouring the emperor and his family. The twelve members of the college were important senators at Rome, including members of the imperial family, holding position for life and replaced by co-option on death. Their acts of worship were recorded on stone inscriptions. While the majority of the plaques are lost, others have survived almost intact, thus providing, for certain periods such as AD 69, a version of official court record.

The numbering used here divides the records according to year and entry, so **A69d** is the fourth preserved record for AD 69. Square brackets indicate a gap in the text. As the rites tend to follow obvious patterns and wordings, and involve a limited number of people, these can usually be filled in with a degree of certainty.

Bibliography: J. Scheid, *Commentarii fratrum arvalium qui supersunt* (Rome 1998; Latin text with French commentary and translation); J. Rupke, Fasti Sacerdotum (Oxford 2008) for definitive lists and biographies of Brothers.

A69a – 1 January, AD 69
(Small fragments for 1 January show Galba and T. Vinius as consuls and L. Salvius Otho Titianus as vice-president of the Arvals (with Galba himself probably president)).

A69b – 3 January, AD 69: vows for Galba
[Under the same consuls, on 3 January in the presidency of Servius Galba Imperator Caesar Augustus, with L. Salvius Otho] Titianus [as vice-president, on behalf of the] co[llege of Arval Brothers, they undertook vows for] the well-being of Servius Galba Imperator Caesar Augustus, *pontifex*] *maximus* [holding tribunician power]. With sacrificial [victims on the Capitol he fulfilled the vows which the previ]ous year's pre[sident had made] and undertook vows for the fo[llowing year at the dictation of L. Salvius O]tho Titi[anus, the vice-president in t]he terms which are [written below: a male] ox [to Jupiter], a cow to Queen Juno, a cow to [Minerv]a, [a cow] to Well-Being; in the new [te]mple, a [male] ox to Div[us] Augustus, a cow to [Div]a Augusta, [a male ox to] D[ivus Claudius]. The following were present [in the coll]ege: L. Salv[ius Oth]o {Titia} Tit[ianus, M. Raecius Ta]urus, L. Maecius Postumus.

[*AFA* 40 column I, lines 7–16]

A69c – 8 January, AD 69:
Under the same [consuls, on 8 January, in the T]emple of Concord, in the pres[ence of the Arval Br]other[s, in the presidency of Servius] Galba Imperator Caesar [Augustus, when L. Salvius Otho Titianus was vice-president, on behalf] of the [c]ollege of Arval Brothers, a sa[crifice] was [an]nounced [to the Dea Dia as d]ictated by L. Maecius Postumus: [on 27] May, in the ho[use; on 29 May], in the grove and in the house; on 30 May, in the house. The following were present [in the college: L. Salvius O]tho Titianus, Q. Tillius Sassius, [M. Ra]ecius Taurus, [L. Maecius P]ostumus.

[*AFA* 40 column I, lines 17–23]

A meeting took place early in January each year to announce the regular sacrifice and games in May. The venue (Temple of Concord) is probably not significant, given that the last such meeting recorded was also there (12 Jan, AD 63).

A69d – 10 January, AD 69: adoption of Piso by Galba

Under the [sam]e consuls, on 10 January, adoption made of L. Li?[cinianus?, in the presiden]cy of Ser. Galba Im[perator] Caesar Augustus, when [L. Salvius Otho Titia]nus was vice-[president], on behalf of the Arval Br[others] sa[crifice was made on the Capitol in honour of] the adoption by [Ser. Sulpicius Gal]ba C[aesar: a male ox to Jupiter, a cow to Juno, a cow to Minerva, a cow to Public Well-Being of the Roman People *(other sacrifices lost)*, a cow] to Provi[dence, a c]ow to [*(deity lost)*, a cow] to *Securi[tas]*, a bull to his [own Divine Spirit, …].

[*AFA* 40 column I, lines 24–31]

The date of the adoption is also given by Tac. *Hist.* 1.18. For L. Calpurnius Piso Frugi Licinianus, see *Hist.* 1.14–19, 29–30, and 48. He took Galba's names (Servius Sulpicius Galba) on adoption. *Securitas* means freedom from anxiety or danger.

A69e – 16? January, AD 69: sacrifices in honour of Otho

[*(exact date lost)*, in the second presidency of Imperator M. Otho Caesar Augustus, the vice-president, L. Salvius Otho Titianus, on behalf of the college of Arval Brothers sacrificed on the Capitol in honour of the reign of Imperator Otho Caesar Augustus: a male ox to Jupiter, a cow to Juno], a cow [to Minerva] a cow to Victory, [a cow] to Well-Being, [a cow to Prosperity, a b]ull [to Mars the Avenger], a bull to his own Divine Spirit. The following were present in the college: L. Salvius Otho Titianus, ~~L. Vitellius~~, son of Lucius, L. Maecius Postumus, M. Raecius Taurus.

[*AFA* 40 column I, lines 35–41]

Galba and Piso were killed, and Otho proclaimed emperor on 15 Jan., Tac. *Hist.* 1.27–45. Otho had been an arval since *c.* 56 and was younger brother of Salvius Otho Titianus. L. Vitellius was brother of the future emperor: consul 48, arval by 63, he attends meetings, before leaving to fight (Tac. *Hist.* 3.58). Executed after his surrender (*Hist.* 4.2), his name is consistently erased from the records, perhaps in error for his brother.

A69f – 26 January, AD 69: Otho elected consul

On 26 January, in the second presidency of Imperator Otho Caesar Augustus, the vice-president L. Salvius Otho Titianus, on behalf of the Arval Brothers sacrificed on the Capitol in honour of the consular elections of Imperator Otho Caesar Augustus: a male ox to Jupiter, a cow to Juno, a cow to Minerva, a bull to his own Divine Spirit. The following were present in the college: L. S[al]vius Otho Titianus.

[*AFA* 40 column I, lines 41–45]

For Otho's consulship, see **B69**. Salvius Otho Titianus, Otho's fellow consul was his elder brother, cos ord 52, arval from *c.* 56, president 58, already vice-president for 69.

A69g – 30 January, AD 69: vows for Otho

When Imperator M. Otho Caesar Augustus and L. Salvius Otho Titianus for the second time, were consuls. On 30 January, when Imperator M. Otho Caesar Augustus was president and L. Salvius Otho Titianus was vice-president, he sacrificed in the name of the college of Arval Brothers for vows being undertaken for the well-being

of Imperator M. Otho Caesa[r A]ugustus for 3 January in the following year: a male
ox to Jupiter, a cow to Juno, a cow to Minerva, a cow to the Public Well-Being of the
Roman People, a male ox to Divus Augustus, and cow to Diva Augusta, a male ox to
Divus Claudius. The following were present in the college: L. Salvius Otho Titianus,
L. Maecius Postumus, P. Valerius Marinus, M. Raecius Taurus, L. Vitellius.

[*AFA* 40 column I, lines 47–53]

These were the usual vows taken on 3 January for the emperor's well-being. Otho had not been emperor then.

A69h – 26 February, AD 69: Tampius Flavianus co-opted
Under the same consuls on 26 February, in the Temple of Divus Julius, in the presence
of the Arval Brothers, L. Tampius Flavianus was co-opted in place of S[er. Sul]picius
Galba, in the [second] presidency of Imperator M. Otho Caesar [Augustus], when L.
Salvius Otho Titianus was [vice-]president. The following were present in the college:
Otho Titianus, P. V[aleri]us Marinus, L. Vitellius.

[*AFA* 40 column I, lines 54–57]

L. Tampius Flavianus, cos I suff 45, cos II suff 76, see **B76** and **U5**.

A69i – 28 February, AD 69: Otho given tribunician power
Under the same consuls on 28 February, in the second presidency of Imperator
M. Otho Caesar Augustus, when L. Salvius Otho Titianus was vice-president, he
sacrificed on behalf of the college of Arval Brothers on the Capitol in honour of the
election to tribunician power of the Imperator: a male ox to Jupiter, a cow to Juno, a
cow to Minerva, a cow to Well-Being, a cow to Victory, a bull to the Divine Spirit of
the Roman People, a bull to his own Divine Spirit. The following were present in the
college: Otho Titianus, Maecius Postumus, Valer(ius) Marin(us), L. Vitellius.

[*AFA* 40 column I, lines 58–62]

The delay in assuming the tribunician power which had come to define the position of emperor may have
reflected Otho's caution in whether he could maintain power (Wellesley, *Year of the Four Emperors,* 3rd
ed. 2000, pp 57–8). It appears that the stone-cutter was feeling overworked, since he has given up on the
praenomina of those present and even abbreviated Valerius Marinus' names. This may also explain mention
of tribunician power of the Imperator – this could just mean 'Victorious Commander', and later means
'emperor' but here the stone-cutter probably just omitted the rest of Otho's official name.

A69j – 1 March, AD 69: laurel wreath on the Capitol
When L. Verginius Rufus, for a second time, and L. Pompeius Vopiscus were consuls,
on 1 March, in the second presidency of Imperator M. Otho Caesar Augustus, when
L. Salvius Otho Titianus was vice-president, he sacrificed on behalf of the college of
Arval Brothers on the Capitol in honour of a laurel wreath being placed: a male ox to
Jupiter, a cow to Juno, a cow to Minerva, a cow to Well-Being, a cow to Victory, a bull
to Mars, a bull to his own Divine Spirit. The following were present in the college:
Otho Titianus, L. Vitellius, L. Maecius Postumus, P. Valerius Marinus.

[*AFA* 40 column I, lines 63–67]

The laurel wreath symbolised a victory over the Rhoxolani, a Sarmatian tribe (Tac. *Hist.* 1.79), won by M.
Aponius, governor of Moesia, himself an arval brother.

A69k – 3 March, AD 69: Otho given priesthoods
Under the same consuls on 3 March, in the second presidency of Imperator M. Otho Caesar Augustus, when L. Salvius Otho Titianus was vice-president, he sacrificed on behalf of the college of Arval Brothers on the Capitol in honour of the election to the priesthoods of Imperator Otho Augustus: a male ox to Jupiter, a cow to Juno, a cow to Minerva, a bull to his own Divine Spirit. The following were present in the college: Otho Titianus, P. Valer(ius) Marin(us).

[*AFA* 40 column I, lines 68–71]

A69m – 9 March, AD 69: Otho made *pontifex maximus*
Under the same consuls on 9 March, in the second presidency of Imperator M. Otho Caesar Augustus, when L. Salvius Otho Titianus was vice-president, he sacrificed on behalf of the college of Arval Brothers on the Capitol in honour of the election as *pontifex maximus* of Imperator Otho Augustus: a male ox to Jupiter, a cow to Juno, a cow to Minerva, a cow to the Dea Dia, a bull to his own Divine Spirit. The following were present in the college: Otho Titianus, Otho Augustus, P. Valerius Marin(us), L. Maecius Postumus, L. Vitellius

[*AFA* 40 column I, lines 72–75]

A69n – 14 March, AD 69: vows for an emperor's safe return
Under the same consuls on 14 March, vows were undertaken for the we[ll-b]eing and safe return of Vitellius Germanicus Imperator, at the dictation of L. Maecius Postumus, in the presidency of Vitellius Germanicus Imperator, when Maecius Postumus was vice-president, on behalf of the college of Arval Brothers: a male ox to Jupiter, a cow to Juno, a cow to Minerva, a cow to Public Well-Being of the Roman People, a male ox to Divus Augustus, a cow to Diva Augusta, a male ox to Divus Claudius. The following was present in the college: L. Maecius Postumus.

[*AFA* 40 column I, lines 76–80]

An interesting entry: Tac. *Hist.* 1.90 tells us that Otho left Rome to the senate on this day before setting out to fight Vitellius' forces. Vows will have been made for his return. In fact he committed suicide on the morning of 16 April after defeat at the battle of Cremona (Tac. *Hist.* 2.46–50). But the records were written up to show vows for Vitellius (the titles Germanicus Imperator are certainly his), before his name was erased.

A69p – 30 April, AD 69: Vitellius given tribunician power
When T. Flavius [Sab]inus and Cn. Arulenus Caelius Sabinus were consuls, on 30 April, in honour of the election to tribunician power of Vitellius Germanicus Imperator, when L. Maecius Postumus was vice-president, he sacrificed on behalf of the college of Arval Brothers, on the Capitol: a male ox to Jupiter, a cow to Juno, a cow to Minerva, a cow to Well-Being, a bull to his own Divine Spirit. The following was present in the college: Maecius Postumus.

[*AFA* 40 column I, lines 81–84]

A69q – 1 May, AD 69: belated sacrifice for the day of Vitellius' accession
Under the same consuls on 1 May, in honour of the day on which Vitellius Germanicus Imperator came to power which was decreed to have been 19 April, in the presidency of Vitellius Germanicus Imperator, when L. Maecius Postumus was vice-president,

he sacrificed on behalf of the college of Arval Brothers, on the Capitol: a male ox to Jupiter, a cow to Juno, a cow to Minerva, a male ox to Jupiter Victor, a cow to Well-Being, a cow to Prosperity, a bull to the Divine Spirit of the Roman People; and in the Forum of Augustus, a bull to Mars the Avenger, a bull to his own Divine Spirit. The following were (*sic*) present in the college: Maecius Postumus.

[*AFA* 40 column I, lines 84–89]

19 April will have been when the garrisons at Rome took an oath to the new emperor (Tac. *Hist.* 2.55), after receiving news by messenger relay from Cremona (*c.* 330 miles) of Otho's suicide on the morning of 16 April.

A69r – May AD 69: Vitellius returns to Rome

[…] for the well-being and a[rrival of Vitellius Germanicus Imperator, in the presidency of Vitellius Ger]manicus Imperator, when L. Maecius Postumus was vice-president, [he sacrificed on behalf of the college of Arval Brothers], on the [Ca]pitol: [a male ox] to Jupiter, a cow to Juno, a cow to Minerva, a male ox to Jupiter Victor, [a cow to] Well[-Being of the Roman People, a cow to Prosperity, a bull to the Divine Spirit of the Roman People; and in the Forum of August]us, a bull to Mars the Av[enger], a bull to his own Divine Spirit. The following was present in the college: Ma[ecius Postumus].

[*AFA* 40 column II, lines 1–5]

For Vitellius' return to Rome, see Tac. *Hist.* 2.87–90 (not giving a date).

A69s – 29 May, AD 69: sacrifices and games

Under the sa[me consuls, on 29] May, in the [third p]residency of Vitellius Ger[manicus I]mperator, when [L. Maecius] Postumus was vice-president, he [sa]crificed [two] sows to make appeas[ement], at the altar of the Dea [Dia on behalf of the] coll[ege of the Arval Brothers], and likewise a cow. Then, after the [sacr]ifice was made [in the temple, on the hearth] he sa[crificed a perfect lamb] to the Dea Dia. After the [sacrifice] was complete, veiled and cr[owned], he [gave] the signal from [the starting-gat]es to [the chariots] and stunt-riders. [The following was present in the college: L.] Maecius Postumus.

[*AFA* 40 column II, lines 6–10]

A69t – 3 June, AD 69: birthday of Galeria, wife of Vitellius

Under the [same] consuls, on 3 Ju[ne, in the third presidency of Vitellius Germanicus Imperator, when L. Maecius Postumus was vice-president, [he sacrificed] on behalf of the [college] of Arval [Bro]thers [on the Capitol in honour of the bir]thday of Galeria, wife of Germanic[us Imperator A]ugustus: a male ox to Jupiter, [a cow] to Juno, [a cow to Minerva, a cow to the Well-Being of the Roman People], a cow to [Co]ncord, a bull to his own Divine Spirit. The following [was] present in the college [L. Maecius Postumus?]

[*AFA* 40 column II, lines 10–13]

A69u – unknown date, AD 69: blue (circus) team

Under the same consuls, on […?... in the grove of the Dea Dia, expiation] was made by the atten[dant and the assistants of the college of Arval Brothers for ….] the blue team: a sow and [perfect] l[amb].

[*AFA* 40 column II, lines 13–15]

Vitellius was a fanatical supporter of the blue chariot team (Suet. *Vit.* 7.1, 14.4). Scheid (Commentary) suggests the organisers needed to atone for having broken the rules, trying to achieve a blue victory in the races of 29 May.

A69v – unknown date, AD 69: sacrifices

Under the same consuls [...? ..., in honour of ... ? ...] in the presidency of Vitellius Germanicus Imperator III, when C. [*(name lost)*] was vice-president, [he sacrificed on behalf of] the college of Arval Brothers, on the Capitol: a male ox to Jupiter, a cow to Juno, a cow to Minerva, [a male ox to Jupiter Victor, a cow to Well-Being of the Roman People; and in the Forum of Augustus], a bull [to Mars the Avenger], a bull to his own Divine Spirit. The following was present in the college: ...

[*AFA* 40 column II, lines 15–18]

The records for the rest of AD 69 are lost, except for three tiny fragments not worth giving.

A70a – unknown date: sacrifices probably for Vespasian's return in AD 70

[...] when Q. Tillius Sassius was vice-president, he sacrificed, [on behalf of the] c[ollege of Arval Brothers] on the Capitol, in honour of the day [when Emperor C]aesar Vespasian Augustus entered [into the city]: a [male] ox to Jupiter, [a cow to Juno], a cow to Minerva, [a cow] to Fortune the Home-Bringer. The following were present in the college: Q. Tillius Sassius, C. Licinius [Mucianus? *(other names lost)*]

[*AFA* 41]

This fragment seems likely to honour Vespasian's return, given the mention of sacrifice to *Fortuna Redux* (Fortune the Home-Bringer).

A72a – early January AD 72

(Small fragments show the promise of sacrifices to the Dea Dia later in the year, on a similar formula to other years, and presumably at the same time in January).

A72b – Spring, AD 72: appeasement for fallen tree

When Emperor C[aesa]r Ves[pasian Augustus] for the fourth time and Titus Caesar Imperator for the second were consuls, on [*(part of date preserved, indicating a date between 14 April and 15 May)*] [a sacr]ifice was carried out [in the grov]e of the Dea Dia, by the attendant and the assistants in appeasement for a tree which had [fallen] in a storm.

[*AFA* 42, lines 12–15]

The listing of the consuls here is unusual as entries usually start with the formula 'Under the same consuls', except where they are different from the previous entry which was not the case here.

A72c – 29 May, AD 72: sacrifices and games

When C. Licinius Mucia[nus for the third time] and T. Flavius Sabinus for the second were consuls, on 29 May, in the presidency of [M.] Trebellius Maximus and when L. Maecius Postumus was vice-president, [on behalf] of the college of Arval Brothers he sacrificed [two] s[ows, at the altar] to the Dea Dia [to make appeasement] and the[n a c]ow. [*(fragments show games on the same pattern as every May, e.g.* **A69p, A80a**

*and indicate the presence of C. Vipstanus Apronianus and Ti. Julius Candidus Marius
Celsus; several other names are lost.)*]

[AFA 42 lines 16–28]

A75a – 3 January, AD 75: vows and sacrifices for Vespasian and Titus

When Emperor Caesar [Ve]spasian Augustus for the sixth time and Titus Caesar
[I]mperator for the fourth time were consuls, on 3 January, the president Ti. Ju[lius
Ca]ndidus [Mar]ius Celsus, [on behalf] of the college of Arval Brothers [un]dertook
vows for the well-being of Emperor Vespasian Caesar [Augustus, *pontifex maximus*,
holding trib]unic[ian] power and of [Titus Caesar] Ves[pasian Imperator] son of
Augustus, with sacrificial victims offered [on the Capitol wh]ich the pre[vious year's
pr]eside[nt had vowed. The following were prese]nt in the college: Emperor Caesa[r
Vespasian Augustus, T. Caesar Vespasian, son of Augustus, Caesar] Domitian, son of
Augustus [*(other names lost)*].

[AFA 43abcdf lines 1–10]

A75b – early January, AD 75

[*(Small fragments show the regular promise made in January of offerings to the Dea
Dia in May)*]

A78a – 3 January, AD 78: sacrifices and vows for Vespasian and Titus

When L. Ceionius Commodus and D. Novius Priscus were consuls, on 3 January in
the presidency of C. Matidius Patruinus, with L. Veratius Quadratus as vice-president,
on behalf of the college of Arval Brothers, they undertook vows for the well-being of
Emperor Vespasian Caesar Augustus, *pontifex maximus*, holding tribunician power,
consul eight times and of Titus Caesar Vespasian, son of Augustus, consul six times.
With sacrificial victims on the Capitol he fulfilled the vows which the previous year's
president had made and undertook vows for the following year at the dictation of L.
Veratius Quadratus in exactly the terms written below: a male ox to Jupiter Greatest
and Best, a cow to Queen Juno, a cow to Minerva, a cow to Well-Being. Likewise
for Titus Imperator Vespasian Caesar, son of Augustus, in the same words which are
written below: a male ox to Jupiter Greatest and Best, a cow to Queen Juno, a cow to
Minerva, a cow to Well-Being. The following were present in the college: L. Veratius
Quadratus, C. Tadius Mefitanus, Q. Tillius Sassius, L. Maecius Postumus, A. Julius
Quadratus, C. Vipstanus Apronianus.

[AFA 44a lines 1–16]

A78b – 8 January, AD 78

Under the same consuls on 8 January, in the Temple of Concord, in the presence of the
Arval Brothers, in the presidency of C. Matidius Patruinus, when L. Veratius Quadratus
was vice-president of the college of Arval Brothers, a sacrifice was announced to the
Dea Dia as dictated by L. Maecius Postumus: on 27 May, in the house; on 29 May, in
the grove and in the house; on 30 May, in the house. The following were present in
the college: L. Veratius Quadratus, C. Vipstanus Apronianus, L. Maecius Postumus,
C. Junius Tadius Mefitanus, A. Julius Quadratus.

[AFA 44a lines 16–22]

A78c – 1 March, AD 78: Salvius Liberalis co-opted on written advice of Vespasian

Under the same consuls on 1 March, in the Temple of Concord, in the presence of the Arval Brothers; in line with the letter sent by Emperor Caesar Vespasian Augustus, we co-opted C. Salvius Liberalis Nonius Bassus in place of the deceased C. Matidius Patruinus. The following were present in the college: L. Veratius Quadratus, C. Vipstanus Apronianus, L. Maecius Postumus, C. Salvius Liberalis Nonius Bassus. In the presidency of C. Salonus Matidius Patruinus, P. Sallustius Blaesus succeeded to his place and undertook the presidency for the same year, under the same consuls, on 1 March.

[*AFA* 44a lines 22–29]

C. Salonus Matidius Patruinus, brother-in-law to Trajan had a very short career as an arval, being only known as president in absence for the start of the year (**A78a–b**). For Salvius, see **B84** and **U26**; for Sallustius, **B89**.

A78d – 11 March, AD 78: Sallustius Blaesus co-opted as president

Under the same consuls, on 11 March, in the Temple of Concord, the president P. Sallustius Blaesus, co-opted in place of C. Matidius Patruinus, summoned the college of Arval Brothers [and nominated] L. Veratius Quadratus as high priest. The following were present in the college: P. Sallustius Blaesus, L. Veratius Q[uadratus, L. Maecius] Postumus, C. Junius Mefitanus, A. Julius Quadr[atus, C. Salvius Liberalis] Nonius Bassus

[*AFA* 44a lines 29–35]

A78e – 29 May, AD 78: games

When Q. Articuleius Paetus and Sex. Vi]tulasius Nep[os were consuls … *(This pair of suffect consuls probably took office on 1 May. What happened in their consulship is lost, until the end of the entry for 29 May)*]

[… Th]en P. Sallustius Bl[aesus, the president, veiled and crowned] gave [the signal, from the starting-gates] to the chariots and the stunt-riders w[hom he presented with silver crowns]. The following were present in the college: P. Sallustius B[laesus … *(one name lost)*, C. Junius] Mefitanus, L. Veratius Quadratus, [*(another name lost)*, C. Salvius] Liberali{u}s Nonius Bassus.

A78f – 30 May, AD 78: feast at the house of the president

[Under the same consuls, on 30 May, likewise the Brothers dining] at the house of the president to complete the sacrifice, and [well-born boys], the sons of [se]nators [with fathers and mother both still alive, receiv]ing fruits from the priests and [bringing them] to the alt[ar].

[When Q. Articulei]us Paetus and [Sex. Vi]tulasius Nepos were consuls … *(This entry and any others for AD 78 are lost – it is not clear why the consular date is repeated, but see above* **A72b***)*]

A79a – unknown date, probably AD 79: special vows and sacrifices

[When … and Caesar] Domitian for the 6th? time [were consuls, *(date and name of president lost)* and when P. Sa]llustius Blaesus [was vice-president, vows were undertaken on behalf] of the college of [Arval] bro[thers, for the well-being of Emperor] Vespasian Caesar [Augustus, consul 9 times and Titus Caesar Vespasian, son of Augustus, consul 7 times, and Caesar Domit]ian, [son of Augustus], consul 6 times: victims [were sacrificed on the Capitol and vows fulfill]ed, [two male] oxen to Jupiter, Greatest and Best, [two cows to Queen Juno, t]wo [cows to Minerva, two cows] to Public Well-Being, [and vows were undertaken for the following year, as dictated by P. Sallustius Blaesus [vice-president … *(the rest lost)*…].

[*AFA* 45]

Though very fragmentary, and lost after being recorded in the 16th century, the inscription may show unusual vows and sacrifices, with plural oxen, almost certainly two cows, and the inclusion of Domitian making it different from **A78a**, and possibly evidence for special response to Vespasian's (last?) illness or the conspiracy of Caecina (**C16b, H50, P2**).

A80a – 29 May, AD 80: games

[Under the same consuls, on 29 May, … L. Venuleius Aproni]anus, [president], cro[wned and veiled] gave the [signal to the chariots and the stunt-]riders [in the starting-gates], whom […]

[The following were present in the college: Emperor T. Caesar] Vespasian Augustus, [son of Divus], Caesar Domitian, son of Divus, [L. Venuleius Apronianus], C. Vipstanus Apronianus, C. Junius Tadius Mefitanus, L. Veratius [Quadratus, L. Po]mpeius Vopiscus Arruntius Catellius Celer, Ti. Julius Candidus Marius [Celsus], Q. Tillius Sassius.

[*AFA* 48, lines 1–7]

A80b – 30 May, AD 80: feast with aristocratic boys in attendance

Under the same consuls, on 30 May, in the house of L. Venuleius Apronianus, president, to complete the sacrifice, through feasting of the Arval Brothers, attended by well-born boys, the sons of senators with fathers and mothers both still alive, bringing fruits to the altar on platters.

[*AFA* 48, lines 8–10]

A80c – 7 December AD 80: vows for restoration of the Capitol

When M. Tittius Frugi and T. Vinicius Julianus were consuls, on 7 December on the Capitol, the priests came to the Temple of Strength (Ops) to fulfil the vows for the restoration and dedication of the Capitol by Emperor T. Caesar Vespasian Augustus. The following were present in the college: L. Venuleius Apronianus, C. Vipstanus Apronianus, L. Veratius Quadratus, L. Pompeius Vopsicus Arruntius Catellius Celer, C. Junius Tadius Mefitanus, P. Sallustius Blaesus.

[*AFA* 48, lines 11–16]

For the Capitol, twice rebuilt by the Flavians, see **K27–K32**.

A80d – 15 January AD 81: ritual for fallen tree in the sacred grove

When L. Flavius Silva Nonius Bassus and Asinius Pollio Verrucosus were consuls, on 15 January, in the grove of the Dea Dia, an act of expiation was carried out with sacrifice of a sow and perfect lamb by the attendant and assistants of the priest, because a tree had fallen through age.

[*AFA* 48, lines 17–19]

The expiation was carried out on 15 Jan, AD 81. But as Scheid (Commentary) explains, a decision to offer appeasement, taken in a previous presidency, as with routine expiation for bringing metal writing implements into the temple at **A80e** and would result in the act of fulfilment being thought of as belonging to the previous year.

A80e: expiation (in May 81) for writing implements used in AD 80

When L. Vettius Paullus and T. Junius Montanus were consuls, on 1 May, in the grove of the Dea Dia, a sacrifice of sow and perfect lamb was carried out by the attendant and the assistants of the priest, for metal having been brought in to the temple to write. Under the same consuls, on 13 May, in the grove of the Dea Dia, a sacrifice of sow and perfect lamb was carried out by the attendant and the assistants of the priest, for metal having been brought out of the temple.

[*AFA* 48, lines 20–24]

A80f – first half of AD 80: seats allocated in the amphitheatre

When L. Aelius Plautius Lamia and Q. Pactumeius Fronto were consuls. Received by Laberius Maximus, procurator, prefect of the corn-supply, when L. Ven{n}uleius Apronianus was president, and Thyrsus the freedman was secretary. For the Arval Brothers: in the first level, twelfth wedge, eight marble steps: on the first step 5 feet and 15/48th, on the eighth step 5 feet 15/48th, making 42½ feet {on the first step 22½ feet}. And on the {top} second level, sixth wedge, four marble steps: on the first step {one} 22½ feet. And on the top level in the wooden seats, in the fifty-third section, eleven steps: on the first step 5 feet 9/24th, on the eleventh step 5 feet and 45/48th. Making 63 feet and 23/24th. The sum total 129 feet and 23/24th.

[*AFA* 48, lines 25–34]

This entry form a sort of appendix to the acts for AD 80, even though the consular date was in the first half of the year (given Plautius Lamia's long consulship, see **B80**, we cannot currently date his partnership with Pactumeius closer than from some point between 14 Jan and 12 June). See note to **K14**.

A81e – 3 January AD 81: vows for imperial family at start of year

When L. Flavius Silva Nonius Bassus and Asinius Pollio Verrucosus were consuls, on 3 January, the president C. Junius Tadius Mefitanus, undertook vows on behalf of the college of Arval Brothers, for the well-being of Emperor Titus Caesar Vespasian Augustus, son of Divus, *pontifex maximus*, holding tribunician power, consul eight times, and for Caesar Domitian, son of Divus, consul seven times, and for Julia Augusta, and for their children; after burning sacrificial victims on the Capitol which the president of the previous year had vowed, he rendered two male oxen to Jupiter Greatest and Best, two cows to Queen Juno, two cows to Minerva, two cows to Public Well-Being, and he undertook vows for the following year, as dictated by L. Pompeius Vopiscus C. Arruntius Catellius Celer, in the exact terms written below:

Jupiter, Greatest and Best, if Emperor Titus Caesar Vespasian Augustus, *pontifex maximus*, holding tribunician power, father of the fatherland, and Caesar Domitian, son of Divus, both of whom we consciously mention are alive and their households safe, on 3 January in the next year for the people of Rome and the Quirites, and if to that day you preserve them safe from any dangers which may be, [or come to be before] that day, and if you [grant] the happy outcome which we consciously mention and preserve [them in the] condition they are now in, or a yet better one, [and if you do this, then], in the name of the college of Arval Brothers, [we vow that you shall have two] golden oxen.

[Queen Juno, on exactly the same terms according to which] we have vowed that Jupiter shall have two golden [oxen, which I have vowed today, if you do this accordingly, then], in exactly the same terms, [in the name of the college of Arval Brothers, we vow that] you shall have [two golden cows …] (*The rest of the entry for this day is missing, but can be assumed to include exactly the same vows for Minerva and Public Well-Being, on the lines of* **A87a**).

[*AFA* 48, lines 35–55]

A81f – Early January, AD 81: promise of sacrifices later in the year
[(*The start of this entry is missing, but contained a meeting to promise a series of sacrifices to the Dea Dia)*] by L. Pompeius Vopiscus Gaius Arruntius Catellius C[eler] on 17 May in the house, on 19 May in the grove and in the house, on 20 May in the house. The following were present in the college: C. Junius Tadius Mefitanus, Ti. Julius Candidus Marius Celsus, L. Pompeius Vopiscus Gaius Arruntius Catellius Celer, L. Veratius Quadratus, P. Sallustius Blaesus.

[*AFA* 49, lines 1–4]

A81g – 29 March, AD 81: trees fallen in snow storm
When M. Roscius Coelius and C. Julius Juvenalis were consuls, on 29 March in the grove of the Dea Dia, a sacrifice of sow and perfect lamb was made by the attendant and the assistants to the priest in appeasement for trees which had fallen in a snow storm.

[*AFA* 49, lines 5–7]

A81h – 17 May, AD 81: brethren dine at president's house
When T. Junius Montanus and L. Vettius Paullus were consuls, and C. Junius Mefitanus president of the college of Arval Brothers, on 17 May, a sacrifice was conducted in the house of Junius Mefitanus by the president and other priests; they also dined at the house of the president; free-born boys who were sons of senators, and with their fathers and mothers both still alive were in attendance with the incense and wine, carrying bowls back to the altar.

[*AFA* 49, lines 8–12]

A81i – 19 May, AD 81: sacrifice and games
Under the same consuls, on 19 May, when C. Junius Mefitanus was president, in the grove of the Dea Dia, he likewise, on behalf of the college of Arval Brothers sacrificed two sows at the altar to the Dea Dia to make appeasement and then a cow to the Dea Dia. Then, when they had taken their seats in the Temple of Caesar, they tasted food from the sacrifice. Then having made the sacrifice, they burnt an offering of a perfect lamb to the Dea Dia in the sanctuary of the temple, and after this sacrifice they dined in the Temple of Caesar in honour of the president. Then the president, C. Junius Mefitanus, crowned and veiled, gave, from the starting-gates the signal to the chariots and stunt-riders, whom he decorated with silver crowns. The following were present in the college: Emperor Titus Caesar Vespasian Augustus, son of Divus Vespasian, C. Fufius Junius Tadius Mefitanus, L. Pompeius Vopiscus Arruntius Catellius Celer, Q. Tillius Sassius, Ti. Julius Candidus Mar[ius Ce]lsus, L. Veratius Quadratus.

[*AFA* 49, lines 13–23]

A81j – 20 May, AD 81: another dinner

Under the same consuls, on 20 May, the Brothers likewise dined at the house of the president to com[plete] the sacrifice; free-born boys who were sons of senators, and with their fathers and mothers still alive, received fruit from the priests and carried it back to the altar.

[*AFA* 49, lines 24–26]

A81k – 14 September, AD 81: sacrifice for Domitian's reign

When M. Petronius Umbrinus and L. Carminius Lusitanicus were consuls, on 14 September, the college of Arval Brothers sacrificed on the Capitol for the reign of Caesar Domitian Augustus, son of Divus, in the magistracy of C. Junius Mefitanus, when L. Pompeius Vopiscus C. Arruntius Catellius Celer was vice-president, a male ox to Jupiter Greatest and Best, a cow to Queen Juno, a cow to Minerva, a cow to Well-Being, a cow to Prosperity, a bull to Mars. The following were (*sic*) present in the college: L. Pompeius Vopiscus C. Arruntius Catellius Celer

[*AFA* 49, lines 27–32]

Titus died on 13 Sept at Aquae Cutiliae, about 56 miles (90km) by road from Rome, (Suet. *Titus* 11).

A81m – 30 September AD 81: Domitian's tribunician power

Under the same consuls on 30 September, on the Capitol, for the tribune election of Caesar Domitian Augustus, son of Divus, the college of Arval Brothers, through the vice-president, L. Pompeius [Vop]iscus C. Arruntius Catellius Celer (acting on behalf of) C. Junius Mefitanus, with sacrificial victims – a male ox to Jupiter Greatest and Best, a cow to Queen Juno, a cow to Minerva. The following were present in the college: L. Pompeius Vopiscus C. Arruntius Catellius Celer, Q. Tillius Sassius, C. Salvius Liberalis Nonius Bassus.

[*AFA* 49, lines 33–38]

A81n – 1 October AD 81: vows for Domitian and family

Under the same consuls, on 1 October, on the Capitol, the college of Arval Brothers sacrificed to commend vows for the well-being and safety of Caesar Domitian Augustus, son of Divus, through the vice-president, L. Pompeius Vopiscus C. Arruntius Catellius Celer (acting on behalf of) C. Junius Mefitanus – a male ox to Jupiter Greatest and Best, a cow to Queen Juno, a cow to Minerva, a bull to his divine spirit. Likewise, on the Capitol, he proclaimed vows for the following year for the well-being of Emperor Caesar Domitian Augustus, son of Divus, in the words which are written below: a male ox to Jupiter, a cow to Queen Juno, a cow to Minerva, a cow to Well-Being. Likewise for the well-being of Domitia Augusta, his wife, in the words which are written below: a male ox to Jupiter, a cow to Queen Juno, a cow to Minerva, a cow to Well-Being. Likewise for the well-being of Julia Augusta, daughter of Emperor Titus, in the words which are written below: a male ox to Jupiter, a cow to Queen Juno, a cow to Minerva, a cow to Well-Being. The following were present in the college: L. Pompeius Vopiscus C. Arruntius Catellius Celer, Q. Tillius Sassius, L. Veratius Quadratus, C. Salvius Liberalis Nonius Bassus.

[*AFA* 49, lines 39–51]

Domitian and Julia, but not Domitia had been included in the vows at the start of the year, **A81e**.

A81o – 30 October, AD 81

Under the same consuls, on 30 October, [in the Temple] of Concord, in the presence of the Arval Brothers … [*(the rest is lost and only one tiny fragment survives from (probably 82/3))*].

[*AFA* 49, line 52]

A84a – 29 May, AD 84: sacrifice and games

[On 29 May], in the presidency of Ti. Tutinius [Severus], a sacrifice to Dea Dia in [her] g[rove]: [Ti. Tutin]ius Severus [sacrificed] two sows [at the altar] to make appeasement to the grove for (wood) [being cut down and work being done]; then he sacrificed a [white] cow at the hearth [to honour the Dea Dia. Then they took their seats in the four-columned (temple) and] feasted on the meat from the sacrifice. Having put [on the toga praetexta and crowned] with wreaths [of co]rn, [they ascended to a remote part] of the grove of the Dea [Dia and], through Ti. Tutinius Se[verus], the president, they [sac]rificed [a perfect lamb to the Dea Dia], and when [the sacrifice] was complete, [they all ma]de [offerings of incense and wine]. Then having [put on] their wreaths and having anointed the statues], they made [L. Pompeiu]s Vopiscus Arrunt[ius Catellius Celer president for the year from] the next [Saturna]lia until [the following] Sa[turnalia, and made *(name lost)* the high priest. Then they [went back to the four-columned (temple), and there], reclining [in the dining-]room, [they feasted in honour of the president Ti. Tutiniu]s Severus. [After the feast, wearing a veil and sandals and with a crown of intertwi]ned roses, [he ascended] from the remote part to above the start[ing-gates and] [gave] the signal to the chariots a[nd stunt-riders], while L. Pompei[us Vopiscus Arruntius] Catellius Celer officiated; he pres[ented] the win[ners with palms and] silver [cr]owns. The following were present in the college of [Arval Brothers: the president, Ti.] Tutinius Severus, Ti. J[ulius Candidus Ma]rius Celsus, A. Julius [Quadratus, L. Vera]tius Quadratus, L. Pom[peius Vopiscus] Arruntius Catellius [Celer, C. Vipstanus Apronia]nus, P. Sallustius Blaes[us, L. Venuleius] Montanus Apronianus, [C. Salvius Libe]ralis Nonius Bassus. On the same day in Rome, those who had been in [the grove had dinner] at the house of the presi[dent, Ti. Tutini]us Severus.

[*AFA* 53, column I.1–16, column II.1–15]

A84b – 30 May, AD 84: feast at the house of the president of the Arval Brothers

On 30 May at the house of the president, Ti T[utinius Severus], the Arval Brothers had dinner to mark off[icially the sacrifice] to the Dea Dia, and during the dinner, Ti. Tutinius Severus, president, Ti. Julius [Candidus Marius] Celsus, A. Julius Quadratus, L. [Veratius Quadratus… *(the rest of this entry, and others for the remainder of AD 84 and 85 are lost)*].

[*AFA* 53, column II.16–20]

A86a – 3 January, AD 86: vows for the new year

[*(the start of the vows are lost)*...] he fulfilled the vows [which] the previous year's president had made: a golden [ox] to Jupiter [Greatest and Best, a go]lden cow to Queen Juno, a golden [cow] to Minerva, a g[old]en cow to Public Well-Being. And they undertook vows for the follow[ing year] in exactly the words [which] are written below:

Jupiter, Greatest and Best, I pray and beseech you that if Em[peror Caesar Domitian Augustus] Germanicus and Domitia Augusta, his wife [and Julia Augusta, and those whom we] consciously mention are alive and their households safe, on 3 January in the next year for the people of Rome and the Quirites, and if to that day you preserve them safe from any dangers which may be, or come to be before that day, and if you grant the happy outcome which we consciously mention and preserve them in the condition they are now in, or a yet better one, and if you do this, then, in the name of the college of Arval Brothers, I vow that you shall have a golden white male ox.

Queen Juno, on [exactly] the same terms according to which [I have vowed] that Jupiter shall have a golden white male ox, [which I have vowed today, if] you do this accordingly, then, in exactly the same terms, in the name of the college [of Arval Brot]hers, I vow that you shall have a golden white female ox.

[Minerva, on exactly] the same terms according to which I have vowed that Queen Juno shall have a golden white female ox, [which] I have vowed today, if you do this accordingly, then, in exactly the same terms, in the name of the [college of Arval Brot]hers, I vow that you shall have a golden white female ox.

[Pub]lic [Well-Being], on exactly the same terms according to which I have vowed that Queen Juno shall have a gol[den white female ox], which I have vowed today, if you do this accordingly, [then, in exactly the same terms], in the name of the college of Arval Brothers, I vow that you shall have [a golden white female ox]. The following were present in the college: L. Veratius [Quadratus, vice-president, Q. Tillius] Sassius, C. Salvius Liberalis Nonius Bassus, [another name lost], L. Venuleius Apronianus, P. Sallustius Blaesus, C. Vipsta[nus Apronianus].

[AFA 54, lines 1–26]

A86b – 6–12 January, AD 86: promise of sacrifices later in the year

Under the same consuls, on [...] January, in the Temple of Concord, in the presence of the Arval Brothers, in the presidency of [Emperor] Caesar Domitian Augustus Germanicus, when L. Veratius Quadratus was vice-president of the college of Arval Brothers, a sacrifice was announced to the Dea Dia by L. Veratius Q[uadratus], vice-president, assisted by Q. Tillius Sassius, on 27 [May], in the house; on 29 May, in the grove and in the house; on 30 May, in the house. The following were present in the college: L. Veratius Quadratus, vice-president, L. Venuleius Apronianus, A. Julius Quadratus, C. Salvius Liberalis Nonius Bassus, Q. Tillius Sassius, P. Sallustius Blaesus.

[AFA 54, lines 27–34]

A86c – 22 January, AD 86: vows for Domitian

In the consulship of Servius Cornelius Dolabella and Gaius Secius Campanus, on 22 January, in the presidency of Emperor Caesar Domitian Augustus Germanicus, when L. Veratius Quadratus was vice-president of the college of Arval Brothers, they undertook vows for the well-being of Emperor Caesar Domitian Augustus Germanicus: "Jupiter of the Capitol, Greatest and Best, if Emperor Caesar Domitian Augustus Germanicus, son of Divus Vespasian, *pontifex maximus*, holding tribunician power, censor for life, father of the fatherland, on whose preservation the well-being of all depends, whom we consciously mention, shall be alive and if his household shall be well for the state and the Roman People, the Quirites on 22 January in the next year for the Roman People, the Quirites; and if you keep him safe that day from dangers which happen or are to happen before that day; and if you grant him as prosperous a situation as we consciously name; and if you see to it that you preserve him in the same condition as at present or better; and if you guard the eternity of empire which he has expanded by taking it up, so that you often make the state share in this vow; if you do these things accordingly, then we vow that it shall be fulfilled with a golden ox."

[*AFA* 54, lines 35–47]

This entry records vows being made but none fulfilled from the previous year. So presumably some significant (but unknown) event took place just before 22 January, AD 86 to prompt this additional set of annual vows recorded for the rest of Domitian's reign, whenever January is preserved (A87d, A89e, A90c). Also new for this entry is Domitian as censor for life (on coins from AD 85) and the phrase that 'on his safety the well-being of all depends'.

A86d – 26 February, AD 86: co-option of Julius Silanus

Under the same consuls, on 26 February in the Temple of Concord to co-opt Gaius Julius Silanus in place of Gaius Vipstanus Apronianus. The following were present in the college: L. Veratius Quadratus, vice-president, Q. Tillius Sassius, L. Venuleius Apronianus, L. Maecius Postumus, A. Julius Quadratus, C. Salvius Liberalis Nonius Bassus, P. Sallustius Blaesus.

[*AFA* 54, lines 48–52]

C. Julius Silanus (Rupke no. 1988, page 732) was consul in 92, dead by 98. This entry is fully preserved at the bottom of its plaque. No trace of the next plaque recording events of the rest of AD 86 survives.

A87a – 3 January, AD 87: vows for the new year

When Emperor Caesar Domitian Augustus Germ[anicus, for the thirteenth time] and Lucius [V]olusius Saturninus [were consuls]. [On 3 January] on the Capitol, in the ves[tibule of Jupiter Greatest and Be]st, Gaius Salvius Liberalis, Arval Brother who was acting as president [in place of Gaius Julius Silanus] reported to the college of Arval Brothers: Since the immortal gods have [listened to] vows of the whole world which had been eagerly undertaken for the well-being of Emperor Caesar Domitian Augustus [Germani]cus, son of Divus Vespasian, *pontifex maximus*, and of Domitia Augusta, his wife, [and of Juli]a Augusta, and of their whole house, it (is fitting) for the college to meet to discharge the previous vows and undertake new ones. The college has decreed: may it [be] good, favourable, fortunate, and beneficial! Since it has come to pass that the previous vows should be discharged and new ones [vowed] for the well-being and safety of Emperor Caesar Domitian Augustus Germanicus, [son] of Divus [Vespasian], *pontifex maximus*, and of Domi[tia Augusta], his wife, [and of Juli]a Augusta, and of their whole house; a male ox to Jupiter Best and Greatest, a cow to Queeen Juno, a cow to Minerva, a cow to Public Well-Being of the Roman People, the Quirites.

On the same day, in the courtyard, Gaius Salvius Liberalis, who was acting in place of the president, with incense and wine on the fire in the hearth, and using wine, spelt and a knife, made a sacrifice of a male ox to Jupiter Best and Greatest, a cow to Queeen Juno, a cow to Minerva, a cow to Public Well-Being of the Roman People, the Quirites. He handed over the organs cooked in the hall.

On the same day, also in the vestibule of Jupiter Greatest and Best, Gaius Salvius Liberalis, Arval Brother who was acting as president in place of Gaius Julius Silanus, in the presence of the college of Arval [Brothers] undertook vows for the well-being and safety of Emperor Caesar Domitian Augustus Germanicus, son of [Divus Vespasian], *pontifex maximus*, holding tribunician power, [censor for] life, father of the fatherland, and of Domitia Augusta, his wife, and of Julia Augusta, and of their [whole h]ouse, on behalf of the college of Arval Brothers, in the following [words]:

"Jupiter, Greatest and Best, if Emperor Caesar Domitia[n Au]gustus Germanicus, son of Divus Vespasian, *pontifex maximus*, holding tribunician power, censor for life, father of the [fatherland, and Domit]ia Augusta, his wife, and Julia Augusta, all of whom I consciously [mention, shall be al]ive and if their household shall be well for the state and the Roman People, the Quirites on [3] of the January in the next year for the Roman People, the Quirites; and if you keep them safe that day from dangers which happen or are to happen before that day; and if you grant him as prosperous a situation as I consciously mention; and if you see to it that you preserve them in the same condition as at present or better; if you do these things accordingly, then we vow that it shall be fulfilled with a golden ox for you."

"Queen Juno, on the same terms according to which I vow to Jupiter Greatest and Best that it shall be fulfilled with a golden ox, which I have vowed today, if you do this accordingly, then I vow, on behalf of the college of Arval Brothers, in exactly the same terms, that it shall be fulfilled with a golden ox for you."

"Minerva, on the same terms according to which I vow to Jupiter Greatest and Best that it shall be fulfilled with a golden ox, which I have vowed today, if you do this accordingly, then I vow, on behalf of the college of Arval Brothers, in exactly the same terms, that it shall be fulfilled with a golden ox for you."

"Public Well-Being of the Roman People, the Quirites, on the same terms according to which I vow to Jupiter Greatest and Best that it shall be fulfilled with a golden ox, which I have vowed today, if you do this accordingly, then I vow, on behalf of the college of Arval Brothers, in exactly the same terms, that it shall be fulfilled with a golden ox for you." The following were present in the college: C. Salvius Liberalis Nonius B[assus, A. J]ulius Quadratus, [L. Maec]ius Postumus, L. Veratius Quadratus, P. Sallustius Blaesus, [L. Venul]eius Apronianus.

[*AFA* 55, column I, lines 1–50]

A87b: 6–11 January, AD 87: promise of sacrifices later in the year

Under the same consuls, on [6–11] January, in the vestibule of the Temple of Concord which is near the [Temp]le of Divus Vespasian. [Gaius Salvius] Liberalis Nonius Bassus, Arval Brother, who was acting as president in p[lace of Julius Sila]nus, in the presence of the [Arval] Brothers, proclaimed a sacrifice in the coming year to the Dea Dia in the following words: may it [be] good, favourable, {favourable}, fortunate, fine, and beneficial! Since it has come to pass that the previous vows should be discharged and new ones [vowed] for the well-being and safety of Emperor Caesar Domitian Augustus Germanicus, *pontifex maximus*, and for Dom[itia A]ugusta, his wife, and for Ju[lia] Augusta, and for their whole house, and for the Roman People the Quirites, and for the Arval Brothers and for me! There shall be a sacrifice to the Dea Dia on (17 May) in the house, on 19 May in the grove and in the house, and [on 20 May] in the house. The following were present in the college: [C. Salviu]s Libera[lis Nonius Bas]sus, L. Veratius Quadratus, L. Mae[cius Postumus, A. J]uliu[s Quadratus, P.] Sallustius Blaesus.

[*AFA* 55, column I, lines 51–63]

A87c – Mid-January, AD 87: vows fulfilled for Domitian's return
When Lucius Volusius Satur[nin]us and Gaius Calpu[rnius Piso were consuls, on ? January, in accordance with a decree of the senate that vows should be fulfilled] on the Capit[ol fo]r the well-being a[nd safe return? of Emperor Caesar Domitian Augustus] Germanicus, [when Gaius Julius Silanus] was preside[nt and Gaius Salvius Liberalis was vice-president,] a male ox [to Jupiter Greatest and Best, a cow] to Queen Juno, [a cow to Minerva …. The following] were present [in the college:] Emperor Caesar Domitian [Augustus Germanicus, C. Salvius Liberalis] Nonius Bassus, L. Maecius Postumus, L. [Veratius Quadratus].

[*AFA* 55, column I, lines 64–69]

We do not know from where Domitian had returned, though his attendance in the college is unusual.

A87d – 22 January, AD 87: vows for Domitian
Under the same consuls on 22 January on the Capitol to fulfil vows [and undertake new ones for] the well-being and safety of Emperor Caesar Domit[ian Augustus Germanicus], when Gaius Julius Silanus was president, and Gaius Salvius [Liberalis Nonius Bassus] was vice-president. The following were present in the college: C. Salvius Liberalis Nonius [Bassus *(and other names, lost)*]

"Jupiter of the Capitol, Greatest and Best, i[f Emperor Caesar Domitian] Augustus Germanicus, [son of Divus Vespasian, *pontifex*] max[*imus*, holding tribunician power, censor for life, father of the fatherland], on whose preservation [the well-being of all depends, whom we] consciously mention, shall be alive [and if his household shall be well for the state and the Roman People, the Quirites on 22 of the January] in the next year for the Roman People, the Quirites; and if you keep him safe [that day from dangers which happen or are to happen before that] day; [and if you grant him as] prosperous a situation as we consciously name; and if you see to it that you preserve him [in the same condition as at present or better; and if] you guard the eternity [of empire which he has expanded by taking it up, so that] you often make the state share in this vow; [if you do these things accordingly], then, on behalf of the college of Arval Brothers, I [vow] that it shall be fulfilled [with a golden ox]."

[*AFA* 55, column I, lines 70–73 and column II, lines 1–12]

A87e – 1 February, AD 87: a new assistant for the Brethren
Under the same consuls, on 1 Febraury, Narcissus Annianus was chosen as assistant to the Arval Brothers in place of Nymphus Numisianus.

[*AFA* 55, column II, lines 13–14]

The '*publicus*' was usually a public slave, here attached to the Brethren (Rupke, *Fasti Sacerdotum*, p.11–12 and no.2501).

A87f – 19 May, AD 87: sacrifices and games
When Gaius Bellicus Natalis Tebianus and Gaius Ducenius Proculus were consuls, on 19 May, in the grove of the Dea Dia, when Gaius Julius Silanus was president, under the agency of Gaius Nonius Bassus Salvius Liberalis, the Arval Brothers made a sacrifice to the Dea Dia. Gaius Salvius Liberalis who was acting as president in place of Gaius Julius Silanus, on an altar in front of the grove sacrificed two sows to make appeasement to the grove for (wood) being cut down and work being done; then he sacrificed a cow to honour the Dea Dia. Gaius Salvius Liberalis Nonius Bassus, L.

Maecius Postumus, A. Julius Quadratus, P. Sallustius Blaesus, Q. Tilius Sassius took their seats in the four-columned (temple) and feasted on the meat from the sacrifice. Having put on the toga praetexta and crowned with wreaths of corn, they ascended to a remote part of the grove of the Dea Dia and, through Salvius Liberalis Nonius Bassus who was acting as president, and Q. Tillius Sassius, who was acting in place of the high priest, they sacrificed a perfect lamb to the Dea Dia, and when the sacrifice was complete, they all made offerings of incense and wine. Then having put on their wreaths and having anointed the statues, they made Q. Tillius Sassius president for the year from the next Saturnalia until the following Saturnalia, and made Ti. Julius Celsus Marius Candidus the high priest. Then they went back to the four-columned (temple), and there, reclining in the dining-room, they feasted in honour of the president C. Julius Silanus. After the feast, wearing a veil and sandals and with a crown of intertwined roses, he ascended from the remote part to above the starting-gates and gave the signal to the chariots and stunt-riders, while L. Maecius Postumus officiated; he presented the winners with palms and silver crowns. On the same day in Rome, those who had been in the grove had dinner at the house of the president, C. Julius Silanus.

[*AFA* 55, column II, lines 15–40]

A87g – 20 May, AD 87: feast at the house of the president of the Arval Brothers

On 20 May at the house of the president, C. Julius Silanus, the Arval Brothers had dinner to mark officially the sacrifice to the Dea Dia, and during the dinner, C. Salvius Liberalis Nonius Bassus, L. Maecius Postumus, A. Julius Quadratus, P. Sallustius Blaesus, Q. Tillius Sassius, L. Venuleius Apronianus made offerings of incense and wine; children with mothers and fathers both still alive were in attendance – the same ones as on 17 May – and the Arval Brothers brought fruit as offerings to the altar, and with lamps lit, laid their hands on Etruscan vessels which they had their servants send from their houses. The children [with mothers and fathers both still alive] who were in attendance at the sacrifice to the Dea Dia [were …]ilius Marcianus, P. Calvisius, son of Ruso, M. Petronius Cremutius, son of Umbrinus [*(two other names lost)*].

[*AFA* 55, column II, lines 41–53]

A87h – 10 September, AD 87: expiatory sacrifice

[When C. Cilnius Proculus and L. Neratius] Priscus were consuls, on 10 September, when C. Julius [Sila]nus was president, in the grove of the Dea Dia, a sacrifice was made by the attendant and the assistants because a branch had fallen from an ilex tree through its age.

[*AFA* 55, column II, lines 54–57]

A87i – 13 September, AD 87: altar dedicated for Silanus' presidency

Under the same consuls, on 13 September, on the Capitol, at the dedication of an altar for the presidency of Julius Silanus, L. Maecius Post[umus] sacrificed a cow. The following were present in the college: L. Maecius Postumus, A. Julius Quadratus, Q. Tillius Sassius.

[*AFA* 55, column II, lines 58–61]

The reason for this unprecedented dedication is not known, though the date chosen was the festival of Jupiter on the anniversary of the dedication of the Capitol to him.

A87j – 22 September, AD 87 – a conspiracy

Under the same consuls, on 22 September, on the Capitol, on account of the detection of crimes of evil-doers, in the presidency of C. Julius Silanus, L. Venu[leius Ap]ronianus sacrificed a male ox {sacrificed} on the Capitol.

[*AFA* 55, column II, lines 62–64]

The conspiracy is unknown: see **P6**.

A87k – expiation (in April 88) for implements used to record the acts of AD 87

When L. Minucius Rufus and D Plotius Gryphus were consuls, on 15 April, a sacrifice [was carried out in the grove of the Dea Dia by the attendant] and the assistants for bringing in metal [for writing and inscribing so that the deeds of the presi]dent C. Julius Silanus [might be inscribed]. [*(names of consuls lost),* a sacrifice was c[arried out] for the De[a Dia by the attendant and the assistants for] metal [...]

[*AFA* 55, column II, lines 65–69]

Compare **A80e**, and for deeds carried out in a following year recorded when they were promised, see **A80d**.

A89a – early January, AD 89: vows for Domitian's well-being

For the well-being of Emperor Caes[ar Domiti]an Augustus Germanicus, A. Julius Quadratus, Arval [Brother] who was acting as president in place of Ti. Julius Candidus, undertook vows.

The following were present in the college: A. Julius Quadratus, P. Sallustius Blaesus, L. Maecius Postumus, L. Venuleius Montanus Apronianus, L. Veratius Quadratus.

[*AFA* 57, lines 1–6]

A89b – 8 January, AD 89: promise of sacrifices later in the year

Under the same consuls, on 8 January in the vestibule of the Temple of Concord, the Arval Brothers proclaimed a sacrifice to the Dea Dia on 17 May at the house of the magistrates, on 19 May in the grove and at the house of the magistrates, on 20 May at the house of the magistrates. The following were present in the college: A. Julius Quadratus, L. Veratius Quadratus, P. Sallustius Blaesus, Q. Tillius Sassius.

[*AFA* 57, lines 7–12]

A89c – 12 January, AD 89: vows undertaken for Domitian (Saturninus revolt)

Under the same consuls, on 12 January, on the Capitol, by decree of the senate, for the well-being, victory and safe return of Emperor Domitian Caesar Augustus Ger[manicus], the Arval [Brothers] undertook vows. [The following were present] in the college: L. Veratius Quadratus, P. Sallustius Bl[aesus, L. Maecius Postumus], A. Julius Quadratus, L. Venuleius Montanus Ap[ronianus].

[*AFA* 57, lines 13–18]

For the Saturninus revolt, see **P8**.

A89d – 17 January, AD 89: more vows undertaken for Domitian (Saturninus revolt)
Under the same consuls, on 17 January, on the Capitol, by edict of the consuls for the undertaking of vows and by decree of the senate for the well-being, victory and safe return of Emperor Caesar Domitian Augustus Germ[anicus], the college of Arval Brothers met. The following were present in the college: A. Julius Quadratus, L. Maecius Postum[us, L. Vera]tius Quadratus, L. Venuleius Montanus Apronianus, P. [Sallustius Bl]aesus, Q. Tillius Sassius.

[*AFA* 57, lines 19–25]

A89e – 22 January, AD 89: vows fulfilled
Under the same consuls, on 22 January, on the Capitol, by decree of the senate, for the fulfilment of vows and the undertaking of new ones [for the well-being] of Emperor Caesar Domitian Augustus Germanicus. The following were pre[sent: A. Julius] Quadratus, L. Maecius Postumus, Q. Tillius Sassi[us, P. Sallustius Blaesus,] L. Veratius Quadratus, L. Venuleius Montanu[s Apronianus].

[*AFA* 57, lines 26–30]

Though the date coincides with the Saturninus revolt, this was a regular date for vows (see on **A86c**).

A89f – 24 January, AD 89: thanksgiving by the senate (Saturninus revolt)
Under the same consuls, on 24 January, on the Capitol, the s{a}enate made an offering with incense and wine. [The following were present]: A. Julius Quadratus, L. Maecius Postumus, P. [Sallustius Blaesus, L. Venuleius] Montanus Apronianus, Q. Tillius S[assius, L. Veratius Quadratus].

[*AFA* 57, lines 31–34]

A89g – 25 January, AD 89: thanksgiving by the Arval Brothers
Under the same consuls, on 25 January, on the Capitol, on account of public happiness, the [Arval Brothers] sacrificed a male ox to Jupiter Greatest and Best in the Temple [of Jupiter Greatest and Best?]. [The following were present]: A. Julius Quadratus, L. Maecius Postumus, P. Sallust[ius Blaesus, L. Venuleius] Montanus Apronianus, Q. Tillius Sassius.

[*AFA* 57, lines 35–39]

A89h – 29 January, AD 89: more vows undertaken for Domitian's safe return
Under the same consuls, on 29 January, on the Capitol, by decree of the senate, the Arval Brothers met for the fulfilment of vows and the undertaking of new ones for the well-being and safe re[turn] of Emperor Caesar Domitian Augustus Germanicus. They made vows to Jupiter, Juno, Minerva, Mars, Well-Being, Fortune, Victory the Bringer-Back, [the Divine Spirit] of the Roman People. The following were present: [A. Julius Quadra]tus, L. [Maec]ius Postumus, Q. Tillius Sassius, P. Sallustius Blaesus.

[*AFA* 57, lines 40–46]

A89i – 12 April, AD 89: expiation for fallen tree in sacred grove
Under the same consuls, on 12 April, [in the grove, a sacrifice] was carried out for a sacred t[re]e which [...], by the assistants and the attendant.

[*AFA* 57, lines 47–49]

A89j – 19 May, AD 89: sacrifices and games

When [P. Sallustius Blaesus and M.] Peducaeus Saenianus [were consuls, on (19)] May, [in the grove of the Dea Dia], when Ti. Julius Candidus Marius Celsus was [president, under the agency of A. Julius Quadratus, the Ar]val Brothers made a sacrifice to the Dea Dia. [(*fragments of the next 19 lines make it clear that sacrifices and games followed the detailed pattern of other years, see* **A87f**)]

[*AFA* 57, lines 50–72]

A90a –3 January, AD 90: vows for the new year

[When Emperor Caesar Domitia]n Augustus Germanicus, [*pontifex maximus*], holding tribunician power for the 9th time, censor for life, father of the fatherland was consul for the fifteenth time, and [M. Cocceius] Nerva was consul for the second time. [When P. Sal]lustius Blaesus was president for the second time, on [3] January, [on the Capitol, in the vestibule of Jupiter Greatest and Best, Ti. Tutinius Seve]rus, Arval Brother, reported to the college of Arval Brothers: "Since the immortal gods [have listened to vows of the whole world which had been eager]ly undertaken [for the well-being] of Emperor Caesar Domitian Augustus [Germani]cus, son of Divus Vespasian, *pontifex maximus*, and [of Domitia Augusta, his wife, and of their whole house], it (is fitting) for the college to meet to discharge the previous vows and [undertake] new ones [for the coming year]. The college has decreed: [May it be good, favourable, fortunate, and beneficial! Since] it has come to pass that the previous [vows] should be discharged and new ones vowed for the well-being and saf[ety of Emperor Caesar Domitian Augustus Germa]nicus, [son of Divus Vespasian], *pontifex maximus*, and of Domitia Augusta, his wife, and of their whole house; [a male ox to Jupiter Best and Greatest, a cow to Queeen Juno, a cow to Minerva], a cow to [Public Well-Being] of the Roman People, the Quirites.

[On the same day, in the courtyard, (*name lost*), with incense and wine on the fi]re in the hearth, and using wine, spelt and a knife, made a sacrifice of a male ox to Jupiter Best and Greatest, a cow to Queeen Juno, a cow to Minerva, [a cow to Public Well-Being of the Roman People, the Quirites. He handed over the organs cooked in the hall].

[On the same day, also in the vestibule of Jupiter Greatest and Best, (*name lost*)], Arval [Brother], in the presence of the college of Arval Brothers undertook vows for the well-being and safety [of Emperor Caesar Domitian Augustus Germanicus, son of Divus Vespasian, pon]*tifex maximus*, holding tribunician power, perpetual [censor for] life, father of the fatherland, and of Domitia Augusta, his wife, and of their whole house, on behalf of the college of Arval Brothers], in the following words:

["Jupiter, Greatest and Best, if Emperor Caesar Domitian Augustus Ge]rmanicus, [son of Divus Vespasian], *pontifex maximus*, holding tribunician power, censor for life, father of the fatherland, and Domitia Augusta, his wife, [whom I consciously mention, shall be alive and if their household shall be well] for the state and the Roman People, the Quirites on 3 January in the next year for the Roman People, the Quirites; and if [you keep] them safe that day [from dangers which happen or are to happen before that day]; and if you grant him as prosperous a situation as I consciously mention; and if you see to it that [you preserve them] in the same condition as at present [or better; if you do these things accordingly, then, on behalf of the coll]ege of Arval Brothers, I vow that a golden ox shall be yours."

[Queen Juno, on the same terms according to which I vow to Jupiter Greatest and Best that it shall be fulfilled with a golden ox, wh]ich I have vowed today, if you do this accordingly, [then I vow], on behalf of the college of Arval Brothers, that a golden cow [shall be] yours.

[Minerva, on the same terms according to which I vow to Jupiter Greatest and Best that it shall be fulfilled with a golden ox, which] I have vowed [today], if you do this accordingly, then I vow, [on behalf of the college of Arval Brothers], in exactly the same [terms], that a golden cow shall be yours.

[Public Well-Being of the Roman People, the Quirites, on the same terms according to which I vow to Jupiter Greatest and Best that it shall be fulfilled with a golden ox, which I have vowed today, if you do this accordingly, then I vow, [on behalf of the college of Arval Brothers], in exactly the same [terms, that a golden cow] shall be yours. [The following were present in the college: (*one or two names lost*)), L]. Venuleius Apronianus, L. Maecius Postumus, Q. Tillius Sassius.

[*AFA* 58, lines 1–28]

The rubric is very similar to (and partly reconstructed from **A87a**). Mention of Julia is omitted.

A90b – early January, AD 90: promise of sacrifices later in the year

[Under the same consuls on ? January], when P. Sallustius Blaesus was [pres]ident for a second time, [in the vestibule of the Temple of Concord, P. Sallustius Blaesus, president] of the [Arval] Brothers, his hands washed and his head covered, under the high open sky, facing East, [proclaimed a sacrifice] to the Dea [Dia, alongside his colleagues]:

[May it be good, favourable, fortunate, fine, and beneficial for Emperor Caesa]r Domitian Augustus Germanicus, *pontifex maximus*, and for Domitia Augusta, his wife, [and for their whole house, and for the Roman People the Quirites, and] for the Arval [Brothers] and for me! There shall be a sacrifice this year to the Dea Dia on 25 May in the house, [on 27 May in the grove and in the house, and on 28 May in the house. The following were present in the college: P. Sallustius Blaesus, L. Maecius Postumus, Q. Tillius Sassius, [(*and possibly several others*)].

[*AFA* 58, lines 29–35]

A90c – 22 January, AD 90: vows for Domitian

[When M. Cocceius Nerva, for the second time, and L. Cornelius Pusio were consuls, on 22 J]anuary on the Capitol, vows were fulfilled and new ones undertaken for the well-being [of Emperor Caesar Domitian Augustus Germanicus, *pontifex maximus*, when P. Sallus]tius Blaesus was president for the second time: ["Jupiter of the Capitol, Greatest and Best, if Emperor Caesar Domitian] Augustus Germanicus, [son of Divus Vespasian], *pontifex maximus*, holding tribunician power, censor for life, father of the fatherland, [on whose preservation the well-being of all depends, whom I con]sciously mention, shall be alive and if his household shall be well [for the state and the Roman People, the Quirites] on 22 of the January in the next year for the Roman People, the Quirites]; and if you keep him safe [that day] from dangers which happen or are to happen before that day; [and if you grant him as prosperous] a situation [as I consciously name; and if] you preserve him [in the same condition as at pres]ent or better; and if you guard the eternity of empire which [he has expanded by] taki[ng it up, so that you often make the state share in this vow]; if you do these things accordingly, then, on behalf of the college of Arval Brothers, I [vow] that [it shall be fulfilled] with a golden ox." [The following were present in the college: P. Sallustius Blaesus, L. Ma]ecius Postumus, Q. Tillius Sassius, L. Veratius Quadratus, L. Venuleuis Apronianus.

[*AFA* 58, lines 36–43]

A90d – 23 April AD 90: expiation for a fallen tree
[When L. Antistius Rusticus and Ser. Julius Servianus were consuls], on 23 April when P. Sallustius Blaesus was president, [in the grove of the Dea Dia a sacrifice was made by the attendant and the assistants, in the form of a so]w and a lamb, for a sacred tree which had fallen down through age.

[*AFA* 58, lines 44–45]

A90e – 25 May, AD 90: feast and sacrifice to Dea Dia
[When Q. Accaeus Rufus and C. Caristanio Fronto were consuls] and P. Sallustius Blaesus was president, on 25 May, [in the house of P. Sallustius Blaesus, president for the second time, the Arval Brothers, recli]ning [to eat] made a sacrifice to the Dea Dia with incense and wine, and boys who were sons of senators, with their fathers [and their mothers both still alive, wearing the *toga praetexta*, went back to the altar with the assistants].

[*AFA* 58, lines 46–48]

A90f – 27 May, AD 90: feast at the house of the president and games
[Under the same consuls], on 27 May, when P. Sallustius Blaesus was president for the second time, [in the grove of the Dea Dia, the Arval Brothers made a sacrifice to the Dea Dia. At the altar], P. Sallustius [Blaesus, president for the second time] sacrificed two sows to make appeasement to the grove for (wood) being cut down and work being done; [then] P. Sallustius Blaesus, president for the second time [sacrificed a cow to honour the Dea Dia] on a hearth in front of the grove. [P. Sallustius Blaesus, president for the second time *(another name lost)*, L. Po]mpeius Catellius Celer, Q. Tillius Sassius, L. Venuleius Apronianus, L. Maecius Postumus, [took their seats in the four-columned (temple) and feasted on the meat from the sacrifice. Having put] on the *toga praetexta* and crowned with wreaths of corn, they ascended to a remote part of the grove of the Dea Dia [and, through P. Sallustius Blaesus, president for the second time they sacrificed a perfect lamb to the Dea Dia], and when the sacrifice was complete, they all made offerings of incense and wine. Then having put on their wreaths and having [anointed] the statues, [they made L. Veratius Quadratus] president for the year [from the next Saturnalia until] the following Saturnalia, and made L. Venuleius [Apronianus the high priest. Then they went back to the four-columned (temple)], and there, reclining in the dining-room, they feasted in honour of the president P. Sallustius Blaesus. After the feast, wearing a veil and sandals and with a c]rown of intertwined roses, he ascended from the remote part to above the starting-gates and [gave] the signal to the chariots [and stunt-riders, while *(name lost)* officiated; he presented the [winners] with palms and silver crowns. [On the same day in Rome], those who had been in the grove had dinner [at the house of the president, P. Sallustius Blaesus].

[*AFA* 58, lines 49–59]

A90g – 28 May, AD 90: feast at the house of the president of the Arval Brothers
[On 28 May at the house of the president, P. Sallustius Blaesus, the Arval Brothers]
had dinner to mark officially the sacrifice to the Dea Dia, and during the dinner, P.
Sallustius Blaesus, *(one name lost)*], L. Maecius Postumus, L. Arruntius Catellius
Celer, L. Veratius Quadratus made offerings of incense and wine; [boys with mothers
and fathers both still alive were in attendance – the same ones as on 25] May – and the
boys, veiled and [wearing the *toga praetexta* brought] fruit as offerings [to the altar],
helped by attendants and assistants; [after lamps had been lit], they laid their hands on
Etruscan vessels which they had their servants send from their houses.

[AFA 58, lines 60–63]

The rubric is very similar to (and gaps are supplied from) that for 20 May, AD 87. The boys in attendance
(known as *camilli*) are explicitly described here as senatorial, but are not named.

A90h – expiation (in April 91) for implements used to record acts of AD 90
[When M'. Acilius Glabrio and M. Ul]pius Traianus were consuls, on 29 April, [a
sacrifice was carried out in the grove of the Dea Dia by the attendant and the assistants
for] bringing [in metal] so that the deeds of P. Sallustius Blaesus, president for the
second might be inscribed.
    [Under the same consuls a sacri]fice was carried out in the grove of the Dea Dia by
the at]tendant and the assistants for metal having been brought out.

[AFA 58, lines 64–66]

A91a – 3 January, AD 91: vows for the new year
["Jupiter, Greatest and Best, if Emperor Caesar Domitian Augustus Germanicus, son of
Divus Vespasian, *pontifex maximus*, holding tribunician power, censor for life, father
of the fatherland, and Domitia Augusta], his wife, whom I con[sciously mention, shall
be alive and if] their household shall be well for the state [and the Roman People, the
Quirites] on 3 [January] in the next year for the Roman People, the Quirites; [and] if
you keep them safe that day from dang[ers which happen] or [are to happen] before
that day; and if you grant him as prosperous a situation [as I consciously menti]on;
and if you [pres]erve them in the same condition as at present [or better]; if you do
these things accordingly, then, on behalf of the college of Arval [Brothers], we vow
that a golden ox shall be yours."
    [Queen Juno], on the same terms according to which I vow to Jupiter Greatest
and Best that a golden ox [shall be his], which we have vowed today, if you do this
accordingly, then we vow, [in exactly the same] terms, on behalf of the college of
Arval Brothers, that a golden cow shall be yours.
    [Mi]nerva, on the same terms according to which we vow to Jupiter Greatest and
Best that a golden ox shall be his, which I have vowed today, if you do this accordingly,
then we vow, on behalf of the college of Arval Brothers, in exactly the same terms,
that a golden cow shall be yours.
    Public Well-Being of the Roman People, the Quirites, on the same terms
according to which we vow to Jupiter Greatest and Best that a golden ox shall be
his, which I have vowed today, if you do this accordingly, then we vow, on behalf of
the college of Arval Brothers, in exactly the same terms, that a golden cow shall be
yours. The following were present in the college: L. Veratius Quadratus, L. Maecius

Postumus, P. Sallustius Blaesus, Q. Tillius Sassius. L. Pompeius Vopiscus Arruntius Catellius Celer.

[*AFA* 59, column I, lines 0–23]

The rubric is very similar to (and partly reconstructed from **A87a**).

A91b – 7 January AD 91: promise of sacrifices later in the year

Under the same consuls, on 7 January, in the vestibule of the Temple of Concord the Arval Brothers, proclaimed a sacrifice to the Dea Dia in the second presidency of L. Veratius Quadratus. In the vestibule of the Temple of Concord, L. Veratius Quadratus, president of the Arval Brothers, his hands washed and his head covered, under the high open sky, facing East, proclaimed a sacrifice to the Dea Dia, alongside his colleagues: May it be good, favourable, fortunate, fine, and beneficial for Emperor Caesar Domitian Augustus Germanicus, *pontifex maximus*, and for Domitia Augusta, his wife, and for their whole house, and for the Roman People the Quirites, and for the Arval Brothers and for me! There shall be a sacrifice this year to the Dea Dia on 17 May in the house, on 19 May in the grove and in the house, and on 20 May in the house. The following were present in the college: L. Veratius Quadratus, L. Maecius Postumus, Q. Tillius Sassius.

[*AFA* 59, column I, lines 24–38]

A91c – 17 May, AD 91: sacrifice, feast and games
[*(several lines are lost from the start of the description of sacrifices to the Dea Dia on 17 May, AD 91, though the outline of the events can be determined from the formula of previous years (especially AD 87)*]

[took their seats in the four-columned (temple) and feasted on the meat from the sacrifice. Having put on the *toga praetexta* and crowned with wreaths of] cor[n, they ascended to a remote part of the grove of the Dea Dia and], through [L. Veratius Quadratus, president, they sacrifi]ced [a perfect lamb to the Dea Dia, and when the sacrifice was] com[plete, they all made offerings of incense and wine. Then having put on] their wreaths [and having anointed the statues], they made [L. Venuleius Apronianus presi]dent [for the year] from the [next] Saturnalia [until the following Saturnalia, and made *(name lost)* the high priest]. Then they [went back] to the four-column[ed (temple), and there, reclining in the dining-room], they feasted with table-linen [in honour of the president L. Veratius Quadratus]. After the feast, wearing a veil and sa[ndals and with a crown of intertwined roses], he asce[nded from the re]mote part to above the starting-gates [and gave the signal to the chariots and stunt-] riders, while L. [*(rest of name lost)*] officiated; he presented the [winners with palms] and silver crowns. [On the same day in Rome, those who had been in the grove had dinner] at the house of the president, L. Veratius Quadratus.

[*AFA* 59, column II, lines 1–13]

A91d – 20 May, AD 91: feast at the house of the president of the Arval Brothers

On 20 May at the house of the presi[dent, L. Veratius Quadratus], the Arval Brothers [had dinner] to mark offici[ally the sacrifice to the Dea Dia], and during the dinner, L. Veratius Qu[adratus, president *(one name lost)*], P. Sallustius Blaesus, L. Pompeius [Vopiscus Arruntius Catel]lius Celer, L. Julius Marinus C[aecilius Simplex] made offerings of incense and wine; boys [with mothers and fathers both still alive] were in attendance – the same ones as on 17 May – and the boys, veiled and [wearing the *toga praetexta* bro]ught fruit as of[ferings to the altar, helped by atte]ndants and assistants; after lamps had been lit, [they laid their hands on] Etru[scan vessels which] they had their servants send from their houses.

[*AFA* 59, column II, lines 14–23]

The rubric is very similar to (and gaps are supplied from) that for 20 May, AD 87. The boys in attendance (known as *camilli*) are not named. L. Julius Marinus Caecilius Simplex (= Rupke, *Fasti Sacerdotum* no.2051) makes his first appearance.

A91e – 5 November, AD 91: expiation for a fallen tree
When Q. Valerius Vegetus and P. Met[ilius Nepos] were consuls, on 5 November, when L. Veratius Quadratus was president for the second time, [a sacrifice was made by the atten]dant and assistants and the sacristan in [the grove of the Dea Dia in the form of a sow and a la]mb, in expiation for a tree which [had fallen down] through age.

[*AFA* 59, column II, lines 24–28]

A91f – ? November, AD 91: Arval Brother co-opted to replace Q. Tillius Sassius
Under the same consuls, [*(date lost)*], when L. Veratius Quadratus was president for the second time, [… in the vestibule of the Te]mple of Concord, the college of [Arval Brothers met] and there co-opted [L. Julius Marinus Caecilius Simplex?] as Arval Brother in place of Q. Tillius Sassius. The following were present: L. Veratius Quadratus, president, L. Venuleius Montanus [Apronianus, L. Julius] Marinus Caecilius Simplex, T. [*(rest of name lost)*].

[*AFA* 59, column II, lines 29–35]

A91g: expiation (in April 92) for implements used to record acts of AD 91
When Q. Volusius Saturninus, L. Venu[leius Apronianus were consuls], on 25 April, a sacrifice was ca[rried out in the grove of the Dea Dia by the at]tendant for bringing in metal [to inscribe and write (the deeds) of the president]. A sacrifice was carried out by the attendant [and the assistants for meta]l having been brought [in] and brought out to inscribe [and write the official acts of the president of the A]rval [Brothers].

[*AFA* 59, column II, lines 36–41]

SECTION B
THE *FASTI CONSULARES* (LIST OF CONSULS)

The consulship. Towards the end of his principate Nero had re-established the Tiberian pattern of six-month consulships. The chaos of AD 69 saw 16 consuls including Vitellius who declared himself perpetual consul. Vespasian did not follow this precedent but one of his formal powers from AD 69/70 was that all candidates for any magistracy whom he recommended should be elected. (Law on the Power of Vespasian, 10–13 = **H20**). Like Augustus at the start of his reign, Vespasian monopolised the *ordinarius* consulship, awarding only four of twenty outside his immediate family in his reign. With this, and the need to reward those who brought him to power (and then their sons a generation later), the Flavians awarded almost the same number of consulships as Tiberius, Gaius, Claudius and Nero combined, in half the time. Two-month consulships became almost the norm. At the same time the honour was differentiated: the six, non-Flavian consuls *ordinarii* in the 12 years of appointments by Vespasian and Titus were, statistically, far more privileged than in the republican system; so too were those who shared a consulship with the emperor. Being chosen as suffect to the emperor was an honour, as was being given a second or even third consulship; the first named consul of a pair also had precedence over his colleague.

The Fasti Consulares. Reference to the consuls remains the standard official way of dating documents within the Roman empire. The official list inscribed in Rome (in the temple of Janus, see **B2**), does not survive for this period. But the information needed to be available in towns around the empire, as confirmed by the partial survival of *Fasti* from Ostia and Potentia, carved on stone, and including historical events and local magistrates. Ordinary documents, especially from Pompeii and Herculaneum show great care being taken to give the correct (suffect) consuls for a given date. Such documents, together with many military discharge certificates (*diplomas*) enable the list that follows to be reconstructed. Even so it certainly has omissions and uncertainties: for example about 30 more men are known to have been consuls in the Flavian period though their consulships cannot be dated.

Bibliography: The Fasti are published in Degrassi, *Inscriptiones Italiae* 13.1 (1947 onwards, with commentary in Latin). Gallivan, *The Fasti for AD 70–96*, (Classical Quarterly 31 = 1981, pages 186–220) is vital, and often quoted below, but sometimes superseded by more recent evidence. An up-to-date list appears in A.E. Cooley, *Cambridge Manual of Latin Epigraphy* (2012) Appendix 1. *Prosopographia Imperii Romani* (ed. E. Klebs *et al.* Berlin 1897–8; 2nd edition 1933 and ongoing: text in Latin) gives biographical details and sources for all the consuls, but some parts of the alphabet are very out of date. [In the list below, the names of *consules ordinarii* appear in bold, with suffect consuls appearing below the consuls they replaced. Names in italics are of men who were certainly consul, but perhaps a year earlier or later than the date given.]

B1–B2: The restored *fasti consulares* forms the bulk of this section, but we begin with two contemporary poems which between them provide much information on how consulships might be regarded. Statius celebrated Domitian's seventeenth consulship which began on 1 January, AD 95, was his first consulship for three years, and proved to be his last. This actually followed one held by the son of Silius Italicus and celebrated by Martial in **B2**. **B3–B5** are the literary sources which help us to establish the naturally complicated fast for AD 69.

B1   **Statius celebrates Domitian's 17th consulship in AD 95**
    In joy the purple toga adds to Caesar's sixteen
    Consulships; Germanicus unveils a famous year
    And rises with new sun and constellations great,
    Shining more brightly himself, more strong than early Dawn.
    Let Latin laws exult, rejoice, o consulships,   5
    Let sevenfold hills of Rome the heavens strike with pride

More great; and more than all the rest, Evander's peak[1] –
The *fasces* new have entered in the Palatine,
Our prayers are heard, the double privilege returns;[2]
The senate-house enjoys surpassing Caesar's modesty.[3]   10
The great renewer of eternal years himself
Uplifts his faces and gives thanks from both his doors –
Janus, tied to neighbouring Peace, whom you bade
To settle every war and swear obedience to
The laws of the new forum.[4] Look he raises hands,   15
Palms up, on either side and speaks with twofold voice:
"Hail, Parent of the World,[5] you who prepare with me
To herald centuries. Your Rome would always wish thus
To see you in my month; thus ages should be born,
Thus new years enter in. Delight the calendar   20
Eternally. Your shoulders many times be clothed,
In toga purple, keenly wrought by your Minerva's hands.[6]
You see new brightness in the temples, higher flames
On altars? My month's stars grow warm for you, and for
Your virtues; cavalry and tribes rejoice, and purpled   25
Senators; each magistrate takes glory reflected
From the consul.[7] How could the previous year compare?
Come, tell me, mighty Rome, count, great Antiquity,
The lists with me, but don't go over trivial ones,
Just those my Caesar gets some credit from surpassing.   30
Augustus thirteen times held Latin *fasces* as the years
Rolled by; but only lately began deserving them:
You surpassed your ancestors while young.[8] Great honours you
Refuse, forbid. But still you'll yield to the senate's prayers
And oft allow this day. A longer sequence remains   35
To come, as lucky Rome as often grants you consulships,
Then three and four times more. You'll found with me another age,
Tarentum's ancient altar will be renewed by you.[9]

---

[1] Evander in legend left Arcadia in Greece and first settled the Palatine hill of Rome.

[2] *fasces* were the axes and rods carried by a consul's *lictores* ('bodyguard') as a symbol of authority. A consul had twelve lictors, but an emperor was given twenty-four, hence the 'double privilege'. Mussolini revived the *fasces* as a symbol of his own 'fascist' authority.

[3] The point is that the senate would have urged Domitian to hold the consulship each year – perhaps sycophantically, perhaps to increase the prestige of the senators who became suffects (see note 7).

[4] For the Temple of Janus, built next to Vespasian's Temple/Forum of Peace, see **K64–K72**. Janus had two faces, hence two voices (line 16) and his temple had two doors (line 12).

[5] 'Parent of the World' is a poetic improvement on the title 'father of the fatherland'.

[6] Minerva was viewed by Domitian as his special patroness (**L44–L49**) and was goddess of crafts, including spinning, hence it would be appropriate for her to make a consular toga for her protégé.

[7] It had long been the greatest honour to share the consulship with the emperor. Statius implies that this honour extended to any magistrate in office in that year. He was certainly right in the sense that they would be able to say they held the magistracy in the year of Domitian's 17th consulship.

[8] The totals are as follows: Augustus 13; Tiberius 5; Gaius 4; Claudius 5; Nero 5; Vespasian 9; Titus 8.

[9] The altar of Tarentum on the Campus Martius was an important site for the *ludi saeculares*, celebrated in AD 88 (**L17–L21**). If Domitian really had celebrated another 17 consulships and then a further three or four times that number, he would almost have lived to celebrate another *ludi saeculares* (due at intervals of 110 years).

A thousand trophies you shall win – if triumphs you allow.[10]
Not subject to new tribute, Bactra, Babylon remain;[11]   40
Nor yet are laurel-wreaths from India in Jove's lap;
Nor yet does China or Arabia yield;[12] nor does all
The year have honour – ten more months desire your name."[13]
So Janus said, and gladly closed the door behind him.[14]
Then all the gods were struck with awe, and gave their signs   45
To happy heaven, while Jove vouchsafed to you, great king,
Eternal youth, and promised his own years.

[Statius, *Silvae* 4.1 (published 95)]

B2   Silius Italicus congratulated on his son's consulship
To Caesar, Muses, render pious incense
And victims, on behalf of your Silius.
Behold the dozen *fasces* again return,
His son is consul and so with noble rod
The bard's Castalian home resounds: so Caesar,   5
One and only safeguard of the world, commands.
Yet in his joy there's still one thing to wish for –
The happy purple and a third consulship.
The senate may have granted Pompey special
Honours, as did Caesar for his son-in-law,   10
That peaceful Janus thrice did celebrate their
Names: but this is how Silius would rather
Number these often repeated consulships.

[Martial, *Epigram* 8.66 (published 94)]

Martial celebrates the consulship in September 94 of Silius Decianus, son of Tiberius Catius Asconius Silius
Italicus, the epic poet, consul in 68, **R20**. A consul was traditionally accompanied by twelve lictors carrying the
fasces (rods and axe symbolic of authority). Livy (6.34.6) tells us that a lictor would ceremonially knock on the
door of the consul's house when he returned home. The Castalian spring at Delphi was traditionally a source
of inspiration. Pompey the Great and Agrippa (Augustus Caesar's son-in-law) each held three (whole-year)
consulships. A third consulship did indeed become the pinnacle of achievement for those outside the imperial
family around this time (Pliny the Younger, *Panegyric* 58.2), and Martial is almost certainly right to see that
prospect as a tribute to Silius Italicus himself, as any achievements of Silius Decianus are unknown and Italicus'
second son actually died shortly afterwards without a consulship (Martial, *Epigram* 9.86).

---

[10] Statius alludes to Domitian's refusal of a triumph in 93 after a campaign against the Sarmatae (see **N48**).
[11] Bactra and Babylon were part of the Parthian Empire and had both been conquered by Alexander the
Great.
[12] India and China are both coupled, hyperbolically, as future conquests by Augustus (Horace, *Odes*
1.12.56). Arabia was the target of an unsuccessful expedition around 25 BC (LACTOR 17, N18–N22),
and a successful one in 106, under Trajan.
[13] i.e. Domitian had renamed September and October as Germanicus and Domitianus, (see **T6–T8**) but
10 months were still available for him to rename. In 192 Commodus did name all the months after his
various names and titles, but neither he nor the names survived the year.
[14] Closing the gates of Janus had been a symbolic Augustan revival denoting peace.

B3   Plutarch on Otho's changes to the consuls for AD 69

In the Senate Otho spoke at length, and in the manner of a generous and popular leader. He said that he would allocate part of the time which he had intended to serve as consul to Verginius Rufus, and that he would observe all the consulships designated by Nero or Galba.

[Plutarch, Otho 1.2]

B4   Tacitus on Otho's changes to the consuls for AD 69

Otho went about his imperial tasks as if peace was assured: some he fulfilled with proper regard for the state; many others in undignified haste for some short-term benefit. He himself became consul up to the first of March with his brother, Titianus. He appointed Verginius for the following months to appease to some extent the armies in Germany. Pompeius Vopsicus was appointed as Verginius' colleague on the excuse of long-standing friendship, but most interpreted it as a tribute paid to Vienne. The other consulships remained as Nero and Galba had intended, with Caelius Sabinus and Flavius Sabinus for July, Arrius Antoninus and Marius Celsus for September. Even when Vitellius won he did not veto these honours.

[Tacitus, Histories 1.77.2]

Plutarch and Tacitus both seem to be using a common source, as is confirmed by the almost identical way in which they both immediately afterwards describe Otho's appointments to priesthoods. G. Townend 'The consuls of AD 69/70' in *American Journal of Philology* 1962, 113–129 explains the changes clearly.

B5   Tacitus on Vitellius' changes to the consuls for AD 69

So as to open some spare months to honour Valens and Caecina, Vitellius shortened the consulships of others, and ignored that of Marcus Macer as having been a leader of Otho's partisans; he also postponed the consulship promised by Galba to Valerius Marinus. He had not offended in any way, but was a mild man, slow to take offence.

[Tacitus, Histories 2.71.2]

Caecina Alienus and Fabius Valens had commanded individual legions in Vitellius' German army and been the most eager to put him on the throne (Tac. *Hist.* 1.52.3, 53.1, 57.1). These two Vitellians are often paired and contrasted by Tacitus (*Hist.* 2.55–6, 2.99, 3.62). Valerius Marinus did in fact take offence sailing from Puteoli to Africa in only 9 days (Pliny, *NH* 19.3 = **M44**) presumably to go over to Vespasian.

The Consul Lists for AD 69–96

69	Ser. Sulpicius Galba Imp. Caes. Aug. II	T. Vinius
	Imp. M. Otho Caesar Augustus	L. Salvius Otho Titianus
Mar.	L. Verginius Rufus II	L. Pompeius Vopiscus
Apr.	T. Flavius Sabinus	Cn. Arulenus Caelius Sabinus
July	P. Arrius Antoninus	Marius Celsus
Sep.	Fabius Valens	A. Caecina Alienus
		Oct 31: Rosius Regulus
Nov.	C. Quinctius Atticus	Cn. Caecilius Simplex
	A. Vitellius Imperator, cos. perp.	

Galba: cos I ord AD 33, emperor June 68 – 15 Jan 69.

T. Vinius: Galba's right hand man (Plut. *Galba* 12ff), killed with him (Tac. *Hist.* 1.42).

M. Otho: emperor 15 Jan, consul 28 Jan (**A69e**).

L. Salvius Otho Titianus: elder brother of the emperor Otho (Tac. *Hist.* 1.77.2).

L. Verginius Rufus II: in 68 put down Vindex's revolt, but refused to put himself forward as emperor. Cos III in 97. Y. Pliny, *Letters* 2.1 and 9.19 (LACTOR 19, P13i–j) suggest a life in retirement under the Flavians.

L. Pompeius Vopiscus: known only from Tac. *Hist.* 1.77.2 above.

T. Flavius Sabinus: Vespasian's nephew, see **J6** and **B72** for his second consulship.

Cn. Arulenus Caelius Sabinus: a distinguished lawyer.

P. Arrius Antoninus: from Narbonese Gaul, governed Asia, cos II 97, grandfather of emperor Antoninus Pius.

Marius Celsus: frequently mentioned by Tacitus and Plutarch, possibly a source for the civil war and on Roman tactics, and governor of Syria in 72 (**M16**). Syme, *Tacitus,* app. 32.

Fabius Valens: first proclaimed Vitellius (Tac. *Hist.* 1.57) and led his forces; death and 'obituary' *Hist.* 3.62.

A. Caecina Alienus: supporter of Vitellius (Tac. *Hist.* 1.53 etc) but defected to Flavian side (Tac. *Hist.* 2.101–1, 3,13), gaining 'honours beyond expectation' (Jos. *JW* 4.644) though no actual posts are known). He fell suddenly AD 78/9 (**C16b, H50, P2**).

Rosius Regulus: consul for 1 day (31 Oct) after Caecina went over to Vespasian (Tac. *Hist.* 3.37).

C. Quinctius Atticus: pro-Flavian consul, captured with Flavius Sabinus, he just escaped execution (Tac. *Hist.* 3.73–75).

Cn. Caecilius Simplex: known from Tac. *Hist.* 2.60 and 3.67.

Vitellius: his 'perpetual consulship' is known from **H7** and Suet. *Vit.* 11, though Tacitus fails to mention it where we might have expected it (*Hist.* 2.91 or 3.55).

70	Imp. Caesar Vespasianus Augustus II	Titus Caesar Vespasianus
July	C. Licinius Mucianus II	Q. Petillius Cerialis Caesius Rufus
Sep.	*T. Aurelius Fulvus*	*Q. Julius Cordinus C. Rutilius Gallicus*
Nov.	L. Annius Bassus	C. Laecanius Bassus Caecina Paetus

Vespasianus: Vespasian's first, suffect, consulship had been in AD 51 as a reward for commanding a legion in the invasion of Britian.

Titus: became consul two days after his 30th birthday, and *in absentia* (Tac. *Hist.* 4.38.1).

Mucianus: Vespasian's chief lieutenant, previously suffect cos *c.* AD 64. See **U3**.

Q. Petillius Rufus: a 'close relation to Vespasian' (Tac. *Hist.* 3.59.2), probably his son-in-law (Dio 65.18.1). Jos. *JW* 7.82 = **H30** gives a (slightly confused) account of Petillius' appointment. He had commanded legion IX in Britain in AD 61 and would return as governor AD 71–74 (Tac. *Ann.* 14.32.3 and *Agr.* 8.2–3, 17.1–2). Cos II 74.

T. Aurelius Fulvus: (*PIR* A[2] 1510) from Nimes. Commander of legion III 'Gallic' in AD 64 (*ILS* 232) winning a victory and consular decorations from Otho in AD 69 (Tac. *Hist.* 1.79). Then presumably joined Vespasian, prospering greatly as cos I, probably in 70 (Gallivan 200), as governor of Nearer Spain 75–78, cos II ord in AD 85, and city prefect. His grandson, Antoninus Pius became emperor.

C. Rutilius Gallicus: see **U10a, b**. This is the probable year for this man's first consulship (Gallivan 200).

L. Annius Bassus: commander of legion XI in AD 69 (Tac. *Hist.* 3.50), active in the Flavian advance on Rome. A biography of him is mentioned by Y. Pliny, *Letters* 7.31.5.

C. Laecanius Bassus Caecina Paetus: his name suggests that he was related to the Laecanii Bassi family, which provided the suffect of 40 and the cos ord of 64, and to A. Caecina Paetus, suffect 37.

71	**Imp. Vespasianus III**	**M. Cocceius Nerva**
Mar.	Caesar Domitianus	Cn. Pedius Cascus
May	"	C. Calpetanus Rantius Valerius Festus
July	L. Flavius Fimbria	C. Atilius Barbarus
Sep.	L. Acilius Strabo	Sex. Neranius Capito
Nov.	Cn. Pompeius Collega	Q. Julius Cordus

M. Cocceius Nerva: the future emperor Nerva. Born *c.* AD 35. Aristocrat, with direct ancestors of the same name consul in 36 BC and *c.* AD 21. See **U11**.

Domitian: aged only 19, hence probably a suffect consulship (Suet. comments on this at *Dom.* 2), but for four months, not just two as all other consulships in AD 71.

Cn. Pedius Cascus: It was possibly his wife, Rectina whom Pliny tried to rescue from Herculaneum (texts give Tascus or Cascus as the name). Prominent consulship early in Vespasian's reign, but otherwise unknown.

C. Calpetanus Festus: son presumably of cos 47. Legate of III Augusta in Africa. 'A young spendthrift, highly ambitious and related to Vitellius' (Tac. *Hist.* 4.49.1), he 'publicly supported Vitellius, but secretly contacted Vespasian, intending to back whoever was stronger' (Tac. *Hist.* 2.98.1). Career in **U12**.

L. Flavius Fimbria: little is known about him (*PIR* F² 269), and no connection is likely with Flavian dynasty.

C. Atilius Barbarus: unknown except for the date of his consulship.

L. Acilius Strabo: sent as praetor by Claudius to adjudicate on land ownership in Cyrene and prosecuted by Cyreneans in 59 (Tac. *Ann.* 14.18). Went on to command army of Lower Germany (*ILS* 6460).

Sex. Neranius Capito: only known as a consular name.

Cn. Pompeius Collega: in charge of legion IV under overall command of Vespasian who appointed him acting-governor before a replacement arrived (Jos. *JW* 7.58–60). Governor of Galatia, *c.* 75. Son cos ord 93.

Q. Julius Cordus: Tacitus, *Hist.* 1.76 mentions a Julius Cordus making Aquitania swear loyalty to Otho, presumably as governor of this public province. He is otherwise unknown.

72	**Imp. Vespasianus IV**	**Titus Caesar II**
May	C. Licinius Mucianus III	T. Flavius Sabinus II
	M. Ulpius Traianus	?
	L. Nonius Calpurnius Asprenas	?

Mucianus: see **B70**.

T. Flavius Sabinus: see **B69**. Nothing further is heard of him, so he must have died soon after 72.

M. Ulpius Traianus: father of emperor Trajan. From Baetica, S. Spain, he commanded a legion under Vespasian and was rewarded with the consulship and patrician status (**U14**). Governed Syria 73/4–78 (**M18, M19**) and Asia (79/80). Fragment of the *fasti* from Ostia naming him probably belongs in this year, though possibly in AD 70.

L. Nonius Calpurnius Asprenas: Son and grandson of consuls (AD 6, AD 29). His full career is known from **U15**. AD 72 seems the most probable year for his consulship (Gallivan). His son was cos 94.

73	**Caesar Domitianus II**	**L. Valerius Catullus Messallinus**
May	L. Aelius Oculatus	Q. Gavius Atticus
	M. Arrecinus Clemens	?
	Sex. Julius Frontinus?	

Caesar Domitianus II: Domitian's only cos ord under Vesp. came at Titus' insistence (Suet. *Dom.* 2.1).

L. Valerius Catullus Messallinus: no official posts are known except this and a second consulship in 85. But he was notorious as an informer (Tac. *Agr.* 45.1 = **P11b**; Y. Pliny, *Letter* 4.22.5 = **T18**; Juv. *Sat.* 4.113–8 = **G1**).

L. Aelius Oculatus: name known only from a diploma, but given his very rare *cognomen*, he must be the father of the Oculatae sisters, Vestal virgins executed *c.* 82 (Suet. *Dom.* 8.3).

Q. Gavius Atticus: nothing else is known of this man.

M. Arrecinus Clemens: see **J20** for this relation by marriage of Vespasian, who had been made praetorian prefect in 70, despite being a senator.

Sex. Julius Frontinus: distinguished general, statesman, writer, administrator. Probably from Gaul. Urban praetor at start of AD 70 (Tac. *Hist.* 4.39), commander of an army in the German/Gallic revolt, AD 70 (**H32**), and governor of Britain 74–77, he must have been consul in 73 or 72. Probably campaigned with Domitian in Germany (**N18–N21**), governed Asia in 86. Water commissioner from AD 97 (**K77**). Cos II 98, cos III ord 100.

74	**Imp. Vespasianus V**	**Titus Caesar III**
Jan.	Ti. Plautius Silvanus Aelianus II	"
Mar.	L. Junius Vibius Crispus II	?
May	Q. Petillius Cerialis Caesius Rufus II	T. Clodius Eprius Marcellus II
Jul.	[...]	[*M. Hirtius Fr*]on[*to Neratius Pansa*] ?
Sep.	C. Pomponius ...	L. Manlius Patruinus

T. Plautius Silvanus Aelianus II: for this distinguished figure, cos I AD 45, city prefect, see **U6**.

Vibius Crispus: on this wit, cos I suff in unknown year, see **U2**.

Q. Petillius Cerialis Caesius Rufus II: see above on AD 70.

T. Clodius Eprius Marcellus II: well known literary figure, cos I suff probably in 62, see **U4**.

M. Hirtius Fronto Neratius Pansa? known as a consul (*ILS* 4537), Pansa's career is now known from the very fragmentary *AE* 1968.145. His consulship should fall around 74, and 'Fronto' would fit the fragmentary ..ON.. from the Ostia *fasti* (above), though he could also have been Domitian's consular partner for 76.

C. Pomponius: known as cos from *AE* 1968, 7 but 'not a word can be said' – Syme *RP* 4.145

L. Manlius Patruinus: known only from a wax tablet from Herculaneum and for having been manhandled in the town of Sena in Etruria (Tac. *Hist.* 4.45).

75	**Imp. Vespasianus VI**	**Titus Caesar IV**
Mar.	Caesar Domitianus III	L. Pasidienus Firmus
?	*Sextus Sentius Caecilianus*	?

L. Pasidienus Firmus: probably the son of the many-named cos ord 65, A. Licinius Nerva Silianus P. Pasidienus Firmus, and grandson of cos ord AD 7. With such ancestry, he might have expected to be cos ord, but a consulship only 10 years after his father, shared with Domitian, and in years when the cos ord were being monopolised by Vespasian and Titus was signal honour. The man himself is unknown, except as consul.

Sextus Sentius Caecilianus: U17, M4, M5 (described as consul designate, either for this year or 76).

76	**Imp. Vespasianus VII**	**Titus Caesar V**
Mar.	Caesar Domitianus IV	?
	L. Tampius Flavianus II	M. Pompeius Silvanus Staberius Flavinus II
Dec.	Galeo Tettienus Petronianus	M. Fulvius Gillo

Tampius Flavianus and **Pompeius Silvanus**: both suffects in AD 45 and paired by Tacitus, *Hist.* 2.86.3 as 'rich and elderly' governors of Pannonia and Dalmatia respectively in AD 69. Both also governed Africa and were Aqueducts Commissioners (**K77**). Silvanus: in Africa 54–57 (LACTOR 19, M69b; Tac. *Ann.* 13.52); aqueducts 71–73. Tampius: see **U5**.

Galeo Tettienus Petronianus: family probably from Assisi where many inscriptions of slaves and freedmen have been found; his younger brother was cos in 81.
M. Fulvius Gillo: from Forum Novum in Sabine hills, 50km north of Rome (*ILS* 3596), was an adopted son cos 98.

77	Imp. Vespasianus VIII	Titus Caesar VI
Jun.	Caesar Domitianus V	
Sept.	C. Arruntius Catellius Celer	M. Arruntius Aquila
	Cn. Julius Agricola	

L. Pompeius Vopiscus C. Arruntius Catellius Celer: (full name given in Arval Records) was arval from at latest 75, and president in 85; governor of Lusitania (MW 104 = **M34**); consul with Aquila MW 460 = **M8**.

M. Arruntius Aquila: *ILS* 980. Son of cos 66, XVvir. See Syme *RP* 4.372.

Cn. Julius Agricola: Tacitus' father-in-law and subject of his biography, see **U21**.

78	D. Junius Novius Priscus (Rufus?)	L. Ceionius Commodus
	Sex. Vitulasius Nepos	Q. Articuleius Paetus
Sep.	Q. Corellius Rufus	L. Funisulanus Vettonianus

D. Junius Novius Priscus: a Novius Priscus, was exiled as a friend of Seneca in AD 65. This could be the same man or his son. In either case it is not clear why he was he was one of the only pair of non-Flavian *ordinarii* consuls in Vespasian's reign. He went on to command the legions of Lower Germany, *c.* 79–81.

L. Ceionius Commodus: from Etruria. Governed Syria *c.* 78–81. See **U18** for imperial descendants.

Sex. Vitulasius Nepos: from Samnium, C. Italy, near where he built an aqueduct, MW 469 = **K80**.

Q. Articuleius Paetus: two generations of Articuleii Paeti are known to have been in the senate in 18 BC (Dio 54.14.3). This man's son and grandson were both cos ord (101 and 123), perhaps because Trajan had been his questor in 78 – Syme, *Tacitus* 31n.

Q. Corellius Rufus: From N. Italy. Legate of Upper Germany *c.* 82 (diploma *ILS* 1995). Y. Pliny paid tribute to him on his death aged 67 under Nerva (*Letter* 1.12).

L. Funisulanus Vettonianus: MW 307 = **U19** gives his whole career.

79	Imp. Vespasianus IX	Titus Caesar VII
	Caesar Domitianus VI	?
Mar.	L. Junius Caesennius Paetus	P. Calvisius Ruso Julius Frontinus
Sep.	T. Rubrius Aelius Nepos	M. Arrius Flaccus

L. Junius Caesennius Paetus: his father, Caesennius Paetus, was cos ord 61, commander in Armenia under Nero (Tac. *Ann.* 15.6–17), governor of Syria 70–72 (Jos. *JW* 7.59, 7.219ff), and married a Flavia Sabina (**J7a**). This son from an earlier marriage served his father in Armenia (Tac. *Ann.* 15.28.2) and eventually governed Asia, *c.* 93/4.

P. Calvisius Ruso Julius Frontinus (Rüpke 1065: *AE* 1914.267; *PIR* C² 350). Proconsul of Asia in 97/8. Governed Cappadocia between 104 and 107.

T. Rubrius Aelius Nepos: (*PIR* R² 124) probably son of T. Rubrius Nepos (*PIR* R² 129), senator and deputy water commissioner under Gaius/Claudius.

M. Arrius Flaccus: name known from diplomas including MW 401 = **N53** and Picenum fasti only.

80	Imp. T. Caesar Vespasianus Aug. VIII	Caesar Domitianus VII
Jan.	A. Didius Gallus Fabricius Veiento II	L. Aelius Plautius Lamia Aelianus
	Q. Aurelius Pactumeius Fronto	"
Jun.	C. Marius Marcellus Octavius P. Cluvius Rufus	"
Nov.	M. Tittius Frugi	T. Vinicius Julianus

A. Didius Gallus Fabricius Veiento II: adopted son of A. Didius Gallus, suffect consul of 39 and governor of Britain. A prominent senator and priest, he wrote a work 'Codicils' mocking his peers which earned his exile in AD 62 (Tac. *Ann.* 14.50), but he was greatly favoured by Flavians, with consulships from each the emperors (date of cos I under Vespasian is unknown), and continued so under Nerva and Trajan (Y. Pliny, *Letters* 12.5 and *Panegyric* 58.1). See **U9** with further refs.

L. Aelius Plautius Lamia Aelianus: Son of Plautius Silvanus Aelianus, cos 45, and adopted by the aristocratic Aelius Lamia family. His was an unusually long consulship, and he is attested as consul with three different co-consuls (with Veiento late Jan/early Feb, *AE* 1948.56; with Pactumeius, date unknown, MW 11; with Cluvius Rufus on 13 June, *CIL* 16.26). The first husband of Domitia, wife of Domitian, he was executed by Domitian (Suet. *Dom.* 10.2; Juv. *Sat.* 4.154 = **G1**).

Q. Aurelius Pactumeius Fronto; (Rupke 856 = *PIR* P² 38) first consul from Africa, see **U23**.

C. Marius Marcellus Octavius Publius Cluvius Rufus: his full name (on a diploma, *CIL* 16.26), makes him some connection to Cluvius Rufus, historian and cos 40.

M. Tittius Frugi: commanded legion XV at fall of Jerusalem (Jos. *JW* 6.237), thus taking the legion over from Titus' command having served under him.

T. Vinicius Iulianus: only known as cos and not necessarily related to five Vinicius consuls known between 33 BC – AD 30 (Syme *RP* 2.531–2).

81	**L. Flavius Silva Nonius Bassus**	**L. Asinius Pollio Verrucosus**
Mar.	M. Roscius Coelius	C. Julius Juvenalis
May	L. Vettius Paullus	T. Junius Montanus
Jul.	C. Scoedius Natta Pinarius	T. Tettienus Serenus
Sep.	M. Petronius Umbrinus	L. Carminius Lusitanicus

L. Flavius Silva Nonius Bassus: from Urbs Salvia (so not a Flavian family member) see **K98**. His cos ord was a reward for service in the Jewish War, where he commanded legion XXI and governed Judaea from AD 73–81, leading the capture of Masada (Jos. *JW* 7.252, 275–407).

L. Asinius Pollio Verrucosus: (Rüpke 746: *PIR* A² 1243) little is known about him, but his cos ord suggests he was a direct descendant of C. Asinius Pollio, cos ord AD 23 and therefore of M. Agrippa.

M. Roscius Coelius: Possibly from Siciliy. Commander of legion XX in Britain by 69, he and his legion were insubordinate and late to come over to Vespasian (Tac. *Hist.* 1.60 and *Agr.* 7.3). This presumably delayed his consulship.

C. Julius Juvenalis: known just as consul (**A81c**) and possibly *sodalis Augustalis* in 69 (Rüpke 2046).

L. Vettius Paullus: known only as a counsul (**A81c**).

T. Junius Montanus: possibly 'Montanus the Belly' of Juv. *Sat.* 4.107 – otherwise only known as a consul.

C. Scoedius Natta Pinarius: known only as a consular name.

T. Tettienus Serenus: from Assisi (see on elder brother, cos 76); imperial legate of Gallia Lugdunensis, 78/9; co-opted into Augustan/ Claudian brotherhood in 92, and *pontifex* in 101 and 102, died in 115.

M. Petronius Umbrinus: propraetorian governor of Cilicia *c.* 79–81, probably grandson of C. Petronius, cos 25. A son is mentioned in **A87g**.

L. Carminius Lusitanicus: his father, cos 51, had governed Lusitania giving this unusual *cognomen* to his son, the elder brother of cos 83: otherwise unknown (*PIR* C² 434).

82	**Imp. Domitianus VIII**	**T. Flavius Sabinus**
	?	[?Q. Servaeus In]noc(ens)?
	?	[...]an(us)
	?	[?M. Mettius Mo]dest(us)
Jul.	P. Valerius Patruinus	L. Antonius Saturninus
Sep.	M. Larcius Magnus Pompeius Silo	T. Aurelius Quietus

T. Flavius Sabinus: Grandson of Vespasian's brother, the city prefect, see **J14**, executed in 82, allegedly because he was announced as emperor in a slip of the tongue (Dio 67.14.1–2).

Small fragments of the Fasti from Ostia show 3 pairs of suffects early in 82, whose identity is very uncertain.

M. Mettius Modestus: see **P9**. Mettius's father of the same name was equestrian procurator of Syria under Claudius.

P. Valerius Patruinus: governed Cappadocia for period around 85, then Syria 87/8–89/90. *Sodalis Augustalis* 91 to 94 (*CIL* 6.1988).

L. Antonius: leader of rebellion in Jan 89, see **P8a–g**, and Syme *RP* 3.1072.

M. Larcius Magnus Pompeius Silo: known from diploma (MW 402) giving his consulship (Gallivan 210).

T. Aurelius Quietus: propraetorian legate of Lycia/Pamphylia in 80/1.

83	Imp. Domitianus IX	Q. Petillius Rufus II
	L. Junius Vibius Crispus III	A. Didius Gallus Fabricius Veiento III
Apr.	M. Annius Messalla	C. Fisius Sabinus
Jun.	L. Tettius Iulianus	Terentius Strabo Erucius Homullus
Sep.	L. Calventius Sex. Carminius Vetus	M. Cornelius Nigrinus Curiatius Maternus

Q. Petillius Rufus II: now thought to be a younger brother of Petillius Cerialis cos I suff 70, cos II suff 74. If so he was probably brother-in-law to Flavia Domitilla, Domitian's (dead) sister. Date of his first cos unknown.

Fabricius Veiento: see on cos II suff, AD 80.

M. Annius Messalla: *IRT* 516 shows adlection by Vespasian and Titus. Son cos 90.

C. Fisius Sabinus: known only as a name on a dated token (*AE* 1969/70, 6 – Gallivan 190).

L. Tettius Julianus: legate of VII Claudia in Moesia in AD 69, winning consular ornaments under Otho (Tac. *Hist.* 1.79.5). Did not follow their defection to Vespasian (Tac. *Hist.* 2.85, 4.39 and 4.40.2) but was restored to favour and legate of III Augusta by AD 81 (*AE* 1954, 137). Won victory at Tapae in AD 88 (Dio 67.10.1; Statius, *Silvae* 3.3.115ff = **S9b** celebrated marriage of his sister to the father of Claudius Etruscus, imperial freedman.

Terentius Strabo Erucius Homullus: 'only a name' Syme *RP* 2.489.

L. Calventius Sex. Carminius Vetus: Son of cos 51, governed Asia late 96 and 97. Younger brother of cos 81. Son and grandson both consuls (116 and 150).

M. Cornelius Nigrinus Curiatius Maternus: From Liria in Baetica, S. Spain. Enlisted to senate by Vespasian and Titus with rank of a praetor (*AE* 1973, 283). Governed Aquitania, around 81, Moesia in 85 and Syria in 90s. May be the Curiatius Maternus of Tacitus, *Dialogus*.

84	Imp. Domitianus X	C. Oppius Sabinus
May?	?	L. Julius Ursus
Sep.	C. Tullius Capito Pomponianus Plotius Firmus	C. Cornelius Gallicanus
	?	[… G]allus

C. Oppius Sabinus: son or nephew of cos 43, but his great prominence as cos ord with Domitian, then immediately governor of Moesia in 85 in charge of four legions, is unexplained. There he was surprised by Dacian incursion and killed (Suet. *Dom.* 6.1, **N32, T2**).

L. Julius Ursus: possibly a relative of Julia, Domitian's niece, unusually promoted to consulship after an equestrian career culminating as prefect of Egypt (Dio 67.3.1 and 4.2), and see also **M29, U43–U44**.

C. Tullius Capito Pomponianus Plotius Firmus: possibly adopted son of Plotius Firmus, Otho's praetorian prefect. Special legate of Vespasian for boundary redistribution in Numidia, named on various boundary stones (**M9**).

C. Cornelius Gallicanus: legate of Lugdunensis 83 (*ILS* 2118), and went on to operate poor-relief under Trajan (*ILS* 6675). A Gallicanus mentioned by Jos. *JW* 3.344 as military tribune in Vespasian's army in AD 67 would have been exactly the right age.

Gallus: the end of a name on a fragment of the Ostia *fasti*. Syme (*RP* 2.767) suggests Raccius Gallus (see **L55**).

85	**Imp. Domitianus XI**	**T. Aurelius Fulvus II**
Jan.	[-----]atus	
Mar.	C. Rutilius Gallic(us) II	L. Valer(ius) Catullus Mess(allinus) II
May	M. Arrecinus Clemens II	L. Baebius Honoratus
Jul.	P. Herennius Pollio	M. Herennius Pollio f(ilius)
Sep.	D. Aburius Bassus	Q. Julius Balbus
Nov.	C. Salvius Liberalis Nonnius Bassus	[... Ore]stes

Aurelius Fulvus: see cos 70

C. Rutilius Gallic(us) II: see cos 70.

L. Valer(ius) Catullus Mess(allinus) II: cos I in 73.

M. Arrecinus Clemens II: cos I in 73, he was put to death by Domitian (Suet. *Dom.* 11.1).

L. Baebius Honoratus: had probably been proconsul of Macedonia *AE* 1900,130

P. Herennius Pollio: the unusual honour of father and son holding joint consulships is only paralleled in the first century by the Flavians.

M. Herennius Pollio: the ex-consul mentioned by Y. Pliny 4.9.14 as an opposing speaker in a trial of AD 103. He seems to have married a daughter of Helvidius Priscus, and owned clay-pits which made roof tiles for Rome.

D. Aburius Bassus: nothing known about this man or family except as dating formula on a diploma.

Q. Julius Balbus: unknown background, but went on to be proconsul of Asia (*ILS* 4051) under Trajan, perhaps 98 or 100 (*PIR* I^2 199).

C. Salvius Liberalis: See **U26** for this man, the anti-hero of the Cambridge Latin Course!

Orestes: the name appears on a fragment of the Ostia *Fasti*. He cannon be identified, but the ending suggests he was Greek.

86	**Imp. Domitianus XII**	**Ser. Cornelius Dolabella Petronianus**
Jan.	C. Secius Campanus	"
Mar.	?	Q. Vibius Secundus
May,	Sex. Octavius Fronto	T. Julius Candidus Marius Celsus
Sep.	A. Bucius Lappius Maximus	C. Octavius Tidius Tossianus
		L. Iavolenus Priscus

Ser. Cornelius Dolabella Petronianus: *ordinarius* for his aristocratic background (ancestors cos 44 BC, AD 10, AD 55) and mother Petronia had been first wife of Vitellius (Tac. *Hist.* 2.64.1). His father was a serious candidate for emperor in 68/9 (Plut. *Galba* 23.1; Suet. *Galba* 12.2; Tac. *Hist.* 1.88, 2.63–4) leading to his death in 69.

C. Secius Campanus: known only as a consular name.

Q. Vibius Secundus: his name, but not that of his partner appear on the Fasti Potentini. Not in *PIR* V^1, but nephew of Vibius Crispus who had saved his father from worse punishment for maladministration of Mauretania in AD 60 (Tac. *Ann.* 14.28).

Sex. Octavius Fronto: proconsul in Chersonese in Bosporus under Dom (MW 310); propraetorian legate of Dom in Lower Moesia in 92 (diplomas); 'Fronto, famously distinguished in war and peace' Martial 1.55.

Ti. Julius Candidus Marius Celsus: From the east (Syme *RP* 4.260). Perhaps son of Marius Celsus, cos 69 (Syme, *Tac.* app. 32). He went on to a prominent career, governing Galatia & Cappadocia 89–92, cos II ord 105, city prefect, arval until after 109.

A. Bucius Lappius Maximus: legate of legion VIII 'Augustan' and governor of Bithynia *c.* 82. After his consulship he crushed the Saturninus rebellion (see **P8**), receiving a second consulship (**B95**).

C. Octavius Tidius Tossianus L. Javolenus Priscus: see MW 309 = **M77**. Prominent as a jurist (*Digest* 1.2.2.53, 36.1.48, 40.2.5, **M78**), though Y. Pliny (6.15) reports a faux pas at a literary recital.

87	Imp. Domitianus XIII	L. Volusius Saturninus
Jan.	C. Calpurnius Piso Licinianus	"
May,	C. Bellicus Natalis Tebanianus	C. Ducenius Proculus
Sep.	C. Cilnius Proculus	L. Neratius Priscus

L. Volusius Saturninus: honoured by a consulship shared with Domitian because three previous generations of the family had been consuls (12 BC, AD 3, AD 56). Not otherwise prominent.

C. Calpurnius (Crassus Frugi?) Piso Licinianus: part of the famous family descended from Crassus and Pompey and probably nephew of Galba's would-be heir. Perhaps too aristocratic, he was suspected by Nerva and Trajan, and finally executed under Hadrian.

C. Bellicius Natalis P. Gavidius Tebianus: (full name on diploma *Scripta Classica Israelica* 2012, no.54) from Vienne in S. Gaul, son of cos 68. For his sarcophagus, see **L37**.

C. Ducenius Proculus: name shows he is from Patavium: otherwise 'only a name and date' – Syme *RP* 4.372.

C. Cilnius Proculus: from the ancient ruling family of Arretium in Etruria (Livy 10.3.2) to which Maecenas belonged. Father of homonymous consul in 100 (*CIL* 11.1833, much decorated by Trajan and Hadrian).

L. Neratius Priscus: From Saepinum in Samnium (C. Italy). Probably brother of Hirrius Fronto Neratius, cos 73/4. Two sons both reached consulships in 95 and 97, Syme *RP* 7.597ff. He is known to have been prefect of the treasury and governor of Pannonia (*ILS* 1034).

88	Imp. Domitianus XIV	L. Minicius Rufus
	D. Plotius Grypus	
May	Q. Ninnius Hasta	Libo Rupilius Frugi
Sept.	M. Otacilius Catulus	Sex. Julius Sparsus

L. Minicius Rufus: some connection with the proconsul of Crete-Cyrene (*PIR* M² 626); legate of Lugdunensis at some point between 83 and 88 (**N64**). Consul with Domitian (**L30**) for the *ludi saeculares* – still in post on 15 April; procos in Bithynia, (Y. Pliny, *Letters* 10.72).

D. Plotius Grypus: son of a naval captain (see note 193) and brother of the city prefect (**U7**). Enlisted by Vespasian to the senate and put in charge of legion VII 'Claudian' and further promoted to praetorship at the start of 70 (Tac. *Hist.* 3.52.3 and 4.39.1).

Q. Ninnius Hasta: unusual *nomen* shows he came from Samnium (*PIR* N²100): held a senatorial post relating to Rome's aqueducts (*ILS* 8682) before his consulship. His son was cos ord in 114.

L. Rupilius or Scribonius Frugi: presumably the son of the immensely aristocratic cos ord 64 M. Licinius Crassus Frugi (see Tac. *Hist.* 4.42). Libo Frugi (Libo was a family name) was named as an ex-consul by Y. Pliny 3.9.33 (referring to a trial of 100/101).

M. Otacilius Catulus: known only as cos and for legal case about his will in 95 (Celsus, *Digest* 31.29 – *PIR* O² 171).

Sex. Julius Sparsus: Y. Pliny addressed *Letters* 4.5, 8.3 to this man, probably the wealthy friend of Martial (12.57).

89	T. Aurelius Fulvus	M. Asinius Atratinus
May	P. Sallustius Blaesus	M. Peducaeus Saenianus
Sep.	A. Vicirius Proculus	M'. Laberius Maximus

T. Aurelius Fulvus: from Nimes. His father had been cos 70, cos II ord 85 alongside Domitian, hence the honour of a cos ord for the son. His own son became the emperor Antoninus Pius. The consul of 89, 'an honest and strict man' (*HA Pius* 1.2) must have died soon after his consulship. There were just three pairs of consuls for the year.

M. Asinius Atratinus: appears on the fasti from Potentia (discovered after *PIR* A² 1319), but his prominence is unexplained, unless his name shows some connection to L. Sempronius Atratinus orator, cos 34, *triumphator* 21 BC, and adoption into Asinius clan.

P. Sallustius Blaesus: active member of arvals, before 78 to after 90, see Section A *passim*. Not clear whether he is the same as Sallustius Lucullus killed by Dom. as governor of Britain (Suet. *Dom.* 10.3).

M. Peducaeus Saenianus: the family was probably Sabine (Syme *RP* 2.599): and it is likely that members of this family were important equestrian officials under Claudius and Vespasian (Peducaeus Fronto, *PIR* P² 223, procurator under Claudius; Peducaeus Colo, *PIR* P² 222, prefect of Egypt under Vespasian). This may well have led to his cos, and to the cos ord of (probably) his brother in 93.

A. Vicirius Proculus: obscure, but family name suggests Etruria or Campania (Syme *RP* 1.459).

M'. Laberius Maximus: His father had been procurator of Judaea in AD 71 (Jos *JW* 7.216); prefect of the corn supply in 80 (**A81c**); prefect of Egypt of 83, (diploma – *ILS* 1996), praetorian prefect, **U44**. He governed Lower Moesia by 100, cos II in 103. Exiled for conspiring against Trajan (Dio 68.9.4).

90	Imp. Domitianus XV	M. Cocceius Nerva II
	L. Cornelius Pusio	"
	L. Antistius Rusticus	Ser. Julius Servianus
	Q. Accaeus Rufus	C. Caristanius Fronto
	P. Baebius Italicus	C. Aquilius Proculus
Oct.	L. Albius Pullaienus Pollio	Cn. Pinarius Aemilius Cicatricula
		Pompeius Longinus
	M. Tullius Cerialis	Cn. Pompeius Catullinus

M. Cocceius Nerva II: Nerva's second *ordinarius* consulship in partnership with an emperor shows how close the future emperor (**U9**) was to the Flavian regime.

L. Cornelius Pusio: from Baetica. His early career is detailed in *CIL* 6.31706, while his brief funerary inscription (*AE* 1915.60) describes him as consul, VII vir and proconsul (of Asia or Africa).

L. Antistius Rusticus: his career is known from an inscription put up in his honour *c.* AD 93, when governor of Pisidia, for having taken measures against famine, see **U27** and **M52**.

Sex. Julius Servianus: From Spain, adopted by Julius Ursus (**B84, U43–U44**). Went to govern U. Germany and Pannonia *c.* 98–101, cos II ord 102, cos III 134. Hadrian's brother-in-law. Committed suicide, aged 90, after opposing Commodus as successor to Hadrian: Dio 69.17.2, *HA Hadr* 15.8, 23.8, 25.8).

Q. Accaeus Rufus: neither he nor any member of his family is mentioned in *PIR* A².

C. Caristanius Fronto: his career, known from **U28** shows rapid rise from equestrian status and commanding a cavalry unit under Vespasian.

P. Baebius Italicus: honoured at Tlos see **U29**.

C. Aquilius Proculus: funerary inscr. at Puteoli to his wife (*AE* 1984, 194) shows he was also XVvir and proconsul. This proconsulship was of Asia, under Trajan, *c.* 103/4 (*ILS* 7193/4).

L. Albius Pullaienus Pollio: proconsul of Asia under Trajan *ILS* 4046, *c.* 104/5.

Cn. Pinarius Aemilius Cicatricula Pompeius Longinus: son of Cn. Pinarius Aemilius Cicatricula, probably cos 71/72 (Gallivan 206). Possibly made tribune of praetorian guard by favouritism under Galba (Tac. *Hist.* 1.31.3); certainly governed Judaea in 86, Moesia Superior between 93–6, and Pannonia in 98 (diplomas *CIL* 16.39, 42).

M. Tullius Cerialis: his name appears clearly on the Fasti Potentini. Y. Pliny, *Letters* 2.11.9 refers to a Tuccius Cerialis as an ex-consul. This may be a mistake for Tullius, cos 90, but see on cos 93.

Cn. Pompeius Catullinus: not known except as a name on the fasti Potentini.

91	M'. Acilius Glabrio	M. Ulpius Traianus
May,	D. Minicius Faustinus	P. Valerius Marinus
Nov.	Q. Valerius Vegetus	P. Metilius (Sabinus?) Nepos

M'. Acilius Glabrio: son of Acilius Aviola, member of Domitian's *consilium* (Juv. *Sat.* 4.94–6). cos. ord. with Trajan in 91 (Dio 67.12.1). During his consulship, however, Domitian forced him to fight a lion at his Alban estate (for this episode see **P13**), and Dio suggests his success prompted Domitian's jealousy and his condemnation for adopting Jewish practices (Dio 67.14.2–3). Suetonius, *Domitian* 10.2 describes him as being put to death in exile for planning revolution.

M. Ulpius Traianus: the future emperor Trajan (Dio 67.12.1) whose father had been cos in 70 (or 72).

D. Minicius Faustinus: known as consul from several diplomas (e.g. *AE* 1962, 264). Father of cos 117.

P. Valerius Marinus: a man of this name was arval in 69 (**A69g–j**), and was denied a consulship by Vitellius, see **B5**. The cos 91 would presumably be his son.

Q. Valerius Vegetus: from Iliberri in S. Spain (*CIL* 2.2074, 2077), his son was cos 112.

P. Metilius (Sabinus?) Nepos: from Novaria in NW Italy. Earlier posts unknown, but governor of Britain in the years before 98, and arval their records from 105, being replaced in 118. See Birley, *Roman Government* 100–2.

92	Imp. Domitianus XVI	Q. Volusius Saturninus
Jan.	L. Venuleius Montanus Apronianus	"
May	L. Stertinius Avitus	Ti. Julius Celsus Polemaeanus
Sep.	C. Julius Silanus	Q. Junius Arulenus Rusticus

Q. Volusius Saturninus: like his brother (**B87**), honoured by a consulship shared with Domitian because three previous generations of the family had been consuls (12 BC, AD 3, AD 56). Not otherwise prominent.

L. Venuleius Montanus Apronianus: on Arval Records as president in 80 and then in 92 (**A80f**).

L. Stertinius Avitus: possibly from Africa, (Syme *Tac.* 597); Martial addressed 7 epigrams to him, esp. book 9 preface, suggesting he wrote poetry. Probably father of consuls of 112 and 113.

Ti. Julius Celsus Polemaeanus: from Ephesus or Sardis, he entered the senate under Vespasian and became the first consul from the Greek East. He governed Asia 105–107. The famous library of Celsus in Ephesus was funded by him and also became his mausoleum (**U30**).

C. Julius Silanus: co-opted as arval 86 (**A86d** but not recorded as present at any meetings thereafter).

Q. Junius Arulenus Rusticus: From N. Italy, as tribune of the plebs he had wanted to veto Thrasea Paetus' condemnation in AD 66 (Tac. *Ann.* 16.26), but was dissuaded. Praetor in 69, and wounded in an attempt at peacemaking (Tac. *Hist.* 3.80). Domitian made him consul at the end of 92 but a year later he was accused of writing laudatory biographies of Helvidius Priscus, condemned and executed, see **P11**.

93	Sex. Pompeius Collega	Q. Peducaeus Priscinus
May?	T. Avidius Quietus	Sex. Lusianus Proculus
Sep.?	C. Cornelius Rarus Naso	[Tuccius Ceria??]lis

Sex. Pompeius Collega: the *ordinarius* consulship was a tribute to this man's father who had fought under and with Vespasian and been cos suff in 71. This man is mentioned by Y. Pliny, *Letters* 2.11.

Q. Peducaeus Priscinus: for the family background, see on (probably) his brother, cos 89. This man's son and grandson were cos ord in 110 and 141.

Avidius Quietus: From Faventia, NE Italy. A friend of the Stoic 'martyr' Thrasea Paetus, executed by Nero in AD 66, so an odd, and perhaps conciliatory choice for consul in AD 93. Friend of Y. Pliny (*Letters* 9.13.15) and Plutarch (*e.g. Moralia* 478B). He could be the 'honest propraetor' of **M51**. Governed Achaia in AD 95 (MW 318) and Britain in AD 98. See also **M41** (requested as patron of a veteran colony). His son was cos in 111.

Sex. Lusianus Proculus: (*PIR* L[2] 372 as Lucianus Proclus) known only from Dio 67.11.5.

C. Cornelius Rarus Sextius Na[...] (Rupke 1365). Fragmentary building inscr. from Lepcis Magna, *IRT* 523 includes career as XVvir, cos, governor of Africa.

[Tuccius Ceria??]lis: from the three letters at the end of a name on the Fasti at Ostia, the ex-consul referred to by Y. Pliny, *Letters* 2.11.9 as Tuccius Cerialis may have been consul in 93, but Pliny may more probably have referred to Tullius Cerialis, cos 90, and [...] lis be someone unknown.

94	L. Nonius Calpurnius Asprenas Torquatus	T. Sextius Magius Lateranus
May	M. Lollius Paullinus D. Valerius Asiaticus Saturninus	C. Antius A. Julius Quadratus
Sep.	L. Silius Decianus	T. Pomponius Bassus

L. Nonius Calpurnius Asprenas Torquatus: (*PIR* N² 133) fourth generation of Nonii Asprenates to be consul, see on his father, cos 72, above. He went on to be cos II ord in 128.

T. Sextius Magius Lateranus: presumed son of the patrician T. Sextius Africanus, cos 59 (on whom Tac. *Ann.* 13.19). Career unknown.

M. Lollius Paullinus D. Valerius Asiaticus Saturninus: aristocrat: his grandfather had been twice consul (35, II ord 48); his father died while consul designate; his long name also proclaimed descent from Lollius Paullinus, father-in-law of Gaius. This man's career was distinguished too, cos II ord 125 and city prefect 134.

C. Antius A. Julius Quadratus: from Pergamum. Arval by 78, and president for the third time in 111. Under Trajan he governed Syria (100–104), was cos II ord in 105 and governed Asia *c.* 109/110. *ILS 8819, 8819a*.

L. Silius Decianus: son of Silius Italicus, cos ord 68, proconsul of Asia in 77, see **B2**.

T. Pomponius Bassus: Y. Pliny, writing to congratulate him on his retirement, perhaps *c.* 103, gives a brief summary of his career (4.23.2). Served as legate of the proconsul in Asia 79–80; career probably delayed under Domitian. Went on to govern Galatia & Cappadocia from 95–100 (*ILS* 5840).

95	**Imp. Domitianus XVII**	**T. Flavius Clemens**
Jan.	L. Neratius Marcellus	"
May	A. Bucius Lappius Maximus II	P. Ducenius Verus
Sep.	Q. Pomponius Rufus	L. Baebius Tullus

T. Flavius Clemens: see **J16**. Domitian's closest male relative, married to his niece, father to his chosen heirs. He did not survive the year (see **D14**).

L. Neratius Marcellus: From Saepinum in Samnium (C. Italy). Elder son of Neratius Priscus, cos 87, adopted son of M. Hirrius Fronto Neratius, cos 73/4. His career is known from a fragmentary inscription at Saepinum, (*ILS* 1032, *AE* 1990.217). He went on to be Water Commisioner before 101 and cos II 129. As governor of Britain, 103, he gave a military tribunate to Suetonius the biographer at the request of Y. Pliny (*Letters* 3.8.1). See Birley, *Roman Government* 104–112.

A. Bucius Lappius Maximus II: cos I in 86, the second consulship was reward for crushing the Saturninus revolt in 89, see **P8b**. He was still a *pontifex* in 102.

P. Ducenius Verus: (*PIR* D² 200). Not prominent.

Q. Pomponius Rufus: His career is known from a building inscription in Libya, **H2**.

L. Baebius Tullus: went on to govern Asia at some point under Trajan.

96	C. Manlius Valens	C. Antistius Vetus
May	Q. Fabius Postuminus	T. Prifernius [Paetus?]
Sep.	Ti. Catius Caesius Fronto	M. Calpurnius [...]icus

C. Manlius Valens: Dio 67.14.5 tells us that he died after becoming consul in his 90ᵗʰ year. He had commanded legions in AD 52 (Tac. *Ann.* 12.40.1) and AD 69 (Tac. *Hist.* 1.64.4). The appointment of such an old man as *cos ord* could have been seen by the senate as insulting (Syme, 'Domitian: The Last Years' in *Chiron* 13, p.135) or reassuring (Jones, *Domitian* 166).

C. Antistius Vetus: his aristocratic family explains his *ordinarius* consulship: direct ancestors of the same name held consulships in 30 BC, AD 23, 46, 50; other relatives in AD 26 and 55.

Q. Fabius Postuminus: went on to govern Moesia (103) and Asia (115/6).

T. Prifernius [Paetus?] Sabine name (Syme *RP* 2.584); nothing else known (Syme *RP* 2.486n) except for recent diploma (*AE* 2008, 1738) showing him in command in Moesia Superior in AD 112.

Ti. Catius Caesius Fronto: consul at Nerva's accession (**T42**), orator known from Pliny letters (2.11.3, 4.9.15, 6.13.2, 9.13.4). Probably related to the poet (T. Catius) Silius Italicus, (see on Silius Decianus cos 94). Arval from at least AD 101–5.

M. Calpurnius [...]icus: cannot be identified from parts of his name on the Fasti at Ostia.

SECTION C

CASSIUS DIO, *ROMAN HISTORY*, BOOK 66
ABRIDGED BY XIPHILINUS

Cassius Dio (born c. AD 160s, died after AD 229) came from a prominent Greek family in the Roman province of Pontus & Bithynia. Although ethnically Greek, he held Roman citizenship, and was thus able to pursue a senatorial career in Rome. He was a successful politician, honoured in 229 with a second consulship held with the emperor, having served as a provincial governor in Africa, Dalmatia and Upper Pannonia during the AD 220s (Dio 80.1.2–3). At the same time he wrote the *Roman History*, tracing the history of Rome from its foundation to his own day. Being a 'senatorial historian' brought advantages, but also a tendency shaped by his own experience (he lived through the tyranny of Commodus and the Civil Wars which followed it, and into the much more measured reign of Septimius Severus), to make strong black-and-white judgements of previous emperors based on how well or badly they treated the senatorial aristocracy. He may also have written his *Roman History* partly with the agenda of creating a blueprint to help guide Septimius and his successors towards what Dio saw as desirable imperial behaviour.

Being comprehensive in scope (originally in 80 books) and written in Greek it seems to have become the standard account of Roman history in the Eastern empire. It also became prime material when the tenth-century Byzantine Emperor Constantine VII wanted collected anthologies of examples of virtue and vice, pithy remarks and embassies. These anthologies often quote whole paragraphs from Dio's *History*. In addition there was demand for abridgements of Dio. In the 1070s the monk John Xiphilinus of Trapezus composed "Epitomes of Dio's *Roman History* ... covering the reigns of twenty-five Caesars from Pompey the Great to Alexander Severus". Xiphilinus' method of working was roughly speaking, to strike out passages of Dio that he thought repetitive or uninteresting (e.g. Claudius' invasion of Britain!) and to copy the rest almost verbatim. In 1118 for his *Epitome of World History* Zonaras used Dio as his main source, paraphrasing Dio rather than quoting. Both Xiphilinus and Zonaras found that the manuscripts they used had parts of Dio's narrative missing (see 70.1.1) and over the next few centuries further books including all the last 20 were lost, so that for the reign of Nero onwards we only have Dio as excerpted or summarised. This reconstituted version is what is presented by standard texts of Dio, such as the Loeb edition (tr. Cary, 1914–1927, easily available online). But "strictly speaking, we have to admit that these books do not exist." (Murison, introducing his superb commentary on books 64–67 (Atlanta, Georgia 1999): many of my notes are obviously endebted to this work, henceforth referred to as Murison, *Commentary*). Instead I present below the text of Xiphilinus while other quotation or summaries of Dio are presented in the thematic sections of the LACTOR. Subheadings are my own and deliberately adhere to the 'chapter' numbers of Dio/Xiphilinus' text.

For the Flavian period, 'Dio' must be used with great caution. The narrative of the eruption of Vesuvius (**C21–3**) might have used Tacitus' account, if not the letters of Y. Pliny (6.16, 6.20), and Xiphilinus clearly reports Dio at length: instead it merely reflects popular superstition. The previous paragraph (**C20.3**) contains a misdating, a demonstrably inaccurate accusation against Domitian, and a likely textual error (note 93). Further uncertainties are created by the way in which the text has survived, described above. But Xiphilinus remains our only chronological narrative of significant length for 70–96!

C1   The start of Vespasian's reign

(66.1.1) That concludes my account of these struggles for power. Once they were over, Vespasian was acknowledged as Emperor by the senate, while Titus and Domitian were given the honorific titles of Caesar. Even though they were still in Egypt and Palestine respectively, Vespasian and Titus appropriated the consulship for themselves.[15]

---

[15]   Vesp. acknowledged by the senate: Tac. *Hist.* 4.3–10; Dom. usurps title of Caesar: Tac. *Hist.* 4.2.1; Vesp. and Titus enter consulship *in absentia* Tac. *Hist.* 4.38.1.

(1.2) A number of omens and dreams had long since signalled that Vespasian was destined to be emperor.[16] On the country estate, where he had spent a great deal of his time, an ox approached him while he was dining, sank to its knees, and placed its head under his feet. And then again, while he was taking a meal, a dog deposited a human hand under his table. (1.3) A magnificent cypress tree, which had been uprooted and felled by a violent gust of wind, righted itself the following day of its own accord and continued to flourish as before. In his dreams he was told that when the emperor Nero lost a tooth, he would himself become emperor. The loss of that tooth actually happened the following day. Then too, Nero himself once dreamed that he had personally driven Zeus' carriage up to Vespasian's house. (1.4) Such omens required expert interpretation; but not the prophecy of a Jew called Josephus. He had been taken prisoner and put in chains by Vespasian, but his only reaction was to laugh aloud. "For the time being you can shackle me," he said; "but in a year's time you will set me free – when you have become emperor."[17]

C2   Mucianus governs Rome (AD 70)

(2.1) Thus it is clear that Vespasian, like a number of others, was born to rule. While he was still away in Egypt, Mucianus carried on the whole administration of government with the help of Domitian.[18] Mucianus was inclined to give himself airs, boasting loudly that he had personally bestowed the emperorship on Vespasian.[19] He was particularly proud of the fact that Vespasian called him his "brother," and had given him authority to take whatever decisions he wished without reference back to himself, and simply to issue written instructions under the emperor's name. (2.2) This was the reason that he wore a ring, which had been sent to him so that he could place the emperor's seal on official documents. Indeed, Mucianus and Domitian handed out offices in all directions, appointing a succession of governors, procurators, praetors and even consuls. (2.3) In fact, they conducted themselves in every way so much as if they were absolute monarchs that Vespasian once sent a despatch to Domitian to this effect: (2.4) "I am grateful, my boy, that you still permit me to be emperor and that you have not yet dismissed me."[20]

(2.5) Mucianus was also all too eager to rake in untold sums of cash from all possible sources, which he piled up in the public treasury. In this way he spared Vespasian the inevitable unpopularity by diverting it to himself. His constant motto was that cash formed the sinews of government, and for this reason he would urge Vespasian to acquire it from every possible source.[21] He himself had never ceased to do so from

---

[16] For these and other portents see Suet. *Vesp.* 5. and **H13–H15**. Tacitus gives a typically intelligent evaluation of such stories at *Histories* 1.10.3, 2.1 and 2.78.2 (the cypress tree) dismissing them as Flavian propaganda, believed by the credulous.

[17] For Josephus' own account of his prediction, see Jos. *Jewish War* 3.400–401 = **H13**.

[18] Gaius Licinius Mucianus: an appraisal of his character by Dio, which may have originally belonged here can be found at **U3d**. For Tacitus' assessment, see **U3c**. For his authority: *Hist.* 4.4.1, 4.11.1, 4.39.2, 4.44.1, 4.46.1–3.

[19] *Hist.* 4.4.1, also describing the boast of having 'given' Vespasian supreme power. But Tacitus' account largely backs up Mucianus' boast (*Hist.* 2.74–78). Suet. *Vesp.* 13.1 condemns Mucianus' morals.

[20] Compare Suet. *Dom.* 1.3, also forgetting Vespasian's well-known sense of humour.

[21] Vespasian declared at his accession that 40,000 million sesterces were required to put the country back on its feet (Suet. *Vesp.* 16) and Tacitus records financial worries being debated in the senate immediately after Vespasian's accession (*Hist.* 4.9.1, 4.47).

the beginning, and had as a result provided massive reserves for the empire – and significant quantities for himself as well.

C3　　　Gallic and German revolts (AD 70)

(3.1) In Germany a number of tribal revolts against Rome took place, none of which need to be recorded in my *Abridgement* at least.[22] But there was one incident, which was certainly surprising. On his own initiative, a leading nobleman of the Lingones, called Julius Sabinus, recruited a private army and, claiming to be a descendant of Julius Caesar, took the name of Caesar. (3.2) He lost a series of battles and escaped to one of his country estates. There he concealed himself in an underground mausoleum, which he first burned to the ground. Everyone assumed that he was dead, but in fact he remained there in hiding for nine years together with his wife, and had two sons by her.[23] (3.3) The revolts in Germany were suppressed by Petillius Cerialis in a long series of battles, in one of which so many Romans and barbarians were slaughtered that the waters of the adjacent river were dammed up by the corpses of the dead.[24]

(3.4) Domitian was becoming frightened of his father, both because of his past actions and even more so because of his future plans, which were ambitious in the extreme. He was spending a great deal of time in the Alban Mount district of Rome, having become obsessed by his infatuation for Domitia, the daughter of Corbulo.[25] He had seduced her away from her husband, Lucius Lamia Aelianus,[26] and at that point made her one of his mistresses, though he married her later.

C4　　　Titus and the siege of Jerusalem, AD 70 [27]

(4.1) Titus had by now been appointed to command the Jewish campaign. He tried to win over the Jews by a combination of negotiation and assurances, but when this proved unsuccessful, he reverted to military action. His early engagements proved indecisive, but in time he gained the initiative and laid siege to Jerusalem. The city was defended by three walls, including the one which surrounded the Temple. (4.2) So the Romans piled up earthworks against the outer wall, wheeled up their siege-engines, and in combat at close-quarters drove back those who sallied out to counter-attack. Meanwhile they kept the walls clear of defenders with covering fire from their archers and slingers, of which they had a large number, supplied by several barbarian kings.[28] (4.3) But the Jews too had considerable support, both from the local area and from the wider Jewish *diaspora*, not only within the Roman Empire, but also beyond the Euphrates. They fired missiles and hurled stones, both by hand and catapults, and with considerable effect, since they occupied the higher position. (4.4) They launched counter-attacks also by night and day, wherever they saw an opportunity, setting fire

---

22　Here Xiphilinus is clearly referring to his own version of Dio, explicitly abridging the original text, and ignoring the whole of the subject matter of Tacitus, *Histories* books 4–5.

23　Tac. *Hist.* 4.67.2 and Plutarch, *Moralia* 770D = **H34**.

24　Cerialis' campaigns: Tac. *Hist.* 4.71–79 and 5.14–24.

25　Dom's licentious behaviour (see Suet. *Dom.* 1.3, Tac. *Hist.* 4.2 and Index of People, Domitian: sexual relations) was often associated with his Alban villa, actually 15 miles SE of Rome.

26　L. Aelius Plautius Lamia Aelianus, cos. 80: see **B80** and further references.

27　Vastly more detail is provided, of course, by Josephus'*Jewish War* (books 5–6), but Dio's account may well be more objective. It may be derived from Tacitus, who had provided a comprehensive introduction to the Jewish people (*Hist.* 5.1–13) just before the *Histories* fails.

28　Dio means the 'friendly kings' of Emesa and Commagene, mentioned by Tacitus as providing support, see **M55**.

to the siege engines and killing large numbers of their enemies. They also undermined the Roman earthwork by digging it out from below and taking the spoil back under the walls. As for the battering rams, sometimes they lassoed them from above and snapped them off, sometimes they dragged them up with hooks, and at other times they dampened the effect of their blows with thick planks, fastened together and reinforced with iron, which they let down in front of the wall. (4.5) But it was the lack of water that inflicted the most severe suffering on the Romans, since it was brackish and had to be transported from a distance. The Jews had another advantage with their underground tunnels. They excavated them from inside the city, under the walls and well out into the countryside; then they would slip out through them to ambush the Roman water-carriers and inflict casualties on their scattered patrols. But Titus had them all blocked up.

C5   Losses on both sides

(5.1) The effect of these activities was to inflict serious casualties and loss of life on both sides. Titus himself was hit by a rock on the left shoulder, which left him with a permanently weakened arm. (5.2) After some time, however, the Romans got over the outer wall, and once they had established a strongpoint between the two walls, proceeded to attack the inner one. But this presented them with a different set of problems. Their enemy had now all retreated behind that inner wall, which gave them a much-reduced perimeter to defend. This proved a great deal easier. (5.3) So Titus issued a second proclamation, offering them all an amnesty. But still they held out. Any that deserted or were taken prisoner still managed secretly to disrupt the Romans' water-supplies, and if anywhere they came across individual soldiers out on their own, they would assassinate them. As a result Titus ceased to take prisoners or accept deserters. (5.4) Meanwhile, parts of the Roman army were becoming demoralised – a typical problem in any long drawn out siege operation. Rumour reinforced their suspicion that the city was impregnable, and desertions began. The Jews, despite their shortage of supplies, treated them well, in order to demonstrate that deserters were coming over to their side also.

C6   The destruction of the Temple in Jerusalem, AD 70

(6.1) Though the siege engines forced a breach in the wall, even this failed to lead to the capture of the city; indeed the Romans suffered severe casualties as they tried to force their way through. The Jews also set fire to some of the nearby buildings, hoping that this would also block the Romans' advance, even if they gained control of the perimeter wall. But the effect was that they damaged the wall itself, and also quite unintentionally burnt down the wall of the temple precinct. This gave the Romans a way into the temple, (6.2) but even so, superstitious fears prevented the soldiers from breaking in immediately. But at last, driven forward by Titus, they forced an entry.[29] This made the Jewish resistance even more ferocious, almost as if they regarded it as a heaven-sent stroke of luck to be able to fight in front of their own temple and to die defending it. The common people were stationed in the front courtyard, members of the Sanhedrin[30] on the steps, and the priests in the temple building itself. (6.3) Their

---

[29]   Dio and Josephus completely disagree on Titus' role, though both intend to praise him: the Jewish Josephus stressed Titus' repeated attempts to prevent the destruction and pillage of the Temple (N5). For Dio and his sources, however, for a commander to lead the assault was a matter for great praise.

[30]   The supreme legal Jewish authority, 71 in number.

numbers were few and they were facing fearful odds, but they were not defeated until a part of the temple itself was set alight. But then they died willingly, some spitting themselves on the Roman swords, some killing one another, some committing suicide, others leaping into the flames. It was clear to all, especially to themselves, that for them it was not death but victory, salvation, and a heavenly blessing that they had perished at the same moment as their temple.

C7 Aftermath of the capture of Jerusalem

(7.1) Nevertheless, some prisoners were also taken, including Bargiora their commander.[31] He was the only one executed as part of the victory celebrations. (7.2) Such was the sack of Jerusalem.[32] The city fell on a Saturday, which for Jews even now is their holiest day.[33] Thereafter, it was decreed that Jews who continued to observe their ancestral traditions should pay an annual two-drachma tax to Jupiter of the Capitoline.[34] In recognition of their achievement, both generals received the accolade of "*imperator*," but neither took the title "Judaicus". All the other trappings appropriate to such a famous victory were voted for them, including even triumphal arches, covered with the trophies of victory.[35]

C8 Vespasian in Alexandria, AD 69–70

(8.1) When Vespasian marched into Alexandria, the Nile overflowed, in a single day rising by three inches more than usual. This was said to have only ever happened once before. Vespasian himself publicly healed two men, who had approached him as a result of visions in their sleep. One was blind; the other had a crippled hand. The latter he cured by standing on his hand, the former by smearing spit on his eyelids.[36] (8.2) Despite these signs of heavenly honour, the people of Alexandria gave him no sign of welcome; rather, they totally detested him, so much so that both privately and in public they poked fun and hurled abuse at him. They had expected to reap great rewards from having been the first to declare him emperor;[37] instead, they got nothing and instead had extra taxes heaped upon them. (8.3) Many and various were the ways in which he extracted revenues; he missed no opportunity, whether arbitrary or disgraceful, and raised cash from sources secular and sacred alike. He renewed many taxes that had been neglected, increased those that were still current, and instituted yet more that were unprecedented. (8.4) Afterwards, he followed the same practice among Rome's other subjects, both in Italy and even Rome itself.[38] This was why

---

[31] Simon ben Gioras was one of two leaders of the revolt, who only surrendered after failing to tunnel his way out of the city, after Titus had already left (Josephus, *Jewish War* 7.25–36).

[32] Dio wrongly treats the destruction of the Temple and the fall of Jerusalem as the same.

[33] The planetary week was not a traditional part of the Roman calendar, but is attested in AD 79 at Pompeii (Cooley[2] H3) and was described by Dio (*c.* AD 220) as 'recently adopted' but 'now very widespread everywhere, including with the Romans' (Dio 37.18–19).

[34] With cynical opportunism, Vesp. decreed that the annual tax formerly paid by Jews for the upkeep of the Temple in Jerusalem should now go to Rome (Jos. *JW* 7.218 = **N15**). Dom's extension and enforcement of the tax was unpopular (Suet. *Dom.* 12.2) and Nerva relaxed it (Dio 68.1.2, coins – Smallwood, *Nerva to Hadrian* 20). For an official in charge of its collection, see **M46**.

[35] For celebrations of the victory, see **E6, N7–N13**.

[36] Tac. *Hist* 4.81 gives considerable detail, and the interesting comment that eyewitnesses still maintain the truth of the miracle, even under a changed dynasty. Suet. *Vesp.* 7.2 also gives the story.

[37] Tac. *Hist.* 2.79.1 'The first move towards putting Vespasian on the throne started at Alexandria', and **H16–H18**.

[38] Vespasian's venality is frequently mentioned: Suet. *Vesp.* 16; Eutropius 7.19; Aurelius Victor 9.

the people of Alexandria were so hostile: they were outraged both at the taxation described above and because he sold off most of the royal palace. Among the many forms of abuse they hurled at him was the chant,

"What do you want? What do you want?"

"Six obols more! Six obols more!"

(8.5) As a result even the easy-going Vespasian got fed up and issued orders for a poll tax of six obols to be levied on every man, and started to plan other forms of punishment as well. The chant itself was somewhat offensive, but there was also something about its rhythm, which simply got under his skin and enraged him. (8.6) But when Titus persuaded him to let them off, Vespasian agreed. The Alexandrians, however, did not know when to stop. At one of their crowded public meetings, they all started together to shout at Titus,

"We grant him a pardon; we grant him a pardon."

"He doesn't know how to be Caesar."

(8.7) And so they continued to chance their luck with such abuse, indulging in these unrestrained displays of disorderly behaviour, which were always likely to work to their disadvantage, and tested to its limits the emperor's goodwill. (9.1) In the end he simply ignored them.[39]

C9   Vespasian as sole ruler of Rome

He sent a despatch to Rome cancelling for all alike, whether living or deceased, the loss of civil rights, which had been imposed by Nero and his successors on those who had been condemned for so-called treason. He also put an end to prosecutions for all accusations of this kind.[40] (9.2) He expelled the astrologers from Rome, even though he himself regularly consulted their leading practitioners.[41] As a compliment to Barbillus,[42] himself an astrologer, he had even allowed the Ephesians to celebrate their sacred games, though he never granted this privilege to any other city.[43]

(9.3) From there Vespasian went on to Rome, having already met up with Mucianus and a number of other notables at Brundisium, and with Domitian at Beneventum. The latter was very much on edge, being all too conscious of his future plans as well as his past misconduct. Sometimes he even pretended to be off his head. (9.4) While spending most of his time residing at his Alban villa, he often indulged in a series of ridiculous activities, including spearing flies on the end of his stylus. This is hardly appropriate material for a serious historical record, but I feel compelled to mention it,

---

[39] Alexandrians had a reputation for disorder and mocking their rulers (Seneca, *Dialogue* 12.19.6) continuing until Dio's time (79.35.1–3) and beyond. Suet. *Vesp.* 19.2 reports one of their insults as 'salted-fish seller'.

[40] Putting an end to treason trials becomes a standard act of a 'good' emperor. But in the context of information on Egypt, Dio may be slightly confusedly reporting the standard practice of a Ptolemaic pharaoh in giving an amnesty to (Egyptian) prisoners (Murison, *Commentary*).

[41] 'A type of person which will always be outlawed in our state and will always be kept busy.' (Tac. *Hist.* 1.22). Astrologers had been banned by Augustus in AD 11 from predicting deaths (Dio 56.25.5); were banished by Vitellius (Dio 65.1.4, Tac. *Hist.* 2.62.2). Tiberius used them (Suet. *Tib.* 62) and they must have been much in demand in the unrest of AD 68/9.

[42] It is not clear whether Barbillus is to be identified with Ti. Claudius Balbillus, prefect of Egypt, *c.* 55 – 59 or a son of the same name (*PIR* C² 812/3).

[43] Zonaras' summary of Dio gives information, probably at this point in the original about Vespasian sending corn from Egypt to Rome and then returning himself, leaving Titus to finish off the Jewish revolt – see **H21**.

both because it is typical behaviour and therefore a useful indication of his character, and above all because he continued to do this sort of thing after he became emperor. (9.5) As a result, someone with a rather nice sense of humour was heard to remark to the man who asked him what Domitian was doing these days, that he was "living on his own, without so much as a fly to keep him company."[44]

C10   Vespasian's personality
(10.1) Vespasian soon cut Domitian down to size, but he treated everyone else as if he himself were still a private citizen and not the emperor. He never forgot his own fortunate beginnings.[45] (10.2) He started at once on the construction of the temple on the Capitoline.[46] He himself carried away the first load of soil, thus making it quite clear to all the other leading citizens that he expected them to do likewise. By this example, he wanted to make it impossible for the rest of the population to avoid what was a sacred duty.[47] (10.3) In all essential public expenditure, he was extraordinarily generous; religious festivals he organised without regard for expense. But in his private life he was economical in the extreme, spending no more than was absolutely essential to his needs. The only cooked food he permitted to be sold even in taverns was green vegetables.[48] As a result of all this he made it absolutely clear to all that he was building up financial reserves not for his own pleasure but to meet the needs of the people.[49]

(10.4) There follows an account of his everyday life and habits.[50] He spent little of his time in the palace, most of it in the area known as the Gardens of Sallust, where he was happy to receive anyone who wished to see him, not only senators but anyone else as well. (10.5) He enjoyed meeting with his close friends, even before dawn while he was still in bed;[51] others would greet him in the streets. The palace doors were always open throughout the day; there were never guards on duty there. He would regularly attend the senate and was open to discussion with its members on every topic. He often dispensed justice in the Forum too. (10.6) Any despatches that he could not read himself, because of his age,[52] and any decisions that he wished to communicate in his absence, he usually asked his sons to read for him, thus showing even in such minor details a meticulous respect for the senate. He daily invited many senators to dine with him, along with others, and would also himself often dine at the homes of his closest friends.

---

[44]   The famous story, told more pithily by Suet. *Dom.* 3.1, and also Aur. Vict. 11.5–6, and Epitome 11.6–8 (**J10g**). The wit was Vibius Crispus (**U2**).

[45]   Zonaras' summary mentions Vespasian's rebuilding of public buildings – see **H24**.

[46]   For this, the most important temple in Rome, burnt down in fighting in Rome at the end of AD 69, see **K27–K31**. Tac. *Hist.* 4.53 gives details of the start of restoration when Vespasian was still away from Rome.

[47]   Zonaras' summary includes a paragraph on Vespasian not confiscating money from his opponents, see **H24**, which editors of Dio place here.

[48]   Several other emperors are known to have made decrees about cooked food being sold, though it is not clear why: (Suet. *Tib.* 34, *Claud.* 38.2, *Nero* 16.2; Dio 60.6.7, 62.24.2).

[49]   For a saying of Vespasian, possibly belonging here in Dio's original work, see **J4i**.

[50]   Suet. *Vesp.* 21 gives a similar account.

[51]   A routine confirmed by Y. Pliny, *Letters* 3.5.9, describing his uncle as receiving briefings from Vespasian before dawn, by Suet. *Vesp.* 21, by Philostratos and by the *Epitome* (**J4b, J4c**).

[52]   Natural long-sightedness in an age before reading-glasses (invented in 13th century, though Seneca (*NQ* 1.6.5) described the effect of letters being enlarged when viewed through water or glass).

C11   Vespasian's toleration of personal insult
(11.1) All in all, he was regarded as an emperor only for the care with which he oversaw the conduct of national affairs. In all other respects he lived like an ordinary citizen and on equal terms with them. For example, he could crack a joke as well as the next man, and would happily accept it when the laugh was on him.[53] As for any of the graffiti, usually anonymous, which were posted around casting abuse at the emperors, he would simply give as good as he got without any evidence of irritation. (11.2) There was one occasion, for example, when Phoebus came up to him to apologise for an episode that occurred during Nero's reign. It was in the theatre in Greece, and Vespasian had apparently once made clear his disapproval by scowling when he saw the emperor behaving improperly for one of his position. Phoebus had lost his temper and told Vespasian to "get lost." "Where to?" he had asked. "To hell," Phoebus replied. When he now offered this apology, Vespasian took no action against him and simply gave him the same answer back: "Go to hell!"[54] (11.3) Again, when Vologaesus sent him a letter addressed as follows, "Arsaces, King of Kings, to Flavius Vespasian, Greeting," he took no offence, but simply replied in the same manner, without adding any of his own imperial titles.[55]

C12   Vespasian and Helvidius Priscus
(12.1) Helvidius Priscus,[56] the son-in-law of Thrasea Paetus, had been brought up on the principles of the Stoic philosophy, and was inclined to ill-timed imitation of his father-in-law's directness of speech.[57] At this particular time he was a praetor,[58] but he made no attempt to do anything that would enhance respect for the emperor. Instead he constantly insulted him. For this on one occasion he was arrested by the tribunes, and placed in custody with their deputies. Vespasian was greatly distressed by this and left the senate-house in tears. His only comment was that, "my son is going to be my successor; no one else."[59]

C13   Vespasian expels philosophers
(13.1) There were many others also, among them Demetrius the Cynic,[60] who were encouraged by so-called Stoic teachings to promote to the public at large many ideas,

---

53   Suet. *Vesp.* 13 gives different examples.
54   Suet. *Vesp.* 14 gives the same story; for other insults tolerated see **J4g, J4n, P1j**.
55   Dio or his source may wrongly have adduced this example of Vespasian's typical unpretentiousness: the offer to Vespasian of cavalry forces by Vologaesus or Vologeses I (AD 51–*c*.78, a member of the Arsacid dynasty, hence 'Arsaces' in his own title) came very soon after news of Vitellius' death (Tac. *Hist.* 4.51.1–2) when he was not yet officially 'Imperator Caesar Vespasianus Augustus'.
56   For Helvidius Priscus and the whole episode of 'philosophical opposition' to Vespasian, see **P1, P11**.
57   P. Clodius Thrasea Paetus was forced to suicide by Nero in AD 66 (Tac. *Ann.* 16.21) for a series of acts of principled independence, most notably walking out of a senate honouring Nero for matricide (Tac. *Ann.* 14.12).
58   Helvidius was praetor in June AD 70 (Tac. *Hist.* 4.53.2–3) when work started on the new Capitoline Temple.
59   Presumably at this point Dio originally included an account of Titus' return and his joint triumph with Vespasian. Zonaras gives a brief summary, see **N8**.
60   Cynic philosophers enjoyed a reputation for challenging all aspects of ancient society, as suggested by their name (see note 64), and by Demetrius' defence in AD 70 of an obviously guilty informer (Tac. *Hist.* 4.40.3). But Demetrius was also a friend of Seneca and Thrasea Paetus (who addressed his dying words to him – Tac. *Ann.* 16.35). Cynic philosophy was not especially like that of the Stoics, though Dio here conflates the two.

wholly inappropriate to current circumstances, under the guise of philosophical instruction. This had an imperceptibly corrupting effect on a number of their listeners. As a result, Mucianus persuaded Vespasian to expel all such persons from the city, though the motive for his lengthy diatribes against them were rather more the result of ill temper than any enjoyment of rational argument.[61] (13.2) Vespasian's immediate reaction was to expel all the philosophers from Rome, except Musonius;[62] with Demetrius and Hostilianus he went further, deporting them to imprisonment on islands. Hostilianus happened to be holding a conversation with someone, when he heard of the decision for his exile. Far from refraining from any further discussion, he continued to denounce autocracy even more vigorously. All the same, he lost no time in leaving Rome.[63] (13.3) Demetrius, by contrast, even then refused to give an inch. Vespasian had a message sent to him to the effect that "you are doing everything you can to make me execute you. But I don't kill yapping dogs."[64]

C14   Caenis, Vespasian's mistress

(14.1) This year also marked the death of Caenis, Vespasian's concubine.[65] I mention her for two reasons, first because she was totally faithful to him, and second because she was blessed with a remarkable memory. Antonia, her mistress and the mother of Claudius, for example, had once used her to write a secret letter to Tiberius about Sejanus,[66] (14.2) but had then ordered her to erase it completely, so that not a single incriminating trace of it remained. "It's no use telling me to do that, Mistress," she replied. "I carry in my head everything you have ever dictated to me, not just this, but everything else as well. They cannot be rubbed out." (14.3) I find this story truly remarkable and no less so the fact that Vespasian absolutely adored her. For this reason she exercised enormous influence and made a large fortune, so that it was even thought that Vespasian had used her to raise money. She received innumerable gifts from many sources, in return for the sale of governorships, procuratorships, army commands, and priesthoods, and on a few occasions even decisions from the emperor himself. (14.4) Vespasian never killed anyone for their money; but he certainly spared many lives in return for payment. Caenis was the one that was given it; but it was

---

61 A lengthy but misguided attack on philosophers by Mucianus, preserved in a collection of sayings by Petrus Patricius, a sixth-century Byzantine lawyer and administrator probably belonged at this point in Dio's original history: see **P1k**. A character-sketch of Mucianus (**U3d**) from a later Byzantine collection *may* belong here.

62 Musonius was an equestrian from Tuscany, a well-known philosopher and associate of the rich and famous. He taught Epictetus, the writers Aulus Gellius and Dio of Prusa, and Nero's potential rival Rubellius Plautus (Tac. *Ann.* 14.59). Nero exiled him after the Pisonian conspiracy of AD 65 (Tac. *Ann.* 15.71.4). He returned to attempt mediation during the civil war (Tac. *Hist.* 3.81.1). Jerome, *Chronicle* 2095 notes 'he [Titus] recalls the philosopher Musonius Rufus from exile.' So he must have fallen out with Vespasian after initially being exempted.

63 Xiphilinus leaves it quite unclear whether Hostilius (identity unclear) suffered deportation to a prison island, or merely exile.

64 Vespasian is punning on Demetrius being a 'cynic' (= 'doglike', see note 60). A lengthier description of Helvidius' faults, preserved in a Byzantine anthology *On Virtues and Vices* probably came at this point in Dio's original narrative. See **P1i**.

65 Antonia Caenis was a slave of Antonia, later freed (Suet. *Vesp.* 3, 21; *Dom.* 12.3) and **J21**.

66 The story would fit with that of Josephus (*JA* 18.180–2 = LACTOR 19, P4e) that it took Antonia to persuade her brother-in-law Tiberius of Sejanus' disloyalty. But perhaps the idea that one of the most fascinating figures of the Flavian dynasty had a role in the downfall of one of the most fascinating figures of the previous dynasty is too good to be believed.

generally suspected on the evidence of his own actions elsewhere that Vespasian willingly allowed her to do this. I will give you a few examples.[67] (14.5) When a number of people voted to put up a statue to him at a cost of 250,000 drachmas, he held out his hand and said, "Give me the money. This hand is the statue-base."[68] Titus once complained about the urine tax on public lavatories, which was one of a number of newly published taxes. Vespasian showed him some gold coins, which this tax had raised, with the words, "Well, son, can you smell anything?" [69]

C15   Temple of Peace and Berenice in Rome, AD 75

(15.1) In Vespasian's sixth consulship and Titus' fourth, the sacred precinct of Peace was dedicated and the Colossus was set up on the Sacred Way.[70] They say that it was a hundred feet high and that it looked like either Nero or Titus, according to different sources. (15.2) Vespasian used to put on wild animal hunts in the theatres, but he did not especially like individual combats between gladiators. Nevertheless on one occasion during a Youth Sporting Festival celebrated in his home city, Titus participated in a shadow-battle in heavy armour with Alienus.[71]

(15.3) When the Parthians were caught up in a war against some enemy or other and asked for his help, he had replied that it was not right to interfere in the affairs of another state.[72] Berenice was by then at the peak of her power and influence, and for this reason she accompanied her brother Marcus Julius Agrippa when he came to Rome.[73] (15.4) He was honoured with praetorian rank, while she became Titus' mistress and lived with him in the palace. She fully expected to marry him and conducted herself in every way as if she were already his wife. But he realised that the Roman people disapproved of this arrangement, so he sent her away.[74] (15.5) This gave rise to a lot of gossip. It was already a hot topic when some Cynic philosophers

---

[67]   Xiphilinus may be indicating that he has chosen two of the anecdotes related by Dio. Suet. *Vesp.* 23.1–3 gives four, including the two here.

[68]   Suet. *Vesp.* 25.

[69]   Public urinals in Paris were colloquially known as *vespasiennes,* and Italians use the term *vespasiani.* Suetonius also tells the story (*Vesp.* 23.3), which gave rise to the expression '*pecunia non olet*' ('money does not stink' in other words, money is money, no matter how it was earned). The 'urine tax' is best explained as one levied on Roman 'fullers' who used urine as part of their process of cleaning cloth (urethric acid present in urine would help break down grease).

[70]   Precinct of Peace – more usually known as 'Temple of Peace' but also 'forum of Peace' or 'forum of Vespasian'. See **K64–K72**. The Colossus was the huge (100+ foot) statue built near the entrance to Nero's Golden House. See LACTOR 19, K44.

[71]   Caecina Alienus (see also below, note 77).

[72]   A very good example of the difficulties posed by our sources: Xiphilinus' abridgement is so brief as to reduce a significant episode between the two world powers of the time into a trivial saying of the emperor, probably misdated. The likely scenario is that in 72 the Alani tribe had swept across the Caucasus through territories of Persia and Armenia (kingdom friendly to Rome) – **M65**. A Parthian-Roman alliance against this common enemy would have made sense, but Vesp. seems to have rejected it, to the disappointment of Dom. (Suet. *Dom.* 2.2). But he did offer help to the friendly king – see **M66**.

[73]   Marcus Julius Agrippa II (AD 28–*c*.92) great-grandson of Herod the Great and son of Herod Agrippa (see **M61**). Like his father he was educated in Rome and ruled various parts of Palestine as a friendly king. Failing to prevent the Jewish revolt (Jos. *JW* 2.345–407), he actively helped the Romans throughout (Jos. *JW* 3.68, Tac. *Ann.* 5.1 = **M55**), accompanying Titus, and being rewarded with expansion of his territories.

[74]   Julia Berenice married three times, and was rumoured to have had a relationship with Agrippa (Jos. *Jewish Antiquities* 20.145–6, Juvenal, *Sat.* 6.156–160). For her relationship with Titus, perhaps 11 years younger than she, see Tac. *Hist.* 2.2.1; Suet. *Tit.* 7.1–2.

somehow contrived to slink back into the city. Diogenes led the way. He entered the crowded theatre and castigated the pair of them in a long and ferocious denunciation; for this he was flogged. He was followed by Heras, who expected nothing worse by way of punishment. He yapped away like a dog in typically Cynic fashion with a wide range of extraordinary allegations, for which he had his head cut off.[75]

C16a Sabinus the Gaul

(16.1) Around this time there were other happenings too. In a local tavern such a large quantity of wine overflowed its container that it flooded the street. Sabinus the Gaul, as already reported, had claimed to be a Caesar, been defeated after staging a revolt, and had hidden himself in that mausoleum. He was discovered and brought back to Rome. (16.2) He and his wife, Peponila, who had at one point saved his life, were both put to death. She cast her children before Vespasian's feet and delivered a heartbreaking plea on their behalf. "These children," she said, "I bore and brought up in that mausoleum, because I wanted to increase the numbers of us to beg you for mercy." She brought tears to the eyes of Vespasian and all around him, but no mercy to her children.[76]

C16b The Caecina conspiracy

(16.3) At this point there was also a conspiracy against the emperor, led by Alienus and Marcellus, two men whom he regarded as the closest of his friends, on whom with unlimited generosity he had heaped every kind of honour. However, their plot to assassinate him failed. They were both detected.[77] Alienus was getting up from dinner in the palace with Vespasian himself, and was immediately killed on the orders of Titus. He wanted to prevent any insurrection that might occur that same night, since a large number of soldiers had been put on stand-by by Alienus and were ready for action. (16.4) Marcellus was tried by the senate and found guilty. He cut his own throat with a razor. All this goes to show, I suppose, that naturally wicked men cannot be won over by kindness, since these two men conspired against one who had been so often so generous towards them.

C17 Death of Vespasian

(17.1) After all this had happened, Vespasian fell ill, not (to tell the truth) from his usual attack of gout, but from a high fever.[78] He died in the Sabine town of Aquae Cutilae.[79] Malicious gossip from many sources, including the Emperor Hadrian,

---

[75] Nothing else is known about Heras or Diogenes (not *the* Diogenes the Cynic, who lived through most of the fourth century BC). Presumably being Greek, not Roman citizens, they were subject to corporal punishment or summary execution. For Cynics as dogs, see note 64.

[76] See above 3.1–2, and Plutarch, *Moralia* 770–771 = **H34**, a very different account from Dio-Xiphilinus.

[77] Aulus Caecina Alienus, cos 69, had been an important and opportunist commander in the civil wars, introduced by Tac. *Hist.* 1.52.3 and 53.1–2 and mentioned a further 80 times. T. Clodius Eprius Marcellus (*OCD* under Eprius), cos 62, cos II 74, proconsul of Asia for an unusual three-year period, see **B74** and **U4**. The plot is mysterious (see **P2**): it may perhaps be best explained as an attempt, as Vespasian's health failed, to pre-empt the otherwise inevitable accession of Titus.

[78] Other accounts, including the various dying quips mentioned by Dio, are given by Suetonius (*Vesp.* 23.4–24), Eutropius 7.20, *Epitome* – see **J4g**, with note.

[79] Aquae Cutiliae is a 'spa town' in Central Italy, 9 miles from Reate, Vespasian's home town.

sought to incriminate Titus by falsely claiming that he was given poison at a dinner.[80] (17.2) But there had been a number of omens pointing towards his impending death, such as a comet, which blazed for a long time, and the fact that the doors of Augustus' mausoleum had opened of their own accord. His doctors ticked him off for failing to adjust his lifestyle to his illness and for continuing to carry out all his usual imperial duties. His only reply was that, "An emperor should die standing up." (17.3) When people raised the subject of the comet, he replied simply that, "it has nothing to do with me. But it has got a message for the King of Parthia. He's got long hair; I am bald."[81] Once he realised that he was indeed dying, he remarked, "I am already becoming a god."

His age was sixty-nine years and eight months; and he had ruled for six days short of ten years.[82] (17.4) The effect of this calculation is to leave one year and twenty-two days from the death of Nero to the accession of Vespasian. I have stated this to avoid any misunderstanding by those who try to calculate the length of rule of the intervening rulers. (17.5) For, you see, they did not succeed one another in an orderly fashion; each of them assumed that he was emperor, from the moment that he got the throne in his sights, even though his predecessor was still alive and in power.[83] It is important not to count up all the days of their individual claims to the title, as if they had followed each other neatly in succession. In the interests of accuracy, one must make a single calculation of the whole period, in the manner I have just explained.

C18   General character of Titus' reign
(18.1) Once he became emperor, Titus committed no act of either murder or lechery. Though the target of conspiracies,[84] he proved honourable; and though Berenice showed up in Rome once again, he kept his passions in check. It is perfectly possible that his character had changed. After all, it is one thing for a man to share power with another; quite a different thing to exercise it on his own. (18.2) In the first case men tend to be indifferent to their good reputation as rulers, abusing their power with a complete lack of restraint, thus incurring envy and malicious slander by many of their actions. But in the latter case they fully realise that everything comes back to their responsibility alone, and so they are careful to preserve their good reputation. (18.3) I suppose that this explains Titus' comment to one of his former close associates to the effect that, "it is not at all the same thing to ask someone else for a favour as to make your own decision, nor to ask for something from someone else as to offer it as a gift.

---

80   Hadrian (born AD 76) cannot have known Titus, so this is an odd statement – but Dio/Xiphilinus' history of Hadrian (book 69) is largely hostile to the emperor.
81   Vespasian's retort seems to contain a double Greek and Latin pun, since the Greek word 'cometes' means 'long-haired' or a 'long-haired star' i.e. a comet. But bald in Latin is 'calvus', from which derives the name Julia Calvina, the great-great-granddaughter of Augustus, whose death, so Vesp. said, the opening of the Mausoleum foretold (Suet. *Vesp* 23.4). Dio's account instead refers to the king of Parthia, Vologeses I who died around this time.
82   Despite Dio/Xiphilinus' apparent precision, his dates do not quite match those given by Suetonius for his life – 17 Nov 9 – 23 June 79 (*Vesp*. 2.1 and 24), nor can they be quite reconciled with the official date of his accession – 1 July 69. Faulty calculations and/or confusion in copying numbers in manuscripts are probably to blame.
83   This is correct in all cases of 68–9, most obviously Vesp's (date of accession 1 July; death of Vitellius 20 Dec).
84   Dio does not detail any conspiracies during his reign. Suet. *Titus* 9.1–2 reports, without names, an episode also in Aur. Vict. 10.3, and in Dio 68.3.2 about Nerva.

Of course he also lived only for a very short time (at least for a ruler) and so had very little opportunity to make mistakes.[85] (18.4) He lived for only two years, two months, and twenty days beyond the thirty-nine years, five months, and twenty-five days of his previous life. People regard his reign as the equal of the long reign of Augustus in this respect, that if Augustus had lived for a shorter period, he would not have been loved; nor would Titus, had he lived any longer. (18.5) Augustus, they argue, was more brutal at the start of his reign, because of the wars and internal struggles he faced; but in time he managed to become a shining example of general benevolence;[86] but Titus had made a very gentle start to his reign, and died at the height of his glory. Had he lived much longer, he might well have soon revealed that he owed more to his good luck than to his good character.

C19   Titus' clemency
(19.1) But the fact remains that in the course of his reign Titus never put a senator to death, nor was anyone else executed while he remained emperor.[87] Charges of treason he ruled inadmissible, refusing to try them himself or allow others to do so, insisting that it was impossible to insult or diminish the emperor's majesty in any way. (19.2) "I never do anything reprehensible," he asserted, "and I am indifferent to false slanders. As for the emperors who are already dead, if they really are semi-divine and possess supernatural powers, they will avenge themselves, if anyone does them wrong."[88] (19.3) He established a number of other measures to render the lives of ordinary citizens more secure and free from anxiety. He issued a decree confirming the right of all recipients of gifts from previous emperors to retain them, thus sparing such people from the trouble of having to petition him individually.[89] He also banished all informers from Rome.[90]

C20   Agricola in Britain
(20.1) In the same period war broke out once more in Britain. The response of the governor, Gnaeus Julius Agricola, was to overrun the whole extent of enemy territory there. He was the first Roman that we know of to establish that Britain is an island. The reason for this is that some of his soldiers mutinied and after murdering their centurions and the military tribune, they escaped in boats and sailed round the western coastline, drifting along wherever the winds and tides happened to carry them. Ultimately, without realising it because they approached from the opposite direction, they put into shore and arrived back at the same camps. As a result, Agricola sent out another team to attempt a circumnavigation, and thanks to their expedition he confirmed that it was indeed an island.[91]

---

[85] Students of politics would now call this the 'honeymoon period', and compare approval ratings of George W. Bush: 70% after 2 years and 2 months in office, 30% near end of second term (Harrup online).

[86] See for example Seneca, *On Clemency* 1.9.1 and 1.11.1 (= LACTOR 17, **H7–H8).**

[87] Suet. *Titus,* 9.1 links this to his becoming *pontifex maximus.*

[88] A similar principle had been established by Tiberius (Tac. *Ann.* 1.73).

[89] Suet. *Titus,* 8.1 and Aur.Vict. 10.2.

[90] Suet. *Titus,* 8.5 gives considerably more detail, as does Y. Pliny, *Pan.* 34–35. Martial, *On the Shows* 4, = **H57** describes a parade of informers at the opening of the Flavian Amphitheatre. Zonaras adds, probably from this point in the original narrative a general summary of Titus' financial prudence (**J8g**) and a paragraph on the emergence of a 'False Nero' (Dio/Zonaras 19.b–c = **P3a**).

[91] Tacitus, *Agricola* 28 gives a similar account of accidental exploration, by recently conscripted Usipi, to be dated three years later. But ancient geographers had long known that Britain was an island.

(20.3) So much for these activities in Britain. As a result, Titus was hailed *imperator* for the fifteenth time,[92] but Agricola spent the rest of his life in disgrace and penury, as a penalty for the fact that his achievements exceeded those deemed appropriate to a general. For the same reasons, he was ultimately murdered by Domitian, despite the fact that he had previously even received triumphal honours from Titus.[93]

C21   The eruption of Vesuvius, Autumn AD 79

(21.1) In Campania there took place an amazing and terrifying event. During the autumn an enormous conflagration suddenly occurred.[94] Mount Vesuvius rises close to the sea across the bay from Naples and has unlimited sources of fire. Once upon a time it was equally high all round, and flames arose from its centre, which was the only source of fire, the outer flanks of the mountain remaining to this day unaffected by the flames. (21.2) As a result those outer parts have never been burned, but the centre is permanently scorched and reduced to ashes. Up till now the surrounding peaks have remained as high as they always were, but the whole section where the fires rage has been burned away, and as a result of subsidence formed into a hollow bowl. In fact, if I may compare great things with small, the whole mountain has come to resemble an amphitheatre.[95] (21.3) Even its higher slopes are covered with innumerable trees and vines, but the central crater is consumed with fire, sending up plumes of smoke by day and fire by night. In fact it is as if every kind of incense was being burnt there. (21.4) To a greater or lesser extent this goes on all the time. Often it throws up ashes, when the piles of debris in the centre are collapsing, and erupts with rocks when violent blasts of air tear it apart. It rumbles and roars, too, because its vents are not concentrated in any one area, but are narrow and hard to detect.

C22   A fantastical description: the eruption

(22.1) So much for the characteristics of Vesuvius. The sort of events I have so far described happen there almost every year. But all such other eruptions as have occurred there since time immemorial, however unexpectedly vast they may have appeared to those who happened to be contemporary witnesses, would pale into insignificance compared with the present manifestation, even if they were all lumped together. (22.2) This is what happened.[96] Many huge figures were seen, far greater in stature than any modern human beings, and in appearance somewhat resembling the paintings of the legendary Giants. Sometimes they were seen on the mountain, sometimes in the surrounding countryside, sometimes again in the cities by day, and wandering about over the earth and flitting through the air by night. (22.3) This was followed by terrible droughts and sudden violent earthquakes, which churned up the whole coastal plain and

---

[92]   IMP XV appears on coins of 79, e.g. *RIC Titus* 36–54. The acclamation should have been later than 8 Sept as Titus is still IMP XIIII on a diploma of that date (*CIL* 16.24 = **N53**).

[93]   Section 20.3 provides a startling example of the dangers of Dio/Xiphilinus: besides the misdating of the circumnavigation (note 91), even Tacitus' bitter account of Agricola's wrongs under Domitian does not suggest murder. The mistake in who gave him triumphal honours is probably one arising from miscopying 'παρα τουτου' (from him) as 'παρα του Τιτου – from Titus'.

[94]   The dating to autumn does not fit easily with the traditional dating on August 24, but does fit well with the flora found in excavations, and with the discovery of a coin *in situ* showing Titus as IMP XV (see note 92). The date from Y. Pliny's letter has quite probably been miscopied, with Oct 24 more likely– see Cooley[2] p.43.

[95]   Dio/Xiphilinus' physical description of Vesuvius is reasonably accurate.

[96]   Vesuvius had erupted within Dio's lifetime, in AD 202, but the account here is of little value.

made the peaks of the mountains leap into the air. There were thunderous subterranean explosions, and on the surface a roaring as of the bellowing of vast beasts, while the sea added to the tremendous noise and the heavens redoubled the volume. (22.4) After that a sudden, unearthly crash was heard, as if all the mountains were collapsing on top of one another. Vast boulders were tossed into the air, as high as the very tops of the mountains, and then vast flames and dense clouds of smoke followed, so that the sky was totally obliterated and the sun blotted out, as in an eclipse.

C23   A fantastical description II: the disaster

(23.1) Day became night and instead of the light there was pitch darkness. Some people believed that the giants were staging another revolt against the gods, because many gigantic shapes were seen at the time amidst the smoke, and trumpet blasts could be heard as well; others thought that Chaos was come again, or fire devouring the whole of creation. (23.2) The result was panic, some people rushing from their houses into the streets, others from the streets back into their houses, from the sea back to land, from land into the sea, everyone imagining that anywhere was bound to be safer than where they were at that moment. (23.3) At the same time, while all this was happening, an unbelievably vast ash cloud was blasted upward which covered the land and sea, and filled the air. The damage it inflicted was enormous and diverse, and utterly random, afflicting people, places and animals alike. The worst casualties were the birds and the fish: they were all completely wiped out. On top of all that, it totally buried two whole cities, Herculaneum and Pompeii, the latter while its population were all seated in the theatre.[97] (23.4) So great was the total extent of the consequent dust cloud that it reached Africa, Syria, and Egypt, as well as Rome, filling the skies overhead and darkening the sun. (23.5) In those places, too, there was widespread terror for many days, since no one knew, nor could they guess, what had happened. They too thought that all creation was being turned topsy-turvy, that the sun was disappearing into the earth, and the earth going up into the sky. The ash cloud itself did them no significant harm immediately, but later it was the cause of terrible plague-borne diseases in Rome itself.

C24   The fire at Rome, AD 80

(24.1) But in the following year there was another fire, this time above ground. It spread over much of Rome, while Titus was away dealing with the disaster in Campania. (24.2) It destroyed the Temple of Serapis, the Temple of Isis, the voting enclosures (*Saepta Julia*), the Temple of Neptune, Agrippa's Baths, the Pantheon, the Ballot-house (*Diribitorium*), the Theatre of Balbus, the stage-building of the Theatre of Pompey, the Portico of Octavia and its library, the Temple of Capitoline Jupiter and the surrounding temples. (24.3) This was no man-made disaster but an act of the gods, as can be readily understood by any one who reckons up the scale of the remaining losses from this catalogue of buildings destroyed.[98] Titus' immediate

---

[97]   Dio, like many later popular writers completely misunderstands the process of Pompeii's destruction, clearly described by Y. Pliny's eye-witness account which should have served as the basis for Tacitus' account (lost), and confirmed by modern archaeology. Instead Dio's account is more the melodrama found in Lytton's, *Last Days of Pompeii* (1834).

[98]   Suet. *Titus* 8.3 tells us that the fire lasted three days. The buildings affected are in a wedge-shape from the Capitol, north-west into the Campus Martius (see Map 2), suggesting that it may have started on the Capitol, hence an 'act of god'. See Map of Rome, page 20.

reaction was to send two men of consular rank to Campania to supervise a programme of total reconstruction. He made cash grants generally, but also allocations of property derived from those who had died without heirs. (24.4) In all this he personally accepted nothing from individuals, communities, or kings despite many offers and promises of assistance. Instead he made good all the ruined areas out of his own existing resources.[99]

C25 The dedication of the Flavian Amphitheatre

(25.1) Broadly speaking and for the most part Titus achieved little remarkable in the course of his reign. But for the dedication of the Hunting Amphitheatre (the Colosseum) and the Baths which were named after him, he did provide many amazing spectacles.[100] There was a battle between cranes and also between four elephants; other battles resulted in the slaughter of anything up to nine thousand animals, both domestic and wild. Women joined in the task of slaughter, though not any women of high rank.[101] (25.2) As for the men, large numbers took part in single combat, many more in teams for both infantry and naval battles. For Titus suddenly filled this amphitheatre with water and then brought in horses, bulls, and other domestic animals trained to act in water exactly as they did on land.[102] He also introduced crews for the ships (25.3) and there in the amphitheatre they staged a sea battle, imitating the one fought between the Corcyraeans and the Corinthians.[103] Others staged similar battles outside the city in the Grove of Gaius and Lucius, which Augustus had had excavated for this very purpose.[104] Here too, on the first day of the festival, the lake in front of the images was covered over with planks, and scaffolding with benches erected around it. The programme included bouts of single-combat and the slaughter of wild-beasts. (25.4) On the second day there was horse-racing, and on the third a naval battle between three thousand men, followed by an infantry battle. The Athenian army defeated the Syracusan army, (these were the names given to the combatants) and made a landing on a tiny island of Ortygia and then launched an attack on the wall which had been built round the monument and captured it.[105]

Such were the spectacles provided for entertainment and they lasted for a hundred days. But Titus also introduced some features, which were intended to be beneficial to ordinary people. (25.5) From on high into the theatre he used to throw down small wooden balls, marked with inscriptions indicating that they were tokens for food, or clothing, or silverware, perhaps, or gold artefacts, or for horses, beasts of burden, cattle or slaves. Anyone who managed to grab one of these was supposed to carry them to the official distributors and collect the item specified.[106]

---

[99] Titus' contribution to the relief efforts is mentioned by Suet. 8.3 and shown in inscriptions in Naples (**K102**), Salerno and Sorrento (**K103**).
[100] For the Flavian Amphitheatre, see **K12–K19**, and for the Baths, **K26**.
[101] Martial, *On the Shows* describes women fighting in poems 7 and 8; elephants in 20 and 22.
[102] For the flooding of the amphitheatre, see Martial, *On the Shows* 27, 28, 30, 34 and **K19**.
[103] Just before the Peloponnesian War, in 433 BC, the greatest sea-battle in terms of number of ships was fought between Corinth and Corcyra. Thucydides 1.46–50 gives the numbers on each side as 150 and 110.
[104] For the grove as setting for naval battles see *Red Gestae* 23, Tac. *Ann.* 12.56 and 14.15.
[105] The historical scenario here is the Athenian invasion of Sicily, 415–413 BC, and their attack on Ortygia, the ancient settlement of Syracuse. In reality the Athenians did not capture Ortygia and the expedition was a disaster.
[106] Caligula and Nero had done similarly (Suet. *Cal.* 37.1, 18.2, Dio 59.9.6–7; Suet. *Nero* 11–12, Dio 61.18.1–2).

C26 The death of Titus, AD 81

(26.1) Once he had completed this programme of spectacles and shed bitter tears on the final day so that the whole populace could see him, he achieved nothing else of any significance.[107] The following year, in the consulship of Flavius and Pollio, having completed the dedications described above, he died at Aquae Cutilae, the same town in which his father had also died. (26.2) Rumour has it that he was murdered by his brother, because he had been the target of a previous plot by Domitian. But other sources state that he had fallen ill.[108] Domitian was said to have accelerated his demise by shutting him in a chest stuffed full of snow, while he was still breathing and had every likelihood of recovering, on the grounds that the fever required some kind of reduction of temperature.

(26.3) Whatever the truth of the story, Domitian rode off to Rome while Titus was still alive, entered the camp of the Praetorian guard, received the title and powers of the emperor, and gave the soldiers all the same donatives as his brother had done before him. Titus' own last words were these: "I only made one mistake." It was not clear what he meant by this and no one could be quite certain that they had heard it correctly. It was all a matter of guesswork, one making this suggestion, another that.[109] (26.4) The most popular suggestion comes from some who say that that he had taken his brother's wife, Domitia. Others, however, suggest (and I incline to agree) that when he caught Domitian manifestly plotting against him, his mistake was not to have killed him, preferring himself to be killed by him instead. In so doing, he had handed over the Roman empire to the sort of man, whose character will be revealed in the next chapters of this history.

As already recorded, Titus ruled for two years, two months, and twenty days.

---

[107] Suet. *Titus* 10.1 also mentions the public tears.

[108] Other accounts are Suet. *Titus* 10.1 (fever), *Epitome* 10.15–16 = **J8i** (fever), Eutropius 7.22 = **T1** (disease), Aur. Vict. 10.5 (murder), Philostratos *Life of Ap.* 6.32 = **P4** (poison).

[109] Suetonius also includes the 'one mistake' story (*Titus* 10.1–2) and also moves to reject the idea that it was a relationship with Domitia.

SECTION D

CASSIUS DIO, *ROMAN HISTORY*, BOOK 67

ABRIDGED BY XIPHILINUS

D1   Domitian's character

(67.1.1) Domitian was aggressive and bad-tempered, but also treacherous and cunning. From the first two characteristics came his impetuosity, from the latter his deviousness. Like a thunderbolt, he would often launch devastating attacks upon people, sometimes humiliating them shamefully, at other times often deliberately inflict physical injuries on them.[110] (1.2) Of the gods, it was Athena (Minerva) that he most honoured, and for this reason he would celebrate the Panathenaea with the most elaborate festivities.[111] At these, held almost every year at his Alban villa, he would conduct competitions of poetry and rhetoric, as well as gladiatorial contests. At the foot of the Alban Mount, from which it took its name, he had chosen to make his estate into a sort of (Athenian) Acropolis.

(1.3) He felt no genuine affection for anyone, except one or two women; but he always put on a great show of affection for anyone whom he most wanted to murder next. He trusted least those who had done him some favour or aided and abetted his most nefarious crimes; as a result, he took care to eliminate anyone who had provided him with generous gifts of cash or given false evidence against large numbers of people, particularly if they were slaves who had laid information of any kind against their masters. (1.4) Such people, even if they received wealth and honours from him, or shared high office with him, spent their lives in a situation neither more honoured nor more protected than their fellow men.[112] Indeed, they tended to be punished for the very crimes which they had themselves committed with Domitian's encouragement, since his purpose was to make it appear that those crimes were their responsibility alone. It was with precisely this same intention that he once issued an announcement to the effect that any emperor who did not punish informers was himself responsible for encouraging their existence.[113]

---

[110] Dio's account of Domitian is as negative as those of Y. Pliny or Tacitus' *Agricola*. It may derive from the lost books of Tacitus' *Histories*. But Dio may also have recalled living under the unpopular Commodus (180–192) and being a senator under Caracalla (211–217: Dio, *History* 78–79.10) – the next two emperors to succeed their fathers, both assassinated.

[111] The Panathenaea was a sporting and cultural festival at Athens, celebrated in early August: Domitian celebrated the *Quinquatrus Minervae* from 19–23 March.

[112] Shared high office: this can only mean the consulship, see Section B. In fact most of the 9 who shared ordinary consulships with Domitian in his reign seem to have done so as tribute to their aristocratic ancestors: the two later to have fallen victim were his cousins. Dio may be thinking of life in the senate under Caracalla, e.g. 78.11.5 '[Caracalla] hated those in any way preeminent and especially those he pretended to love most.'

[113] The whole paragraph (1.3–4 and also 2.1–7) is preserved in the 10th-century, Byzantine selection, *On Virtues and Vices*. Independently, when Xiphilinus came to make his excerpts, he chose all of this but omitted 1.4, presumably as containing roughly the same material as 1.3.

D2 Domitian's resentment of his brother

(2.1) This was the way he treated everyone, throughout his reign. But he surpassed himself in the way in which he contrived the disgrace and ruination of the friends of his father and brother. It is true that he issued a proclamation confirming all the gifts bestowed on anyone by either of them, or by any of the other emperors. (2.2) But this was an entirely futile gesture, designed to make a good impression. In fact he hated them, both for their failure to grant all his demands, however many or inappropriate they were, and because they had been held in high esteem. He regarded as his enemy any for whom his father or brother had shown unusual affection, or to whom they had granted significant powers.[114] (2.3) That was the reason why he decreed that in future no one within the Roman Empire should be castrated. Domitian himself was in fact in love with a eunuch called Earinus; but Titus had very much enjoyed the company of eunuchs generally, and this ban was intended as an insult to his brother.[115] His whole philosophy was summed up by his habit of saying that emperors who failed to execute large numbers were not so much virtuous as lucky.

(2.4) This, too, was the same emperor who was entirely dismissive of those who praised Titus for never having put to death a single senator; nor was he impressed that the senate had passed frequent resolutions to the effect that it should be illegal for the emperor to put to death any member of their order. Did they really imagine that it made a lot of difference whether he did away with one of their number on his own initiative or with their authority, as if they actually had the power to gainsay him in any matter or to refuse to condemn someone to death?[116] (2.5) There were, of course, some who praised Titus, but only when Domitian was not listening, for that was just as grave an offence as to abuse him in his presence and in his hearing. But [he hated them just the same],[117] because he was fully aware that they were secretly doing this. It was all a complete charade – and there was another similar feature in all of it. (2.6) He himself put on a great show of love for his brother and grief at his loss. With tears in his eyes he delivered the funeral address over his body, insisting with great enthusiasm that he should be accorded the status of a god, making a great pretence of the very opposite to what he really wanted. In fact he could not have cared less for him, and even abolished the horse race, which was part of Titus' birthday celebrations.[118] (2.7) In fact everyone else was in grave danger, whether they shared his grief or his delight. If they grieved, they would offend his true feelings; if they rejoiced, they would simply convict him of hypocrisy.

---

[114] Dio paints a picture of the younger brother (12 years younger than Titus) resenting that he was unlikely to succeed to the throne and jealous of powers being given to others. But he had received 6 consulships, and was the obvious successor especially in the absence of any sons to Titus.

[115] For Earinus see **J23**. While personal reasons are likely for the ban, attributing it to the wish to insult his dead brother rather than sympathy for Earinus is implausible in the extreme.

[116] Domitian had made the senate at least acquiesce in condemnation of his senatorial opponents, and the knowledge of such complicity adds considerably to the bitterness of Tacitus and Y. Pliny (e.g. *Agr.* 45.1–2 = **P11b**; *Panegyric* 76.3–6 = **T22**; *Letters* 8.14.8 = **T24**) and quite possibly Dio, recalling and comparing his time as a consular under Caracalla.

[117] This phrase or similar needs to be added for the text to make sense.

[118] Honours for Titus: deification was not immediate as is shown by the Arval Records (**A81j**) dating from 1 Oct, 18 days after Titus' death, which refer to Julia as daughter of Titus (not Divus Titus). Domitian was, of course, already 'Divi filius'.

D3a   Domitian and Domitia

(3.1) He planned to execute his wife, Domitia, for adultery, but was dissuaded by Lucius Julius Ursus and instead sent her away, having murdered Paris the pantomime actor in the middle of the street.[119] Many people laid tributes of flowers and perfumes on the spot, so Domitian gave orders for them to be murdered too.[120] (3.2) After this he lived quite openly with his own niece (that is to say, Julia), as if she was his wife. Then, by popular request, he made it up with Domitia, but continued his relationship with Julia just as before.[121]

D3b   Domitian and the Vestals

(3.3.1) Whether by murder or exile, he was getting rid of many of the leading aristocrats on a range of pretexts,[122] (3.3.2) and he did not even spare Vestal Virgins, but punished them on a charge of having had sexual intercourse with men. So harsh and savage were their judicial examinations, and so great the numbers of those accused and punished, that it is even said that Helvius Agrippa, one of the Pontifices, found it utterly intolerable and died of shock then and there in the senate house.[123]

D4   Domitian and the Chatti, AD 83

(4.1) He then led an expeditionary force into Germany, and without having even set eyes on any warfare, he returned home.[124] There is little point in mentioning the honours that were heaped upon him for this achievement, (as they had been on a number of previous occasions on other similar emperors). The purpose was simply to prevent those emperors from becoming dangerously angry, if they once came to suspect that honours, which were both limited in number and trivial in importance, showed only that their pretensions had been seen for what they were worth.[125] (4.2) But one of Domitian's least attractive qualities was that he longed to be flattered, yet was equally irritated by both types of people, those that fawned upon him and those that did not, the former because they were clearly seeking to ingratiate themselves with him, the latter because they seemed to view him with contempt. All the same, he made a great show of delight at the honours which the senate voted for him, and almost put Ursus to death for not showing manifest delight at his emperor's achievements. But then he made him a consul, because Julia asked him to.[126]

(4.3) However, since by now he lacked any sense of reality, he became yet more arrogant. He was voted consul for ten years in succession and censor for life, an

---

[119] For Paris see **Q11**. For Ursus see **U43–U44**.

[120] This may correspond to a conspiracy in 83 known only from Eusebius *Chron.* under AD 83 – see **P5**.

[121] For Julia see **J15**. Despite the Domitia/Domitian/Julia episode being used to condemn Domitian in all our sources, it is worth noting that Domitian could simply have married Julia (as Claudius had married Agrippina, under the law permitting marriage with a niece).

[122] Further details, cut by Xiphilinus, are given in the Byzantine collection *On Vices and Virtues*, (see **P5c**).

[123] Again Xiphilinus has cut further detail from Dio preserved in the Byzantine collection *On Vices and Virtues*, see **L11**.

[124] This is Xiphilinus' version of the same expedition against the Chatti which Zonaras summarized in **N22**, also describing the army pay rise as a direct result. On Frontinus' good evidence (**N18–N21**), Dio/Xiphilinus is quite wrong to say (4.1) that he did nothing in person, and the whole account is exceptionally tangential: it does not even name the honours (the title 'Germanicus' and the triumph).

[125] One may suspect that this bitter judgement was influenced by Dio's own experience as senator (e.g. under Caracalla 78.17.3) as well as by his study of the emperors.

[126] On L. Julius Ursus see **U43–U44** – he may have been a relation of Julia.

honour unprecedented for any private citizen or emperor, and was granted an escort of twenty-four lictors and the right to wear triumphal dress whenever he entered the senate.[127] (4.4) Having been born in October, he changed its name to Domitianus.[128] He established two new factions of charioteers, called Gold and Purple.[129] He gave many gifts to spectators by means of the little wooden balls mentioned above,[130] and once he gave them a feast while they stayed in their seats, and supplied them with wine, which flowed in abundance all night everywhere. (4.5) All this of course won him great popularity with the mob, but for the upper classes it spelt ruination. For he had no reserves of cash from which to fund his generosity, and so he murdered many of them, dragging some before the senate, prosecuting others even in their absence, and treacherously murdering some others by dosing them secretly with drugs.[131]

D6[132]   The Dacian War
(6.1) For the Romans, the greatest war that they waged in this period was with the Dacians.[133] Their king at the time was Decebalus, a brilliant military strategist and in the field a canny tactician. His attacks were masterly; his retreats perfectly timed; his ambuscades were cunning; his set-piece battles exemplary. He could exploit a victory superbly, yet in defeat he never lost control. In fact he was for a long time Rome's most formidable antagonist.[134] (6.2) I call these people Dacians, which I believe is the name they use themselves and the Romans likewise. I am well aware that some Greeks call them Getae, whether rightly or wrongly I cannot say. The people that I know of as the Getae live beyond the Haemus mountain range and along the Danube.[135] (6.3) So Domitian launched a campaign against them but without involving himself personally in the campaign. He stayed in one of the cities of Moesia living it up in the usual way. He was physically soft and at heart a coward. He was debauched and licentious in the extreme, equally depraved in his taste for women or young boys. He was content to send out others to command his wars, and as a result usually came off worst.[136]

---

[127] Domitian was not consul for ten successive years (see Section B). Coins from 85 proclaim Domitian as having censorial power (*RIC* Domitian 318–390) and then as censor for life (*RIC* Domitian 391–423); thereafter it is a usual part of his titulature (e.g. L17, L18, L35) as for subsequent emperors. Lictors accompanied Roman magistrates, bearing their *fasces* (symbols of office). Julius Caesar employed 24 lictors as *dictator* and also wore triumphal garb in the senate.

[128] For the calendar changes, see **T6–T8** (Suet. *Dom.* 13.3, Aur. Vict. 11.4, Jerome under AD 87, MW 405).

[129] For Purples and Golds, see **Q14**, Suet. *Dom.* 7.1.

[130] 66.25.5 = **C25**.

[131] This idea, and the similar one at 67.11.6 may be an attempt to explain outbreaks of food-poisoning or disease, or may even be derived from Caracalla's stockpiling of poison in Dio's day (79.6.3).

[132] For section 5, restored to Dio's narrative from a Byzantine collection on *Embassies – Foreign*, see **N29**.

[133] Dio's original account included campaigns in Africa, preserved by Zonaras (**N30**), and thought to predate the Dacian campaigns.

[134] Decebalus is more famous as the opponent of Trajan's Dacian Wars eventually resulting in the creation of the province of Dacia, after Decebalus' death in AD 106; all commemorated in the frieze of Trajan's column.

[135] Getae were the same people, living further south, in Thrace, and thus closer to the Greeks who called them and their Dacian kindred further north by the same term.

[136] Various parts of Dio's narrative cut by Xiphilinus, but preserved in other collections may be placed here: a very generic criticism (67.6.4); a detail about an embassy from Decebalus (67.6.5 = **N34**); a request from Fuscus' soldiers to Domitian (67.6.6 = **N38**) and a punitive expedition to Pannonia (67.7.1 = **N42**); final peace treaty with Decebalus, crowning of his brother Degis, and celebrations in Rome (67.7.2 = **N39**).

D8   Celebrations in Rome

(8.1) So many honours were voted for him that almost all the world, or at least that part of it which he ruled, was filled with gold and silver images and statues of him. He put on an extravagant spectacle, in which we have no record of anything happening that was historically significant except for a girls' foot-race.[137] After that he put on innumerable contests as part of what he presented as victory celebrations. (8.2) These included battles in the Circus, both between infantry and cavalry, and in a newly constructed location he staged a naval battle also. There almost every one of the combatants lost their lives, along with many of the spectators. (8.3) For a cloudburst occurred and a sudden violent storm, but he allowed no one to leave the spectacle. He himself changed into several thick Persian cloaks, but he forbade any other change of clothing for the spectators, and as a result quite a few of them fell sick and died.[138] (8.4) As some sort of consolation for this misfortune, I suppose, he laid on at public expense an all-night dinner party. There were often all-night games, as well, and on some occasions he would stage fights between women and dwarfs.[139]

D9   A black joke

(9.1) So that was the way in which he feasted the people. But on another occasion he entertained the leading senators and equestrians in the following way. He prepared a room with ceiling, walls and floor all totally jet black, and then on the bare floor laid out couches of the same colour and devoid of any cushions, and then he invited his guests to come at night and without their normal retinues. (9.2) Then at each one's place he set up a stone slab, rather like a grave stone, with their name engraved upon it, together with a small lamp such as are usually hung up in mausoleums. Then good looking boys, naked and all similarly painted black, came in like ghosts, and performed a menacing dance routine round and round the guests before taking up their positions at their feet. (9.3) After that all the things that are dedicated in offerings to the dead were brought in,[140] all black and set out in black dishes, so that every one of the guests was scared out of his wits, and trembling with fear that at any moment they could all expect to have their throats cut. The atmosphere was intensified by the deathly silence of all concerned, as if they were already in the land of the dead, while only Domitian himself chattered away about anything that had to do with death and murder.

(9.4) In the end he let them go. But before that, he had exchanged their own slaves, who had been waiting for them in the vestibule, for others whom they did not know, to be taken home in their carriages or litters. This greatly increased their terror. But scarcely had each of them reached home and felt able to breathe again, so to speak, when he was informed that a messenger had come from the emperor himself. (9.5) At that every one of them thought his last hour had finally come. But then the first messenger came in with the grave stone, wrought in silver, then another and another, each carrying something different, including the items which had been set before them at the dinner tables, and all of them fashioned from very expensive materials. In each case the final gift was the particular boy who had been the guest's attendant spirit, but

---

[137] This should match the girls' race mentioned by Suet. *Dom.* 4.4, though that is explicitly connected with the Capitoline Games of AD 86 (see **Q16–Q19**).
[138] For the naval battle in the thunderstorm, see Suet. *Dom.* 4.2.
[139] This or a similar Saturnalian party is described by Statius, *Silvae* 1.6.
[140] Romans made offerings to the dead each year at festivals of Lemuria and Parentalia.

now washed and attractively dressed. And so, having spent the whole night in a state of absolute terror, they took delivery of their gifts.

(9.6) Such were the triumphal celebrations, which Domitian laid on for those who had died in Dacia or in Rome.[141] The people called them funeral rites. And even at this time Domitian had some of the leading citizens murdered, and went so far as to confiscate the goods of someone who buried the body of one of his victims, on the grounds that he had died on that man's property.

D10   The Dacian War continued

(10.1) There are also a number of other events in the Dacian war, which are worth recording. Julianus,[142] whom Domitian had appointed as supreme commander for the campaign, made a series of excellent regulations. The best was that every soldier should inscribe on his shield his own name and that of his centurion, so that it would be easier to identify those whose conduct had been especially courageous or despicable.[143] (10.2) He brought the enemy to battle at Tapae, and slaughtered them in great numbers.[144] Among them Vezenas, Decebalus' second in command, found that he could not get away alive; so he fell down deliberately as if he were dead and thus passed unnoticed before slipping away in the night. (10.3) Decebalus was now alarmed that the victorious Romans might attack his capital, and so he cut down all the trees in the area and put armour on their stumps, in the hope that this would frighten the Romans into retreating. It worked!

D11   Revolt of Saturninus

(11.1) In this period a certain Antonius was the governor of Germany. He staged a revolt against Domitian, but Lucius Maximus attacked and destroyed him. In itself this victory was of little merit or significance – after all, unexpected success is not unusual in military campaigns, and of course Lucius' soldiers were part and parcel of that victory. (11.2) But Lucius also burnt all the documents that were found in Antonius' storage chests, an act which showed that he was relatively indifferent to his own safety compared with his desire to protect others from being informed against.[145] Such an action seems to me so wholly admirable that I cannot find words with which to express my admiration. Nevertheless, with or without such evidence, it gave Domitian an excellent excuse for embarking on a series of murders, and no one can tell how many people he killed.[146] (11.4) One young man called Julius Calvaster, a military tribune with senatorial ambitions, had a remarkably unexpected reprieve. When it became clear that he had had a large number of private meetings with Antonius, he could not think of any way of escaping a charge of conspiracy. So he stated that they had in fact met for sexual intercourse – and certainly his looks made the claim plausible. And so he was acquitted.[147] Let me record just one more

---

[141] It's not clear what Dio is referring to, or when. He may be making the point that the triumphs were won at the cost of much Roman blood, or that Domitian was wrong to be joking in Rome while troops were dying in Dacia.

[142] L. Tettius Julianus, cos 83, see **B83** and **S9b**.

[143] More probably to be able to identify bodies.

[144] The victory at Tapae, obviously preceding the final victory/peace was in AD 88.

[145] For the revolt of Antonius Saturninus, see **P8** and Suet. *Dom.* 6.2 and 7.3. 'Lucius' Maximus was actually A. Bucius Lappius Maximus, whose name was misread as L. Appius Maximus.

[146] Xiphilinus here cut a passage preserved in the Byzantine collection '*On Virtues and Vices*' see **P8a**.

[147] Presumably he was the same as the nameless tribune mentioned by Suet. *Dom.* 10.5. Antonius goes down in history as a pervert – *Epitome* = **P8b**, Aelian fr. 112 = **P8c**.

episode from the events of this period and I then I shall say no more. (11.5) An elderly senator named Lucianus Proclus who spent most of his time on his country estate had accompanied Domitian when he set out from Rome to confront Antonius. He felt he had little choice, since it might otherwise look as if he was deserting his emperor in his hour of danger, and this would certainly lead to his own death. But when the news of his victory came, he said to Domitian, "Yours is the victory I have been praying for, my Emperor. So now, please give me back to my own countryside." He then left Domitian and returned to his estate, and never again went near him, even though he lived for many years more.[148]

(11.6) During this period, among a number of people a craze developed for smearing needle points with poison and then injecting them at random into anyone that took their fancy. Many of them died totally unaware of the source of their affliction. But many of the poisoners were executed thanks to information laid against them. This was not just a local phenomenon in Rome; it happened almost everywhere throughout the known world.[149]

D12   Various conspiracies, AD 91
(12.1) When Ulpius Traianus and Acilius Glabrio became consuls at this time, identical portents are said to have taken place. For Glabrio, they foretold death; for Traianus, imperial power.[150] Many men and women among the wealthy classes were punished for adultery, some of the women being the victims of rape by Domitian himself. Many others were fined or murdered on a variety of charges.[151] (12.2) One woman was tried and put to death for undressing in front of a statue of Domitian; another man for consorting with astrologers.[152] Among the innumerable victims of that period was one, Mettius Pompusianus, whom Vespasian had not ill-treated, when he heard a report that he would one day be a king. In fact, he had treated him with honour, observing that "he will certainly remember me and do me honour in return." But Domitian first of all exiled him to Corsica and then put him to death, after a number of charges were laid against him, including the allegation that on the walls of his bedroom he had had painted a map of the world, and that he made a habit of selecting and reading the speeches of kings and other prominent figures, which are recorded in the works of Livy.[153] (12.5) Then there was a sophist called Maternus, whom Domitian executed for criticising tyrants as part of a rhetorical exercise.[154] The emperor used to associate with would-be prosecutors and witnesses, and helped them to put together their cases and advised them on everything that needed to be said. He would often cross-examine

[148] It is inexplicable, given the extreme haste of operations, that an elderly senator (perhaps the cos 93, Lusianus Proculus) should have accompanied Domitian.
[149] A repeat of the story at Dio 67.4.5 = D4 and note 131.
[150] Their consulships were March-April AD 91, see **B91**.
[151] The charges against Domitian are hypocrisy (perhaps inevitable for someone who tried to reform public morals) and greed, since financial penalties for adultery were severe – one third or half of the adulterer's property.
[152] Astrologers and their predictions of people's life-spans were of great interest and suspicion to emperors (e.g. Dio 56.25.5: Augustus' ban; Suet. *Tib.* 14.4, 62.3: Tiberius and Thrasyllus).
[153] Mettius Pompusianus also features in Suet. *Vesp.* 14, *Dom.* 10.3 and *Epit.* 9.14 (**P9**). Several other Mettii are known and the scandal may have brought down the whole family.
[154] It is not at all clear whether this is the same person as Curiatius Maternus who hosts Tacitus' *Dialogue* on the decline of oratory, and/or the governor of Moesia and Syria (see **B83**).

prisoners in private, holding their fetters in his hands. He did not trust anyone else to hear what was going to be said, and was frightened of the prisoners themselves, even though they were in chains.

D13 Persecution of the philosophers

(13.1) As censor some of Domitian's actions also deserve a mention. He expelled Caecilius Rufinus from the senate for acting in pantomimes, and gave Claudius Pacatus back to his master even though he was now a centurion, because it was proved that he had been a slave.[155] (13.2) But that part of his record as emperor which I am now going to relate bears no resemblance to the above whatsoever. He killed Arulenus Rusticus for being a philosopher and for calling Thrasea Paetus "holy"; and Herennius Senecio, because in the whole of a long life he had failed to campaign for any office after his quaestorship, and had written a biography of Helvidius Priscus. (13.3) Many others died for the self same offence of philosophising, and any that remained were all exiled from Rome once more.[156] But Juventius Celsus, a leading member of one of the conspiracies against Domitian, was charged with this offence but managed a remarkable escape. (13.4) When he was about to be found guilty, he asked for a private audience with the emperor. Here he grovelled before him, repeatedly addressed him as "master" and "my god" (already familiar terms used by a number of people). "As for me," he declared, "I have done none of things I am accused of; but if I am granted a reprieve I shall conduct a thorough investigation into all these matters, and will name names and secure convictions for you against a large number of conspirators." For this he was released, but subsequently failed to reveal a single name. Time and again he offered various excuses, and managed to spin out his own survival until the death of Domitian.[157]

D14 Further executions, AD 95

(14.1) During this period the road from Sinuessa to Puteoli was paved with stone.[158] In the same year, among the many other victims of Domitian's executions was the consul, Flavius Clemens, even though he was a first cousin of the emperor and had married one of his relatives, Flavia Domitilla. (14.2) They were both charged with atheism, an offence which had shipwrecked many of those who had been condemned for sailing too close to Jewish customs. Some were executed; for the others the minimum penalty was confiscation of property. Domitilla herself was merely exiled to the island of Pandateria.[159] (14.3) But Glabrio, Traianus' fellow consul, was charged with the same offences as many others, but specifically also with fighting in the arena with wild animals, and executed. Indeed, it is likely that the primary source of the emperor's

---

[155] Both these actions were in line with Roman law (actors were subject to *infamia* – in other words had no status). Suet. *Dom.* 8.3 refers to an unnamed quaestor (i.e. senator).

[156] For the trial of Helvidius Priscus II and associates, in AD 93, see **P11**.

[157] Juventius Celsus is the name of two distinguished Roman jurists, father and son, and it is not certain which one is meant here.

[158] See Statius, *Silvae* 4.3 = **K92** for the *via Domitiana*, completed in AD 95.

[159] T. Flavius Clemens was Domitian's cousin, (see family tree), and shared the consulship of 95 with him. Suet. *Dom.* 15.1 suggest the execution 'of this despicably lazy man, occurred suddenly on the flimsiest of pretexts and virtually during his consulship.' His wife, Flavia Domitilla was Domitian's niece. A later, Christian tradition took the charge of atheism as implying Christianity, claiming Flavia Domitilla as a martyr, but this is unlikely. Pandateria, now Ventotene, was an island of exile, 25 miles off the coast of Italy.

anger against him was jealousy. During his consulship Domitian had invited him to his Alban villa for the so-called Festival of Youth and had challenged him to slay an enormous lion. Glabrio managed to do so with an arrow-shot of the most deadly accuracy and without suffering so much as a scratch.[160]

(14.4) As a result of all these crimes the emperor was becoming paranoiac.[161] He no longer trusted anyone and felt his safety threatened by both his freedmen and his prefects of the guard, whom he usually managed to have charged and tried while they were actually still in office. Epaphroditus, Nero's freedman, he had originally exiled, but now had him executed, charged with failure to protect the emperor, Nero. Such a punishment, exercised on behalf of Nero, was intended to terrify his own freedmen from risking any such failure.[162]

D15   The final conspiracy, AD 96
(14.5) All this was no help to him whatever. The following year there was a conspiracy against him, in which he was murdered, during the consulship of Gaius Antistius and Gaius Valens. The latter had become consul at the age of eighty nine and himself died in that same year.[163]

(15.1) Those who had planned the deed and then attacked him were as follows: Parthenius, his chamberlain, despite the fact that he had been highly honoured by him in being allowed to wear a sword; Sigerus, also one of the team of chamberlains; Entellus, his petitions secretary; and a freedman, Stephanus.[164] (15.2) If we are to believe what is said, his wife Domitia, the prefect Norbanus, and his colleague, Petronius Secundus, were all in the know.[165] Domitia herself had always been loathed by Domitian and for this reason lived in fear for her life; the rest of them no longer felt any affection for him, some because they were already the targets of complaints, the others because they expected to be. (15.3) I myself have also heard the following story: Domitian had already become suspicious of the conspirators and had decided to kill them. So he wrote their names on a twin-page tablet of lime wood and hid it under his pillow on the couch where he usually took a nap.[166] One of his naked boys, the so-called "Whisperers", stole it while the emperor was asleep during the day and kept it without knowing what it was all about. (15.4) Domitia happened to come across it, read it, and told the conspirators about it. They were already making their

---

[160] For Glabrio see **B91**.
[161] See Suet. *Dom.* 14: but perhaps he was paranoid because people *were* plotting against him!
[162] Epaphroditus, Nero's *a libellis* (petitions secretary), accompanied his final flight and helped him commit suicide (Dio 63.29.2, Suet. *Nero* 49.3) and *that* was why Domitian had him killed, according to Suetonius (*Dom.* 14.4).
[163] See **B96**.
[164] Of the four freedmen listed, all but Stephanus are known from poems of Martial (e.g. 4.78.8, 5.6 = **R21**, 8.48), and all but Entellus are mentioned in Suetonius' account (*Dom.* 17).
[165] Suet. *Dom.* 14.1 asserts the involvement of Domitia, but does not mention her in the actual account. She still referred to herself 30 years later as Domitia wife of Domitian (**J11h**). Petronius was killed later – see Suet. *Dom.* 23, while Norbanus (presumably promoted for his loyalty in the Saturninus revolt) is not heard of further.
[166] The story of a death-list written on two pieces of lime-wood also occurs in Herodian's account (1.17.1– 7) of the death of Commodus in AD 192, within Dio's lifetime, and later in accounts of Aurelian's death in AD 275. This doesn't make any of the accounts automatically untrue, but does make the motif dubious.

plans and as a result accelerated the plot. But they took no positive action until they had a clear idea about who was to inherit the imperial position. (15.5) They sounded out a number of possible candidates, but none of them was willing to take it on, since they all feared that their loyalty was being tested. In the end they turned to Nerva, an aristocrat of the noblest birth and most genial disposition,[167] whose own life had also been in danger as a result of slanderous predictions by astrologers that he would one day be monarch.[168] This factor enabled them to persuade him to accept the office more readily. (15.6) Domitian always took particular care to scrutinise the date and hour of birth of the leading citizens, and as a result he eliminated a significant number of them as a precaution, even though they had no ambitions for high office. He would have killed Nerva as well, had not an astrologer friend of his declared that he would be dead within a few days.[169]

D16   Portents of Domitian's death

(16.1) It is impossible for such important events to happen unexpectedly, and there were indeed a number of unfavourable omens at the time.[170] Domitian himself had a dream in which Rusticus had approached him with a sword, and the statue of Minerva, which he kept in his bedroom, had thrown away her weapons and plunged into an abyss in her chariot drawn by two black horses.[171] But of all the manifestations the most remarkable was this one. (16.2) Larginus Proculus made a public declaration in the province of Germany that the emperor would die on the very day on which he actually did so. He was sent under arrest to Rome by the governor, and when hauled in front of the emperor even under those circumstances insisted on the truth of his prophecy. He was condemned to death, but the execution was postponed so that his death would take place once the emperor had survived the threat. But then Domitian was murdered and Proculus' life was saved. He was also given 400,000 sesterces by Nerva. (16.3) Earlier someone else had once told Domitian when and how he would die. The speaker was then asked by the emperor how his own life would end, and he replied that he would be devoured by dogs. So Domitian ordered him to be burned alive. The pyre had already been set alight around him, when there was an enormous cloudburst, which quenched the flames. A pack of dogs later found him lying on the pyre with his hands still tied behind his back. They tore him to pieces.[172]

D17   Domitian's death

(17.1) I have one more very remarkable item of information, which I shall divulge after describing Domitian's death. He had risen from presiding over his court of justice and was about to take his usual afternoon nap. But Parthenius had first removed the blade

---

[167] Nerva had been a close friend of Nero, rewarded by him after the failure of the Piso conspiracy in AD 65 (Tac. *Ann.* 15.72), and survived the civil war to be cos ord with Vespasian in 71 and cos II ord with Domitian in 90. He certainly must have been a smooth operator (Murison, page 266).

[168] Evidence that even, or especially, the next emperor had to justify his actions or inactions under Domitian.

[169] This sentence of Dio adds little, so was cut by Xiphilinus, though preserved by Zonaras.

[170] Dio, like Suetonius, and indeed the whole historiographical tradition except for Tacitus, takes omens and portents of great events for granted. Dio gives fewer than Suet. *Dom.* 14–16.

[171] For Domitian's special relationship with Minerva see **L44–L49**.

[172] The same story is told by Suet. *Dom.* 15.3, but with the revealing difference that Suet. has Dom. have the astrologer, Ascletarion killed immediately with orders for careful cremation of the body. Dio embellishes with the torture of burning alive.

from the sword which was always kept under his pillow, so that it would be no use to him. He then sent Stephanus, who was stronger than the rest of them, into the room (17.2) and he struck Domitian, not fatally but with sufficient force to knock him to the floor where he lay unconscious. Terrified that he might yet escape, Parthenius rushed in (or according to some reports, sent in a freedman called Maximus). That was the end of Domitian, but Stephanus was also immediately killed by a concerted attack on him by those who were not part of the conspiracy.[173]

D18 Apollonius of Tyana's vision

(18.1) I mentioned above one item of information which I regard as more remarkable than any other. On the very day and at the very hour on which Domitian was murdered, as was confirmed later by the events which occurred in both locations, in Ephesus (or somewhere else like that) a certain Apollonius of Tyana called a meeting of the whole population. He climbed onto a high rock and then shouted, "Well done, Stephanus, hooray, Stephanus. Strike that bloody murderer. You have struck; you have wounded; you have killed him." (18.2) Those are the true facts, even if you don't believe them ten thousand times.[174]

Domitian lived for forty four years, ten months, and twenty six days. His reign lasted fifteen years and five days. His nurse, Phyllis, stole his body away and buried it.[175]

---

[173] Suet. *Dom.* 17.1–2 gives considerably more detail including the source, a slave-boy who was present.
[174] Dio had presumably read Philostratos' biography of Apollonius, see **P16c**.
[175] More details are given by Suet. *Dom.* 17.3.

SECTION E

JOSEPHUS, *JEWISH WAR*

Introduction: Yosef ben Mattityahu (Joseph son of Matthias) was born in Jerusalem in AD 37/8 to an aristocratic family of priestly class. He led Jewish forces around Galilee in the Jewish revolt where he failed to prevent the Roman commander Vespasian from capturing Jotapata in AD 67 and was besieged in a cave with forty others. Having survived a suicide pact (**E3**) he surrendered to the Romans, and predicted the accession of Vespasian and Titus. When Vespasian was indeed hailed emperor two years later, Josephus was released from captivity (**E5**), and attached to the entourage of Vespasian and Titus. He was with them in Alexandria, before returning with Titus to Judaea for the capture of Jerusalem (AD 70, **E8**) and his triumphant return to Rome (**E6**). Granted Roman citizenship and considerable patronage by Vespasian (**E8**), Titus Flavius Josephus (as he now became) began to write histories in Aramaic which he then translated into Greek (**E1a**). His seven-book account of the Jewish War was written 'when the deeds were virtually still before our eyes' (**E7**), probably starting after the building of the Temple of Peace in AD 75 and completed after the death of Caecina Alienus *c.* AD 79 whom he disparages. He then went on to write a twenty-book account of all Jewish history, *Jewish Antiquities* which he completed in AD 93/94, aged 55. It seems that he appended a one-book '*My Life*' to a later edition of the *JA*.

It will be obvious that Josephus owed everything in the second half of his life to the Flavians, and that he was a strong supporter of the Flavian dynasty. It is also clear from his writings that he was a very controversial figure (**E7–E9**). But attacks on him seem to have been made, not just from those accusing him of being a Roman 'collaborator' but from other 'pro-Roman' Jews. It is also worth remembering that a number of other Romanised or Hellenised Jews were important Flavian figures: Ti. Julius Alexander, King Agrippa, Berenice. Josephus is a uniquely important source for the Flavian period because of his closeness to many important events, and because not being a Roman writing for other Romans, he describes in detail things other Romans may have taken for granted, providing our best accounts of a Roman triumph (**E6**), and of the Roman imperial army (**N2**).

The best current accounts of Josephus and his times are T. Rajak, *Josephus* (2ⁿᵈ ed. London 2002) and edd. Edmondson, Mason and Rives, *Flavius Josephus and Flavian Rome* (Oxford 2005). The *Jewish War* is available in a Penguin Classics translation (1959, revised 1980). All his works are readily available online in the inevitably antiquated translation by the remarkable William Whiston, Lucasian professor of mathematics at Cambridge 1702–1710.

This section presents extracts from Josephus' *Jewish War* which are relevant to his life and/or historical works. Other extracts of more specific relevance to particular topics can be found in part II.

E1 Josephus' preface, apology and summary of his work

Josephus prefaces his work, which he began around AD 75, with a promise to report all the facts accurately with no embellishment, although he admits that at times he may succumb to his emotions whilst relating the destruction of his city. He establishes himself as an eyewitness and participant who began the war fighting against the Romans but ended as a supporter of the Flavian dynasty. His preamble is quick to lay the blame for the destruction of Jerusalem with the leaders of the various Jewish factions and with in-fighting amongst the Jews, exonerating Titus Caesar and the Romans from censure.

E1a Josephus introduces his account

[1] The war which the Jews made against the Romans was not only the greatest of our time but also greater almost than any ever heard of, whether city against city or nation against nation. However, some who were not present themselves have collected baseless and contradictory tales and have written down twisted accounts, [2] and some eyewitnesses have falsely reported things, either from a desire to flatter the Romans or to show their hatred to the Jews, and their accounts contain slanderous accusations and flattering praise instead of the exact truth. [3] For the sake of those living in the Roman Empire, I have decided to translate into Greek those books which I wrote earlier in my native tongue and circulated among the non-Greek speakers. I, Josephus,

son of Matthias, a Jew from Jerusalem by birth and a priest, who at first fought against the Romans and was forced to witness what happened afterwards, wrote this account.

[4] This, as I said, was the greatest disturbance of all time and happened when the affairs of the Romans were themselves in great disarray. Jewish revolutionaries, strong in resources and wealth, arose from the disturbance. The state of affairs in the East was so tumultuous that some were motivated by hope of gain and others from fear of loss in such troubles; [5] for the Jews hoped that all of their countrymen beyond the Euphrates would rise with them, while the Gauls who neighboured the Romans were becoming inflamed and the Celts were not quiet. In fact, after the death of Nero, there was chaos everywhere. The opportunity persuaded many to aspire to the imperial throne, while the soldiers, in hope of gaining money, were eager for change.

E1b   Criticism of contemporary historians

[6] I thought it absurd to see the truth distorted in affairs of such great consequence and ignore it. The Parthians, the Babylonians, the Southern Arabians, those of our countrymen beyond the Euphrates and the Adiabeni, on account of my labours, knew accurately the causes of the war, the sufferings it bought upon us, and its terrible ending, yet the Greeks and those Romans who were not in the wars, remained ignorant, reading either flatteries or fictions. [7] Some writers claim to write histories, yet fail in their purpose and reveal nothing that is sound. For they wish to show the greatness of the Romans, and always diminish and belittle the actions of the Jews. [8] However I do not see how men can show themselves to be great by conquering feeble opponents! And they are not ashamed of overlooking the length of the war, the great number of Roman troops who suffered hardships, the might of their commanders, whose great toils in Jerusalem will be considered inglorious if what they achieved is reckoned to be a small matter. [9] However, I do not intend to show opposition to the champions of the Romans nor to exaggerate the deeds of my countrymen; but I will reveal the deeds of both with accuracy.

E1c   Difficult for Josephus to remain detached

However the language with which I shall record the affairs I describe, will reflect my own passions and I must allow myself to lament the miseries of my country. [10] For the country was destroyed by our own internal factions and the Romans, who unwillingly attacked us and burnt our Temple, were bought in by Jewish faction leaders, as Titus Caesar, who destroyed the Temple, has himself testified. During the war, he pitied the people who were kept down by the leaders of the factions, and he often delayed taking the city and prolonged the siege in order to let the ringleaders have the opportunity to yield. [11] But if anyone criticises my accusations against the Jewish leaders or their gangs, or my lamentations over the misfortunes of my country, I must beg his pardon for my weakness, although it runs contrary to the rules for writing history. For our city had reached the highest degree of prosperity of any other city in the Roman Empire and yet fell into the depths of misfortune. [12] And so it seems to me that the misfortunes of all men, from the beginning of the world, when compared to those of the Jews, are small; and yet we ourselves were the authors of these. This makes it impossible for me to master my passions. But if anyone is hard-hearted enough to censure me for this, let him distinguish between the facts, which belong to the history, and the lamentations, which belong to the writer.

E1d   Contemporary history to be preferred

[13] However, I may justly censure the Greek scholars who, knowing that such great actions in their own times eclipse the old wars, sit in judgement and bitterly criticise those who devote their attention to the period; although their eloquence may be superior, their historical sense is not. They write new histories about the Assyrians and the Medes, as if the ancient writers had not described their affairs as they ought to have. [14] However their writing is as inferior as their thinking. For the old historians wrote about what happened in their own time and their immediate participation in the events gave validity to their accounts and made it shameful to write lies, when they must be known by the readers to be such. [15] However, seeking to preserve the memory of what has not been recorded before and to present contemporary events to future generations is really worthy of praise. The man who not only records what has not been recorded before but also composes a new historical work of his own should be esteemed, not the man who does no more than change the arrangement and order of other men's works. [16] And so, at great expense and through great endeavours, although I am a foreigner, I dedicate this work as a record of the great deeds of the Greeks and the Romans. Some native Greek writers, their mouths wide open and their tongues loosened when they have the chance to gain from lawsuits, when writing history, where they must speak the truth and gather together the facts diligently, appear to be gagged. Thus they leave the writing of history to inferior writers who are not acquainted with the actions of the great men. I will endeavour to present the real truth of the historical facts, although the Greek historians have neglected this.

[17] I do not think it fitting to write here about the antiquities of the Jews, who they were and how they revolted from the Egyptians, what countries they travelled over and what countries they conquered, and how they were removed from them. This would be, in any case, superfluous. For many Jews before me have composed accurate histories of our ancestors and some have been translated into Greek with very few mistakes.

E1e   Josephus outlines his history

[18] I shall begin my story where the Greek historians and our prophets leave off. I shall relate in great depth, and with all the thoroughness I am capable of, the events of the war which happened in my own time; but I shall run over briefly the events which preceded my own time.

[19] I shall relate how Antiochus Epiphanes stormed Jerusalem and held it three years and three months and was then ejected out of the country by the Hasmonaeans. After that, I shall relate how their descendants quarrelled about the throne and brought in Pompey and the Romans to settle their affairs. Then how Herod, Antipater's son, ended the Hasmonaean line and brought in Sosius. [20] Next, how our people revolted upon Herod's death, while Augustus was the Roman Emperor, and Quintilius Varus the local governor. I shall relate how the war broke out in the twelfth year of Nero's reign, the fate of Cestius and the places the Jews attacked in the first encounters of the war.

[21] I shall also relate how they built fortifications around neighbouring cities; the decision, after Cestius' defeat, of Nero who feared for the empire as a whole, and

made Vespasian general in this war; and how Vespasian, with his eldest son, invaded Judaea; the size of the Roman army and auxiliaries with which he over-ran Galilee; and how he took some cities by force, and others by negotiation. [22] At this stage, I shall describe the good order of the Roman army and the discipline of the legions; the dimensions and nature of the two Galilees and the limits of Judaea; the peculiarities of the country and the lakes and fountains found in them; I shall give an accurate account of the misfortunes that befell every city as they were taken, based on what I saw done or endured. For I shall not conceal any of the misfortunes I myself suffered, which my readers are familiar with.

[23] Next I shall relate how, when the Jews' affairs were worsening, how Nero died and how Vespasian, when he was advancing on Jerusalem, was called back to take the throne; the signs he received from portents and the upheavals in the government at Rome [24] and how the soldiers made him emperor despite his protests; and how, on his departure to Egypt to settle the affairs of the empire, internal strife broke out among the Jews; how the tyrants rose up against them and fell into in-fighting amongst themselves.

[25] Moreover, I shall record how Titus marched to Judaea from Egypt for a second time; the method, location and size of his forces; the state of the in-fighting in the city when he arrived, the attacks he made, the ramparts he erected; the measurements of the three walls which encompassed the city; the defences of the city and the layout of the Temple and the sanctuary; [26] the exact measurements of these and of the altar; certain festivals, the seven grades of purity, the ministrations of the priests, their attire and that of the high priests; and the nature of the most holy place of the Temple. I shall conceal nothing or add anything to the known facts.

[27] Next, I shall report the barbarism of the Jewish leaders towards their own people as well as the clemency of the Romans towards foreigners, and how often Titus, desiring to preserve the city and the Temple, invited the rebels to come to terms. I shall distinguish between the sufferings and misfortunes of the people that led to their defeat and how far they were afflicted by the war, the in-fighting and by starvation. [28] Nor shall I neglect the misfortunes of the deserters, nor the punishments inflicted on the prisoners, the burning of the Temple, without Caesar's consent, the number of sacred treasures snatched from the fire, the destruction of the whole city, with the signs and portents that preceded it; the capture of the faction leaders, the number of people enslaved and the fates that befell them; [29] what the Romans did to the remains of the war and how they demolished the fortifications that were in the country; and how Titus advanced through the whole country, establishing order, and his return to Italy and triumphal celebrations.

[30] All these things I have enclosed in seven books and I have left no cause for complaint or accusation among those who participated in the war or have been acquainted with the facts. I have written it down for those who love the truth, not those who seek to entertain themselves. I will begin my record of these things from the start of my summary.

[Josephus, *Jewish War* 1.1–30]

E2 Josephus intends to surrender himself to the Romans (July AD 67)

(As a young man, Josephus had travelled to Rome to meet Nero about the release of some Jewish prisoners (My Life, 13–16). On his return to Judaea he was made commander of the Jewish forces in Gallilee against the Romans (JW 2.568). Vespasian marched against this area (see N3) and captured the city in July AD 67 (JW 3.141–339). Josephus eluded capture and was besieged in a cave with forty others. The Romans repeatedly sent guarantees of his safety if he surrendered, including through his friend, Nicanor (JW 3.340–349).

[350] As Josephus considered Nicanor's proposal, the Roman soldiers were so angry that they hurried to set fire to smoke him out of the cave, but the tribune would not permit them to do so in his determination to take the man alive. [351] And as Nicanor entreated Josephus to comply, and the threatening attitude of his amassed enemies was clear, Josephus recalled those dreams which he had dreamed in the night, in which God had forewarned him about both the future calamities of the Jews, and the fortunes of the Roman emperors. [352] Now Josephus was able to give shrewd interpretations about the meanings of such dreams which have been ambiguously delivered by God. Also, as a priest himself and a descendant of priests, he was not unacquainted with the prophecies contained in the sacred books. [353] At this moment, he was divinely inspired; setting before him the terrifying images from the dreams he had recently had, he sent up a secret prayer to God: [354] 'Since it pleases you, the creator of the Jewish nation, to crush them, and since all their good fortune has passed to the Romans, and since you have chosen this soul of mine to foretell what will come to pass hereafter, I willingly give myself into their hands and am content to live. And I openly declare that I do not go over to the Romans as a deserter of the Jews, but as your servant.'

[Josephus, *Jewish War* 3.350–354]

(The other men perceive Josephus' intention and turn on him. He reports a speech he then made urging them that suicide is a sin (JW 3.355–382)).

E3 Josephus survives (July AD 67)

[383] Josephus used these and many similar arguments to prevent the men from killing themselves. [384] However desperation had closed their ears; they had long ago devoted themselves to death and they were furious with Josephus. They ran at him with swords in their hands from all directions and called him a coward, all appearing ready to strike him. [385] But he called one of them by name, he glared at another like a general, a third he took by the hand and pleaded with a fourth until that man was ashamed of himself; and distracted by various passions, as well he might in the great distress he was in, Josephus kept all their swords away from him, turning like a cornered animal to each attacker in turn. [386] In these fatal moments, some of their right hands were weakened by the reverence they bore for their general and their swords dropped from their hands and many, when they aimed to strike him with their swords, were not willing or able to do it.

[387] However, in this predicament, his wisdom did not fail him and, putting his trust in God, he risked his life in the following way: [388] 'And now,' he said. 'Since you have chosen to die, come on, let us draw lots to kill one another. [389] Whoever draws the first lot shall be killed by whoever draws the second and thus shall fortune make its progress through us all. And none of us shall perish by his own hand, for it

would be unfair if, when the rest are gone, somebody should change his mind and save himself.' This proposal seemed to them to be very just. [390] When he had persuaded them to determine the matter by lot, he drew one of the lots for himself also. The man who drew the first lot offered his throat to the man who had the next, believing that the general would die amongst them too in due course. Death, they thought, was sweeter than life, if Josephus might die with them. [391] Yet, whether by chance or divine intervention, Josephus was left to the last. And because he did not desire to be condemned by the lot nor to stain his hand with the blood of a fellow countryman, he persuaded him to make a pact and both remained alive.

[Josephus, *Jewish War* 3.383–391]

It remains debateable whether Josephus rigged the lot to ensure his survival, and if so, how. The situation is the basis for the 'Josephus Problem' in mathematics and computer science.

E4   Josephus prophesies Vespasian's accession (July AD 67)

[399] When Josephus heard Vespasian give those orders, he said that would like to speak to him in private. Vespasian ordered everyone to withdraw except Titus and two of his friends and Josephus said: [400] 'Vespasian, you think that you have merely secured a prisoner. However I come to you as a messenger of greater tidings; for I have been sent to you by God. I know the Jewish law and how a general should die. [401] Will you send me to Nero? Why? Will Nero and those who succeed him before you remain on the throne? You, Vespasian, are Caesar and Emperor, you and your son here. [402] Bind me tighter, and keep me for yourself, Caesar, for you are master not only of me but also over the land and the sea and all of mankind. And I ask to be kept in closer custody in order to be punished [403] if I take the name of God in vain.' When he had said this, Vespasian did not immediately believe him but supposed that Josephus was using a cunning trick to save himself. [404] However, after a while he grew convinced and believed that what he had said was true, as God himself raised his ambitions so that he began to think of gaining the empire and foreshadowed his rise with other signs. [405] He also found that Josephus' prophecies had proved true on other occasions.

[Josephus, *Jewish War* 3.399–405]

E5   Josephus freed by Vespasian and Titus (July AD 69)

[622] Everywhere Vespasian's good fortune was evident and, for the most part, everything was coming together for him. He now thought that he had government in his hands through divine providence and that a just fate had brought imperial power to him. [623] For, as he recalled the other omens, which everywhere had foretold that he should obtain the throne, he remembered in particular what Josephus had told him, when he dared to foretell his accession while Nero was still alive. [624] He was concerned that this man was still a prisoner; so he sent for Mucianus, together with his other officers and companions, and, after firstly informing them of Josephus' bravery and how hard he had made life for them during the siege of Jotapata, [625] he went on to relate Josephus' predictions, which he had initially suspected were invented out of fear, but which had been proven to be true over time. [626] 'It is a shameful thing,' he said. 'That the man who foretold my rise to power and who delivered a divine message to me should still be a prisoner and endure the life of a captive.' So he called for

Josephus and commanded that he should be freed. [627] From this requital Vespasian had made to a stranger, the officers were expecting great things for themselves. Titus was then present with his father and said: [628] 'Father, it is right that Josephus' disgrace be removed along with his chains. For if we cut them to pieces, instead of loosening them, he will be like a man who was never bound at all.' For that was the usual procedure for those chained up without a cause. [629] Vespasian agreed and a man came in and cut the chain to pieces. Josephus gained his privilege as a reward for his past prophecies and was believed to be capable of foretelling the future.

[Josephus, *Jewish War* 4.622–629]

The cutting of Josephus' bonds meant that he avoided the legal status of an ex-slave. For discussion of this episode see Rajak, *Josephus*[2] 186–7.

E6 The Jewish triumph of Vespasian and Titus

The triumph of Vespasian and Titus over the Jews, held in AD 71 was the first since Claudius' triumph over the Britons, 28 years before. This, by contrast was celebrated by the actual commanders, and was the first ever joint triumph. In addition, Josephus' account is the only surviving account of any Roman triumph by an eye-witness.

E6a Titus returns to Rome

[7.116] And so, resuming his journey into Egypt, Titus crossed the desert very quickly and came to Alexandria, [117] intending to sail to Rome by sea. He sent the two legions accompanying him back to where they had been stationed before; the Fifth to Moesia and the Fifteenth to Pannonia. [118] As for the leaders of the prisoners, he ordered Simon and John, along with seven hundred men, selected as exceptional for their height and physique, to be sent to Italy, to be displayed in his triumph.

E6b Preparations for the triumph

[7.119] When his journey had gone as smoothly as he could have wished, the city of Rome welcomed him in the same way as his father and met him from a distance. But what made the occasion more glorious for Titus was when his father himself met and received him. [120] The crowd of citizens was overjoyed to see all three together. [121] A few days later, they decided to hold a single triumph for both of them, to celebrate their glorious exploits, although the senate had decreed each a separate triumph. [122] When notice was given of the day appointed for the victory procession, not a single person out of the immense population was left in the city. Everyone came out so that there was standing room only, leaving only enough space for the procession to advance. [123] All the soldiers had marched out the night before in their centuries and cohorts under their commanders and were all around the gates, not of the Upper Palace, but the ones near the Temple of Isis, which was where the emperors had rested the previous night. [124] As soon as the day came, Vespasian and Titus came out with laurel wreaths and clothed in the traditional purple robes of their ancestors and went as far as the Portico of Octavia; [125] for it was there that the senate, the senior magistrates and the equestrians waited for them.

For the route of the triumphal procession, and Josephus' account, see Beard, *The Roman Triumph*, 93–96 and Millar, "Last Year in Jerusalem: Monuments of the Jewish War in Rome" in edd. Edmondson, Mason & Rives, *Flavius Josephus & Flavian Rome* (Oxford, 2005). See also Map of Rome, page 20.

E6c   The start of the triumph

[7.126] A tribunal had been set up in front of the colonnades and ivory chairs had been placed upon it. When they came and sat on them, the soldiers at once shouted acclamations, giving full attestation of their valour. They themselves sat unarmed, dressed in silk robes and laurel wreaths. [127] Vespasian received their acclamations and gave them the signal for silence, although they were disposed to go on shouting them. [128] All were silent and the emperor stood up, covered most of his head with his cloak, offered the customary prayers, as did Titus too. [129] Then, after the prayers, Vespasian made a short speech to all the people and then sent away the soldiers to the dinners which victorious generals were accustomed to provide. [130] Vespasian himself retired to the gate which took its name from all the triumphal processions passing through there. [131] There they tasted some food, put on their triumphal robes and made sacrifices to the gods that stand on either side of the gate. They then resumed their triumphal procession, advancing through the theatres so that they might be more easily seen by the crowds.

E6d   Magnificence of the display

[7.132] It is impossible to do justice to the number of shows, and their magnificence in every respect, whether as performances, works of art, variety of riches or the rarities of nature. [133] For almost all such priceless treasures that the most fortunate men ever get piece by piece were here all heaped on one another; and all that was brought together on that day demonstrated the greatness of the Roman Empire. [134] For there were masses of silver and gold and ivory, crafted into every shape, and these poured forth more like a flowing river than as if carried in a procession. In some parts the rarest purple tapestries were carried along and others were embroidered with life-like representations by the Babylonian artists. [135] Precious, transparent stones, some set in crowns of gold, some in other mounts, were carried in such vast numbers that we could see how foolish we had been to suppose that any of them were rare. [136] Images of the gods were also carried, wonderful in their size and artistic merit, each made from nothing but the most costly materials. Also many species of animals were paraded, each in their own natural trappings. [137] Accompanying all parts of this parade was a large group of men, wearing purple garments, all interwoven with gold; those chosen to take part in the procession had such magnificent ornaments, which were both extraordinary and astonishing. [138] In addition, not even the great number of captives went unadorned; the deformity of their bodies was concealed from sight by the variety and fine textures of their garments.

E6e   Scenes depicting events of the war

[7.139] But what was most surprising of all was the structure of the stages which were carried along; for so great was their size that anyone who met them would be afraid that the bearers might not be able to support them firmly enough. [140] Indeed, many of them were three or even four storeys high and their magnificence of their decoration brought both pleasure and surprise. [141] Many of them were covered in gold tapestries and all were framed in gold and ivory. [142] There were numerous tableaux showing the different stages of the war, portrayed in a most lively way. [143] For here a happy country laid waste could be seen, and there entire squadrons of the enemies slain; some of them ran away and some were led away into captivity; walls of great size were overthrown and destroyed by engines; great strongholds were taken and the walls of heavily populated cities upon hills were seized [144] and an army streaming in through the walls; every place was full of slaughter and supplications by the enemy who were no longer able to raise their hands in opposition; temples set on fire were represented, and houses which were overthrown and collapsing upon their owners. [145] After desolation and misery, rivers also flowed neither into cultivated fields nor to bring drink for men or cattle, but through a land ablaze on every sides. Such were the agonies which the Jews had suffered during the war. [146] The craftsmanship and art of these constructions was so magnificent that it showed, to those who had not seen it, what had been done as clearly as if they had been really present. [147] On top of every one of these stages was placed the commander of a captured town and the manner in which he was taken. Furthermore, a number of ships followed.

E6f   The spoils from the Temple

[7.148] The majority of the spoils was carried in a great heap but those taken from the Temple in Jerusalem were more prominent than all the rest. There was a golden table weighing many talents and a candlestick also made of gold although constructed differently from those used nowadays; [149] for its central shaft was fixed to a base and from this extended smaller branches placed like the forks of a trident. At the end of each was a socket made of brass for a lamp. There were seven of these representing the honour of the number seven among the Jews. [150] After these was carried the Law of the Jews, the last of the spoils. [151] Next came past very many men carrying images of Victory made from either ivory or gold. [152] Behind them Vespasian went first in a chariot, with Titus following him. Domitian also rode along with them, magnificently adorned himself, riding on a horse worthy of admiration.

E6g   End of the procession: death of Simon ben Gioras

[7.153] The procession ended at the Temple of Jupiter Capitolinus, where they came to a halt. For it was ancestral Roman custom to remain there until somebody brought news that the general of the enemy was dead. [154] This was Simon, the son of Gioras, who had been led in the procession with the prisoners. A noose had been thrown around his head and he had been dragged to the usual spot in the forum, tormented continually by those who led him. This was the place where the laws of Romans required condemned men to die for their crimes. [155] And so, when his death was announced, and all the people had raised a shout for joy, the sacrifices were begun and the customary prayers offered. The omens proved favourable. When they had finished this, they went away to the palace. [156] The emperor and his sons entertained some of the spectators at their own feast and for all the rest, luxurious banquets had been prepared at home for feasting. [157] This was a festival day for the City of Rome and celebrated the victory their army won against the enemy, the end of civil strife and the beginning of hopes for a prosperous and happy future.

[Josephus, *Jewish War* 7.116–157]

This passage continues in **K64** with an account of the Temple of Peace, housing some of the spoils from Jerusalem.

E7   Josephus on the publication of his *Jewish War*

[358] But perhaps you will say that you have written an accurate account of the things inflicted on Jerusalem. How can that be, when you had no part in that war, and have not even read Caesar's commentaries. That can be clearly demonstrated, since you have written the opposite of Caesar's commentaries. [359] But if you are confident that what you have written is better than everything else, why did you not put your history in the public domain when Vespasian and Titus were still alive, the commanders throughout the war, or when King Agrippa and his family were still around, people who has reached the heights of Greek scholarship? [360] You have had it written for more than twenty years and could have won testimonials for your accuracy from those with knowledge: but as it is, you are only confident now, since they are no longer with us, and you think that you cannot be contradicted. [361] Whereas I had no such fears about my own writing, but gave my books to the commanders themselves, when their deeds were virtually still before our eyes: I knew well, as an eye-witness, that I had reported the truth, and I was not wrong in anticipating their testimonials for what I reported. [362] I also immediately gave my history to many others, several of whom had played a part in the war, including King Agrippa and his relations. [363] The Emperor Titus was so keen that information about the events should be passed down to people from my books alone that he put his own signet seal on my books and ordered them to be published. [364] King Agrippa sent me sixty-two letters supporting the accuracy of my report.

[Josephus, '*My Life*' 358–363]

Josephus' '*Vita*' seems to have been published as a sort of appendix to his *Jewish Antiquities* in AD 93/4. Not a full account of his life it concentrates on justifying his actions, not as we might have expected against charges of collaboration with the Romans, but against charges of fellow pro-Roman Jews that when fighting in Galilee he had been incompetent and too aggressive. In particular he responds at length to written criticisms by Justus of Tiberias, whose works do not survive. In so doing he writes much of interest about his *Jewish War* and contemporary historiography, including the fact that Caesar (i.e. Vespasian) wrote commentaries – see **R1**. For more on his Josephus' '*My Life*' see Rajak, *Josephus²*, chapter 6.

E8   Josephus set up in Rome by Vespasian …

[422] … When Titus was about to sail away to Rome, he welcomed me as a fellow passenger and gave me every honour. [423] When we came to Rome, I received great attention from Vespasian: he gave me rooms in the house which was his before he became emperor, and honoured me with Roman citizenship; gave me a salary and continued to honour me until he changed from this life, without his generosity to me diminishing at all.

[Josephus, '*My Life*' 422–3]

E9   … and his continued protection by the Flavian family

[428] My treatment by the emperors remained the same: for when Vespasian died, Titus succeeded as emperor, and continued to uphold my reputation as his father had, in disbelieving accusations often made against me. [429] Domitian succeeded Titus and increased the honours paid to me, by punishing the Jews who had brought an accusation against me and by ordering that a eunuch slave, who was helping teach my son but had also brought an accusation against me, should be punished. He also gave me exemption from tax for my land in Judaea, which is a very great honour for the person who obtains it. And Domitia, the wife of Caesar, continued to do much to help

me. [430] These then are my achievements during my life: from them let others judge my character, as they wish. To you, Epaphroditus, best of men, I dedicate the whole work of my *Antiquities* and for now here conclude my writing.

[Josephus, *'My Life'*, 428–430]

Epaphroditus is probably not Nero's freedman, executed in AD 95, but rather the scholar and bibliophile, **R34**.

SECTION F
FLAVIAN MUNICIPAL LAW IN SPAIN

By the start of the Flavian period, Spain already had several towns (*municipia* and *coloniae*) whose inhabitants were Roman citizens. Vespasian's grant of the Latin right (*ius Latii*) in AD 73/4 (**M32**) meant that other communities could apply to establish, by town charter, a system of local government which meant that the magistrates became Roman citizens at the end of their year in office (**M33**). Several communities in Baetica (the law may only have applied to this province) set up detailed statutes clearly following a model (with very minor local variations). Parts of these statutes have been found for Malaca (Malaga: the *Lex Malacitana*) and Salpe(n)sa (near Utrera: the *Lex Salpensana*). Much more significant are the 6 large tablets of the *Lex Irnitana*, found in 1981 near a completely unknown Roman settlement, not mentioned any other source, nor included by Pliny in his list of 127 settlements in Baetica 'worth mentioning or easy to express in Latin' (*NH* 3.7). This, when supplemented by one section of the *Lex Malacitana*, gives us about two thirds of the whole charter (see figure below). The statute is complex but reveals much about how local government operated, both in Spain and elsewhere, since many provisions are clearly modelled on practice at Rome. It also suggests that provincial communities were already conforming to Roman practice. Some parts, including the first fifth of the lex are unknown. Missing sections probably legislated for the organisation of public cults and priesthoods (perhaps especially of imperial cult: here we might compare **L57** establishing rules for imperial cult at Narbo in Gaul) and for the constitution of the citizen body.

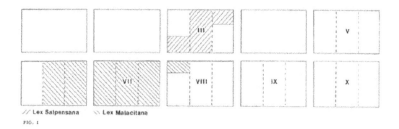

FIG. 1

The *Lex Irnitana* was almost certainly originally laid out in three columns on ten bronze tablets. Those labelled above in Roman numerals have been discovered, almost complete. About two thirds of tablet III corresponds to the previously known *Lex Salpensana*, while the *Lex Malacitana* duplicates tablet VII and also provides text corresponding to the middle and right-hand columns of Irni's sixth tablet (undiscovered).

The key publication of the *Lex Irnitana* is J. González and M.H. Crawford, 'The Lex Irnitana: A New Copy of the Flavian Municipal Law' in *The Journal of Roman Studies,* 76 (1986), pages 147–243, giving introduction, Latin text, English translation, commentary, pictures of the whole inscription and the figure above. Minor corrections are in *JRS* 98 (2008). I am very grateful to Cambridge University Press for permission to reproduce material from *JRS* and most especially to Professor Crawford for providing me with some further updates to his translation and for setting me right on many points about the text. His translation is intended to be as far as possible literal, and reproduces Latin terms. I have provided a glossary of terms used more than once: where a Latin term is used only once in the text, I have given an approximate translation or explanation in brackets.

The headings in bold are those of the statutes which summarise each chapter of the law. The *Lex Irnitana* does not provide chapter numbers but these can be matched to numbers given in other surviving versions, except for tablet V which has been attributed letters by the modern editors. I have not changed these for the LACTOR.

Glossary of Latin terms used in the Flavian Municipal Law

apparitor (pl. *apparitores*): a magistrate's attendant: his pay is *aes apparitorium*.

cognitor (pl. *cognitores*) in chapters 63–65, someone who vouched for another person (see note on ch.63 and Cicero, *II Verrines*, 1.13, 5.16–7). In ch.70 the word is used in its normal meaning of legal representative.

conscriptus (pl. *conscripti*): a traditional term for a Roman senator, hence, at a local level, a member of the town council.

curia (pl. *curiae*): the electorate was divided into *curiae* for voting purposes (see further note on ch.L). All elections in the Roman world depended on votes of voting groups.

decuriones (pl): the normal word for town councillors (collectively).

decuria (pl. *decuriae*): were groups of town councillors.

duumvir (pl. *duumviri*): 'duumvirs' (lit. 'two men') were the two chief, annually elected magistrates of the town.

incola (pl. *incolae*): this term, meaning 'inhabitants' designates residents of the town who were not *municipes* 'citizens'. They had mostly the same rights and responsibilities.

iudex (pl. *iudices*): a iudex judged a legal case, but was a non-paid layman, selected from a list, so was like a modern juror rather than a judge.

municeps (pl. *municipes*): a citizen of the *municipium*.

municipium: the proper designation of the town/settlement of Irni.

munus: a civic duty for rich inhabitants to spend money on their town(speople).

praeiudicium: a decision made in a trial with impact on another trial.

praes (pl. *praedes*), *praedia*: terms used in legal guarantees that money would be available to pay a fine or make up a shortfall. So if Quintus might be liable for a payment, his friend Gaius might be a *praes*, whereas Quintus' villa might be a *praedia* offering security against Quintus not paying.

praefectus: in this context, a person taking the place of a duumvir, either temporarily (ch 25) or as effective duumvir after the election of the emperor as honorary duumvir (ch.24).

recuperatores: members of a small panel of *iudices* which gave judgements in some law-cases.

sponsio: a sort of wager taken by the two parties of a case, over a sum of money to be paid by the loser to the winner.

Tablet IIIA
[Ch. 19]
The aediles, who have been appointed in that *municipium* according to an edict of
the Emperor Vespasian Caesar Augustus or the Emperor Titus Caesar Vespasian
Augustus or the Emperor Caesar Domitian Augustus and now hold that aedileship,
those aediles and those who are hereafter appointed aediles there under this statute
are to be aediles of the *Municipium Flavium Irnitanum*, in both cases until the date to
which their appointment runs. They are to have the right and power of managing the
corn-supply, the sacred buildings, the sacred and holy places, the town, the roads, the
districts, the drains, the baths and the market and of checking weights and measures;
of managing *vigiliae* (local watchmen) when occasion arises; and of seeing to and
doing whatever else the *decuriones* or *conscripti* decide is to be done by the aediles;
likewise of seizing a pledge from *municipes* and *incolae*, which may not be more
than 10,000 sesterces per person per day; likewise of imposing a fine on them or
pronouncing a condemnation against them not over 5,000 sesterces per person per
day. And those aediles (already in office) and those who are hereafter appointed under
this statute are to have jurisdiction and the right of granting or assigning a *iudex*
or *recuperatores* in those cases and between those parties where the duumviri have
jurisdiction, up to 1,000 sesterces, according to the rules in this statute. And those
aediles are to be allowed to have common slaves of the *municipes* of that *municipium*
as to attend on them as *limo cincti*. And as long as none of all those duties which are
listed above is carried out contrary to statutes, plebiscites, decrees of the senate, edicts,
judgments or constitutions of the Divine Augustus or Tiberius Julius Caesar Augustus
or the Emperor Galba Caesar Augustus or Tiberius Claudius Caesar Augustus or the
Emperor Vespasian Caesar Augustus or the Emperor Titus Caesar Vespasian Augustus
or the Emperor Caesar Domitian Augustus, chief priest, father of his country, those
aediles are to have rights and powers.

The original rubric is not preserved, but this section sets out the rights and powers of aediles. These were
the two annually elected magistrates, junior to the duumvirs (whose rights and powers must have been set
out in the previous chapter). Their duties included supervision of public buildings and they had the right to
levy fines up to certain limits. They were accompanied by *limo cincti* – slaves wearing a purple bordered
apron. This chapter gives a list of 'good emperors' whose decrees are to be regarded as valid. Galba appears
out of order here, but correctly in ch. 20 below.

[Ch. 20] Rubric. **Concerning the rights and powers of quaestors.**
The quaestors, who have been appointed before this statute according to an edict,
judgment or order of the Emperor Caesar Vespasian Augustus or the Emperor Titus
Caesar Vespasian Augustus or the Emperor Caesar Domitian Augustus and now
hold that quaestorship, likewise those who are appointed under this statute, are to be
quaestors, in both cases until the date to which their appointment runs. And they are to
have the right and power of collecting, spending, keeping, administering and looking
after the common funds of the *municipes* of that *municipium* at the discretion of the
duumviri. And they are to be allowed to have common slaves of the *municipes* of that
municipium with them in that *municipium* to attend on them. And as long as none of
all those duties which are listed above is carried out contrary to statutes, plebiscites,
decrees of the senate, edicts, judgments or constitutions of the Divine Augustus or

Tiberius Julius Caesar Augustus or Tiberius Claudius Caesar Augustus or the Emperor Galba Caesar Augustus or the Emperor Vespasian Caesar Augustus or the Emperor Titus Caesar Vespasian Augustus or the Emperor Caesar Domitian Augustus, chief priest, father of his country, they are to have rights and powers.

These local quaestors seem to have been modelled on those at Rome whose duties were mainly financial.

[Ch. 21] Rubric. **How they may acquire Roman citizenship in that *municipium*.**

Those among the senators, *decuriones* or *conscripti* of the *Municipium Flavium Irnitanum* who have been or are appointed magistrates, as is laid down in this statute, when they have left that office, they are to be Roman citizens, along with their parents and wives and any children who are born in legal marriages and have been in the power of their parents, likewise their grandsons and granddaughters born to a son, who have been in the power of their parents, provided that no more may become Roman citizens than the number of magistrates it is appropriate to appoint under this statute.

The locals could thus acquire full Roman citizenship for themselves and their immediate descendants by serving in their local town council. See *ILS* 1981 = **M33** for an example of this happening.

[Ch. 22] Rubric. **That those who acquire Roman citizenship should remain in the *manus* and *mancipium* and power of the same persons (as before).**

Whoever, male or female, acquires Roman citizenship under this statute or according to an edict of the Emperor Caesar Vespasian Augustus or the Emperor Titus Caesar Vespasian Augustus or the Emperor Caesar Domitian Augustus, father of his country, he or she is to be (as before) in the power and *manus* and *mancipium* of the person who has become a Roman citizen under this statute, in whose power and *manus* and *mancipium* he or she would be if he or she had undergone no change of citizenship. And he or she is to have that right of *tutoris optio* (choice of legal guardian) which they would have if they were born from a Roman citizen and had undergone no change of citizenship.

The purpose of this chapter (and the next) is that new grants of citizenship should not alter the existing (Roman) legal status within families whereby wives and children would legally be still under the control of the father of the household. Gaius, *Institutes* 1.108 explains *manus* as being a man's legal power over his wife, and *mancipium* (1.116–7) as his power over children.

[Ch. 23] Rubric. **That those who acquire Roman citizenship should retain rights over freedmen.**

[Tablet IIIB] Whoever, male or female, acquires Roman citizenship under this statute or according to an edict of the Emperor Caesar Vespasian Augustus or the Emperor Titus Caesar Vespasian Augustus or the Emperor Caesar Domitian Augustus, is to have the same right and the same position, as they would have if they had undergone no change of citizenship, over their own and their parents' freedmen and freedwomen, who have not acquired Roman citizenship, also over their goods and the obligations imposed in return for freedom.

[Ch. 24] Rubric. **Concerning the *praefectus* of the Emperor Caesar Domitian Augustus.**

If the *decuriones* or *conscripti* or *municipes* of that *municipium*, in the common name of the *municipes* of that *municipium*, confer the duumvirate on the Emperor Caesar Domitian Augustus, father of his country, and the Emperor Caesar Domitian Augustus, father of his country, accepts that duumvirate and orders anyone to be *praefectus* in his place, that *praefectus* is to have the same rights as he would have if it had been appropriate for him to be appointed sole duumvir under this statute and he had been appointed under this statute sole duumvir for the administration of justice.

Pompeii honoured the emperor Gaius in AD 40/1 by making him chief magistrate (*CIL* 10.904), but with a prefect to carry out his duties, as envisaged here.

[Ch. 25] Rubric. **Concerning the rights of a *praefectus* who has been left (in charge) by a duumvir.**

Whichever of the *duumviri*, who are in charge of the administration of justice in that *municipium*, hereafter leaves that *municipium* and does not think that he will return to that *municipium* on that day, he is to see that the person whom he decides to leave in charge as *praefectus* of the *municipium*, being over 35 and one of the *decuriones* or *conscripti*, swears by Jupiter and the Divine Augustus and the Divine Claudius and the Divine Vespasian Augustus and the Divine Titus Augustus and the genius of the Emperor Caesar Domitian Augustus and the Penates, that he will do what it is appropriate for a duumvir who is in charge of the administration of justice to do under this statute, while he is *praefectus*, as long as it can be done in that time, and that he will not knowingly and with wrongful intent do anything contrary to these rules. And when he has sworn in this way, he (the duumvir) is to leave him as *praefectus* of that *municipium*. And, until one or other of the *duumviri* returns to that *municipium*, the person who has been left as *praefectus* in this way is to have those rights and those powers in everything, except over the leaving of a *praefectus* and the acquisition of Roman citizenship, as is given under this law to the *duumviri* inasmuch as they are in charge of the administration of justice. And that person, while he is *praefectus* and on every occasion that he goes outside the *municipium*, is not to be away for more than one day at a time.

[Ch. 26] Rubric. **Concerning the oath of the *duumviri* and aediles and quaestors.**

The *duumviri* who are in charge of the administration of justice in that *municipium*, likewise the aediles who are in that *municipium*, likewise the quaestors who are in that *municipium*, each of them within five days after the granting of this statute, and those are hereafter appointed *duumviri*, aediles or quaestors under this statute, each of them within five days after he has begun to be duumvir, aedile or quaestor, before a meeting of the *decuriones* or *conscripti* is held, is to swear in a *contio* (public speech) by Jupiter and the Divine Augustus and the Divine Claudius and the Divine Vespasian Augustus and the Divine Titus Augustus and the genius of the Emperor Caesar Domitian Augustus and the Penates that he will do properly whatever he may believe to be according to this statute and according to the common good of the *municipes* of the *Municipium Flavium Irnitanum* and that he will not knowingly and with wrongful intent do anything contrary to this statute or to the common good of the *municipes* of that *municipium* and that he will restrain those whom he is able to restrain, and that he will neither initiate a course (of action) nor advise it nor express an opinion otherwise than he believes to be according to this statute and according to the common good of the *municipes* of that *municipium*. Anyone who has not sworn in this way is to be condemned to pay 10,000 sesterces to the *municipes* of that *municipium*; and the right of action, suit and claim of that money and concerning that money is to belong to any of the *municipes* of that *municipium* who wishes and who is entitled under this statute.

[Ch. 27] Rubric. **Concerning intercession amongst *duumviri* and aediles and quaestors.**

Whoever are *duumviri* or aediles or quaestors of that *municipium*, those *duumviri* are to have the right and power of interceding against each other and when anyone appeals to one or other or both, of them from one or more aediles or from one or more quaestor, likewise the aediles against each other, provided that the intercession takes place within three days from when the appeal [Tablet IIIC] has been made and from when intercession is possible, insofar as nothing is done contrary to this statute, and provided that none of them is appealed to more than once in the same case; and no-one is to do anything contrary to these rules when intercession has taken place.

The right of intercession was one of the most obvious 'checks and balances' of the traditional Roman constitution, and follows the pattern of equal magistrates at Rome, e.g. consuls being able, tradionally, to block each other.

[Ch. 28] Rubric. **Concerning the manumission of slaves before the *duumviri*.**

If any *municeps* of the *Municipium Flavium Irnitanum*, who is a Latin, in the presence of a duumvir of that *municipium* in charge of the administration of justice manumits his male or female slave from slavery into freedom or orders him or her to be free, provided that no ward or unmarried or married woman may manumit or order to be free anyone, male or female, without the authority of a guardian, any male slave who has been manumitted or ordered to be free in this way is to be free, any female slave who has been manumitted or ordered to be free in this way is to be free, in the same way as Latin freedmen with the fullest rights are or shall be free; provided that someone who is under 20 may only manumit if the number of *decuriones* necessary for decrees passed under this statute to be valid decide that the grounds for manumission are proper.

[Ch. 29] Rubric. **Concerning the granting of guardians.**

If anyone does not have a guardian or their guardian is uncertain, if he or she is a *municeps* of the *Municipium Flavium Irnitanum* and if he or she is not a ward, and if they request of a duumvir of that *municipium* in charge of the administration of justice to grant a guardian to them and nominate the person whom they want granted, then the person from whom the request has been made in this way, whether he has one or more colleagues, according to the advice of all his colleagues who are then in that *municipium* or within the boundaries of that *municipium*, once the case has been examined, if it seems right to him, is to grant as guardian the person who has been nominated. If the person, male or female, in whose name a request is made in this way is a ward or if the person from whom the request is made does not have a colleague or no colleague of his is in that *municipium* or within the boundaries of that *municipium*, then the person from whom the request has been made in this way, once the case has been examined, within ten days, according to a decree of the *decuriones* which has been passed when not less than two-thirds of the *decuriones* are present, is to grant as guardian to him (or her) the person who has been nominated, with the proviso that guardianship may not pass from the proper guardian. Whoever is granted as guardian under this statute, he is to be as proper a guardian to the person to whom he has been granted, with the proviso that guardianship may not pass from the proper guardian, as if he was a guardian as a Roman citizen and a nearest agnate to a Roman citizen.

[Ch. 30] Rubric. **The position of *decuriones* and *conscripti*.**
Whoever are now senators or substitute senators, or *decuriones* or *conscripti* or substitute *decuriones* or *conscripti* in the *Municipium Flavium Irnitanum* and those who are hereafter chosen or chosen in replacement under this statute (to be) counted as *decuriones* or *conscripti*, whoever of all of these ought to be *decuriones* or *conscripti* under this law are to be *decuriones* or *conscripti* of the *Municipium Flavium Irnitanum*, with the fullest rights and highest status as of the *decuriones* or *conscripti* of any Latin *municipium*.

This chapter formalises that existing councillors ('senators') will become councillors ('*decuriones*') of the new *municipium*.

[Ch. 31] Rubric. **Concerning the summoning by edict of the *decuriones* for the purpose of choosing *decuriones* in replacement.**
In any year in which there are fewer than 63 *decuriones* or *conscripti* in that *municipium*, which was the number by the law and custom of that *municipium* before the passage of this statute, unless choice or choice in replacement of *decuriones* or *conscripti* has already taken place in that year, the *duumviri* in charge of the administration of justice in that year, either or both of them at the earliest possible opportunity, as they may think proper, are to raise with the *decuriones* or *conscripti*, when no less than two thirds of them are present, on what day they wish to carry out the choice or choice in replacement or substitution of those whose addition to the number of *decuriones* or *conscripti* will lead to the presence of 63 *decuriones* or *conscripti* in that *municipium*, which was the number by the law and custom of that *municipium* before the passage of this statute. And when this matter has been raised with them, they are at the earliest possible opportunity to fix a day for this matter, provided that it is not one of those days on which it is the case that business is postponed in that *municipium* or which are feast-days or in the category of festivals in connection with the worship of the Imperial house and provided that nothing will take place for 30 days from the day on which the decree concerning this matter is passed, (a day for this matter) which is the next after the thirtieth day on which it is possible for justice to be administered and on which the majority has decided. The *duumviri*, either or both of them at the earliest possible opportunity, are to act in such a way that on that day the *decuriones* or *conscripti* and whoever by age ...

One whole tablet (IV) is lost here, but since tablet V still deals with decurions, that must have been the subject of the missing tablet – probably who was eligible or ineligible for that role.

Tablet VA
[Ch. A]
... he is to raise ... [insofar as] nothing is done contrary to this statute. And he is to grant the right of speaking about the matter to those who have requested that the matter be raised, likewise to anyone who wishes to speak against, before he begins to take votes. And he is to take votes, as is appropriate under this statute. And he is to declare what the majority of the *decuriones* or *conscripti* has decided about this matter and he is to take action and see that the decision is carried out. If there are any further matters, which a duumvir of that *municipium* thinks should be raised with the *decuriones* for the public good, nothing is enacted in this statute to prevent him raising it with the *decuriones*, according to the rules in this statute.

This chapter shows how decisions are taken under the chairmanship of (presumably) the duumvir.

[Ch. B] Rubric. **Concerning the order in which votes may be taken.**
Whoever holds a meeting of the *decuriones* or *conscripti* under this statute, provided that he does not do anything in this connection contrary to statutes or decrees of the senate or edicts or judgments of the Divine Augustus or of Tiberius Julius Caesar Augustus or of Tiberius Claudius Caesar Augustus or of the Emperor Galba Caesar Augustus or of the Emperor Vespasian Caesar Augustus or of the Emperor Titus Caesar Vespasian Augustus or of the Emperor Caesar Domitian Augustus, chief priest, father of his country, or against this statute, is to take the vote, according to the rules in this statute, from the *decuriones*, first (from those who have children), *ordo* by *ordo*, in the sequence determined by the number of children born to each in legal marriages, or from those who are, or would be if they were Roman citizens, in the same position as they would be if they then had children. If two or more are in the same position or do not have children and do not have the *ius liberorum* as mentioned above, he is to take the vote first from those who have been *duumviri*, in order of tenure, then among the rest in the order in which each was first chosen to be a *decurio* or *conscriptus*.

Roman senators voted by giving their opinion orally and in order of their political seniority. So here the local councillors are to express their opinions by *ordo* (rank), but with the next determinant being number of children – a result of Augustan marriage legislation aimed at rewarding larger families among the upper classes with a range of incentives.

[Ch. C] Rubric. **Concerning the reading out of decrees of the *decuriones* and their placing in the archives of the *municipium*.**
Any decree of the *decuriones* or *conscripti* which has been passed in that *municipium* under this statute, the person who passed it or his colleague or whichever of them is acting on behalf of the other is to read it out in the presence of the *decuriones* or *conscripti* on the day on which it was passed. If it is not read out on that day, he is to read it out on the next day on which a meeting of the *decuriones* or *conscripti* is held before any other matter is dealt with; or if the person on whose proposal the decree was passed has ceased to be duumvir the person who is then duumvir is then to read it out. And he is then to place it in the common records of the *municipes* of that *municipium*, as it has been read out and approved, within the next ten days.

[Ch. D] Rubric. **If it is appropriate for any decrees of the *decuriones* to be annulled, how they may be annulled.**
Any decree of the *decuriones* or *conscripti* which has been passed in that *municipium* under this statute, no-one is to raise with the *decuriones* or *conscripti* the annulment or erasure or rendering void of that decree, except when not less than two thirds of them are present. When the matter has been thus raised, if not less than three quarters of those who are thus present decide that the decree should be annulled or erased or rendered void, it is to be void. And the person who raised the matter or his colleague or the prefect nominated and left (in charge) under this law is to see in the presence of the *decuriones* or *conscripti* that it is erased and annulled and be or be rendered void.

[Ch. E] Rubric. **That the *decuriones* may not be dismissed or called away.**
When a duumvir holds a meeting of the *decuriones* or *conscripti* summoned under this statute in that *municipium*, his colleague is not to dismiss them or call them away to another place unless dismissed by the person who first summoned them.

[Ch. F] Rubric. **Concerning the distribution of *decuriones* into three *decuriae* which are to undertake embassies in turn.**
The *duumviri* who are the first in that *municipium* after this statute, likewise those who are in charge of the administration of justice in each year in which it is appropriate for there to be a new distribution of those who [Tablet VB] are to undertake the *munus* of performing embassies according to this statute, either or both at the earliest possible opportunity is to distribute the *decuriones* or *conscripti*, who are under 60, as equally as possible into three *decuriae*; and he is to draw lots among those *decuriae* and those who are in them for the order in which each *decuria* and the order in which those who are in each *decuria* are to undertake the *munus* of an embassy. And in whatever order the *decuriae* and those who are in them come out by lot, they are thereafter to perform the *munus* of an embassy in that order in rotation, until there is another distribution according to this statute.

Embassies could be expensive, time-consuming and nerve-wracking (see Millar, *ERW* 364, 375–85). Plutarch, *Moralia* 602C even suggests not having to do this as a consolation of being exiled. Municipalities frequently gave honours to those who undertook these tasks, and chapter G suggests men may have tried to avoid the task.

[Ch. G] Rubric. **Concerning the sending of ambassadors and the accepting of excuses.**
When it is necessary for one or more ambassadors to be sent anywhere on the common business of the *municipes* of the *Municipium Flavium Irnitanum*, then the duumvir who is in charge of the administration of justice is to raise with the *decuriones* or *conscripti* the sending of ambassadors. When the matter has been thus raised, he is to send and depute so many ambassadors, to such a destination, on such business, as the *decuriones* or *conscripti* have decided are to be sent, (namely) those who are then obliged to undertake the *munus* of an embassy in their turn, provided he does not send or depute anyone, who then or in the previous year is or has been duumvir, aedile or quaestor in that *municipium* and has not presented the accounts of the duumvirate, aedileship or quaestorship which has been held and had them approved by the *decuriones* or *conscripti* of that *municipium*; or anyone who has had in his

possession funds which are the common funds of the *municipes* of that *municipium* or who has handled or managed the finances or common business of the *municipes* of that *municipium* and has indeed not restored those funds to the common account of the *municipes* of that *municipium* or presented his accounts to the *decuriones* or *conscripti*, or to the person or persons to whom the commission has been given of receiving those (funds) and checking those (accounts), according to a decree of the *decuriones* or *conscripti* which has been passed when not less than two thirds of them were present, and had them approved, unless not less than two thirds of all the *decuriones* or *conscripti* decided that any of them was to be sent or deputed. Whoever has been deputed under this statute, unless the *decuriones* or *conscripti* have accepted his excuse or he has sworn in the presence of the *decuriones* or *conscripti* by Jupiter and the Divine Augustus and the Divine Claudius and the Divine Vespasian Augustus and the Divine Titus Augustus and the genius of the Emperor Caesar Domitian Augustus and the Penates that he is 60 or over or that illness is a reason why he cannot perform that embassy, he is to perform that embassy or he is to provide a substitute at the discretion of the *decuriones* or *conscripti*, from that *ordo*, who is to perform that embassy, provided that he does not provide someone who is obliged to perform the burden of that embassy in his own name. Whoever knowingly and with wrongful intent does not perform an embassy in this way and does not provide a substitute according to this statute who may perform the embassy for him and does not swear as laid down above and does not have his excuse approved by the *decuriones* or *conscripti*, is to be condemned to pay 20,000 sesterces to the *municipes* of that *municipium*; and the right of action, suit and claim for that money and concerning that money is to belong to any of the *municipes* of that *municipium* who wishes and who is entitled under this statute.

[Ch. H] Rubric. **How much may be given to ambassadors.**
A duumvir is to give to each ambassador under the heading of daily expenses as much as the *decuriones* or *conscripti* decided was to be given.

[Ch. I] Rubric. **Concerning anyone who undertakes an embassy other than according to the decree of the *decuriones*.**
No ambassador is to act or speak contrary to the instructions of the *decuriones* or *conscripti* [Tablet VC] nor is he to apply wrongful intent so that anything happens contrary to the instructions of the *decuriones* or *conscripti* or that the embassy is completed or makes its report late. Anyone who knowingly and with wrongful intent acts contrary to these rules is to be condemned to pay the value of the case in which he did anything contrary to these rules. And the right of action, suit and claim for that money and concerning that money is to belong to any *municeps* of that *municipium* who wishes and who is entitled under this statute.

[Ch. J] Rubric. **Those who may not rent or buy or be partners when public (contracts) are offered for rent or sold.**
Whenever public (revenues) or contracts or anything else is offered for rent or sold in the *Municipium Flavium Irnitanum*, no duumvir or aedile or quaestor or son or grandson or father or grandfather or brother or scribe or attendant of any of them is to rent or buy anything, nor is he to be a partner in any such affair, nor is he to take a share in any such affair or with reference to such an affair or on account thereof, nor is

he to do anything else knowingly and with wrongful intent in such a way that anything accrues to him thereafter from any such affair or with reference to any such affair or on account thereof. If anyone acts contrary to these rules, he is to be condemned to pay twice the sum involved on each occasion on which he acted contrary to these rules to the public account for the *municipes* of the *Municipium Flavium Irnitanum*; and the right of action suit and claim for that money and concerning that money is to belong to any *municeps* of the *Municipium Flavium Irnitanum* who wishes and who is entitled under this statute.

These contracts might include collection of taxes ('rented' for a fixed period) or a building contract ('sold' for a specific occasion). Building inscriptions from Pompeii record the local magistrates awarding a contract with the approval of the council (e.g. *ILS* 6354, 5636 = Cooley[2] B9, B11).

[Ch. K] Rubric. **Concerning the postponement of business.**
The *duumviri* who now hold office in that *municipium* and those who shall hold office hereafter are to raise with the *decuriones* or *conscripti* at the earliest possible moment, one or both, for what period within their term of office they wish business to be postponed for the harvest or the vintage. For the period during which the *decuriones* or *conscripti* decree that they wish business to be postponed, provided that they do not decree more than twice or for more than twice thirty days in one year that they wish business to be postponed, for that period concerning which they have passed that decree business is to be postponed. The *duumviri*, one or both, when the decree of the *decuriones* or *conscripti* has been passed on this matter, are to announce by edict at the earliest possible moment that business has been postponed for that period. And during that period, the *duumviri* are not to summon the *decuriones* or *conscripti*, they are not to hold an assembly, they are not to administer justice except concerning those matters concerning which it is customary to administer justice at Rome when business has been postponed for the harvest or the vintage; they are not to allow matters to be judged during that period, unless it is agreed between everyone who will be a party to that trial and their *iudex* or *recuperatores*; and they are not to allow *vadimonia* to be entered into for appearance in that period except concerning those matters concerning which it is customary to administer justice at Rome when business has been postponed for the harvest or the vintage; likewise concerning [other matters], they are not to allow them to take place, except for those days which follow immediately after that period which is the period of postponed business; nor is any *iudex* or *recuperator* to hear or judge cases on any other basis during that period.

This chapter reminds us that in a pre-industrial society, grain and grape-harvest and would be a vital and labour-intensive process.

[Ch. L] Rubric. **That the *duumviri* in charge of the administration of justice should establish *curiae*, provided that there are eleven.**
The *duumviri* in charge of the administration of justice, who shall first hold office in the *Municipium Flavium Irnitanum*, within the first ninety days after this statute has been conveyed to that *municipium*, are to see to it that *curiae* are established, at the discretion of the greater part of the *decuriones*, when not less than two thirds of the *decuriones* are present, provided that not more than ...

Curiae were the division of the electorate into voting-groups which determined the outcome of elections in the Roman world more than the individual votes. Here tablet V of *Lex Irnitana* ends, and tablet VI is lost. However the *Lex Malacitana* survives for the equivalent of the middle and right hand columns of tablet VI, thus providing us with an equivalent text for this tablet (chapters 51–59). The missing part (roughly equivalent to about a page of modern text) probably set out dates of elections, provision for suffect magistrates and how candidates would formally apply.

[Ch. 51] [Rubric. Concerning nomination of candidates.]
[Column 1] [If on the day by which application] must be made, application has been made in no-one's name or in the names of fewer persons than it is necessary to appoint, or if among those in whose names application has been made there are fewer persons whom it is proper to regard as eligible for election under this statute than it is necessary to appoint, then the person who must hold the election is to display, in such a way that they can be read properly from ground level, as many names of persons who are entitled to seek that office under this statute as are lacking to make up the number which it is necessary to appoint according to this statute. Those who(se names) are thus displayed are each, if they wish, in the presence of the person who must hold that election, to nominate one person in the same position (as themselves), and those persons in turn who have then been nominated by them are each, if they wish, in the presence of the same person, to nominate one person in the same position (as themselves); and the person, in whose presence this nomination has been made, is to publish the names of all of them in such a way that they can be read properly from ground level. And he is further to hold the election as between all of them, as if application had been made according to this statute on behalf of them also, for the seeking of office, within the prescribed day and they had begun to seek that office of their own accord and had not abandoned that intention.

Ch. 52 Rubric. **Concerning the holding of the election.**
Whoever is the older of the *duumviri* who now hold office, likewise of those who are *duumviri* in the future in that *municipium*, or if any reason prevents him from being able to hold the election then the other of them, is to hold the election under this statute for choosing or choosing in replacement *duumviri*, likewise aediles, likewise quaestors; and as the votes must be cast according to that distribution of *curiae* which has been laid down above, so he is to see that they are cast by ballot. And those who are thus appointed are to hold that office which they have achieved in the voting for one year, (but) if they are appointed in replacement of someone else, for the remaining part of that year.

Ch. 53 Rubric. **In which *curia incolae* may cast their votes.**
Whoever holds an election in that *municipium* for choosing *duumviri*, likewise aediles, likewise quaestors, is to draw one of the *curiae* by lot, in which *incolae* who are Roman or Latin citizens may cast their votes, and the casting of their vote is to take place in that *curia*.

Incolae (= 'inhabitants, residents') did not enjoy all the rights of *municipes* (= 'townsmen', e.g. chs.28, 29, 77, 79, 82). The first (lost) part of the law may have defined *incolae*.

Ch. 54 Rubric. **Whom it is appropriate to regard as eligible at the election.**
The person who must hold an election is to see first to the appointment of *duumviri* to be in charge of the administration of justice, from that class of freeborn men which is prescribed and laid down in this statute, next thereafter of aediles, likewise of quaestors, (both) from that class of freeborn men which is prescribed and laid down in this statute, provided that he does not accept in the election the eligibility of anyone seeking the duumvirate who is under 25 or who has held that office within the last five years, likewise of anyone seeking the aedileship or the quaestorship who is under 25, or (in all three cases) of anyone who is in such a position that [Col. 2] it would not be lawful for him to be a *decurio* or *conscriptus* if he were a Roman citizen.

The minimum age of 25 for holding local office had been set by Augustus (Dio 52.20).

Ch. 55 Rubric. **Concerning the casting of the votes.**
The person who holds an election under this statute is to summon the *municipes* by *curia* to cast their votes, in such a way that he summon all the *curiae* to the vote with one summons and that each of them cast its votes by ballot in separate enclosures. And he is likewise to see to the presence beside the ballot box of each *curia* of three people, from the *municipes* of that *municipium*, not from that *curia*, to watch and count the votes; and he is to see that before they do this each of them swear that he will make and report the count of the votes in good faith. And he is not to restrain those who are seeking office from also stationing one scrutineer each beside each ballot-box. And those scrutineers stationed by the person who holds the election, likewise by those who are seeking office, are each of them to cast their votes in that *curia* beside whose ballot box they have been stationed as scrutineers, and their votes are to be legal and valid just as if each had cast his vote in his own *curia*.

Ch. 56 Rubric. **What it is appropriate to do in the case of those who have an equal number of votes.**
The person who holds this election, as and when anyone has more votes than the others in any *curia*, is to announce that he has been elected and appointed before the others for that *curia*, until the number which it is necessary to appoint has been reached (in that *curia*). In any *curia* in which two or more have the same number of votes, he is to place ahead and announce before the others a man who is married or who counts as married, over a man who is not married, without sons, who does not count as married; a man who has sons over a man who does not; a man who has more sons over a man who has fewer, provided that two children lost after the giving of the name or one male child over puberty lost or one female child over puberty lost are to count as one surviving child. If two or more have the same number of votes and are in the same position, he is to draw lots with their names and announce before the others the one whose name has been drawn by lot.

Ch. 57 Rubric. **Concerning the drawing of lots between the *curiae* and (concerning) those who are equal in the number of *curiae* (carried).**
The person who holds the election under this statute, after the lists of all the *curiae* have been reported, is to draw lots with the names of the *curiae* and is to draw out

the name of each *curia* by lot, and as the name of each *curia* comes up by lot, he is to order those whom that *curia* has elected to be declared. And as soon as anyone gets a majority of the number of the *curiae*, once he has sworn an oath and given security in relation to common funds according to this statute, he is to announce that he has been elected and appointed, until there are as many magistrates as it is necessary to appoint under this statute. If two or more have the same number of *curiae*, he is to act in the case of those who have the same number of *curiae* as is laid down above in the case of those who were equal in the number of votes, and in the same way is to announce that each one has been appointed before (the others).

Randomising the order in which the *curiae* declared their results cannot have affected outcomes, but will have made the *curiae* seem equally important.

Ch. 58 Rubric. **That nothing may be done to prevent the election being held.**
No-one is to intercede or do anything else to prevent the election being held and completed in that *municipium* under this statute. Whoever acts otherwise or contrary to these rules knowingly [Col. 3] and with wrongful intent, is to be condemned to pay 10,000 sesterces to the *municipes* of the *Municipium Flavium Malacitanum* for each case and the right of action, suit and claim of that money and concerning that money is to belong to any *municeps* of that *municipium* who wishes and who is entitled under this statute.

Ch. 59 Rubric. **Concerning the oath of those who have won a majority of the number of the *curiae*.**
The person who holds this election, as each of those who is seeking the duumvirate [*The Lex Irnitana resumes at this point*: Tablet VIIA] or the aedileship or the quaestorship wins a majority of the number of the *curiae*, before he announces that he has been elected and appointed, is to administer an oath openly in a *contio* (public speech) by Jupiter and the Divine Augustus and the Divine Claudius and the Divine Vespasian Augustus and the Divine Titus Augustus and the genius of the Emperor Caesar Domitian Augustus and the Penates, that he will do what it is necessary to do under this statute and that he has not done and will not do anything against this law knowingly and with wrongful intent.

[Ch. 60] Rubric. **That those who seek the duumvirate or the quaestorship shouldgive security in relation to common funds of the *municipes*.**
Those who in that *municipium* seek the duumvirate or the quaestorship or are forced into that position by being nominated, on the grounds that application has been made in the name of fewer than is necessary, in such a way that it is appropriate for votes to be cast for them also under this statute, each of them, on the day on which the election is held, before the votes are cast, is to provide at the discretion of the person who holds that election *praedes* to the common account of the *municipes*, that their common funds which he handles in the course of his office will be kept safe for them. If it appears that too little has been secured for that purpose with those *praedes*, he is to register *praedia* at the discretion of the same person. And that person is to accept *praedes* and *praedia* from them without wrongful intent, until everything has been properly secured, as he may think proper. Anyone of those for whom it is necessary for votes to be cast at the election for *duumviri* or quaestors, whose fault it is that

everything has not been properly secured, is not to be regarded as eligible by the person who holds the election.

Here the charter stipulates sureties in the form of people offering bail (*praedes*) or properties (*praedia*) which will guarantee against financial misconduct on the part of the magistrates.

[Ch. 61] Rubric. **Concerning the co-opting of a patron.**
No-one is publicly to co-opt a patron for the *municipes* of the *Municipium Flavium Irnitanum* or to confer the power of patronage on anyone, except by a decree of the majority of the *decuriones*, which has been passed when not less than two thirds of the *decuriones* are present and they have cast their votes by ballot on oath. Whoever publicly co-opts otherwise or contrary to these rules a patron for the *municipes* of the *Municipium Flavium Irnitanum* or confers the power of patronage on anyone, is to be condemned to pay 10,000 sesterces to the public account of the *municipes* of the *Municipium Flavium Irnitanum*; and whoever has been co-opted a patron against this statute or had the power of patronage conferred on him, is not thereby to be a patron of the *municipes* of the *Municipium Flavium Irnitanum*.

Patrons of a colony were expected to have wealth and influence. At Pompeii, prior to its destruction a normal town, Publius Sulla (nephew of the *dictator*), and Marcellus (Augustus' nephew) were patrons, as were the less well known M. Holconius Rufus and Sallustius. For patrons of towns see Index of Themes, patron.

[Ch. 62] Rubric. **That no-one is to destroy buildings which he is not going to replace.**
No-one in the town of the *Municipium Flavium Irnitanum* or where buildings are continuous with that town, is to unroof or destroy or see to the demolition of a building, except by resolution of the *decuriones* or *conscripti*, when the majority of them is present, unless he is going to replace it within the next year. Whoever acts against these rules, is to be condemned to pay to the *municipes* of the *Municipium Flavium Irnitanum* as much money as the case is worth, and the right of action, suit and claim of that money and concerning that money is to belong to any *municeps* of that *municipium* who wishes and who is entitled under this statute.

Similar municipal legislation was enacted at Tarentum (Lex Tarentina, lines 32-38). A decree of the Roman senate against demolition of buildings for greater profit was copied and preserved at Herculaneum (*ILS* 6043 LACTOR 19, K33–K34).

[Ch. 63: Tablet VIIB] Rubric. **Concerning the publishing and entering in the records of the *municipium* of offerings for rent and conditions for offerings for rent.**
Whoever is duumvir in charge of the administration of justice, is to offer for rent the revenues and the contracts and whatever else it is necessary to offer for rent in the common name of the *municipes* of that *municipium*. And he is to have entered in the common records of the *municipes* of that *municipium* whatever offerings for rent he has held and whatever conditions he has laid down, and for how much anything has been rented and who have been accepted as *praedes*, and what *praedia* have been furnished and registered and pledged, and who have been accepted as *cognitores* of the *praedia*, and he is to have them published for the whole of the rest of his time in office, in such a way that they can be read properly from ground level, in the place in which the *decuriones* or *conscripti* decide that they should be published.

On 'renting' see ch.J and ch.76. Roman collection of taxes was 'privatised'. So a 'tax-farmer' (*publicanus*) would bid for the right to collect a local tax, guaranteeing that sum to the *municipium*. Any excess would represent his profit, any shortfall would be covered by the people who had offered to provide bail (*praedes*) or the properties (*praedia*) he had pledged. It is not clear how the *cognitores* ('people aware') helped secure this. The importance of this is shown by the detailed requirements for publishing the contracts and sureties in ch.63, and the longer details for the pledging of sureties (ch.64) involving the same procedure as in the main Treasury (*Aerarium*) in Rome and possible recovery of money (ch.65). Caecilius' wax-tablets at Pompeii show him paying moneys to the public slave for a farm, fullery, pasturage and a market (*CIL* 4.3340.138–151; Cooley[2], H114–5): the last is explicitly said to be on behalf of a third party (the stall holder paying rent or tax on a space).

[Ch. 64] Rubric. **Concerning the pledging of *praedes* and *praedia* and *cognitores*.**
In respect of whoever have been or are appointed as *praedes* in the *Municipium Flavium Irnitanum* for the common account of the *municipes* of that *municipium*, and of whatever *praedia* have been or are accepted, and of whoever have been or are appointed as *cognitores* of those *praedia*, all of those persons, together with whatever then belongs to each of them when he is or shall be appointed *praes* or *cognitor* and whatever comes or shall come to belong to them after they are pledged, that is those of them who have not been or are not discharged by payment or otherwise, or at any rate not without wrongful intent, and all of those *praedia* which have not been or are not discharged by payment or otherwise, or at any rate not without wrongful intent, are to be pledged to the common account of the *municipes* of that *municipium*, just as the men and the property would be pledged to the Roman people if they had been appointed *praedes* and *cognitores* and those *praedia* had been furnished or registered or pledged in the presence of those who are in charge of the Aerarium at Rome. And the *duumviri* who are in charge of the administration of justice there, both or either of them, are to have the right and power of selling up and laying down the conditions for those sales in the case of those *praedes* and those *praedia*, as well as those *cognitores*, if any of those *praedia* for which they have been appointed *cognitores* is not so (???), that is those persons and properties which have not been or are not discharged by payment or otherwise, or at any rate not without wrongful intent, following a decree of the *decuriones* or *conscripti* which has been passed when not less than two thirds of them are present; always provided that they lay down the conditions for those sales which it is appropriate for those who are in charge of the Aerarium at Rome to lay down under the *lex praediatoria* for selling up *praedes* and *praedia* or which it would be appropriate for them to lay down for sales in *vacuam* if they do not find a purchaser under the *lex praediatoria*; and always provided that they lay down the conditions in such a way that the money is produced and handed over and paid in the forum of the *Municipium Flavium Irnitanum*. And whatever conditions are so established are to be legal and valid.

[Ch. 65: Tablet VIIC] Rubric. **That justice should be administered according to the conditions laid down for the selling up of *praedes* and *praedia*.**
Whatever *praedes* and *praedia* and *cognitores* the *duumviri* of the *Municipium Flavium Irnitanum* sell up according to this statute, whoever is in charge of the administration of justice, if an approach has been made to him for justice in this case, he is so to administer justice concerning them and grant a trial, that those who have bought up those *praedes* and *cognitores* and *praedia* and their *praedes*, partners and heirs and those who have an interest in the case may properly have a right of action, suit and claim in such cases.

[Ch. 66] Rubric. **About any fine which is imposed.**
The *duumviri* who are in charge of the administration of justice are to order to be
entered in the common records of the *municipes* of that *municipium* the fines imposed
in that *municipium* by the *duumviri* or the prefect, likewise by the aediles, provided
that the aediles have declared before the *duumviri*, both or either of them, that they
have imposed them. If the person on whom the fine is imposed or someone else in his
name demands that it should be raised with the *decuriones* or *conscripti*, there is to be
a trial of the case by the *decuriones* or *conscripti*. And whatever fines have not been
judged unjust by the *decuriones* or *conscripti*, the *duumviri* are to collect those fines
for the public account of the *municipes* of that *municipium*.

[Ch. 67] Rubric. **Concerning common funds of the *municipes* and their accounts.**
Whoever has received common funds of the *municipes* of that *municipium*, he or his
heir or whoever has an interest in the case is to deliver it to the public account of the
municipes of that *municipium* within the next thirty days after he has received those
funds. And whoever runs and handles the common accounts or any common business
of the *municipes* of that *municipium*, he or his heir or whoever has an interest in the
case, within the next thirty days after he has ceased to run and handle that business or
those accounts, provided that there is a meeting of the *decuriones* or *conscripti*, is to
produce his accounts and render them to the *decuriones* or *conscripti* or to the person
to whom the commission has been given of accepting and checking them, according
to a decree of the *decuriones* and *conscripti* which has been passed when not less than
two thirds of them are present. Anyone whose fault it is that the money is not collected
or delivered or the accounts not rendered as laid down, he or his heir or whoever has
an interest in the case which is at issue is to be condemned to pay to the *municipes* of
that *municipium* as much as is at issue and as much again and the right of action, suit
and claim of that money and concerning that money is to belong to any *municeps* of
the *Municipium Flavium Irnitanum* who wishes and who is entitled under this statute.

This chapter obliges magistrates to render financial accounts, with further details of the legal processes in
chapters 68–71.

[Ch. 68] Rubric. **Concerning the appointment of advocates for the case, when
accounts are rendered.**
When accounts are rendered as laid down, the duumvir who holds the meeting of the
decuriones or *conscripti* is to raise with the *decuriones* or *conscripti* what persons
they wish to plead the public cause; and those *decuriones* or *conscripti* are to decree
on that matter by ballot under oath, when not less than two thirds of them are present,
in such a way that three men, whom the majority have chosen by ballot, may plead the
public cause; and those who have been chosen in this way are to request time from the
decuriones and *conscripti* in which they may get to know the case and prepare their
plea, and when the time which has been granted to them is up they are to plead that
cause, as they may think proper.

[Ch. 69] Rubric. **Concerning a trial over common funds.**
Whatever is sued for in the name of the *municipes* of the *Municipium Flavium
Irnitanum* from someone who is a *municeps* or *incola* of that *municipium* or whatever
is the subject of an action against him, which is worth more than 500 sestertii and

not worth so much that if it were a private action no action could take place there if either party were unwilling, even if the person against whom the action is brought is unwilling for it to be brought there, the right of hearing the case and judging it and fixing the penalty is to belong to the *decuriones* or *conscripti*, provided that when the action takes place not less than two thirds of the *decuriones* or *conscripti* are present and the votes are cast by them by ballot and those who are about to cast their votes, before they cast their votes, swear each of them by Jupiter and the Divine Augustus and the Divine Claudius and the Divine Vespasian Augustus and the Divine Titus Augustus and the genius of the Emperor Domitian Augustus and the Penates, that his judgment will be what he believes to be fair and right and most for the common good of that *municipium*. As the majority of them has judged and estimated the value of the case, so is the judgment and the estimation of the value of the case to be legal and valid. Whatever is worth 500 sestertii or less, the right of hearing the case and judging it and fixing the penalty, which would belong to the *decuriones* or *conscripti*, if the sum which was being sued for or over which the action was being brought were greater than 500 sestertii, is to belong to those five who are left, after every alternate *decurio* or *conscriptus* of those who are then present has been rejected in such a way that the person who brings the action or sues rejects first from an uneven number, the person against whom the action or the suit is brought (rejects) from an even number, until five are left. And as the majority of them has judged and estimated the value of the case, so are the judgment and the estimation of the value of the case to be legal and valid.

A summary of this rather convoluted regulation is that cases worth over 1,000 sesterces would be tried elsewhere (compare ch.84); cases worth 500 to 1,000 sesterces are to be tried before the full council of *decuriones*; cases worth less than 500 are to be tried by panel of 5 *decuriones* selected by a process in which each side alternately rejects a *decurio* from the full panel. The median of the sums of money recorded as paid or loaned on Caecilius' wax tablets at Pompeii is for over 4,000 sesterces (Cooley[2] page 278), well above the limit for local judgement at Irni. But the limits recorded by the *Lex Malacitana* for the bigger town of Malaca are double.

[Ch. 70] Rubric. **Concerning the appointment of a legal representative of the** *municipes* **and his reward or fee.**
The *decuriones* or *conscripti*, when not less than two thirds of them are present, are to have the power of vetting and appointing the person or persons to whom it may be entrusted or allowed to bring an action or sue in the name of the *municipes* or accept trial in their name if an action or a suit is brought against them, so long as they choose a person who is allowed to be a legal representative or *cognitor* for them under the edict of the person who governs the province; and they are to appoint how much it is appropriate to give as reward or fee to the person or persons who sue or shall sue or shall have sued for the *municipes* of the *Municipium Flavium Irnitanum* or shall have accepted or shall accept trial in their name.

[Ch. 71] Rubric. **That those who are to be legal representatives in the matter of common funds should have the right of summoning witnesses.**
Whoever in the name of the *municipes* of the *Municipium Flavium Irnitanum*, in that *municipium*, under this statute or under a decree of the *decuriones* or *conscripti* brings an action against a *municeps* or *incola* of that *municipium* or sues from him, is to have the right and power of summoning as witnesses *municipes* and *incolae* of

that *municipium* up to ten. The duumvir in charge of the administration of justice, to whom the request is made, is to order by edict to be present those whom he has been informed have been summoned and is to force them to give testimony under oath and is to coerce them by (the threat of) a fine and (the seizure of) pledges, provided that he may not force anyone or impose a fine on anyone or seize a pledge for this reason from anyone who would not be forced to give testimony at Rome in a *iudicium publicum* (public law-suit) against the person against whom a suit or an action is being brought.

[Ch. 72] Rubric. **Concerning the manumission of public slaves.**
If any [duumvir] wishes to manumit a male or female public slave, he is to raise with the *decuriones* or *conscripti* when not less than two thirds of the *decuriones* or *conscripti* are present, concerning him or her, whether they believe that he or she should be manumitted. If not less than two thirds of those who are present decide that the manumission should take place and if he or she gives and pays to the public account for the *municipes* of the *Municipium Flavium Irnitanum* the sum which the *decuriones* decide should be received from him or her or gives security for it, then that duumvir in charge of the administration of justice is to manumit that male or female slave and order him or her to be free. Whatever man or woman has been manumitted and ordered to be free in this way is to be free and a Latin and they are to be *municipes* of the *Municipium Flavium Irnitanum*, nor is anyone to receive from them for their freedom more than the *decuriones* decide nor act in such a way that anyone receives anything for this reason or on this account; and the rights of the *Municipium Flavium Irnitanum* in claiming the inheritance or the possession of the goods of the man or woman who has been manumitted in this way or over their *operae* or gifts or services are to be the same as if he or she were a freedman or freedwoman of a *municipium* of Italy. Whoever knowingly and with wrongful intent does anything contrary to these rules is to be condemned to pay to the public account for the *municipes* of the *Municipium Flavium Irnitanum* as much as is at issue and the right of action, suit and claim of that money and concerning that money is to belong to any *municeps* of that *municipium* who wishes and who is entitled under this statute.

A former master could expect legally expect half the estate of a freedman who died without a child (Gaius, *Institutes* 3.41). So the *municipium* acts to claim inheritance rights in a similar way.

[Ch. 73] Rubric. **Concerning scribes and their oath and the *aes apparitorium*.**
The scribes who are to write and prepare the common records, books and accounts in that *municipium*, whom the *decuriones* or *conscripti* of that *municipium*, the majority, have approved, are to attend on the *duumviri*; and they, before they see the common records of their *municipes* or enter anything in them are to swear, each of them, by Jupiter and the Divine Augustus [and the Divine Claudius] and the Divine Vespasian Augustus and the Divine Titus Augustus and the genius of the Emperor Domitian Augustus and the Penates that they will write the common records of their *municipes* in good faith and that they will not knowingly and with wrongful intent enter anything false in those records or with wrongful intent leave out anything which should be entered in them. Anyone who does not swear in this way is not to be a scribe. The *decuriones* or *conscripti* are to appoint how much *aes apparitorium* it is appropriate to give to each kind of *apparitor*. It is to be allowed for the *duumviri* to spend from the

common funds of the *municipes* of that *municipium* the sum which has been appointed in this way and for *apparitores* to receive it in this way, without incurring liability.

The chapter deals with how magistrates' attendants and (*apparitores*) are to behave and how much pay (*aes apparitorium*) they are to receive. Other local decrees exist which stipulate the level of pay, but here, as in other matters (ch.H, ch.70), payment is left at the discretion of the town council.

[Ch. 74] Rubric. **Concerning illegal gatherings, societies and colleges.**
No-one is to take part in an illegal gathering in that *municipium* or to hold a meeting of a society or college for that purpose or to conspire that it be held or to act in such a way that any of these things occur. Anyone who acts contrary to these rules is to be condemned to pay 10,000 sesterces to the *municipes* of the *Municipium Flavium Irnitanum* and the right of action, suit and claim of that money and concerning that money is to belong to any *municeps* of that *municipium* who wishes and who is entitled under this statute.

Julius Caesar and Augustus had both introduced (unknown) legislation on meetings of 'colleges' or associations (Suet. *Iul.* 42.3; *Aug.* 32.1). The Roman senate's response to the riot at Pompeii's amphitheatre in AD 59 was to crack down on 'illegal associations' (*collegia*) in the town (Tac. *Ann.* 14.17).

[Ch. 75] Rubric. **That nothing may be bought up or hoarded.**
No-one in that *municipium* is to buy up or hoard anything or join with another or agree or enter into a partnership in order that something may be sold more dearly or not be sold or not enough be sold. Anyone who acts contrary to these rules is to be condemned to pay 10,000 sesterces to the *municipes* of the *Municipium Flavium Irnitanum* for each case and the right of action, suit and claim of that money and concerning that money is to belong to any *municeps* of that *municipium* who wishes and who is entitled under this statute.

At around this period Dio of Prusa was, apparently, almost lynched by his fellow townsmen on suspicion of having hoarded grain in a food-shortage (*Oration* 46).

[Ch. 76] Rubric. **Concerning the visiting and inspection of the territories and the sources of revenue, whether it seems to be appropriate or not, and, if it is agreed that they should be visited and inspected, by whom and how it is to be agreed that they should be visited and inspected.**
A duumvir of the *Municipium Flavium Irnitanum*, each in his year, is to raise with the *decuriones* or *conscripti* of that *municipium*, when not less than two thirds of them are present, whether it is to be decided that the territories and fields and sources of revenue of that *municipium* are to be visited and inspected that year; and on this matter he is to have a decree of the *decuriones* or *conscripti* passed according to this statute. Whatever commission the *decuriones* or *conscripti* have given and decreed to anyone in this way, he is to undertake it and see that it is undertaken without wrongful intent, as it is appropriate for any of them to undertake it according to a decree of the *decuriones* or *conscripti*.

This chapter concerns public land owned by the town as a source of revenue. Vespasian had been much concerned with ownership of land (see **N6–N9**). A farm, fullery, pasturage and market-space are all attested from Caecilius' wax tablets as providing revenue at Pompeii (see note on ch.63).

[Ch. 77] Rubric. **Concerning expenses for religious observances, games and dinners which are to be provided.**
The *duumviri* who are in charge of the administration of justice in that *municipium* are to raise with the *decuriones* or *conscripti* at the earliest possible moment how much should be spent for expenses on religious observances and games and how much on dinners which are offered to the *municipes* or the *decuriones* or *conscripti* in common, and they are to spend as much as the majority of them decides, as they may think proper.

[Ch. 78] Rubric. **That the *decuriones* should be consulted concerning what type of business each public slave should be assigned to.**
Whoever is duumvir, in the first five days in which he holds office in the *Municipium Flavium Irnitanum*, is to raise with the *decuriones* or *conscripti*, as many as possible, which public slaves should be assigned to each type of business, and he is to get the *decuriones* or *conscripti* to pass a decree on that matter, and see that what the majority has decreed is carried out without wrongful intent.

[Ch. 79] Rubric. **How large a quorum of *decuriones* or *conscripti* is appropriate when the spending of common funds of the *municipes* is raised.**
No duumvir of that *municipium* is otherwise to consult the *decuriones* or *conscripti* on or raise with them distributing or dividing up or allotting to the *municipes* or the *decuriones* or *conscripti* the funds which are the common funds of the *municipes* of that *municipium*, nor is he to propose it to the *municipes* of that *municipium*, nor is he to distribute or divide up or allot their common funds to the colonists or the *decuriones* or *conscripti*, nor is he to raise with the *decuriones* or *conscripti* alienating, reducing, spending or lending in the name of the *municipes* the funds which are the common funds of the *municipes* – except for those reasons which are allowed in this chapter or are expressly laid down in another part of this statute – or allowing a remission to someone who is under an obligation to give, carry out or provide something for the *municipes* of that *municipium*, when fewer are present than could make up three quarters of the whole number of *decuriones* or *conscripti*; and even then in such a way that a decree is not passed except if the *decuriones* or *conscripti* cast their votes by ballot and before they cast them swear by Jupiter and the Divine Augustus [and the Divine Claudius] and the Divine Vespasian Augustus and the Divine Titus Augustus and the genius of the Emperor Caesar Domitian Augustus and the Penates that they will cast their votes as they believe most for the common good of the *municipes*. If anything is raised or decreed in any other way [Tablet IXA] it is to be neither legal nor valid. Nothing is enacted in this statute to prevent the raising with the *decuriones* or *conscripti*, provided it is not with less than half, of what sums must be spent on religious observances, games or dinners to which the *decuriones* and *conscripti* or *municipes* are invited; *aera apparitoria*, embassies and the building or repair of works in that *municipium*; the protection of sacred buildings and monuments; food and clothing for and purchase of those who are the slaves of the *municipes*; likewise on those things which it is appropriate to be provided for the *duumviri*, aediles and quaestors in order to perform religious observances in the name of the *municipes*, likewise in order to carry out the duties which must be performed on account of the office which someone has begun; or to prevent the spending of whatever funds the

decuriones or *conscripti* decide should be spent on these things after the granting of this statute, even if they have not sworn and the votes have not been cast by ballot.

This chapter describes, more generally than the rubric states, what *decuriones* are and are not permitted to spend public money on. 'Regular' spending, set out in the second half of this chapter has to be approved with at least half the *decuriones* present; any special spending requires three-quarters.

[Ch. 80] Rubric. **Concerning the raising of a public loan.**
If the *decuriones* or *conscripti* of that *municipium* decide under oath by ballot, when not less than three quarters of them are present, that any loan is to be raised for the use of the *res publica* ('community') of the *Municipium Flavium Irnitanum* and those funds are entered as spent for the *municipes*, provided that not more than 50,000 sesterces are entered as spent for them in one year, except with the authorisation of the person who governs that province, the *municipes* of the *Municipium Flavium Irnitanum* are to owe those funds which have been entered as spent in this way.

[Ch. 81] Rubric. **Concerning the arrangement of (spectators at) games.**
Whatever games are given in that *municipium*, in whatever seats each group of men was accustomed to watch those games before this statute, they are to watch them in the same seats, as it is or shall be allowed there under a decree of the *decuriones* or *conscripti* or under statutes or plebiscites or decrees of the senate or edicts or judgments of the Divine Augustus or Tiberius Julius Caesar Augustus or Tiberius Claudius Caesar Augustus or the Emperor Galba Caesar Augustus or the Emperor Vespasian Caesar Augustus or the Emperor Titus Caesar Vespasian Augustus or the Emperor Domitian Caesar Augustus.

Augustus had legislated to reintroduce seating by *ordo* in the theatre. See **S19, S21, S22** for Domitian's reinforcement of the law in AD 90.

[Ch. 82] Rubric. **Concerning roads, ways, rivers, ditches and drains.**
The *duumviri*, either or both, are to have the right and power of creating, or altering the course of, whatever roads, ways, rivers, ditches or drains of that *municipium* the *duumviri*, either or both, wish, provided that this takes place by decree of the *decuriones* or *conscripti* and within the boundaries of that *municipium* and without damage to private interests. Whatever is created or altered in this way, it is to be right for it so to be and remain.

[Ch. 83] Rubric. **Concerning building.**
Whatever work or building the *decuriones* or *conscripti* of that *municipium* decide should be undertaken, provided that not less than three quarters of the *decuriones* or *conscripti* are present and of those who are present not less than two thirds agree, and provided that not more than five days of work each should be exacted or decreed in one year from one man and one yoke of animals who are within the boundaries of that *municipium*, and provided that if any loss is inflicted on anyone in the course of that work or that building compensation should be provided from common funds, and provided that days of work should not be imposed on or exacted from anyone who is under 15 or over 60 against their will; whoever is a *municeps* or *incola* of that *municipium* or lives or has a

field or fields within the boundaries of that *municipium*, all of them are to be obliged to give, carry out and provide those days of work. The aediles or those who are in charge of that work or building by decree of the *decuriones* or *conscripti* are to have the right and power of imposing or exacting those days of work and of seizing a pledge or imposing a fine, as is prescribed and laid down in [other] chapters.

The requirement for citizens to provide labour is also known from the *Digest of Roman Law*, 50.2.2.8.

[Ch. 84] Rubric. **Over what matters and up to what sum there may be jurisdiction in that *municipium*.**
[Tablet IXB] Whichever *municipes* or *incolae* of that *municipium* wish privately within the boundaries of that *municipium* to bring an action against or sue or claim against each other on any matter in their own names or in that of someone else who is a *municeps* or *incola*, provided that the matter is worth 1,000 sesterces or less and has not been or is not divided in order to evade this statute, and provided that there will not be a *praeiudicium* concerning a free person or a larger sum than 1,000 sesterces, and provided that there has not been and will not be a *sponsio*, and provided that the matter at issue is not one in which there has been *vis* other than under the interdict, judgment or order of the person who is in charge of the administration of justice, and provided the case is not over freedom, or over partnership or *fiducia* or mandate, involving an accusation of wrongful intent, or *depositum* or *tutela*, against someone who is accused of having done any of those things in his own name, or under the Lex Laetoria, or over a *sponsio* which is said to have been made in *probrum*, or over wrongful intent, or over *fraus*, or over theft against a free man or woman or against a slave so long as it relates to his master or mistress, or over harm against a free man or woman, or concerning a matter in which there would be a *praeiudicium* concerning a free person, the duumvir who is in charge of the administration of justice there is to have jurisdiction and the right of granting and assigning a *iudex* or arbiter or *recuperatores* from those who(se names) are published there, and a trial; and even about these matters if each of the two parties is willing, and about all other matters about which actions are brought privately and in which there will not be a *praeiudicium* concerning a free person; and he is to have jurisdiction [at any rate] over the promise of a *vadimonium* concerning all matters for the place in which the person who governs that province will be or is expected to be on that day for which the request for the promise of the *vadimonium* is made. And likewise the aedile who is there is to have jurisdiction and the right of granting and assigning a *iudex* or arbiter or *recuperatores* from the same group and a trial, under the same conditions, concerning anything which is 1,000 sesterces or less.

The range of court cases regarded as too serious for the local magistrates (and therefore to be referred to the governor unless both parties consent) are essentially those where condemnation would result in *infamia* (loss of reputation and of some legal rights and status).

A *sponsio* was a sort of wager taken by the two parties of a case, offering a sum to be paid by the loser to the winner; *vis* is violence (e.g. assault); *fiducia* – a legal pledge or mortgage; *depositum* – a trust; *tutela* – legal guardianship; *Lex Laetoria* protected people under 25 years old from entering into an agreement not in their interests; *fraus* is not just fraud or cheating, but any form of injury or damage; *probrum* is insult, libel; *vadimonium* is 'bail money' – specifically pledged to guarantee an appearance in court; *praeiudicium* – some form of judgement in a previous case.

[Ch. 85] Rubric. **That the magistrates should have in public the *album*
(published legal decisions) of the person who holds the province and administer
justice according to it.**
Whatever edicts or formulae for trials or *sponsiones* or stipulations or *satis acceptiones*
or prescriptions or exceptions or interdicts the person who governs that province
has published in that province, whichever of them relates to the jurisdiction of that
magistrate who is in charge of the administration of justice in the *Municipium Flavium
Irnitanum*, he is to have all of them published and displayed in that *municipium* in his
magistracy every day for the greater part of each day so that they may be properly read
from ground level, and justice be administered in that *municipium* according to those
interdicts, edicts, formulae, *sponsiones*, stipulations, *satis acceptiones*, exceptions
and prescriptions, and trials be granted and take place and be carried into effect, and
what is not against this law take place without wrongful intent, as is allowed under
this statute.

This chapter, quite reasonably, formalises the duty of the local magistrate to publish decrees by the
provincial governor: *satis acceptiones* were an accepted level of security.

[Ch. 86] Rubric. **Concerning the choosing and displaying (the names) of *iudices*.**
The *duumviri* who are in charge of the administration of justice in that *municipium*,
by joint decision, or one if the other of them is absent or it happens to him for any
other reason that he cannot carry out that business, within five days after he has begun
to be in charge of the administration of justice and is able, is to choose from the
decuriones or *conscripti* as many *iudices* as seems good to the person who governs
that province, who must not in that year undertake [any other *munus* at the same time];
(he is to choose) from the other *municipes*, apart from the *decuriones* or *conscripti*,
who are free born, as many as seems good to the person who governs that province,
not younger than 25, whose own property is worth not less than 5,000 sesterces, or
whose father or paternal grandfather or paternal [Tablet IXC] great-grandfather or
father in whose power they are has such property, whom he thinks most suitable and
whom he has sworn in the presence of not less than ten *decuriones* or *conscripti* to be
being chosen as *iudices* for the common good of the *municipes* of that *municipium*;
provided that he does not choose anyone who will be prevented by illness from being
able to attend to judging matters in that year, or who will be over 65, or who will
be aedile or quaestor, or who will be absent on public business or on the common
business of the *municipes* of that *municipium*, or who will without wrongful intent not
be in that area and therefore not be able in that year to attend to judging matters, or
who will be in such a position that he cannot be chosen as or be one of the *decuriones*
or *conscripti*, unless he cannot be chosen as or be (one of the *decuriones* or *conscripti*)
because his own property or his father's or his paternal grandfather's or his paternal
great-grandfather's or his father's, in whose power he is, is such that he cannot be
chosen as or be one of the *decuriones* or *conscripti*. And he is to distribute them into
three *decuriae* as equally as possible. Those who are chosen as *iudices* and distributed
in this way, are to be the *iudices* of private cases for that year in that *municipium* under
this law; and the person who is in charge of the administration of justice is to have
published by his tribunal for all the remaining days of that year, for the greater part of
each day, all their *praenomina*, *nomina*, fathers' *praenomina*, tribes and *cognomina*,
written on tablets, so that they may be properly read from ground level. And for those

cases for which it is not appropriate for *recuperatores* to be granted, he is to order the person from among those *iudices*, who is appropriate under this statute, to be granted and assigned as *iudex* or arbiter and to judge; and he is not to grant anyone else as *iudex* or arbiter nor order anyone to judge against the will of any one of the two or more parties between whom any dispute exists.

The *iudices* 'judges' were laymen, unpaid and without any legal training, hence the *iudex* appointed to judge a case was much more like a one-man jury. *Decuria* was the special term for groups from which the *iudices* were drawn.

[Ch. 87] Rubric. **Concerning the rejection and granting of *iudices*.**
If it is not agreed between two people, between whom there is a case or controversy in a private matter, in which it is appropriate for a *iudex* or arbiter to be granted under this statute, whom they should have as *iudex* or arbiter, the person who is in charge of the administration of justice is to see to it that in a rejection of *decuriae* the person who is bringing the action or the suit, or if both are bringing the action or the suit the person who is bringing the action over the greater matter or suing for the greater amount, should have the first right of rejection; and that from the *decuria* which remains they should have the right of rejection in turn, provided that the person who is bringing the action or the suit, or if both are bringing the action or the suit, whichever is bringing the action over the greater matter or suing for the greater amount, should reject first from an uneven number; and that the person against whom the action or the suit is being brought, or if both are bringing the action or the suit, the person who is bringing the action over the lesser matter or suing for the lesser amount, should reject first from an even number, until one of them is left; or if either of them is unwilling to reject *decuriae* or *iudices*, he is to grant as *iudex* or arbiter between them for that matter and assign and order to judge the person whom his adversary wishes to have as *iudex* or arbiter from the *iudices* (whose names are) published; or if it is agreed between them about some *municeps* (whose name is) not published and who is neither duumvir nor aedile nor quaestor that they should have him as *iudex* or arbiter, except if, in the case of the person about whom it is agreed, illness is a reason preventing him from being able to attend to judging matters or he is over 65 and does not wish to judge that matter. The person who been granted and assigned and ordered to judge in this way is to judge and estimate the value of the case, and whatever he has judged under this law and however he has estimated the value of the case, [Tablet XA] that is to be legal and valid.

[Ch. 88] Rubric. **Concerning the rejection and drawing by lot and granting of *recuperatores*.**
If it is appropriate for *recuperatores* to be granted to anyone, the person who is in charge of the administration of justice is to grant under this statute as many *recuperatores* drawn by lot as it is appropriate to grant under this statute in each case, [from among those who] are among the *iudices*, (either) when [the *iudices*] have been rejected similarly and in the same way (as above) until there are seven left of them or when an option has been given similarly and in the same way (as above) for seven *recuperatores* or if it is agreed between them that they wish seven from among the

iudices to be drawn by lot as *recuperatores*; and he is to force them to hear the case and judge. Whoever are then granted as *recuperatores* are to judge and estimate the value of the case in these matters. And whatever they have judged and however they have estimated the case, that is to be legal and valid.

[Ch. 89] Rubric. **In which cases single *iudices* or arbiters and in which cases *recuperatores* are to be granted and how many.**
The *duumviri* who are in charge of the administration of justice in that *municipium* are to grant a *iudex* or arbiter in any case which is 1,000 sesterces or less and concerning which no *sponsio* for more than 1,000 sesterces has been or is being made, and in which there will be no *praeiudicium* for more than 1,000 sesterces, and which is not being or has not been divided in order to evade this statute, and which is not such that if it were being heard at Rome it would be appropriate for *recuperatores* to be granted, irrespective of how much it was for. And they are to grant as many *recuperatores* as it would be appropriate to grant if the matter were being heard at Rome in a matter in which if it were being heard at Rome it would be appropriate for *recuperatores* to be granted, irrespective of how much it was for.

Recuperatores were members of a small panel which gave judgements especially in law-cases about property or where it was felt public interest was concerned.

[Ch. 90] Rubric. **Concerning the granting of notice 'for the third day' (*intertium*).**
Whatever duumvir is in charge of jurisdiction in that *municipium*, is to grant notice for the third day for all those days on which it is lawful and appropriate for trials to take place there under this statute. And he is to have that fact displayed in that place in which he administers justice for the greater part of each day on all those days on which it is right for notice to be granted for the third day, so that it may be properly read from level ground. Likewise, if it is agreed between the parties and the *iudex* who is obliged to judge between them that notice for them for the third day should be granted for a certain day, and that day is not a feast-day because of the worship of the Imperial house or ought to be placed in the category of festivals for the same reason, he is to grant notice for the third day for them for that day. Whoever is obliged to grant notice for the third day and does not grant it or who knowingly and with wrongful intent does not have it displayed according to this statute, is to be condemned to pay to the *municipes* of the *Municipium Flavium Irnitanum* 1,000 sesterces for each day on which he ought to have granted it or did not have it published, and the right of action, suit and claim of that money and concerning that money is to belong to any *municeps* of that *municipium* who wishes and who is entitled under this statute.

The concept of *intertium* 'notice for the third day' was unfamiliar within Roman law before the discovery of the *Lex Irnitana,* and no firm agreement has been reached as to what it means. Possibilities include a three day adjournment when the case is already before a *iudex*; the setting of a date for a trial (with the original meaning of 'three days' having been lost); notice to the parties to a case that judgement will be given. (Crook, Johnston and Stein, 'Intertiumjagd and the Lex Irnitana: A Colloquium' in *Zeitschrift für Papyrologie und Epigraphik* 1987, 173–184 available in JSTOR).

[Ch. 91] Rubric. **According to what law notice for the third day may be served, the day may be postponed or have been postponed, a matter may be judged, a case may be at the peril of the *iudex*, a matter may cease to be under trial.**

In whatever private matter *iudices* or arbiters have been granted, substituted or assigned in that *municipium* under this statute, for those *iudices* and arbiters and those between whom those *iudices* or arbiters have been granted, substituted or assigned under this statute, in that matter, in serving notice for the third day to an adversary, *iudex* or arbiter within the two previous days, in postponing the day, in swearing that the days have been postponed, before they (the *iudices*) judge, in judging and valuing the case, during those days and in that place which are lawful and appropriate under this statute; and if the day has not been postponed and judgment has not taken place, so that the suit may be at the peril of the *iudex* or arbiter; and if judgment has not taken place within that time which is laid down in Chapter XII of the Lex Julia which has been most recently passed concerning *iudicia privata* and [Tablet XB] in the decrees of the senate which relate to that chapter of the statute, so that the matter is no longer under trial; the statute and law and position is to be as it would be if a praetor of the Roman people had ordered that matter to be judged in the city of Rome between Roman citizens and it was appropriate, under whatever statute or *rogatio* (bill) or plebiscite *iudicia privata* (private cases) shall take place under in the city of Rome, for that matter to be brought or dealt with, or for it (*intertium*) to be served, or for the day to be postponed or have been postponed, or for judgment to take place, or for the case to be at the peril of the *iudex*, or for the matter not to be under trial; except insofar as it is appropriate under this statute for it (*intertium*) to be served or for a matter to be judged or for the day to be postponed during other days and in another place. And so for all of them, in that matter and during those days which are lawful under this statute, in serving (notice for the third day) within that *municipium* and within one mile from that *municipium* or where they agree, in postponing the day, in judging in the forum of that *municipium* or where they agree, provided that it is within the boundaries of that *municipium*; and so that the day may be postponed or have been postponed for the same reasons; and so that the case may be at the peril of the *iudex* or arbiter if there has been no postponement under statute and judgment has not taken place during the days and in the place which are lawful and appropriate under this statute; and so that the matter may not be under trial if it has not been judged within the time which is laid down above; the statute and law and position is to be as if a praetor of the Roman people had ordered judgment to take place between Roman citizens and it was appropriate for a trial to take place there about that matter, under whatever statute or *rogatio* (bill) or plebiscite it is appropriate for *iudicia privata* (private cases) to take place under in the city of Rome; except insofar as it is appropriate under this statute for (notice for the third day) to be served or for a matter to be judged or for the day to be postponed during other days and in another place. Whatever has been done in this way is to be legal and valid.

The Julian Law on private cases set a limit of 18 months for proceedings (Gaius, *Institutes* 4.104).

[Ch. 92] Rubric. **On what days matters may not be judged and for what days notice for the third day may not be granted.**

Whoever is in charge of the administration of justice in that *municipium* is not to allow a *iudex* or arbiter or *recuperatores* to judge a private matter on those days nor is he to grant notice for the third day for those days which it is or will be appropriate to have or regard as feast-days or in the category of festivals because of the worship of the Imperial house, and on the days on which games are given in that *municipium* by decree of the *decuriones* or *conscripti* or a meal or distribution of meat is given to the *municipes* or a dinner to the *decuriones* or *conscripti* at the expense of the *municipes*, and on the days on which there are assemblies in that *municipium*, and on the days which are fixed under this statute as the days on which business is postponed because of harvest or vintage; except if the *iudex* or arbiter or *recuperatores* and those whose matter is being heard all wish it to be heard then and it is not a day which it is appropriate to have or regard as a feast-day or in the category of festivals because of the worship of the Imperial house. No *iudex* or arbiter or *recuperator* is to judge a private matter on those days which have been laid down above or value a case or devote attention for the sake of judging or express an opinion for the sake of judging, except if the *iudex* or arbiter or *recuperatores* and those whose matter is being heard all wish it to be heard then and it is not a day which it is appropriate to have or regard as a feast-day or in the category of festivals because of the worship of the Imperial house. And no-one is to serve notice for the third day for those days to an adversary or a *iudex* or arbiter within the two previous days for the sake of judging, except if the *iudex* or arbiter and those whose case is being heard all wish it to be heard then and it is not a day which it is appropriate to have or regard as a feast-day or in the category of festivals because of the worship of the Imperial house. Whatever is done contrary to these rules, is not to be legal or valid.

Festivals of the imperial cult are here given higher status in terms of mandatory suspension of legal business than any other religious festivals.

[Ch. 93] Rubric. **Concerning the law of the *municipes*.**

On whatever matters there is no explicit provision or rule in this statute, concerning the law under which the *municipes* of the *Municipium Flavium Irnitanum* should deal with each other, they are to deal with each other in all these matters under the civil law under which Roman citizens deal or will deal with each other. Whatever does not take place contrary to this statute and whatever is done in such a way that it does not take place or is not done with wrongful intent, is to be legal and valid.

[Ch. 94] Rubric. **Concerning *incolae*.**

As the *municipes* should obey this statute, so the *incolae* of that *municipium* are to obey it.

[Ch. 95] Rubric. **Concerning the inscription of the statute on bronze.**

Any duumvir who is in charge of the administration of justice in that *municipium* is to see that this statute is inscribed on bronze at the earliest possible moment and affixed in the most prominent place in that *municipium* so that it may be properly read from level ground.

[Ch. 96] Rubric. **Sanction.**
One is to do whatever it is appropriate to do under this statute and is not to act knowingly and with wrongful intent against this statute or in such a way that this statute may be evaded. Whatever is done against this statute or in such a way that this statute may be evaded is not to be valid; and whoever acts knowingly and with wrongful intent against these rules or evades this law is to be condemned to pay 100,000 sesterces to the *municipes* of the *Municipium Flavium Irnitanum* for each offence, and the right of action, suit and claim of that money and concerning that money is to belong to any *municeps* of that *municipium* who wishes and who is eligible under this statute.

[Ch. 97] Rubric. **That patrons should have the same rights as they had before over freedmen or freedwomen who have obtained Roman citizenship as a result of the offices of their sons or husbands.**
If any freedmen or freedwomen have obtained Roman citizenship under this statute as a result of the offices of their sons or husbands, the persons who manumitted them are to have the same rights over them and their goods, even if they themselves have not obtained Roman citizenship, as they would have had if they had not been made Roman citizens. If the patrons, male or female, have (also) obtained Roman citizenship, they are to have the same rights over those freedmen and freedwomen and their goods as they would have if they had been manumitted by Roman citizens.

This addendum, written in smaller letters than the rest of the statute, acts similarly to ch. 22–23 in ensuring that the new statute does not disrupt pre-existing relationships within the larger Roman *familia* including freedmen.

Letter
I know full well that some marriages are covered by the Latin statute; and if your anxiety indicates in any way that you have entered into some unions later with too little thought, those of you to whom I give forgiveness for the past I demand that in future you remember the statute, since now every avenue of indulgence has been used up.

Letter given on the fourth day before the Ides of April at Circeii, recited on the fifth day before the Ides of the month of Domitian.

In the year of M . Acilius Glabrio and M. Ulpius Traianus, consuls.

[.] Caecilius Optatus duumvir and Caecilius Montanus ambassador saw to the inscription.

The dates are 10 April and 11 October, AD 91. For Circeii on the Tyrrhenian coast of Italy see Juv. *Sat.* 4.141 (**G1.141**) and note. Domitian's letter (or extract from a letter – the formal ending contrasts with the lack of formal beginning) is distinctive in its expression. Marriage laws provided that a man of Junian Latin status could marry a woman of Roman or Latin status, and on proof of their having a child of one year old, the whole family became Roman citizens. The whole process was carefully documented by Venidius Ennychus at Herculaneum (*AE* 2006.304–7 = Cooley[2] G1–G4 and is known from Gaius, *Institutes* 1.28–29). There is nothing to indicate that the letter (in the same size as the main statute (see note on ch.97)) was engraved later than the rest of the statute. Domitian's name is not erased anywhere on the *Lex Irnitana* or *Salpensana* but is, in the only place he is named in the preserved parts of the *Lex Malacitana*.

SECTION G

JUVENAL, *SATIRE* IV
DOMITIAN'S COUNCIL MEETS TO DISCUSS A FISH

"Juvenal's Satire is of the utmost importance in the understanding both of the *consilium* and of Flavian politics. Here are jurists, soldiers, diplomats, aged and venerable counsellors – a most respectable and capable body, once we have penetrated beyond the screen of prejudice with which their careers have been overlaid. ... Of the eleven, the only *equites* seem to be praetorian prefects, and one of the senators is *praefectus urbi.*" J.A. Crook, *Consilium principis,* 51 – the major work on the emperor's council.

The ***consilium principis***, effectively the emperor's cabinet, was certainly a very important group, though only scattered pieces of evidence exist for how it operated: Josephus describes a *consilium* of Augustus' 'friends and the most prominent Romans' to decide what to do with Judaea after Herod's death (*JA* 17.300–323) while a papyrus reveals Augustus and named advisers meeting an embassy from Alexandria (LACTOR 17, M14). Nero seems to have asked for a written judgement from each adviser, but made the decision himself (Suet. *Nero* 15). Juvenal's portrayal, though intended satirically, fits with everything we know about the *consilium* at this period, especially with a letter of Domitian to Falerio of AD 82, (MW 463 = **K110**) in which he wrote, 'After summoning distinguished men from both classes [i.e. senators and equestrians] and hearing the case, I have pronounced as follows:...' That meeting also took place at his Alban villa. So the members of *consilium* were called, when required, to the emperor's house to give advice (as the word *consilium* implies) in some form, while the decision, of course, remained the emperor's. Not until the time of Marcus Aurelius (Millar, *ERW*, 94–5) did the *consilium* seem to have had legal experts as standing members.

Juvenal's fourth satire attacks the selfish and arbitrary nature of Domitian's reign, the sycophancy and self-serving nature of his advisers, as well as the personal faults of particular individuals. Finally, and in a much more direct way he deplores the cruelty and killings of Domitian's reign. It is also clear that there is a literary parody of Statius' epic poem on Domitian's German Wars, or at least the *consilium* as depicted there (see **G2**).

The Juvenal scholia: the name given to various ancient commentators on Juvenal's *Satires,* themselves preserved in a complicated manuscript tradition (see Braund & Osgood, *Blackwell Companion to Juvenal and Persius,* chapter 19). The scholia are of very variable quality. We are misinformed (line 141) that the Lucrine Lake is in Britain, not Italy; on Crispus (line 80 and note 195) we are given valuable information about the wrong 'Crispus'). Sometimes they 'explain' things that are obvious from the text anyway (lines 110–2, where Fuscus is explained as having been killed in war by the Dacians). Often they pass by names which neither they nor we can readily explain (Montanus, 107; Pompeius 109). Yet occasionally they provide nuggets of genuine historical information. These appear in the footnotes in ***bold italics***. Even more valuably they also preserve four lines of Statius' poem which Juvenal parodies, given here as **G2**.

Further reading: S. Braund, *Juvenal Book 1* (CUP 1996) provides an excellent modern commentary on *Satire* 4, including an essay on the satire as a whole.

Oh hell! It's Crispinus again.[176] I've got to put him on stage
For another encore – he's type-cast for the role. He's vicious,
A monster redeemed by no virtue, a pox-ridden pervert, who's fit for
Nothing but sex; a lecher from whom no woman is safe – unless
She's unmarried.[177] He has vast covered drive-ways, down which   5

---

[176] Crispinus, one of Domitian's courtiers, had been cited as someone who made it hard not to write satire, **U8**. This poem starts (1–33) with an attack on his morals and extravagance in buying a fish before moving on to attack at much greater length Domitian and his council (of which Crispinus is a member) being summoned to discuss a fish, and the emperor generally.

[177] Hostile sources say the same about Domitian, e.g. Suet. *Dom.* 1.3, and the point of this first section of the poem is perhaps to show Crispinus as a miniature Domitian (Braund, *Comm.* p.274).

He can gallop his panting nags; yet he has no use for them; no use
For his woods with their shades stretching onward forever; no use
For that monster estate and mansion palatial bought near the forum.
No crook is ever content – least of all some godless adulterer, who
Has recently ravished a Vestal, ribbons and all – she'll now be buried alive.[178]   10
But now let's turn to more innocent vices – yet if anyone else had been guilty
Of these sorts of crimes, he'd have fallen foul of the censor. Good blokes,
Such as Seius or Titius,[179] would have blushed to commit them; but he,
Crispinus, was proud to have done it. But what's to be done when a man
Is more vile and more foul than even the filthiest crimes?

                                           A mullet[180]   15
He bought, for six thousand sesterces, at roughly a thousand per pound –
Or so people say who are keen to make a good story better. Well you might,
I suppose, admire financial acumen, if such an investment were used
To win for himself in the will of an elderly, childless old man, nomination
As prime beneficiary. Better still, had he sent it straight off to his mistress,   20
The fat one, who rides in her wide-windowed, cavernous carriage,
In curtained seclusion. No chance! Get real! He bought it, but just for himself.
We see many things these days, which even the gourmand, poor, prudent Apicius[181]
Could never imagine. As for you, Crispinus, did you really pay that for a fish,
When not long ago you went about naked, but for your loin cloth
   of native papyrus?   25
I bet that for less than you paid for that fish, you'd have bought the whole fisherman.
It's the price of a decent estate in any old province; in Apulia the price of a big one.
But can you imagine what sort of dinner our Sovereign Imperial Majesty gorged on,
When his purple-clad Palace buffoon, Crispinus, (now Head of the Order of
   Knights,[182]
But once just a screeching street-seller of shop-soiled sardines, foreign
   like himself,   30
Can belch out a fortune, though it's worth little more than a tiny proportion,
An *hors d'oeuvre,* to what is served up at the emperor's table?

                                     Come now, Calliope, begin!
But there's no need to stand; and for god's sake, don't sing; we're after the truth,
Not an epic. Come, tell us your tale, holy Muses, Pierian maidens – and
   grant me   35

---

[178] The Vestal Virgin Cornelia was buried alive in AD 93, see **L10–L15**, but Juvenal is not saying that Crispinus had an affair with her.

[179] These names are used in Roman legal texts to refer to 'Joe Bloggs' (like the US use of John/Jane Doe).

[180] Proverbially expensive, like caviar nowadays: a variety of writers record absurd prices, including Pliny, *NH* 9.64–68 and Suet. *Tib.* 34.1

[181] M. Gavius Apicius lived at the time of Tiberius. His name became proverbial for fine cuisine and extravagant living and was attached to a later cookbook. Juvenal is being sarcastic in describing him as poor and prudent.

[182] This description suggests that he had reached the very top of the equestrian *cursus* as praetorian prefect, which would explain his presence on the *consilium.*

Your blessing for calling you maidens.[183]
           When Domitian, the last of the Flavians, was lashing
The world half to death while Rome cringed before this bald-headed Nero,[184]
By chance, right in front of the Temple of Venus, which stands on the headland
Of Doric Ancona,[185] a turbot of wondrous proportions, *Rhombus Adriaticus*, fell   40
Right into a fisherman's net, which could hardly contain it. As big as a tunny it was,
One of those which the ice-bound Sea of Azov keeps trapped in its waters,
Till it finally melts in the spring-sun's rays, and disgorges them down
To the mouths of the boiling Black Sea, still sluggish with sloth, and fat
From their long hibernation. This monstrous catch, surely an omen, our Captain   45
Of vessel and line is minded to give to our *pontifex maximus*. No one else
Would dare to sell such a fish – or to buy it – when even the shores are awash
With hordes of informers. The ubiquitous Seaweed Inspectorate[186] would
  quickly converge
From all sides with a writ for our fisherman, before he could even get into
  his clothes,
Alleging, beyond dispute that this was a runaway, fattened long since and fed   50
In the emperor's fish-ponds; he must, like a fugitive slave, be restored
To his previous owner. After all, if we can believe one word legal eagles assert,
Armillatus, perhaps, or Palfurius,[187] then every fine, beautiful creature that swims
In the whole of the Ocean, wherever it's found, belongs to His Majesty's Treasury.[188]
So of course he will make it a gift – to prevent its going to waste.   55
Disease-ridden Autumn was ending; the frosts were returning; now the sick
Were hoping for 'flu to take the place of malaria; wild winter's winds were howling,
But at least the cold kept the cargo still fresh, while the fisherman sped off to Rome
As if on the wings of the wind. And then, in the valley below as he hurried along
The Lakes could be seen, where Alba, though ruined, remains still guarding
  the flame   60

---

[183] Juvenal marks the main part of his satire by calling on the Muses, the goddesses of the arts who lived in Pieria, near Mount Olympus, and especially Calliope, goddess of epic poetry. As they had been invoked by poets for about 900 years (since Homer) and several had children in mythology (e.g. Orpheus, son of Calliope), they were not really 'maidens'! Juvenal is probably mocking Statius' epic poem on Domitian's German campaign, see **G2**.

[184] Domitian was bald and sensitive about it, Suet. *Dom.* 18.2: associated explicitly with Nero as a 'bad emperor' and last of his dynasty – probably the meaning of Martial 11.33.

[185] Ancona was a town on the Adriatic coast of central Italy, founded by settlers from Syracuse in Sicily, itself a Doric Greek colony.

[186] There was, of course, no such thing, as seaweed was proverbially worthless: Juvenal satirises the intrusion of the informers into every aspect of life.

[187] *Palfurius Sura, the son of a former consul fought under Nero with a Spartan girl in games. Later, removed from the senate by Vespasian, he converted to the Stoic sect, in which he excelled in eloquence and poetic glory. Abusing his close friendship with Domitian he carried to extremes the practice of informing. On Domitian's death he was put on trial and condemned by the senate for having been amongst the informers.* [Scholia (Probus) on Juvenal 4.53]. Palfurius is also mentioned by Suetonius, *Domitian* 13.1, while Armatillus is not otherwise known.

[188] British readers may be aware that certain 'royal' fish washed up on the beaches of Cornwall do, legally, belong to the Duchy of Cornwall, i.e. to HRH Prince Charles. Under Roman law, there was no such rule (*Digest* 47.10.13.7 shows that even much later, the sea was common property). But Y. Pliny praises Trajan for not regarding everything as his (*Panegyric* 50.2) implying that Domitian did do so.

Brought here by the Trojans, and tending the shrine of Vesta the Less.[189]
For a moment he halted, his progress obstructed by wondering crowds. But then,
As he paused, the hinges surrendered, the great doors gave way, and the Lords
   of the Senate,
Excluded, saw their right of precedence claimed – by a fish.
                                                    Into the Presence it came, right up
To 'Agamemnon' himself, the Son of Atreus.[190] Then our man from Picenum[191]   65
Spoke out, "I pray you, accept this my gift, too large for a citizen's kitchen;
Let this day celebrate your own *genius*.[192] Make haste; and purge your intestines of
Previous dinners; now feast on this turbot, divinely preserved for your era's glory;
It longed to be caught." Transparent flattery, of course. But His Majesty's crest
   rose up,
As he preened, for there's nothing imperial power cannot believe of itself,   70
When its power is likened to that of the gods. But now there's a crisis!
There isn't a dish big enough. A summons goes out for the Emperor's
   Security Council,
Noblemen all, and all of them hated.[193] They come, faces pallid and drawn
   with their fear
Of his dangerous friendship. "Hurry up! He is seated. The conclave's begun,"
   cries the
Chamberlain slave from Illyricum.
                                          First to arrive, still clutching his cloak, is lately   75
Promoted Pegasus, Bailiff of the terrified City. But in those days
What else was the prefect of Rome but a Bailiff?[194] Yet of all of them
He was the best, a totally scrupulous doctor of law, although he believed
In times as dreadful as these that Justice was better dispensed with less than
The so-called "full force of the Law." The next to arrive was Vibius Crispus.[195]   80
He was old, but a genial cove, with a kind disposition and morals to match,
He could talk the hind leg off a donkey and argue all sides of a case. He would

---

[189] Alba Longa was in Latium (Lazio), 13 miles south of Rome (but for the fisherman, *c.* 150 miles from
       Ancona). It was traditionally founded by Ascanius, son of Aeneas (Virgil, *Aeneid* 1.271), but destroyed
       (*c.* 650 BC) by Rome's third king, Tullus, except for the temples (Livy 1.29). Domitian built himself a
       palace there, now the pope's summer residence (Castel Gandolfo) see **K95**.
[190] Agamemnon was leader of the Greek forces at Troy, killed on his return by his wife, Clytemnestra.
       Juvenal's reference to Agamemnon fits the mock-epic poem and the bullying nature of the king as
       depicted by Homer's *Iliad*; it *may* also suggest death at the hands of his wife caused partly by adulterous
       affairs on both sides (Agamemnon as in the play by Aeschylus; Domitia's alleged involvement as in Dio
       67.15, Suet. *Dom.* 22, **P16b**).
[191] Picenum was one of the eleven Augustan regions of Italy, midway along the Adriatic coast, and
       including Ancona where the fish was caught, line 39. So Juvenal just means 'the fisherman'.
[192] *genius* – 'divine spirit'. A Roman would worship an emperor's *genius* rather than the man himself.
       See **L28**.
[193] Juvenal makes it clear that Domitian hated them – ironically, since the advisers were usually known as
       amici principis – 'friends of the emperor'.
[194] *Pegasus: he was the son of a naval captain, and got his name from one of his father's warships. His
       deserved fame from his knowledge of law meant that he was popularly known as 'a book', not a man.
       He achieved every honour and after governing several provinces took on the role of city prefect.*
       [Scholia on Juv. 4.77] For more on Plotius Pegasus, see **U7**.
[195] Quintus Vibius Crispus see **U2**. He is not to be confused with another noted wit of an earlier period,
       Sallustius Passienus Crispus, though this is exactly the mistake made by the scholia in their comments,
       accidentally preserving vital information about the wrong Crispus (see LACTOR 19, U5).

Have been an ideal confidential adviser to one who was ruler of seas,
Lands, and nations, if under that pestilential disaster it had just been permitted
To tender honest advice and condemn actions savage and cruel. But what   85
Can be more inclined to violent extremes than the ear of a tyrant, who holds
In his hands the fate of some friend, who only wanted to talk of the weather,
The rain, or the heat-wave, or even the showers of spring? That was why
Crispus would never go swimming upstream, against the force of the current,
Nor was he one of the public-spirited kind, who would freely offer opinions   90
Or risk his life for the truth. Thanks to that he survived many winters, and reached
His eightieth year, preserved even in such a court, by his safety-first system.

The next to arrive was his equal in age, Acilius Glabrio, hurrying in with
His son, who little deserved the cruel death that would soon overtake him,   95
Brought about all too soon by the swords of imperial assassins.[196] But old age
In a nobleman has for so long been so little short of a miracle that I would prefer
To be puny, some 'little brother of some great nobody'. Poor fellow,
It did him no good, when dressed like some lightly-clad hunter he fought
Hand to hand in the Alban arena as he speared those Numidian bears.   100
But who nowadays doesn't see through the tricks those patricians get up to?
Is anyone, now, remotely impressed by old-fashioned Brutus' pose as a
    simpleton?[197]
Back then by such tricks it was easy to take in a hairy old king with a beard.

Rubrius Gallus came next, a plebeian, but still none the happier for it. [198]
Long ago he was charged with a crime we had better pass over in silence,[199]
    but still   105
With less sense of shame than you'd find in some dirty old sod that writes satire.
Next enters Montanus' belly, slowed up by the size of its gut.[200] And Crispinus,
Simply sweating out morning deodorants, smelling more like the incense
You'd need for a couple of funerals. Then Pompeius arrived, more vicious even
Than he, who could slit a man's throat with a whisper.[201] Fuscus followed,
    a general   110

---

[196] Juvenal seems wrongly to give father and son the same name. Manius Acilius Aviola was consul under Claudius in 54. His son was M'. Acilius Glabrio, cos. ord. with Trajan in 91 (Dio 67.12.1). During his consulship, however, Domitian forced him to fight a lion at his Alban villa (for this episode see Fronto, **P13**), and Dio suggests his success prompted Domitian's jealousy and his condemnation for adopting Jewish practices (Dio 67.14.2–3). Suetonius, *Domitian* 10.2 describes him as being put to death in exile for planning revolution.

[197] M. Junius Brutus was alleged to have kept himself safe under the tyrannical Tarquin the Proud, by pretending to be stupid (Lat = '*brutus*').

[198] Rubrius Gallus (Jones, *Domitian* 58) commanded forces under Nero (Dio 63.27.1), and Otho (Tac. *Hist.* 2.51). He acted as intermediary between Caecina (then lieutenant of Vitellius) and Flavius Sabinus (Tac. *Hist.* 2.99), and governed Moesia for Vespasian (Jos. *JW* 7.92).

[199] The crime is mentioned only in the scholia on Juvenal: *This fellow Rubrius had seduced Domitia when she was a girl.* [Scholia on Juv. 4.105]

[200] Montanus (Jones, *Domitian* 54): identity not certain, but probably either T. Junius Montanus cos 81 or Curtius Montanus (Tac. *Ann.* 16.28, 29, 33).

[201] Pompeius (Jones, *Domitian* 55–56): probably M. Pompeius Silvanus Staberius Flavinus, cos 45, cos II 76, legate of Dalmatia in 69 (MW 451), water commissioner 71–73. Tacitus describes him as a rich old man (*Hist.* 2.86.3), 'useless in war, wasting the moment for action by talk' (*Hist.* 3.50).

Who, safe in his marble-built halls, had dreamed of battles to come,
But the only things he kept safe were his guts, as food for the Dacian vultures. [202]
In came Veiento the crafty survivor,[203] with blind Catullus,[204] the deadly informer
Still burning with passionate love for the girl he had never set eyes on.
A monster he was, unparalleled even today, for his huge, notorious crimes.   115
Now a courtier, raised from his pitch at the bridge as a beggar, he cringed with
    the best,
But was dangerous, though blind, fit only to beg at Aricia's coach wheels,
And throw kisses to vehicles as they went creeping downhill.[205]
His was the finest performance, gazing amazed at the turbot, gabbling his praise
While he looked to the left at the prodigy placed to his right. It was an old trick,   120
Which he used when clapping Cilix, the gladiator's left thrust and right parry,
Or the stage-device which would fly boy acrobats up to the awnings.[206]
But Veiento would not be outdone. Like some crazed devotee of Bellona,
Goddess of War, he bursts into prophecy: "See, you have here an omen prodigious –
Some great and glorious triumph is coming. You shall capture a king,   125
Or perhaps from the pole of a British war-chariot Arviragus shall tumble.[207]
After all the monster is also a foreigner; see how the spines on its back
Face in the wrong direction." Fabricius Veiento got just
One single thing wrong: he left out the age of the beast and its provenance.
"What then is the opinion of council?"[208] the Emperor asked, "Chop it up?"
    Montanus   130
Replied, "Heavens, No! Such a course is unworthy. Rather let preparation
Be made for a dish so vast it will gather within its thin walls such a mighty
Circumference.[209] We need a Prometheus, at once, a potter great enough to contrive
Such a dish.[210] Make haste, bring us clay and the wheel of a potter. Great Caesar,
Henceforth from this time, let potters be part of your army's auxiliary forces."   135
The motion was carried. Its dignity matched its proposer, a courtier familiar
With the luxury known of old in the Palace of Nero,[211] and the orgies at midnight
With gluttony piled upon hunger by appetites fired by Falernian wine. For none
In my time knew better than he the true art of the gourmet. With an oyster,
For instance, his connoisseur's taste buds could tell at first nibble the place   140
Of its birth, whether native of Circeii, rocky Lucrine, or the deep oyster-beds

---

[202] Cornelius Fuscus, praetorian prefect, see Tac. *Hist.* 2.86.3 and **N34, N35, N41**– his death in Dacia.
[203] A. Didius Gallus Fabricius Veiento, cos II 80, cos III 83, see **U9** and further refs there.
[204] L. Valerius Catullus Messallinus: a notorious informer (**P11b, T18, B73**).
[205] Aricia, mentioned with great topicality as only 2 miles SE of the Alban villa, was at a steep slope of the via Appia, so carriages would have to travel very slowly (in either direction).
[206] So though blind, Catullus would attend the emperor's shows to flatter him.
[207] Arviragus is only known from Geoffrey of Monmouth, twelfth-century *History of the Kings of Britain*, according to which unreliable source, he was a son of Cymbeline.
[208] Juvenal uses a regular formula of question from Roman political life (*OLD* under *'censeo'*).
[209] The making of a dish may recall one of Vitellius' acts, see **H8**.
[210] In Greek mythology, Prometheus moulded the first humans from clay.
[211] Tacitus gives one example of feasts under Nero at *Ann.* 15.37.

Of Richborough's farm;[212] he'd know at a glance from what shores a mere
  sea urchin came.
They stood. The Council dismissed. The noblemen told to depart. Yet these
Were the men whom their Glorious Leader had dragged from their beds
To his fortress up on the Alban, in panic and ordered to hurry, as if   145
There were urgent despatches,[213] with some news of the Germans, the Chatti,
Or savage Sygambri,[214] or again, as if from all over the Empire had come
Frantic messages, borne on the wings of precipitate birds.[215]
And yet, I could well have wished that he'd spent all his days
On such trivial matters, instead of those inhuman crimes, by which   150
With total impunity he robbed hapless Rome of those famous, illustrious lives,
Which none could defend, none avenge. But once the Workers of Rome
Took alarm, he was done for. That's what finished him off, the one
Who was dripping with blood from upper class toffs like Lamia.[216]

G2   Domitian's council from Statius' epic poem on the German War
Eyes; the gentle prudence of Crispus, Nestor's equal in years
And Fabius Veiento (their power shown by the purple each wears),
The Fasti they have filled will thrice their names recall,
And close by, Acilius, neighbour of the emperor's great hall.

                           [Scholia on Juvenal 4.94 = Statius, *On the German War,* fragment]

The scholiast quotes the four lines of Statius given above to elucidate Juvenal's mention of Acilius: "Acilius Glabrio, the son, was consul under Domitian and is mentioned in Papinius Statius' epic poem about the German War which Domitian waged …"

The lines quoted also fit perfectly with Juvenal's theme of the emperor's council, since they mention three of the same advisers as Juvenal. Statius presumably included an epic-style council meeting in his poem, maybe modelled on the meeting of the gods at the start of Homer's *Odyssey* (1.26ff). The word 'Eyes' at the start of the first line quoted seems to belong to the previous clause (the original quotation gives no punctuation), and is possibly a reference to the blind Catullus mentioned in Juvenal's council.

---

[212] Circeii, now Monte Circeo is a headland on the Tyrrhenian coast of Italy roughly halfway between Rome and Campania. The Lucrine Lake is in Campania (not Britain as the scholia say). Both were popular areas for luxury villas. Richborough is in Kent (UK), the landing-place of the Roman invasion and an important harbour.

[213] Nero had apparently summoned an emergency council to announce an innovation to water-organs (Dio 63.26.4).

[214] Domitian awarded himself a triumph for campaigns against the Chatti in 83. This will have formed part of Statius' poem on the Germanic War, whose description of the council is parodied by Juvenal. No campaigns against the Sygambri are known, and this may be the point.

[215] News could travel very fast on the *cursus publicus* which provided regular staging posts for fresh horses. For remarkable speed of news and action in this period, see **P8d** or Plutarch, *Galba* 7.

[216] L. Aelius Plautius Lamia, cos 80, see **B80**. He was the first husband of Domitia and executed by Domitian (Suet. *Dom.* 10.2).

SECTION H
ESTABLISHING THE FLAVIAN DYNASTY

Vespasian alone, out of all the emperors before him, changed for the better.

[Tacitus, *Histories* 1.50.4]

This section gives sources which show how Vespasian set about establishing stability and the Flavian dynasty after the chaos of the Year of the Four Emperors. Several of the problems and solutions were quite similar to those of Octavian/Augustus. Material is arranged by theme and chronologically.

THE YEAR OF THE FOUR EMPERORS: H1–H12

H1   A very brief account of the year of the four emperors
[494] I might report also how the war in Gaul ended and how Galba was made emperor and returned out of Spain to Rome; and how he was accused of meanness by the soldiers, and killed by treachery in the middle of the Roman Forum, and how Otho was made emperor; [495] I might report on Otho's campaigns against the commanders of Vitellius, and his defeat, and what disturbances there were under Vitellius, and the fighting around the Capitol; also on how Antonius Primus and Mucianus destroyed Vitellius and his German legions and thereby ended the civil war. [496] I have omitted to give a detailed account of them because they are well known by all and have been described by many Greek and Roman authors; yet for the sake of the continuity, and so that my history may not be incoherent, I have summarised everything briefly.

[Josephus, *Jewish War* 4.494–496]

'Many ... authors': at the time Josephus was writing the *Jewish War*, Pliny's history had been written but not published (see **R12**); Tacitus' *Histories* had not been written nor the presumed source for Plutarch's biographies of Galba and Otho (see Syme, *Tacitus* 181). Tacitus cites Vipstanus Messalla (*Hist.* 3.25, 3.28). Plutarch suggests that he had many sources available for the second battle of Cremona (*Otho* 9).

H2   Galba's 'war for the state'
Quintus Pomponius Rufus, consul, *pontifex*, *sodalis Flavialis*, commissioner for public works, imperial propraetorian legate of the provinces of Moesia, Dalmatia, and Spain, commander of Legion V, prefect of the sea coast of Nearer Spain and Gallia Narbonensis in the war which the emperor Galba fought for the state, proconsul of the province of Africa, through L. Asinius Rufus, propraetorian legate [... *the rest lost* ...]

[MW 31 = *IRT* 537 = EDCS–14200137]

The interest here is in the unique description of Galba's war from someone who prospered under the Flavians (e.g. *flavialis* and cos 95) and beyond. The inscription was from the Arch of Trajan in Lepcis Magna, set up in 110 (*IRT* 353) during Pomponius' governorship of Africa (http://inslib.kcl.ac.uk/irt2009/IRT537.html).

H3   Funerary altar of Piso and his wife, AD 69? and *c.* 96–100.
To the divine spirits of [L.] Calpurnius Piso Frugi Licinianus, [quindecim]vir for sacrifices and of Verania Gemina, daughter of Q. Veranius, consul and augur, and wife of Piso Frugi.

[MW 76 = *ILS* 240 = EDCS–19500121*]

Tacitus tells us that Verania had to search for and ransom Piso's head after his murder (*Hist.* 1.47). His epitaph makes no mention of his ill-fated adoption by Galba. Verania's death is mentioned in Y. Pliny *Letters* 2.20.2–6 (*c.* AD 96–100) when her name was added (the letters are very slightly different). Her loyalty and devotion are rewarded in the sense that their marble funerary altar is still well-preserved in Rome's 'Terme' museum while those of their ememies are lost.

H4   Otho's suicide praised by Martial

> While civil war's goddess was still unsure
> And gentle Otho might have had a chance to win
> He turned his back on war that would have caused much bloodshed
> And with unflinching hand he pierced right through to his heart.
> Let Cato in his life be greater than was Caesar   5
> But in his death not greater, surely, than was Otho.

> [Martial, *Epigram* 6.32 (published December 91)]

Otho committed suicide on the morning of 16 April after defeat at the battle of Cremona (Plut. *Otho* 15–18; Tac. *Hist.* 2.46–50: the accounts agree as do their evaluation with praise for his death balancing condemnation of his life/murder of Galba). M. Porcius Cato 'Uticensis' a descendant of the censor fought against Julius Caesar in the civil war and committed suicide in 45 BC rather than accept Caesar's pardon. His idealism was made even more famous in Flavian times and beyond by Lucan: "the victors' cause was favoured by the gods, but that of the vanquished by Cato" (*Civil War* 1.128).

H5   Otho's epitaph

> To the spirits of Marcus Otho

This very simple epitaph to Otho does not survive but is mentioned by Tacitus (*Histories* 2.49), Plutarch (*Life of Otho* 18.1) and Suetonius (*Vitellius* 10.3), and quoted as MW 34.

H6   Vitellius with two children on *aureus*, Rome AD 69

Obv: Head of Vitellius, laureate, right
> A VITELLIVS GERMAN IMP TR P (Aulus Vitellius Germanicus, Emperor, tribunician power)

Rev: Busts of Vitellius' son (left) and daughter (right), facing each other
> LIBERI IMP GERMAN (Children of Emperor Germanicus)

> [*RIC* 1² Vitellius 78]

Vitellius treated his 'infant son' as of imperial rank making his armies salute him as 'Germanicus' (Tac. *Hist.* 2.59) and parading him on his 'abdication' on 18 December (*Hist.* 3.67). This was the despicable excuse for Mucianus to execute the boy in AD 70 (*Hist.* 4.80). The girl, Vitellia, was given a dowry by Vesp. (Suet. *Vesp.* 14, **J4g**). *Denarii* were also issued from both Lugdunum and Rome with this design (*RIC* 1.2, Vitellius 57 and 79).

H7 Vitellius as perpetual consul
Aulus Vitellius, son of Lucius, Imperator, perpetual consul

[MW 81 = *ILS* 242 = EDCS–17301048*]

This inscription was mentioned several times by 16th-century antiquarians, but is now lost. Suet. *Vit.* 11.2 mentions his perpetual consulship. The innovation was not followed by Flavians or later emperors.

Reputation of previous emperors: H8–H12
'The mob went for him as viciously when he was dead as they had flattered him when alive.' Tacitus' description of Vitellius' death (*Hist.* 3.85) could almost apply to his reputation, except that he had hardly reigned long enough for any sources to praise him (coins and individual records of the Arval Brothers being the only exception). For writers immediately afterwards, to criticise Vitellius was to praise, at least implicitly, his successor. Similarly, criticism of Nero would also justify the new dynasty. Pliny the Elder's support for the Flavians was probably genuine (see **R13**). The case of Philostratos is more complicated, given that we know so little about the author. What he writes about the meeting between his idol, Apollonius, and Vespasian is invented, but plausibly the sort of thing promoted by the Flavian writers, perhaps especially the idea of Vespasian stressing that he did not revolt against Nero (who, however bad, was clearly an emperor legitimately in power).

H8 Vitellius' luxury
When we said (when writing about ornithology) that one dish cost Aesop the tragic actor 100,000 sesterces, I am sure my readers were indignant. Yet, by Hercules, Vitellius as emperor had a dish made costing 1,000,000 sesterces. A kiln had to be built in the countryside to make it, taking luxury to the point where even pottery cost more than crystal.

[Pliny, *Natural History* 35.163]

H9 An invented account of Vespasian in Egypt justifying his actions
"I do not think that I was a slave to wealth even when a young man, and I fulfilled the magistracies and honours relating to Roman government with such good sense and moderation as to seem neither arrogant nor again timid. I meditated no rebellion against Nero; instead (since the power he held had been received, even if not constitutionally, from an undisputed emperor) I obeyed him for the sake of Claudius who made me consul and his adviser. I swear by Athene that whenever I saw Nero doing something disgraceful, I wept, thinking of Claudius and of the dregs which had inherited his greatest possession."

[Philostratos, *Life of Apollonius of Tyana* 5.29.1–2]

H10 Criticism of Vitellius
"But even now Nero is out of the way, I see that human affairs have not changed for the better; rather the empire is faring so disgracefully as to be in Vitellius' power. So I am confident in aiming for it, firstly because I wish to make myself of great value to mankind. Then again, my competitor is a drunkard: Vitellius uses more perfume to wash in than I use water – I think if he were struck with a sword he would spout perfume not blood. He is out of his mind going from one drinking bout to another. He

plays dice and dreads the dice falling badly, and risks the empire in sport. Lying under prostitutes, he leaps on top of married women, saying that love-making is more fun for having an element of danger."

[Philostratos, *Life of Apollonius of Tyana* 5.29.3]

H11 'Official Flavian attitude to predecessors?'

"Today let us join in philosophical discussion of my plans, so that I may do all that is best and in the interests of mankind. Consider first Tiberius, how he turned power into something inhuman and savage. Then after him, Gaius, like a man possessed by Dionysus and Persianizing his dress, and winning imaginary wars, making all state affairs into a disgusting orgy. Next the good Claudius, how he was dominated by women and forgot to rule, and even to live, since they killed him, so people say. Why should I attack Nero when Apollonius has summed him up in a word talking about the 'flats and sharps' with which he disgraced his reign. Why should I mention the arrangements put in place by Galba who was killed in the middle of the forum after adopting as his sons his former lovers, Otho and Piso? And if we were to hand over power to Vitellius, the most disgusting of them all, Nero would come back to life.

[Philostratos, *Life of Apollonius of Tyana* 5.32.2]

H12 Vespasian hears reports of Rome under Vitellius

[585] While this was happening, Rome suffered heavy calamities. [586] For Vitellius had arrived from Germany with his army and a vast mob of other men as well. And when the accommodation allotted to the soldiers could not contain them, he turned all of Rome itself into his camp and filled all the houses with his armed men. [587] When these men saw the riches of Rome, with eyes unaccustomed to such wealth, and found themselves with the glint of silver and gold all round them, they could barely contain their covetous desires, and turned to plunder and to slaughter any who should stand in their way. Such was the state of affairs in Italy at that time.

[588] But when Vespasian had overthrown all the places in the neighbourhood of Jerusalem, he returned to Caesarea, and heard of the troubles that were at Rome, and that Vitellius had become emperor. [589] Although he knew very well how to obey as well as to rule, this news caused him indignation, since he could not accept for his master one who had acted so madly, and seized upon the empire as if it were absolutely destitute of a commander. [590] And in his sorrow, he could not bear the torments he was suffering, nor could he focus on other wars, while his fatherland was being devastated. [591] However, while his passion aroused him to avenge his fatherland, he was restrained by the thought of the distance involved; for fortune might hamper and play tricks on him before he himself could sail over the seas to Italy, especially as it was still the winter season. So he restrained his anger, despite its vehemence.

[Josephus, *Jewish War* 4.585–591]

PROMOTING VESPASIAN: H13–H18

Flavian supporters were clearly effective at presenting Vespasian's rise as divinely sanctioned: Suetonius, *Vespasian* 5 gives a list of eleven prophecies. Dio 65.1.2–4 (**C1**) gives a shorter list. Tacitus gives a typically intelligent evaluation of such stories at *Histories* 1.10.3, 2.1 (= **H15**) and 2.78.2. For Silius Italicus' epic 'prediction' of Flavian rule, see **H62**. Even today, politicians, no matter how ambitious, generally insist they are only standing for office because others have urged them to do so. Rather than quote a real politician, here is the fictional Jim Hacker from the brilliant political satire, *Yes, Prime Minister:* 'All I've ever wanted to do is serve my country. I've never sought office. But I suppose that if my colleagues were to persuade me that the best place to serve it was Ten Downing Street, then I might reluctantly have to accept the responsibility, whatever my own private wishes might be.' J. Lynn & A. Jay, *The Complete Yes, Prime Minister* (BBC, 1987, p.56). So too Vespasian chose to be portrayed as reluctantly accepting the purple (**H16–H18**).

H13   Prediction of Vespasian's rule by Josephus (=E4)

You, Vespasian, are Caesar and Emperor, you and your son here. [402] Bind me tighter, and keep me for yourself, Caesar, for you are master not only of me but also over the land and the sea and all of mankind. And I ask to be kept in closer custody in order to be punished [403] if I take the name of God in vain.'

[Josephus, *Jewish War* 3.401–3]

H14   Statue of Gaius Caesar turns to the east

Everyone saw that the statue of Gaius Caesar on Tiber Island had turned from west to east, and without any earthquake or storm. This is said to have happened at the time when Vespasian was finally, openly, aiming to take over.

[Plutarch, *Otho* 4.5–6]

H15   Prophecies believed

Things were going well for Vespasian, prophecies had been received, and chance events were greeted as omens by people with a mind to believe such things.

[Tacitus, *Histories* 2.1]

H16   An imagined account of Vespasian's men urging him to claim the purple

[592] But now his generals and soldiers met in groups and openly discussed revolution and cried out in indignation: 'In Rome there are soldiers who are living in luxury and, fearing the word 'war', they vote whoever they fancy to the throne, making them emperors in the hope of personal gain. [593] We, who have gone through so many labours, and who have grown old under our helmets, allow others to use such a power, when we ourselves have in our midst one more worthy to rule. [594] Now what better opportunity shall we have of properly repaying his kindness to us, if we do not make use of this chance? Vespasian's claims for becoming emperor are far stronger than Vitellius' – just as we are far more deserving than those other troops who have made the other emperors. [595] For we have undergone wars as great as the troops who come from Germany; nor are we inferior fighters to those who have brought that tyrant to Rome! [596] But a contest will not be necessary; for neither will the senate nor the people of Rome tolerate such a lustful emperor as Vitellius in place of a disciplined man like Vespasian; nor will they endure a barbaric tyrant over a kindly leader, nor choose a childless man to rule above a father. For the legitimate succession of princes is the most certain guarantee of peace. [597] If we estimate the ability to govern well from the experience of years, we should have Vespasian; if from the vigour of youth, we ought to have Titus. For we shall have the advantages of both their ages combined. [598] The strength we afford to those we appoint will not only be our three legions and other auxiliaries from the neighbouring kings, but also the support of all the armies in the east and also those in Europe, which are out of the reach of Vitellius, besides the allies in Italy itself, as well as Vespasian's brother, and

his other son. [599] One will bring in a great number of distinguished young men and the other has already been entrusted with the government of the city – this will be an immense asset to Vespasian's gaining the throne. [600] All in all, if we make further delays, the senate may choose as emperor the man whom the soldiers, after helping him to safeguard the empire, have passed over.'

[Josephus, *Jewish War* 4.592–600]

This speech represents a very long indirect speech in Vespasian's Greek ('they cried out that there were soldiers in Rome … and that there was no better opportunity … and that' (etc.)), but which can only be translated sensibly in English by use of direct speech. There was, of course, no single speech given by 'the men' and reported by Josephus, who was still a prisoner at this point in his narrative. But it does represent plausible gossip of the time by men praising their own legion and commander. As for rumours about Vitellius, he *did* have children (see **H6** and note) but not adult sons. And since the winners write history, Vitellius appears in all our sources as cruel, greedy, lustful and degenerate (Suetonius has no word of praise, e.g. *Vit.* 4.1 'guilty of every vice': Tacitus, deliberately aiming at a more balanced judgement, *Hist.* 3.85–6). Reports of similarly disgraceful behaviour from his troops may have arisen as reflections of their commander (and billeted troops are never going to be popular), but are also reported at Tac. *Ann.* 2.93.1.

H17 Vespasian 'forced' to accept being hailed 'Caesar'

[601] These were the arguments of the soldiers in their various companies. After this, they joined together into one body, and, encouraging each other, they declared Vespasian emperor, and urged him to save the empire, which was now in danger. [602] Although Vespasian had been concerned about the whole state for a long time, he did not intend to set himself up as emperor, for although his actions showed that he deserved it, he preferred the safety of a private life to the dangers of high office. [603] However, when he refused the empire, the officers insisted more earnestly that he accept and the soldiers surrounded him, armed with their drawn swords, and threatened to kill him if he refused the life he deserved. [604] In the end, after he had protested strongly and had tried to thrust away this office, but without success, he yielded to them and accepted their nomination. [605] Mucianus and the other commanders encouraged him to accept the throne and the rest of the army loudly cried out that they were willing to be led against all who opposed him. His first intention was to gain control over Alexandria, as he knew that Egypt was of the greatest importance to obtaining the entire empire because it supplied corn to Rome. [606] Once master of Egypt, he hoped to depose Vitellius, even if things dragged on; for the latter would not be able to hold out if the people at Rome were hungry. Secondly, he wished to join the two legions that were at Alexandria to his other legions. [607] Lastly, he planned to make that country a defence for himself against the uncertainties of fate; for Egypt is hard to enter by land, and has no good harbours on the coast.

[Josephus, *Jewish War* 4.601–607]

H18 Vespasian gets the support of Ti. Julius Alexander, prefect of Egypt

[616] Naturally Vespasian wanted to gain control there in order to strengthen his claims upon the whole empire. And so he immediately wrote to Tiberius Alexander, who was then the governor of Egypt and of Alexandria, and informed him of the insistence of the army, and how he, after being forced to accept of the burden of the empire, wanted to have his help and support. [617] Alexander read this letter in public and enthusiastically called on the soldiers and the civilians to take an oath of loyalty to Vespasian. Both willingly obeyed him, already knowing the courage of the

man from his nearby campaigns. [618] Already entrusted with the matters concerning the accession, he prepared everything for his arrival. Rumour, quicker than thought, carried news abroad that he was emperor over the east. Every city celebrated festivals, and offered sacrifices for him.

[Josephus, *Jewish War* 4.616–618]

For a papyrus recording Vespasian's acclamation at Alexandria, mentioning Tiberius Alexander and referring to Vespasian as Serapis, see **L22**. The importance of Tiberius Julius Alexander, prefect of Egypt is amply shown by the date on which he hailed Vespasian being later taken as his official accession date (Tac. *Hist.* 2.79). Though Josephus has Vespasian soliciting his support, Tac. *Hist.* 2.74.1 simply says that Ti. Alexander 'had made common cause', suggesting some length of planning (R. Ash's commentary, p.286).

THE FLAVIANS RETURN TO ROME, AD 70: H19–H29

Like Octavian after Actium, Vespasian seems to have chosen to return to Rome slowly, allowing his supporters to mop up any resistance (e.g. Tac. *Hist.* 4.1–4, 46, 80) and deal with the senate (*Hist.* 4.5–11, 40–44) before he returned in triumph.

H19   Mucianus in charge

[7.2] Mucianus ruled over the beginnings of the principate and the state of the city, while Domitian was just a young man, using his father's position as an excuse for behaving without any restraint.

[Tacitus, *Agricola* 7.2]

For Mucianus in control of Rome, see Tac. *Hist.* 4.11.1 and 4.39.1. For Domitian, *Hist.* 4.2.1.

H20   Law on the power of Vespasian, AD 69/70, Rome

[…………..] or that it be lawful to make a treaty with whomever he wishes, just as it was lawful for Divus Augustus, Tiberius Julius Caesar Augustus, and for Tiberius Claudius Caesar Augustus Germanicus.

[3] And that it be lawful for him to convene the senate, to introduce or send back a motion, and to pass senatorial decrees by motion and by voting, just as it was lawful for Divus Augustus, Tiberius Julius Caesar Augustus, and Tiberius Claudius Caesar Augustus Germanicus.

[7] And that, when the senate is convened by his will or authority, order or command, or when he is present, the legality of everything be regarded and preserved just as if the senate had been declared and convened as the result of a statute.

[10] And that all candidates for a magistracy, power, post, or curatorship of anything whom he recommends to the senate and people of Rome, and to whom he gives and promises his support, an extraordinary reckoning is to be held for them at their elections.

[14] And that it be lawful for him to advance and enlarge the city's sacred boundary, when he judges it to be in the state's interest, just as it was lawful for Tiberius Claudius Caesar Augustus Germanicus.

[17] And that whatever he judges to be to the state's advantage and in keeping with the majesty of things divine and human, public and private, let him have the legal power to perform and do this, just as it was for Divus Augustus, Tiberius Julius Caesar Augustus, and Tiberius Claudius Caesar Augustus Germanicus.

[22] And that in those statutes or plebiscites it has been written, that Divus Augustus, or Tiberius Julius Caesar Augustus and Tiberius Claudius Caesar Augustus

Germanicus are exempt, let Emperor Caesar Vespasian be released from those statutes and plebiscites, and whatever in accordance with any statute or bill Divus Augustus or Tiberius Julius Caesar Augustus or Tiberius Claudius Caesar Augustus Germanicus had to do, all these things it be lawful for Emperor Caesar Vespasian Augustus to do.

[29] And that whatever has been performed, accomplished, decreed or commanded by Emperor Caesar Vespasian Augustus before this statute was proposed or by anyone commanded acting by his order or command, these things are to be lawful and binding just as if they had been performed by command of the people or commoners.

Sanction.

[33] If anyone in consequence of this statute has acted or will act contrary to the statutes, bills, plebiscites or senatorial decrees, or if in consequence of this statute he does not do what he ought to do in accordance with a statute, bill, plebiscite or senatorial decree, let him not be liable for this, nor because of this is he to be obliged to give anything to the people, nor is there to be a legal process or settlement concerning this against him, nor is anyone to allow a case to be pleaded before him concerning this matter.

[M.H. Crawford, ed. *Roman Statutes* I (London 1996) no. 39 = *ILS* 244]

A large bronze tablet, displaying the final section of the bill put before the people of Rome granting powers to Vespasian on his accession as emperor following the civil wars of AD 68/9. The first part must have appeared on a separate tablet. In the extant text, Augustus is repeatedly cited as the first precedent for the powers being granted, followed by Tiberius and Claudius, the other 'good' Julio-Claudians (omitting the 'bad' Gaius Caligula and Nero, as well as the other three emperors of 69).

H21   Vespasian's journey back to Rome, AD 70

[9.2.a] As for Egypt, it did not take him long to settle the situation, and from there he sent massive supplies of corn back to Rome. He had left his son, Titus, with the task of sacking Jerusalem, and was himself waiting for its capture, so that he could return to Rome accompanied by him. But faced with the protracted length of the siege, he left Titus in Palestine, and himself boarded a merchant ship and sailed to Lycia, whence he travelled on to Brundisium, partly by land and partly by sea.

[Zonaras, *Summary of Dio*, 11.17 = Dio 66.9.2a]

Vespasian's plan to wrest the empire from Vitellius may initially have involved cutting off corn supplies to Rome (Tac. *Hist.* 2.48.3). Josephus, *Jewish War* 7.21–22 gives details of Vespasian's return, via Asia Minor and Greece – the usual route, staying near to the coast, but also allowing visits to the main cities. The voyage probably took the greater part of the autumn of AD 70. Rather like Octavian's slow return to Rome from Alexandria in 30/29 BC it probably allowed the emperor's subordinates to get the blame for unpopular decisions, such as the murder of Vitellius' young son (Tac. *Hist.* 4.80 and note on **H6** above).

H22   Reception of Vespasian in Rome

[64] For the whole of Italy showed the great joy in their hearts even when Vespasian was some way off, as if he had already been there. Their eager expectations made them mistake the prospect of his arrival for his actual arrival and their goodwill to him was free and spontaneous. [65] It was desirable for the senate, who could recall only too well the disastrous rapid succession of emperors, to receive an emperor who possessed the dignity of mature age and enjoyed the highest skill in warfare, whose

accession would be, as they knew, a source of safety for his subjects. [66] The people, exhausted by the miseries of civil war, were even more eager for his coming. For they believed that now they could finally be freed from their sufferings and could again enjoy their former peace and prosperity. [67] Above all, the soldiers had the highest regard for him, having seen at first hand his great exploits in war and also having experienced the incompetence and cowardice of the other emperors, they desired to be free from the great shame that they had undergone and wholeheartedly wanted to receive a leader who could restore security and honour to them. [68] Among this universal goodwill towards Vespasian, distinguished men could not endure the wait in Rome and made haste to meet him at a great distance from the city. [69] Nor indeed could any of the others bear the delay in seeing him and, believing that it was better for them to go than to stay behind, they poured out of the city in such numbers that the city itself joyfully found itself almost empty of citizens! For those who stayed within the city were fewer than those who went out. [70] When the news of his impending arrival was announced, and those who had met him first reported the friendly welcome with which he had received all who had come to him, the rest of the people who had remained in the city, with their wives and children, came into the road and waited for him. [71] As he passed them by, each group overwhelmed by their delight in seeing him and by his gentle countenance, uttered every type of acclamation, greeting him as 'benefactor', 'saviour' and 'the only worthy emperor of Rome'. The whole city was like a temple, full of garlands and incense. [72] It was difficult for him to reach the palace due to the crowds of people standing in his way but at last he offered sacrifices to his household gods in thanksgiving for his safe return to the city. [73] The crowd then turned to celebrations and feasting in their tribes, families and neighbourhoods, and offered prayers and libations to God, asking that Vespasian be granted a long reign as emperor and that his throne be preserved for his sons and their descendants. [74] And it was in this manner that the city of Rome joyfully welcomed Vespasian and then moved on to great prosperity.

[Josephus, *Jewish War* 7.63–74]

Vespasian arrived in Rome in mid-AD 70. Since Vitellius' death, Mucianus aided by Domitian had day-to-day control of Rome. Josephus reports, with some exaggeration, the general relief at the accession of Vespasian and the end of the war. Tacitus' narrative *Hist.* 4.6–8 includes the senatorial debate on the delegation to be sent to welcome Vespasian, but fails before his description of the actual return.

H23   Vespasian's handout, AD 70
He gave a handout of 85 denarii [= 340 sesterces]

[*Chronicle of 354*: Section 16, Vespasian]

The *Chronicle* is interested in handouts given by the emperors: 75 denarii = 300 sesterces is perhaps a more likely round number, with an extra X creeping into LXXV. Though not dated here, the handout doubtless coincided with Vespasian's return, as suggested by Dio/Zonaras below.

H24   Vespasian's entry to Rome, AD 70

[10.1a] Once he got to Rome, he distributed donatives to the soldiery and the common people. He made good the damage to all sacred and public buildings and rebuilt those that were already ruined. Once that was done he restored the original inscriptions, putting up the names of the original benefactor instead of his own. [10.2a] He renounced any claim to the property of his enemies who had fallen in their many battles, and left it to their children or other relatives; long-standing promissory notes for debts which were owed to the Treasury, he destroyed.

[Zonaras, *Summary of Dio*, 11.17 = Dio 66.10.1a, 10.2a]

H25   Vespasian putting Rome back on her feet, *aureus* AD 69–70 (Illyricum)

Obv: Head of Vespasian, laureate, right.
         IMP CAESAR VESPASIANVS AVG
Rev: Vespasian standing left, raising Roma from her knees.
         ROMA RESVRGENS (Rome rising up again)

[*RIC* 2.1, Vespasian 1360 = *BMCRE²* 425, p.87 = BM no. 1924,0308.15]

H26   Citizenship granted to sailors in the Ravenna fleet, 26 Feb., AD 70

Emperor Vespasian Caesar Augustus, holding tribunician power, twice consul, grants citizenship to the *beneficiarii* whose are serving in the fleet at Ravenna under Sextus Lucilius Bassus, whose names are written below, and also to their children and their descendants. He also grants right of marriage with their wives whom they had at the time when citizenship was granted, or, if they were unmarried, to those whom they married afterwards, each individually. On 26 February, when Emperor Vespasian Caesar Augustus, for the 2nd time, and Caesar Vespasian, son of Augustus, were consuls. Dernalus Dacus (or 'the Dacian'), son of Derdipilus. Written down and validated from a bronze inscription which is fixed at Rome on the Capitol on the base of the wall in front of the Temple of the *Genius* of the Roman People.

[*RMD* 4.203 = *JRA* 1996.247 = *AE* 1997, 1771 = EDCS–24400402*]

The defection of the Ravenna fleet under Lucilius Bassus is mentioned several times by Tacitus, and presented as crucial in persuading Caecina to change sides too (*Hist.* 2.100 and especially 3.12–13). Comparisons with a 'normal' diploma (e.g. **N53**) are revealing: sailors or auxiliaries normally had to have served around 25 years and been honourably discharged. Sailors of the Ravenna fleet were rewarded for their timely change of sides – some by transfer to legions in November 69 (Tac. *Hist.* 3.50) and the more privileged *beneficiarii* (men exempted from 'fatigue' duties) with citizenship. Bassus' reward was being given command of Judaea (Jos. *JW* 7.163 and **N14**).

H27   Early coin of Vespasian and sons as *principes iuventutis, denarius* of AD 69, Rome

Obv: Head of Vespasian, laureate, right.
         IMP CAESAR VESPASIANVS AVG
Rev: Titus and Domitian riding right, with right hands outstretched.
         TITVS ET DOMITIAN CAES PRIN IV (Titus and Domitian Caesar, leaders
         of the younger generation (*principes iuventutis)*
                                                      [*RIC* 2.1 Vespasian 5 = BM no. 1978,0920.1]

This coin was found as part of the Cirencester hoard in 1978. The portrait is not recognisably that of
Vespasian (who did not return to Rome until AD 70, thus posing obvious difficulties for the makers of the
coin die).

H28   Vespasian's sons as senators on *as* of AD 70 (Tarraco, Spain)

Obv: Head of Vespasian, laureate, right.
         IMP CAESAR VESPASIANVS AVG (Emperor Caesar Vespasian Augustus
Rev: Heads of Titus, bare, right and Domitian, bare, left, confronting.
         CAESAR AVG F COS CAESAR AVG F PR (Caesar son of Augustus,
         consul; Caesar son of Augustus, praetor)
                                  [*RIC* 2.1 Vespasian 1321 = *BMCRE*² Vespasian 748B = BM no. R.10649]

For Vitellius' coin showing his potential heirs, see **H6**. But they were young whereas Vespasian could boast
adult sons, already in the senate. The minting of this low value, copper alloy coin, will have ensured that
the message was very widely circulated around the empire.

H29   Family group of Vespasian and sons – Rome, AD 72
(Left): To Titus Caesar Vespasian, hailed *imperator* 3 times, *pontifex*, holding tribunician power for the 2nd time, consul twice
(Centre): To Emperor Caesar Vespasian Augustus, *pontifex maximus*, holding tribunician power for the 4th time, hailed *imperator* 8 times, consul 4 times
(Right) : To Caesar Domitian, son of Augustus, designated consul for the second time, leader of the younger generation
Gaius Papirius Aequos, centurion of Legion III 'Augustan' ordered (this) to be set up in his will, from 10 pounds of gold.

[MW 84 = *ILS* 246 = EDCS–17301051]

CIVILIS/CLASSICUS/SABINUS/VELEDA REVOLTS, AD 70–1: H30–H34
Tacitus gives a full account of these interconnected revolts in *Histories* 4.12–37, 4.54–80, 5.14–26 where the narrative breaks off with the story almost complete. For a modern version, Wellesley, *Year of the Four Emperors*, 168–183.

H30   German revolt suppressed by Petillius Cerialis and Domitian
[82] When a large number of the Germans had agreed to rebel, and the rest followed suit, Vespasian, as if guided by divine providence, sent letters to Petillius Cerialis, who had previously held command in Germany. He gave him the rank of consul and commanded him to take up the position of governor in Britain. [83] Cerialis went where he was ordered to go. However, when he was informed of the revolt of the Germans, he fell upon them as soon as they assembled their troops and, putting his army into battle formation, killed so many of them in the battle that they were forced to abandon their mad schemes and learn sense. [84] Even if Cerialis had not come upon them in such a timely fashion, it would not have been long before their punishment. [85] For, as soon as the news of their revolt came to Rome and reached the ears of Domitian Caesar, he, despite his youthful years, undertook the great burden of responsibility without delay. [86] He had inherited his courage from his father and had advanced beyond his years in his knowledge of warfare. Thus he marched against the barbarians immediately. [87] Their courage failed as they learned the rumour of his approach, and they submitted to him without a battle. Although terrified, they were happy to be brought back under the old yoke again without suffering further consequences. [88] After Domitian had settled the affairs in Gaul, ensuring that there would be no further disturbances, he returned to Rome with great honour and glory, having performed such great exploits, which were far above his own age, but worthy of such a great father.

[Josephus, *Jewish War* 7.82–88]

Josephus gives brief accounts of the outbreak of the revolt (7.75–81) and its course. Tacitus' account is far more detailed and accurate. Here Josephus is certainly wrong to imply Cerialis (cos 70: **B70**) had governed Germany (command of *one* of the legions in Germany is possible) and that he suppressed the revolt *en route* to govern Britain – this was a subsequent appointment. Cerialis emerges as a commander of dubious competence from Tacitus' account of his role in Boudica's revolt (*Ann.* 14.32–33) and the German one. But Josephus inevitably gives a favourable account of this important Flavian (probably Vespasian's son-in-law), and even more so of Domitian's role in the revolt. Tac. *Hist.* 4.85–86 tells a very different, and more credible story.

H31   Tombstone of the general, Dillius Vocula, killed in Civilis Revolt AD 70
To Gaius Dillius Vocula, son of Aulus, of the Sergian tribe, military tribune of Legion
I, on the board of four for roads, quaestor of the province of Pontus & Bithynia,
tribune of the people, praetor, commander of Legion XXII 'First-born' in Germany.
Helvia Procula, daughter of Titus, his wife, had this made.

[MW 40 = *ILS* 983 = EDCS–17900079]

This tombstone was copied at Rome once before the ninth century and is now lost. Dillius Vocula played
an important role in the campaign taking over command of the troops of Upper Germany from the old
and incompetent Hordeonius Flaccus (Tac. *Hist.* 4.25) and conducting operations doggedly but without
imagination (4.34). He was murdered in his camp at Novaesium (Neuss) by a Roman deserter sent by
Classicus, and his troops went over to the rebels, swearing allegiance to the 'Empire of the Gauls' (4.59).

H32   Frontinus in command at Lingones (Langres) during the Civilis revolt
In the war waged under the auspices of Emperor Caesar Domitian Augustus
Germanicus, which Julius Civilis had started in Gaul, the very wealthy city of the
Lingones, which had defected to Civilis, feared that it would be plundered at the
arrival of Caesar's army. When, however, it was left undamaged, and had lost none
of its possessions, it returned to obedience and handed over seventy thousand armed
men to me.

[Frontinus, *On Stratagems* 4.3.14]

The campaign was assigned to the command of Mucianus and Domitian: Tac. *Hist.* 4.68, 4.80, 4.85–6.

H33   Oracle to Vespasian about Veleda
[Oracle granted to Emperor] Vespasian [Caesar Augustus concerning] Veleda: Do you
ask what you should do, [Augustus, concerning this] tall maiden whom the Rhine-
drinkers revere, they who bristle [horribly] with the horns of the golden [moon]? So
as not to keep her in idleness, [let her work] and clean a [little lamp] of bronze.

[MW 55 = *SEG* 16.592]

Greek inscription at Ardea in Latium, 20 miles south of Rome, suggesting that Veleda, a priestess among
the German tribes (Tac. *Hist.* 4.61, 4.65) lived out her life as a temple attendant after being captured by
the Romans.

H34   Julius Sabinus and his wife live in hiding for years
Civilis, who stirred up the revolt in Gaul, had, it seemed, many associates including
Sabinus, a young man of good birth who excelled all men in wealth and prestige.
Their attempt at a great undertaking failed, and, expecting to pay the penalty, some
committed suicide, others fled but were captured. [770e] Sabinus was given every
opportunity possible to escape to the barbarians. He, however, had married an
excellent woman, whom they called Empone in the local language, or as we would
say in Greek, 'Hero', and he was unable to leave her behind or take her with him.
So, since he had in the country some underground storage areas dug out which only
two of his freedmen knew about, he dismissed his other household slaves, as if being

about to poison himself, and went to his underground hideout, taking his two trusted freedmen. [770f] Then he sent a freedman called Martialius to tell his wife that he had died of poison and that his cottage had been burnt together with his body. So he intended to use his wife's unfeigned grief to confirm his own reported death. This was what indeed happened, since when she heard, his wife threw herself down and persisted in mourning and lamenting the death for three whole days and nights without food. Sabinus, on learning this, was afraid that she might actually kill herself, so told Martialius to tell her in secret that he was alive and in hiding, [771a] but that she should continue her grief for a while and not stop being convincing in her pretence. And so this woman feigned suffering as if playing a role in a tragic festival: but, in her desire to see him, she went at night, and came home again. No one else noticed her doing so and almost living in the Underworld with her husband for more than seven months at a stretch. During this time she disguised Sabinus with clothing and haircut and false head of hair so that he was unrecognisable, and took him with her to Rome with high hopes. But she returned without any success and stayed with him for a long time underground, but after a while went to the city, and was seen by her friends and female relations.

[771b] Yet the most incredible thing of all was that even though she went to the women's baths, they did not notice that she was pregnant. This was because of a medicament which women use on their hair to make it golden or reddish-coloured: it also makes flesh look fatter and plumper so as to produce some sort of expansion or swelling. By applying this freely to the other parts of her body, which rose and filled out, she hid the swelling of her belly. As for her labour, she went through it by herself, like a lioness crouching in the den with her mate, and bringing up in secret the male cubs she bore – [771c] there were two of them. Of her sons, one died, killed in Egypt, but the other, named Sabinus, was until very recently, still among us at Delphi. As a result Caesar had her killed: but was punished for having done so by having his whole race utterly removed. For his reign carried out no more vindictive act nor one more likely to make the gods and divinities turn their gaze from him. As it was, her courage and defiant words aroused the pity of those watching, and was what most especially annoyed Vespasian, when she gave up hope of her husband's survival, calling on him to take her life in exchange, and saying that she would rather have lived in darkness underground than to have been king like him.

[Plutarch, *Amatorius* 25 = Moralia 770d–771c]

Plutarch, a long-serving priest at Delphi, clearly knew Sabinus the son (771c), probably the source of the story. The brief summary by Tacitus (*Histories* 4.67) has the deaths of both parents being faked, and the promise to return to the story at the appropriate point in his narrative (AD 79, now lost).

PEACE AND OTHER VIRTUES: H35–H48
After fighting in Rome itself, Vespasian was keen to proclaim peace, as shown by coins, dedications and the symbolic closing of the gates of Janus after the Jewish triumph. For the Temple of Peace see **K64–K72**.

H35   Vespasian and Pax on *aureus* of AD 70 (Lyons)

Obv: Head of Vespasian, laureate, right.
          IMP CAES VESPASIAN AVG P M TR P P P COS III (Emperor Caesar
          Vespasian Augustus, *pontifex maximus*, tribunician power, father of the
          fatherland, consul 3 times)
Rev: Nemesis (the goddess Vengeance) advancing right, holding caduceus over snake.
          PACI AVGVSTI (to the Peace of Augustus)

                              [*RIC* Vespasian 1130 = *BMCRE*[2] 399, p.82 = BM no. 1864,1128.39]

H36   Birthday dedication to Eternal Peace of Vespasian's house, 7 Nov 70
Sacred to the Eternal Peace of the house of Emperor Vespasian Caeesar Augustus
and his children. The Sucusana tribe – young men. Dedicated on 17 November in the
consulship of L. Annius Bassus and C. Caecina Paetus [AD 70]
*[Then on other sides, names of 8 'centuries' of named individuals, followed by between
70 and 100 names in each century]*

                                          [MW 513 = *ILS* 6049 = EDCS–17200127*]

Large square marble block inscribed on all sides. The front bears the dedication and the left side the date,
which was Vespasian's birthday, while back and right side are covered all over with around 700 names,
arranged in alphabetical order after a leader of each 'century' The Sucusana was the older and more
traditional name (also 'Suburana') of the first of Rome's tribes.

H37   Dedication to Augustan Peace, by permission of Arrecinus Clemens
Sacred to Augustan Peace, L. Caesilius Tauriscus Tarquiniensis, C. Portumius Phoebus
II, L. Silius Carpus, L. Statius Patroclus II, D. Novius Priscus, P. Suillius Celer, Ti.
Claudius Helius, freedman of Hermes, P. Agrasius Marcellus, son of Publius, curators
of the younger members of the Sucusana tribe, gave this gift out of their own money,
with the permission of Marcus Arricinus Clemens. L. Faenius Euanthes, a younger
member of the tribe, saw to its setting up.

                                          [MW 514 = *ILS* 6050 = EDCS–17200126]

Marble base by members of the Sucusana tribe (Rome's first tribe) found in Rome alongside a larger
dedication by the whole tribe (**H36**), and other bases sacred to 'Fortune the Restorer of the Imperial House',
'Victory of Emperor Caesar Vespasian Augustus' (MW 515 and 516 = *ILS* 6051 and 6052). For Arrecinus
Clemens, related to Vespasian by marriage (see **J21**): at the (unknown but probably early) date of the
dedication Arrecinus was probably praetorian prefect (Tac. *Hist.* 4.68 = **J20a**).

H38 Peace of the Roman People, Sestertius, AD 71

Obv: Vespasian, laureate, right
IMP CAES VESPASIAN AVG P M TR P P P COS III (Emperor Caesar Vespasian Augustus, *pontifex maximus,* tribunician power, father of the fatherland, consul 3 times)

Rev: S C (by decree of the senate) around Pax standing, branch and cornucopia
PAX P ROMANI (Peace of the Roman People)

[*RIC* 2.1 Vespasian 188 = *BMCRE*² 773, p.187 = BM no. 1924,0509.8]

H39 Pax Romana

The boundless majesty of the Roman peace brings into view in turn not only human beings with their different environments and peoples, but also mountains and ranges that reach up into the clouds, the living beings they bring forth, and their plants as well. May that gift of the gods last for ever, I pray! For they seem to have given the Romans as a second source of light for the affairs of human beings.

[Pliny, *Natural History* 27.3]

Pliny's *Natural History* was published around the same time as the dedication of the Temple of Peace (for which see **K64–K72**)

H40 Titus, preserver of Augustan Peace, Valencia, Spain

[Caesar] T(itus) Emperor Vespasian Augustus, son of Vespasian, preserver of the Augustan Peace.

[MW 103 = *ILS* 259 = EDCS–09100013]

H41   Vespasian's Jewish Triumph on *aureus* AD 71 (Lyons)

Obv: Head of Vespasian, laureate, right.
         IMP CAESAR VESPASIANVS AVG TR P
Rev: Vespasian standing right in *quadriga* right, holding branch in right hand and sceptre in left hand,
         crowned by Victory and accompanied by trumpeter, soldier and captive.
         TRIVMP AVG (imperial triumph)
                                         [*RIC* 2.1 Vespasian 1127 = *BMCRE²* 397, p.81 = BM no. 1864,1128.255]

H42   Gates of Janus closed by Vespasian for the first time since Augustus
Then, to quote the words of Cornelius Tacitus, when Augustus was old, Janus was opened once again, since fresh conquests were sought along the outer boundaries of the world, often profitably, but sometimes at considerable cost, right until the reign of Vespasian. This is according to Tacitus. But then the city of Jerusalem was captured and overthrown, as the prophets had foretold, and the Jews were eliminated by Titus, who had been chosen by God's judgement to avenge the blood of the Lord Jesus Christ. He celebrated a triumph with his father Vespasian and closed the gates of Janus.
                                                                [Orosius, *Histories against the Pagans* 7.3.7]

H43   Gates of Janus closed after the Jewish Triumph, June AD 71
[8] Vespasian and Titus entered the city, celebrating a magnificent triumph over the Jews. The spectacle was beautiful and previously unknown to all men amongst the three hundred and twenty triumphs which had been held from the foundation of the city until that day – a father and son, carried in one triumphal chariot by those who had sinned against the Father and the Son, brought back the victory. [9] Vespasian and Titus immediately announced that there was peace throughout the world, since all wars and domestic unrest had been subdued, and decreed that double Janus should at last be closed and barred, for the sixth time since the founding of the city. Rightly this same honour was counted as vengeance for the suffering of the Lord, as it had been attributed to his nativity.
                                                                [Orosius, *Histories against the Pagans* 7.9.8–9]

H44 Gates of Janus opened again

Gordian while still a boy and about to set out for war against Parthia in the East, opened the gates of Janus, according to Eutropius' account. I do not know of any historian who records whether anyone closed the gates after Vespasian and Titus: Cornelius Tacitus records that they were opened by Vespasian himself after one year.

[Orosius, *Histories against the Pagans* 7.19.4]

Gordian III declared war on Parthia, *c.* AD 242. Orosius (fifth century) was able to use Tacitus' *Histories* in full.

H45 Vespasian honoured as having asserted freedom, AD 71

Obv: Head of Vespasian, laureate, right.
         IMP CAESAR VESPASIANVS AVG P M T P P P COS III (Emperor Caesar Vespasian Augustus, *pontifex maximus,* tribunician power, father of the fatherland, consul 3 times)
Rev: Inscription within oak-wreath.
         S P Q R ADSERTORI LIBERTATIS PVBLIC (The Senate and People of Rome, champion of the Public Freedom)

[*RIC* 2.1 Vespasian 121 = *BMCRE²* 805, p.198 = BM no.1846,0910.202]

The oak wreath was the civic crown, awarded to Augustus for saving the life of citizens (by ending the civil wars). Another sestertius with the same obverse carries the legend within the oak wreath 'for saving citizens' lives' (*ob cives servatos* – *RIC* 2.1 Vespasian 125). An *adsertor libertatis* 'champion of freedom' was the legal term for someone who upheld a slave's claim to be free man.

H46 Vespasian restores freedom, *sestertius*, AD 71

Obv: Head of Vespasian, laureate, right.
        IMP CAESAR VESPASIANVS AVG P M T P P P COS III (Emperor Caesar
        Vespasian Augustus, *pontifex maximus,* tribunician power, father of the
        fatherland, consul 3 times)
Rev: Vespasian standing left, with right hand raising kneeling Libertas; behind, Roma standing right.
        LIBERTAS RESTITVTA S C (Freedom Restored. (Coin issued) by decree
        of the senate)

                    [*RIC* 2.1 Vespasian 88 = *BMCRE²* 549, p.118 = BM no. 1846,0910.204]

H47   Senate crowns Vespasian, *sestertius,* AD 71

Obv: Head of Vespasian, laureate, right.
        IMP CAESAR VESPASIANVS AVG P M T P P P COS III (Emperor Caesar
        Vespasian Augustus, *pontifex maximus,* tribunician power, father of the
        fatherland, consul 3 times)
Rev: Senate, represented as elderly man wearing a toga, standing left, holding branch in right hand,
        crowning Vespasian standing left.
        CONCORDIA SENATVI (full agreement with the senate) S C

                                [*RIC* 2.1 Vespasian 67 = BM no. 1950,1006.973]

H48   Altar of Providence, *as* of AD 71 (Lugdunum)

Obv: Head of Vespasian, laureate, right; globe at point of bust.
        IMP CAES VESPASIAN AVG COS III (Emperor Caesar Vespasian
        Augustus, consul 3 times)
Rev: Altar.
        PROVIDENT(ia). S C (Providence. By decree of the senate)

                    [*RIC* 2.1 Vespasian 1166 = *BMCRE²* 810A = BM no. 1959,0305.11]

This altar also appears on *asses* of AD 71 minted at Rome. Vespasian (frequently, e.g. *RIC* 2.1 313), Titus (*RIC* 2.1 449) and Domitian (*RIC* 2.1 823) all followed previous emperors in minting coins with this altar, perhaps minted to celebrate Augustus' adoption of Tiberius, and thus imperial providence (forward-seeing) in assuring Rome's future.

TITUS AS PRAETORIAN PREFECT: H49–H50
This post had been held by equestrians (compare Suet. *Titus* 6.1), but its importance amply demonstrated by Sejanus and praetorians in the succession of AD 41. With the exception of Cornelius Laco (e.g. Suet. *Galba* 14.2, Tac. *Hist.* 1.6), praetorian prefects had not had a critical impact in 69. But Vespasian quickly appointed a relation, Arrecinus Clemens (Tac. *Hist.* 4.68, see **J20**) before appointing Titus in 71. Pliny, himself an equestrian, praises the appointment.

H49 Titus' praetorian prefecture honours all equestrians
Everyone should know that the empire lives on equal terms with you, even though you have held a triumph, and been censor, consul six times, and sharer of tribunician power. It is even more notable that you have been praetorian prefect, as in doing so you have equally honoured your father and the equestrian order. All this in your public life – and for us what a mess-mate you were in the camp! Nor has the greatness of your fortune changed you at all, except in enabling you to do every good deed you wish.

[Pliny, *Natural History,* Preface 3]

H50 Titus a ruthless praetorian prefect
[4] For when he took the post of praetorian prefect when his father was emperor, he crushed anyone suspected of opposing him, by sending *agents provocateurs* into the theatres and army camps who would demand their punishment as if they had been convicted of a crime. Amongst these victims was Caecina, a former consul, who had been present at a dinner, and had only just left the dining-room when Titus ordered that he be murdered on the suspicion of his debauched wife, Berenice.

[*Epitome de Caesaribus* 10.4]

H51 Coin of Titus' first handout, *sestertius* AD 72 (Rome)

Obv: Head of Titus, laureate, right.
T CAES VESPASIAN IMP PON TR POT COS II (Titus Caesar Vespasian, hailed *imperator*, *pontifex,* tribunician power, consul twice)
Rev: Titus seated left on platform; to left, attendant and citizen; behind, statue of Minerva.
CONGIAR PRIMVM P R DAT (Gives a first handout to the Roman People)
[*RIC* 2.1 Vespasian 420 = *BMCRE²* 629, p.139 = BM no. R.10568]

THE CENSUS, AD 73/4: H52–H55
Traditionally a census was held every four years, recording population numbers, and property valuations. The last known republican census was in 70/69 BC. Octavian (Augustus) and Agrippa were given censorial power to conduct a census in 29/8 BC (*Res Gestae* 8.1, Suet. *Aug.* 27.5) and conducted two more censuses. Claudius had been censor in AD 47. As well as providing the chance to make significant additions to the ranks of senators (**H52** and see **U23–U47** for some of many senatorial careers which began with this census), Vespasian may also have welcomed the chance for the *lustrum* (ceremony of purification) which closed the census to draw a line under recent events.

H52   The powers of censors under the principate

Through their powers as censors, they examine our lives and morals and take the census, enrolling some into the equestrian or the senatorial order, but removing others, as they see fit.

[Dio 53.17.7]

Dio when dealing with Augustus' establishment of the principate explains the various powers taken by Augustus and later emperors.

H53   The first and last census and *lustrum*

The same [period] was for the Romans the time of the 'Great Year', which they called the *lustrum* (ritual purification), such as was instituted by Servius Tullius, so that in each fifth year, when a census of the citizens had been held, a *lustrum* would be established; but this was not continued in the same way by later generations. For between the first *lustrum* established by King Servius and that which was carried out by Emperor Vespasian, consul for the 5th time and Titus Caesar, consul for the 3rd time, slightly fewer than 650 years passed, but throughout all that time, no more than 75 were held and at some later point they ceased to take place.

[Censorinus, *On the Birthday* 18.15]

For the first census and *lustrum* of Servius Tullius (reigned *c.* 578–534), see Livy 1.42–44. Vespasian's was the last known census in Italy, since it was no longer really required for citizenship, voting or taxation purposes.

H54   Pliny uses records from the recent census

More evidence has been provided by the very recent census held within the last four years by the Emperors Caesar Vespasian, father and son, as censors.

[Pliny, *Natural History* 7.162]

Pliny is talking about human life-spans and quotes some (not entirely credible) figures for great ages of residents, male and female of Italy's region 8. The census is datable to AD 73 (and probably into 74) by another passage of Pliny (*NH* 3.66 = **K1**).

H55   One thousand senatorial families in Vespasian's census

One thousand families established, since very many had been abolished by the savagery of the tyrants, and he had only found two hundred with great difficulty.

[*Epitome de Caesaribus* 9.11]

H56 Vespasian expands the *pomerium*
Emperor Caesar Vespasian Augustus, *pontifex maximus*, holding tribuncian power for the 6th time, hailed *imperator* 14 times, father of the fatherland, censor, consul 6 times, and designated for a 7th, and Titus Caesar Vespasian, son of Augustus, hailed *imperator* 6 times, *pontifex,* holding tribuncian power for the 4th time, censor, consul 4 times, and designated for a 5th. Having extended the boundaries of the Roman people, they extended and delimited the *pomerium* (boundary of the city of Rome).
(On the left side) 158

[MW 51 = EDCS–00900596]

Boundary marker in travertine stone found still in its original position in Rome in 1930. The *pomerium* traditionally marked the boundary of the city and could be extended only with new conquests of land for the Roman empire. Claudius extended the *pomerium* after his conquest of Britian (see LACTOR 19, N24) and the *Lex de imperio Vespasiani* **H20** explicitly granted Vespasian power to do the same, citing Claudius as precedent. Three other stones have been found (*CIL* 06, 31538a–c = *AE* 2003, 181), each marked by a number.

H57 Informers paraded in the amphitheatre
>That threat to peace and enemy to placid quiet,
>That crowd which always harassed wretched wealth, has now
>Been put on show: the guilty fill the vast arena
>Informers get the exile they once gave to others.

[Martial, *On the Shows* 4]

Martial celebrates the parade in the amphitheatre of the hated informers who profited under Nero. Vespasian swore to abolish them on accession (Tac. *Hist.* 4.41.1); Suetonius records Titus parading informers in the arena (Suet. *Titus* 8.5). Informers would typically accuse wealthy senators of treason: if successful they claimed a significant proportion of their victim's estate, with the emperor potentially claiming the rest while the victim was forced into exile. Martial's next epigram praises the emperor for foregoing this source of revenue.

H58 Titus punishes informers
[4] Divus Titus had, it is true, shown his great virtue by taking measures to reassure and to avenge us, and by doing so was made equal to the gods: but how much more will you deserve a place in heaven some day, for having added so much to those measures for which we made Titus a god!

[Pliny the Younger, *Panegyric to Trajan* 35.4]

The context (see **T17**) is Y. Pliny praising Trajan for having punished Domitianic informers.

H59   Restoration coinage, *sestertius* AD 80–81

Obv: Head of Nero Drusus, bare, left
         NERO CLAVDIVS DRVSVS GERMANICVS IMP (Nero Claudius Drusus
         Germanicus, hailed *imperator*)
Rev: S C (by decree of the senate)
         IMP T CAES DIVI VESP F AVG P M TR P P P COS VIII; REST (Emperor
         Titus Caesar Augustus, son of Divus Vespasian, *pontifex maximus,* tribunician
         power, father of the fatherland, consul 8 times. Restoration.

[*RIC* 2.1 Titus 416 = *BMCRE²* 292, p.288 = BM no. 1902,0403.1]

In 80–81 a series of coins was issued, mainly of lower values, with busts, not of Titus (though they carried his name and titles) but of various members of the Julio-Claudian family: Augustus (*RIC* 2.1 'Titus' 399–404, 445–469), Livia (405–9, 424–430), Tiberius (410–413, 431–6, 471), Drusus (Tiberius' son: 414–5, 437), Nero Drusus (Tiberius' brother: 416), Germanicus (Tiberius' nephew/adopted son: 417–8, 438–443), Agrippina Elder (419), Claudius (420, 472–490), Galba (421, 496–7), Agrippa (470). For the coins, see *RIC* 2.1, pages 192–3. It is not certain why they were issued, but it certainly appears to show great confidence in the Flavian dynasty.

H60   Domitian, Romulus and Remus and the she-wolf, *aureus*

Obv: Laureate head of Domitian, right.
         CAESAR AVG F DOMITIANVS (Caesar Domitian, son of Augustus)
Rev: She-wolf & twins; boat below
         COS V

[*RIC* 2.1 Domitian 960 = BM no. 1996,0316.22]

This coin was found as part of the Didcot hoard (Oxfordshire) in 1996.

H61   Handouts by Domitian in AD 84 and 93

[*(fragments of consuls' names for AD 84)*]
[Emperor Domitian distributed a handout of] LXXV (*denarii*) (300 sesterces)

[*(fragments of consuls' names for AD 93)*]
[Emperor Domitian distributed a handout of LX]XV (*denarii*) (300 sesterces)

[Fasti Ostienses: MW 56 = *Inscr. It.* 13.1.192–3 = EDCS–20200012]

Part of the *Fasti Ostienses*, the official record at Ostia listing consuls at Rome and other significant events at Rome and Ostia in double columns. Though these entries are very fragmentary, they can be assigned to these years based on fragments of names of consuls known from other sources to have held office. A similar imperial donative is fully recorded for AD 37. The handouts presumably went to each member of the urban plebs. For Vespasian's **H23**; Titus' **H51** and for Flavian ones, **K2**, attributing one to Vespasian, three to Domitian.

H62   Silius Italicus' epic poem predicts Flavian rule over Rome

(At this point in Silius' epic about the Punic Wars between Rome and Carthage, the Carthaginian general Hannibal has reached the summit of the Alps with his army. Venus asks Jupiter whether the Romans are doomed to defeat and exile. Jupiter reassures Venus that Rome will come through the Punic War: various heroes of the war are mentioned by name, and the eventual conqueror, P. Cornelius Scipio Africanus is alluded to. The whole exchange, is, of course, deliberately modelled on the similar prophetic passage of Virgil, Aeneid 1.257–296, with its flattering 'divine prediction' of Augustus' exploits.)

Then, Venus, long your sons shall reign	
'Til heav'nly virtue from Cures, again	
Shall raise still more the Julian name revered,	595
A warlike race, on Sabine berries reared.	
Rome shall grant the father to beat the unknown North,	
'Gainst Scottish woods be first to lead his columns forth;	
Restrain the Rhine, with vigour rule Africa's shore	
In old age vanquish Judah's palms in war.	600
Not Hades' waters, the kingdom without light	
But heaven's home, our honours be his right.	
Next a youth, in strength of mind excelling all	
Shall take his father's burden, yet stand tall	
A match for the power he wields: still a boy	605
He shall fierce tribes in Palestine destroy.	
Yet you, Germanicus, shall surpass your race,	
A boy the gold-haired Teutons dread to face.	
Though impious flames high on the Capitol leapt	
Fear not: safe for the world you shall be kept	610
To join me and long rule the sky. And so	
Ganges' tribes to him shall offer unbent bow,	
In time shall Parthia empty quivers show,	
From North shall Rome see his triumphal car	
And Bacchus yield to triumphs from afar.	615
The Danube, loth to let the Romans through,	
In its Sarmatian lands he will subdue.	
The sons of Rome who for their eloquence won fame	
He conquers with his voice. In music, 'tis the same –	

Surpassing him who mountains moved and rivers stayed,   620
While even Phoebus marvelled when he played.
What's more, a golden Capitol he will have made,
Its temple roof-tops joining to our skies.
Where on Tarpeian rock you see my ancient palace rise.
O'er happy lands, paternal power he'll wield,   625
Both son and sire of gods. So, Romulus, yield
Your throne, when heavens greet him finally.
Placed between father and brother, while close by
The forehead of his son shall light the sky.   629

[Silius Italicus, *Punic Wars* 3.593–629]

594	*Cures*: birthplace of Vespasian; *virtue*: Jupiter had just criticised the luxury of generations of Romans after the Punic War. Vespasian claimed the regions of Italy as where traditional Roman virtues still could be found.
596	*Sabine berries*: the olive. Virgil, *Georgics* 2.532 made the Sabines typical of old-fashioned Roman virtue.
597	*North*: Silius actually refers to 'Thule', perhaps to be identified with Iceland, but proverbially the furthest place North (Virgil, *Georgics* 1.30, hyperbolically describing it as paying tribute to Augustus). A sighting from the Orkneys was claimed by Agricola's fleet (Tac. *Agr.* 10) but this will have been the Shetland Isles, not Iceland. But since Silius is referring to Vespasian, he more likely means to praise, with hyperbole, Vespasian's involvement in Claudius' initial invasion of Britain.
598	*Scottish*: Silius refers to Caledonia: combining hyperbole for Vespasian's role in the invasion of Britain with more recent Roman advances towards Scotland (Tacitus' account of Agricola's campaigns, (*Agr.* 25–27)).
599	*Rhine*: Vespasian commanded legion II based at Argentorate, (Strasbourg) on the Rhine. See **J4c** (Josephus) for similar exaggeration of some unknown engagement.
600	*palm-trees*: the typical symbol of Judaea, regularly appeared on coins of Vespasian and Titus, see **N11**.
601–2	*not Hades ... heaven*: Vespasian's deification.
606	*Palestine*: Titus took command of legion XV in AD 67, at 27 years of age.
607	*Germanicus*: Silius now switches to Domitian, using, appropriately one of his titles. But Domitian's first campaigns, when he was 18 were abortive according to Tacitus (*Histories* 4.86) and Suetonius (*Domitian* 2.1), though Josephus made more of it (*JW* 7.85 = **H30**).
609	*flames on the Capitol*: the burning of the Temple of Jupiter in the fighting in Rome in December 69.
611	*join me*: Silius makes Jupiter predict Domitian's deification.
612	*Ganges' tribes*: there was no basis for this prediction, except that it was frequent in the Augustan poets, e.g. Virgil, *Aeneid* 6.795.
613	*Parthia*: another favourite theme of Augustan poetry (e.g. Propertius 3.4) with more basis for Augustus than Domitian whose Parthian expeditions feature only in poetry (Statius 4.4).
614–5	*North ... triumphal*: Silius refers to Northern and Eastern triumphs. The former could describe Germany, the latter is imaginary. *Bacchus*: traditionally arrived in the Greco-Roman world from the East.
617	*Sarmatia*: see **N16**, **N42–N49** for wars in Pannonia (and Jones, *Domitian* 15–155)
618	*eloquence*: Suetonius, *Dom.* 2 and 20, and **R5, R6** for praise from Quintilian and Martial.
620	*him who ...*: Silius alludes to the mythical Orpheus.
624	*ancient palace*: The Temple of Jupiter, thought to have been begun by Rome's last king (c. 534–509 BC) would already have been ancient at the dramatic date of Jupiter's speech (218 BC). Domitian's rebuilding was the fourth. See **K27** (Plutarch, *Publicola* 15).
626	*son and sire*: Domitian was son of Divus Vespasian and had his baby son deified, see **J12**. *Romulus*: mentioned as the first Roman to be deified.
627	*finally*: sycophants had to be careful in welcoming deification since this would follow death, as of course best shown by Vespasian's dying joke (**C17**, **L55–L75** intro).

SECTION J
IMPERIAL FAMILY

Neither legions nor fleets were ultimately
as strong a safeguard of imperial power
as a number of children.

[Tacitus, *Histories* 4.52]

This section presents personal and family information on members of the Flavian dynasty, including the emperors, with a brief introduction to each. A family tree appears at the end of the book. Repeated use of family names can cause confusion (including sometimes for ancient writers) so Roman numerals are used as well as alphanumeric references to this section, so Flavia Domitilla (II), daughter of Vespasian = **J13** to distinguish her from her mother and daughter. Direct descendants of Vespasian's parents are placed first and arranged in roughly chronological order, followed (**J20–J23**) by four people who had relationships with members of the Flavian dynasty.

J1   T. Flavius Sabinus (I) (dates unknown)
All we really know about Vespasian's father comes from the first chapter of Suetonius' biography. According to this he may been a senior centurion. He collected taxes in Asia and acted as money-lender among the Helvetii (modern Switzerland). See Levick, *Vespasian* 4–6.

J1a
Vespasian was certainly an emperor of obscure birth.

[Eutropius, *Brief History* 7.19]

J2   Vespasia Polla (*c.* 15 BC – after *c.* AD 35)
Again we have to rely on Suetonius for information about Vespasian's mother. She was of higher status than Vespasian's father. Suetonius tells us that her father was three times military tribune and prefect of the camp. Her brother reached the senate and the praetorship. Vespasia's approximate dates can be worked out from the birthdate of her younger son, and Suetonius' story that she prompted Vespasian to aim to follow his brother into the senate well after he came of age (Suet. *Vesp.* 2).

J3   T. Flavius Sabinus (II), before AD 8 – December AD 69
Vespasian's elder brother had a very distinguished career, starting on the senatorial cursus well before Vespasian (Suet. *Vesp.* 2.2), serving alongside him in the invasion of Britain and becoming consul and city prefect. See Birley, *Roman Government* 231–2.

J3a   Legionary commander in Britain, AD 43
Plautius now sent across his legionary legates, Flavius Vespasian (the future emperor) and his brother Sabinus. They also managed somehow to get across the river and killed many of the barbarians in a surprise attack.

[Dio 60.20.3–4]

Dio's Greek text, corrected above, wrongly has Sabinus as subordinate to his younger brother, either as a natural mistake arising from hindsight or from a tiny miscopying of the text in the manuscript trandition.

J3b   Flavius Sabinus' consulship

... dedicated on 1 August in the consulship of Cn. Hosidius Geta and T. Flavius Sabinus.

[*CIL* 6.40414 = Smallwood 131 = EDCS–00900118*]

This beautiful marble inscription records a dedication to Claudius: Sabinus' consulship can be fixed to AD 47.

J3c   Tacitus on the two brothers

There were some who spread their secret suspicions that his delay was due to jealousy and envy of his brother's good fortune. For when they were both private citizens, Flavius Sabinus, being the elder, had enjoyed greater prestige and wealth than Vespasian. It was also believed that Sabinus had been cautious in his help when Vespasian was in financial difficulties, loaning money against Vespasian's house and property. Therefore, despite the appearance of good relations, it was feared that ill-feeling lay underneath. The kinder interpretation was that Sabinus' gentle nature shrank from bloodshed and slaughter, hence the frequent interviews with Vitellius to discuss peace and the conditions for laying down arms.

[Tacitus, *Histories* 3.65]

The context is December 69, with Flavian armies marching on Rome. Flavius Sabinus as city prefect had been urged to use his urban cohorts to rise against Vitellius who was still clinging on to power. Sabinus' refusal to turn to violence was to cost him his life (Tac. *Hist.* 3.74).

J3d   Tacitus' 'obituary'

This was the death of a man not to be underestimated. For thirty-five years he had served the state with distinction at home and abroad. His integrity and fairness were beyond question; he talked too much – that was the only slander voiced about him in the seven years he governed Moesia and the twelve in which he was prefect of the city. At the end of his life some thought he was indecisive, but most that he was a moderate who wished to avoid civilian bloodshed. Everyone agreed that before Vespasian became emperor, the most distinguished in his family was Sabinus.

[Tacitus, *Histories* 3.75]

See Tac. *Hist.* 4.47 and **J3e** for the state funeral and Levick, *Vespasian* p.80.

J3e   Statue base from Roman forum

[…] propraetorian legate of Divus Claudius in the provin[ce of Moesia, he conducted the census] in Gaul and was [twice] prefect of the city. [To him] the senate, under the authority of his brother, Emperor Caesar Vespasian set [up an honorific portrait-bust], decreed an overdue state funeral to honour him, and [voted] that a sta[tue should be placed in the for]um of Augustus.

[MW 97 = *ILS* 984 = EDCS–18700462]

This statue base was actually found in the forum Romanum.

J4 T. Flavius Vespasianus (Nov 17 AD 9 – 23 June 79)

The emperor Vespasian. Suetonius gives an account of his early years *Vespasian* 2–4. Josephus (*Jewish War*) gives full details of his command in the Jewish revolt, from AD 66, as does Tacitus, *Histories* of his rise to power in AD 69. Evidence for the major part of his reign is provided far more anecdotally by Suetonius and Dio/Xiphilinus. For a full-length modern biography, see Levick, *Vespasian*.

J4a Portrait bust of Vespasian, British Museum

[BM no. 1850,0304.35: portrait bust, 45.72cm high, found at Carthage, Tunisia]

Vespasian, aged 60 at accession, seems consciously to have turned away from the 'idealising' style of much Julio-Claudian portraiture in favour of a return to the more traditional republican style, usually described as 'warts-and-all', and in keeping with his age and bluff, matter-of-fact image (though there is some evidence that this bust was recarved from an image of Nero). For a witty comment on his usually strained expression, see Suet. *Vesp.* 20.

J4b   Vespasian conquers the Isle of Wight

Vespasian, who was emperor after Nero, was sent by Claudius himself to Britain, and subjected to Roman rule the Isle of Wight, the most southerly part of Britain. This island is around 30 miles from east to west, 12 from north to south, and on its east coast six miles distant from the southern shore of Britain, and three on the west coast.

[Bede, *Ecclesiastical History of the English People* 1.3]

The Venerable Bede (*c.* 673–735) followed Eutropius 7.19 (**J4n**), adding dimensions which are fairly accurate. Vespasian commanded Legion II 'Augustan' in the invasion of Britain under Claudius. Despite exaggerations by Flavian writers, his achievements were real enough, including more than the capture of the Isle of Wight.

J4c   Vespasian's military career

[3] Nero was deliberating to whom he should entrust the care of the East in its current disturbed state, and who might punish the Jews for their rebellion and prevent the spread of this discontent to the surrounding nations. [4] He found no one except Vespasian equal to the task and able to undertake the responsibility of such a great war. Vespasian was a veteran and had been a soldier from his youth. Long ago he had calmed the West and quelled the rebellion which the Germans stirred up; he had also gained Britain, which had escaped notice previously, for the Romans by force of arms, [5] procuring a triumph for Nero's father, Claudius, without the need for any sweat or labour of his own. [6] Nero considered these circumstances highly fortuitous and saw that Vespasian's age gave him great skill and experience. Moreover, he had sons who could be used as hostages to ensure his loyalty and, being in their prime, they could carry out their father's plans. Perhaps also God was paving the way for the future of the world.

[Josephus, *Jewish War* 3.3–6]

Josephus naturally exaggerates. Vespasian had commanded Legion II 'Augustan', stationed at Argentorate (now Strasbourg) and presumably faced some sort of German unrest early in Claudius' reign ('calmed the West'), before being part of the three-legion invasion force of Britain, under A. Plautius ('gained Britain').

J4d   Vespasian working hard early morning

On the following day Apollonius came to the palace around dawn and asked the guards what the commander was doing. They replied that he had long been awake and was dealing with correspondence. Hearing this he went away and said to Damis, "The man will rule."

[Philostratos, *Life of Apollonius of Tyana* 5.31.1]

J4e   Vespasian like Elder Pliny worked at night

Before dawn, he used to go to the Emperor Vespasian – for he also used his nights to work – then he would go to his appointed duties. When he returned home, he used what remained of the time for his studies.

[Pliny the Younger, *Letters* 3.5.9]

Y. Pliny is writing about his uncle doing all he could to maximise time available for his literature, see **R14**.

J4f Vespasian's personal routine

[15] Indeed what he had started, he kept unchanged for his whole reign. He would be awake when it was still night, complete his public duties, and admit his close friends, putting on his shoes and royal clothes while they were greeting him. But later, having heard whatever cases had come up, he would exercise by riding, then rest; finally, when he had bathed, in a more relaxed frame of mind, he would preside at a banquet. [16] Enthusiasm makes one say much about a good emperor, who was caught, as if by fate, some fifty-six years after the death of Augustus, by the Roman state, exhausted by the savagery of tyrants, so that it should not be utterly ruined.

[*Epitome de Caesaribus* 9.15–16]

This forms the culmination of the Epitome's account of Vespasian, followed only by his death.

J4g Vespasian's clemency

[1] Vespasian reigned for ten years. [2] Amongst his other good qualities, was a special readiness to forget personal animosities, so much so that he gave the daughter of his enemy Vitellius an enormous dowry and married her to a husband of the noblest birth. [3] He used patiently to put up with the political manoeuvrings of his friends, responding to their insults with humour, since he was very witty.

[*Epitome de Caesaribus* 9.1–3]

For Vitellius' children and their treatment, see **H6**. Vitellia's husband is unknown.

J4h Vespasian's stinginess

[7] Yet some people think that he had a weakness about money – wrongly since it is quite clear that there was deficit in the treasury, cities in ruins, and that the taxes were not exacted for very much time after they were imposed.

[*Epitome de Caesaribus* 9.7]

Vespasian's stinginess is a theme of most of our accounts: Tac. *Hist.* 2.5.1; Suet. *Vesp.* 16.1–3, 19.2; Dio 66.2.5, 8.2–5, 14.5; Eutropius 7.19 (**J4n**); Aur. Vict. 9.1.6, though it is often, as here, excused or justified.

J4i "At my own expense"

Vespasian was often mocked for his habit of declaring that he was "paying for this at my own expense," whenever he made a purchase of some kind.

[Petrus Patricius, *Sayings, Vatican Excerpts* 100 = Dio 66.10.3a]

Petrus Patricius was a Byzantine lawyer and administrator of the 6th century whose *Sayings* seem to preserve *verbatim* statements from Dio's history.

J4j Vespasian and the new morality

At the same time, the new men admitted in large numbers to the senate from Italian towns and colonies, and even from the provinces, brought with them prudence in their household management, and, though good fortune or their own hard work saw very many through to a wealthy old age, their former habits remained. Even so the person who was most influential in this more restrained way of life was Vespasian himself, with his old-fashioned habits and lifestyle. For deference to the *princeps* and a desire to imitate him proved more powerful than legal penalties and fear.

[Tacitus, *Annals* 3.55]

Tacitus digresses from mention of sumptuary legislation proposed in AD 22 to explain how luxurious banquets in the century between Actium and Galba went out of fashion. In Tacitus' praise of the new (or old) morals, it should be noted that he and many of his circle (e.g. Y. Pliny) came from Italian towns or the provinces, and he praises the 'provincial prudence' of Marseilles where his father-in-law, Agricola, was brought up (*Agricola* 4.2). Y. Pliny sought to flatter Trajan in his *Panegyric* 45.4–6 by suggesting that an emperor's own example would do more to encourage good morality than a censorship.

J4k   Moral reforms

[5] He soon restored a world long damaged and worn out. For at first he preferred to reform rather than torture and destroy those supporters of tyranny, unless they happened to have gone too far in evil-doing. This was because he very sensibly realised that most crimes are carried out by agents acting out of fear. [6] In addition, by the fairest laws, by giving advice and, most effectively, by the example of his own life, he eliminated most vices.

[Epitome de Caesaribus 9.5–6]

J4m   Vespasian's death

[17] And so when he was one year short of his seventieth, he passed away mixing the jokes which delighted him with serious matters: [18] for when a long-haired comet first appeared, he said, "That's to do with the king of Persia," who had more hair than he did. Then, worn out by diarrhoea but standing up, he said, "An emperor should leave this earth on his feet."

[Epitome de Caesaribus 9.17–18]

Accounts of Vespasian's death are given by Suetonius (*Vesp.* 23.4–24), Dio (66.17.1–3) and Eutropius 7.20 below. The Epitome omits the third and final joke on becoming a god recorded by Suetonius and Dio, and taken by them as evidence of his down-to-earth humour. In fact Schmidt (*Chiron* 18, 83–89, followed by Levick, *Vespasian* p.197) has shown that it was actually a joke at Vespasian's expense, recalling, in the context of Vespasian dying of diarrhoea, that Claudius, the previous emperor to have been deified, voided his bowels in dying of poison.

J4n   Eutropius' summary of Vespasian

[19] Vespasian succeeded Vitellius having been hailed as emperor while in Palestine. He was certainly an emperor of obscure birth, but one to be compared with the very best. Before his accession he was well known for having been sent by Claudius to Germany and then to Britain; for having fought thirty-two engagements with the enemy; and for having acquired for the Roman empire two very valiant nations, twenty towns, and the Isle of Wight which lies right next to Britain. Once in power in Rome he behaved with great self-restraint. He was rather greedy simply for money, but in such a way that he took it from nobody without good reason. Though he paid the greatest attention to the careful collection of money, he was also very keen for it to be given away, especially to those in need. No other emperor before him can be found to have been greater or fairer in his generosity. Very easy-going and lenient, he was very reluctant to give any punishment greater than exile even to those found guilty of treason against him. Under him, Judaea became part of the Roman empire, as did Jerusalem, the most famous city in Palestine. Greece, Lycia, Rhodes, Byzantium, Samos, all of which had been free before his time, and also Thrace, Cilicia, and Commagene which had been under friendly kings, were reduced to the status of provinces.

[20] Vespasian took no notice of those who offended or hated him, and easily put up with insults aimed at him by lawyers and philosophers, though he was much more keen to enforce military discipline. He celebrated a triumph over Jerusalem together with his son Titus. For these reasons he was loved by and popular with the senate, the people, and in short with everybody: he died of diarrhoea on his own country estate in Sabine territory in his sixty-ninth year, after a reign of nine years and seven days, and was deified. So familiar was he with the horoscopes of his sons that, though there were many conspiracies which he disregarded with great contempt when they were revealed, he said in the senate that either his sons would succeed him or no one.

[Eutropius, *Brief History* 7.19–20]

J5 Flavia Domitilla (*c.* AD 20 – before 69)

This was the name of Vespasian's wife as well as their daughter and grand-daughter. According to Suet. *Vesp.* 3 she died while Vespasian was still a 'private citizen' which ought to mean before he had been consul, but more probably means simply before he became *princeps* (compare **U11b**).

J5a Statue at Herculaneum

To Flavia Domitilla, wife of Emperor Vespasian Caesar Augustus.

[*CIL* X 1419 = *ILS* 257 = Cooley[2] F143 = EDCS–11500353]

A life-size bronze statue of Domitilla was set up (posthumously) in the large portico at Herculaneum along with other members of the Flavian family.

J5b Domitilla wrongly described as a freedwoman

[10.1] Titus, known also by the name of his father as Vespasian, was the son of a freedwoman called Domitilla.

[*Epitome de Caesaribus* 10.1]

The Epitome is certainly wrong here and at **J10c**. It is only the source to suggest this; the marriage would have been illegal (see note on **J21**); confusion may have arisen from Vespasian's liaison with the freedwoman Caenis.

J5c In memory of Domitilla, wife of Vespasian, *sestertius*, AD 80/1

Obv: Carpentum drawn right by two mules.

DOMITILLAE / IMP / CAES VESP / AVG ((In memory) of Domitilla, wife of Emperor Caesar Vespasian Augustus); SPQR (Senate and People of Rome)

Rev: Inscription: S C (By decree of the senate)
            IMP T CAES DIVI VESP F AVG P M TR P P P COS VIII (Emperor Titus
            Caesar Augustus, son of Divus Vespasian, *pontifex maximus*, tribunician
            power, father of the fatherland, consul 8 times)

[RIC 2.1 Titus 264 = BMCRE² 229, p.271 = BM no. 1902, 0403.2]

Travel in a *carpentum* was 'an honour formerly given to priests and sacred relics' but which had become associated with female members of the imperial family: Livia in AD 23 (*RIC* Tiberius 51 = LACTOR 19, J1d); for the ashes of Agrippina the Elder (*RIC* Gaius 55 = LACTOR 19, J9d); for Agrippina the Younger to travel in, in person (Tac. *Ann.* 12.42). Domitilla, who died before Vespasian was emperor, cannot herself have travelled in a *carpentum*, so the senate perhaps decreed that a statue of her be transported in a *carpentum*. Another *carpentum* coin commemorated Julia's deification, but Domitilla does not appear as 'Diva' in any source. The coin type illustrated above exists more commonly with the phrase 'MEMORIAE DOMITILLAE' appearing in full.

J6   T. Flavius Sabinus III (cos suffect 69, cos suffect II 72)
Son of the city prefect, thus nephew to Vespasian. Orignally chosen to be *consul ordinarius* for 69 by Nero, his consulship was postponed by the need for Galba and then Otho to hold consulships (Tac. *Hist.* 1.77.2). Sent to command Otho's troops, he handed them over to Vitellius' side after Otho's suicide (Tac. *Hist.* 2.36.2 and 2.51.8). Nothing further is heard of him after his second suffect consulship in AD 72 and it cannot be established whether the inscription for a curator of public works (**J6a**), relates to him or his father (see (*PIR* F² 353–4)).

J6a   Flavius Sabinus, curator of public works
On the authority of Emperor Caesar Titus Vespasian Augustus, in the place which had been designated by Flavius Sabinus, curator of public works, the corn merchants built a temple.

[MW 429 = CIL 6.814 = EDCS–17300952]

J7   Flavia Sabina
Daughter of the city prefect, so niece of Vespasian. Her marriage to Caesennius Paetus, cos 61, is all that is known about her. He probably had two sons, L. Junius Caesennius Paetus, cos 79 and L. Caesennius Sospes, cos 114 (Syme *RP* 3.1062ff), but it is not clear if either was by Flavia Sabina (Syme, *Domitian: the Last Years = RP* 4.264).

J7a   Inscription of Flavia Sabina
Of Flavia Sabina, daughter of Titus, wife of Caesennius Paetus

[Near Praeneste, Latium: ILS 995 = MW 285 = EDCS–05800811]

J8   TITUS Flavius Vespasianus: (30 Dec AD 39 – 1 Sept 81) Emperor 79–81
Josephus, *Jewish War* and Tacitus, *Histories* contain extensive accounts of his generalship. Other sources contain a great deal of information on Titus, mostly adulatory. Traces of more hostile versions, especially before he became emperor appear in Suet. *Titus* 7.1, and **J8e, J8f** below and Dio was surely right that his reputation would not have survived a longer reign. Titus married twice: firstly Arrecina Tertulla (**J9**); then Marcia Furnilla, daughter of Q. Marcius Barea Sura (Suet. *Titus* 4.2) whom he divorced after the birth of a daughter, probably because family had fallen into disgrace with Nero after the Piso conspiracy of AD 65. For his daughters, see **J15**. There is no easily available modern biography.

J8a   Head from marble statue of Titus from Utica, Tunisia

[BM no. 1909,0610.1; head from statue at Utica, 30.48 cm high.]

J8b   The young Titus
Titus was happy to spend his youth in pursuit of pleasures, and showed more restraint
in his own reign than he did in his father's. ... His own talents, which made him
suitable for whatever came him way, increased his reputation, as did his good looks
and deportment.

[Tacitus, *Histories* 2.2]

Tacitus is explaining rumours that Titus might have been chosen as Galba's successor instead of Piso in
early 69.

J8c   Titus' courtesy and approachability
He won loyalty by his courtesy and approachability, while very often on campaign
and on the march he associated with rank and file soldiers, without damaging his
status as commander.

[Tacitus, *Histories* 5.1]

The context is Titus being selected to put an end to the Jewish revolt at the start of AD 70.

J8d   Titus' qualities

He reigned for two years, two months and twenty days. [2] From his boyhood he was thoroughly dedicated to honourable pursuits of honesty, soldiering and literature, showing mental and physical abilities in everything he turned to. [3] After undertaking responsibility for the country, he surpassed the man he was imitating to an incredible extent, especially in clemency, generosity, distribution of honours, and contempt for money; these traits were appreciated all the more, since from some of the things he did while still a private citizen, it was believed that he would be more harsh and devoted to luxury and greed.

[*Epitome de Caesaribus* 10.1–3]

J8e   Titus turns out well

[5] He was accused, under his father of selling legal judgements through his great liking for plunder: because of this everyone thought and said that they had unfortunately been given a Nero to take supreme command. [6] But all this turned for the better and brought him such everlasting glory that he was called the darling and the love of the human race.

[*Epitome de Caesaribus* 10.5–6]

J8f   Titus' clemency

Then, since it was customary that grants or concessions made by previous emperors should be confirmed by their successors, he had no sooner assumed imperial power than he willingly made an edict guaranteeing such grants for the future to those who held them. [9] One day, remembering in the evening that he had done nothing for anyone, he made the following praiseworthy and godlike remark, "Friends, we have wasted a day" because his generosity was impressive. [10] He went so far in his clemency that when two men of highest rank were unable to deny the crime that they had plotted, and the senators had decided that the punishment for the crimes they had admitted should be carried out, Titus warned them first, then ordered that they should be taken to a gladiatorial show and seated on either side of him; then he deliberately asked for the sword of a gladiator whose fights they were watching, and handed it to each man in turn as if to see how sharp it was. They were struck by amazement at his courage, and he asked them "Do not you see that powers are given by fate and that it is useless to attempt a crime in the hope of achieving something, or in fear of losing it?"

[*Epitome de Caesaribus* 10.8–10]

Titus' clemency, mentioned in all sources (Suet. *Titus* 9.1–3, Eutropius 7.21 (**T1**), Aur. Vict. 10.1–4) has also been immortalised in Mozart's last opera, *La Clemenza di Tito.* Dio 66.18 (**C18**) perceptively suggests that this reputation was mainly an effect of his having reigned a very short time.

J8g   Titus' fiscal prudence

He was himself prudent in money matters, never one for extravagance; but he never sought to impose his own principles on others by punishment.

[Zonaras, *Summary of Dio,* 11.18 = Dio 66.19.3a]

J8h   Titus and Domitian

[11] He often implored his brother in tears, when Domitian was hatching plots and fomenting disloyalty amongst the soldiers, not to desire to obtain by parricide what Titus was happy would come to him and which he already had as his partner in power.

[Epitome de Caesaribus 10.11]

J8i   Titus' death

[15] He lived forty-one years and passed away from a fever on the same farm in Sabine territory as his father. [16] News of his death was barely believed: grief so filled Rome and the provinces that men, calling him 'the people's darling' as we have said, wept for a world that had been orphaned.

[Epitome de Caesaribus 10.15–16]

J9   Arrecina Tertulla

Daughter of M. Arrecinus Clemens, prefect of the guard at the time of Gaius's assassination. Married Titus, after his military service (*c.* AD 63: Suet. *Titus* 4.2) but must have died in time for Titus to marry and then divorce Marcia Furnilla around AD 65 (see intro. to Titus). Julia was almost certainly her daughter by Titus, but despite her importance, the only surviving record of her is the mention by Suetonius (above) and a tombstone she set up, probably (from the age of Melior) to the son of a freed slave-woman.

J9a   Tombstone set up by Arrecina

To the divine spirits of Marcus Arrecinus Melior; Arrecina Tertulla made this for her darling. He lived 9 years and 10 days.

[MW 109 = *CIL* 6.12355 = EDCS–14800568]

J10   Titus Flavius DOMITIANUS (24 Oct 51 – 18 Sept 96)

Domitian exemplifies the dangers of having sources which either flatter the emperor while he is alive or vilify him by writing shortly after his death, under a new regime, with animosity still fresh. Suetonius' biography is relatively fair, but disappointingly brief. Contemporary poets provide mere flattery, historians writing after his death create or perpetuate a stereotype of a bad emperor, partly out of guilt.

Modern accounts: Jones, *Domitian;* Southern, *Domitian, the Tragic Tyrant*

J10a   Portrait of Domitian, plaster cast

[Museum of Classical Archaeology, Cambridge no.618. (Original: Munich, Residenz 157)]

J10b   Domitian honoured at Athens
The Areopagus Council and the Council of Six Hundred and the people honour ~~Domitian~~ the younger son of Vespasian Caesar.

[MW 488 = *IG* 2², 3283b]

J10c   A fairly positive start to his reign
[11.1] Domitian, the son of Vespasian and the freedwoman Domitilla, and the brother of Titus, reigned fifteen years. [2] To begin with, he feigned clemency and being not, as yet, lazy seemed quite tolerable in political and military affairs. Therefore he crushed the Chatti and the Germans. [3] He gave justice very fairly. At Rome he built or completed many works.

[*Epitome de Caesaribus* 11.1–3]

For the epitome's confusion of Vespasian's wife, Domitilla and freedwoman mistress, Caenis, see **J5b** note.

J10d Domitian's archery skills

[5] He was such an expert archer that he could shoot arrows between the spread-out fingers of a man standing a great distance away.

[*Epitome de Caesaribus* 11.5]

J10e Domitian's sea-sickness

[1] How different is Trajan from that man who could not bear the calm of the Alban Lake, or the still and quiet waters of the lake at Baiae, and could not endure even the sound and splash of oars without shuddering in shameful terror as every single stroke! [2] So, far from all noise, protected from any jolt or movement, with his vessel carefully held in tow, he was transported like a sacrificial animal. [3] What a disgraceful scene, as the emperor of the Roman people follows behind as if in a captured ship while someone else leads and someone else steers. [4] Rivers too had a part in his deformity – Danube and Rhine were delighted to convey something that so disgraced us.

[Pliny the Younger, *Panegyric to Trajan* 82.1–4]

Domitian had lakeside homes at Alba and Baiae. Horatio Nelson, probably the most famous admiral in English history, suffered from sea-sickness (Letter to Earl of Camden, October 1804).

J10f Domitian's dinner parties

[49.6] For you do not stuff yourself with a dinner eaten on your own before noon and then loom over your banquets, watching and noting everything. Nor, yourself full and belching, do you put before, or even throw at your hungry and starving guests, food which you find it beneath you to touch. Or, having barely put up with that arrogant mockery of a shared meal, take yourself back to secret grub and private extravagance.

[Pliny the Younger, *Panegyric to Trajan* 49.6]

Y. Pliny's unsubtle implication is that Trajan's predecessors, no doubt especially Domitian, *did* do all this. Suetonius writes that Domitian had large lunches but very small dinners (*Dom.* 21). The idea that Domitian enjoyed watching senators is mentioned by Tacitus, *Agricola* 45.2.

J10g Domitian's bad behaviour

[6] Thereafter he was terrifying for slaughtering the upper classes and began to mete out punishments and, like Gaius Caligula, began to insist on being called 'Lord and God': ridiculously idle, he used to pursue swarms of flies, when everyone had been sent out; [7] disgracefully lustful, he referred to his disgraceful exercise, by the Greek term 'wrestling in bed'. [8] So when someone was asked whether anyone was in the palace, the reply was "Not even a fly".

[*Epitome de Caesaribus* 11.6–8]

The Epitome here combines three stories to illustrate Domitian's bad behaviour well known from other authors. The form of address 'Lord and God' is mentioned by Suet. *Dom.* 13.2; Dio 67.4.7 and 13.4; Eutropius 7.23; Aur. Vict. 11.2 and see **T9–T12**. 'Pursuing swarms of flies' or stabbing at them as they ran around with wings removed, is Suet. *Dom.* 3.1 (naming the wit as Vibius Crispus); Dio 65.9.5; Aur. Vict. 11.5–6. 'Greek wrestling' is mentioned by Suet. *Dom.* 22; Dio 67.12.1; Aur. Vict. 11.5.

J10h   Domitian the monster

[48.3] The palace is not left empty and abandoned after the morning greeting, we stop and linger as if we are all at home though it was not long ago that the abhorrent monster had made it a fortress with his reign of terror. As if shut up in some cave he would lap up the blood of his nearest kindred, or set forth to slaughter and massacre the most distinguished citizens. [4] Dread and threats kept watch at his doors: those who were admitted and those who were excluded were equally afraid. In addition the man himself was appalling to see and to meet: arrogance in his expression, anger in his eyes, a feeble whiteness in his body, but his face blushed deep red with shamelessness. [5] No one dared to approach him or speak to him, and he always sought darkness and secrecy; he never came out from his solitude except to make more solitude.

[Pliny the Younger, *Panegyric to Trajan* 48.3–5]

Suetonius attests to Domitian's ruddy complexion (18.1) and his liking for solitude (*Dom.* 3.1, 21) also implicit in the most famous story about him 'No one, not even a fly,' see above. Despite Y. Pliny's first-hand familiarity with Domitian, the passage is almost worthless for its denigration of Domitian and implied flattery of Trajan.

J10i   Domitian's hypocrisy in sexual matters

This was just the case recently when that adulterer, polluted
By a sexual relationship worthy of a tragic play, then brought back   30
Those strict laws which terrified everyone, even Venus and Mars.
Yet at the same time, Julia was purging her fertile womb
By abortions, and spewing out lumps that look just like her uncle.
Isn't it then right and proper that the worst faults should
Condemn pious hypocrites and bite back when criticised?   35

[Juvenal, *Satire* 2.29–35]

Juvenal's second satire attacks hypocrisy especially in sexual matters. Greek and Roman mythology, the subject matter for tragic plays, often dealt with incestuous relationships, deliberate or accidental. The Oedipus myth is merely the most famous example: in **R21** Juvenal also mentions Pelopea and Philomela in context of drama and sexual abuse. The famous relationship of Venus and Mars was adulterous as Venus was married to Vulcan (Homer, *Odyssey* 8.266–366). Other sources reporting the alleged adultery are Suetonius, *Domitian* 22 and Y. Pliny *Letters* 4.11.6.

J11   Domitia Longina (early 50s – *c.* 130)

Daughter of Gnaeus Domitius Corbulo, famous general under Nero, driven to suicide in AD 66. Her first marriage was to Aelius Lamia Plautius (Dio 66.3.4, Suet. *Dom.* 1.3), but she divorced him to marry into the new imperial family, *c.* 70. She is alleged to have had affairs with Titus (Suet. *Titus* 10) and the actor Paris (*Dom.* 3.1) and to have been involved in the assassination of her husband, see **P15b**. All these are probably slanders aimed at denigrating Domitian. Josephus thanks her for patronage (**E9**). She is still referred to as wife of Domitian, 25 years after his assassination and *damnatio memoriae*, (**J11h**) and seems to have inspired enormous loyalty in her freedmen and women (**J11i**). There is an excellent and readable article on Domitia by Levick, B.M., 'Corbulo's Daughter' , *Greece and Rome* 49 no.2 (2002) 199–211; see also Jones, *Domitian* 33–38. Several portrait busts of Domitia are known with examples in the Louvre, and Copenhagen's Ny Carlsberg Glypotek.

J11a   Statue at Herculaneum
To Domitia, daughter of Gnaeus, wife of Domitian Caesar, by decree of the town
councillors

[*CIL* 10.1422 = *ILS* 271 = Cooley² F145 = EDCS–11500356]

Bronze statue at Herculaneum. Reference to Domitia Longina's father reflects that she was an important
person as daughter of the famous Neronian general Gnaeus Domitius Corbulo, as well as wife of Domitian.

J11b   College of the hero Corbulo and Longina at Vestini in Central Italy
To Phoebus, slave of Domitia, wife of Domitian. Domitia Athenais to her brother and
Januarius, his relative from the college of the hero Corbulo and Longina, set this up.

[MW 225 = *ILS* 9518 = EDCS–16300361*]

J11c   Domitia, mother of Divus Caesar on *sestertius* of AD 81/2 (Rome)

Obv: Bust of Domitia, draped, right, hair massed in front and coiled in chignon on back of head.
        DOMITIAE AVG IMP CAES DIVI F DOMITIAN AVG (To Domitia
        Augusta, wife of Emperor Caesar Domitian Augustus, son of Divus)
Rev: Domitia seated left, extending right hand to child standing left holding sceptre.
        DIVI CAESAR MATRI (to the mother of Divus Caesar)

[*RIC* 2.1 Domitian 132, *BMCRE²* 501, p.413 = BM no. R.11462]

The child was born in AD 73, the year after Domitian's second consulship (Suet. *Dom.*3), and see **J12**.

J11d   Domitia, peacock, Concordia Augusti on *aureus* of AD 82–83

Obv: Bust of Domitia, draped, right, hair massed in front and in long plait behind.
        DOMITIA AVGVSTA IMP DOMIT (Domitia Augusta, wife of the Emperor
        Domitian)
Rev: Peacock right.
        CONCORDIA AVGVST(I) (Unanimity of Augustus)

[*RIC* 2.1 Domitian 150 = *BMCRE*² 60, p.311 = BM no. R.10759]

The peacock was symbolic of Juno. Thus the coin flatters the emperor as well as his consort by suggesting a link to Jupiter (compare **L50–L54**).

J11e   Imperial women honoured in Pinara, Lycia
Julia Augusta, daughter of god Titus: honoured by the council and people of Pinara.
Domitia Augusta: honoured by the council and people of Pinara.

[*IGRR* 3.573]

For Domitia, honoured alongside the dead and deified Julia in Noricum see **L74**.

J11f   An expected child for Domitian
Be born, name promised once to Trojan Julus,
True offspring of the gods; be born, great boy, to whom
In centuries to come your father will entrust
Eternal reins to rule the world, an old man, beside
His older sire. Julia herself shall draw golden threads   5
With snow-white thumb, spinning you the whole golden fleece.

[Martial, *Epigram* 6.3 (published December 91)]

Martial's sixth book seems to have been published in December 91. This poem seems to expect the birth of a child. Line 1 contains a clear echo of the first reference in Virgil's *Aeneid* to Augustus (1.288), by his adopted family name Julius, linked to Aeneas' Trojan son, Julus. Martial attempts to predict the boy inheriting the empire without predicting Domitian's death. Julia is imagined as having taken over from the fates in spinning the child's thread of life. Golden threads from (Jason's) Golden Fleece symbolise the boy's immortality. In the event, though, no birth is known, and the poem may therefore represent a pious hope rather than a pregnancy for Domitia.

J11g   Domitia honoured at Brycus in Rhodes

The people of Brycus and all those living in Brycus, on behalf of the people of Rhodes honour goddess Domitia Augusta, wife of Emperor Caesar ~~Domitian~~ Vespasian, son of Augustus, their benefactress.

[MW 491 = *IG* 12.1.995 = *IGRR* 4.1152: Greek]

J11h   Brickstamp, AD 123

From the Sulpician brickyards of Domitia, wife of Domitian, when Paetinus and Apronianus were consuls

[*CIL* 15.548,02 = EDCS–32803400]

This is probably the correct official version of her name, 25 years after the death and *damnatio memoriae* of her husband. But **J11i** shows that she could perhaps have reverted to being daughter of Corbulo.

J11i   Freed slaves sponsor a memorial to Domitia, AD 140

To honour the memory of the house of Domitia Augusta, daughter of Gnaeus Domitius Corbulo, Domitius Polycarpus and Domitia Europe, in a place granted by decree of the order of town councillors built a temple and adorned it with statues and other things at their own expense, and gave an endowment of the same to the state for perpetuity under the terms inscribed below.

(Detailed terms follow, agreed at a meeting of the whole town council on 23 April AD 140, for an annual celebration of Domitia's birthday on 11 February with a feast for town councillors and religious figures provided by an endowment from Domitius Polycarpus and Domitia Europe.)

[Gabii, Central Italy, *ILS* 272]

J12   Divus Caesar (AD 73 – ?)

The child, whose name is unknown, was born in AD 73, the year after Domitian's second consulship (Suet. *Dom*.3).

J12a   Domitian's baby son on *aureus* of AD 82–83

Obv: Bust of Domitia, draped, right, hair massed in front and in long plait behind.
DOMITIA AVGVSTA IMP DOMIT (Domitia Augusta, wife of Emperor Domitian)
Rev: Domitian's son as naked infant boy on globe surrounded by seven stars.
DIVVS CAESAR IMP DOMITIANI F (Divus Caesar, son of Emperor Domitian)

[*RIC* 2.1 Domitian 152 = *BMCRE²* 62, p.311 = BM no. R.10760]

Coins between AD 81 and 83 (*RIC* Dom. 132–136 (see **J11c**) and 152–5) mark the boy's deification once Domitian became emperor. His death cannot be dated. Domitian's son is also one of his deified relatives said to visit his equestrian statue in Statius, *Silvae* 1.1.91–98, see **L72**.

J12b   Lament for Domitian's dead son
Look how thick a fleece of silent waters
Flows down on Caesar's face and chest.
And yet he humours Jove and keeps his head still
And laughs at waters frozen by hard frost,
So used to tire Boötes' northern stars,   5
And ignore Helice's dripping locks.
Who's up to tricks in heaven with dry waters?
I think these snows belong to Caesar's boy.

[Martial, *Epigram* 4.3 (published December 89)]

Martial concludes that a presumably recent snowfall must be Divus Caesar creating the weather. He also praises Domitian's fortitude in dealing with the loss of his son and in having had to deal with such weather on previous campaigns to northern areas (Helice and Boötes being northerly stars).

J13   Flavia Domitilla (II)
Only daughter of Vespasian and Domitilla (I), she died while her father was still a 'private citizen' (Suet. *Vesp.* 3), probably meaning before AD 69. Statius' poem on Domitian's *equus maximus* (**L72**) lists the members of Domitian's family to have been deified – brother, father, son, sister. So the deified Domitilla was his sister not his mother. See **L71** for a priestess of Diva Domitilla.

J13a   Vespasian and Domitilla, on *aureus* of AD 82–83

Obv: Head of deified Vespasian, radiate, right.
        DIVVS AVGVSTVS VESPASIANVS
Rev: Bust of deified Domitilla, draped, right, hair in long plait behind.
        DIVA DOMITILLA AVGVSTA

[*RIC* Domitian 146 = *BMCRE*² 68, p.312 = BM no. 1864,1128.256]

Domitian had these coins minted in AD 82–83 in honour of his deified father, brother, sister and son as part of a series that also includes **J12a**.

J14   T. Flavius Sabinus (IV) (*c.* 52 – 82)
Son of T. Flavius Sabinus III, probably by an Arrecina. He married his cousin Julia. His date of birth can be roughly established by those of his father and grandfather and his consulship in AD 82. Suet. *Dom,* 10.4 says this caused his death as he was accidentally announced as emperor rather than consul. Eutropius 7.23 (**T2**) also refers to Domitian killing cousins.

J14a   Flavius Sabinus (II) with his grandchildren on the Capitol, Dec. AD 69
In the middle of the night Sabinus had managed to get his children and Domitian, his brother's son, to him on the Capitol.

[Tacitus, *Histories* 3.69]

These children must have been his grandsons, Flavius Sabinus (IV) and Flavius Clemens, since his only known son, Flavius Sabinus (III) recently consul can hardly have been described like this.

J14b   Domitian kills Sabinus
When he had killed Sabinus, one of his own relations, and was marrying Julia (this was Julia, the wife of the murdered man, the niece of Domitian, and one of Titus' daughters), Ephesus was making sacrifices in honour of the marriage, but Apollonius stood there at the rituals and said, "O night of the Danaids of old, how unique you were."

[Philostratos, *Life of Apollonius of Tyana* 7.7]

In the famous Greek myth, Danaus, king of Argos and Aegyptus, king of Egypt were brothers with respectively 50 daughters and 50 sons. Initially they ruled jointly, but soon quarrelled. Marriage between the 50 pairs of cousins was meant to resolve the quarrel, but Danaus received an oracle predicting his death at the hands of a son-in-law, so ordered his daughters to murder their new husbands on their wedding night. One only disobeyed (the rest were condemned to exemplary punishment in the underworld). Apollonius alludes, it seems, to fraternal discord, killing of kindred, and ill-fated marriage.

J15   Flavia Julia or **Julia Titi (Julia, daughter of Titus) c. 63 – before 91.**
Almost certainly a daughter of Titus by his first wife, Arrecina Tertulla, **J9**, whose mother was a Julia.
Offered in marriage by Titus to Domitian, her uncle – Suet. *Dom.* 22 (permissible by the legislation which
allowed Claudius to marry Agrippina). For alleged relationship with her uncle despite rejection of the
marriage, see **J15e–f** and Dio 67.3.2. She is included in vows by arvals for the imperial family from the
start of 81 (**A81e**). For her deification, see **K54, L73–L75.**

J15a   Marble portrait bust of Julia in John Paul Getty Museum

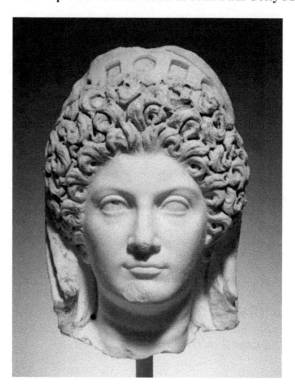

[John Paul Getty Museum no. 58.AA.1]

The bust is 33 cm high: traces of paint suggest Julia's hair was a reddish colour.

J15b   Statue of Julia at Herculaneum
To Julia Augusta, daughter of Titus Caesar, by decree of the town councillors.

[*AE* 1979.176 = Cooley[2] F144]

Julia's title 'Augusta' suggest that this bronze statue was set up between Titus' accession on 23 June and the
destruction of Herculaneum in autumn of the same year (probably on 24 October).

J15c   Julia and Divus Titus, *aureus* AD 82/3

Obv: Head of deified Titus, radiate, right.
         DIVVS TITVS AVGVSTVS
Rev: Bust of Julia, draped, right, hair massed in front and plaited in bun behind.
         IVLIA AVGVSTA DIVI TITI F (Julia Augusta, daughter of Divus Titus)
                    [*RIC* 2.1 Domitian 147 = *BMCRE²* 69, p.312 = BM no. R.10761]

J15d   Julia Augusta on *aureus* of AD 88/9?

Obv: Bust of Julia, draped, right, hair massed in front and in long plait behind.
         IVLIA AVGVSTA
Rev: Peacock facing, with tail spread.
         DIVI TITI FILIA (daughter of Divus Titus)
                    [*RIC* 2.1 Domitian 683 (type) = *BMCRE²* 250, p.350 = BM no.1864,1128.45]

The peacock was associated with Juno (compare **J11d** above)

J15e   Julia's abortion and death
He himself had not only violated with incest his brother's daughter but had even
brought about her death, for she died of an abortion while a widow.
                                                             [Pliny the Younger, *Letters* 4.11.6]

For the whole letter, a posthumous attack on Domitian's condemnation of the Vestals, see **L15**. For Juvenal's
similar accusation, see **J10i**.

J15f   **Statue of Julia**

Who would not think that Pheidias made you,
Julia, or else Minerva's artistry?
In marble white your statue seems to speak
And living beauty shines in your calm face.
Its hand plays gently with the belt of Venus,   5
Which from your neck it snatched, young Cupid.
To win back love from Mars, or mighty Jove,
Let Juno or Venus ask it back from you.

[Martial, *Epigram* 6.13 (published December 91)]

Martial celebrates a statue of Julia as Venus by comparing it to the work of Pheidias, responsible for the statue of Zeus at Olympia, as well as that of Athene in the Parthenon. Venus was the mythical founder of the Julian family (celebrated by Julius Caesar as Venus Genetrix, 'Ancestress' Venus). The belt or girdle of Venus acted as a love charm in her affair with Mars, and was borrowed by Hera (Juno) to charm Zeus (Jupiter) in Homer, *Iliad* 14.21ff). Julia had appeared as Augustan Venus on *denarii* of AD 81 (*RIC* Titus 385–390, *BMCRE*² 143, p.247 = R.10998), and linked with Juno, above, **J15d**.

J16   T. Flavius Clemens (AD *c.* 60 – 95, cos 95)

Younger brother of **J14** but 'a far more shadowy figure' (Jones, *Domitian* 47–8). He was with his grandfather the city prefect on the Capitol just before its destruction in AD 69 (see **J14a**). Married Flavia Domitilla (III), daughter of Domitian's sister (**J13**) – Philostratos (**J16a**) confuses mother and daughter. Dio is more accurate and gives the exact year by his reference to the *via Domitiana*, Dio 67.14.1 (**D14**). By his death he was Domitian's closest male relative; married to his closest relative; and father of his designated heirs.

J16a   Clemens killed by Domitian

He had just had Clemens killed, an ex-consul, to whom he had married his own sister, and had given an order about two or three days after the murder that she should join her husband.

[Philostratos, *Life of Apollonius of Tyana* 8.25.1]

Philostratos confuses Flavia Domitilla (III) and (IV). He attributes to this murder the final spur for Domitian's assassination by Stephanus, freedman of Clemens.

J17   Flavia Domitilla (III)

She was Domitian's niece and married Flavius Clemens, Domitian's first cousin once removed. She had seven children, the two eldest boys being made Domitian's heirs (**J18**). But in AD 95 she was condemned alongside her husband (Dio/Xiphilinus 67.14.1–2) for impiety. This gave rise to a tradition of making her one of the earliest Christian martyrs, see **J17c**, but in reality she is very unlikely indeed to have been a Christian.

J17a   Funerary inscription for freedwoman of Flavia Domitilla, Rome

[…] the daughter of Flavia Domitilla, grand-daughter of [Divus Vespasi]an, made this for her freedwoman Glycera and […]

[*CIL* 6.948a = EDCS–17301066*]

J17b   Nurse to Flavia Domitilla's seven children, Rome

Tatia Baucylis, nurse of seven children [...] of Flavia Domitilla [...] granddaughter of Divus Vespasian, [...] for her services this tomb [...] for my freedmen and freedwomen and their descendants.

[MW 221 = *ILS* 1839 = EDCS–18900009]

J17c   St Flavia Domitilla

In the fifteenth year of Domitian, amongst many others they investigated Flavia Domitilla, daughter of the sister of Flavius Clemens, one of the then consuls at Rome, and for her witness to Christ she was punished by being exiled to the island of Pontia.

[Eusebius, *Church History* 3.18.4]

This tradition from Christian authors elaborating on Dio/Xiphilinus' mention of atheism or Jewish sympathies, arising from wishful thinking from Christian authors. She was beatified and her feast-day celebrated on 12 May (Greek orthodox, and formerly Catholic) now moved to 7 May (Catholic – *Martyrologium Romanum* 2nd edition (Vatican Press 2004), p. 274).

J18 & J19   T. Flavius Domitianus (b. 81) and T. Flavius Vespasianus (b. 82)

Sons of Flavius Clemens and Flavia Domitilla (III), so Vespasian was their great-great-uncle via their father's side and their great-grandfather via their mother's. They were designated Domitian's heirs at an unknown date (Suet. *Dom.* 15.1). It is not known what happened to them after the fall of their parents and then the assassination of Domitian.

J18a   Epitaph to one of the boys' teachers, Rome

To the Shades of Pierus, imperial freedman, teacher of the boys of our Caesar. To this well-deserving man, Flavia Nice his wife set up this inscription with bronze door from her own money, by permission of Hermes, imperial freedman, chamberlain of Domitia Augusta.

[MW 224 = *ILS* 1834 = EDCS–18900045]

J18b   Quintilian as tutor to Domitian's great-nephews

Since Domitian Augustus has entrusted to my care the grandsons of his sister, I would not sufficiently appreciate the honour of such divine judgement if I did not thereby measure the magnitude of my task. [3] For what limit can I have in improving character to deserve the approval of that most righteous censor? Or in improving scholarship so as not to seem to have thereby failed a *princeps* who is as pre-eminent in literature as in all other fields? [4] Now since no one is surprised that the best poets have often invoked the Muses not only at the start of their works, but after making considerable progress and reaching some significant point, have renewed their vows and offered fresh prayers, as it were. [5] So, I can surely be forgiven if I now do what I did not do when I started this work, and invoke all the gods and especially that divine being who is closest of all and most favourable to scholarship: may he inspire me with genius equal to his new expectations of me, and be there, ready and willing to help, to make me what he believed me to be.

[Quintilian, *The Orator's Education* 4 preface 2–5]

The inclusion of this passage shows that the whole work was published before the fall and death of Flavius Clemens in summer 95. For Quintilian's flattery of Domitian's skills as a poet, see **R5**.

J20   M. Arrecinus Clemens (cos I suff 73, cos II suff 85)

For his family, see Levick, *Vespasian* page xxiii. He was the son of the homonymous praetorian prefect of AD 41. It seems that his two sisters married Titus and T. Flavius Sabinus (III). As a family member he was trusted with key appointments including as praetorian prefect in AD 70 (**J20a**) and city prefecture, *c.* 85 including during Domitian's absence on the Danube together with the praetorian prefect, Fuscus. But he fell soon afterwards (Suet. *Dom.* 11.1), implying his execution, perhaps for an alleged conspiracy (see **P6**) or for inefficiency in dealing with it as city prefect (see Jones, *Domitian* 42–44).

J20a   Arrecinus Clemens put in charge of the praetorians

Mucianus put in charge of the praetorians Arrecinus Clemens, who was related to Vespasian's family by marriage and an especial favourite of Domitian's. He repeated that Arrecinus' father had performed the same role with distinction under Gaius Caesar and that the soldiers would be pleased to have the same family name, and that the man himself was capable of both functions, even though of senatorial rank.

[Tacitus, *Histories* 4.68]

J20b   Arrecinus Clemens' career, Pisaurum in Umbria

[M. A]rrecinus [Clemen]s, son of Marcus, of the Camilia tribe, twice consul, city *praet(or) OR praef(ect)*, [imperial] propraetorian [legate] of the province of N[ea]rer [Spai]n had this made at his own expense.

[*AE* 1947, 40 = Supp. It. I (1981), 67 = EDCS–10700687*]

Though the PRAET appears clearly on this building inscription from Pisaurum, Umbria on the NE coast of Italy (near modern San Marino) it is now accepted that it has been remodelled from PRAEF (Syme *RP* 5.613; Jones, Suet. Comm. p.151).

J21   Antonia Caenis (died *c.* AD 71–5)

Antonia Caenis was a freedwoman of Antonia the Younger, the mother of Claudius. She was Vespasian's long-term mistress after the death of Flavia Domitilla. 'He brought Caenis back to live with him and even as emperor treated her almost as his lawful wife.' (Suet. *Vesp.* 3). He could not marry her as Augustan marriage legislation specifically forbade marriage between those of senatorial rank and freed persons (LACTOR 17, S1). For Dio/Xiphilinus' account of her personal qualities, almost certainly embroidered with the passing of time, see 66.14 = **C14**. Modern treatment: Freisenbruch *First Ladies of Rome*, page 168–170.

J21a   Caenis' tombstone, Rome

To the Divine Spirits of Antonia Caenis, imperial freedwoman and best patron. Aglaus the freedman with his children Aglaus, Glene and Aglais [dedicated this].

[MW 210 = *CIL* 6.12037 = EDCS–14800257*]

This beautiful and ornate marble funerary altar tombstone makes no mention of Vespasian.

J22   Berenice (AD 28 – after 80)

Julia Berenice was daughter of M. Julius Agrippa I (= King Herod Agrippa) the friend of Claudius. After marriages to Marcus, brother of Tiberius Julius Alexander (later prefect of Egypt), and to her uncle, Herod, king of Chalcis, she lived with her brother M. Julius Agrippa II who succeeded his uncle as king of Chalcis. She and her brother supported the Romans in the Jewish revolt and Titus fell in love with her in Judaea, and openly lived with her when she came to Rome in 75, but did not marry her and dismissed her on his accession, '*invitus invitam*' as Suetonius elegantly puts it (*Titus* 7.2, 'though he was unwilling and she was unwilling'). Dio/Xiphilinus also gives details 65.15.3–4, 66.8.1.

J22a   Titus in love with Berenice

There were people who believed that his burning desire for Berenice made him change his journey; the young man's spirit certainly did not object to Berenice, but this did not prevent his management of public affairs.

[Tacitus, *Histories* 2.2]

Berenice unsurprisingly supported Vespasian's cause in 69 – Tac. *Hist.* 2.81.

J22b   Titus sends Berenice home

[7] Finally, when he accepted the weight of royal responsibility, he instructed Berenice to return home, **though she was hoping for their marriage OR though he was rejecting their marriage**, and banished the crowd of eunuchs. [8] He did this as if signalling a change to his lack of responsibility.

[*Epitome de Caesaribus* 10.7]

Unfortunately medieval scribes in copying the manuscript were divided between whether to read and copy 'sperabat' (she was hoping) or 'spernebat' (he was rejecting).

J22c   Berenice in court

There have been people who have been involved in judging their own case … and I myself represented Queen Berenice before the woman herself.

[Quintilian, *The Orator's Education* 4.1.19]

The nature of the case is unclear. It must have involved Berenice while in Rome (AD 75–79). Quintilian uses the word for '*iudex*' but these were not 'judges' in the modern sense of a presiding judge, but members of a large panel, more like jurors. Crook, *AJP* 72 (1951) 162–176.

J22d   Berenice & Agrippa

In the winter …
she picks up great crystal vases, and ones made of   155
Semi-precious stones, then a world-famous diamond, more expensive
For being worn on the finger of Berenice. Some foreigner once gave it
As a token of incest, Agrippa gave it to his sister,
Where kings keep that Sabbath as a holy day, barefoot,
And by custom, clemency is granted to pigs to live to old age.   160

[Juvenal, *Satire* 6.153 and 155–160]

Juvenal's sixth satire attacks behaviour of women, here the age-old topic of profligate spending. He implies that Agrippa and Berenice might have had an incestuous relationship; Josephus, *Jewish Antiquities* 20.145 also reports this as a rumour.

J23   Earinus (T. Flavius Earinus, *c.* 78 – *c.* 95)

He was a young castrated slave then freedman of Domitian, and his homosexual lover. Dio mentions the relationship (67.2.1–3) and it is prominent in the contemporary poets (Martial 9.11–13, 16–17, 36, and Statius 3.4) who make much of the potential equivalence between Jupiter's relationship with his cup-bearer, the Trojan prince, Ganymede and Domitian's with Earinus (also from the area of Troy). Two poems (**J23b, c**) celebrate his dedication of locks of hair in his home temple at his coming of age. The poems are very strange, despite the potential for flattering comparison with Jupiter/Ganymede, Earinus' name does not fit in Latin verse metre (**J23a**), and the poets had to write about a eunuch dedicating his hair for an emperor very sensitive about his baldness who had outlawed castration! Nevertheless the poems are not satire, as is clear from other works of the poets. All the poems about Earinus were published in 93/4 and nothing more is heard about him.

J23a   **Tribute to Earinus**
        Name, born together with roses and violets,
        Name which designates the best part of the year,
        Redolent of honey and Attic flowers,
        And carrying the flavour of the phoenix' nest,
        Name that is sweeter still than blessed nectar,   5
        Which Attis would have wanted to be known by
        And he who mixes wine for the Thunderer.
        Call it out loud in the Palatine palace
        And Venuses and Cupids will make reply.
        Name that is noble and delicate and soft,   10
        Which I wished to put in elegant verse.
        But the rude syllables rebel.
        And yet some poets can say "Eiarinios"
        But they are Greeks, and anything goes for them,
        Pronouncing Ares' name any way they like: 15
        But *we* are not allowed to be so clever,
        Since our Latin Muses are stricter by far.
                                        [Martial, *Epigram* 9.11 (published December 94)]

Earinus' Latin name is a transliteration of ἐαρινός meaning 'of spring'. This epigram plays with the idea that Earinus' name (four short syllables) does not fit any of the metres normally used by Roman poets. The next two poems play with the 'spring-like' meaning of his name.

J23b   **Earinus' lock of hair**
        Sweet locks of hair and a mirror, beauty's counsellor
        Are placed as sacred offerings to Pergamum's god,
        By the boy, whose name denotes the time of spring,
        His master's greatest favourite in all the palace.
        Blessed the land thought worthy of such a gift, which
        Would not prefer to have the hair of Ganymede.
                                        [Martial, *Epigram* 9.16 (published December 94)]

J23c   **Statius on Earinus dedicating a lock of hair**
Statius introduced this poem as follows: "Meanwhile Earinus, freedman of our emperor Germanicus, knows how long I delayed his great desire when he asked that I should dedicate in verse his hair which he was sending to healing-god Asclepius at Pergamum with a jewelled box and mirror."

        Go, locks, I pray, make easy crossing of the sea,
        Go, lying gently on a coronet of gold,
        Go! Gentle Venus guarantees a prosperous voyage,
        She'll calm the southern winds, and maybe take you from
        The dangerous boat across the waters in her shell.   5

        Receive, young son of Phoebus, famous curls of hair
        That Caesar's lad presents to you. Receive them gladly,
        And show your long-haired father. Let him see their lovely
        Lustre, and long mistake them for his brother's hair.
        Perhaps he'll even trim his beautiful, immortal   10

Locks, and give you them, enclosed in other gold.
Pergamum, more blessed by far than pine-treed Ida,
(True, Ida claims her cloud of holy rape did give
The gods that Ganymede, yet angry Juno always
Glares at him, shrinks from his hand, rejects the nectar).   15
But, Pergamum, held dear by gods and famous for your
Lovely boy, you've sent a servant welcome both to
Italian Jove and Roman Juno both alike, who
See him and approve: such pleasure for the mighty
Lord of earth fulfils the intention of the gods.   20

(Statius now explains at considerable length that Venus sees the boy, as lovely as her
own son Cupid, and insists that only Asclepius should perform the castration.)

Boy dear to the gods, and picked to taste the holy nectar   60
And often touch that mighty hand which tribes from Getae,
Armenia, Persia, India seek to know and touch.
Boy, brought to birth under a favourable star,
The gods have truly shown the greatest favour to you.
For once your country's god had left high Pergamus,   65
And crossed the sea so that first facial hair should not
Make rough your shining cheeks and spoil your perfect beauty.
No other was vouchsafed the power to soften the boy,
But the son of Phoebus, silently, with gentle skill
Bids the body leave its sex, without inflicting   70
Any wound. Yet Cytheran Venus still is gnawed
By anxious fears of what the boy might suffer yet.
Our leader's splendid clemency had not begun
To keep males safe from birth; but now it is forbidden
To alter sex and change a man. Nature is pleased   75
To see men only as she made them: no perverse law
Makes female slaves the burden dread of bearing sons.
Had *you* been later born, you too would be a youth
With darker cheeks and stronger, fully developed limbs.
You would have gladly sent to Phoebus' shrine not just   80
One lock of hair now sailing to your country's shores.

[Statius, *Silvae* 3.4.1–20, 60–81 (published 93/4)]

One of **Apollo's** spheres was medicine, a function fully attributed to his son **Asclepius**, worshipped at **Pergamum** (NW Turkey). **Venus** features in her roles as goddess of love, ancestress of the Roman people, through Aeneas, and mother of Cupid. **Ganymede** was snatched from Troy, near Mount **Ida** to be Jupiter's lover, or cup-bearer (15, 59–60), to the great offence of Juno (14–15). Lines 73–79 refer to Domitian outlawing male castration (see also **S28–S29**), perhaps as a result of what Earinus had suffered. The final 24 lines of the poem, not included here, refer in great detail, and with many mythological comparisons to the actual dedication of hair and a prayer by Cupid for long life for Earinus, granted in the poem, but perhaps not in reality, since we hear no more of Earinus.

SECTION K
ROME AND ITALY

The City devastated by fires, its most venerable shrines burnt, the Capitol itself burnt by the hands of its own citizens.

[Tacitus, *Histories* 1.2.2]

Introduction: The Flavians were responsible for the amphitheatre which has epitomised Rome for almost two millennia, but also for a great deal else besides. In part this was because they had the need or opportunity to rebuild Rome after three major fires – the Great Fire of AD 64; the burning of the Capitol at the end of the civil war; and a major fire in AD 80. Suetonius typically gives sections on the emperors' building projects: these are disappointingly short for the Flavians – *Vespasian* 9.1 and *Domitian* 5, though fortunately a variety of other sources help fill the gap. Most of this chapter presents written sources for Flavian buildings in Rome: since many of these are at least partially visible today, frequent reference is made to Claridge, *Rome: An Oxford Archaeological Guide* (2nd edition, Oxford 2010). These buildings are presented in (English) alphabetical order since many were built by more than one of the emperors. The section starts with some general descriptions of Rome (**K1–K6**), and concludes with building projects in Italy under the Flavians.

GENERAL DESCRIPTIONS OF ROME: K1–K6

K1   Pliny's general description of the streets of Rome, AD 73
[66] The city had 3 gates when Romulus left it, or, if we believe the greatest figure quoted by authorities, 4. The circumference of its walls at the time when the Vespasians were censors, in the 826th year since the city was founded [AD 73], was 13 miles and 200 yards, enclosing seven hills. Rome is divided into fourteen regions, and has 265 crossroad shrines. If straight lines are drawn from the milestone at the head of the Roman forum to each individual gate (these today number 37, counting the twelve double gates as one each but omitting 7 old gates no longer in use), the result is 20 miles 765 yards, in a straight line. [67] But from the same milestone to the edge of buildings including the Praetorian Camp through the locations of all the roads amounts to slightly over 60 miles. If anyone were to add in the heights of the buildings, he would get a very good estimate and confess that no city in the whole world could compare with Rome in size. It is enclosed on the East by the rampart of Tarquin the Proud which stands as one of the most remarkable of all works, for he made it equal the walls where the city lay most open to attack across a level approach. From other sides Rome was defended by high walls or steep hills, except that expanding buildings have added many cities to it.

[Pliny, *Natural History* 3.66–67]

Pliny's figures are no doubt meant to sound impressive, but are problematic. Rome did not build (or have any need for) walls between the Servian Wall (sixth-fourth century BC) and the Aurelian Wall (started AD 270) which has a circumference of about 12 miles. So Pliny's figures must relate not to a single defensive wall but to the built-up area of the city. It is also hard to see how the combined distance from Rome's centre to its 37 gates could be as little as 20 miles (the distance from forum to Praetorian camp was about 1.5 miles). To give a better comparison, ancient Rome, with a population estimated at about 1 million (Augustus, *RG* 15.2 gave a gift to 320,000 members of the urban plebs, i.e. male citizens) held the all-time record for population, for around 18 centuries, until it was overtaken by London early in the 19th century. London's increase to almost 2 million in 1841 was supported by the Industrial Revolution, the advent of railways and canals, as well as a huge empire and navy (merchant and royal).

K2 'Chronicle of 354' summary of Flavian building works

Divus Vespasian reigned 12 years, 8 months and 28 days. He gave a handout of 85 *denarii*. He dedicated the first three storeys of the amphitheatre. He died at Cures in Sabine territory.

Divus Titus reigned [*figures lost*]. At the amphitheatre he added two storeys to the three of his father. He died at Cures in Sabine territory in his father's bedroom.

Domitian reigned 17 years, 5 months and 5 days. He gave three handouts of 75 *denarii*. By this emperor many public works were constructed. 7 halls, the pepper warehouses where the basilica of Constantine now is, and the granaries of Vespasian, the Temple of Castor and Minerva, the Capena Gate, the Temple of the Flavian Family, the Temple of the Divi, the Temples of Isis and Serapis, the Temple of Minerva of Chalchis, the Odeum, the Old Minucia, the Stadium, the Baths of Titus and Trajan, the amphitheatre up to its shields, the Temple of Vespasian and Titus, the Capitolium, the Senate House, 4 gladiatorial training schools, the Palatine palace, the *Meta Sudans* and the Pantheon. He was killed in the Palace.

[*Chronicle of 354*, part 16]

The Chronicler of AD 354 is an unknown author who compiled a sort of almanac for his patron. One section includes lists of kings, dictators and emperors of Rome. The chronographer records length of reign, distributions of money and place of death. Other than this he sporadically records prodigies of various sorts, including acts of gluttony (under Nero and Alexander), natural and man-made disasters, and information about buildings in Rome. This too is very sporadic: the only building projects recorded for the Julio-Claudian emperors are decorations to the Circus Maximus. But for the Flavians he appears well-informed and comprehensive. The 'Old Minucia' probably relates to a portico (location unknown) where corn distributions took place. He provides the only reference to 'Seven Halls' and to Granaries of Vespasian, and is more helpful than the various summary historians (for Vespasian, Aur. Vict. 9.1.7 and *Epit.* 9.8; for Domitian: Eutropius 7.23 = **T2**).

K3 The huge scale of Flavian building works

So, unlike previously, the roofs of the city have stopped shaking as enormous blocks of stone pass by; our homes stand firm and the temples no longer totter.

[Pliny the Younger, *Panegyric to Trajan* 51.1]

An ingenious attempt by Y. Pliny to condemn Domitian/the Flavians even for the magnificence of building work.

K4 Ammianus Marcellinus, fourth-century visitor to Rome

Finally, surveying the parts of the city spread out between the heights of the seven hills, among the slopes and flat areas of the city and the suburbs, whatever he saw first he thought surpassed everything else: the Temple of Jupiter on the Tarpeian Rock, as far superior as divine things excel things on earth; baths built like provinces; the solid mass of the amphitheatre made out of Tiburtine stone, whose summit the human eye could barely see; the Pantheon, like a whole region with the beautiful height of its curved dome; lofty heights climbed by spiral staircases carrying statues of great emperors; the Temple of Rome; the Forum of Peace; the Theatre of Pompey; and the Odeum; and Stadium, amongst other glories of the eternal city. But when he came to the Forum of Trajan…

[Ammianus Marcellinus 16.14–16]

Ammianus is describing the first visit to Rome in 357 of Emperor Constantius II. The historian himself first visited Rome in 378, and chooses to ignore recent Christian buildings, concentrating on those of the past. Though he saves greatest praise for the Forum of Trajan, five of the other eight buildings especially singled out were Flavian (in bold below): **Temple of Jupiter Capitolinus** AD 82; various Baths, (especially of Trajan AD 109, Caracalla AD 216, Diocletian *c.* AD 302, Constantine *c.* AD 313;); **Flavian Amphitheatre,** AD 80; Pantheon, *c.* AD 125; Columns, e.g. Trajan AD 113, Marcus Aurelius *c.* AD 185; Temple of Venus and Rome, AD 135; **Forum of Peace AD 75**; Theatre of Pompey 55 BC and **Odeum** and **Stadium,** AD 86 (restored by Trajan and Severus respectively).

K5   Street Regulations of Domitian
The thrusting shopkeepers had long been poaching
Our city space, front premises encroaching
Everywhere. Then, Germanicus, you commanded
That the cramped alleyways should be expanded,
And what were footpaths became real roads.   5
One sees no columns, now, festooned with loads
Of chained flagons; the praetor walks the street
Without the indignity of muddy feet;
Razors aren't wildly waved in people's faces;
Bar-owners, butchers, barbers, cooks know their places,   10
And grimy restaurants can't spill out too far.
Now Rome is Rome, not just one huge bazaar.

                                          [Martial, *Epigram* 7.61 (published Dec. 92)
                                          (translated Michie (1972), slightly adapted)]

K6   Martial's view of Life in Rome (after his retirement to the country)
You ask why I head for seek my small farm
At dry Nomentum and my home's dingy hearth?
There's no place in the city, Sparsus, to think
Or sleep, if you are poor. Schoolmasters deny
You life in the morning; bakers in the night;   5
The hammers of bronzesmiths do so all day long.
Here the idle money-changer shakes his
Dirty table with Neronian coins.
There the beater of Hispanic gold-nuggets
Pounds at the worn stone with his shining mallet.   10
The crowd possessed by Bellona never stops;
The bandaged castaway rabbits on and on;
As does the Jew taught to beg by his mother,
And the half-blind hawker of sulphur matches.
Who can count how much lazy sleep has been lost?   15
Easier to say how many Romans bang bronze pots
When a magic circle eclipses the moon.
You, Sparsus, know nothing of this; how could you,
In luxury on your Petilian kingdom?
Your ground floor looks down on the summits of hills,   20
There's country in town and a vineyard in Rome
A greater vintage than Falernus' slopes.
Within your walls there's a drive fit for chariots,

> Sleep in its depths and rest unspoilt by any
> Chatter; daylight comes only when allowed in.   25
> While we are woken by the crowd pushing past,
> And Rome is at my bedside. When, sick and tired
> Of it, I want some sleep, I go to my farm.
>
> [Martial, *Epigram* 12.57 (published 101)]

This epigram dates from Martial's retirement to his native Spain after the death of Domitian and then Nerva. Sullivan, *Martial* 52 describes the decision as prudent, given that Martial will have been identified with the old order. Here Martial writing to Sparsus, probably Sextus Julius Sparsus, cos 88, makes the best of having to leave Rome. Juvenal's famous, long, and scathing *Satire* 3 on life in Rome was written about eleven years later.

FIRES: K7–K9

Fire was an ever-present risk in a Rome lit by oil lamps, with buildings crowded together, even with the presence of *vigiles* whose job it was to watch out for fires. Rome had been devastated by the Great Fire of AD 64, and Nero had probably never recovered politically from rumours that he had started the fire (see Tac. *Ann.* 15.38–44). Introducing the Flavian period, Tacitus describes the destruction caused in AD 69, quoted at the start of this section. He later described this in detail, *Hist.* 3.71–2; narrative of the huge fire of AD 80 is lost in Tacitus, but provided by Dio 66.24.1–2; Suetonius *Titus* 8.3 – 3 days and 3 nights. This fire affected large swathes of the Campus Martius (see map of Rome, p 18). Juvenal famously described (*c.* AD 115) the dangers of fires in Rome in *Satire* 3.197–222.

K7   Huge fire at Rome in Titus' reign

At this period, Mount Vesuvius in Campania began to burn, and a fire at Rome continued unabated for three whole days and nights.

[*Epitome de Caesaribus* 10.12]

K8   Rome rises phoenix-like from fires

> Just as fire renews Assyrian nests, when that
> Amazing bird has passed ten centuries of life,
> Just so has Rome, renewed, cast off her own old age
> Assuming in its place the looks of her protector.
> Please now, Vulcan, lay aside your ancient grudge   5
> And spare us: we are Mars' people, but Venus' too.
> Spare us, father: so may your wanton wife forgive
> Your putting her in chains and love you patiently.
>
> [Martial, *Epigram* 5.7 (published December 90)]

Vulcan caught his wife Venus having an affair with Mars (Homer, *Odyssey* 8.266–366). Rome claimed Mars and Venus as parents of its founders Romulus and Aeneas. Martial, writing in AD 90 may still be thinking mainly of the huge fire of AD 80 (Dio 66.24) and the 'Great Fire' of AD 64 (Tac. *Ann.* 15.38–41).

K9   Domitian dedicates altar and enclosure vowed during Great Fire of AD 64
This area within the stones which mark it out and enclosed by stakes, and the altar
below has been dedicated by Emperor Caesar Domitian Augustus Germanicus, in
accordance with a vow undertaken, but long neglected and unfulfilled, to stop the
fires, when the city was on fire for nine days in the time of Nero.

It was dedicated by this law that nobody should be permitted, within these
boundaries, to erect a building, loiter, do business, plant a tree or sow anything else;
and that the praetor to whom this region was allotted, or another magistrate, should
make sacrifice of a red calf and red boar at the festival to Vulcan, on 23 August every
year, with prayers.

Written below: temple … (*date lost*) August […] to be given […] what Emperor
Caesar Domitian Augustus Germanicus, *pontifex maximus* decided should be done
y[early?]

[MW 442 = *ILS* 4914 = EDCS–17300964]

BUILDINGS OF ROME: K10–K73

ALTARS (K10–K11)
For altars vowed during the Great Fire of AD 64, but erected by Domitian, see **K9**. An altar appears on a
denarius of Domitian, apparently in connection with military victory. All three Flavian emperors carried on
the traditional minting of coins depicting the Altar of Providence, see **H48**. For other altars see **L30, L31,
L38, L68, Q1**.

K10   Altar to the Well-being of the Emperor, *as* AD 84

Obv: Head of Domitian, laureate, right, with aegis.
          IMP CAES DIVI VESP F DOMITIAN AVG GER COS X (Emperor Caesar
          Domitian Augustus Germanicus, son of Divus Vespasian, consul 10 times)
Rev: Altar.
          SALVTI AVGVST S C (To Imperial Well-being, by decree of the senate)
                    [*RIC* 2.1 Domitian 209 = *BMCRE*[2] 286A, p.359 = BM no. 1958,1101.21]

The altar presumably celebrated Domitian's safe return from German wars.

K11   Altar built by Domitian, *denarius* AD 95/6

Obv: Head of Domitian, laureate, right.
IMP CAES DOMIT AVG GERM P M TR P XV (Emperor Caesar Domitian Augustus Germanicus, *pontifex maximus,* son of Divus Vespasian, consul 10 times)

Rev: Altar, with two figures of soldiers, flanked by legionary standards; under each standard on top of the altar is a seated captive.
IMP XXII COS XVII CENS P P P (hailed *imperator* 22 times, consul 17 times, censor for life, father of the fatherland)

[RIC 2.1 Domitian 784 = BMCRE² 237D = BM no. 1980,0706.1]

AMPHITHEATRE (COLOSSEUM) (K12–K19)

Whole books have been written about the most famous of all Roman buildings, now visited by an estimated four million tourists each year. Politically it is the most significant of all Flavian building projects, making a hugely symbolic statement about the new dynasty compared with the old (**K13**); a constant reminder of military success (**K12**); and a token of populism. Vespasian began the building (Suet. Vesp 9.1) and it was inaugurated by Titus in AD 80 (Suet. Titus 7.3 – brief mention; Dio 66.25.1–5 with considerable detail; Martial *On the Shows* – whole book of poems, including **K13**, **K17–K19**, **Q4**, **Q5**).

It is 189m long, 156m wide, 48m high, with an outer perimeter of 545m requiring an estimated 100,000 m^3 of travertine marble. Even more vast amounts of tufa and brick-faced concrete were used for the infrastructure. Internally the arena measured 83m x 48m. Estimated capacity was 50,000. Finishing touches seem to have been added by Domitian.

K12   Reconstructed dedication inscription

[Emperor <Titus> Caesar Vespasian Augustus ordered the construction of the new amphitheatre from his spoils]

[ILS 5633 (reread by G. Alföldy) = AE 2009,464 = EDCS–00900162*]

Drawing after G. Alföldy: the black dots show the peg-holes, the grey letters the metal inscription Alföldy restores.

Part of a marble fifth-century inscription (*CIL* 6.40454a) survives, recording repairs to the amphitheatre. In addition to, and older than the lettering are peg-holes which show that the marble had previously been used for an inscription in bronze letters attached to the marble, which had either fallen off or been melted down and reused. The peg-holes enable a guess to be made as to the original letters. Alföldy (*Zeitschrift für Papyrologie und Epigraphik* 109 (1995) 195–226) suggested a reading of an original inscription by Vespasian, but also that a later insertion of the letter T, (shown by new peg-holes) enabled Titus to claim the entire credit for the building.

So this inscription, perhaps showed Vespasian and then his son, Titus claiming credit for the building, while also reminding readers of their conquest of Judaea and their use of spoils for the public benefit in a way traditionally used by republican generals. One or other reading has been widely accepted (e.g. Claridge, *Rome²* (2010), p.314 (Vespasian); Coleman, *Martial Liber Spectaculorum* (2006); Levick, *LACTOR* 18, 115 (2002) but not only has not a single letter survived, but Alföldy himself admitted that some of the peg-holes are not really in the right place! A.E. Cooley, *Manual of Latin Epigraphy* (2012, p.437) and Hopkins & Beard, *The Colosseum* (2011 pp.33–4) are much more sceptical.

K13   Nero's Golden House replaced

Here where Colossus, heaven's neighbour, more closely sees the stars,
And lofty scaffolding the central highway bars,
The hated palace of a savage king once gleamed,
The entire city his one single dwelling seemed.
Where upward soars the Amphitheatre's great, prodigious mass,   5
An emperor's ornamental lakes we used to pass;
Where now we marvel, and on the Baths' instant blessings have gazed,
The hovels of hapless poverty Nero's proud acres razed.
Where now the portico of Claudius spreads its generous shade,
A palace's final footprints were once laid.   10
Now Rome is restored to Romans. By Great Caesar's patronage we see
A tyrant's pleasure-domes belong to you and me.

[Martial, On the Shows 2]

K14   Allocation of seats
Seats were allocated in the amphitheatre.

When L. Aelius Plautius Lamia and Q. Pactumeius Fronto were consuls [AD 80]. Received by Laberius Maximus, procurator, prefect of the corn-supply, when L. Ven{n}uleius Apronianus was president, and Thyrsus the freedman was secretary. For the Arval Brothers: in the first level, twelfth wedge, eight marble steps: on the first step 5ft and 15/48th, on the eighth step 5ft 15/48th, making 42½ feet {on the first step 22½ feet}. And on the {top} second level, sixth wedge, four marble steps: on the first step {one} «*words and figures accidentally omitted*» 22½ feet. And on the top level in the wooden seats, in the fifty-third section, eleven steps: one the first step 5ft 9/24, on the eleventh step 5ft and 45/48th Making 63ft and 23/24th. The sum total 129ft and 23/24th.

[*AFA* 48, lines 25–34]

The figures are complicated by the Roman method of giving fractions as a compound sum and using a range of symbols. The stone-cutter has, understandably, blundered, mistakenly adding letters, words and numbers {thus} and omitting others «*thus*». For the first level (*maeanium primum*) he has correctly given the number of rows, the width of seating allocated on top and bottom steps, i.e. rows (the same figure) and produced a correct total. For the second level (*maeanium secundum*) he has given the number of rows, but then jumped from mention of the first row to suddenly giving the total for this area of seating. (Assuming equal widths of seating, the arvals were allocated 5ft and 15/24th on each row here. On the top row he has again given figures for widths allocated on the top and bottom rows, though these figures differ slightly. The total is perfectly plausible and gives an average (in decimal!) of 5.81, compared to 5.375 for the first row and 5.94 for the top. The sum total has been correctly added. Modern stadium seats might be about 46cm (18 inches) wide. This would have given the arvals (twelve in number) room for 84 people, but on the simple benches we should assume a much higher number. The seating was hierarchical, with Arvals and guests seated on the first level, and figures like the freedman secretary, Thyrsus, mentioned here on a higher level.

K15   Capacity of the Amphitheatre
Amphitheatre which holds 87,000 places.

[Regionary Catalogues, Region 3]

Modern estimates suggest that the capacity might have been more like 50,000.

K16   Flavian Amphitheatre on *sestertius* of AD 80/81, Rome

Obv: Titus seated, facing left, on magistrates' chair with branch and scroll; weapons all around
        IMP T CAES VESP AVG P M TR P P P COS VIII (Emperor Titus Caesar
        Vespasian Augustus, *pontifex maximus,* tribunician power, father of the
        fatherland, consul 8 times) S C (by decree of the senate)
Rev: Detailed representation of amphitheatre in centre. *Meta Sudans* to left. Columned building
        to right.

[RIC 2.1 Titus 184 = BMCRE² 190, p.262 = BM no. 1844,0425.712]

A great many details visible in this coin help us to reconstruct original features of the amphitheatre. Statues
can be seen in the arches of the second and third storeys, with shields on the attic storey. Above the central
arch is a four-horse chariot, presumably driven by the emperor. These external features are also to be seen
on the 'Haterius relief'. Internally, a gallery can be seen at the top of the seating area as well as two other
tiers and some attempt to represent the imperial box. To the left of the amphitheatre is the *meta sudans*,
and to the right an unidentified building. The weapons on the obverse are probably an allusion to the
amphitheatre being built by Jewish slaves and possibly from Jewish spoils. Domitian issued (*c.* 81/82) very
similar *sestertii* (*RIC* Domitian 131) but with the legend 'To Divus Titus'.

K17   The One Wonder of the World
        Let barbarous Memphis mention wondrous pyramids
        No more; Assyrian toil not boast of Babylon;
        Diana's temple win no praise for camp Ionians;
        Let not the altar's many horns proclaim Delos;
        Nor Carians exalt to heaven with praise o'erblown   5
        Their Mausoleum which seems to hang in empty air.
        All labour is surpassed by Caesar's Amphitheatre,
        Fame shall speak of just one work instead of all.

[Martial, On the Shows 1]

Pyramids, Hanging Gardens of Babylon, Temple of Diana at Ephesus, and Mausoleum at Halicarnassus
form four of the standard wonders of the ancient world. An altar supposedly built by Apollo at Delos from
horns of animals slain by his sister, Diana, was included on the list by Plutarch at around the same time
(*Moralia* 983E). Martial claims there is now only one wonder of the world, the Flavian Amphitheatre.

K18   The World comes to Rome for the games
What tribe so barbarous or so remote, o Caesar
That there is no spectator from it in your city?
The farmers come from Thracian mountains known to Orpheus,
Sarmatians too, well fed on horses' blood, have come,
And those who drink the Nile's water where it rises,   5
With others who are struck by Ocean's farthest waves.
The Arab hurries here, Sabaeans hurry here,
And here Cilicians drip with clouds of their own perfume.
With hair curled in a knot, the Sugambri have come,
With hair curled differently, the Ethiopians.   10
Languages diverse are heard, but all unite
In calling you true Father of the Fatherland.

[Martial, *On the Shows* 3]

Though the Flavian Amphitheatre is not actually mentioned in this epigram, the nature of the attraction is shown by the previous two poems, and in particular it fits in with the idea of the amphitheatre as a wonder of the world. Cilicia was famous for saffron which could be used to make perfume and sprayed on spectators (see Coleman, *Martial*). Exotic names and customs from all round the boundaries of empire give the impression of world domination.

K19   Naval Displays in the Flavian Amphitheatre
Spectator, if you've got here late from far-off shores,
And this was your first day to watch the sacred show,
Don't let the boats and naval warfare lead you astray,
Or waves like sea: it *was* land here a moment since.
You don't believe it? Watch while water wears out war: 5
And very soon you'll say, "Just now this all was sea."

[Martial, *On the Shows* 27]

This poem provides clear evidence that the Flavian Amphitheatre could somehow be used for naval battles. This is supported by the accounts in Dio 66.25.2–3 and Suet. *Dom.* 4.1, but is not compatible with the network of brick passages and rooms now seen below the arena floor: presumably then these were later additions, maybe installed by Domitian to replace earlier wooden structures. Some trace of waterproofing has been found in the perimeter wall. See Coleman, *Martial*, pages lxviii–lxx.

ARCHES (K20–K25)
Arches were intended as a permanent reminder of a triumph, built afterwards but along the route, as both the arches for the Jewish triumph below. Pliny is one of very few Romans to mention arches (**K20**), though according to a joke reported by Suetonius (*Dom.* 13), the Greek word ἄρκι (*arci*) meaning 'enough' was eventually scrawled on one of Domitian's arches in Rome. Given Domitian's *damnatio memoriae* and the comment of Dio (**K25**), it is not surprising that nothing remains of any of his arches.

K20   The purpose of arches
The purpose of columns was for statues to be lifted above other mortals, which is also the message arches convey in their new reinvention.

[Pliny, *Natural History* 34.27]

K21   Arch of Titus in Circus Maximus, AD 80
The Senate and People of Rome to Emperor Titus Caesar Vespasian Augustus, son
of Divus Vespasian, *pontifex maximus*, holding tribunician power for the 10th time,
hailed *imperator* 17 times, consul 8 times, father of the fatherland, their *princeps*.
For having subdued the Jewish race, under his father's command, and following his
example and advice, and for having destroyed the city of Jerusalem which all previous
generals, kings and peoples had attacked in vain or left untouched.

[MW 53 = *ILS* 264 = EDCS–17301062]

The inscription comes from an arch erected at Rome in the Circus Maximus: it was recorded in the ninth
century but no longer survives. See further Levick, *Vespasian*, page 71.

K22   Arch of Titus in Roman Forum
The Senate and People of Rome to Divus Titus Vespasian Augustus, son of Divus
Vespasian.

[MW 108 = *ILS* 265 = EDCS–17301063*]

Probably the best-known Roman triumphal arch, standing at the East end of the Roman forum, and with
its inscription still clearly legible and its scenes from Titus' Jewish triumph still immediately recognisable.
On the underside, is a scene of apotheosis – Titus carried up to heaven on the back of an eagle. The
concentration on Titus alone here, in scenes and on inscription, shows that the arch was more of a memorial
to Titus than one actually erected for, or immediately after, the joint triumph. In fact much of the arch is a
modern rebuilding (by Valadier in 1822) once the arch had been disengaged from the medieval buildings
that had been built on to it, still clearly visible in prints by Piranesi (mid 18th-century). The inscription
above is repeated on each side of the arch.

K23   Arch of Domitian on *sestertius* AD 95/6, Rome

Obv: Bust of Domitian, laureate, draped and cuirassed, right.
           IMP CAES DOMIT AVG GERM COS XVII CENS PER P P (Emperor
           Caesar Domitian Augustus Germanicus, consul 17 times, censor for life,
           father of the fatherland)
Rev: Triumphal arch, showing two archways, surmounted by two elephant *quadrigae*.
           S C (by decree of the senate)

[*RIC* 2.1 Domitian 796 = BM no. 1978,1018.1]

K24   Triumphal arch with elephants
Other gifts witness the great merit of this place:
A sacred arch stands rejoicing over conquered races;
Here double chariots number many an elephant
He alone, in gold, is strong enough for the huge yoked beasts.   10
This gate is worthy of your triumphs, Germanicus:
Is it fitting for Mars' city to have such an entrance.

[Martial, *Epigram* 8.65.7–12 (published January 94)]

For the start of the poem on the Temple of *Fortuna Redux*, see **K57**, with note on Temple and arch.

K25   Destruction of Domitian's arches
The very many arches erected to one man were taken down.

[Dio 68.1.1]

K26   Baths of Titus
These baths probably remodelled Nero's private baths for public use, as suggested by Martial's poem, *On the Shows* 2.7–8 (**K13** above). They are mentioned by Suetonius (*Titus* 7.3) and by Dio (66.25.1) and Martial twice mentions them as an alternative to the Baths of Agrippa (3.20.15, 3.36.6). The chronicler of 354 and Jerome both attribute the baths to Domitian: it is not unlikely that further work was needed after their hasty inauguration by Titus. The site has been established, but remains are very meagre.

THE CAPITOLIUM (K27–K32)
The Capitolium or Capitol was properly the name for the south summit of the Capitoline Hill, occupied by the Temple of Jupiter Optimus Maximus Capitolinus and the *Area Capitolina*, a sacred area containing several other temples, altars and shrine. Tacitus describes the burning of the Capitol in December AD 69, in fighting between supporters of Vespasian, including Flavius Sabinus and Domitian who had taken refuge there, and those of Vitellius, as 'the most appalling and abhorrent crime ever to have happened to the Roman state and people since the founding of the city.' (*Histories* 3.72). Naturally the rebuilding was a priority for Vespasian (Tac. *Hist.* 4.4; Suet. *Vesp* 8.5; Dio 65.10.2). Tacitus, *Histories* 4.53 gives considerable detail about the ceremony initiating the rebuilding work on 21 June 70. It is already depicted on coins from AD 71. But this temple was destroyed again in the serious fire of AD 80 (Dio 66.24.1–2 = **C24**). Titus made vows to restore it (**A80c**). Suetonius records the rebuilding without any detail (*Dom* 5). Luckily we do have an eyewitness account by Plutarch (**K27**). The treasures of the temple were plundered over time; meagre archaeological remains are partly buried beneath Michelangelo's magnificent development of the Campidoglio (1536–1546).

K27   Plutarch's account
[2] When this second temple was again destroyed in the unrest at the time of Vitellius, Vespasian built the third temple, with the same good fortune in this as in all his other deeds. He saw it being built from start to finish, but did not see it being destroyed shortly afterwards, and in this respect he surpassed Sulla in good luck since the latter died before his work was dedicated, the former before it was destroyed. When Vespasian died the Capitol was burnt. [3] The current, fourth temple was completed and dedicated by Domitian. It is said that Tarquin spent forty thousand pounds (weight) of silver on the foundations: on the temple we see, the greatest private fortune calculated in Rome would not pay for the cost of gold which was more than twelve thousand talents. [4] The columns were cut from Pentelic marble and were of a width that was beautifully in

proportion to their height, as we know from seeing them at Athens. But when they were further worked and polished in Rome they did not gain as much in polish as they lost in proportion and beauty, appearing thin and hollow. [5] However if anyone, amazed at the great expense on the Capitol, were to see in Domitian's palace one portico or colonnade or bath-building or the room of one of his mistresses, then just as Epicharmus said to the spendthrift, 'you are not charitable, you just have an addiction to giving,' so someone brought before Domitian might say something like 'you are not pious or keen to be honoured, you just have an addiction to building; and just like the well-known Midas you want all your possessions to be of gold and marble.'

[Plutarch, *Life of Publicola*, 15]

Plutarch in his life of one of the figures of the very start of Rome's republic related how he wanted to be in charge of dedicating the first Temple of Jupiter which had been built by the Tarquins. He then digressed to give the history of the various buildings which replaced the original, including the two built in his own time, Vespasian's and Domitian's which he obviously saw in preparation and when complete. Pentelic marble is mined near Athens and was used to build the Parthenon. Epicharmus was a comic playwright active in the early fifth century BC.

K28   (Third) Temple of Jupiter Capitolinus, *sestertius* AD 76 (Rome)

Obv: Head of Vespasian, laureate, right.
        IMP CAES VESPASIAN AVG P M TR P P P COS VII (Emperor Caesar Vespasian Augustus, *pontifex maximus*, tribunician power, father of the fatherland, consul 7 times)
Rev: Temple of Capitoline Jupiter with six columns, statues in and around temple.
        S C (by decree of the senate)

[*RIC* 2.1 Vespasian 886 = *BMCRE²* 722, p.168 = BM no. 1872,0709.480]

Coins depicting the temple are known to have been minted from AD 71 to 77/8.

K29   (Fourth) Temple of Jupiter Capitolinus, *tridrachm,* Rome AD 82

Obv: Laureate head of Domitian, right.
         IMP CAES DOMITIAN AVG P M COS VIII (Emperor Caesar Domitian
         Augustus, *pontifex maximus*, consul 8 times)
Rev: Temple enclosing Jupiter seated between Juno and Minerva, standing.
         CAPIT RESTIT (Capitolium rebuilt)

                         [*RIC* 2.1 Domitian 841 = *BMCRE²* 251, p.351 = G.2219]

These coins, issued at Rome but for circulation in Asia make prominent the Capitoline triad (Jupiter, Juno
and Minerva) as well as coin legend, at the cost of accuracy of the image (compare below).

K30   (Fourth) Temple of Jupiter Capitolinus, *denarius,* AD 95/6

Obv: Head of Domitian, bare, right.
         DOMITIANVS AVG GERM (Domitian Augustus Germanicus)
Rev: Temple of Capitoline Jupiter, six columns, with Jupiter seated and two figures flanking him,
         between columns.
         (On temple architrave) IMP CAESAR (Emperor Caesar)

                         [*RIC* 2.1 Domitian 815 = *BMCRE²* 242, p.346 = BM no. R.11170]

K31   Roof of Temple of Jupiter Capitolinus
Gizeric sacked the Temple of Jupiter Capitolinus, and took off half the roof. This roof
was made of bronze of the finest quality, with thickly-plated gold on top, so that it
shone out most magnificently and as a great wonder.

                         [Procopius, *Vandal War*, 3.5.8 (AD 455)]

K32   Domitian's statues in the *Area Capitolina*

And so we see only one or two statues of yours in the vestibule of the Temple of Jupiter Greatest and Best, and these are made of bronze. Yet a short while back, every step of the approach, and the whole precinct shone here and there with gold and silver, or rather was polluted, since the statues of the gods were sullied by being mixed with those of an incestuous emperor.

[Pliny the Younger, *Panegyric to Trajan* 52.3]

Suetonius' version (*Dom.* 13.2, also supported by Dio 67.8.1 = **D8** and Eutropius 7.23.2 = **T2**) is that statues of Domitian on the Capitol had to be gold or silver and of a specified weight (perhaps 100 Roman pounds, the weight of the statue mentioned by Statius 5.1.191).

EQUUS MAXIMUS (K33–K35)

The *equus maximus* (massive horse) or *equus Domitiani* was a large, bronze equestrian statue of Domitian in the centre of the Roman forum, later destroyed as part of his *damnatio memoriae*. Traces of the base may be represented in the paving of the forum seen today (Claridge, *Rome*² page 91 and fig. 27.12). Statius devoted the first of his occasional poems, *Silvae* 1.1, to the dedication of the statue, and introduced the poem as follows, 'The first portion of the book has an unassailable witness [to the fact that each of Statius' poems took only a day or two to compose]: I had to adopt the rule 'Start with Jupiter'. These hundred lines which I composed on the great horse, I dared to give to our most indulgent emperor on the day after he had dedicated the work.' (Statius, *Silvae* 1 – introduction).

K33   The massive horse

What is this stands encompassing the Latin forum,
Its great size doubled by the colossus it bears?
Did it descend from heaven fully formed? Or moulded
In Etna's smithy, Vulcan's Cyclopes exhaust?
Or were you made, Germanicus, by hands of Pallas,   5
So that we could know just how the Rhine and mountain
Home of Dacian stunned, saw you with reins in hand.

[Statius, *Silvae* 1.1.1–7 (published 93/4)]

Vulcan, god of fire and blacksmiths was thought to work with the Cyclopes in Mt. Etna. Pallas Athene or Minerva was goddess of art as well as wisdom and Domitian's special patron (**L44–L49**).

K34   The position of the horse in the forum

From here, the Julian building views the spread-out flanks
From there, the lofty palace warlike Paullus built;   30
Your father and smiling Concord view it from behind.
While you outshine the temples, and, with head held high,
Enclosed by purest air alone, seem to gaze out.
Does the rebuilt Palace rise, in spite of flames,
More beautiful than ever? The Trojan fire keep guard   35
With secret torch, and Vesta praise her proven servants?
Your right hand forbids wars; your left is not weighed down
By virgin Pallas holding Medusa's severed neck,
As though to spur the horse. No better home the goddess
Could ever choose, not even the hand of the Father himself.   40

[Statius, *Silvae* 1.1.29–40 (published 93/4)]

So the statue stood facing south-east with the Julian Basilica to its right, to its left that of Aemilius Paullus. Behind it were the Temples of Vespasian (**K73**) and Concord. The rider would be able to see Domitian's new palace on the Palatine Hill, ahead and to his right and below the hill, the Temple of Vesta (where the flame traditionally brought by Aeneas from Troy was permanently kept alive) and the House of the Vestals. Statius alludes positively to the condemnation and horrific execution of the Vestal Virgin (see **L14**). The statue clearly depicted Domitian stretching out his right hand in commanding fashion ('forbidding war' – doubtless like the surviving statue of Marcus Aurelius on the Capitol) and carrying in his right hand a statuette of Minerva equipped with an *aegis* (shield decorated with picture of Medusa's head). For a further extract from the poem, see **L72**.

K35   Equus Maximus on *sestertius* of AD 95/6, Rome

Obv: Bust of Domitian, laureate, draped and cuirassed, right.
    IMP CAES DOMIT AVG GERM COS XVII CENS PER P P (Emperor Caesar Domitian Augustus Germanicus, consul 17 times, censor for life, father of the fatherland)
Rev: Equestrian statue of Domitian, right
    S C (by decree of the senate)

[*RIC* 2.1 Domitian 797 = BM no. 1978,1021.5]

FORUM OF PEACE *see* TEMPLE OF PEACE (K64–K72)

FORUM TRANSITORIUM (K36–K40)
Suetonius (*Domitian* 5) reports that Domitian built a forum, later renamed after Nerva. The long, narrow forum (about 120m x 40m) was between the Forum of Augustus and Vespasian's forum, the Temple of Peace (see below, and map of Rome, page 20). Effectively Domitian monumentalised the *argiletum*, a major road leading north from the Roman Forum, hence its name, '*transitorium*' or 'Passageway'. The sole part now visible consists of two columns, and a sculptured panel in a recess. This is known, after discovery of an identical, but labelled figure found at Aphrodisias, to show a personification of the Piroustae, a people from the Danube area. The forum, therefore, is likely to have shown a series of such figures, represented also in Domitian's triumph. The forum also featured a temple to Domitian's chosen patron goddess, Minerva, which may originally have given her name to the forum; and a Temple of Janus.

K36   Pallas' Forum
… look for Secundus, behind the entrance of Peace and Pallas' Forum.
[Martial, *Epigram* 1.2.7–8 (published *c.* 86)]

Secundus was a bookseller with copies of Martial's poems. Martial is the only writer to refer to the Forum as Pallas Athene's.

K37   Temple of Four-faced Janus in Domitian's forum
Most lovely father of the years and the bright world,
Whom public vows and private prayers do first invoke,
You used to have a tiny house on a thoroughfare
With all of Rome wearing a path through your midst.   5
Now your entrance is surrounded by gifts of Caesar,
And, Janus, you count as many fora, as faces.
But, holy father, in gratitude for such a gift,
Keep shut and bolted evermore your iron doors.
[Martial, *Epigram* 10.28 (published December 95)]

Janus was usually two-faced, but a statue from the town of Falerii, captured by Rome in 241 BC, showed him with four faces, thought to be linked with four points of the compass (Macrobius, *Saturnalia* 1.9.13). Domitian's square shrine allowed the statue to look at the *fora* of Julius, Augustus, Vespasian (Peace) and Domitian (*Transitorium*). But Martial also alludes to the more famous shrine and gates of Janus.

K38   Entrance of Janus
He who encircles with just laws and a forum
The warlike entrance of Janus.
[Statius, *Silvae* 4.3.9–10 (published 95)]

K39   Dedicatory inscription from Temple of Minerva, AD 97
Emperor Nerva Caesar Augustus Germanicus, *pontifex maximus*, holding tribunician power for the second time, consul three times, father of the fatherland, made the Temple of Minerva.
[*CIL* 6.953 = EDCS–17301071]

K40   Nerva dedicates forum and Temple of Minerva
He abdicated in the sixteenth month of his reign, after dedicating the forum which is known as 'Through-road' in which the Temple of Minerva rises rather loftily and magnificently.
[Aurelius Victor, 12.2]

K41   *Ludus Magnus* (The Large School for training gladiators)
Listed in one of the two 'Regionary' catalogues of buildings in the fourteen regions of Rome (Region III in 'Curiosum' not listed in 'Notitia') this was discovered only in 1937 and excavated in 1957, though the half of the structure visible today represents a restoration by Trajan rather than the original building built by Domitian and connected (literally, by underground passage) with the Flavian Amphitheatre. Its arena, only one quarter smaller than the amphitheatre's, provided space for gladiators to train and could be watched from seating for about 3,000 spectators. Barracks have also been excavated in the building.

Meta Sudans (K42)

The *Meta Sudans* or 'Sweating Post' is mentioned by the Chronicler of 354 (**K2** above), and appears next to the amphitheatre coins (**K16**). Its position can still be clearly seen, marked by shallow remains of a fourth-century colonnade. The concrete core still stood to a height of 9 metres until demolished in 1936. Domitian's monument probably replaced an earlier Augustan one, positioned at the intersection of several districts of Rome, but then turned into part of Nero's 'Golden House' estate. See Claridge, *Rome²* 307.

K42   Meta Sudans on *sestertius* of 80–81, possibly forged!

Obv: Head of Titus, laureate, right

       IMP T CAES VESP AVG P M TR P P P COS VIII (Emperor Titus Caesar Vespasian Augustus, *pontifex maximus*, tribunician power, father of the fatherland, consul 8 times)

Rev: Fountain on plinth (Meta Sudans).

       S C (by decree of the senate)

[RIC 2.1 Titus 165 = BMCRE² 189, p.261 = BM no. 1913,0614.12]

The coin has been tooled, with this reverse design possibly created in modern times.

K43   Obelisk of Domitian

This has now been incorporated into Bernini's magnificent *Four Rivers* fountain (1651) in the Piazza Navona. The obelisk is of Egyptian stone (Aswan granite) but the hieroglyphs were cut by Roman stonecutters, making them even harder to decipher! It is thought that the message is a hymn to Divus Vespasian, Divus Titus and Domitian and may refer to something being restored. Bernini took the obelisk from the race-track of Maxentius' villa, just outside Rome, built early in the fourth century, but it is not clear where it was originally (see Claridge, *Rome²* page 237).

Odeum (K44)

This building is listed by Suetonius (*Domitian* 5) and the Chronicler of 354 (**K2**) among Domitian's works. The term is used for a roofed theatre, staging musical and literary events, and Domitian's Odeum, like the Stadium immediately to its north, was presumably built for his Capitoline Games (see **Q16–Q19**). It was restored or possibly completed by Trajan's chief architect, Apollodorus (Dio 69.4.1), and greatly admired by Ammianus writing in the 4ᵗʰ century (**K4** above). Less spectacularly than the Stadium (see below), its shape has also left a mark on present-day buildings and streets, and an 8.6m green marble column from the stage-building has been set up almost *in situ*.

K44   Capacity of the Odeum

       Odeum holds 10,600 places

[Regionary Catalogues, Region 9]

PALATINE PALACE (K45–K48)

Domitianic buildings dominate Rome's Palatine Hill, to the extent of creating words such as 'palace' or 'palatial' in English and many European languages. The remains visible today (parts remain unexcavated) cover more than 3 hectares. Parts of the palace are 10 metres below the main ground level and some of the main rooms are thought to have been originally 30 metres in height (see **K47** note). Meanwhile the vast arcades still visible from where 200,000 Romans would have gathered to watch races in the Circus Maximus, are actually only substructures to support the parts of the palace that would otherwise have been on the slopes of the hill. Small wonder, then, that the contemporary accounts appear filled with hyperbole, **K45–K48**, also Martial 7.60. For an excellent account of the visible remains together with plans and reconstructions, see Claridge, *Rome²*, pages 124–8 and 145–156.

K45   Rabirius' Palatine palace

Rabirius, your pious mind has captured stars and sky,
Constructing Palatine home with wondrous skill.
If Pisa wants to give a temple fit for Pheidias' Jove
She'll seek Rabirius' hands from *our own* Thunderer.

[Martial, *Epigram* 7.56 (published December 92)]

Martial praises Rabirius' building of the Palatine palace as surpassing the Temple of Zeus at Olympia which housed Pheidias' statue of Zeus, a Wonder of the Ancient World. The Greek town of Pisa was responsible for the organising of the Olympic festival. Martial also equates Domitian ('our Thunderer') with Olympian Zeus in that he has a bigger home (critics pointed out that if Pheidias' seated statue Zeus were to rise, he would take the roof off his temple!).

K46   The Palatine Palace outdoes the pyramids

Caesar, laugh at those royal wonders, the pyramids;
Foreign Memphis now keeps quiet on Eastern buildings:
Egyptian toil is matched by one small part of Rome –
The palace. Day sees nothing finer in the world.
You'd think Rome's seven hills were rising together;   5
Ossa was smaller even with Pelion piled on it.
Heavenwards it goes so far that deep in the shining
Stars, its summit thunders clear above the level
Of the clouds, and bathes in Phoebus' hidden light,
Before Circe sees the face of her reborn parent.   10
Yet, Augustus, though the house roof strikes the stars
And equals heaven, it is smaller than its master.

[Martial, *Epigram* 8.36 (published January 94)]

Memphis was the capital of ancient Egypt, and where the Ptolemaic dynasty was crowned. The giants of Greco-Roman legend piled Mt Pelion on Mt Ossa in Thessaly in an attempt to reach Mt Olympus and dethrone Zeus. In Homer's *Odyssey* (10.135–9 and 12.3–4) Circe was daughter of the Sun, and lived at the extreme east of the world, thus being the first to see the sun each morning.

K47   Statius' description of the banqueting hall of the palace
A building huge, august, renowned for columns numb'ring
No mere one hundred, but as would support the sky
Were Atlas freed. The Thunderer's neighbouring palace gawps,   20
The gods rejoice that you are housed in like abode.
(May you be slow to climb the very heights of heaven!)
So wide extends the massive sweep of far-flung hall,
More spacious than a field, enclosing so much open
Sky, yet smaller than its master. He fills the house   25
And weighs it down with mighty spirit. There, rocks
Of Troy and Libya try to outshine each other, and dark
Syenan, Chian, stones that match the blue-grey sea,
And Lunan, only fit to be the base of columns.
Great views stretch high above: you scarcely see the roof   30
With faltering gaze; or think the ceiling that of golden heaven.

[Statius, *Silvae* 4.2.18–31 (published 95)]

For the start of the poem, thanking Domitian for the dinner invitation, see **T5**. Domitian's great dining room can be identified on the Palatine, though very little survives above floor level. The hall was square, its sides just over 30 metres long, and its height may have matched this. There was an apse at one end, opposite the great courtyard, and with smaller fountain courtyards on either side. For a fuller description and reconstruction, see Claridge, *Rome²*, pages 149–151.

Statius lists different types and colours of marble used in the palace. Rock of Libya = Numidian (orange/red); Rock of Troy = Synnadian (white with purple spots (Statius *Silvae* 2.2.88–9)); Syene = rose-coloured granite (Pliny *NH* 36.63); Chios marble was multi-coloured (*NH* 36.46); blue-grey sea (Statius names Doris, daughter of Oceanus and Thetis) = Carystian. Carraran marble, quarried at Luna in Etruria (N. Italy) was the type usually used at Rome (Strabo 5.2.5). It was brilliant white (Pliny *NH* 36.135), but since coloured marble was rarer and more expensive, it was thought in Domitian's palace (or Statius' poem) to be only fit for column bases. The coloured effect was clearly popular at the time as is clear from Statius' own description of Pollius Felix's villa at Sorrento (*Silvae* 2.2.85–94).

K48   The Palatine's dining-room, fit for the gods
Before this time no place could hold the banquets or
Ambrosian feasts of tables Palatine: But here,
Germanicus, you rightly drink the sacred nectar
And the cups mixed by the hand of Ganymede.
Long be it, pray, before you wish to dine with Jove;
But, Thunderer, come in person, if *you* can't wait.

[Martial, *Epigram* 8.39 (published January 94)]

K49   Romulus' hut restored
With you as guardian, ancient temples still are honoured,
The Hut's held sacred, midst the worship paid to Jove;
You found the new, Augustus, reinstate the old:
Things of present and of past owe debts to you.

[Martial, *Epigram* 8.80.5–8 (published January 94)]

In this poem, Martial praises Domitian (referred to as Augustus) for restoring traditions: these include (probably) some form of unarmed combat to the arena (lines 1–4) and, here, Romulus' hut on the Capitol, clearly honoured despite being overshadowed by the rebuilding of the Temple to Jupiter. The emperor Augustus had paid careful attention to Romulus as Rome's founder.

STADIUM (K50–K51)

Domitian's stadium now forms one of Rome's most beautiful and popular piazzas, the Piazza Navona, with the race-track now crowded with cafes, tourists, and artists, and medieval and renaissance buildings built on the solid foundations of the stands (275m x 106m overall). The length of the race-track (192m), was very similar to that of the stadia at Olympia and Delphi, and the stadium was built for the Greek-style games in honour of Jupiter Capitolinus, initiated in AD 86 (Suet. *Dom.* 5). It remained a venue for athletic games (Dio 75.16 for games of AD 200), and seen on the coin below. Domitian's stadium is also mentioned by Eutropius 7.23 (**T2**) and Jerome, and was still a prominent marvel in the fourth century (**K4**). It may be the stadium, rather than the amphitheatre, that is depicted on the 'Haterius relief'.

K50   The Stadium's capacity
Stadium holds 30,088 places

[Regionary Catalogues, Region IX]

This is an entirely plausible figure, given the known overall dimensions of the stadium.

K51   Stadium of Domitian on aureus of Septimius Severus, AD 201–210

Obv: Head of Septimius Severus, laureate, bearded, right.
           SEVERVS PIVS AVG
Rev: View of building, in shape of circus: double row of arches, with central arch (featuring statue group?) and another entrance on curve. Inside: runners, wrestlers, standing figures, wrestlers, seated figures.
           P P COS III (father of the fatherland, consul 3 times)

[*RIC* 4 260, p.124 (type) = *BMCRE*⁵ 319, p.216 = BM no. 1844,1015.170]

TEMPLES (K52–K73)

The Flavians and especially Domitian were responsible for the building of many temples in Rome. Some of these were restorations or rebuildings of temples destroyed by fire, especially the large fire of AD 80.

K52   The gods' debt to Domitian for all their temples
If, Caesar, you claimed back what you've already given
The gods, and heavens, and wished to be repaid; then even
If a great big auction were held in high Olympus
And gods were forced to sell all that they owned; then Atlas
Would be bankrupt and the father of the gods   5

Would not be able to pay one twelfth of what he owes.
What payment could he make for temples Capitoline,
Or the honour of the wreath on the Tarpeian Rock?
What could the Thunderer's wife pay for her two huge homes?
Minerva, as your agent, I pass by. No need   10
To mention Hercules, Apollo and the loving
Twins. Or Flavian temple new to Latium's sky.
Augustus, you will have to wait most patiently:
The treasuries of Jove have not the means to pay.

[Martial, *Epigram* 9.3 (published December 94)]

Martial refers to Temples of Jupiter Optimus Maximus (also one of the homes of Juno) and Jupiter Custos (line 7 and Suet. *Dom.* 5.1); Juno Moneta (line 9); Hercules on the Via Latina (line 11, see **K58**); Castor and Pollux in the forum (Lines 11–12, see **K2**); Temple of the Flavian Gens (line 12 – **K54–K56**). The poem attests a restoration of a Temple of Apollo, presumed to be that on the Palatine, built by Augustus.

K53   Temple/Portico of the Divi
Eutropius (**T2**) mentions the Portico as one of Domitian's main building projects, while the Chronicler of 354 lists it as a temple (**K2**). Though there are no visible remain above ground, excavations in the Campus Martius show a large portico (200m x 55m) surrounding individual temples to Vespasian and Titus.

TEMPLE OF THE FLAVIAN FAMILY (K54–56)
On the Quirinal, but the site has not been identified for certain (Claridge, *Rome²* p.391). Domitian made the family house where he had been born into a temple to the *gens Flavia* (Flavian family/tribe), as reported by Suetonius (*Domitian* 1.1) who also mentioned the temple in passing at 5.1 and 15.2, and tells us that Domitian's ashes were secretly placed there after his assassination (17.3). Book 9 of Martial's *Epigrams* contains many poems in praise of Domitian and the temple, suggesting a completion date of 94 for the temple, which also fits references in Statius, *Silvae* 4.3.18–19 and 5.1.239–241 (**K56**). Martial is able to liken the new temple to that on Crete built where, in mythology, the Curetes had nursed the infant Zeus, (**K55**, also epigram 9.34).

K54   Temple of the Flavian family
As long as the yearly cycle links Janus with winter,
Domitian with autumn, summer with Augustus,
As long as the great Kalends of Germanicus
Asserts its title grand of Rhine-enslavement day;
While still stands the Tarpeian rock of Father Supreme,   5
While suppliant matrons still placate, with hymns of praise
And incense, Diva Julia's sweet godhead:
So long stands tall that glory of the Flavian race,
With sun and stars and with the Roman day.
What's founded by invincible hand belongs to heaven.   10

[Martial, *Epigram* 9.1 (published December 94)]

This poem is in an unusual metre, possibly because Martial wanted to use 'Domitianus' here, alone in all his poems, as the name does not fit his two usual metrical schemes (Henriksen, *Commentary*).

K55   Domitian's birthplace monumentalised
This ground, which lies quite open and is being covered
With marble and gold, was once aware of the infant Lord.
That blessed ground resounded then with mighty wails,
Saw crawling hands and raised them up.
Here once stood the hallowed home which gave the world   5
What Rhodes and holy Crete gave to the starry sky.
Jove was once concealed by Curetes who clashed
Such weapons as unmanly Phrygians can bear:
But the father of gods protected you, and for you, Caesar,
Thunderbolt and aegis replaced spear and shield.   10
[Martial, *Epigram* 9.20 (published December 94)]

K56   Flavius Abascantus, imperial secretary
'Yes, I know this man, the servant of someone
Who has just founded a shrine for his eternal family.'
[Statius, *Silvae* 5.1.239–241]

For this poem see **S10**. Here Statius praises Abascantus for his monument to his wife by claiming that a
passer-by could tell from the magnificence of her tomb that it must have been made by an imperial freedman.

K57   Temple of Fortuna Redux (Fortune the Home-Bringer)
Here where shines the gleaming Temple of Fortune
The Bringer-Home, was recently a sacred space:
Here Caesar stood, adorned with dust from Northern war,
With purple radiance shining from his countenance;
Here Rome her hair with laurel crowned, and clothed in white   5
Did greet her leader with her voice and with her hand.
[Martial, *Epigram* 8.65.1–6 (published January 94)]

For the rest of the poem, describing an arch, see **K24**. *Fortuna Redux* or 'Fortune the Bringer-Back' had
been famously celebrated with an altar built by the senate in 19 BC in honour of Augustus' return from the
East. This temple and arch celebrated Domitian's return from his Sarmatian campaign and triumph in 93.
The temple and arch may be those shown on a relief panel of Marcus Aurelius also returning to Rome in
triumph over Sarmatians in 176 to be greeted by Roma: the panel was reused by Constantine on his arch.

K58   Temple to Hercules on the Via Appia
Caesar deigned come down to appear as Hercules
The Great and grants a new temple to the Latium Way,
Just where the traveller seeks Diana's wooded kingdoms
And reads the eighth marble milestone from the city.
He used, before, to receive vows and numerous victims,   5
Now, the lesser Hercules worships the greater.
The latter gets requests for great wealth, or for honours,
To the former, men, undaunted make their minor vows.
[Martial, *Epigram* 9.64 (published December 94)]

The temple is also included in Martial's list of temples built by Domitian, 9.3 (**K52**), but is not otherwise referred to in literature or known archaeologically. The 'Latium Way' is, presumably, Martial's unique designation for the Via Appia (which led to Latium, past Domitian's Alban Villa and the *Nemorensis Lacus* ('Wooded Lake' now Lake Nemi, with a Temple to Diana on its shore). This is the first of a pair of poems in honour of Hercules/Domitian: for the start of 9.65, see **L42**.

K59 Temple of Honour and Virtue restored by Vespasian

Cornelius Pinus and Attius Priscus made paintings for the Temple of Honour and Virtue which Vespasian was restoring.

[Pliny, *Natural History* 35.120]

The temple near the Circus Maximus was dedicated originally in 205 BC.

K60 Temple of Isis

Domitian rebuilt a temple to the Egyptian goddess Isis in Rome's Campus Martius after it had been destroyed by the fire of AD 80 (Dio 66.24.2; Eutropius 7.23; Jerome *Abr.* 2110). A monumental entrance arch to the temple area was also built, as recorded and labelled on the tomb relief of the Haterii. For personal links between the Flavians and Isis-worship, see **E6b**, **L24**, **L50** note.

K61 Monumental archway to Temple of Isis complex built by Haterii

Arch to/near Isis

[*CIL* 06, 19151 = EDCS–12101060*]

This very short, but ungrammatical, text (*arcus ad Isis*) is clearly carved as part of the detailed relief of five Flavian buildings on the Haterii tomb.

Temple of Jupiter the Guardian *see* L50

TEMPLE(S) OF MINERVA? (K62–K63)

Domitian associated himself closely with Minerva, see **L44–L49**, and **K52** above where Martial implies that Minerva is one of many gods who owes a debt to Domitian for his temple-building. Besides the Temple of Minerva in his forum, and the Temple of Jupiter, Juno and Minerva on the Capitol, various other temples are thought or known to have been built by Domitian in Rome for his patron goddess. The Chronicler of 354 (**K2**) mentions a Temple of Minerva of Chalcis and a Temple of the Castors and Minerva as being built by Domitian and both are mentioned in one of the two 'Regionary Catalogues' (**K62**). No satisfactory explanation has been found for why Castor and Pollux should have had a joint temple with Minerva, or where exactly it could have been. That of Minerva of Chalcis appears on a fragment of the Severan Marble Plan (see note on Temple of Peace, **K64**) as linked to the Portico of the Divi by a flight of stairs. A *denarius* from late in Domitian's reign shows a round temple with a cult statue which seems to be Minerva, and possibly represents one of these temples or else a temple that Domitian planned but did not live to complete.

K62 Temples of Minerva listed in catalogue of the city's buildings

Region VIII, 'The Great Roman Forum' contains … Temple of the Castors and Minerva …

Region IX, 'Circus Flaminius' contains … Iseum, Serapeum, Minerva of Chalcis, Of the Divi …

[Regionary Catalogue, *'Curiosum'* Regions 8 and 9]

K63   Temple of Minerva?, *denarius,* AD 95/6

Obv: Head of Domitian, bare, right.
        DOMITIANVS AVG GERM
Rev: Temple, round with four columns, with Minerva standing, helmeted, right hand raised and
        holding spear in left hand.
        IMP CAES (Imperator Caesar)

[*RIC* 2.1 Domitian 814 = *BMCRE²* 241, p.346 = BM no. 1925,0602.10]

TEMPLE OF PEACE (K64–K72)

The Temple of Peace (or really 'Pacification') was a large complex, containing the temple itself, a large
Latin library, and huge courtyard, each side more than 100m long, forming a forum area. The complex
took over a market area and celebrated victory in the Jewish War with treasures taken from Jerusalem
displayed there (**K64**). The complex also had the aspect of a public gallery for various genres of art, making
a deliberate contrast with works taken by Nero to decorate his Golden House (**K66**). The temple was badly
damaged around 190 (**K72**), and restored by Septimius Severus who had a detailed, huge marble plan of
Rome made and displayed there. By chance, fragments showing much of the complex, labelled 'Peace',
survive, so the general layout is quite well known. The complex was destroyed by serious earthquakes
(in 408) and/or lightning (Procopius, *Gothic War* 4.21) and thoroughly pillaged through the subsequent
centuries, as well having Mussolini build his six-lane road right through the middle, leaving little to be
found by recent archaeological excavations (Claridge, *Rome²* pp. 172–3). One hall of the complex does
survive, converted in 527 into the church of St Cosmas and Damian (with amazing sixth-century mosaics).

K64   Building of the Temple of Peace

*(For the account of the triumph itself, see **E6**)*

[158] When these triumphal processions were over and the affairs of the Romans
settled on steady foundations, Vespasian decided to build a Temple to Peace, which he
completed in such a short time and in such a glorious manner that it was beyond all
human expectations. [159] For he had a vast amount of wealth now, on top of what he
had gained in his other exploits, and had this temple decorated with masterpieces and
great statues. [160] For in the temple were collected and deposited all the works which
men had previously wandered all over the world to see, longing to see them one after
the other. [161] He had also placed there those golden vessels and instruments taken
from the Jewish Temple as symbols of his glory. [162] However he ordered their Law
and the crimson curtains of the Inner Sanctuary to be placed in the palace itself, for
safe-keeping.

[Josephus, *Jewish War* 7.158–162]

K65   The beauty of the Temple of Peace
We must surely include the following in our catalogue of outstanding architectural
works: for sheer magnificence there is the Basilica of Paullus, so famed for its
Phrygian columns, the Forum of the Deified Augustus, and the Emperor Vespasian's
Temple of Peace, the loveliest buildings the world has ever seen.

[Pliny, *Natural History* 36.102]

Pliny dedicated his *Natural History* to Titus shortly after the inauguration of the building, but his artistic
judgement was confirmed 250 years later by Ammianus (**K4** above).

K66   Temple of Peace displays publicly Nero's pillaged art works
Out of all these statues in bronze which I have mentioned, the most famous have now
been dedicated in Rome by the *princeps* Vespasian in his Temple of Peace and other
buildings. Nero had stolen them by force and arranged them in the lounges of his
Golden House.

[Pliny, *Natural History* 34.84]

Despite this 'nationalisation' of art from the Golden House, it seems the Flavians continued to use the
palace and kept some of the best items of art there – see *NH* 34.55 and 36.37 = **R32**.

K67   Temple of Peace displays paintings by old masters
[72] Timanthes painted a *Hero* of consummate artistry, embracing the whole skill of
painting men: this work is now at Rome in the Temple of Peace ... [102] Protogenes'
prized painting is his *Ialysus* which has been dedicated at Rome in the Temple of
Peace ... [109] Nicomachus painted ... a *Scylla* now at Rome in the Temple of Peace.

[Pliny, *Natural History* 35.74, 102, 109]

Pliny tells us that the *Ialysus* (founder of Rhodes) was so famous that in 305 BC King Demetrios lost his
chance to capture Rhodes through being unwilling to risk setting fire to the part of the city where the
painting was.

K68   Anonymous statue of Venus in Temple of Peace
We do not even know who made the [statue of] Venus, dedicated by Emperor Vespasian
in his Peace buildings, which deserved to be as well known as the old masters.

[Pliny, *Natural History* 36.27]

K69   Greywacke statue of Nile in Temple of Peace
The Egyptians discovered in Aethiopia a stone of the same hardness and colour
of iron, hence its name, 'basanites'. The very largest example of this stone is that
dedicated in the Temple of Peace by Emperor Vespasian. It depicts the Nile, with his
sixteen children playing around him, representing the number of cubits that the river
rises for the optimum fertility.

[Pliny, *Natural History* 36.58]

Basanites or greywacke is a hard, dark grey type of sandstone, quarried in the eastern deserts of Egypt.
Ancient Egypt officially fixed annual levels of taxation depending on that season's flood levels as measured
by 'nilometers'. A rise of 16 cubits (24 feet, 7.2m) was just right: too high a flood receded too slowly to
allow planting (Pliny *NH* 5.58).

K70   Vespasian dedicates cinnamon crowns in the Temple of Peace

The very first person to dedicate crowns of cinnamon, surrounded by embossed gold was Vespasian Augustus in the Temple of the Capitol and the Temple of Peace.

[Pliny, *Natural History* 12.94]

Cinnamon, obtained by the Romans from Ethiopia was extremely expensive.

K71   Library of Peace

We searched diligently for the *Commentary on Axioms* of L. Aelius, a learned man who taught Varro, and found and read it in the Library of Peace.

[Aulus Gellius, *Nights in Attica* 16.8.2]

Gellius also mentions the letters of Sinnius Capito found 'in the Temple of Peace' (5.21.9). Both these works being on grammar, the library may have specialised in works of grammarians.

K72   Destruction of the Temple of Peace

A small earthquake took place, then either a lightning strike happened during the night or fire broke out somewhere as a result of the earthquake, and the whole Temple of Peace burnt down, the largest and most beautiful of the buildings in the city. It was also the richest of all temples, decorated with gold and silver offerings because it was a safe place. Everyone used it as a place to keep their treasures.

[Herodian 1.14.3]

Herodian's history covers the period from AD 180 to 238 (his own day). The early parts of his work are sometimes unreliable: here he writes about a serious fire in Rome shortly before the death of Commodus in AD 191.

K73   Temple of Vespasian and Titus

To Divus Vespasian Augustus, the Senate and People of Rome
The Emperors Severus and Antoninus, both 'Caesar Pius Felix Augustus' restored (this)

[*CIL* 6.938 = 6.31210 = *ILS* 255 = EDCS–17301057*]

Three 14.2m columns and the end of the word 'restored' can still be seen at the north-west end of the Roman Forum. The full inscription was seen and copied for the Einsiedeln Itinerary. Despite the inscription, all the remains are Flavian in date (see Claridge, *Rome²* p.82, with figures 22 and 23), and the temple was described by the Chronicler of 354 (**K2**) and by both Regionary Catalogues (Region VIII) as 'Temple of Vespasian and Titus'.

AQUEDUCTS: K74–K81

K74   Vespasian and Titus restore the Claudian aqueduct, AD 71 and 81

Emperor Caesar Vespasian Augustus, *pontifex maximus*, holding tribunician power for the 2nd time, hailed *imperator* 6 times, consul for the 3rd time and designated for the 4th, father of the fatherland, restored to the city, at his own expense, the *aqua Curtia* and *aqua Caerulea*, created by Divus Claudius but afterwards interrupted and allowed to fall into disrepair for nine years.

Emperor Titus Caesar Vespasian Augustus, son of Divus, *pontifex maximus*, holding tribunician power for the 10th time, hailed *imperator* 17 times, father of the fatherland, censor, consul 8 times, oversaw at his own expense the complete remaking to a new design of the *aqua Curtia* and *aqua Caerulea*, created by Divus Claudius and afterwards restored to the city by his own father, Divus Vespasian, when they had fallen into disrepair through age right from their source.

[MW 408 = *ILS* 218 = EDCS–17800161*]

The original aqueduct, built by Claudius in AD 52, was 69 km long with the last 14.5 km carried on arches to reach Rome at a height sufficient to supply even the hillier parts of Rome (Frontinus, *Aq.* 18). Claudius celebrated its building with an inscription (LACTOR 19, K27) on the aqueduct above arches, which became a major gate in Rome's Aurelianic Walls (AD 271–5) now known as the Porta Maggiore. Vespasian and Titus in turn commemorated their efforts to maintain the aqueduct with inscriptions below Claudius'.

K75 Vespasian builds an aqueduct at Ostia, AD 77

Emperor Caesar Vespasian [Augustus, *pontifex maxmus,* holding tribunician power] for the 8th time, hailed *imperator* 1[7? times, father of the fatherland, consul 8 times, built] an aqueduct in the colony of Ostia.

[*AE* 2006, 00262 = EDCS–44100242]

K76 Titus repairs the Marcian aqueduct, AD 79

Emperor Titus Caesar Vespasian Augustus, son of Divus, *pontifex maximus*, holding tribunician power for the 9th time, hailed *imperator* 15 times, censor, consul 7 times, designated for the 8th time, father of the fatherland, rebuilt the channel of the *aqua Marcia*, fallen into disrepair through age, and restored the aqueduct which had stopped being in use.

[MW 409 = *ILS 98c* = EDCS–17700628*]

On arch of *aqua Marcia* crossing the *via Tiburtina* in Rome.

K77 Frontinus' list of Water Commisioners

Succeeding Fonteius Agrippa, when Silius and Galerius Trachalus were consuls [AD 68], Vibius Crispus. Succeeding Crispus, when Vespasian for the 3rd time and Cocceius Nerva were consuls [AD 71], Pompeius Silvanus. Succeeding Silvanus, when Domitian for the 2nd time and Valerius Messalinus were consuls [AD 73], Tampius Flavianus. Succeeding Flavianus, when Vespasian for the 5th time and Titus for the 3rd time were consuls [AD 74], Acilius Aviola. After him, when Emperor Nerva for the 3rd time and Verginius Rufus for the 3rd time were consuls [AD 97], the commission was passed to us.

[Frontinus, *On Aqueducts, 102.13–17*]

Frontinus was an exceptionally careful and accurate writer and administrator, in the best possible position to know the information he relates. So the dates he gives for Acilius Aviola as commissioner (AD 74–96) seems odd: either Aviola (cos. 54) served 23 years and died in a post which seven different men had held in the previous 14 years, all but one going on to other posts; or the apparently important and prestigious post fell vacant; or Frontinus is being discreet in not naming the men who served under Domitian and apparently allowed poor administration of the aqueducts; or, finally, some names have been accidentally omitted.

K78   Martial asks Domitian for an aqueduct branch to his home
I have – and pray it long be mine, while you reign, Caesar, –
A tiny farm, and a little place in Rome.
But from the narrow valley a crooked pump struggles
To draw up any water to give the thirsty garden,
My arid house complains no moisture nourishes it,   5
Although the aqua Marcia's fountain sounds near me.
The water that you give my household gods, Augustus,
Shall be to me the Castalian spring or shower of Jove.

[Martial, *Epigram* 9.18 (published December 94)]

The right to draw water from aqueducts was a direct gift from the emperor (Frontinus, *Aqueducts of Rome* 103, 105 = LACTOR 17, K59, K60). Martial's house in Rome was on the Quirinal hill (10.58.10, 11.1.9).

K79   Imperial freedman's career, including procurator of aqueducts
Ti. Claudius Bucolas, imperial freedman, taster of the head of table, procurator for public shows, procurator of aqueducts, procurator of the camp. He gave this as a gift along with his son, Q. Claudius Flavianus, and his mother, Sulpicia Cantabra.

[MW 205 = *ILS* 1567 = EDCS–22600426]

Inscription from Caere in Etruria. Bucolas is also named as procurator and freedman of Domitian on two water pipes (*CIL* 15.7279 and 7280). Frontinus reports that a freedman procurator was first appointed under Claudius and that the water commissioner would delegate to him the task of putting into effect grants of water from the emperor (Frontinus, *Aqueducts* 105). The inscription also shows a sort of career progression for an imperial freedman in Rome.

K80   New aqueduct for Peltuinum built by Vitulasius, cos AD 78.
Sextus Vitulasius Nepos, son of Lucius, of the tribe Quirina, consul, at his own expense brought the nearby Augustan aqueduct here with new sources and made new arches.

[MW 469 = *ILS* 9368 = EDCS–16700080*]

Vitulasius was consul in AD 78. Peltuinum was a town on the Via Claudia Nova in central Italy, presumably Vitulasius' home town as it was to Domitius Corbulo, Nero's general.

K81   Aqueduct at Lilybaeum (Marsala) in Sicily, AD 84
Emperor Caesar ~~Domitian~~ Augustus Germanicus, *pontifex maximus*, holding tribunician power for the 3rd time, hailed *imperator* 7 times, censor, consul 10 times, father of the fatherland, [saw to] the work of the aqueduct being constructed above ground and built anew with stone blocks …

[MW 410 = *ILS* 5753 = EDCS–22000813]

Found at Lilybaeum (modern Marsala) in Sicily and so showing a new aqueduct being brought to this important and prosperous town.

THE CORN-SUPPLY: K82–K85

The efficient supply of grain was of obvious importance to an emperor and his family living in a city of around one million people, 200,000 of whom at the time of Augustus were in receipt of free public supply, largely coming across the Mediterranean from North Africa (see Josephus, *Jewish War* 2.382 and 386 = LACTOR 19,.N1k and N1m). Claudius' various measures (LACTOR 19, K10–K21) had probably improved the situation, but Vespasian will have been fully aware of the potential vulnerability of the corn-supply, having himself at least threatened to cut off Rome in AD 69 (Tac. *Hist* 3.48). Thereafter, though, there is no record of shortages, although, unlike Claudius, the Flavians' only known building project relating to grain was the 'Granaries of Vespasian' (Chronicle of 354, under Domitian, (**K2** above). It was left to Trajan to carry out vast works at Portus/Ostia.

K82   Rome dangerously short of corn at start of AD 70

[38] Meanwhile Vespasian, for the second time, and Titus entered the consulship while away [in Egypt] … Because severe winter weather was delaying the ships, the common people who usually bought their food supplies on a daily basis, and whose one and only concern regarding public life was for the corn supply, was afraid that the coast was closed and the supply held up. … [52] [Vespasian said to Titus], that he would take care of peace and domestic affairs himself. Then he sent to sea his fastest ships, laden with corn, even though the seas were still rough: this was because Rome was tottering so dangerously that no more than ten days' corn supply was in the granaries, when supplies from Vespasian relieved the situation.

[Tacitus, *Histories* 4.38 and 52]

The normal sailing season was marked in Egypt on 5 March by the festival to the goddess Isis. Seneca, *On the shortness of life* 18.5 reported that only 7 or 8 days' supply was left at the time of Gaius' death. Such stories are possible, since the huge population of Rome relied heavily on corn imported from North Africa, but also make political points of the new emperor rescuing the situation just in time.

K83   Vespasian and the corn-supply, *aureus* of AD 77/8 (Rome)

Obv: Head of Vespasian, laureate, right.
        CAESAR VESPASIANVS AVG
Rev: Annona seated left, with sack of corn-ears.
        ANNONA AVG (Imperial corn-supply)

[*RIC* 2.1 Vespasian 963 = *BMCRE²* 290, p.51 = BM no. 1864,1128.37]

K84   Urban plebs in receipt of public corn
To Emperor Titus Caesar, son of Divus Vespasian, the urban *plebs* in receipt of public
corn and the [35] tribes.

[MW 468 = *ILS* 6045 = EDCS–17301061*]

Well preserved honorific inscription found in Rome. Fragments of two other inscriptions with the same text
have also been found.

K85   Domitian and the corn supply, *dupondius* AD 85

Obv: Head of Domitian, radiate, right.
           IMP CAES DOMITIAN AVG GERM COS XI (Emperor Caesar Domitian
           Augustus Germanicus, consul 11 times)
Rev: Annona (Corn-supply) seated right, with bag of corn-ears; to right, small figure standing left and
           in the background, stern of ship.
           ANNONA AUG S C (Imperial corn-supply; by decree of the senate)

[*RIC* 2.1 Domitian 286 = *BMCRE²* 304, p.365 = BM no. R.11313]

K86   Works on the Tiber's banks, AD 73
By the authority of Emperor Caesar Vespasian Augustus, *pontifex maximus*, holding
tribunician power for the 4th time, hailed *imperator* 10 times, father of the fatherland,
consul 4 times, and designated for a 5th time, censor. C. Calpetanus Rantius Quirinalis
Valerius Festus, curator of the banks and river bed of the Tiber, marked the boundaries
with a straight line.
           Next marker-stone 52 ½ feet
           Next marker-stone 174 feet

[MW 443 = *ILS* 5927 = EDCS–17700589]

Calpetanus Rantius had been consul in AD 71. A bad flood of the Tiber had occurred in 69 (Tac. *Hist.* 1.86.2).

ROADS IN ROME AND ITALY: K87–K94
Flavian road-building included works of restoration (**K87**, like the inscription on the *aqua Claudia* **K74**,
implying the negligence of the previous regime), as well as some new roads in Italy. There was also much

building of roads in the provinces, see **M11–M15**.

K87 Vespasian restores roads within Rome, altar, AD 71

Emperor Caesar Vespasian Augustus, *pontifex maximus*, holding tribunician power for the 3rd time, hailed *imperator* 8 times, father of the fatherland, consul for the 3rd time and designated for the 4th, by decree of the senate, because he restored to the city, at his own expense, the streets of the city, fallen into disrepair by the negligence of former times.

[MW 412 = *ILS* 245 = EDCS–17301050*]

K88 Tunnels on the Flaminian Way (under Vespasian)

[10] In addition mountains were cut through along the Flaminian Way to make its route level and this was popularly known as the 'Hollowed Rocks'.

[*Epitome de Caesaribus* 9.10]

K89 Via Appia repaved, AD 76 and 97

I

Emperor Caesar Vespasian Augustus, *pontifex maximus*, holding tribunician power for the 7th time, hailed *imperator* 17 times, father of the fatherland, censor, consul for the 7th time and designated for the 8th.

  Emperor Nerva Caesar Augustus, *pontifex maximus*, holding tribunician power, consul for the 3rd time, father of the fatherland remade [the via Appia].

[MW 413 = *ILS* 5819 = EDCS–21700021*]

Fine white column with decorated top and base and bands separating the three levels of text. The 'I' on the first line indicates that it was the first milestone of the *Via Appia* or Appian Way. This was Rome's first great road, built by Appius Claudius Caecus, who was censor in 312 BC. It was fully paved by *c.* 130 BC.

K90 Bridge on *via Cassia*, restored AD 77

Tiberius Claudius Caesar Augustus had this made.

Emperor Caesar Vespasian Augustus, *pontifex maximus*, holding tribunician power [for the 9th time], hailed *imperator* 18 times, father of the fatherland, consul for the 8th time and censor, restored it.

[MW 414 = *CIL* 11.2999 = EDCS–22200907]

Found on the still surviving *Ponte San Nicolao*, 50 miles north of Rome on *via Cassia*, now in Viterbo museum.

K91 Milestone at Pola on *via Flavia*, AD 78

Emperor Caes[ar] Vespasian [Augustus], *pontifex maximus*, holding [tribunician] power for the 10th time, [...] consul [for the 8th time and designated] for the 9th time, [built] the *via Flavia* [...]

[MW 415 = *ILS* 5831 = EDCS–05401240*]

The *via Flavia* on the coast of Istria connected Tergeste to Pola (Trieste to Pula – about 90km) and required impressive cuttings (Levick, *Vespasian* p.131). 4 milestones are known including *AE* 2006.459 found in Borgo San Mauro, near Udine, which shows a road to the north of Tergeste was built three years earlier.

Via Domitiana: K92–K94

'Third, I marvel at the *via Domitiana* which has removed a very lengthy delay caused by the sands.' Statius, *Silvae* 4 introduction. The *via Appia* was the main route South from Rome to Campania and beyond. It was built by Appius Claudius Caecus, (censor in 312 BC) from Rome to Capua, with paving begun in 295 BC. Later the main *via Appia* was extended all the way to the heel of Italy and a branch to Puteoli. The *via Domitiana* took a straight line along the coast from Sinuessa where the Appia diverted inland to Capua and Puteoli. As Sinuessa-Capua-Puteoli form virtually an equilateral triangle, Domitian's road halved the distance from Sinuessa to the popular resort of Baiae and the important towns of Puteoli and Misenum. The route, according to Dio 67.14.1, was completed at the same time as the execution of Flavius Clemens, securely dateable to 95. It measured around 30 miles. Parts of the road, and an arch are still visible, just north of Puteoli (pictures and much excellent detail in Coleman, *Statius Silvae IV,* (Oxford 1988) pages 102–135). Statius' poem is in a metre (hendecasyllables) unusual for him, but probably designed to convey speed.

K92   **Statius celebrates the *via Domitiana***
What mighty sound of hardened flint
And toughened iron has filled the side
Of Appian, paved along the coast?
Not the noise of Libyan hordes
Nor foreign duke with treacherous wars   5
Who shakes unquiet Campanian fields.
Nor Nero cutting through mountains,
Disturbing shallows, channeling swamps.
No – he who rings the warlike steps
Of Janus with just laws and forum;   10
Returns to Ceres chaste those acres long
Purloined and sober fields; who stops
The stronger sex from dying out;
As censor won't let adult males
Fear they'll pay for their good looks;   15
The Capitol to Thundering Jove
Restores, and Peace to her own home;
Who consecrates to his father's race
Eternal home and Flavian heaven;
Who irked by people's slow journeys   20
And plains that hold back every trip
Cuts out long detours and by adding
A new base shores up wet sand;
Pleased to bring the Sibyl's home,
Baiae's hot springs and Gauran lakes   25
Closer to the seven hills of Rome.
(The next nine lines describe the slowness of the previous route)
But now the road is made, what used
To take all day takes just two hours.   37

[Statius, *Silvae* 4.3.1–37 (published 95)]

3–6: Hannibal the famous Carthaginian general campaigned in Italy between 217 and 203 BC and would certainly have marched his troops along the Appian Way.

7–8: Nero had attempted to build a canal from Campania to Rome (Tac. *Ann.* 15.42).

9–10: For Domitian's temple of Janus within his forum, see **K37–K38**.

11–12: Domitian banned the planting of vines in Italy in 91/2: hence fields became 'sober' – see **S29–S30**.

13–15: Domitian's legislation banning male castration – see **S28–S29**.

16–19: Domitian's building in Rome: the Temple of Jupiter, Temple of Peace, Temple of Flavian Gens.

24–26: Statius mentions three well-known areas near the terminus of the *Via Domitiana* at Puteoli, namely the Sibyl's cave at Cumae, Mons Gaurus (now Monte Barbaro), and Baiae, a favourite Roman bath-town. The Puteolans' inscription (**K93**) also describes the road as bringing their town closer to Rome.

38ff: the poem continues with description of the road-laying process and comparison to other world-famous engineering projects (38–60); the river Volturnus, crossed by a new bridge, blessing the enterprise (67–94) and also the Sybil at Cumae predicting long life for Domitian (124–163).

K93   Puteoli moved closer to Rome

~~To Emperor Caesar Domitian Augustus Germanicus, son of Divus Vespasian, *pontifex maximus*, holding tribunician power for the 15th time, hailed *imperator* 22 times, consul 17 times, censor for life, father of the fatherland; the Flavian Augustan Colony of Puteoli, having been moved closer to his city, through the condescension of the greatest and divine Princeps.~~

[*AE* 1941, 73 = *AE* 1955, 283 = *AE* 1973, 137 = *AE* 2001, 842 = EDCS–15100073]

An attempt was made to erase the whole inscription, dating to AD 95, but almost all can be clearly read. Puteoli was 'moved closer to' Rome as the *via Domitiana* cut from the journey a detour of about 30 miles.

K94   Curator of the *via Domitiana*

[(*Name and first posts of honorand lost*) … curator] for the construction of the new [road] as far as Puteoli, prefect of the tr[easury] of Saturn, c[onsul].

[*AE* 1961, 282 = *AE* 1992, 661 = EDCS–10900042]

Though we don't know who was honoured, this Latin inscription from Albintimilium (modern Ventimiglia in Liguria (NW Italy) shows that Domitian created a special position of responsibility for his new road.

K95   The Alban Villa

This, Caesar, is for you, perhaps enjoying the hills of Pallas' Alba,
Looking out at Diana Trivia on one side, at Thetis on the other.

[Martial, *Epigram* 5.1.1–2 (published December 90)]

Martial dedicates his book to Domitian in his Alban villa. Alba was Pallas' because Domitian used to celebrate Minerva's annual festival on 19 March there (Suet. *Dom.* 4.4, Dio 67.1.2 = **D1**). Diana's temple was on the shore of Lake Nemi, 5 miles south-east of the villa, which overlooked the Alban Lake, referred to here as Thetis, the sea-goddess.

K96   Water supply to the Alban villa

[In centre of pipe] Alb[an villa]
[On either side] Of Emperor Caesar Domitian Aug., under the care of Alypus procurator, Esychus and Hermeros, slaves, made this.

[MW 227 = *ILS* 8680 = EDCS–05800270]

BUILDING AND RESTORATION WORK IN ITALY: K97–K101

Emperors would assume that buildings outside Rome were the responsibility of the local community itself, or of a local magnate, or politician. This pattern can be seen very clearly in Pompeii and Herculaneum and in **K97–K98** below. Direct interventions are exceptional, those below being explicable through Vespasian intervening in an area where *he was* the local magnate (**K99**), or through a major disaster, such as the eruption of Vesuvius and associated earthquakes (**K100, K102,** Suet. *Titus* 8.3–4). Cremona, sacked by Vespasianic troops after the second battle of Cremona, had its 'temples and forums restored by local townspeople: Vespasian provided encouragement.' (Tac. *Hist.* 3.34).

K97   Puteoli's amphitheatre
The Flavian Augustan colony of Puteoli, at its own expense.

[MW 470 = EDCS–59900061]

The amphitheatre at Puteoli (modern Puzzuoli) on the Bay of Naples was built under the Flavians. It seated around 20,000 and offers the best preserved examples of the subterranean passageways also provided for the Flavian Amphitheatre at Rome. Four examples of this inscription, variously preserved have been found.

K98   Amphitheatre at Urbs Salvia built by Flavius Silva
[Lucius Flavius] Silva Nonius Bassus, [son of …], of the Velina tribe, consul, pontifex, [propraetorian imperial legate of the p]rovince of Judaea, co-opted amongst the patricians [by Divus Vespasian and] Divus Titus as censors and co-opted amongst the praetorians by the same; legate of Legion XXI 'Plunderer', [tribune of the plebs, quaestor, mi]litary tribune of Legion IIII 'Scythian', on the board of three for capital charges, twice quinquennial praetor, patron of his colony. In his own name and that of his mother, […]tta and also that of his wife, […]milla, with his own money, and on his own land, he oversaw [the making of the amphitheatre] and dedicated it with 40 pairs of normal gladiators. 650 places to the plebs of Urbs Salvia from those hono[ured? …]

[*AE* 1961, 140 = *AE* 1995, 434 = EDCS–30301637]

Two identical monumental inscriptions from the ruins of the amphitheatre at Urbs Salvia in Italy, which Flavius Silva, cos ord 81, conqueror of Masada in Judaea, built for what was presumably his home town.

K99   Restoration of Temple of Victory in Sabine territory, AD 73–79
Emperor Caesar Vespasian Augustus, *pontifex maximus*, holding tribunician power, censor, restored at his own expense the Temple of Victory, fallen into disrepair through age.

[MW 432 =*ILS* 3813 = EDCS–05801474]

Varia (modern Vicovaro) is about 25 miles south of Reate, where Vespasian used to spend the summer. He might have felt it appropriate to restore a temple to Victory in his home territory.

K100   Restoration of Temple of Magna Mater at Herculaneum, AD 76
Emperor Caesar Vespasian Augustus, *pontifex maximus,* holding tribunician power for the 7th time, hailed *imperator* 17 times, father of the fatherland, consul 7 times, designated for the 8th time, restored the Temple of the Mother of the Gods which had collapsed in an earthquake.

[MW 433 = *ILS* 250 = Cooley[2] C6 = EDCS–11500340*]

Large marble building inscription, broken into 5 pieces, but well preserved. The same year also saw Vespasian complete another restoration of earthquake damage (Cooley[2] E32).

K101 Disaster relief by Titus

[12] At this period, Mount Vesuvius in Campania began to burn, and a fire at Rome continued unabated for three whole days and nights. [13] There was also a plague, almost as great as any previous one. [14] But no one else suffered in the face of these disasters, since he used his own money and all sorts of remedies, now helping the sick in person, now consoling those mourning the deaths of their family.

[*Epitome de Caesaribus* 10.12–14]

K102 Restoration of earthquake damage at Naples, second half of AD 80

Emperor Titus Caesar Vespasian Augustus, son of Divus Vespasian, *pontifex maximus*, holding tribunician power for the 10th time, hailed victorious general 15 times, consul 8 times, censor, father of the fatherland, restored buildings that had collapsed in the earthquake [at Naples] when he had been [leader of the people], president of the games for the third time, and gymnasiarch.

[MW 54 = *CIL* 10.1481 = EDCS–11500415]

A large stone, with inscription in both Greek and Latin. The Greek inscription lists Titus' Roman titles and the honorary Greek titles he held at Naples. Emperors were regularly made honorary local magistrates as shown in various inscriptions at Pompeii. Naples had obviously honoured Titus as *agonothetes* (president of the games) prior to the eruption and was happy to give him further honorary titles in the wake of the eruption of Vesuvius and his (considerable) rebuilding efforts (Dio 66.24; Suet. *Titus* 8.3).

K103 Sun-dial at Sorrento restored AD 80

Emperor Titus Caesar Vespasian Augustus, son of [Divus] Vespasian, *pontifex maximus,* holding tribunician power for the [9th] time, [hailed *imperator* 15 times], consul 8 times, censor, father of the fatherland, [restored] the sun-dial [with its] decorations [which had collapsed] because of earthquakes.

[*Epigraphica* 2002.141 = *AE* 1902.40 = EDCS–16800221*]

K104 Temple to Bona Dea near Tivoli rebuilt by imperial contractor

To Bona Dea the most holy and heavenly, L. Paquedius Festus, contractor of public and imperial works, rebuilt her ruined temple because by her assistance he completed the channel of the Claudian Augustan aqueduct under Mount Aeflanus. On 3 July in the 14th consulship of Domitian Caesar Augustus Germanicus [AD 88].

[MW 165 = *ILS* 3512 = EDCS–05801519*]

Marble plaque found at Aefula (modern San Gregorio da Sassola) on Mt Aeflanus (now Monte Cerella) which overlooks Tibur (Tivoli). Four aqueduct channels pass nearby on the way to Rome (15 miles distant).

PUBLIC LAND RESTORED IN ITALY: K105–K110

'In Italy Vespasian restored to communities lands that had illegitimately passed into private possession. That did not directly benefit his exchequer: but cities with adequate revenue were less likely to call for imperial aid.' (Levick, *Vespasian* p.99)

K105   Vineyard in Rome restored to public ownership, AD 75

Emperor Caesar Vespasian Augustus, *pontifex maximus*, holding tribunician power for the 6th time, hailed *imperator* 14 times, father of the fatherland, consul for the 6th time, designated for the 7th time, censor, restored, through the college of *pontifices*, an area of public vineyard occupied by private individuals.

[MW 430 = *ILS* 249 = EDCS–17301052*]

K106   Boundaries restored at Canusium in Apulia, AD 76

Emperor Caesar Vespasian Augustus, consul 7 times restored the borders of the public fields of the town of Canusium, from public plans.

[*AE* 1945.85 = EDCS–12800112*]

Canusium is near the Adriatic coast of S. Italy

K107   Boundaries restored at Capua in Campania, AD 77

Emperor Caesar Vespasian Augustus, consul 8 times restored the borders of the fields consecrated to Diana Tifatina by Cornelius Sulla on the plan of Divus Augustus.

[MW 444 = *ILS* 251 = EDCS–17800441*]

Stone marker at Capua in Campania (AD 77). The Tifata was the mountain ridge north of Capua (modern Monte Maddaloni). Cornelius Sulla was very prominent in the area of Campania in the 'Social War', *c.* 90 BC.

K108   Suedius Clemens inquires into land ownership at Pompeii

By the authority of Emperor Caesar Vespasian Augustus, T. Suedius Clemens, tribune, made an inquiry into public lands appropriated by private individuals, carried out a survey and restored them to the Pompeian state.

[MW 339 = *ILS* 5942 = Cooley² F148 = EDCS–11401108*]

The actions of his agent at Pompeii, who undertook to investigate the usurpation of public lands by individuals and to reassign them to the town, was typical of Vespasian's initiatives as a whole. Multiple copies of this inscription were set up outside various city gates. Suedius Clemens' support was also invoked by one candidate for local elections (Cooley² F149, F151).

Tacitus gives attention to Suedius Clemens in his *Histories* as being Otho's commander, responsible for the raid on Narbonese Gaul in which Agricola's mother (Tacitus' wife's grandmother) was killed (*Hist.* 2.12 and *Agr.* 7). Despite this he served Vespasian (**K108**) and was promoted to prefect of the camp in Egypt (*CIL* 3.33), writing his name on the Memnon monument (see **M28** and note) on 11 November, AD 80.

K109   Frontinus

Land allocated to no one could not belong to anyone except the person entitled to allocate it.

[Frontinus, *Contr. Agr.* in *Grom. Vet.* 1.54 Lachman]

Levick, *Vespasian* p.99 suggests that Frontinus could conceivably be using Vespasian's words in this except from a work on land ownership.

K110   Domitian reverts to the position that 'possession is nine tenths of the law' AD 82

Emperor Caesar ~~Domitian~~ Augustus Germanicus, son of Divus Vespasian, *pontifex maximus*, holding tribunician power, hailed *imperator* 2 times, consul 8 times and designated for the 9th, father of the fatherland, greets the magistrates and councillors of Falerio in Picenum.

What I have decided about the unclaimed land, after hearing the case between you and the Firmani, I have ordered to be appended to this letter, so that you might take note.

On 19 July, when P. Valerius Patruinus and ~~L. Antonius Saturninus~~ were consuls. I, Emperor Caesar Domitian Augustus, son of Divus Vespasian, after summoning distinguished men from both classes and hearing the case between the Falerienses and the Firmani, have pronounced as follows: The long-standing dispute which after so many years has been reopened by the Firmani against the Falerienses, disturbs me greatly, since for the peace of mind of those in possession, it could have taken many fewer years. Furthermore, a letter of Divus Augustus, a *princeps* most painstaking and gracious towards his men of Legion IIII, advises them to gather together all their unclaimed land and to sell it, and I am sure that they obeyed such helpful advice; therefore I confirm the rights of those in possession. Farewell.

Given on 22 July in the Alban Villa, under the care of T. Bovius Verus; the envoys were P. Bovius Sabinus, P. Petronius Achilles. Made public by decree of the town council.

[MW 462 = *CIL* 11. 00095,1 = EDCS–16100770*]

This bronze tablet found at Falerio in Italy (Picenum) monumentalises a letter from Domitian about a local land dispute. His decision ties in exactly with what Suetonius states, (*Domitian* 9.3), that plots of land left over after allocation to veterans should continue to be held by those in possession of them. That possession was ten tenths of the law was enshrined in Rome's earliest laws, the 'Ten Tables', but Vespasian's actions had probably encouraged some disputes.

SECTION L

RELIGION

Holy rites desecrated, adultery in high places.

[Tacitus, *Histories* 1.2.2]

Introduction: material in this section is arranged by theme, moving roughly from traditional republican practice towards worship of the emperor. **L1–L9** show the Flavians holding traditional priesthoods and rebuilding temples. **L10–L16** concern the trials of the vestal virgins. **L17–L21** are about the Centennial Games. **L22–L27** display the Flavian interest in Eastern religions while **L28–L40** show ways in which indirect worship of the emperors was continued along the lines established under Augustus. One aspect in which Domitian seems to have expanded on precedents is in adopting a patron goddess, Minerva, and links between emperors and gods, **L41–L54**. Worship of living members of the imperial family is shown by **L55–L61**, while the final section, **L62–L75** contains documents relating to official deification. Latin uses the word *divus* (feminine *diva*) to refer to deified mortals, rather than the related word for 'proper' gods or goddesses (*deus/dea*). Greek, however, uses θεός/θέα for both. Throughout the volume 'Divus/Diva' is left in the original Latin; *deus/dea* is translated as god(dess) when simply referring to an Olympian deity, but is explicitly noted when referred to a mortal; 'god' translates the Greek θεός, whether for men or Olympian gods.

THE FLAVIANS AND TRADITIONAL RELIGION: L1–L9

L1   Four symbols of priesthoods on *denarius* of AD 71 (Rome)

Obv: Head of Vespasian, laureate, right.

[IMP] CAES VESP AVG [P M] (Emperor Caesar Vespasian Augustus, *pontifex maximus*)

Rev: Priestly implements (*simpulum* (ladle), aspergillum or sprinkler, jug and *lituus* (*augur's* staff).

AVGVR / PON MAX (Augur, *pontifex maximus*)

[*RIC* 2.1 Vespasian 42 = *BMCRE²* 48, p.8 = BM no. R.10374]

The coin recalls ones minted by Augustus in 16 BC showing him with four symbols of different priesthoods he held (*RIC* Augustus 367 = LACTOR 17, L1). Rüpke, *Fasti Sacerdotum* suggests Vespasian (no. 1720) was augur and *sodalis Titii* (soon after receiving triumphal ornaments for success in Britain in AD 44), and arval and *pontifex maximus* by his return to Rome in AD 70, but not co-opted into all priesthoods, unlike his sons (**L3** and **L5**).

L2 Titus appointed as additional *sodalis Augustalis Claudialis*, AD 71

Section 28. T. Caesar Imperator, son of Augustus, was appointed to our number, by decree of the senate, when Emperor Caesar Vespasian Augustus for the 3rd time and M. Cocceius Nerva were consuls, 824 years after the founding of Rome.

[MW 152 = *ILS* 5025 = EDCS–18100802]

The lists of the *Sodales Augustales Claudiales*, Rome, a socially-prestigious priesthood instituted at the death of Augustus with 21 leading citizens (Tac. *Ann.* 1.54.1–2) to establish dynastic cult. Later they increased to 27 in number and included Claudius (Suet. *Claud.* 6.2). A 28th priesthood was specially created for Titus, and not filled again for 100 years after his death (Rüpke, *Fasti Sacerdotum* T. Caesar Vespasianus, no. 1017).

L3 Titus as priest of all colleges, AD 71

To T. Caesar Vespasian, [son] of Augustus, hailed *imperator*, holding tribunician power, consul, censor-designate, priest of all the colleges.

[MW 102 = *ILS* 258 = EDCS–00900158*]

Statue base found at Rome

L4 Temple of Vesta, *aureus* AD 73 (Rome)

Obv: Laureate head of Vespasian, right.
IMP CAES VESP AVG CEN (Emperor Caesar Vespasian Augustus, censor)
Rev: Round Temple of Vesta, with four columns and podium of four steps; statues to left, right and in centre.
VESTA

[*RIC* 2.1 Vespasian 515 = BM no. 1996,0316.13]

Coin found as part of the Didcot hoard (Oxfordshire, 1996). Vesta coins in various denominations were frequently issued under Vespasian, especially around 73 and by Titus throughout his short reign. Vesta's flame symbolically safeguarded Rome.

L5 Domitian priest of all colleges, AD 73–76

To Domitian, consul [2/3/4] times, priest of all the colleges, leader of the younger generation.

[MW 115 = *ILS* 267 = EDCS–15300004*]

A dedication from Cures, the home town of Vespasian.

L6   Nero's colossus converted to the Sun-god

Zenodorus was summoned by Nero to Rome where he made the colossus, over 100 feet tall, intended as a statue of the emperor, but now dedicated to the Sun, after condemnation of the crimes of that *princeps.*

[Pliny, *Natural History* 34.45]

Martial twice mentions the colossus (*On Shows* 1.2.1 and *Epigrams* 1.70,7–8), while Suetonius, *Vesp.* 18 mentions the artist responsible for the remodelling being generously paid.

L7   Vespasian and Sun-god (Sol), on *denarius* (Rome)

Obv: Head of Sol, facing (no legend)
Rev: Vespasian standing left with right arm raised and transverse spear in left hand.
        VESPASIA NVS

[*RIC* 2.1 Vespasian 689 = *BMCRE²* 47, p.8 = BM no. 1897,0305.82]

Only the specimen in the British Museum is known, and the coin is undated and undateable, but could relate to Vespasian converting Nero's colossus into the sun. The long hair suggests a traditional view of sun-god as Apollo or Helios, rather than as *sol invictus* which later became extremely popular.

L8   Vespasian celebrated for upholding traditional religion, AD 78?

[To the emperor] Caesar Vespasian Augustus, *pontifex maximus,* holding tribunician power for the [9th] time, hailed *imperator* 17 times, consul 8 times, designated for a 9th time, censor. He preserved the public ceremonies and restored the sacred temples: erected by the *sodales Titii* (members of the fraternity of Titius).

[MW 151 = *ILS* 252 = EDCS–17301053]

This stone was seen and recorded in the 15th century near the Capitol in Rome, but is now lost. As recorded, the consul and 'Imperator' numbers are inconsistent. It has been suggested (*AE* 1980.41 and given in EDCS) that the dedication is to Titus, which works for the other numbers, but Titus was not designated consul for 81. The *sodales Titii* were an ancient order of priests revived by Augustus, of uncertain significance, but socially prestigious.

L9   Domitian rebuilds the Temple of Apollo at Delphi, AD 84

Emperor Caesar Domitian Augustus Germanicus, son of Divus Vespasian, chief priest, holding tribunician power for the 3rd time, father of the fatherland, hailed *imperator* 7 times, consul 10 times and designated for the 11th time, rebuilt the Temple of Apollo at his own expense.

[MW 463 = *ILS* 8905 = EDCS–30000399]

This Latin inscription is preserved as part of a dossier of inscriptions also including an inscribed letter from Domitian expressing support for the Pythian Games – see **Q22**. Delphi was one of the most important religious sites in the ancient world.

PUNISHMENT OF VESTAL VIRGINS FOR BREAKING THEIR VOWS: L10–L16

This episode (actually episodes) is often taken as proof of Domitian's malevolent cruelty. In fact the several near contemporary sources suggest Domitian was severe but just, and piously concerned with upholding religious law and moral values. Suetonius, *Domitian* 8.3–4, though without indicating dates, gives a clear account of the two separate trials and various punishments, which he includes in a long section about Domitian's fair giving of justice. Jerome's *Chronicle* provides the only explicit dating: his dates for the Flavian period are mostly accurate and the dates he gives are entirely plausible. Statius mentions Vesta's 'proven servants' (*Silvae* 1.1.35–6 = **K34**). Tacitus was presumably thinking of the Vestals when he characterised the period of his *Histories* as including 'religious rites profaned, adultery amongst the great' (1.2); his main narrative is, of course, lost. Plutarch's factual and contemporary account shows why the affair attracted so much attention. Pliny the Younger used the second case to vilify Domitian in a letter written well after Domitian's death ('The whole letter is a remarkable example of special pleading.' Sherwin-White, *Commentrary* on 4.11.5). Dio 67.3.2 and 4.1 (**D3, D4**) takes a negative and sensationalist view, while Philostratos takes Domitian's behaviour as so outrageous as to justify sarcasm. But compare Jones, *Domitian* 101–2, concluding 'the entire affair exemplifies the attention Domitian paid to the letter of religious law.'

L10   Jerome's Chronicle, for AD 83
Three Vestal virgins condemned for adultery.

[Jerome, *Chronicle*, year 2099 after Abraham = AD 83]

L11   The first Vestal trial
Domitian was in fact rather proud of the fact that he did not follow tradition and bury alive those Vestals who were convicted of having intercourse with men, but had them put to death in other ways.

[*On Virtues and Vices*, Valesius' Excerpts 278 = Dio 67.3.4.1]

This represents the 'First Vestal Trial', see Suet. *Dom.* 8.3. For the second, see **L14**.

L12   How a Vestal Virgin is punished for breaking her oath
[4] A Vestal virgin who has broken her vow of virginity is buried alive near the Colline Gate. In this place there is a mound of earth stretching out beyond the wall within the city. It is called a bank in the language of the Latins. [5] There a small underground house is prepared with a way down from above. In it are placed a bed with bed-clothes, a lighted lamp, offerings of the necessities of life in small measure, such as bread, a bowl of water, milk, and oil, as if to absolve the blame of starving to death a body consecrated to the holiest of rituals. [6] They place the woman being punished in a litter, cover it over from the outside and fasten it down with straps, so that no cry can be heard outside; then they carry it through the forum. All people stand aside for it in silence and follow it without a sound with a terrible sense of shame. No other sight is more frightful, nor does the city pass any day more hateful that this. [7] When the litter has been brought to the place, the attendants take off the bonds, and the *pontifex maximus* makes some prayers whose words are kept secret, and stretches out his hands to the gods before the final deed. Then he leads out the woman, completely veiled and places her on the ladder leading down to the chamber. Then he himself turns away,

together with the other priests. When she has gone down the ladder is removed and the chamber is hidden by a great deal of earth thrown down from above, so that the area becomes the same height as the rest of the bank. This is how those who break their vow of virginity are punished.

[Plutarch, *Life of Numa* 10.4–7]

Romans traditionally ascribed many of their civic and religious traditions to Numa, their second king (traditionally 715–673 BC). Plutarch follows this in his 'Parallel Life' of Numa (paired with Lycurgus of Sparta), giving much attention to priesthoods and religious traditions established by Numa. Given Plutarch's residence in Rome at around this time and his profound interest in history and religion, it is impossible to believe that this account was not based very closely on Cornelia's death, and perfectly possible that Plutarch was an eye-witness to the event.

L13   Jerome's *Chronicle* for AD 91

The Chief Vestal virgin, Cornelia, convicted of adultery and buried alive in accordance with the law.

[Jerome, *Chronicle*, year 2107 after Abraham = AD 91]

L14   Pliny the Younger's later account of the second trial

Have you heard that Valerius Licinianus is teaching Sicily? I do not think you can have done, for the news is recent. He is of praetorian rank, and he used at one time to be considered among the most eloquent lawyers; but now he has sunk to the level that he is an exile rather than a senator, and a teacher instead of a practitioner of rhetoric. [2] Therefore in his introduction he stated, in sadness and sorrow: "O Fortune, you make fun of us for you own pleasure! For you turn senators into teachers, and teachers into senators." There is so much indignation and bitterness in that expression that it seems to me that he became a teacher for the very purpose of saying it. [3] Then again, when he entered the hall wearing a Greek cloak – for those who have been banished from 'fire-and-water' no longer have the right to wear the toga – he first composed himself and then, looking down at his clothing, he said, "I shall make my speeches in Latin." [4] You will say that this is sad and deserving our pity, but he deserves it, a man who dishonoured the study of rhetoric by the crime of incest. He did confess to the crime of incest, but it is uncertain whether he did so because he was guilty or because he feared a worse punishment if he denied it. For Domitian was very angry and burning with great rage because he had been robbed of his witnesses. [6] For he desperately wanted to bury alive Cornelia, the chief priestess of the Vestal Virgins, since he thought to make his age memorable by examples of this kind. He intended to use his rights as *pontifex maximus*, or rather the monstrous savagery of a tyrant and the freedom of a master; so he summoned the rest of the *pontifices* not to the *Regia* but to his Alban villa. There, with no less a crime than the one he pretended to be avenging, he condemned her on a charge of incest, while absent and unheard, despite the fact that he himself had not only violated with incest his brother's daughter but had even brought about her death, for she died of abortion while a widow. [7] He immediately sent some of the *pontifices* to see that his victim was buried alive and killed. Cornelia held out her hands to Vesta and of the rest of the gods, and repeatedly shouted many things but this most frequently: "How does Caesar think me guilty of incest, when it was through my performance of the sacred rites that he conquered and triumphed?" [8] Whether this was to soften him or to make fun of him, is not known, or whether she said this out of confidence in herself or contempt for the emperor. She carried on saying this until she was led to her execution; whether she was innocent or not, she was led away without doubt looking as if she was. [9] Indeed even when she was being let down into the underground room and her dress caught as she was being lowered, she turned and readjusted it, and when the executioner offered her his hand she turned away and shrank back, as though rejecting his foul touch from her chaste and pure body in a final act of piety, and with perfect modesty, like Polyxena "taking great care to fall in a decent manner." [10] Besides, when Celer, the Roman equestrian who was involved with Cornelia, was flogged with rods in the Forum, he persisted in crying out, "What have I done? I have done nothing."

[11] Therefore Domitian burned with anger at his notoriety for both cruelty and injustice. He seized upon Licinianus for hiding a freedwoman of Cornelia on one of his farms. Friends of Licinianus, who were concerned for his safety, advised him, if he did not want to be flogged in the Forum, to escape it by making a confession and asking for pardon. He did so. [12] Herennius Senecio spoke for him in his absence in that sort of way as, "Patroclus lies dead"; for he said, "Instead of being a lawyer, I am a messenger: Licinianus has abandoned his defence." [13] This was so pleasing to Domitian that he was betrayed by his joy into saying, "Licinianus has cleared us." He even added that a man who admitted his shame in doing wrong should not be pressed for his reasons; he allowed him to take what he could of his possessions before his goods were confiscated, and granted him a pleasant exile as if a reward. [14] Afterwards, however, by the kindness of the Emperor Nerva, he was removed to Sicily, where he now is a teacher and takes his revenge upon Fortune in his introductory remarks.

[15] You see how obediently I obey you, when I not only write to you about city matters, but also foreign matters, and so carefully that I tell the story in such detail. I thought clearly that, because you were away from Rome at the time, you had heard only that Licinianus had been banished for incest. For rumour only gives the main points of the matter, not the various events in the right order. [16] I deserve a letter in return; so write and tell me what is going on in your town and neighbourhood, for some things usually do happen which are worth telling. Finally, write whatever you wish, provided the letter is as long as mine to you. I shall count up not only the pages, but the lines and the syllables as well. Farewell.

[Pliny the Younger, *Letters* 4.11]

The datable letters in book 4 are from 104 and 105. This letter was to a wealthy equestrian from Bergamum who received 3.9, 8.12 and was prompted by news of Licinianus now teaching rhetoric in his exile. Y. Pliny tells us much about the second trial of Cornelia (Suet. *Dom.* 8.4; Dio 67.3), all intended to make the readers condemn Domitian. But as a recent study concludes, 'had such action been taken by Trajan, we can be sure Pliny would have reported it as a return to ancient Roman values.' (Carlon, *Pliny's Women* (Cambridge 2009) p.200). It is notable that Nerva did not cancel Licinianus' sentence, and Suetonius had no doubt about the guilt of the vestals. A trial at Domitian's villa rather than at the *Regia*, the traditional 'palace' in the Roman forum does not seem to have been irregular either, though Cornelia's absence must have been. The equestrian Celer is not mentioned in other accounts. Herennius Senecio's involvement helps date the trial as before his execution late in 93.

L15   'A splendid purification'
News came that Domitian had made a splendid purification of Roman Vesta, since he had killed three of the Vestal Virgins on an accusation of sexual intercourse and not keeping pure as regards marriage as they should have done in dutifully serving Trojan Athene and the fire there.

[Philostratos, *Life of Apollonius of Tyana* 7.6]

L16   Domitian grants special permission to a *flamen dialis* for divorce
A *flamen* was not allowed to divorce his wife and this is still the case; however, in my
lifetime, Domitian once granted it when petitioned. The priests were present at the
dissolution of the marriage performing many horrible, weird and gloomy rites.

[Plutarch, *Roman Questions* 50]

In this work, Plutarch asks and then answers 113 questions on Roman customs, especially religious ones.
Here the question is why the *flamen dialis* had to step down if his wife died. It is not known who held this
prestigious but tedious priesthood in the first part of Domitian's reign. From the early 90s it was L. Subrius
Dexter L. Cornelius Priscus (Rupke no. 1362) who went on to be consul 104 and proconsul of Asia 120/1.

DOMITIAN AND THE *LUDI SAECULARES* (CENTENNIAL GAMES): L17–L21
Augustus had resurrected the idea of celebrating *ludi saeculares,* games to be held once in a lifetime. By
manipulating figures and history he was able to claim they were due in 17 BC. Claudius, ignoring Augustus'
figures, decided to hold the *ludi saeculares* to celebrate the 800th anniversary of the founding of Rome in
AD 47 (Tac. *Ann.* 11.11; Suet. *Claud.* 21.2). Domitian decided on AD 88, reverting to the Augustan scheme
and an apparent original intention to celebrate them in 23 BC (Suet. *Dom.* 4.3). Alone of the short histories,
the *Epitome* mentions Domitian's games as the last item in his reign (11.14).

L17   Tacitus on the board of fifteen for Domitian's *ludi saeculares*
Under the same consuls, Centennial Games were seen, in the eight hundredth year
after the founding of Rome, and the sixth-fourth since Augustus had held them. I omit
the calculations of each of these emperors, having explained them sufficiently in the
books I have written on the emperor Domitian. For he also held Centennial Games
which I attended with considerable interest having been granted the position of priest
of the board of fifteen and also praetor.

[Tacitus, *Annals* 11.11.1]

For Tacitus' career progression under the Flavians, see **U32a–b** and **U33f**.

L18   Fragment of the Capitoline Consul List
In year 841 after Rome was founded [… 3 lines erased …] by decree of the senate the
Centennial Games were held.

[MW 61 = Inscr It 13.1, pp 62–3 = EDCS–57500001*]

L19   The seventh Centennial Games
Domitian held the seventh Gentennial Games in his own 13th consulship and that of
L. Minucius Rufus, in year 841.

[Censorinus, *On the Birthday* 17]

Censorinus was a Roman grammarian of the third century. His work preserves a great deal of accurate
information on time and the Centennial Games (see LACTOR 17, L20–L22).

L20   Domitian receives offerings at the Centennial Games, *as*, AD 88

Obv: Head of Domitian, laureate, right.

IMP CAES DOMIT AVG GERM P M TR P VIII CENS PER P P (Emperor Caesar Domitian Augustus Germanicus, *pontifex maximus,* holding tribunician power for the 8th time, censor for life, father of the fatherland.

Rev: Domitian seated right on platform, approached by two citizens with open sacks; in background, four-column temple.

(around edge): COS XIIII LVD SAEC A POP; (on platform) FRVG AC; (on exergue) S C (At the) Centennial Games he received crops from the people. By decree of the senate.

[*RIC* 2.1 Domitian 606 = *BMCRE²* 419, p.392 = BM no.1872,0709.507]

The reverse shows one of the ceremonies connected with the *ludi saeculares*, with Domitian receiving *fruges* – corn, barley and beans – from the people (Zosimus 2.5.2 = LACTOR 17, L24).

L21   Domitian makes sacrifice at the *ludi saeculares, dupondius,* AD 88

Obv: Head of Domitian, radiate, right.

IMP CAES DOMIT AVG GERM P M TR P VIII CENS PER P P (Emperor Caesar Domitian Augustus Germanicus, *pontifex maximus,* holding tribunician power for the 8th time, censor for life, father of the fatherland.

Rev: Domitian standing left, sacrificing over altar; to left, *victimarius* with goat and lamb, flute-player and lyre-player standing right; in background, six-column temple, eagle in pediment.

COS XIIII LVD SAEC FEC S C (when consul for the 14th time he held Centennial Games by decree of the senate).

[*RIC* 2.1 Domitian 619 = *BMCRE²* 430, p.395 = BM no. R.11403]

The reverse shows the sacrifice of a black lamb and a goat to the Moirae on the first night of the games as described in inscriptions detailing the ceremonies of 17 BC (*CIL* 6.32323, lines 90–99 = LACTOR 17, L27j).

IMPERIAL FAMILY AND EASTERN RELIGION: L22–L27

Despite having inherited a Greek pantheon, Romans were traditionally suspicious of eastern or mystic religions involving some sort of personal initiation. Evidence can be seen ranging from the senate's suppression of Bacchic worship in 186 BC (Livy 39.8–18, *ILLRP* 511) to Tiberius' repression of Egyptian cults (Tac. *Ann.* 2.85) or Juvenal's attack in *Satire* 6.508–541. The Flavians however established and proclaimed links to several non-traditional Roman religions: Vespasian claimed Serapis worked a miracle through him (Suet. *Vesp.* 7.2; Tac. *Hist.* 4.81; Dio 66.8.1 = **C8**) and may have been hailed as the new Serapis (see below, **L22**). Domitian's escape from Vitellian forces dressed as a follower of Isis (see **L50** note) is perhaps why his father and brother spent the night before their Jewish triumph in Isis' temple (Jos. *Jewish War* 7.123 = **E6b**).

L22   Vespasian hailed as new Serapis in Alexandria

…Tibe]rius Alexa[nder …] the emperor [… came into] the city and the cro[wds gathered to fill] the whole racetrack [...] "Lord Caesar, [may you come] in good health [… Vesp]asian, saviour and b[enefactor …] rising up [...]. Keep him safe for us [...]. O Augustus, benefactor, [new?] Sar[apis …?] Son of Ammon, and together [...] we thank Tiberius [Alexander]." Tiberius [...] God Caesar [...] good health [...] God Caesar Vespasian [...] Lord Augustus V[espasian].

[MW 41 = Fouad Papyrus 8 = Sherk 81]

See Levick, *Vespasian* 69. Vespasian as new Sarapis, accepted by *OCD³* under 'Sarapis'

L23   Vespasian and Titus and *cista mystica* on *aurei* of AD 75 (Rome)

Obv: Head of Vespasian / Titus, laureate, right.
IMP CAESAR VESPASIANVS AVG / T CAESAR IMP VESPASIAN

Rev: Victory standing left on cista mystica, holding wreath in right hand and palm in left hand, flanked by snakes.
PON MAX TR P COS VI / PONTIF TR P COS IIII (*pontifex maximus, holding tribunician power, consul 6 times / pontifex,* holding tribunician power, consul 4 times).

[*RIC* 2.1 Vespasian 775 & 785 = *BMCRE²* 168, p.31 & 173, p.33 = BM nos. R.10310–1]

Cistae mysticae or 'mystic chests' were used to keep snakes as part of the initiation to Bacchic and perhaps Isis worship.

L24   Vespasian and Temple of Isis on *sestertius* AD 71 (Rome)

Obv: Head of Vespasian, laureate, right, with aegis and globe at point of bust.
IMP CAESAR VESPASIANVS AVG P M T P P P COS III (Emperor Caesar Vespasian Augustus, *pontifex maximus,* tribunician power, father of the fatherland, three times consul)

Rev: Temple of Isis.
S C (by decree of the senate)

[*RIC* 2.1 Vespasian 117, *BMCRE²* 780, p.189 = BM no.1852,0609.1]

For the Flavian family's personal links to Isis see **E6b** and **L50**. The temple burnt down in AD 80 (Dio 66.24.2 = **C66**) and was restored by Domitian (Eutropius 7.23.5 = **T2**). The coin shows a temple with Corinthian columns and a round pediment with the figure of Isis on a dog.

L25   Domitian and Temple of Serapis, *denarius*, AD 95/6

Obv: Head of Domitian, bare, right.
        DOMITIANVS AVG GERM
Rev: Temple with four columns, with Serapis seated left, with Cerberus.
        IMP CAES

[*RIC* 2.1 Domitian 812 = *BMCRE*² 238, p.345 = BM no. R.11168]

L26   Domitian and Temple of Cybele, *denarius*, AD 95/6

Obv: Head of Domitian, bare, right.
        DOMITIANVS AVG GERM
Rev: Temple with four columns, with Cybele standing left.
        IMP CAES

[*RIC* 2.1 Domitian 813 = *BMCRE*² 239, p.346 = BM no. R.11169]

The two coins above share the same obverse die, as does a third obverse type, showing a Temple of Minerva (**K63**). All three show distinctive temples with likely but not certain identifications. The Temple of Serapis was part of the complex involving the Temple of Isis (**K60–K61**) rebuilt by Domitian after the fire of AD 80, see Chronicler of 354 (**K2**).

L27   Domitian's liking for foreign cults
Nor are there now, at the emperor's banquets, members of foreign cults in attendance all over the place or obscene behaviour: instead generous hospitality, easy-going wit, and appreciation of scholarship.

[Pliny the Younger, *Panegyric to Trajan* 49.8]

INDIRECT WORSHIP OF THE EMPEROR: L28–L40

Augustus and especially Tiberius had been clear in his dislike of direct worship of a living emperor (Suet. *Tib.* 26.1; Tac. *Ann.* 4.37–8; his own decree at Gytheion, EJ 102b = LACTOR 19, L4b). Many of the formulae of indirect worship of the emperor still continued under the Flavians: prayers to the *genius* (divine spirit) of an emperor, rather than the emperor himself; vows for his well-being. Domitian proclaimed a close relationship with one particular goddess, Minerva. But so had Julius Caesar with Venus, and Augustus with Apollo. Meanwhile poets continued to praise the emperor as equivalent to the gods (see **H62, K48, K58, T5**), just as Virgil and Horace had done from the inception of the principate.

L28 A witness at Herculaneum takes an oath by the *genius* of Vespasian, AD 75/6

I [?] Mammius [?] have written at the request of Marcus Calatorius Marullus, in his presence, because he says he does not know how to write, that he has sworn by the *genius* (divine spirit) of Emperor Vespasian Augustus and his children that I know that Calatoria Themis manumitted the girl as well as me: from this I know that the girl is a freedwoman of Calatoria Themis. This is the matter under discussion.

[Arangio-Ruiz (1959) 241: Tab. XXIV]

This was part of a legal case in Herculaneum in AD 75/6 about whether a woman was free or a freedwoman. For the case being referred to Rome, see **M45**, and for other documents about the case, Cooley[2] G5–G11. The significance here is that the witness' oath is by the *genius* of Vespasian and his sons (compare oaths to be taken in the Flavian Municipal Charter (**F25, F26, FG, F59, F69, F73, F79**).

L29 Dedication, AD 83, by presidents of the cult of the Augustan Lares

To the Augustan Lares and the *genii* (divine spirits) of the Caesars, [to Emperor Caesar Domitian Augustus, consul 9 times], designated for the 10th, father of the fatherland, by permission of A. Annius Camars, tri[bune of the people], the presidents of year 92, at their own expense, restored from its f[oundations the shrine of region I, neighbourhood of Honour] and Virtue. C. Julius Zosimus, freedman of Gaius, M'. Birrius Hierus, freedman of Manlius, [*(other names lost)*]

[MW 145 = *ILS* 3617 = EDCS–17300602*]

Large marble inscription, from Rome, broken into several pieces. The cult of the Augustan Lares (household or local gods) had been introduced under Augustus and provided a way for freedmen and slaves, excluded from traditional worship, to take a role and show loyalty to the princeps. Domitian's ninth consulship was in AD 83. Year 92 counts from the start of the cult, apparently on 1 August 9 BC (see LACTOR 17, L12 for an inscription from the start of the cult).

L30 Dedication to the imperial house, AD 88

Sacred to the *numen* (spirit) of the Augustan House, the local councillors who gather in this senate-house laid down this altar and flint courtyard from their own money. Dedicated on 5 January when Emperor Caesar Augustus Germanicus for the 14th time and Q. Minucius Rufus were consuls, under the stewardship of Ti. Claudius Januarius and Ti. Claudius Excellens with lifetime exemption from the presidency.

[MW 150 = *ILS* 7357 = EDCS–17300687*]

The stone plaque was found in Rome, but refers to a local town council. It is not well carved, with letters poorly spaced and of irregular height. 'Caesar Augustus' has clearly been re-inscribed over an erasure, presumably of 'Domitian'.

L31   Altar ? for Titus' well-being, Rome

For the well-being of Titus Caesar Imperator Vespasian, son of Augustus. Tiberius Claudius Clemens had this made. Titus Naevius Diadumenus, curator of the college of diggers, worshippers of Silvanus, had it remade with his own money.

[MW 431 = *CIL* 6.940 = EDCS–17301059]

L32   Success of the Emperor, 'Rochester Road' *denarius*, AD 79–80

Obv: Head of Titus, laureate, right.
        IMP TITVS CAES VESPASIAN AVG P M (Emperor Titus Caesar Vespasian Augustus, *pontifex maximus*)
Rev: Bonus Eventus standing left, holding patera in right hand and corn-ears and poppy in left hand.
        BONVS EVENTVS AVGVSTI (Success of the Emperor)

[*RIC* 2.1 Titus 89, p.204 (type) = BM no. 1937,1107.5]

Coin found on Rochester Road, Bristol in 1937. *Bonus Eventus* ('Good Outcome' or 'Success') was an established personification, appearing on coins of 62 BC. Pliny *NH* 36.23 mentions two statues on public display in Rome by Greek masters of Bonus Eventus (or some Greek equivalent). Here 'Success' is effectively made an imperial quality.

L33   Tombstone of Vitellia Rufilla, priestess of Augustan Well-Being, after AD 85

To Vitellia Rufilla, daughter of Gaius, wife of C. Salvius Liberalis, consul; high priestess of Augustan Well-Being; C. Salvius Vitellianus, in his lifetime, to the best of mothers.

[MW 173 = *ILS* 1012 = EDCS–16200616]

Tombstone from Urbs Salvia in Picenum, Italy, of Rufilla (she of Cambridge Latin Course, book 2!). The only indication of date is that Rufilla's husband Salvius had already held his consulship.

L34   Vows for Domitian, AD 93/4

> Yea! What huge gathering of the world at Latium's altars
> Discharges vows and undertakes them for its leader!
> It's not just men that thus rejoice, Germanicus,
> But, I think, the gods themselves give worship now.

> [Martial, *Epigram* 8.4 (published January 94)]

For vows fulfilled and fresh ones undertaken for the well-being of the emperor, on 3 January each year, see the Acts of the Arval Brothers, e.g. **A87a**.

L35   A *Flavialis*

For the well-being of the colony, and the order of town-councillors, and the people of Tuder, in honour of Jupiter Greatest and Best, the Guardian and Preserver, because, by his divine power he rescued and vindicated from the unspeakable robbery of an utterly evil public slave the names of the order of town-councillors, fixed on monuments, and freed the colony and its citizens from fear and peril. L. Cancrius Primigenius, freedman of Clemens, on the board of six, *Augustalis* and *Flavialis*, first of all to be granted these honours by the order (of town-councillors), discharged his vow.

> [MW 154 = *ILS* 3001 = EDCS–22900416]

Altar from Tuder (modern Todi, 90km north of Rome). The interest is in Cancrius Primigenius being made a *Flavialis* as an honour (known from Suetonius, *Domitian* 4) and obviously modelled on the idea of *Augustales* created as a focus for emperor-worship among slaves and freedmen (contrast the socially prestigious *sodales Flaviales* **L36, L37**). Primigenius had presumably exposed corruption in a public slave responsible for keeping records of membership of the local classes.

L36   Veiento, a *sodalis Flavialis*

A. Didius Gallus Fabricius Veiento, thrice consul, on the board of fifteen for carrying out sacrifices, *sodalis Augustalis, sodalis Flavialis, sodalis Titialis*, and his wife Attica, willingly and deservedly fulfilled their vow to Nemetona.

> [MW 155 = *ILS* 1010 = EDCS–11001342*]

While a *Flavialis* like an *Augustalis*, was a freedman, a *sodalis Flavialis*, like the equivalent *sodalis Augustalis* was a member of a socially prestigious fraternity, as shown by this very prominent Flavian, Veiento (Rüpke no. 1451, and see **B80** and **U9**), who put up an offering to Nemetona (ancient goddess assimilated to Mars) in Mogontiacum (Mainz in Germany) with this accompanying elegant plaque. The priestly orders of *Flaviales* and *Titiales* were later combined.

L37   A marble sarcophagus at Pisa

C. Bellicus Natalis Tebanianus, consul, *quindecimvir* of the *Flaviales*

> [MW 312 = *ILS* 1009 = EDCS–20402900]

Bellicus was consul in 87. His elaborate marble sarcophagus, now in the Campo Santo at Pisa shows that he was proud of the new honour of being *sodalis Flavialis* since the inscription omits a host of other offices he held, but also, it seems that the stone-cutter was less familiar with the priesthood since he has wrongly inscribed '*quindecimvir* of the *Flaviales*' rather than '*quindecimvir, sodalis Flavialis*'(see notes to **L35, L36**).

L38 A soldier tired of war's alarms, Philippi
To Augustan *Quies* of the Colony of Philippi, Lucius Tatinius Cnosus, son of Lucius of the Voltinian tribe, centurion of military police, had this put up with his own money.

[MW 368 = EDCS–16100271*]

A stone altar dedicated at Philippi, W. coast of Greece, to an unusual personification of *quies* as a goddess and linked to the emperor – (though there was a shrine to *Quies* on the Via Labicana, leading east from Rome: Livy 4.41.8). It can mean 'quiet' or 'rest'; or be effectively a synonym for 'peace' which is presumably its use here. It can also refer to a life free of political interference. The dedicator's military service is known from **N65**.

L39 Mercury Augustus
[To Merc]ury August[us ... for the well-being of emp]eror Titus Caesar [Vespasian Augustus ....] the temple from its foundat[ions ... an enclosing-w]all in the area all round and for the buildings [...]

[MW 171 = *ILS* 3191 = EDCS–01200074*]

Large fragment of monumental inscription from Cologne, Germany.

L40 Ephesian Artemis and Domitian
For Ephesian Artemis and Emperor ~~Domitian~~ Caesar Augustus ~~Germanicus~~, the city of the Ephesians, Warden of the Temple, established from its own resources the paving of the Embolos; M. Atilius Postumus Bradua the proconsul consecrated it, with M. Tigellius Lupus Philocaesar negotiating the business and bringing it to completion.

[Greek: MW 142]

In provinces such as Asia where imperial cult had been established from the beginning of the Principate, cities vied with each other for the honour of being selected as Warden of the Temple (*neokoros*) of the cults established for each new emperor. The Embolos was the great colonnade leading from the Temple of Domitian towards the theatre. The year of Atilius' consulship is not known.

ASSOCIATION OF THE EMPEROR WITH PARTICULAR GODS: L41–L54
The tendency for an emperor to identify himself with a particular god can be traced back at least to Julius Caesar claiming Venus as the ancestor of his Julian family. Augustus had cultivated an association with Apollo. Efforts to make the natural association with Jupiter may have been a step too far for many (see Suet. *Cal.* 22.2, Seneca, *On Anger* 1.20.9) but poets had done so since Ovid. Vespasian did not promote any particular association, but Domitian certainly did with Minerva.

L41 Domitian as Dionysus of the Fine Fruit, AD 92/3
To Emperor Caesar Domitian Augustus Germanicus, son of God Vespasian, chief priest, holding tribunician power for the 12th time, hailed *imperator* 22 times, consul 16 times, censor for life, father of the fatherland, Dionysus of the Fine Fruit. Lucius Valerius Niger, having been local magistrate and priest of the goddess Roma, and Lucius Valerius Varus Pollio, having been priest of God Titus Caesar Augustus and having been local magistrate and priest of the goddess Roma, this pair, father and son built the temple in return for their magistracies and priesthood, as they promised the people. Quintus Gellius Longus, legate and propraetor of Domitian Caesar Augustus Germanicus dedicated it.

[Greek: MW 317]

The inscription dedicated a temple in Anazarbus (in Cilicia) to Domitian equated with Dionysus 'Kallikarpos' – 'of fine fruit' – a cult title not otherwise known. The dedicatees, though local magistrates, have obviously Roman names.

L42 *Hercules as Domitian in his new temple*
The Latin Thunderer will acknowledge Hercules,
Now he bears the handsome face of god Caesar

[Martial, *Epigram* 9.65.1–2 (published December 94)]

For Martial's previous poem on the temple, see **K58**. Martial explicitly likens Domitian to Hercules in Epigram 5.65 where he praises Domitian's gladiatorial shows as more than matching Hercules' labours: Hercules was quickly deified for his labours; Martial expressed the hope that Domitian's deification will only take place after a lengthy life.

L43 Apollo and Raven on *semis* of AD 90–91, Rome

Obv: Bust of Apollo, draped, right; to right, branch.
IMP DOMIT AVG GERM COS XV (emperor Domitian Augustus Germanicus, consul 15 times)
Rev: Raven standing right on laurel-branch.
S C (by decree of the senate)

[*RIC* 2.1 Domitian 710, *BMCRE²* 453, p.401 = BM no. R.11424]

Various classical myths associate Apollo with ravens: the laurel is symbolic of victory.

DOMITIAN AND MINERVA: L44–L49

For Dio, Domitian's association of himself with Minerva ((Pallas) Athene in Greek) is the second thing he mentions in his book on Domitian (67.1.2 = **D1**), while a portent involving Minerva is one of those presaging his death (67.16.2 and compare Suet. *Dom.* 15.3). For Romans, Minerva was one of the three gods – the Capitoline Triad celebrated at the heart of Rome in the Temple of Jupiter Capitolinus (**K27**–**K32**); she was also a goddess powerful in war, usually depicted with helmet, spear and aegis; finally, of course, a patron of the arts and culture. See **K36**, **K39**–**K40** for the Temple of Minerva that formed the main feature of Domitian's forum, and **K62**–**K63** with note for other temples to Minerva.

L44   Domitian and Minerva on *aureus*, AD 82 Rome

Obv: Head of Domitian, laureate, right.
        IMP CAES DOMITIANVS AVG P M (emperor Caesar Domitian Augustus,
        pontifex maximus)
Rev: Bust of Minerva left, with aegis, wearing helmet, with transverse sceptre over right shoulder.
        TR POT IMP II COS VIII DES IX P P (tribunician power, hailed *imperator* 2
        times, consul 8 times, designated for a 9th, father of the fatherland)
                            [*RIC* 2.1 Domitian 138 = *BMCRE*[2] 33, p.304 = BM no. R.10756]

L45   Gift label on a silver statuette of Minerva
        Warlike maiden, since you have your spear and helmet,
        Tell me why you lack your aegis. "Caesar has it."
                                            [Martial, *Epigram* 14.179 (published *c.* 84/85)]

Martial's book 14 (published before book 1) consists of two-line epigrams apparently meant as labels for Saturnalia presents. Minerva and Domitian are also linked in 7.1 (**L46**) and 7.2, 8.1 (**T3**), 9.3 (**K52**), 9.23.

L46   Domitian wears Minerva's aegis to campaign
        Receive the breastplate fierce Minerva wears to war.
        Which even the fury of Medusa's hair does dread.
        When not in Caesar's use, it may be termed cuirass:
        An aegis, when it shall bedeck his sacred chest.
                                            [Martial, *Epigram* 7.1 (published Dec. 92)]

An aegis was a weapon peculiar to Minerva and Jupiter of uncertain function but usually portrayed in ancient art as covering Minerva's upper body, sometimes with a gorgon's head. The armour, further described in the next epigram was either taken from or modelled on one in a Temple of Minerva to emphasise her divine favour and protection of the emperor (compare Suet. *Dom.* 15.3 and Dio 67.1.2 and 67.16.1).

L47   Domitian and Minerva's owl on *semis* (copper alloy coin) AD 88/9

Obv: Bust of Minerva, helmeted, draped, right.
           IMP DOMIT AVG GERM COS XIIII (emperor Domitian Augustus
           Germanicus, consul 14 times)
Rev: Owl standing left, head facing.
           S C (by decree of the senate)

[RIC 2.1 Domitian 651 = BMCRE² 418, p.391 = BM no. R.11395]

Athenian tetradrachms (silver coins) were known throughout ancient Greece as 'little owls' and to modern
numismatists as 'owls' because of the owls depicted as symbolic of Athene/Athens.

L48   Imperial freedman's dedication to Minerva, AD 92, near Regium, S. Italy
To Minerva, T. Flavius Narcissus, when Emperor Caesar Augustus for the 16th time
and Q. Volusius Saturninus were consuls.

[MW 192 = CIL 10.7 = EDCS–11400094]

L49   Domitian wishing to be known as child of Athene
Another man said that he was facing a charge because when he was making a sacrifice
at Tarentum, where he was magistrate, he had not included in the public prayers that
Domitian was the son of Athene.

[Philostratos, Life of Apollonius of Tyana 7.24]

This is one of several statements apparently made by those awaiting trial under Domitian with Apollonius.

DOMITIAN AND JUPITER: L50–L54
From the inception of the principate under Augustus it was natural for poets, amongst others, to equate the
king of the gods with the emperor. Domitian claimed a special and specific link as a result of events at the
end of the civil war (**L50–L51**).

L50   Domitian and Jupiter the Preserver/Guardian
Domitian, when the attackers first burst in, hid in the home of a temple caretaker.
Then a quick-thinking freedman got him to sneak away unnoticed in a linen cloak
and mixed in with a crowd of priests to the house in the Velabrum district, belonging
to Cornelius Primus, a client of his father's. So when his father came to power, he
demolished the caretaker's lodge and erected a small shrine to Jupiter the Preserver
and an altar with a marble relief showing what had happened to him. Presently after

attaining power, he dedicated a huge Temple to Jupiter the Guardian with himself in
the lap of the god.

[Tacitus, *Histories* 3.74]

Suetonius, *Domitian* 1.2–3 gives a similar account adding the detail that he was dressed as a follower of
Isis amongst priests of the cult.

L51   Domitian celebrates Jupiter his preserver, *aureus* AD 82–3

Obv: Head of Domitian, laureate, right.
         IMP CAES DOMITIANVS AVG P M (emperor Caesar Domitian Augustus,
         pontifex maximus
Rev: Eagle standing front on thunderbolt, wings outspread, head left.
         IVPPITER CONSERVATOR (Jupiter the Preserver)

[*RIC* 2.1 Domitian 143 = *BMCRE²* 51, p.309 = BM no. R.10757]

Asses were also minted in AD 85 with the legend IOVI CONSERVAT (to Jupiter the Preserver) and with a
statue of Jupiter rather than his eagle on the obverse. Single examples of *sestertii* of AD 86 and AD 88–9,
neither well-preserved, show the legend 'Jupiter Custos' and a seated figure of Jupiter.

L52   Domitian as Zeus the Liberator, Athens
To Good Fortune. When Emperor Caesar Domitian Augustus Germanicus, Zeus
Eleutherios (the Liberator), son of Divus Vespasian was chief magistrate, the director
Stratonos Epikepheisios enrolled the teachers under him and the ephebes under him.

[Greek: *IG* II², 1996 = MW 121]

L53   Better to ask favour of Domitian than Jupiter
         When asking Jove just now for but a thousand or two,
         He said, "That shall he give, who gave temples to me."
         He did indeed give Jove the temples, but gave to me
         No thousands: I'm ashamed I asked Jove for so little.

[Martial, *Epigram* 6.10.1–4 (published December 91)]

Martial plays here with the equivalence of Jupiter and Domitian. In line one the poet describes himself as
asking (the 'real') Jupiter for cash. By line 4, he has followed the god's advice to ask the emperor for money
instead and it is Domitian who is referred to as Jove in this line. The poem goes on to flatter Domitian
further and to have Minerva assuring Martial that his petition has not necessarily been denied. Martial
also refers to Domitian as Jupiter at 4.8.12, 7.74.10, 9.24, 9.28.10, 9.36.2, 9.86.8, 9.91 (**L54**), and suggests
equivalence at 7.60 and 8.24, 8.49

L54 Better to dine with Domitian than Jupiter

If I were asked to dine in different heavens – here
By Caesar's messenger or there by that of Jove
And if the heavens were closer, the palace further off
I'd give this answer to be taken back to the gods:
"Search on for one who'd rather be the Thunderer's guest:
For look, my Jupiter keeps me here on earth."

[Martial, *Epigram* 9.91 (published December 94)]

Henriksen (Commentary Martial 9, pp. 353–4) suggests that this poem, unlike Statius *Silvae* 4.2 does not celebrate a real invitation to dine at Domitian's palace, but simple praise of emperor and his newly completed dining room on the Palatine (as also 8.39).

IMPERIAL CULT: L55–L75

The famous last words, *"vae me, puto deus fio"* "Oh dear, I think I'm becoming a god" were taken by Suetonius and Dio (Suet. *Vesp.* 23.4; Dio 66.17.3) as indicative of Vespasian's down-to-earth humour (but see **J4m** note for a more likely explanation). At any rate deification *was* inevitable as Pliny shows in flattery, and because Titus, and then Domitian, could hardly have done otherwise.

L55 Perpetual high priest of Vespasian at Tarraco, Spain

[M. Ra]ecius Gallus, [son of] Taurus, of the Galerian tribe, mil[itary tribune] of Emperor Galba, perpetual [high pri]est of Emperor Vespasian Caesar Augustus, by decree of the town council, [high p]riest of PHC (province of Hispania Citerior), quaestor of the province of Baetica, tribune of the people, praetor, *sodalis Augu[stalis]*. M. Minatius […], to his excellent and most dis[tinguished] friend.

[*CIL* 2.14.2, 992 = *RIT* 145 = EDCS–03400070]

Tarraco (Tarragona), the provincial capital of Hispania Tarraconensis was keen on emperor cult (Quintilian 6.3.77) and built a terraced complex of temple/precinct for provincial cult around this period (compare **L70** below). Raecius (Rüpke, *Fasti Sacerdotum* no. 2894) was son of an Arval Brother serving in January 69. Syme (*RP* 2.767) describes a high priest entering on a senatorial career as 'a striking anomaly' but suggests that as *sodalis Augustalis* he may even have gone on to be consul, since a 'Gallus' is attested for AD 84.

L56 Priest of Vespasian at Pisidian Antioch

T. Flavius Calpurnianus Hierocles, in honour of [*(praenomen and nomen lost)*] Paullinus, soldier of Legion XII 'Thunderer', priest of Emperor Caesar Vespasian Augustus, twice duumvir, four times quinquennial.

[MW 132 = EDCS–16300051]

Legion XII served Vespasian in the Jewish War before being transferred to Cappadocia and based at Militene, 400 miles east of Pisidian Antioch.

L57 Establishment of rules for emperor worship at Narbo under Vespasian

[Honours due to the high priest ... at Na]rbo
[... when the high priest performs the rites] and [sacrifices], the lictors [who attend on magistrates are to attend on him. ... According to the law] and right of [...] the province he [is to have the right of giving his opinion and voting] among the members of the council or senate; likewise [... he is to have] the right of viewing [public games of the province] from the front seats [among members of the council] or senators [... . The wife] of the high priest, clad in white or purple garments [on festal day ...] nor is she to take an oath against her will or [touch] the body of a dead person nor [... unless] it is of a person [related to her]. And [it is to be permitted] for her [to be present ...] at public shows in that [province].

Honours due to one who [has been] high priest.
If a man who [has been] high priest has done nothing in breach of this law, then the incumbent high priest [is to ensure ... that ... by ballot] and under oath they decree and make it their pleasure that a man who has vacated the high priesthood should be permitted [to set up] a statue [of himself. The man to whom they have so decreed that he has the right of setting up a statue] and [of inscribing] his own name and that of his father; his place of origin and the year of his high priesthood is to have the right of setting up the statue [at Narbo] within the confines of the temple, unless Emperor [Caesar ?Vespasian Augustus] has accorded someone else the right. And he] is to have the right in his city council place and in the provincial council of Narbonensis of giving his opinion and voting among men of his rank according to the law [...]; likewise, when a public show [is given] in the province, of [attending among members of the council] in a magistrate's toga, and on those days on which he made sacrifices when he was high priest [of wearing in public] the dress [which he wore when making them].

Possible lack of high priest in the community.
If there ceases to be a high priest in the community and no substitute has been elected for him, then as each [high priest ... is at Narbo] within three days of his being informed and being able, he is to perform the rites at Narbo and is to conduct [all those rites throughout the rest] of the year [according to the law] in the order in which [the rites] of the annual high priest [are conducted, and if he conducts them for not less than thirty days] the same law, right and claims are to apply [to him] as apply to one [who has been elected] high priest of Augustus [according to the prescription of this law].

Place in which the [provincial] council is to be held.
Those who assemble for the provincial council in Narbo are to hold it there. If any business is transacted at a council held outside Narbo or the boundaries of the people of Narbo it [is not to be held] lawful and valid.

Money [earmarked for rites].
A man who has vacated the high priesthood is to use [the surplus] of the money [which has been earmarked for rites, to dedicate] statues and images of Emperor Caesar [?Vespasian Augustus] within the said temple [at the discretion of the] incumbent governor of the province [... And he is to prove] before the official who [computes

the finances of the province that he has] in this respect done [everything as provided in this law ...] temple [...]

[MW 128 = ILS 6964 = EDCS–09303050*]

Under the Flavians, imperial cult spread to new provinces and became consolidated, embracing the cult of previously deified emperors, and bringing Vespasian and his sons within the fold. Vespasian may have taken the initiative in extending the cult to Narbonensis, Baetica, Africa and other provinces. Alternately, provinces that had found themselves backing other candidates in the Year of the Four Emperors may have decided to ingratiate themselves with Vespasian on his success.

L58   Dedication to Emperor Titus God, AD 79–81, in Moesia

To Emperor Titus Caesar Augustus, son of Emperor Vespasian, chief priest, holding tribunician power, Heracleon, chief priest of Dionysus, from his own private money first erected this statue, having also given a distribution to citizens, Romans and foreigners.

To Emperor Titus Flavius Vespasian God Augustus, Heracleon, chief priest of Dionysus, from his own private money first erected this statue, having also given a distribution to citizens, Romans and foreigners.

[Greek: MW 138]

From Odessus (now Varna on Black Sea in Bulgaria): inscription in Greek on left and right sides of the base of a statue of Titus, while he was emperor, but describing him as θεός (god).

L59   Dedication to Emperor Domitian God, Ephesus

To Emperor ~~Domitian~~ God Caesar Augustus ~~Germanicus~~ Vespasian when Lucius Mestrius Florus was proconsul, the people of Synaeitai ? for the Temple of the Caesars in Ephesus, by the state of Asia, by the agency of Philippus ...

[Greek: MW 139]

L60   Diva Domitia in Termessus

When the chief priest and priest of Zeus Solumis was Laertes, son of Nan[itoos], grandson of Laertes, the priestess of the goddess Augusta Domitia, Artemis, daughter of Nannamoos, granddaughter of Laertes honoured her husband in gratitude and to preserve his memory.

The people honoured Laertes, son of Nanitoos, the six-times chief priest of emperor Caesar Augustus and the priest for life of Zeus Solumis, friend of his city and father of his city. The people honoured the three-times chief priestess of Augusta, Artemis, daughter of Nannamoos, wife [...]

[Greek: IGRR III.444–5 = MW 148 and 149]

These inscriptions from Termessus (Lycia, SW Turkey) show Artemis, priestess of Domitia honouring her husband, priest of Caesar Augustus (i.e. Domitian), and the local people in turn honouring them both (presumably with statues). They must have been priests of the living imperial couple.

L61   *Dominus et Deus*

Domitian first orders that he be called 'master and god'

[Jerome, Chronicle, year 2102 after Abraham = AD 86]

For this, see **T9–T11**.

L62   Vespasian becoming a god by his benevolence

For mortal to aid mortal, that is what it is to be a god, and this is the route to eternal glory. On this route went our Roman founders; on this route now, with heavenly step, together with his children proceeds the greatest ruler of all time, Vespasian Augustus, bringing help to our exhausted times. This is the oldest tradition of recording our gratitude to those who deserve it, to enrol such men amongst the divinities.

[Pliny, *Natural History* 2.18–19]

Pliny has just described belief in the traditional Greco-Roman gods as 'virtually childish fantasies' and 'utterly disgraceful' to accept the traditional stories of their immoral behaviour.

L63   Motives for deification I

Praise is due to some because they have been born immortal, to some because they have achieved immortality by virtue: the piety of our emperor has provided an outstanding example of this for our time.

[Quintilian, *The Orator's Education* 3.7.9]

'Piety' (*pietas*) is usually doing one's duty to one's father or family. The emperor Antoninus (reigned AD 138–161) became known as Pius through insisting that the senate deified his (adopted) father, Hadrian. So Quintilian is really praising Domitian for doing the right thing in deifying his brother, Titus.

L64   Motives for deification II

The being (Nerva) whom you (Trajan) first mourned as a son should, you proceeded to honour with temples. You were not imitating those who did the same, but had quite different intentions. Tiberius consecrated Augustus to heaven, but with the purpose of introducing the charge of diminishing the majesty of the Roman People, and Nero consecrated Claudius just to make fun of him. Titus consecrated Vespasian, Domitian consecrated Titus, but the first did so with the object of appearing as the son of a god, the second of appearing as brother of one. [2] You gave your father a position amongst the stars, not to frighten your fellow-citizens, insult the gods, or extol yourself, but because you believed him to be a god.

[Pliny the Younger, *Panegyric to Trajan* 11.1–2]

Y. Pliny, in flattering Trajan, cannot mention the obvious similarity and reason for all the deifications (except Domitian's of Titus) in enabling the current emperor to style himself '*Divi filius*' or 'son of God', as Augustus had done. Domitian, of course, was already '*Divi filius*'. He may have been motivated by the other reason, also not mentioned, that of wishing to appear '*pius*' i.e. doing one's duty to one's family (see note above).

L65   Divus Vespasian with double Capricorn, *denarius* AD 80–1, Rome

Obv: Head of deified Vespasian, laureate, right.
       DIVVS AVGVSTVS VESPASIANVS
Rev: Two capricorns, back-to-back, supporting shield inscribed S C; below, globe.

[*RIC* 2.1 Titus 357 = *BMCRE²* 132, p.245 = BM no. 1911,0414.6]

Augustus had issued coins depicting Capricorn, globe and rudder (LACTOR17, L8). Vespasian followed suit in coins issued in his name (e.g. *RIC* 2.1 Vespasian 769), and that of Titus (*RIC* 2.1 Vespasian 781). Titus issued several Capricorn types after his accession (*RIC* 2.1 Titus 4–5, 17–20, 36–38), and this double-capricorn after his father's deification by the senate in AD 80. For another coin by Domitian showing Divus Vespasian, see **J13a.**

L66   Dedication in Blaundus, Phrygia, to Titus and the god his father, AD 79–81

The people (dedicated this) to [Emperor Ti]tus Caesar Augustus and the god his father

[Greek: MW 107 = *IGRR* 4.715]

Greek makes no distinction between '*divus*' and '*deus*', using θεος (god) for both.

L67   High priest of Vespasian, Aquinum, Italy

Sacred to Ceres. [D. Ju]nius Juvenalis, [tribune] of the 1st cohort of Dalmatians, quinquennial duumvir, priest of Divus Vespasian vowed and dedicated this at his own expense.

[*ILS* 2926 = EDCS–20401175]

Aquinum lay 75 miles south-east of Rome along the Via Latina

L68   High priest of Vespasian, Lepcis Magna, AD 92

When Emperor Caesar ~~Domitian Augustus Germanicus~~, son of Divus Vespasian, ~~pontifex maximus, was holding tribunician power for the 11th time, hailed imperator 21 times, consul 16 times, censor for life (and) father of the fatherland~~ .

Tiberius Claudius Sestius, of the Quirina voting tribe, son of Tiberius Claudius Sestius, prefect in charge of sacred things, high priest of Divus Vespasian, magistrate, perpetual high priest, lover of his fatherland, lover of its citizens, adorner of his fatherland, lover of concord, who was the first to be granted permission by the city council and the people to wear a broad purple band at all times, on account of his own merits and those of his ancestors.

He saw to the making of the base and the altar at his own expense.

[*IRT* 347* = EDCS–06000343]

This vast inscription runs round the parapet of the *orchestra* of the theatre at Lepcis Magna, on 65 slabs in letters 22–14cm high. [Text and pictures at http://irt.kcl.ac.uk/irt2009/]

L69   Divus Titus on *sestertius, c.* 81–82, Rome

Obv: Divus Titus, sitting left, holding branch and sceptre, with garlanded altar to left.
        T DIVO AVG DIVI VESP F VESPASIANO (To Titus Divus Augustus Vespasian, son of Divus Vespasian)
Rev: Inscription: S C (by decree of the senate)
        IMP CAES DIVI VESP F DOMIT AVG P M TR P P P (by decree of the senate: emperor Caesar Domitian Augustus, son of Divus Vespasian, *pontifex maximus,* tribunician power, father of the fatherland)

[*RIC* 2.1 Domitian 126 = *BMCRE*² 284, p.358 = BM no. 1872,0709.495]

L70   High priest of Divus Titus and Tarraco, Spain
To C. Egnatuleius Seneca of Tarraco, son of Gaius, of the Galerian tribe, aedile, quaestor, duumvir, high priest of Divus Titus, granted the public horse, prefect of Thracian Mounted cohort IV, high priest of the province of Nearer Spain. Egnatuleia Sige to her most generous patron.

[MW 344 = EDCS–05503243]

For Tarraco, see on **L55** above.

L71   Priestess of Diva Domitilla at Patavium
Asconia, daughter of Gaius, husband of Augurinus, priestess of Diva Domitilla; to her brother, C. Asconius Sardo, of the Fabian tribe, quattuorvir with judicial power, prefect of builders; to her mother, Cusinia, daughter of Marcus, husband of Sardus; and to herself.

[MW 146 = *ILS* 6692 = EDCS–04201876*]

Well-preserved stele, found at Patavium now in Padua Museum. For Flavia Domitilla, Domitian's sister, see **J13**, and also **L72**.

L72   Domitian's deified family visit his equestrian statue
This work does not fear winter rains, nor triple fires
Of Jove, nor Aeolus' pent-up cohorts, nor the years'
Slow march. It shall stand as long as earth and heaven;
As long as Roman day. In quietness of night,
When gods do love the earth, a crowd of your relations   95
Shall leave the sky, and gliding here exchange kisses.
To your embrace will come your brother, father, son,
And sister; one neck providing room for all the stars.

[Statius, *Silvae* 1.1.91–98 (published 93/4)]

Statius' poetic conceit is that the deified members of Domitian's family (his infant son, Titus, Vespasian, and sister Domitilla) will return to earth to embrace his colossal statue in the forum (see **K33–K35**). Domitian seems to have deified his sister and his son at about the same time as his brother. Deification was equated with becoming stars or constellations (like Castor and Pollux (Gemini) or Caesar's comet).

L73   Deified Julia, *sestertius*, AD 90/91

Obv: Carpentum drawn right by two mules.
         DIVAE IVLIAE AVG DIVI TITI F (of/for Diva Julia Augusta, daughter of
         Divus Titus): (below): SPQR (the Senate and People of Rome)
Rev: Inscription: S C (by decree of the senate)
         IMP CAES DOMIT AVG GERM COS XV CENS PER P P

[*RIC* 2.1 Domitian 717 = *BMCRE²* 458, p.402 = BM no. 1867,0101.2038]

For the *carpentum* see **J5c**. Sestertii of the same design were also issued when Domitian was 'cos XVI' i.e. between 92 and 94 (*RIC* Domitian 760).

L74   Statues to Diva Julia and Domitia Augusta at Celeia in Noricum
(Left) For Diva Julia: Lucius Cassius Maximus of the Claudian voting-tribe, centurion of Legion VI 'Ironclad', ordered this to be made in his will.

   (Right) For Domitia [Augusta]: Lucius Cassius Maximus of the Claudian voting-tribe, centurion of Legion VI 'Ironclad', ordered this to be made in his will. Lucius Cassius Eu[odus? oversaw] their construction.

[MW 112 = *ILS* 8906 = EDCS–14600332*]

This base found at Celeia in Noricum (modern Celje in Slovenia). Domitia and Julia are regularly included by name in prayers made by the Arval Brothers, e.g. 81, 86. Domitia but not Julia is named on records for 90.

L75   High priestess of Diva Julia at Aeclanum (central southern Italy)
To Cantria Longina, daughter of Publius, priestess and high priestess of Diva Julia Pia
Augusta and of the mother of the Gods ?of Mount Ida? and of Isis the Queen. These
monuments she gave to the community, on account of the office of her priesthood, and
50,000 sesterces. Set up at public expense and by decree of the councillors.

[MW 147 = *ILS* 6487 = EDCS–12400657]

SECTION M

ADMINISTRATION OF EMPIRE

The provinces without troops ... would be given up as the prize for war.

[Tacitus, *Histories* 1.11.3]

Introduction: This section collects sources relevant to how Rome administered her provinces, a task famously described by Augustus as greater than mere conquest. He, of course, had created the basic pattern of dividing provinces into public or imperial ones. Cassius Dio, 53.12–15 gives a detailed account of this and of the different names and seniority of governors and officials. Dio presents the situation established by Augustus in 28/27 BC combined with a few changes made by his own day. Changes under the Flavians in provincial structure had been minor (**M1–M9**). Direct imperial building tended to be for large infrastructure projects carried out by the army (**M10–M16**) or disaster relief (**M23**). But provinces differed vastly in character: Egypt continued to be governed in a distinctive way, confirmed perhaps by its importance in Vespasian's accession and by the flourishing trade routes to the East (**M24–M31**); Antioch in Syria also benefited from direct imperial knowledge (**M17–M21**); Spain flourished in this period as shown by **M32–M38** as well as the local charters of Section F, and other communities across the empire sought to improve their status (**M39–M43**). Britain provides a good example of an area becoming a province, with its resources exploited by continuing military expansion, but legal officers being appointed to administer. Friendly kings in the East of the empire had helped Vespasian to the throne: their use continued (**M54–M71**).

PROVINCIAL REORGANISATION: M1–M9
Soon after accession, Vespasian sent out a series of magistrates to reorganise the territories, 'and doubtless to increase the taxes' (CAH XI², page 515). In addition to making free or friendly territories into directly ruled provinces, a significant item for state revenue was the clarification of boundaries. For the state it simplified collection of revenue and for the cities it secured their finances, especially if their public property had been taken over by private individuals and was now recovered.

M1 New provinces created by Vespasian
Achaia, Lycia, Rhodes, Byzantium, Samos, Thrace, Cilicia, and Commagene which had previously been free under friendly kings, were reduced to provinces.

[Jerome, *Chronicle*, year 2090 after Abraham = AD 74]

Suet. *Vesp.* 8.4 provides the same list as Jerome, omitting Thrace. In all cases, the change was to direct rule from status as free cities, free provinces, or friendly kingdoms. The changes actually happened over the course of Vespasian's reign, not in AD 74.

M2 Nero frees, but Vespasian re-enslaves Greece
Nero released Achaia from all duties. ... However the Greeks were not to benefit from this gift: in the reign of Vespasian, who followed Nero, they fell into civil war, and Vespasian ordered them to pay taxes once more and to obey a governor, saying that the Greek nation had forgotten freedom.

[Pausanias, *Guide to Greece* 7.17.3–4]

M3 Letters of Apollonius on Vespasian revoking Greece's freedom
Nero had set Greece free, showing better sense than usual, and the cities had returned to their Doric and Ionic customs, and all was flourishing with good relations between the cities, such as Greece did not have of old. But when Vespasian arrived he took away this freedom, using their quarrels as an excuse and other things quite out of

proportion to his anger. This seemed to those affected and to Apollonius to be harsher than the proper behaviour of a king, so he wrote to the king in the following terms:

[2] Apollonius to King Vespasian, greetings: You have enslaved Greece, so they say, and you think you possess more than Xerxes, ignoring the fact that you possess less than Nero. For Nero possessed it and gave it up. Farewell."

"To the same: Since you have treated the Greeks so badly as to enslave them when they were free, what need have you of my presence? Farewell."

"To the same: Nero freed the Greek in jest, but you have enslaved them in earnest. Farewell."

That was what Vespasian did which annoyed Apollonius, but hearing how Vespasian conducted the rest of his reign after this, Apollonius rejoiced openly and considered that what he had done would be to his own benefit too.

[Philostratos, *Life of Apollonius of Tyana* 5.41]

M4　Caecilianus sets out boundaries along the line of the Royal Ditch, before AD 75

On the authority of Emperor Vespasian Caesar Augustus, father of the fatherland, boundaries of the new and the old province have been set out where the royal ditch was, through Rutilius Gallicus, consul and *pontifex*, and Sentius Caecilianus, praetor, both propraetorian imperial legates.

[MW 449 = *ILS* 5955 = EDCS–16300372]

The royal ditch (*fossa regia*), built by the Romans after the destruction of Carthage in 146 BC marked the boundary of the province of Africa. 12 boundary-stones with the same inscription have been found in modern Tunisia. The division will have eased tax-collection and maximised revenue from fertile land (Levick, *Vespasian* p.100).

M5　Caecilianus appointed to regulate both Mauretanias, AD 75

When Emperor Caesar Vespasian Augustus was consul for the 6th time and Titus Imperator, son of Augustus, consul for the 4th time, the colonists of the Colony of Julia Valentia Banasa from the new province of Mauretania Africa co-opted as patron for themselves, their offspring and their descendants, Sextus Sentius Caecilianus, son of Sextus of the Quirina tribe, legate of Augustus of praetorian rank for the regulation of both provinces of Mauretania, consul designate.

Sextus Sentius Caecilianus, son of Sextus of the Quirina tribe, legate of Augustus of praetorian rank for the regulation of both provinces of Mauretania, consul designate, receives into his protection and formal patronage, and into that of his kin, the colonists of the Colony of Julia Valentia Banasa from the new province of Mauretania Africa themselves, their offspring and their descendants. The envoys L. Caecilius Calvus, son of Quintus, of the Fabian tribe, L. Sallustius, son of Lucius, of the Fabian tribe, and [...]

[MW 277 = EDCS–08800110]

Caecilianus' complete career is known from U17. After conducting boundary administration in Africa Proconsularis (see above) he was then given further administrative duties further east: Mauretania represents the area of the Atlas Mountains – modern Morocco and North-West Algeria. Previously ruled by friendly kings, Caligula had annexed the area, dividing it into two provinces, but prompting a revolt, crushed by Claudius (LACTOR 19, N8–N11). Banasa had been founded for veterans of Actium. A very similar inscription (*AE* 1969/70, 747) has been found at Volubilis (modern Walili, 50 miles SE of Banasa) showing the people there also making Caecilianus their patron at the same time.

M6   Boundary dispute in French Alps resolved by Pinarius Cornelius, AD 74

On the authority of Emperor Caesar Vespasian Augustus, *pontifex maximus*, holding tribunician power for the 5th time, consul 5 times, designated for a 6th time, father of the fatherland; Cn. Pinarius Cornelius Clemens, his legate of the Upper German army, set the boundary stones between the people of Vienne and the Ceutrones.

[MW 446 = ILS 5957 = EDCS–08400689*]

Cippus (boundary stone) from Col de la Forclaz, between Chamonix and St Gervais les Bains in the French Alps. Pinarius' career is known from **U13**.

M7   Public land restored at Orange, S. France, AD 77

[Emperor] Caesar [Vespasian] Augustus, *pontifex maximus*, holding tribunician power for the [8th] time, hailed *imperator* [18] times, father of the fatherland, consul 8 times, censor.

[For the restoration of sites belonging to the public] which [Divus Augustus] had given [to the troops of] the 'Gallic' Legion [which had been in the possession of private individuals] for a number of years.

[He ordered the table] to be displayed in public with the yearly tax in each [century of land noted down, with *(name lost)* overseeing the procedings], when the proconsul of the province was [Ummid]ius Bassus.

[MW 447 = EDCS–13302625*]

A decorative architrave now much broken, from Arausio (Orange, S. France). It was accompanied by large marble maps showing the division of public land ('centuriation' – see, e.g. *Oxford Classical Dictionary*).

M8   Letter of Vespasian about a land dispute in N. Corsica, AD 77

Emperor Caesar Vespasian Augustus gives greeting to the magistrates and senators of the Vanacini.

"I am delighted that Otacilius Sagitta, my friend and procurator has earned a testimonial from you for being in charge of you. Regarding the boundary dispute which you currently have with the Mariani about the fields which you bought from my procurator Publilius Memorialis, I have written that my procurator Claudius Clemens should fix the boundaries and have sent him a surveyor. I confirm the privileges granted you by Divus Augustus after his seventh consulship and retained until the time of Galba."

The following were the ambassadors: Lasemo, son of Leucanus, priest of the emperor, and Eunus, son of Tomasus, priest of Augustus. When C. Arruntius Catellius Celer and M. Arruntius Aquila were consuls [AD 77], on 12 October.

[MW 460 = EDCS–22500815]

Stone inscription at Vanacini, N. Corsica. Of more interest than the land dispute is the fact that the Vancini have bought land from Vespasian's procurator, raising money for the exchequer.

M9 Public lands allocated to tribes in Numidia (modern Algeria)

[On the authority of Emperor] Vespasian Caesar Augustus, public lands of Cirta have been allocated to the Suburbures Regiani and the Nicibes through Tullius Pomponianus Capito, legate of Augustus.

[MW 448 = EDCS–13600222*]

C. Tullius Capito Pomponianus Plotius Firmus became consul in 84. For Cirta, see **U23**.

M10 Vespasian's building around the empire

And equally, through all lands in Roman jurisdiction, cities were restored with exceptional care, roads were built at enormous expense.

[*Epitome de Caesaribus* 9.9]

M11 Road-restoration in Sardinia, AD 74

[5]6 [miles] from Turris. Emperor Caesar Vespasian Augustus *pontifex maximus*, holding tribunician [power for the 5th time], hailed *imperator* 13 times, father of the fatherland, consul 5 times, designated for a 6th time, censor; he remade and restored (the road) when [Sex.] Subrius Dexter was procurator and prefect of Sardinia.

[MW 337 = *CIL* 10. 8024 = EDCS–22500801]

Milestone, AD 74, on road from Caralis (Cagliari) to Turris Libisonis (Porto Torres) in Sardinia.

M12 Road building in Eastern Turkey, AD 76

Under Emperor Vespasian Caesar Augustus, *pontifex maximus,* holding tribunician power for the 7th time, hailed *imperator* 14 times, consul 7 times, father of the fatherland; Emperor Titus Caesar, son of Augustus, consul 5 times; and ~~Domitian Caesar, son of Augustus~~, consul 4 times. Gnaeus Pompeius Collega, propraetorian legate of Augustus. 3 miles.

[MW 86 = *ILS* 8904 = EDCS–26900094]

Milestone from modern Yurtbasi in Eastern Turkey.

M13 Bridge over R. Calycadnus, Rough Cilicia, built AD 77–8

Emperor Caesar Vespasian Augustus, father of the fatherland, consul 8 times, and Emperor Titus Caesar, son of Augustus, consul 6 times, both censors, built the bridge from public funds. Through L. Octavius Memor, propraetorian legate, proconsul and consul designate.

[Greek: MW 438 = *IGRR* 3.507]

Parts of the limestone Roman bridge still survive in Silifke, S. Turkey, just north of Cyprus.

M14   Road-building all across Asia Minor under Titus, AD 80

Emp(eror) [T(itus)] Caesar Augustus, son of Divus Vespasian, *pontifex maximus*, holding tribunician power for the 10th time, *imperator* 15 times, consul 8 times, censor, father of the fatherland [and] Caes(ar) ~~Domitian, son of Divus~~, consul 7 times, leader of the younger generation, [through] the agency of Aulus Caesennius Gallus, propraetorian legate, built the roads of the provinces of Galatia, Cappadocia, Pontus, Pisidia, Paphlagonia, Lycaonia and Armenia Minor. 71.

[MW 105 = ILS 263 = EDCS–24100197]

Marble milestone on the road between Ancyra and Dorylaeum (Phrygia, central Turkey), recorded by Hamilton in the 18th century. Domitian's name, though not his titles was erased. 71 represents the distance of the milestone.

M15   Domitian restores road in Corduba, S. Spain, AD 90

Emperor Caesar Domitian Augustus Germanicus, son of Divus Vespasian, *pontifex maxsumus*, holding tribunician power for the 9th time, hailed *imperator* 21 times, consul 15 times, censor for life, father of the fatherland, [restored] the Augustan road from the arch where Baetica starts […]

[MW 122 = *ILS* 269 = EDCS–05600090]

Milestone (damaged at end) from Corduba in Baetica. The inscription misspells *pontifex maximus.*

M16   Engineering work on the River Euphrates in Asia Minor, AD 72–3

[Emperor Ca]esar Vespasian Augustus, *pontifex maximus,* holding tribunician power for the 4th time, hailed *imperator* 10 times, [consul] 4 times, designated for the 5th, [father of the fatherland, and Titus] Caesar Vespasian, son of Augustus, hailed *imperator* 3 times, holding tribunician power for the 2nd time, consul 2 times, designated for the 3rd, censors designate, under [Publius] Marius Celsus, propraetorian legate of Augustus […] and Legion? […] carried out the work of the mechanical screw from communal [expense?] (*picture of the River Euphrates*) Legion [III] 'Gallic'.

[MW 93 = *ILS* 8903 = EDCS–16700312]

Found by R. Euphrates in Ayni, S. Turkey, an area now under the Ataturk Dam Lake. The mechanical screw will presumably have been an Archimedes screw, used for irrigation.

INFRASTRUCTURE PROJECTS AT ANTIOCH IN SYRIA: M17–M21

Antioch in Syria (*OCD*: Antioch (1) = modern Antayka, Turkey, at the NE corner of the Mediterranean, near the Syrian border) was a Seleucid royal capital, founded 300 BC which was made a free city by Julius Caesar in 47 BC and capital of the Roman province of Syria. Together with its harbour town, Seleucia in Pieria (*OCD*: Seleucia (2)) it received considerable attention under Vespasian who had known the area well as governor of Syria. The range of sources show infrastructure projects being undertaken through direct intervention of emperor or governor but also by the local population. The town also receives contemporary notice from Josephus because of its large Jewish population (*Jewish War,* 7.41–62).

M17   Vespasian at Antioch, AD 67

Vespasian had taken command of his forces at Antioch, which is the capital of Syria, and as regards size and general prosperity, undoubtedly holds third place in the Roman world.

[Josephus, *Jewish War* 3.29]

M18   Canal built for fullers by locals in Antioch, Syria, AD 73/74

Under Emperor Titus Flavius Vespasian Caesar Augustus and Emperor Titus Caesar and Emperor Domitian Caesar, sons of Augustus. The work of constructing the canal for fullers, and barriers diverting water from the same river, having been first conceived by Marcus Ulpius Traianus, legate of Caesar Augustus, was carried out by the Metropolis of the Antiochians by means of embedded blocks in the year 122. From the River Orontes up to the [mouth under] Mount Amanus is a length of fourteen stades, the area of each block is [forty]-one square feet; the assignment of the work was [equal] according to the proportion of the number of men engaged to the length, breadth and depth of each block. Each block which has been worked on will be kept as clean as it was when it was handed over. There are on this pillar the rest of the names of the men in the sector of Damas the high priest: length in feet 33.75; the block of Bagrades 38.25 feet in length (etc.) ... 720 feet in all.

[D. Feissel, *Syria* 62 (1985), pages 79–84]

One of a pair of limestone *stelai* in Greek showing the leaders of the citizen groups responsible for each 720 foot section of the canal (slightly under two miles in total length). Fulleries (ancient laundries) naturally required large amounts of water, but were perhaps the sort of private amenity to be built by citizens rather than Roman soldiers, like the canal below. It is unusual to find Vespasian's full name as given here. For Ulpius Traianus, father of the emperor Trajan, see **B70**.

M19   Canal built by legionaries in Antioch, Syria, AD 75

Emperor Vespasian Caesar Augustus, *pontifex maximus*, holding tribunican power for the 6th time, hailed *imperator* 12 times, father of the fatherland, consul 6 times, designated consul for the 7th, censor; Emperor Titus Caesar son of Augustus, *pontifex maximus*, in his 4th year of tribunician power, consul 4 times, designated consul for the 5th, censor; ~~Domitian~~ Caesar son of Augustus, consul 3 times; Marcus Ulpius Traianus as legate of Augustus with praetorian rank, took care of [the construction] of the course of the Dipotamia ("Double River") Canal for three miles, with bridges, by soldiers of four legions: III 'Gallic', IIII 'Scythian', VI 'Ironclad', XVI 'Flavian', likewise of twenty cohorts and [likewise?] of the people of Antioch. One mile.

[*AE* 1983, 927 = EDCS–08500619]

The stonecutter has made Vespasian imperator twelve times instead of fourteen and awarded Titus a priesthood he held only as Emperor.

M20   Canal at Antioch

The river Orontes in Syria does not flow down to the sea in a completely smooth course, but is carried there over cliffs and rapids and waterfalls. The Roman king wanted to sail ships from the sea up to the city of Antioch, and so with much labour and monetary expense he had a navigable canal dug and diverted the river into it.

[Pausanias, *Guide to Greece* 8.29.3]

M21   Inscription at the start of the canal/tunnel at Antioch

Divus Vespasian and Divus Titus (oversaw the building)

[*CIL* 3.6702 = EDCS–27800552]

The mile-long canal still mostly survives, including a sizable portion through a tunnel engineered by Legion X 'Straits' and completed only under Antoninus Pius [*CIL* 3.189].

M22   Arch to Vespasian at Lepcis Magna, Libya, AD 77–78

To emperor Caesar Vespasian Augustus, *pontifex maximus*, holding tribunician power for the [9th time, hailed *imperator*] 19 times, father of the fatherland, consul 8 times, (and) Titus Emperor Caesar Vespasian, son of Augustus, *pontifex*, [hailed *imperator* ? times], consul 6 times; Gaius Paccius Africanus, pontifex, consul, proconsul of Africa, patron, through the agency of Gnaeus Domitius Ponticus, praetor, legate with propraetorian powers, patron of the municipality, dedicated (this).

[MW 485 = *IRT* 342* = EDCS–14200133]

Grey limestone blocks with the same text on front and back. Probably from an archway (text is visible front and back) later incorporated into a Byzantine gateway. Paccius Africanus is known from Tacitus, *Histories* 4.41 to have been criticised in the senate for prosecuting fellow senators under Nero.

M23   Restoration of stoa at Megalopolis, Greece AD 93/4

Emperor Caesar ~~Domitian~~ Augustus ~~Germanicus~~, son of Divus Vespasian, *pontifex maximus*, holding tribunician power for the 13th time, hailed *imperator* 22 times, consul 16 times, censor for life, at his own expense completely restored the portico for the people of Megalopolis which had been destroyed by fire.

[Latin and Greek: MW 436 = EDCS–29601651]

EGYPT AND BERENICE: M24–M30

Egypt had been a separate and special administrative area since the time of Augustus (Tac. *Ann.* 2.59, *Hist.* 1.11 = LACTOR 17, M6, M8). Its importance was confirmed in AD 68/9 by the attempt of Clodius Macer in Africa to seize control of the grain supplies, and by the important declaration for Vespasian of Tiberius Julius Alexander, prefect of Egypt. Under the Flavians, trade with India seems to have been increasingly important and the period shows development of Berenice. This harbour (modern Medinet-el-Haras in Egypt) was founded by Ptolemy II on the western coast of the Red Sea. Goods travelling between the Indian Ocean and Roman empire would be transported from Berenice across by road to Coptos and the navigable Nile. A *praefectus Berenices* or 'prefect of {Mount} Berenice', first attested in this period, was responsible for the port and the whole road. The area around Berenice was also rich in emeralds. In AD 92 Domitian ordered *horrea piperataria* (Pepper Warehouse) to be built in Rome, for pepper coming from India via Egypt.

M24   Trade with India

It will be useful to set out the whole of the route from Egypt, now that for the first time reliable knowledge of it is available. It is a worthwhile subject since each year India takes up no less than 50 million sesterces from our empire, in return for products which sell for a hundred times their original cost.

[Pliny, *Natural History* 6.101]

Pliny then (*NH* 6.102–3) describes the journey from Alexandria to Coptos (Keft – 309 miles or 12 days, down the Nile) and then another 257 miles by road with camels, taking 12 days, travelling at night, stopping by day at designated watering stations, to reach Berenice on the Red Sea. He then gives the various routes and ports to Arabia and India (*NH* 6.104–106).

M25   Riches from Arabia

What has made Arabia 'happy' (*Arabia Felix)* is the extravagance of human beings even in their death, when they burn over the deceased spices that they know perfectly well to have been created for the benefit of the gods. ... [84] But the Arabian Sea is even 'happier': out of it come the pearls that it exports; and on the lowest estimate a hundred million sesterces every year are taken from us by India, the Chinese and the peninsula of Arabia. That is the high price of our fancy tastes and our women.

[Pliny, *Natural History* 12.82, 84]

M26   *The Voyage around the Red Sea*

[1] Of the known harbours of the Red Sea and the trading posts around it, the first is the Egyptian port of Myos Hormos (Mouse Harbour), and after that, sailing 1,800 stades on the right is Berenice. Both harbours are at the edges of Egypt, and lie on the Red Sea. ...

[19] On the left of Berenice, after two or three days' run from Myos Hormos if you sail eastwards through the Gulf along the coast, there is a second harbour and port which is called Leuke Kome ('White Village'). This provides access to Petra and Malichas, king of the Nabataeans. This has some means of trading for those who equip and dispatch ships of no great size to it from Arabia. Therefore it is the seat of a collector of the 25% tax on imported goods, and for the sake of security a centurion is settled there with a force.

[*Voyage around the Red Sea*, 1 and 19]

The *Periplous Maris Erythraei* (*Voyage around the Red Sea*) is by an unknown first-century AD author, but 'a source of the highest importance for the really extensive knowledge of the routes to southern India and south along the East African coast that had been opened up.' (*Oxford Classical Dictionary³*, under '*periploi* ').

M27   Vespasian confiscates inheritances

The deified Vespasian confiscated inheritances left in trust by Greeks to Romans or by Romans to Greeks; however, those who have acknowledged the trust have received one half.

[*Gnomon of the Idios Logos* – '*Regulations of the Special Accountant'* 18]

Egypt also had special financial regulations which survive in the form of 115 clauses of regulations of the 'Special Accountant'.

M28   Prefect of Mount Berenice

I, L. Junius Calvinus, prefect of Mount Berenice, heard Memnon, with my wife Minicia Rustica, at 8 o'clock on 18 March in the fourth year of our Emperor Vespasian Augustus.

[MW 521 = *CIL* 3.32 = EDCS–21200091]

Memnon was the name wrongly given by Greeks and Romans to one of two colossal statues of Amenhotep III (1417–1379 BC) in the necropolis of Thebes in Egypt. After being damaged in an earthquake in 27 BC, the more northerly statue was alleged to 'sing' (Tac. *Ann.* 2.61.2; Pliny *NH* 2.101) or to sound like a broken harp-string (Pausanias 1.42.3). Some 107 Roman graffiti record individual visitors, including Germanicus in AD 19, and Petronius Secundus, prefect of Egypt on 14 March AD 92 (MW 523). The sound, presumably caused by something in the damaged statue expanding in the heat of the sun stopped when emperor Septimius Severus mended the statue (*SHA Severus* 17.4).

M29 Julius Ursus orders provision of water for the Coptos-Berenice road, AD 76/7

In year 8 of Emperor Caesar Augustus Vespasian, L. Julius Ursus, prefect of Egypt, returning from Berenice, ordered a watering-place to be sought in this area and when it was discovered he ordered a fort and cisterns to be built. M. Trebonius Valens, prefect of Mount Berenice oversaw the work.

[Bagnall, Bulow-Jacobsen & Cuvigny, *JRA* 14 (2001) pages 325–333 = EDCS–24800741*].

This well-preserved Latin inscription was found at Sikayt, *c.* 7km WNW of Berenice. It can be recognised as equivalent to another fragmentary inscription (*AE* 1956.57) found at Didymoi on the Berenice-Coptos road (described earlier by Pliny, *NH* 6.102–3) and similar to MW 335, found at Aphrodites on the same road which showed Ursus expanding a watering-place and strengthening the fort. The *JRA* article republishes both other inscriptions too and helpfully shows how this affects our knowledge of Ursus' career (**U43–U44**).

M30 Prefect of Egypt's decree on record-keeping, AD 89

Proclamation of Marcus Mettius Rufus, prefect of Egypt. Claudius Areius, officer of the Oxyrhynchite district, has demonstrated to me that neither private nor public affairs are suitably organised because for many years the official abstracts in the property record office have not been kept in the proper way, even though there were frequent decisions on the part of my predecessors that they should receive the necessary correction. It is not feasible to do this properly without copies going back to the past. I therefore order all property owners to register their own possession with the property record office within six months; creditors any mortgages they have, and others any claims they may have. When they make their return they are to declare the source of each item of property or possession that has come to them.

Wives too are to be appended to the declaration of their husbands if in accordance with local law his property is liable to a claim by them, and children likewise in the property declarations of their parents where usufruct has been guaranteed to the parents through public contracts but ownership after their death has been secured to the children, so that those who enter into contracts with them are not misled by ignorance.

I also enjoin the clerks who draw up contracts and the recorders to [finalise] nothing without instructions from the property record office. They are informed that anything of that kind will not be valid and further that they themselves if they act contrary to instructions will have to expect the appropriate penalty. If in the property record office there are registrations from earlier times, they are to be most carefully protected and likewise the abstracts, in order that if there is any further investigation into those who have made irregular registrations, they may be convicted by these means.

[Therefore in order that] the use of the abstracts may be secure and preserved in perpetuity, making a second registration unnecessary, I enjoin the keepers of the record office to review the abstracts every five years, transferring to freshly made ones those of the most recent property statement of each individual by village and by category. In the ninth year of Domitian, 4th day of the month Domitian.

[Oxyrhyncus Papyrus II 237, col. 8, 27–43]

M31   Bridge over the Nile at Coptos built by Domitian, AD 90

Emperor Caesar ~~Domitian Augustus Germanicus~~ *pontifex maximus* with tribunician power, consul 15 times, censor for life, father of the fatherland made the bridge from the ground up [... *(one line deleted)*...] when Q. Licinius Ancotius Proculus was prefect of the camp, L. Antistius Asiaticus was prefect of Berenice, under the supervision of C. Julius Magnus, centurion of Legion III 'Cyrene'.

[Latin: MW 411 = *CIL* 3.13580 = EDCS–17100167]

For a picture of this inscription, see **T31**. Domitian's name has been erased, and almost certainly that of a prefect of Egypt, M. Mettius Rufus (**P9**).

CITIZENSHIP IN SPAIN AND ELSEWHERE: M32–M43

Spain already had several *municipia* and *coloniae* whose citizens had Roman citizenship. Vespasian's grant of the Latin right (*ius Latii*) meant that other communities in Spain could apply to establish by town charter a system of local government which meant that the magistrates became Roman citizens at the end of their year in office. Thus the two generations after AD 69 can be described as 'in many respects the zenith of Roman Spain' (Alföldy on Spain in *CAH²* XI, chapter 13). Several otherwise unknown communities set up detailed statutes which show how closely provincial communities were already conforming to Roman practice, how closely their charters made them follow it, and how anomalies were dealt with. For the *Lex Irnitana* (supplemented by statutes from Salpensa and Malaca) see **Section F**. For the benefits of Roman citizenship, see the case of St Paul who, as a Roman citizen, escaped flogging and could appeal directly to Caesar when dragged before the Roman military by his opponents (*Acts* 22.22–29 and 25.6–12 = LACTOR 19, M76 and M37).

M32   Vespasian extends Roman citizenship in Spain

To the whole of Spain the Emperor Vespasian Augustus granted the Latin right, which had been tossed about in the storms that the state underwent.

[Pliny, *Natural History* 3.30]

M33   Local magistrates in Igabrum (Cabra in S. Spain) gain citizenship AD 75

To Augustan Apollo. The townspeople of Igabrum, having, by the gift of Emperor Caesar Augustus Vespasian, obtained Roman citizenship, together with their families, by holding office, when Vespasian was consul for the 6th time. Marcus Aelius Niger, son of Marcus, aedile, gave this as a gift.

[MW 481 = *ILS* 1981 = EDCS–08700321*]

M34   Gold statue put up to Titus by Emerita in Lusitania, AD 77

To Titus Caesar Vespasian, son of Augustus, *pontifex,* hailed *imperator* 12 times, holding tribunician power for the 7th time, consul 6 times. The province of Lusitania, under C. Arruntius Catellius Celer, propraetorian legate of Augustus, and L. Junius Latro Conimbricesis, high priest of the province of Lusitania, made this from 5 pounds of gold.

[MW 104 = *ILS* 261 = EDCS–05600561*]

M35 Settlement rebuilt on the plain, in Spain, AD 77

Emperor Caesar Vespasian Augustus, *pontifex maximus*, holding tribunician power for the 9th time, hailed *imperator* 18 times, consul 8 times, father of the fatherland, gives greeting to the 4 chief magistrates and the councillors of the Saborenses.

"Since you indicate that you are in an unsatisfactory condition and labouring under many difficulties, I give you permission to construct a town centre, bearing my name as you wish, on level ground. I guarantee the income from indirect taxes which you say were assigned to you by Divus Augustus; if you wish to add any new ones you will have to approach the proconsul about them. I can make no decision when there is no one to present the other side of the case. I received your decree on 25 July; and dismissed your ambassadors on 29 July. Farewell."

The duumvirs C. Cornelius Severus and M. Septimius Severus had the inscription cut in bronze at public expense.

[MW 461 = *ILS* 6092 = EDCS–08700935]

Levick, *Vespasian* p.140 mentions this case. The area is now Cañete, Eastern Spain.

M36 Dedication from a new municipality in N. Portugal, AD 79

To Emperor Caesar Vespasian Augustus, *pontifex maximus*, holding tribunician power for the 10th time, hailed *imperator* 20 times, father of the fatherland, consul 9 times; to Emperor T. Vespasian Caesar son of Augustus, *pontifex*, holding tribunician power for the 8th time, hailed *imperator* 14 times, consul 7 times; [Domitian's name and titles erased]; To Gaius Calpetanus Rantius Quirinalis Festus, of the Valerian tribe, propraetorian legate of Augustus; to Decimus Cornelius Maecianus, legate of Augustus; to L. Arruntius Maximus, procurator of Augustus. Legion VII, 'Fortunate and Twinned'. The 10 settlements: Aquiflavians, [Aobrigens,] Bibali, Coelerni, [Equaesi], Interamici, [Limici, Aebisocii], Quarquerni, Tamagani.

[MW 87 = *ILS* 254 = EDCS–05501843]

This inscription from Aquae Flaviae = modern Chaves in N. Portugal marks the settlement becoming a municipality in AD 79. Legion VII was raised by Galba in Spain (Tac. *Hist.* 2.86), and returned to Spain to be stationed at Legio, now Leon in NW Spain (about 100 miles away).

M37 Failed appeal against tax assessment, Munigua, Baetica, 7 September, AD 79

Emperor Titus Caesar Vespasian Augustus, *pontifex maximus*, in his 9th year of tribunician power, hailed *imperator* 14 times, 7 times consul, father of the fatherland gives greetings to the four-man board and councillors of Munigua. Since, then, you have appealed against paying the money that you owed to Servilius Pollio according to the judgement of Sempronius Fuscus, it was appropriate that the penalty for making an unjustified appeal should be exacted from you. But I have put what I say on the basis of my own forbearance rather than on your lack of prudence, and I have remitted the HS 50,000 to your treasury, given its fragile state, which you have offered in your own defence. I have written, moreover, to my friend Gallicanus, the proconsul, that the money that has been adjudged due to Pollio you shall pay, but that he should free you from payment of the interest from the day the judgement was delivered. It is fair that the income from your indirect taxes, which you indicate that Pollio had, should be taken into account, to prevent anything being lost to the community on this head. Farewell. Issued on 7 September.

[*AE* 1962, 288 = EDCS–10102150*]

Bronze inscription, dated 7 September AD 79, and showing Titus had been hailed as *imperator* 14 times at this date. A coin has been found *in situ* at Pompeii showing Titus with 15 salutations (still only published in a popular Italian archaeology magazine, G. Stefani, *La vera data dell'eruzione*, in "Archeo" n. 10 (260), ottobre 2006, pp 10–13). This would show that the eruption of Vesuvius was later in 79 than the date of 24 September usually found in manuscripts of Pliny *Letters*.

M38   Local magistrates in Iluro (Aluro in S. Spain) gain citizenship under Domitian

To Emperor Domitian Caesar Augustus Germanicus. Lucius Munius Novatus of the Quirina tribe and Lucius Munius Aurelianus, son of Lucius, of the Quirina tribe, who obtained the Roman citizenship by holding the office of duumvir, presented this monument as a gift at their own expense.

[MW 480 = *ILS* 1982 = EDCS–05501644]

M39   Caesarea in Palestine becomes *Colonia Prima Flavia*

Caesarea, founded by King Herod, now the colony Prima Flavia, established by the emperor Vespasian.

[Pliny, *Natural History* 5.69]

Caesarea Maritima, between modern Tel Aviv and Haifa in Israel was an ancient town rebuilt by Herod the Great. Nero's judgment against the minority Jewish community in AD 66 led to riots, a massacre of Jews and the Jewish revolt. (Jos. *JW* 2.266–270, 284–5). After the war, Vespasian refounded the city as a Roman colony.

M40   Coinage from the Flavian Colony of Corinth

Obv: Emperor Caesar Domitian Augustus Germanicus
Rev: Horseman with spear, galloping. Julian Flavian Augustan Colony of Corinth

[MW 489 = *BMC, Corinth* 580, p.72]

The circumstances in which Corinth became a 'Flavian' colony as well as the 'Julian' one founded in 44/43 BC are not clear, but it may relate to an earthquake there in the 70s, and the city's gratitude for imperial aid (or even the hope of aid). Corinth and other Achaian cities had been deprived of their right to mint coinage by Vespasian (along with their freedom see **M2**), but this was restored by Domitian from around 84.

M41   A colony on the Black Sea seeks a senatorial patron, AD 82

When Emperor Domitian [Augustus for the 8th time] and Titus Flavius Sabinus were [consuls], on 13 June, in [the senate-house?] in the Flavian Colony of Peace, Deultum, [...]talca and Gaius Occeius Niger, the duumvirs made speeches [...] for patronage being granted to our colony by Avidius Quietus, imperial legate, a most distinguished man; they decided that the following should be done about the matter in hand. Since we have served in Legion VIII 'Augustan' and ear[ned 25 years of pay], and have been settled by the most hallowed emperor in the Deultum colony, it was sought from him (*i.e. Avidius*) that according to his great humanity [he might deign] to undertake the patronage of our colony and that it be permitted that a tablet recording that matter be placed in his home, so that he himself might rejoice in his humanity and that the status of our promotion and his dutifulness might be recorded.

The following were present when this was written: (*list of names not given here*)

[MW 486 = *ILS* 6105 = EDCS–19000538]

Bronze tablet, found in Rome on Esquiline Hill (presumably where Quietus lived). Pliny *NH* 4.45 refers to 'Develcon, a veteran colony, with a marsh, now called Deultum' (Black Sea coast of Bulgaria). Avidius Quietus, sought as patron by the colony, was presumably the legate of legion at the time. For his career, see **B93**.

M42   Bronze coin from Domitian-city, Sala in Lydia (Turkey)

Obv: Laureate head of Domitia, right.
ΔΟΜΙΤΙΑ [C]ΕΒΑCΤΗ (Domitia Augusta)
Rev: Cybele holding large, shallow bowl and resting left arm on tympanum
ΔΟΜΙΤΙΑΝΟΠΟΛΕΙΤΩΝ ΣΑΛΗΝΩΝ (of the people of the Domitian-city of Sala).

[MW 503 = *RPC* 1341]

The coin shows Sala in Lydia (Turkey) renaming itself Domitianopolis (Domitian-city). Another town in Lydia was named Flaviopolis (MW 506).

M43   Award of citizenship in Cilicia

To Titus Flavius Alexander, son of Castor, of the Quirina tribe. His freedman Hermes made this after Emperor Caesar Vespasian gave him citizenship.

[MW 520 = *ILS* 1979 = EDCS–27800573]

Site of Palaea Isaura in Taurus Mountains, central southern Turkey. It is not known what the dedication was or how Alexander had gained citizenship.

OFFICIALS AND GOVERNORS: M44–M53

Vespasian was keen to maximise imperial revenues (e.g. **J4h**, **M1–M9**), and seems to have created new methods of accounting as well as new taxes (**M46**). A *fiscus Asiaticus* and a *fiscus Alexandrinus* (**M47–M48**) came into being to collect revenues from those two wealthy provinces, instead of the traditional *aerarium* (treasury). Suetonius described Domitian as an emperor responsible for an unprecendentedly high standard of honesty and justice among his provincial governors (Suet. *Dom.* 8) and this can be seen in **M49**, **M52–M53**, nothwithstanding Pliny's accusations and those prompted by Domitian's reputation (**M50–M51**).

M44   Record sailing times

15 summers later [in AD 69], praetorian senator Valerius Marinus made Alexandria from Puteoli on the ninth day, under a very gentle breeze. Gaius Flavius, deputy of proconsul Vibius Crispus made Africa from Cadiz within two days, under the lightest breeze.

[Pliny, *Natural History* 19.3]

Pliny praises the use of flax in sails. Alexandria is 1,800 km from Puteoli by the most direct route. More normally ships would stay close to the coast in case of storms, but Marinus was in a hurry to defect to Vesp. (**B5** note).

M45   Legal dispute at Herculaneum sent to the urban praetor at Rome

An appointment is made for Calatoria Themis, on 3 December next at Rome in the forum of Augustus in front of the platform of the urban *praetor*, at the second hour. The woman who claims that she is Petronia Iusta, daughter of Spurius, has exacted a promise for 1,000 sesterces to be given. Calatoria Themis, under the authority of her guardian Gaius Petronius Telesphorus has made a pledge. An appointment is made for Gaius Petronius Telesphorus for the stated day, place, and hour. Petronia Iusta, daughter of Spurius, has exacted a promise for 1,000 sesterces to be given. Gaius Petronius Telesphorus has made a pledge. Transacted 6 September in the consulship of Gaius Pomponius and Lucius Manlius Patruinus [AD 74].

[*AE* (1951) 213 = *AE* (1951) 215 = *AE* (1952) 163 = *AE* (1956) 265 = EDCS–13900594]

The dispute was about whether Calatoria Themis was free or a freedwoman with ongoing duties towards her former owner. For a witness statement in the case, see **L28**, and for other documents about the case, Cooley² G5–G11.

M46   Funerary altar of procurator of the Jewish poll-tax, Rome

To Titus Flavius Euschemon, imperial freedman, secretary of correspondence and likewise procurator in charge of the Jewish poll-tax. Flavia Aphrodisia made the monument for her well-deserving patron and husband.

[MW 203 = *ILS* 1519 = EDCS–18500251*]

M47   Funerary inscription of imperial freedman, procurator of Alexandrian treasury

To Ulpia Euhodia his excellent wife, T. Flavius Delphicus, imperial freedman, clerk managing the account of the procurator in charge of the chests of inheritances of the Alexandrian treasury.

[MW 202 = *ILS* 1518 = EDCS–30200479]

M48 Funerary inscription of imperial freedman, procurator of Asian treasury

To Hermes, imperial freedman, chamberlain of Domitia, wife of Augustus. Fortunatus (made this) for his most dutiful and generous father, procurator of the Asian treasury.

[MW 200 = *ILS* 1517 = EDCS–18500217]

M49 Letter of Domitian against requisitioning

According to the instructions of Emperor ~~Domitian~~ Caesar Augustus, son of Augustus, to Claudius Athenodorus, procurator. Among the prime subjects, and ones demanding much care from my father Divus Vespasian Caesar, I am aware that the privileges of the cities received much concern. With keen attention to these, he gave instructions that the provinces should be oppressed neither by hiring out beasts of burden nor by troubles caused by entertaining strangers. But nevertheless, through complacency or because it did not meet with any correction, this set of rules has not been observed: a long-standing and well-established practice survives to this day which is gradually passing into law, if force is not used to prevent it prevailing. I instruct you to pay attention to prevent anyone taking a beast of burden if he does not possess my warrant. For it is the height of injustice either to do a favour to certain people or, because of their standing, that warrants should be written out when it is permitted to no one to grant them except myself. Nothing then is to be done which will infringe my instruction and will nullify my extremely beneficent attitude towards the cities. For it is just to come to the aid of the provinces when they are not in good condition and hardly adequate to necessary impositions. Nobody is to bring force to bear on them contrary to my wish. Nobody is to take any conveyance except one which has my warrant. If agricultural workers are dragged off, the countryside will remain uncultivated. And you, either using privately owned beasts of burden or hiring them, will do your best [to --- . ---] send signed warrants to you.

[MW 466 = *SEG* 17.755]

Inscribed in Greek at Hama (Syria). Requisitioning was a persistent complaint of provincials, and emperors seem to have made repeated (and therefore ineffectual) decrees setting out what was (not) allowed. For decrees under Tiberius and Claudius, see LACTOR 19, M59–M63.

M50 Requisitioning

There was no rumpus in commandeering vehicles, no fuss about billets; rations were the same as for the rest; in all this your entourage was alert and obedient. One would have said that some great general was going out to his army, very probably yourself, since there was no, or very little difference between you as future emperor and actual emperor. How different was the journey of another emperor a short while ago! If indeed it was a 'journey' not a raid when homes were emptied to provide billets, when all land to left and right is burnt and trampled, as if some force of nature or even those very barbarians from whom he was fleeing had fallen on it. The provinces had to be convinced that that was how Domitian travelled, not every emperor. Therefore, not so much for your own reputation as for the common good, you added a proclamation of your expenditure and his.

[Pliny, *Panegyric to Trajan* 20.3–5]

M51 An honest praetor under Domitian

Titus Quietus the praetor had recently returned from his province, having shown the greatest integrity in his praetorship – which was extremely noteworthy in Domitian's era.

[Macrobius, Saturnalia 7.3.15]

Name, date and description would all fit T. Avidus Quietus, see **B93**. Macrobius, writing in the fourth century is only aware of Domitian's general reputation as a 'bad emperor' rather than that given by Suet. *Dom.* 8.

M52 Edict of governor of Pisidia, ensuring winter corn supply to Antioch, *c.* AD 93

Edict of Lucius Antistius Rusticus, propraetorian legate to Emperor Caesar Domitian Augustus Germanicus. Since the duumvirs and members of the council of the most splendid Colony of Antioch have written to me saying that the harshness of winter has caused the price of corn to flare up, and have requested that the mass of ordinary people should have some means of buying it {Hooray!}, all persons who are either citizens or resident aliens of the Colony of Antioch are to declare before the duumvirs of the Colony of Antioch within thirty days of the posting of my edict how much corn each has and where it is, and how much he is drawing for seed or for the annual supply of his household; and he is to make all the rest of the corn available to the buyers of the Colony of Antioch. I appoint a period for selling to end on 1 August next. If anyone fails to act accordingly, let him know that for whatever is kept contrary to my edict, I shall impose penalties for the offence, establishing an eighth share as the reward for informers. Further, since it is declared to me that before this persistently cold winter weather the price of corn in the colony was eight or nine *asses* per *modius*, and since it would be the height of iniquity that anyone should make a profit out of the hunger of his fellow citizens, I forbid the sale price of corn to rise above one *denarius* [i.e. 10 *asses*] per *modius*.

    [...] Rufus, imperial procurator

[MW 464 = EDCS–12700147]

Latin inscription from Antioch in Pisidia (modern Turkey) on a base honouring Antistius Rusticus, whose career inscription appears on the same stone (see **U27a**).

M53 Baebius Massa prosecuted in AD 93 for extortion in Baetica

[4] The senate had appointed Herennius Senecio and myself as counsels for the province of Baetica, in their prosecution of Baebius Massa. He was convicted; and the House decreed that his property be kept in public custody. Senecio investigated and discovered that the consuls were about to give time to his requests to reclaim his property. So he came to me, and said, "Let us go and seek from the consuls, with the same unanimity with which we conducted the prosecution, not to allow his property to be squandered by those who ought to be protecting them." [5] I answered, "Since we were given the duty of prosecutors, by the senate, reflect whether or not you think that we have completed our task, now the enquiry is finished." He said "You set what limits you wish for yourself, since you have no links with the province, except from

this service you have recently given; I myself was born there, and served as quaestor there." [6] So I said, "If that is what you have decided and are fixed upon, I will follow you, so that if any ill-will comes of this, it will not be yours alone." [7] We went to the consuls; Senecio said what was needed, and I added some comments. We had only just finished, when Massa complained that Senecio had discharged his duty as a prosecutor but had satisfied his enmity and bitterness towards himself; he demanded to be allowed to prosecute him for impiety. [8] Horror all round. But I spoke up: "Most noble consuls, I am afraid that Massa has charged me with collusion and a dereliction of my duty by his silence, since he has not asked permission to prosecute me as well." What I said was taken up at once, and soon afterwards praised and talked about everywhere. [9] Divus Nerva (for he, while still a private citizen, paid attention to any public action that was right and good) wrote a most serious letter to me, congratulating not only me, but the age, which had the good fortune to have an example (for that is what he wrote) so like that of the ancients.

[Pliny the Younger, *Letters* 7.33.4–9]

For the start and finish of the letter, which Pliny wrote in the hope of appearing in Tacitus' *Histories*, see **R31**.

FRIENDLY KINGDOMS: M54–M68
Tacitus (almost alone) refers to local monarchs as 'client kings' (**M54**). They *were* dependent for their position on Rome (**M59**), but friendly kings helped Vespasian to the throne (**M54–M56**) and could expect help in return (**M66–M68**). Most were Roman citizens, and in the next generation become Roman senators (**M59** note).

**M54   Friendly kings of Emesa and Commagene support Vespasian's bid
        for power**
Before 15 July, the whole of Syria had made the same oath. Sohaemus had come on board with his kingdom and his considerable resources; so had Antiochus with his vast ancestral wealth, the richest of all the client kings.

[Tacitus, *Histories* 2.81]

M55   Friendly kings support Titus in siege of Jerusalem
'The kings Agrippa and Sohaemus also accompanied him, and there was strong military support from King Antiochus...'

[Tacitus, *Histories* 5.1]

M56   Altar in honour of Sohaemus, King of Emesa
To great king Gaius Julius Sohaemus, son of great king Samsigeramus, friend of Caesar, friend of the Romans, awarded the [insignia] of a consul [...], patron of the colony, quinquennial duumvir. Lucius Vitellius Sossianus, son of Lucius, of the Fabian tribe [erected this].

[MW 239 = *ILS* 8958 = EDCS–17700163*]

Altar from Heliopolis (= Baalbek in Lebanon). Sohaemus of Emesa (centred around Homs in Syria) supported Vespasian's bid for power, provided troops for Titus' attack on Jerusalem (**M55**, Jos. *JW* 3.68) and against Antiochus (Jos. *JW* 7.227 = **M59**).

COMMAGENE (M57–M60)

Commagene is the area of modern southern Turkey to the north of Syria. Tiberius had annexed the kingdom in AD 17, but Gaius restored its status as a friendly kingdom in 38, under Antiochus IV. He declared support for Vespasian's bid for empire by 15 July 69 (**M54**) and sent his son, Epiphanes, to help Titus in the siege of Jerusalem in AD 70. But in AD 72 Rome took Commagene over as a province (**M59**) when the Syrian governor Paetus accused the Commagene royal family of plotting to help the Parthians. They were deposed and brought back to Rome (**N58**) but Commagene, incorporated into Syria, remained loyal to Rome.

M57   Antiochus of Commagene

Much the most prosperous of all the kings under the Romans was the king of Commagene, at least before he experienced a change of fortune. He too showed in his old age that one should call no man blessed before his death.

[Josephus, *Jewish War* 5.461]

On the wealth of Antiochus Epiphanes (IV), compare **M54.** Josephus (5.460–465) is describing the courage of Epiphanes' son in bringing 'Macedonian' forces to help Titus in the siege of Jerusalem in AD 70.

M58   Princes of Commagene on coin

Obv: Two young horsemen (Epiphanes and Callinicus)
          ΒΑCΙΛΕΩC ΥΙΟΙ (Sons of the king)
Rev: Capricorn, stars and anchor, in wreath
          ΚΟΜΜΑΓΗΝΩΝ (of the people of Commagene)

[MW 240 = BMC Syria p.110, no1]

M59   Annexation of Commagene, AD 73

Caesennius Paetus, then governor of Syria, whether truthfully or acting out of hatred for Antiochus (for a clear conclusion was never really reached), sent letters to Caesar [221] saying that Antiochus with his son Epiphanes had decided to revolt from the Romans, and had an agreement with the king of the Parthians … [225] Paetus was believed, and received permission to act as he thought advantageous. He did not hesitate, but suddenly, when Antiochus and his court were expecting nothing, invaded Commagene, leading the Sixth Legion and some cohorts and cavalry squadrons to reinforce them. [226] Aristobulus, king of the region called Chalcidice, and Sohaemus, king of Emesa, as it is named, were alongside him too. [227] The invasion met no opposition: none of the natives wanted to raise a hand against them. [228] Antiochus, when the news reached him without warning, cherished no intention of war with the Romans. He decided to leave the entire realm as it was and withdraw in a chariot with his wife and children. He thought that that way he would clear himself in the eyes of the Romans of the charge that had been brought against him … [232] For his sons, however, who were young, experienced in war and exceptionally strong, it was not easy to bear the disaster without putting up a fight. So Epiphanes and Callinicus resorted to force. [233] The struggle was violent and lasted the whole day. The young men displayed conspicuous bravery and their force was in no way diminished when they disengaged in the evening. [234] But Antiochus, even though this was the outcome of the battle, thought he could not bear to remain. He picked up his wife and daughters and took flight with them to Cilicia, and by doing that he broke the morale of his own troops … [236] Before they were completely deprived of their allies, then, Epiphanes' suite had to save themselves from the enemy; a total of ten horsemen crossed the Euphrates with them. [237] From there they then rode under safe-conduct to Vologeses, king of the Parthians, and were not received arrogantly as if they were exiles, but were accorded every honour, as if they still enjoyed their previous good fortune. [238] Paetus sent a centurion to Tarsus, where Antiochus had arrived, and sent him in chains to Rome … [240] Vespasian then gave orders, while Antiochus was still on the road, that he should be released from the chains, abandon Rome as his goal, and stay for the present in Sparta … [243] Caesar graciously gave Epiphanes and Callinicus safe conduct and they arrived in Rome, while their father immediately came to them from Sparta, and they settled there, treated with every sign of respect.

[Josephus, *Jewish War* 7.220–1, 225–8, 232–4, 236–8, 240, 243]

L. Junius P. Caesennius Paetus had been consul in 61, commander in Armenia (Tac. *Ann.* 15.6–17). Vespasian made him governor of Syria, 70–2 (Jos. *JW* 59). At some point he married Flavia Sabina (**J7a**). Antiochus and Callinicus fade from history at this point, presumably living out their lives in comfortable exile. Epiphanes clearly moved to Athens and his two children arguably achieved greater prominence within the Roman Empire than they would have as friendly rulers of Commagene: Gaius Julius Antiochus Epiphanes Philopappos, cos 109, is still famous in Athens today, thanks to his monument and the hill in Athens named after it. His sister, Julia Balbilla was a close friend of Hadrian's empress, Sabina. **N58** records the career of the centurion who brought the princes to Rome.

M60   1st Flavian cohort of Commagenians

To [Gaius] Betitius Pietas, son of Gaius, of the Cornelian tribe, prefect of the first Flavian cohort of Commagenians, quaestor, magistrate [with judicial power], quinquennial magistrate. Betitius Pius, his son, made this for his excellent father and Neratia Procilla for her excellent husband.

[MW 353 = EDCS–12400636]

This tombstone from Aeclanum (central southern Italy) erected to a local magistrate shows the existence of an auxiliary cohort from Commagene, presumably created soon after the annexation of the province in 73.

M61   Agrippa and Berenice restore baths of Herod the Great at Beirut

[Great King Agrippa Philocaesar and] Queen Berenice [children] of great king A[grippa, at their own expense restored the bath-building of the Julian Augustan Fortunate Colony of Berytus wh]ich King Herod, their great-grandfather had made, which through ol[d age had collapsed to the ground, and adorned it] with marble and six columns.

[MW 244 = EDCS–15300229]

M. Julius Agrippa II was son of 'Herod Agrippa' (properly M. Julius Agrippa I), and great-grandson of Herod the Great. His names show the family's long association with Augustus, Marcus Agrippa and the Julio-Claudians. He was brought up in Rome. Under Nero his kingdom included much of Palestine, but he was expelled from Jerusalem in AD 66 for being perceived as too pro-Roman. Having failed to prevent the Jewish revolt, he supported the Roman side (see **M55**) and was rewarded with further extension of his territory. In 75 his sister, Berenice (**J22**), went to live with Titus in Rome and Agrippa II received praetorian status there.

M62   Berenice honoured at Athens

The Council of the Areopagus and the Council of 500, and the people (honour) Julia Berenice, great queen, daughter of King Julius Agrippa, descendant of great kings and benefactors of our city, through the providence of the curator of the city, Tiberius Claudius Theogenes Paianeus.

[MW 243]

M63   King Rhescuporis of Bosporus, AD 71

[In honour of] Emperor Vespasian Caesar [Augustus, chief priest, hailed *imperator*] for the 6th time, father of the fatherland, [3 times consul, designated consul for the 4th], lord of the entire Bosphorus [...] piously, justly, of the hereditary king Tiberius Julius Rhescuporis, son of King Julius [...], friend of Caesar, friend of the Romans, high priest of the Augusti for life, and benefactor of his fatherland [...]

[MW 233 = *IGRR* 1.903]

The kingdom of Bosporus consisted of the area of modern Crimea and an area to the east of the Sea of Azov. Settled of old by Greek colonists, it had become a kingdom long friendly to Rome. Tiberius Julius Rhescuporis (I) was son of Tiberius Julius Cotys who may have been deposed by Nero *c*. AD 63. If so, Rhescuporis regained the kingship and ruled until *c*. 90. He was a direct descendant of Mark Antony (for family tree, see LACTOR 19, page 267). He was succeeded by his son, Sauromates I who reigned until *c*. 122 (Pliny, *Letters* 10.63–64).

M64   **Gold coin showing King Rhescuporis of Bosporus and Domitian, AD 84/5**

Obv: Bust of Rhescuporis, right, laureate
       ΤΙΒΕΡΙΟC ΙΟΥΛΙΟC ΡΗCΚΟΥΠΟΡΙC ΒΑCΙΛΕΥC (King Tiberius Julius Rhescuporis)
Rev: Bust of Domitian, right, laureate
       ΔΠΤ (year 384 (of Bosporan era = AD 87))

[*RPC* 2.461 = MW 236]

M65   Incursions by the Alani tribe into Armenia
The tribe of the Alani, Scythians living round the River Tanais and Lake Maeotis, as I have shown in a previous passage, [245] took it into their heads at this period to go on a plundering expedition into Media and even the country beyond it. They entered into negotiations with the king of the Hyrcanians; he commanded the pass which King Alexander had closed with iron gates … [248] They made their plundering expeditions with complete ease, then, and advanced as far as Armenia, laying waste to everything. [249] Tiridates was ruling it, and he met them and in the battle he fought with them came close to be taken alive in the conflict … [251] The brutality of the Alani was still further increased because of the battle. They ruined the countryside, drove off a large number of people and other forms of booty from both the kingdoms, and took themselves back to their own country.

[Josephus, *Jewish War* 7.244–5, 248–9, 251]

Tanais is the River Don, Lake Maeotis the Sea of Azov, currently shared between Ukraine and Russia. The raid worried Parthia since Tiridates was the brother of King Vologeses of Parthia who appealed to Rome for help. Vespasian declined (Dio 66.15.3 = **C15**) but acted in support of the friendly kingdom of Iberia (**M66**).

M66   Vespasian fortifies the capital of the friendly kingdom of Iberia

[Emperor Caesa]r Vesp[asian Aug]ustus, chief [priest], holding tribunician power for the 7th time, hailed *imperator* 14 times, consul 6 times, designated for a 7th time, father of the fatherland, censor, and Emperor Titus Caesar, son of Augustus, holding tribunician power for the 5th time, consul 3 times, designated for a 4th time, fortified these wall for King Mithridates of the Iberians, son of King Pharasmanes, and for Iamaspus his son, friend of Caesar, friend of the Romans, and for the tribe [of the Iberians].

[MW 237 = *ILS* 8795]

The kingdom of Iberia was roughly modern Georgia. It had come under Roman influence since Pompey's conquest of Pontus, remaining a client kingdom of Rome. This inscription from Harmozica (mod. Mtskheta) and **M67** below show how this worked, with Roman fortifications providing a buffer against raids by the Alani (**M65**).

M67   Fortress on the Black Sea, modern Turkey/Georgia border

On the coast before Trapezus is the River Pixites, and beyond Trapezus is the tribe of the Sanni Heniochi, the River Apsarus with its fortress of the same name on the gorge, 140 miles from Trapezus.

[Pliny, *Natural History* 6.12]

Trapezus = modern Trabzon (Trebizon) on the Black Sea in NE Turkey. Apsarus is on the border between Turkey and Georgia, usually marked as the north-eastern-most limit of the Roman empire.

M68   A centurion near Baku in Azerbaijan

Under Emperor Domitian Caesar Augustus Germanicus, L. Julius Maximus, centurion of Legion XII 'Thunderer'.

[MW 369 = EDCS–13900611*]

Inscription near modern Baku (capital of Azerbaijan) on the Caspian Sea. Pollard and Berry, *The Complete Roman Legions* (pages 164–5, with illustration) suggest that it probably attests the temporary presence of an advanced outpost under the centurion's command, perhaps to support allied Iberian and Albanian rulers.

PARTHIAN KINGS: M69–M71

Nero had established good relations with the Parthians under Vologeses I. He offered Vespasian military support in 69 or 70 (Dio 66.11 = **C11**; Tac. *Hist.* 4.51), though Vespasian declined this and a request for help against the Alani tribes attacking Armenia *c.* 72 (**C15** and **M65**). Vologeses I seems to have died about the same time as Vespasian (see **C17** and note). He was succeeded by his son, Vologeses II (**M69**), about whom little is known, but who clearly fell victim to rival claimants: Artabanus III (**M70**) issued coins and harboured a 'false Nero' in Titus' reign (Dio (**P3a**) described Artabanus as leader (*archegos*) of the Persians). But Pacorus II, brother of Vologeses I, eventually established himself. Tacitus, *Histories* 1.40 described Otho's soldiers setting out to murder the old and defenceless emperor, Galba, as if deposing Vologeses or Pacorus from the ancient Arsacid throne.

M69   Vologeses II on silver tetradrachm, AD 78/9, Seleucia on Tigris

Obv: Short-bearded Vologeses II facing left, with earring visible, wearing tiara with hooked crest and torque. Letter delta (unexplained).

Rev: Enthroned king, facing left, with Tyche (Fortune) standing before him holding diadem and sceptre.

[ΒΑ]ΣΙΛ[ΕΩΣ] ΒΑΣΙΛΕ[ΩΝ] [...] ΟΛΑΓΑ[ΣΟΥ] [...] ΕΠΙΦΑΝ[ΟΥΣ] [ΦΙ]ΛΕΛΛΗΝ[ΟΣ]: Of the King of Kings, [Arsaces] Olagases, [the just], the illustrious, the Philhellene.

[BMC Parthia p.210, no.5 = BM no.1848,0803.85]

The Greek alphabet struggles to represent the name of this king whom Tacitus calls Vologeses/Vologaesus. The full legend and Seleucid year 380 appears on other coins (e.g. BMC Parthia p.209, no.4).

M70   Artabanus III, silver tetradrachm, AD 80

Obv: Bearded Artabanus III facing left, with earring visible, wearing diadem and torque, and with hair in distinctive waves above diadem.

Rev: Enthroned king facing left, receiving untied diadem from standing Tyche (Fortune).

[... ΒΑ]ΣΙΛΕΩ[Ν] [ΑΡ]ΣΑΚΟ[Υ] ΑΡΤΑΒΑΝΟ[Υ] ΔΙΚΑΙΟΥ [Ε]ΠΙΦΑΝΟΥ[Σ] [...] Β-Τ [Α]ΠΕΛΛΑ[ΙΟΥ]: [Of the King] of Kings, Arsaces Artabanus, the just, the illustrious, [the Philhellene]. Apellaois 392 = November 80.

[MW 246 = BMC Parthia p.203 no.1 = BM no. 1900,0405.59]

M71   Pacorus II on silver tetradrachm, AD 82

Obv: Beardless Pacorus II facing left, wearing diadem and torque.
Rev: King on horseback facing left, and receiving diadem from Tyche (Fortune), standing with
         sceptre. Man stands behind goddess holding untied diadem.
         ΒΑΣΙΛΕΩ[Σ] ΒΑΣΙΛΕΩ[Ν] ΑΡΣΑ[ΚΟΥ] ΠΑΚΟ[ΡΟΥ] ΔΙΚΑΙ[ΟΥ]
         [Ε]ΠΙΦΑΝΟ[ΥΣ] [Φ]ΙΛΕΛΛΗΝΟ[Σ]: Of the King of Kings, Arsaces
         Pacorus, the just, the illustrious, the Philhellene). Δ-Τ ΠΕΡΙΤΙ[ΟΥ]: Year
         394 (AD 82) month of Peritios (Feb).

         [MW 247 = Parthia, p.197, no.33 = BM no. 1891,0603.42]

ESTABLISHING BRITANNIA: M72–M79

Theoretically the empire paid for Rome's armies, buildings, and citizens' benefits, since Roman citizens
were exempt from poll tax, and natives of Italy and some specially privileged communities were exempt
from land tax. The immediate gain of conquest was spoils, the permanent one taxation, in a variety of forms.
Natural resources may also have been a motive for conquest, and were certainly a welcome benefit from
invasion and expansion in Britain. Metals were the property of the emperor. Pliny's comments (**M72**) and
even the word 'plumbing' show the importance of lead (*plumbum*): in addition silver is often present in lead
ore. The smelting process (cupellation) serves to separate the two metals and several lead 'pigs' (the name
from the moulds for the individual ingots being arranged around a central area like piglets suckling on a
sow!) have been found in various areas of Britain (**M73–M75**).

M72   British lead

We use black lead for pipes and sheets: it is mined with difficulty in Spain and all the
Gallic provinces, but in Britain it is on the upper layers of the earth in such abundance
that a law prohibits its production beyond a certain level.

[Pliny, *Natural History* 34.164]

M73   Lead pig from Staffordshire

When Emperor Vespasian Augustus, for the 7th time, and Titus Emperor, for the 5rd time, were consuls. The Deceangli.

[MW 439 = *ILS* 8710 = EDCS–25100852]

This lead ingot was found in 1771 in Staffordshire on the line of Watling Street, having probably been lost in transport from the area of the Deceangli tribe, around Chester (Cheshire/N. Wales). Length: 57.2 cm: Weight: 68.3 kg: BM no. P&EE 1856.6–26.1

M74   Lead from Mendip silver–mines
Of Emperor Vespasian Augustus. British (lead), from silver works, *VEB*

[MW 440 = *RIB* 2.1 no.2404.04 = EDCS–48800583]

Lead pig from Charterhouse-on-Mendip, Somerset. The letters VEB have been found on many lead pigs from Britain but are unexplained.

M75   Lead pig from Heyshaw Moor, near Ripley, Yorkshire, AD 81
Emperor Caesar Domitian Augustus, consul 7 times. The Brigantes.

[MW 441 = *CIL* 7.1207 = EDCS–48800561]

M76   "Romanisation" of Britain
The winter that followed was spent on some very constructive schemes. To let people who were scattered, backward, and therefore given to fighting have a taste of the pleasures of a peaceful and untroubled existence, and so to accustom them to it, Agricola gave encouragement to individuals and assistance to communities in the construction of temples, markets and private houses. If they showed willing he had praise for them, if they hung back, a rebuke. In that way, instead of being put under duress they were spurred on by rivalry for marks of his esteem. [2] Not only that: he was having the sons of the chieftains educated in the liberal arts, and Agricola preferred the keen-witted Britons to the Gauls, cultured though these were; so that the very people who a short time before would have nothing to do with Latin were eager for the training of an orator. Then our way of dressing came to be held in regard, and

the toga was often to be seen. Little by little they went astray, taking to the colonnades, bath-houses and elaborate banquets that make moral failings attractive. They were naive: they called it 'civilisation' when it helped to ensure the loss of their freedom.

[Tacitus, *Agricola* 21]

M77   Javolenus Priscus as *iuridicus* in Britain

To C. Octavius Tidius Tossia{a}nus L. Ja«v»olenus Priscus, legate of Legion IIII 'Flavian', legate of Legion III 'Augustan', *iuridicus* of the province of Britain, consular legate of the province of Upper Germany, consular legate of the province of Syria, proconsul of the province of Africa, *pontifex*. P. Mutilius Crispinus, son of Publius of the Claudian tribe, ordered this inscription to be put up to his very dear friend.

[MW 309 = *ILS* 1015 = EDCS–28400116]

Inscription from Nedinum in Dalmatia (Nadin in Croatia). Discussed in Birley, *Roman Government* 270–2. *Iuridici* seem to have been appointed in Britain in periods when the governor was too preoccupied with military affairs to deal with legal business. The two Flavian appointments, perhaps the first to be created, were fairly senior praetors. Javolenus was a famous jurist, frequently cited in the *Digest of Roman Law*. Pliny (*Letters* 6.15 (around AD 104) describes him as being involved in the senate, meetings of the imperial council, and giving judgements on civil law.

M78   Javolenus on a legal dispute in Britain

Seius Saturninus, the chief helmsman of the British fleet, in his will left Valerius Maximus, a trireme captain as heir in trust, asking him to return the inheritance to Seius Oceanus when he reached the age of sixteen. Seius Saturninus died before reaching that age.

[Javolenus, *Letter* 11, in *Digest of Roman Law* 36.1.48]

M79   Carvoran corn measure

When Emperor ~~Domitian~~ Caesar Augustus Germanicus was consul for the 15th time. Measured to hold 17½ pints, 38 pounds in weight.

[*RIB* 2.2, 2415.56 = MW 527 = EDCS–48900166]

Beautiful bronze jar, with Domitian's name carefully removed, found near Hadrian's Wall, now in Chesters Museum. The jar actually holds more than is stated, perhaps suggesting an attempt to deceive local farmers. Another suggestion is that the irregular figure 17½ represents a week's corn for legionaries, at 2½ pints per day – close to a figure quoted for legionaries in the republican period.

SECTION N

WAR AND EXPANSION

*Unrest in the Balkans, Gaul wavering, Britain no sooner conquered
than lost: Sarmatian and Suebian tribes rising against us, the Dacian
distinguished by major victories and defeats.*

[Tacitus, *Histories* 1.2.1]

Introduction: We are uniquely well informed about military matters at the start of the Flavian period thanks to surveys of Rome's strength in AD 66 and 69 given by Josephus (*JW* 2.363–387) and Tacitus, *Histories*, (tabulated in LACTOR 19, N2). This section begins with the priceless, first-hand, information written by a commander defeated by the Roman army (Josephus) about the army he faced and about Roman military discipline in general. The section does not repeat Tacitus' detailed account of the Roman civil wars of AD 69, but deals with revolts and wars of conquest in chronological order. Our evidence is far less good for these later conflicts, consisting mainly of contemporary poetry and posthumous criticism of this and every aspect of Domitian's reign.

THE JEWISH REVOLT: N1–N15

The Jewish Revolt, AD 66–73 made the Flavians. Vespasian was given command of three legions to deal with the uprising as well as support from friendly kings (Tac. *Hist.* 5.1.2). His troops provided the means for claiming the purple; his victories the prestige; his plunder the resources. Josephus, of course, provides a full-length narrative of the war: passages in this volume are those of a wider significance for the empire. Tacitus, *Histories* 5.1–13 gives background to the sack of Jerusalem.

N1   The size of Vespasian's army

[64] Meanwhile Titus sailed from Greece to Alexandria, and sooner than the winter season usually permitted. There he took with him the forces he was sent to fetch and, marching at a great pace, he quickly reached Ptolemais. [65] There he found his father with two legions, the fifth and the tenth, the most distinguished legions of all, and he joined them with his own fifteenth. [66] Attached to these legions were eighteen cohorts and these were joined by five cohorts and one troop of cavalry from Caesarea, and five other troops of cavalry from Syria. [67] Ten of these cohorts had 1,000 infantry, the other thirteen had 600 infantry and 120 cavalry. A considerable number of auxiliaries were also contributed by the kings, [68] Antiochus, Agrippa and Sohaemus, each providing 2,000 un-mounted archers and 1,000 mounted. Malchus, the king of Arabia, sent 1,000 cavalry and 5,000 infantry, most of whom were archers. [69] Therefore the whole army, including the auxiliaries sent by the kings and the cavalry and infantry, amounted to 60,000, not including the servants who should not be distinguished from the fighting men, as they followed in great numbers and had been trained in war with the rest. For in times of peace, they took part in the same exercises as their masters and in times of war shared the dangers, so that only their masters surpassed them in skill and prowess.

[Josephus, *Jewish War* 3.64–69]

Vespasian had been appointed in 67 by Nero (see **J4c**) to counter the Jewish uprising, with legion V 'Macedonian' and X 'The Straits' from the four legions of Syria and legion XV 'Apollo's' from Egypt. The passage shows the importance of 'friendly kings' – see **M54–M71**.

N2   Digression on the contemporary Roman army

Josephus led an armed group against the Romans in the early part of the Jewish War. In this long digression on the merits of the Roman Army, prompted by the mention of Vespasian's forces above (**N1**) Josephus shows a genuine respect and admiration for the skills, training and ethos of the Roman military. Roman authors tend to take for granted their readers' knowledge of their own legions and military system, so this digression provides easily our most valuable source on the Roman imperial army.

N2a   The importance of training

[70] Now one cannot but admire the foresight of the Romans, in making their domestic servants useful not only in the services of everyday life, but also in war. [71] Indeed, if anyone were to look at the organisation of the army, he would realise that their obtaining so large an empire has been a prize of valour rather than the gift of fate. [72] For they do not wait for war to begin before they use their weapons, nor do they keep their hands idle in times of peace and take action only when an emergency comes. Instead, as if born with weapons, they never have a truce from training nor do they remain still until war is declared. [73] For their drills are no different from real warfare and each soldier trains as hard each day as if on active campaign. [74] This is why they bear the fatigue of battle so easily. For indiscipline cannot move them from their regular formation, no fear can move them and no toil can tire them. And this discipline always allows them to conquer those not trained in this way. [75] It would not be wrong to call their exercises 'bloodless battles' and their battles 'bloody exercises'.

N2b   The legionary camp

[76] Nor can their enemies easily catch them off-guard. For as soon as they have invaded an enemy's land, they do not begin to fight until they have fortified their camp. [77] And the walls they raise are not haphazard or uneven; nor do their men tackle the tasks without organisation – if the ground is uneven, it is firstly levelled and the camp is rectangular. [78] To this end, great numbers of engineers are ready with their tools to construct their buildings. [79] The area within the camp is divided for huts but around the outside, the appearance is of a wall adorned with evenly-spaced towers. [80] Between the towers stand spear-throwers, catapults, stone slingers and other engines, all ready for operations. [81] They set up four gates, one on each side of the wall, large enough for the entry of baggage-animals, and wide enough for armed excursions, if necessary. [82] They divide the camp into accurately marked-out streets and place the huts of the commanders in the middle. In the midst of this is the general's own hut, which resembles a shrine. [83] It all seems like a city built instantly, with a market place, workman's quarters, and places where senior and junior officers can hear and settle differences which arise. [84] The camp, the buildings inside and the wall around is set up sooner than one would imagine due to the number and skill of the workers. If the occasion should arise, a ditch is dug all around the walls, six feet deep and six feet wide.

N2c   Organisation within the legion

[85] When they have completed the fortifications, they live together in companies, quietly and decently. All other duties are carried out in good order and securely. Each company brings in wood, food and water as required. [86] They do not eat supper or dine individually as they please, but all together. Times for sleeping, guard-duty

and rising are announced by the sound of the trumpets and nothing is done without such a signal. [87] In the morning the soldiers each go to their centurions, and these centurions go to their tribunes to offer greetings. The tribunes go with their superior officers to the general, [88] who then gives them the password and other orders to pass on to those under their command. They act in the same way when they go to fight, changing direction suddenly when necessary and always moving as a unit, whether attacking or retreating.

N2d   Striking camp

[89] When they are about to leave their camp, the trumpet gives a sound and no man is idle. At the first signal they take down the huts and prepare everything for their departure. [90] The trumpets sound again to order them to get ready for marching. Then they load their baggage on their mules and pack-animals and take their places for marching. Then they set fire to the camp because it will be easy for them to erect another and so that it may not be of future benefit to their enemies. [91] When the trumpets sound a third time, they go out and encourage those who may be loitering, so that no man may be out of his correct place when the army marches. [92] Then the herald, standing at the commander's right hand, asks them three times, in their own tongue, whether they are ready for war. They reply three times, loudly and cheerfully: 'We are ready!' They do this almost before the question is asked and filled with a kind of warlike fervour. As they cry out, they raise their rights hands as well.

N2e   The legionaries' armour

[93] As they leave the camp, marching silently and in good order, everyone keeps to his own rank, just as in a war. The infantry are armed with breastplates and helmet and a sword on each side. [94] The sword on the left is the longer by far, for that on the right is no longer than nine inches. [95] Those infantrymen chosen to guard the general himself have a spear and a small shield. The others have a javelin and a long shield, with a saw and a basket, a pick and an axe, a strap, a meat-hook and provisions for three days; in fact, they are as burdened as a baggage-mule. [96] The cavalry have a long sword on their right hip, and a lance in their hand. A shield lies across the side of their horses. They have three or more darts in their quiver, with wide tips and as large as spears. [97] Like the infantrymen, they also have helmets and breastplates. The armour of the general's bodyguard differs in no way from that of the cavalry or the other troops. The legion at the head of the column is always chosen by lot.

N2f   The importance of planning

[98] This is the routine for the Romans while marching and resting and the various equipment they use. In battle, nothing is left to chance, nor done spontaneously; careful planning precedes any action and all actions conform to the decisions taken. [99] Because of this, errors are rarely made and if slips occur, they are soon corrected. [100] They also consider a victory due to luck to be less desirable than an unsuccessful but well-planned effort in that a fortuitous advantage might tempt them to neglect their planning, while planning, despite the occasional failure, makes men plan more carefully in the future. [101] A commander gains no credit from advantages arising from chance; but there is at least the comfort when unexpected misfortunes happen that he has taken the best precautions to prevent them.

N2g   Roman military discipline the key to success

[102] Their military drills not only strengthen the bodies of the soldiers, but their souls too. Fear also hardens them for war; [103] for their laws inflict the death penalty not only for deserting a post but also for less serious offences. Their generals are feared more than the laws; for by greatly rewarding the valiant soldiers, they avoid seeming cruel towards the men they punish. [104] The desire to obey their commanders is so great that in peace they are a credit to Rome and in war they move as one body, [105] so co-ordinated are their ranks, so sudden their manoeuvres, so sharp their hearing of orders, so quick their eyes for signals, and so nimble their hands for completing tasks. [106] Therefore they are quick to act and very slow to be worsted, and we cannot find any examples of engagement with the enemy where the Romans have been vanquished in battle, either due to the greater numbers of the enemy, or their tactics, or the difficulties of locale, or fortune itself, for their victories have been truer than fortune could have granted them. [107] When planning precedes the action and where the best advice is followed by so effective an army, it is little wonder that the Euphrates in the East, the ocean on the West, the most fertile regions of Libya in the South and the Danube and Rhine in the North are the limits of empire! Indeed, the Roman conquests are no less remarkable than the Romans themselves.

[108] This account I have given the readers has been less to commend the Romans than to console those who have been conquered by them and to deter others from attempting revolts. [109] This digression on Roman military conduct may also perhaps be useful to those who are curious and unaware of it, but wish to know it. I return now to the main subject.

[Josephus, *Jewish War* 3.70–109]

N3   A Roman army on the march

[115] Vespasian, keen to invade Galilee, marched out from Ptolemais, having arranged his army in the order normal for the Romans for marching. [116] He ordered the lightly-armed auxiliaries and the archers to march first in order to prevent any sudden unexpected assaults from the enemy and to reconnoitre the woods suspected of being potential sites for ambushes. After them came a contingent of Roman heavily-armed troops, both infantry and cavalry. [117] They were followed by a detachment of ten men from each century, carrying their own kit and equipment for measuring out a camp-site. [118] After them came engineers to straighten out irregularities in the road, level difficult places, and to cut down the woods that hindered their march, so that the army should not be worn out by a difficult march. [119] Behind these he set his own baggage and that of his staff-officers, with a great number of cavalry by them for their security. [120] Behind these he rode himself, with an elite body of infantry, cavalry and spear-men. Behind these came the particular cavalry of his own legion, for there were a hundred and twenty horsemen that were attached to every legion. [121] Next to these came the mules that carried the siege towers and other devices. [122] Then came the commanders of the cohorts and the tribunes, escorted by elite troops. [123] Next came the standards surrounding the eagle, which the Romans have in front of every legion, because it is the king of the birds and the most courageous. They take it as a sign of empire and an omen that they will be victorious, whoever their opponents may be. [124] Behind these sacred objects were the trumpeters and behind them the squadrons and battalions, six men in depth, which were followed by a centurion who,

in the customary way, observed the rest. [125] The servants of every legion followed the infantry in a single group, bringing the troops' baggage on mules and oxen. [126] Behind all the legions came a mass of mercenary forces and behind them followed a rearguard of infantry, lightly and heavily armed, and cavalry.

[Josephus, *Jewish War* 3.115–126]

Josephus is describing Vespasian's army setting out against Josephus' own forces in Galilee in AD 67. But like the digression on the Roman army above, it also provides superb evidence of how the Roman army operated in general.

N4 Vespasian attacks on Sabbath

Divus Augustus Vespasian attacked and conquered the Jews on a Sabbath, a day on which it is sinful for them to do any business.

[Frontinus, *On Stratagems* 2.1.17]

Dio 65.7.2 says Jerusalem fell on a Saturday, though his account conflates the destruction of the Temple with the fall of the city. Josephus laments a massacre of Jews in Caesarea by locals at *Jewish War* 2.456–7. In 1973 Egypt and Syria attacked Israel on Yom Kippur, the holiest day in the Jewish Calendar.

N5 Burning of the Temple not Titus' fault

Titus withdrew to the Antonia fortress. He had decided to attack in full force at dawn the following day and surround the Temple. [250] But God had long since condemned it to be burnt, and in the passing of the ages the fated day had arrived, 10 Lous [*c.* 10 August], on which it had been burnt before by the king of Babylon. [251] However, the Temple's own people were responsible for the flames and they were started by them: when Titus withdrew, the rebels, after a short rest, attacked the Romans again. There was an encounter between the Temple guards and soldiers putting out the fire, who put the Jews to flight and pursued them up to the shrine. [252] That was when one of the soldiers, without waiting for instructions and without shrinking from such an action, was driven by some uncanny impulse to snatch a piece of wood from the fire and, lifted up by one of his fellow-soldiers, to hurl the torch through a golden door which led to other buildings round the shrine on its northern side. [253] The flame went up and a shriek arose from the Jews that did full justice to the disaster. They rushed together to help, giving up all thought of saving their own lives or saving their energy: the object of their previous care was lost. [254] Someone came running to bring the news to Titus who happened to be resting in his tent after the battle. He leapt up, as he was, and ran towards the Temple to put out the fire. [255] All his generals followed him, with the legions behind them, in a state. The shouting and din was that inevitably caused by the rushed movement of a force of that size. [256] Caesar called and signalled to those fighting to extinguish the fire, but they did not hear his shouts which were drowned out by the greaten noise, nor did they heed his hand-signals because of the fighting or being distracted by their anger.

[Josephus, *Jewish War* 6.249–56]

The responsibility for the destruction of the Temple in 70 is shifted from Titus by his admirer Josephus who goes on to stress, at length, the efforts Titus immediately took to extinguish the fire. Compare also *JW* 1.28 (= **E1e**); 6.124–8 and 214–16 where Titus promises to save the Temple. But in *Jewish Antiquities,* 20.250, written AD 93/94, he says that Titus captured and set fire to the Temple.

N6   Temple deliberately destroyed by Titus

[4] Therefore the Romans burst in on the exhausted defenders. This chanced to be on the day of the Passover, when the whole population of Judaea had come together from the countryside; for so it had pleased God that the wicked race should be given over to slaughter at that time of year when it had crucified the Lord. [5] The Pharisees for some while fought very fiercely to defend the Temple until, their minds set on death, they intentionally threw themselves on the flames. The number killed is claimed as eleven hundred thousand, with 100 thousand actually captured and sold. [6] Titus is reported to have held a meeting before this to decide whether the Temple was of such great worth. To some it seemed that a building sacred and famous beyond all human endeavour should not be destroyed, when its preservation would be a testament to Roman moderation while its destruction would be a permanent reminder of cruelty. [7] Others, however, including Titus himself, thought that the Temple should be overthrown especially to remove more completely the religion of Jews and Christians, since these religions, though opposite, had arisen from the same sources: Christians had sprung up from the Jews and the offshoot would die easily once the root was taken away. [8] So, in accordance with God's will, spirits were enflamed and the Temple destroyed, three hundred and thirty-one years ago.

[Sulpicius Severus, *Chronicle* 2.30.4–8]

Sulpicius' account shows clearly its late and Christian standpoint, but his account of the destruction may have value in being derived from the lost account in Tacitus' *Histories*. Rajak argues that Josephus' account is to be preferred (*Josephus* 206–9), but others prefer Sulpicius, e.g. Goodman in *CAH²* X, 758. The number given for those killed is impossible: Tac. *Hist.* 5.13 says 'we are told that 600,000 were besieged in the city'.

N7   Titus captured Jerusalem, awarded 'crowns'

When Titus had taken Jerusalem, and everywhere was full of corpses, the neighbouring people gave him crowns. But he did not think he deserved it, not having done it himself, but having given a hand when god was showing his anger. Apollonius approved of this, since judgement and understanding of things human and divine was shown by his conduct, and a great measure of self-restraint not to be crowned in blood. So he sent a letter to him, making Damis the messenger, writing as follows: "Apollonius to Titus, Roman general, greetings. You did not want to be proclaimed for war or for enemy blood, but I give you a crown for self-restraint, since you realise what crowns should be awarded for. Farewell." Overjoyed at this, Titus wrote in a letter, "On my own behalf and that of my father I thank you, and shall remember what you said. I have captured Jerusalem and you have captured me."

[Philostratos, *Life of Apollonius of Tyana* 6.29.1–2 = *Letter* 77d]

N8   Jewish triumph

After the capture of Jerusalem Titus returned to Italy, and he and his father celebrated a triumph, riding in the traditional four-horse triumphal chariot. Domitian, as consul, joined the procession, mounted upon a racing stallion.

[Zonaras, *Summary of Dio,* 11.17 = Dio 66.12.1a]

For a full length description of the Jewish triumph, see **E6**. Pliny the Elder may well have ended his *History* with an account of the triumph and the closing of the gates of Janus to show peace, known from **H42–H43**.

N9 Balsam trees carried in the Jewish triumph
Balsam is ranked above every other scent, a plant unique to Judaea in the whole world, and previously known only to two gardens, both royal, one no bigger than 13 acres, the other smaller still. The emperors Vespasian and Titus exhibited this tree to Rome, and it is remarkable to note that trees have been led in triumphs since the time of Pompey the Great. This tree is now enslaved and pays tribute with the race it comes from. ... [113] The imperial treasury now plants it and it has never been as widespread; its height has remained at a maximum of two cubits.

[Pliny, *Natural History* 12.111, 113]

Commiphora gileadensis/opobalsamum or Balsam of Mecca: its sap was used as perfume or medicine. Tacitus refers to balsam tree in his excursus on Jewish customs, *Histories* 5.6.1.

N10 Arch of Titus celebrates the destruction of Jerusalem
The Senate and People of Rome to Emperor Titus Caesar Vespasian Augustus, son of Divus Vespasian, *pontifex maximus*, holding tribunician power for the 10th time, hailed *imperator* 17 times, consul 8 times, father of the fatherland, their *princeps*. For having subdued the Jewish race, under his father's command, and following his example and advice, and for having destroyed the city of Jerusalem which all previous generals, kings and peoples had attacked in vain or left untouched.

[MW 53 = *ILS* 264 = EDCS–17301062]

The inscription from an arch erected at Rome in the Circus Maximus in AD 80 was recorded in the ninth century but no longer survives. The triumph may have passed through the Circus (Josephus **E6c** speaks of the route allowing more people to view the procession in the 'theatres'). The better known arch of Titus still standing on the Sacred Way in the Roman Forum with its famous Jewish scenes was on the route of the triumph but was erected to commemorate Titus. See **K22**.

N11 Judaea Captured, *sestertius* AD 71

Obv: Head of Vespasian, laureate, right.
         IMP CAES VESPASIAN AVG P M TR P P P COS III (Emperor Caesar Vespasian Augustus, *pontifex maximus,* holding tribunician power, father of the fatherland, thrice consul)
Rev: Palm tree; to left, Vespasian standing right holding spear in right hand and dagger in left hand, foot on helmet; to right, Judaea seated right on cuirass.
         IVDAEA CAPTA (Judaea captured)

[*RIC* 2.1 Vespasian 167 = *BMCRE*[2] 765, p.186 = BM no. R.10658]

Dozens of variations on this coin-type were minted throughout Vespasian's reign. The basic design has a female figure, Judaea personified sitting beneath a palm-tree in an attitude of dejection. Variations show another figure of a defeated old man; weapons; victory attaching to the palm-tree a shield with SPQR. The legend sometimes reads 'Judaea conquered' (*devicta*).

N12   Vespasian celebrates naval victory, *dupondius* AD 71

Obv: Head of Vespasian, radiate, right.
         IMP CAES VESPASIAN AVG COS III
Rev: Victory standing right on prow, holding wreath in right hand and palm in left hand over left shoulder.
         VICTORIA NAVALIS S C (naval victory, by decree of the senate)

[RIC 2.1 Vespasian 284 = BMCRE² 597, p.129 = R.10549 = MW 47]

The battle had taken place in AD 67 on Lake Gennesareth and is described in full by Jos. *JW* 3.522–531, with 6,700 slain in either the naval battle or the earlier fight for the town of Tarichaeae *JW* 3.462–502. Many ships featured in the triumph (*JW* 7.147 = **E6e**), hence its widespread celebration especially on copper *asses* from 71–3 (e.g. *RIC Vesp.* 335–9, 406–7, 650)

N13   Individual soldiers benefit as well

All the soldiers were so stuffed with plunder that throughout Syria the value of gold for sale was down to half its former price.

[Josephus, Jewish War 6.317]

N14   Roman colony established at Emmaus

About the same time Caesar sent to Bassus and to Laberius Maximus, who was the procurator of Judaea, ordering them to lease out all the land belonging to the Jews. [217] For he founded no city there, keeping the land in his own control, although to eight hundred men discharged from the army he did exceptionally give a place to settle, called Emmaus, which was four miles from Jerusalem.

[Josephus, Jewish War 7.216–217]

Sex. Lucilius Bassus had commanded the Ravenna fleet, and defected to Vespasian (see **H26**). He was rewarded by being given command of Judaea (Jos. *JW* 7.163). This passage also shows the traditional use of colonies: veterans settled to keep an eye on the local population.

N15   Jewish tax

[218] He imposed tribute on the Jews wherever they lived, demanding two drachmas from each person every year to be paid to the Capitol, just as they used formerly to contribute it to the Temple in Jerusalem.

[Josephus, Jewish War 7.218]

There were numerous stories of Vespasian's own venality (Suetonius, Vesp. 23.2). The ending of the Jewish revolt of 66–73 brought great booty, which paid for the construction of the Flavian Amphitheatre (*JW* 7.115). But the cost of the war, of restoring the substructure of the country, and of maintaining a senatorial governor and a complete legion in garrison at Jerusalem had to be set against it. After 70 Vespasian found a new, Roman, use for the Jewish poll-tax previously paid for the upkeep of the Temple in Jerusalem (see **M46**), namely to rebuild the Capitolium in Rome.

N16   Sarmatian attack, AD 70

At the very same time as the revolt of the Germans that I have described, there coincided a bold attack on the Romans made by the Scythians. [90] For the section of the Scythians called the Sarmatians, who are very numerous, crossed the Danube to the Roman side without being noticed. The incursion was very violent and they were hard to deal with because their arrival was totally unexpected. They massacred large numbers of the Romans on guard, [91] including the legate and ex-consul Fonteius Agrippa who came up to meet them, and whom they killed fighting valiantly. They overran the whole adjacent country, plundering and pillaging whatever they fell on. [92] Vespasian heard what had happened and of the devastation of Moesia and sent Rubrius Gallus to bring the Sarmatians to justice. [93] At his hands numbers of them fell in the fighting and the remnant fled in terror to their own territory. [94] The general, having put an end to the war in this way, took thought for future security. He distributed larger garrisons in the area and at more frequent intervals, so as to make the crossing completely impossible for the barbarians. [95] The war in Moesia, then, reached a quick resolution in this way.

[Josephus, Jewish War 7.89–95]

Hostile incursions over the Danube had begun in the winter of 67–68: in February 69 an expedition of up to 9,000 tribesmen had been destroyed (Tac, *Hist.* 1.79.1–4.). But the Flavian leadership withdrew troops and in late September 69 the Dacians moved against Oescus and Novae. Mucianus' task-force, en route for Italy, turned north, and legion VI 'Ironclad' went to repel the Dacians (Tac, *Hist.* 3.46). In late autumn, C. Fonteius Agrippa was brought up from Asia with additional forces, to co-ordinate defence.

N17   Milestone, Offenburg, *c.* AD 73

When Caesar ~~Domitian, son of Augustus~~ was consul for the [3rd?] time, and Cn. Cor[nelius Cleme]ns was [imperial] legate [with praetorian rank], the route was la[id down from Arge]ntorate to R[aetia (*or,* to the R[iver Danube's bank]).

[MW 416 = ILS 5832 = EDCS–12400396*]

A worn, originally cylindrical milestone in sandstone, found at Offenburg near Argentorate (Strasbourg). The road was built as part of an attempt to renew the advance in Germany, aiming at the area between the sources of the Rhine and Danube. A town was built to serve as a centre for the area, Arae Flaviae (meaning Flavian Altars: modern Rottweil in SW Germany).

DOMITIAN AND THE WAR AGAINST THE CHATTI, *C.* AD 83–87: N18–N28
This campaign against a tribe (Tac. *Germ.* 30–31) on the far side of the Rhine, (roughly between modern Bonn and Frankfurt) is hard to reconstruct from the hostile and unclear accounts derived from Dio (67.3.5–67.4.5), Suetonius' lack of interest in military affairs (6.1), hyperbolic poetry, coins and inscriptions and chance references in Tacitus and Frontinus. Unlike his father or brother, Domitian had no military experience prior to becoming emperor, so, like Claudius, wanted to gain success. This he did in the form of a triumph and by taking the name Germanicus late in 83, though hostile sources belittle the success.

Frontinus on Domitian's stratagems in the Chatti War (N18–N21)
Frontinus describes his *Stratagems* as conveniently summarising examples of military strategy from Greek and Roman history. He also adds several from contemporary campaigns, including one of his own direct involvement (**H32**). His governorship of Britain *c.* 72–75 saw successful military campaigns and he may have accompanied Domitian on his Chatti campaign of 83, providing the following examples which 'sound authentic and were presumably chosen to demonstrate the emperor's qualities as a general and competence in fieldcraft' (B. Campbell, "Teach yourself how to be general", *The Journal of Roman Studies* 77 (1987): 13–29).

N18   'On concealing one's plans'
When Emperor Caesar Domitian Augustus Germanicus wished to crush the Germans who were at arms, he was aware that they would make even greater preparations for war if they were forewarned of the arrival of such a great general. Therefore he pretended that he was leaving Rome to conduct a census in Gaul, and thus plunged suddenly into war, crushed these fierce and savage peoples, to the benefit of the provinces.

[Frontinus, *On Stratagems* 1.1.8]

N19   'On establishing the type of warfare'
Emperor Caesar Domitian Augustus, when the Germans adopted their usual custom of coming out from pastures and unseen hiding-places to attack our men and then retreating far into the woods, by making paths one hundred and twenty miles long, changed not only the state of war but brought his enemy under his power by exposing their hideouts.

[Frontinus, *On Stratagems* 1.3.10]

Frontinus seems to mean that Domitian had paths or roads built across enemy territory. (Latin = *limites* – the word seems to mean 'boundaries' or 'frontiers' only later, see Jones, *Domitian* 130 with notes (but he seems to reverse the mile/km conversion)).

N20   Guerilla tactics of the Chatti
Emperor Caesar Domitian Augustus, when the Chatti kept disrupting cavalry battles by fleeing into the forests, ordered his cavalrymen to dismount and fight on foot as soon as they reached the baggage carts. By this tactic he ensured that no terrain would delay his victory.

[Frontinus, *On Stratagems* 2.3.23]

N21 **'On keeping the loyalty of the waverers'**
Emperor Caesar Domitian Augustus, in the war in which he deservedly acquired
the name 'Germanicus' from his defeated foe, was setting up forts in the territory of
the Ubii. He ordered payment to be made for the crops in areas enclosed within the
rampart. As a result his reputation for justice gained the loyalty of all.

[Frontinus, *On Stratagems* 2.11.7]

The text given is 'Cubii', but these people are unknown, whereas the Ubii had been settled on the left bank
of the Rhine opposite the Chatti (Tac. *Germ.* 28.3).

N22 **War against the Chatti**
After this he set out for Gaul and launched a campaign of pillage against some of the
tribes beyond the Rhine, who enjoyed treaty rights with Rome. This success gave him
a swollen head, as if it was a mighty achievement, and perhaps it was his "victory"
which encouraged him to give his soldiers an increase in pay.

[Zonaras, *Summary of Dio,* 11.19 = Dio 67.3.5]

This sentence in Zonaras and 4.1 in Xiphilinus (**D4**) is all that remains of Dio's account of Domitian's war
against the Chatti. Frontinus' contemporary (perhaps eyewitness) account shows that Zonaras accurately
preserves a detail of Domitian's concealing his intentions (**N18**). For Zonaras on the increase in pay, see
N51.

N23 **Domitian takes name Germanicus**
Crete bestowed a name, and Africa one greater,
Victorious Scipio has the one, Metellus the other;
Germany gave one nobler still when Rhine was conquered,
This title, Caesar, you deserved when still a boy.
Your brother earned his Jewish triumphs with your father
But the laurel given for the Chatti is yours alone.

[Martial, *Epigram* 2.2 (published 85)]

Two members of the Cornelius Scipio family took the name 'Africanus' after victories in the Punic Wars
(against Carthage) in 204 and 146 BC. Q. Caecilius Metellus conquered Crete for Rome in 69–67 BC,
taking the name 'Creticus'. Domitian took the name 'Germanicus' in AD 83, after his triumph over the
Chatti. He had taken part in an expedition in Germany in AD 70. Titus and Vespasian celebrated a joint
triumph, but refused the title 'Judaicus' which could have made them sound like Jewish converts (Titus'
arch does not name his opponents, and Martial here actually refers to Idumaean triumphs). The name
'Germanicus' had been given to Drusus' son in honour of the campaigns of his father, and taken by Caligula
and Claudius (Germanicus' son and brother respectively).

N24   Aureus of 84 with Minerva and title 'Germanicus'

Obv: Head of Domitian, laureate, right.

         IMP CAES DOMITIAN AVG GERMANICVS

Rev: Minerva standing right on top of podium with ships' prows, holding spear in right hand and
         shield on left arm; to right, owl.

         P M TR POT III IMP V COS X P P (*pontifex maximus,* tribunician power
         for the 3rd time, hailed *imperator* 5 times, consul 10 times, father of the
         fatherland)

                             [*RIC* 2.1 Domitian 173 = *BMCRE²* 46, p.308 = BM no. 1896,0608.19]

All known coins of Domitian minted at Rome in 84 carry the title Germanicus (*RIC* Domitian 172–254:
the exception, no. 202 instead has a captive, a trophy, and the legend *DE GERMAN* (over the Germans)).
Reverses are of Minerva on *aurei* and *denarii* and of other gods on lower value coins. More triumphant
reverses appear on lower value coins in 85, such as the captured Germans below, or Germans being ridden
down by Domitian e.g. *RIC* 2.1 Vespasian 280 = BM 1970, 0803.1.

N25   Germania Capta, *sestertius* **AD 85**

Obv: Head of Domitian, laureate, right, with aegis.

         IMP CAES DOMIT AVG GERM COS XI CENS POT P P (Emperor Caesar
         Domitian Augustus Germanicus, consul 11 times, censorial power, father of
         the fatherland)

Rev: Trophy; to right, German captive standing right, hands bound, head left; to left, Germania seated
         left; around, arms.

         GERMANIA CAPTA (Germany captured)

                             [*RIC* 2.1 Domitian 351 = *BMCRE²* 326, p.369 = R.11329]

N26   Domitian's sham triumph
Domitian was conscious that his recent false triumph over Germany had exposed him to mockery, with men having been bought at markets whose clothes and hair had been made to look like that of captured prisoners.

[Tacitus, *Agricola* 39.1]

Tacitus' point here is to contrast Domitian's victories with those of Agricola, especially the battle of Mons Graupius (late in AD 83; *Agr.* 35–37).

N27   Triumphs rather than conquest in Germany
Soon the great threats of Gaius Caesar turned farcical. [5] Then followed peace, until the opportunity of our conflicts and civil war led to the storming of the legionaries' winter-quarters, and an attack on Gaul, before they were repulsed. In very recent times they have been more triumphed over than conquered.

[Tacitus, *Germania* 37.4–5]

N28   Domitian's sham triumph
And so, some day, the Capitol shall welcome no sham chariots or faked images of some false victory, but a commander returning with real and substantial glory, bringing back peace and quiet and a surrender of his enemies that is so obvious that none shall remain to be conquered. This will be finer than any triumph; for never has it been the case that we have won, except after some breach of our sovereignty.

[Pliny the Younger, *Panegyric to Trajan* 16.3–4]

Y. Pliny looks forward to military triumph under Trajan, simultaneously playing down Domitian's triumphs as either sham ones (compare Tac. *Agr.* 39.1 = **N26**) or resulting from (to a Roman mind) shameful need for self-defence rather than glorious imperial expansionism (such as Claudius' conquest of Britain). Pliny may well have rewritten the passage after Trajan's Dacian triumph, celebrated two years after the delivery of his speech.

N29   Embassies from kings of German tribes
Chariomerus, the king of the Cherusci, had been hounded out of his kingdom by the Chatti for being a friend of the Romans. His initial response was to get together a group of supporters and to make a successful return. But then they deserted him, because he had sent hostages to the Romans, so he turned to Domitian and begged for help. Domitian sent him money, but refused any sort of military alliance.

[*On Embassies – Foreign* = Ursinus' Excerpt 43 = Dio 67.5.1]

This excerpt from Dio is undatable.

N30   War against the Nasamones
Many of Rome's tributary allies, such as the Nasamones, revolted after being compelled by force to pay taxes. They butchered all the tax-gatherers and when Flaccus, the governor of Numidia, hurried to attack them, they so utterly defeated him that they even sacked his camp. But in the camp they discovered all his supplies, including quantities of wine; they feasted on both and then fell asleep. News of this reached

Flaccus, and he immediately launched a second attack against them and wiped them out, including all their civilian camp followers. Domitian was enchanted by the news and declared to the senate that, "I have forbidden the Nasamones to exist."

[Zonaras, *Summary of Dio*, 11.19 = Dio 67.4.6]

Zonaras alone preserves the account of the campaign against the Nasamones in N. Libya. Domitian's comment was untrue as well as odious as the Nasamones are attested in Byzantine times. Suellius Flaccus was legate in N. Africa in AD 87, (MW 450).

N31   Nasamones and Dacians defeated in AD 86
Nasamones and Dacians defeated fighting against Rome

[Jerome, *Chronicle*, year 2102 after Abraham, = AD 86]

DACIAN WARS, AD 85–89: N32–N41
Dacia was roughly the area of modern Romania. Despite the many sources (Tac. *Agr.* 41–2–3; Suet. *Dom.* 6.1; Eutropius 7.23.4; Orosius 7.10.3–4; Jordanes *Getica* 13.76–78; Statius *Silvae* 3.3.168–171; Martial 5.3, 7.8.6) 'an adequate picture of these campaigns is scarcely achievable' (Murison, *Dio Commentary*, page 230). This is because the main account, Dio's, is very hostile to Domitian, and has to be put together from five separate sets of excerpts. The war seems to have been started by a surprise (pre-emptive?) Dacian attack in AD 85/6. After an apparent change of leadership (but the relationship between Dorpaneus, Duras and Decebalus is impossible to determine), the Romans rejected a treaty offer and sent a force under Fuscus in 86 which was also defeated. Domitian took command for a time. In 89, after a Roman victory under Tettius Julianus at Tapae in 88 (Dio 67.10.1–3), the war was ended by 'a generous peace by which Decebalus was established as a king friendly to Rome … and received an annual subsidy' (*OCD* under Decebalus).

N32   Dacians invade Moesia and defeat Sabinus, AD 85
After a long interval, when Emperor Domitian was on the throne and they feared his greed, the Goths broke the treaty that they had long since struck with other emperors. They laid waste the Danubian bank, which had long been in the possession of the Romans, crushing the troops along with their generals. Oppius Sabinus was governing the province at that time, after Agrippa, while the Goths were under the rule of Dorpaneus. The Goths embarked on the war, defeated the Romans, cut off the head of Sabinus, took over numerous forts and settlements, openly plundering what belonged to the emperor.

(This passage continues in N35)

[Jordanes, *Gothic History* 13.76]

N33   Decebalus takes over military command from Duras
For the Romans, the greatest war that they waged in this period was with the Dacians. Their king at the time was Decebalus, since Duras who had possessed the leadership had willingly surrendered it to Decebalus, king of the Dacians, because he was a brilliant military strategist and in the field a canny tactician.

[*On Virtues and Vices*, Valesius' Excerpts 284 = Dio 67.6.1]

Xiphilinus' abridgement of Dio cut detail that Duras has ceded sovereignty to Decebalus.

N34   Embassies from Decebalus

The Dacian king, Decebalus, sent an embassy to Domitian offering promises of peace. Domitian's response was to despatch Fuscus against him with an enormous army. When he heard the news, Decebalus sent off a second embassy with a new proposal, hardly intended to be taken seriously, in which he said that if every Roman would agree to pay him two obols per annum, he would make peace with the emperor. Otherwise he would make war on them and inflict vast damage on their state.

[Petrus Patricius, *Embassies* = Dio 67.6.5]

This is preserved in a selection compiled in 6ᵗʰ century Byzantium by Petrus Patricius, senior administrator of the emperor Justinian.

N35   Dacians defeat Fuscus, AD 86
(This passage continues N32)

[77] This was a crisis for his people, and Domitian hastened with all his forces into Illyricum, with soldiers drawn from almost the entire state. Fuscus as general was sent on ahead, along with the cream of the soldiery, and making a pontoon bridge of boats he forced them to cross the River Danube beyond the army of Dorpaneus. [78] Then the Dacians, proving no slouches, took up their weapons, and, armed as they were, in the first encounter lost no time in defeating the Romans. The commander Fuscus was killed, and they stripped the camp of the soldiers' valuables. Having won an important victory in the region, they now began to call their leading warriors, as men who had won their victory with fortune's favour, not simple men, but demigods – 'Anses' in their language.

[Jordanes, *Gothic History* 13.77–78]

Jordanes was a sixth-century historian, probably writing in a monastery in Constantinople. Descended from Goths (tribe from area of modern Poland), he wrote a Gothic history, *Getica,* closely based on a lost work of his contemporary, Cassiodorus.

N36   Rome needs Agricola as general in face of military disasters

[41.2] And there followed a period for the state which did not permit Agricola to be silent, when a great number of armies, in Moesia and Dacia and Germany and Pannonia, were lost through their leaders' rashness or cowardice; a great number of professional soldiers and their cohorts were taken by storm and captured. It was no longer the frontiers and banks of the empire that were in doubt, but the winter quarters of the legionaries and Rome's provinces. [41.3] So loss followed loss and the whole year was marked out by deaths and disasters: popular opinion demanded Agricola as general, as everyone compared his vigour, fortitude and mettle tested in wars, with the lethargy and cowardice of the others.

[Tacitus, *Agricola* 41.2–3]

N37   Orosius quotes Tacitus' account in his *Histories*

[3] He waged war against the Germans and Dacians through legates which was equally destructive to the state: in Rome he tore apart the senate and people, while abroad the enemy finished off the badly defended army in continual slaughter. [4] I would like to turn out a long description of the magnitude of the battles that took place between Diurpaneus, King of the Dacians and the general Fuscus, and of the magnitude of the

Roman disaster – but Cornelius Tacitus who has described this history very carefully has said that Sallustius Crispus and a very great number of other historians have hallowed the tradition of keeping silent about the numbers of those killed, and that he had chosen to do the same. Domitian, however, bloated by the most disgraceful arrogance, held a triumph for the legions which had been wiped out, claiming that the enemy had been defeated.

[Orosius, *Histories against the Pagans* 7.13.3–4]

N38   Domitian takes command
Dio in book 67 [records that] ..., when the soldiers of Fuscus' army asked him (Domitian) to take over command of their army.

[*On Syntax* = Dio 67.6.6]

The Byzantine collection, *On Syntax* contains quotations from Dio including book-number references.

N39   Treaty with Decebalus, AD 89
Domitian was defeated by the Marcomanni and beat a hasty retreat. He then sent an urgent message to Decebalus, king of the Dacians, and enticed him into accepting the very truce which he had previously refused to grant him, despite repeated requests. Decebalus had suffered dreadful hardships, and so he agreed to make a treaty. But he himself had no desire to hold face to face negotiations, so he sent Diegis with an entourage to hand over weapons and a few captives, pretending that they were all he had. (7.3) Domitian's response was to "crown" Diegis with a diadem, as if to demonstrate that he had really defeated him and could give the Dacians any king he liked. He handed his own soldiers battle honours and donatives, and then, as if he had secured a genuine victory, he sent a series of despatches back to Rome, together with a delegation from Decebalus, as well as a letter allegedly from the king himself, though rumour had it that Domitian had forged it. (7.4) He then celebrated a festival, which he adorned with many of the trappings of a triumph, not spoils captured from his enemies, but taken from the imperial furniture stores, which he always treated as if they were spoils of war for his own use – after all he had enslaved the whole empire. It was, in fact, the exact opposite of a real triumph, because his peace treaty had come at a price: he had paid large sums of money to Decebalus on the spot, but also supplied him with craftsmen, who were experts both in military ordnance and peacetime trades of every kind, and promised him lots more for the indefinite future.

[*On Embassies – Roman* = Ursinus' Excerpts 14 = Dio 67.7.2–4]

This whole paragraph is from a Byzantine compilation on embassies. Diegis (also 'Decis' or 'Degis' was Decebalus' brother (**N40**). Diadem: Domitian will have been acting like Nero in crowning Tiridates king of Armenia in AD 66, implying that the Romans could chose who should rule a 'friendly' or 'client kingdom'. Battle honours: several inscriptions to soldiers show the military honours awarded, see **N61**. Trappings of a triumph: in fact Suet. *Dom.* 6.1 shows it was a triumph or double triumph over Chatti and Dacians, though not one widely commemorated on coinage.

N40   Degis, brother of Decabalus of Dacia
Degis, who used to live on what is now our bank,
Approached Germanicus from Hister's captured waters
And, when he saw the ruler of the world, is said
To have remarked in joyous amazement to his friends,
"I am more lucky than my brother, being allowed
To see in person the god he worships from afar.
[Martial, *Epigram* 5.3 (published December 90)]

N41   Fuscus' death in Dacia now avenged
The guard beside the holy one, the togate Mars,
To whom was given an army of the greatest leader,
Fuscus lies here. Fortune, this may be confessed:
This tombstone now has nought to fear from enemy threats.
Subdued Dacia's neck now wears slavery's yoke
The victor's shade possesses the wood that he enslaved.
[Martial, *Epigram* 6.76 (published December 91)]

Aulus Pudens, a close friend of Martial's, campaigned in Dacia (6.58, 1.31.3 etc) which may explain his interest.

THE PANNONIAN/SARMATIAN WARS, AD 89–92: N42–N49

These wars were fought against Suebian tribes the Quadi and Marcomanni (modern Czechoslovakia) and the Sarmatian tribes, Iazyges and Roxolani (modern Hungary/Romania), in two campaigns of 89 and 92. There may have been a third campaign in 95 (Jones, *Domitian* 153–5). They were sufficiently significant for Tacitus to include in his introduction (see chapter heading), but are very poorly known. Fragments of Dio only cover the first war, though Martial highlights the second war: several poems in book 7 (published in December 92) predict an easy victory for Domitian (poems 1, 2, 5, 6, 7, 8) without giving any actual information. By chance we know that Velius Rufus led an expeditionary force consisting of vexillations from nine legions through Dacian territory thanks to the recent treaty (**N39**). But the Sarmatians destroyed a whole legion (Suet. *Dom.* 6.1). Martial nonetheless cheerfully marked Domitian's return and various celebrations for his victory (Epigram 8.8, also 8.11, 8.15, 8.21, 8.49) in an eight-month campaign (Martial *9.31*). The celebrations stopped short of a triumph (Suet. *Dom.* 6.1, Martial **N48**).

N42   First Pannonian War, AD 89

Domitian wanted to punish the Quadi and the Marcomanni for their failure to help him in his Dacian campaign, so he marched into Pannonia to make war on them. They sent two sets of envoys to him with peace proposals; he put both to death.
[*On Embassies – Foreign* = Ursinus' Excerpts 42 = Dio 67.7.1]

Despite Dio's account, news of unrest in these tribes may have preceded or even prompted Domitian's peace treaty with Decebalus.

N43   Negotiations with the Semnones
Masyus, king of the Semnones, and Ganna (a virgin priestess who practised divination among the Germanic tribes in succession to Veleda) paid an official visit to Domitian, was received with honour, and then returned home.

[*On Embassies – Foreign* = Ursinus' Excerpt 45 = Dio 67.5.3]

This passage, extracted from Dio's original narrative for the Byzantine compilation *On Embassies – Foreign* cannot be dated for certain. But the Semnones were a tribe of the Suebi and could have been useful allies against other Suebi tribes further east, such as the Quadi and Marcomanni so this embassy may have been 'hardly coinicidental' (Jones, *Domitian* 151) to plans for the Second Pannonian War.

N44   Force sent to help the Lugii
In Moesia the Lugii got involved in a war with some of the Suebi, and sent an embassy to Domitian to ask for his help. They received a force that was not large numerically, but of high status: a hundred knights was the response – nothing more. This infuriated the Suebi who persuaded some Iazyges to join them, and with them they began to make preparations for a crossing of the Danube.

[*On Embassies – Foreign* = Ursinus' Excerpts 44 = Dio 67.5.2]

Section 5.2 comes from the Byzantine collection *On Embassies – Foreign*. The Lugii inhabited the area of southern Poland, not Moesia (ex-Yugoslavia). This attack was probably the one which destroyed a legion (Suet. *Dom.* 6.1) probably XXI 'Plunderer' which had been moved to Pannonia after its involvement in Saturninus' revolt, and brought Domitian to Pannonia (Martial 7.8.3–4, 8.2, 9.31.3–4, 8.15.5–6, 8.65; Statius, *Silvae* 3.3.170–1; Suet. *Dom.* 6.1.

N45   Sarmatian expedition, AD 92
Breastplate of our lord, against Sarmatian arrows
Proof; more trusty than the Getic shield of Mars
Woven from the polished hooves of countless boars
To protect against the blows of Aetolian spears.
Happy you are, allowed to touch the sacred chest,   5
And be warmed by our god's heart. Accompany him,
To win, unscathed, triumphs great and well-deserved.
But restore our general soon to togas edged with palms.

[Martial, *Epigram* 7.2 (published December 92)]

N46   Over by Saturnalia?
Does Caesar turn away from Northern lands towards us,
Prepare so soon to travel on Italian roads?
Though certain news is lacking, every voice proclaims it:
Rumour, I believe you mostly tell the truth.
Victorious messages do witness public joy,   5
Spears of Mars are decked with tips of laurel leaves.
Hurray, once more: Rome shouts out your triumphs great,
'Invincible Augustus' rings out in your city.
But that the happy news may still be trusted more,
Come in person to announce Sarmatian triumph.   10

[Martial, *Epigram* 7.6 (published December 92)]

N47 **… or actually soon after**
But you are better pleased with this, that in your month,
Janus, Rome was blessed to see her god return.

[Martial, *Epigram* 8.8 (published January 94)]

N48 **'Private triumph' for Pannonian war**
While new glories of the Pannonian War are counted,
While each altar prays to Jove the Bringer-home,
The people, senate, grateful equestrians, all alike give
Incense, while third gifts enrich the Latin tribes.
Rome shall not forget these private triumphs too, 5
And this your laurel of peace shall count no less. Since you
Yourself can trust the pious devotion of your people.
The leader's greatest virtue is to know his subjects.

[Martial, *Epigram* 8.15 (published January 94)]

Domitian clearly celebrated his return with a third handout of money to the *plebs*), see **H51, H61, K2.**

N49 **Public banquet held to celebrate Domitian's triumph**
Great as the banquets held in triumph o'er the giants,
Great as that night, we're told, for all the heavenly ones,
When the good father once reclined with common gods
And did permit the fauns to demand Jove's wine;
As great, o Caesar are the feasts to celebrate 5
Your victories; our joys make glad the gods themselves.
Equestrians all, and people, senate, dine with you.
Rome now eats with you a banquet of gods' food.
You promised much, yet how much more you've given us!
A handout meal was promised, a dinner true was given. 10

[Martial, *Epigrams* 8.49 (published January 94)]

N50 **Domitian's triumph recalled on aureus AD 90–2 (Rome)**

Obv: Head of Domitian, laureate, right.
DOMITIANVS AVGVSTVS
Rev: Domitian riding left in triumphal quadriga, holding branch and sceptre
GERMANICVS COS XV

[*RIC* 2.1 Domitian 700, p.315 = *BMCRE*² 175, p.335 = BM no. R.10768]

Aurei showing Domitian in triumphal chariot are known to have been issued in AD 88 (*RIC* 2.1 Domitian 561), AD 90–1 (above) and AD 92–4 (*RIC* 2.1 Dom 748–50). Datings are only possible by Domitian's consulship number, but it is possible that the coins coincide with German campaigns for which Domitian might have claimed a full triumph but chose not to do so.

THE SOLDIERS: N51–N66
Suetonius tells us that the soldiers took the news of his death very badly (*Dom.* 23.1). Nerva was later forced by the praetorian guards to punish Domitian's killers (Dio 68.3.3, *Epitome* 12.6–8, Pliny, *Pan.* 6.1).

N51   Legionary pay
He ordered each payment to be raised from 300 to 400 sesterces. Later he changed his mind, but instead of reducing their pay, he reduced the overall size of the army. Both these decisions did serious damage to the national interest, since the army was no longer large enough to defend the state, and its soldiers were overpaid.

[Zonaras, *Summary of Dio,* 11.19 = Dio 67.3.5]

Zonaras puts the increase in pay in the context of Domitian's victory against the Chatti, see **N22**. Roman legionaries were paid three times a year. Domitian increased annual pay from 900 to 1,200 sesterces, see Suet. *Dom.* 7.3. Though Suet. *Dom.* 12.1, also describes a reduction in the number of legions there is no evidence to support it.

N52   Domitian with soldiers, *sestertius* AD 85

Obv: Head of Domitian, laureate, right, with aegis.
        IMP CAES DOMITIAN AVG GERM COS XI
Rev: Domitian standing right, clasping hands over altar with officer standing left; behind officer, one soldier with standard and one soldier at right with spear and shield.
        S C (by decree of the senate)

[*RIC* 2.1 Domitian 281, p.285 = *BMCRE*[2] 301, p.364 = BM no. R11310]

DIPLOMAS (N53–N54)

From the mid-first century AD, auxiliaries in the Roman army could be granted full Roman citizenship on their retirement after years of loyal service. This award was inscribed on a bronze tablet displayed in public in Rome, where they could be checked, and each individual beneficiary was given (or could request) an official copy of the document for his personal use, on a small portable bronze tablet. Many copies from around the Roman empire have been found, and tend to be known by the modern term 'diploma'. They are also a good source of information about consulships, since they give imperial titles and names of consuls on a particular date.

N53a   Picture of diploma in British Museum, 8 September AD 79

BM no. 1923,0116.1. First of two sheets of bronze, 16cm high, 19 cm wide. © Trustees of the British Museum.

N53b   Diploma granted by Titus, 8 September AD 79

Emperor Titus Caesar Vespasian Augustus, *pontifex maximus*, holding tribunician power for the 9th time, hailed *imperator* 14 times, father of the fatherland, censor, consul 7 times, grants citizenship to the veterans who have served in the fleet which is in Egypt, who have earned 26 or more years' pay, and have been given an honourable discharge, whose names are written below, and also to their children and their descendants. He also grants right of marriage with their wives who they had at the time when citizenship was granted, or, if they were unmarried, to those whom they married afterwards, one for each individual.

On 8 September, when T. Rubrius Aelius Nepos and M. Arrius Flaccus were consuls. To Marcus Papirius of Arsinoite, son of Marcus; and to his wife Tapaia, daughter of Tryphon; and to his son Carpinius.

Written down and validated from a bronze inscription which is fixed at Rome on the Capitol on the base of the statue of King Pompilius, near the Altar of the Julian Clan.

[MW 401 = *CIL* 16.24 = EDCS–12300228*, from Arsinoite district

(Al Fayyum, Egypt)]

N54   Diploma proving citizenship of a legionary and his three children

(*Written on the outside*) When L. Nonius Calpurnius Torquatus Asprenas and T. Sextius Magius Lateranus were consuls, on 2 July, in the 13th year of Emperor Caesar Domitian Augustus Germanicus [AD 94], on the 8th day of the [Egyptian] month Epeiph, at Alexandria in Egypt. M. Valerius Quadratus, son of Marcus, of the tribe Pollia, released with honourable discharge from Legion X 'The Straits' witnessed that he had made a written and validated copy, from a bronze inscription which is fixed on the Great Caesareum, under the portico on the right as one climbs the second stairs, beside the marble Temple of Venus, in the wall on which is written what is written below:

"Emperor Caesar Domitian Augustus Germanicus, son of Divus Vespasian, *pontifex maximus*, holding tribunician power for the 8th time [AD 88/89], hailed *imperator* 16 times, censor for life, father of the fatherland says:

'I have decided, to proclaim by edict, that all of your military veterans should be exempt from all public taxes and import duties; and that they, their wives who married them, their children, and their parents, may be Roman citizens, to the full extent of the law, and shall be given complete and absolute immunity, and those abovementioned parents and children shall have the very same rights and status as regards full immunity, and that estates, houses, shops [...] veterans who do not want [...]

(*Written on the inside*) [...] of the veterans with their wives and children, inscribed above in bronze, or, if they were unmarried, to those whom they married afterwards, one for each individual, who have served at Jerusalem, in Legion X 'The Straits' and who have earned their pay, and have been given an honourable discharge, through Sextus Hermetidius Campanus, propraetorian imperial legate, on 28 December when Sex. Pompeius Collega and Q. Peducaeus Priscinus were consuls [AD 93] – they began their service when P. Galerius Trachalus, Ti. Catius [AD 68] and T. Flavius, Cn. Arulenus [AD 69] were consuls.'

By the permission of M. Junius Rufus, prefect of Egypt, when L. Nonius Calpurnius Torquatus Asprenas and T. Sextius Magius Lateranus were consuls, on 1 July, in year 13 of Emperor Caesar Domitian Augustus Germanicus [AD 94], on the 8th day of the [Egyptian] month Epeiph.

There M. Valerius Quadratus, son of Marcus, of the Pollian tribe, in front of those who were present and about to set their seals, swore an oath and stated by Jupiter Greatest and Best, and the Spirit of the most sacred Emperor Caesar Domitian Augustus Germanicus that while he was a soldier, L. Valerius Valens and Valeria Heraclus and Valeria Artemis – all those three named above – were born, and that those inscribed on the bronze above had gained Roman citizenship by the grant of that greatest emperor.

[MW 404 = *ILS* 9059 = EDCS–12500247]

This diploma, like **N53** was found in the Arsinoite area of central Egypt. Early in July AD 94, a veteran Roman legionary attests formally (quoting the original document, under oath and in the presence of witnesses) that an auxiliary served with him and gained Roman citizenship for himself and his children at his discharge.

N55   Centurion cashiered by Galba

To [L.] Antonius Naso, son of Marcus of the Fabian tribe, [centurion of Le]gion III
'Cyrene', [centurion of Le]gion XIII 'Twin', [honour]ed with the *'White Parade'*
by the emperor, [...] of the town of the Colaphiani, [*primi*]*pilus* of Legion XIII
'Twinned', tribune of Legion I 'Italian', [tribune] of Watch [Cohort] IIII, tribune of
Urban Cohort XV, [tribune of] Urban [Cohort] XI, tribune of Praetorian Cohort IX,
[decorated] by Emperor [Nero] with the rampart crown, golden crown, two banners,
two special spears; [put in charge of Le]gion XIV 'Twinned' by Emperor [Otho],
tribune of Praetorian Cohort I and put in charge of the veterans of several armies
staying at Rome, imperial procurator of Pontus & Bithynia.

[MW 355 = *CIL* 3.14387 = EDCS–17700182*]

Latin inscription from Heliopolis (Baalbek in Syria). Antonius Naso is mentioned by Tacitus, *Histories*
1.20.3 as one of four tribunes dismissed by Galba from the 9th Praetorian Cohort. In the chaos of 68/9 it is
not surprising that this did not end his long career which ranged from Egypt to Pannonia. As procurator of
Pontus & Bithynia, he is attested building roads in AD 77/8 – MW 421 – and *PIR* A² 854. The significance
of the 'White Parade' is unknown. (Pollard & Berry, page 40)

N56   Legionary tombstone from Lincoln, AD 71–78

Titus Valerius Pudens, son of Titus of the Claudian tribe,
from Savaria, soldier of Legion II 'Helper, Faithful and
Loyal', in the century of Dossennius Proculus, aged 30,
[6] years' pay. His heir set this up at his own expense.
Here he lies.

[MW 384 = *RIB* 258 = EDCS–07800507 = BM no. 1853,1108.1]

Tombstone found in Lincoln in 1849, now in British Museum. Legion
II was raised in AD 69 from sailors of the Ravenna fleet (see **H26** and
note). The dolphins and trident on the gable of the tombstone allude to
this origin. It came to Britain in AD 71 with Cerialis, replacing legion
IX at Lincoln, and was transferred to Chester around 78. Valerius'
years of service are partly lost, [?]I, but XI would have seen the legion
based at Chester so VI is likely. Height 1.86m, width 0.66m. Drawing
© Trustees of the British Museum.

N57   Veteran enrolled as town councillor at Aquileia

To L. Arrius Macer, veteran, served 36 years, inscribed on bronze by Divus Vespasian
as town councillor of Aquileia. Arria Trophime, freedwomen of Lucius, made this for
her patron while she lived, and for herself and her descendants.

[MW 379 = *CIL* 5.889 = EDCS–01600167*]

Aquileia, NE Italy: Lovely funerary monument, with beautifully carved image of a matron grieving on the
left-hand side. The text shows a veteran being enlisted on the local town council by the emperor.

N58   Velius Rufus, veteran of many Flavian campaigns

To Gaius Velius Rufus, son of Salvius, chief centurion of Legion XII 'Thunderer', commander of detachments of 9 legions (I 'Helper', II 'Helper', II 'Augustan', VIII 'Augustan' IX 'Spanish', XIV 'Twinned', XX 'Victorious', XXI 'Plunderer'), tribune of Urban Cohort XIII, commander of the African and Mauretanian army for subduing the tribes in Mauretania, decorated in the Jewish War by Emperor Vespasian and Emperor Titus with the rampart crown, and with collars, medallions and bracelets; also decorated with the wall crown, with two spears and two banners, and in the war against Marcomanni, Quadi and Sarmatae, for making an expedition against them through the territory of Decebalus, king of the Dacians, with wall crown, with two spears and two banners; procurator of Emperor Caesar Augustus Germanicus of the province of Pannonia & Dalmatia, and likewise procurator of the province of Raetia with power of life and death. He was sent to Parthia and brought back Epiphanes and Callinicus, sons of King Antiochus to the Emperor Vespasian together with a vast band of his subjects. M. Alfius Olympiacus, son of Marcus, of the Fabian tribe, standard-bearer and veteran of Legion XV 'Apollo's' erected this in his honour.

[MW 372 = *ILS* 9200 = EDCS–16300627*]

This statue base from Heliopolis (Baalbek) in Syria gives a remarkably long and detailed inscription of a much decorated soldier, and almost a military history of the Flavian period, as elucidated by D. Kennedy, "C. Velius Rufus", in: *Britannia* 14 (1983) 183–196. The decorations obtained in the Jewish War suggest that Velius then ranked as a centurion. Notice by the Flavians and perhaps personal acquaintance with Antiochus' sons presumably led to his being given the task of escorting them to Rome in around 73 (see **M59**). After being appointed senior centurion he was given the prestigious command of urban cohort XIII in Carthage, and then the irregular command of an army against Mauretania, probably at roughly the same period, but distinct from the Nasamones war (**N31–32**). The campaign in which he commanded detachments from 9 legions (the inscription lists only 8: probably legion XI 'Claudian' has been accidentally omitted) was probably some stage of the Pannonian War. A Martial poem (**N59**) probably, but not certainly, refers to Velius Rufus having a role in the second war. At some point he achieved equestrian status, required for governorships of Pannonia/Dalmatia and then Raetia.

N59   Velius' vows for Caesar's success fulfilled within eight months

When Velius was Caesar's close comrade-in-arms
In Northern lands, on his behalf he vowed
A bird to Mars. The full moon had not yet come round
Eight times, when god claimed payment of his vows.

[Martial, *Epigram* 9.31 (published December 94)]

N60   Epitaph of soldier honoured in Commagene War, AD 72

[… *Name of man honoured is lost* …] In the war against Commagene he was decorated with honours given by the emperors, a golden crown, collars, bracelets and medallions; honoured in a dress parade by the emperor as *primipilus* of Legion III 'Gallic'; granted honorary local magistracy by decree of the town council. M. Antonius Hennunes, freedman of Hoplo, for his great merits.

[MW 49 = *ILS* 9198 = EDCS–17700196*]

Found at Heliopolis (Baalbek, Lebanon). For Commagene, see **M59**.

N61 Tombstone of veteran of Dacian and German wars

To the divine shades: Quintus Vilanius Nepos, son of Quintus, of the Voltinian tribe, citizen of Philippi, centurion of Urban Cohort XIII, decorated by Domitian in the Dacian war, also by him in the German war, also awarded collars and bracelets in the Dacian war. He lived for 50 years, and served in the army for 32. Marcus Silius Quintianus, *optio,* set this up; he deserved well.

[MW 58 = *ILS* 2127 = EDCS–17700850*]

Tombstone with crown inscribed above the inscription and cavalryman below. Found at Carthage, now in Algiers Museum, where Urban Cohort XIII was based before serving in the Pannonian Wars (see **N57** and note).

N62 Soldier of 'Domitian's own' legion (AD 89–96)

L. Magius Dubius, <son> of Lucius, of Oufentian tribe, from Milan. Soldier of Legion I 'Flavian Minervan, Domitian's own, Faithful and Loyal'. Custodian of the armoury, in the century of Aufidius Martial. 31 years old, 13 year's pay. His heir saw to this being made.

[MW 387 = *ILS* 2279 = EDCS–11100294*]

Tombstone with floral decoration at the top found near Rome to a soldier of Domitian's new legion (Dio 55.24.3), probably raised for the emperor's campaigns against the Chatti in AD 83. It was probably named 'Flavia Minervia'. Together with the other legions sent to put down the Saturninus revolt in 89, it received the names 'Pia Fidelis Domitiana' in addition, abbreviated to FMPFD on this inscription. After his assassination, the names Flavian and Domitian were dropped.

N63 A clearly dated military career

M. Carantius Macrinus, created centurion of Urban Cohort I. A soldier in the same cohort when Domitian was consul for the second time [73]; assistant of Tettienus Serenus, imperial legate, when Vespasian was consul for the tenth time [79?]; adjutant of Cornelius Gallicanus, imperial legate, with cavalry-level pay when Domitian was consul for the ninth time [83]; likewise of Minicius Rufus, imperial legate. Recalled when Augustus Domitian was consul for the fourteenth time [88], centurion when Emperor Nerva was consul for the second time [90]. He ordered this to be erected in his will.

[MW 361 = *ILS* 2118 = EDCS–09201054*]

Funerary inscription with decorated gable in relief from Genava (Geneva, Switzerland). Vespasian was actually only consul 9 times.

N64 A very long-serving veteran and army doctor

L. Pellartius Celer Julius Montanus, son of Gaius, of the Lemonian tribe, discharged after 43 years' military service as a veteran and army doctor of Legion XV 'Apollo's' by Domitian Caesar Augustus and received for his public service 300 sesterces, which no one else had previously received for his service. Also decorated by Divus Titus in the Jewish War with awards and the golden crown, he lived his life for 73 years. L. Pellartius Anthus, to whom permission was granted, gave this tomb with its inscription to his daughters as well. Space of the monument 55 feet wide, and 45 feet deep.

[MW 374 = EDCS–01401130*: tombstone Aquileia, NE Italy]

N65   A Domitianic veteran

To Lucius Tatinius Cnosus, son of Lucius, of the Voltinian tribe, soldier of the 4th praetorian cohort, orderly and *beneficiarius* of the tribune, *optio, beneficiarius* of the praetorian prefect, veteran recalled by the Emperor; awarded the torque, bracelets, medallions, golden crown ~~by Emperor Domitian Caesar Augustus Germanicus~~ centurion of Watch Cohort IIII, centurion of military police, centurion of Urban Cohort XI: the veterans who served under him in the Watch and received honourable discharge.

[MW 367 = Philippi 00202 = EDCS–15800368*]

Statue base at Philippi, Greece. For the stone altar erected by this man to celebrate his retirement and 'Augustan *Quies*', see **L38**.

SECTION P
CONSPIRACIES, REVOLTS AND SCANDALS

The sea filled with exiles, rocky islands stained with blood.

[Tacitus, *Histories* 1.2.2]

Having reached power after a series of revolts, it is hardly surprising that the Flavian emperors should have been wary of, and alert to, discontent in others. **P12** and **P15** sum up a paranoiac attitude of Domitian, also recorded by Suetonius (*Dom.* 21). In particular the Flavians are sometimes said to have faced 'Stoic opposition', especially from the extended family of Thrasea Paetus, under Vespasian and *c.* AD 93. Sources for this are given in **P1a–n** and **P11a–g**. The best modern account and explanation remains C. Wirszubski, *Libertas as a Political Idea at Rome during the Late Republic and Early Principate,* (CUP 1950). All conspiracies, revolts and scandals are arranged here in likely chronological order, each under one number, with lettered subsections.

P1   Helvidius Priscus and 'the Stoic opposition' AD 70s
Towards the end of his reign, Nero had persecuted various influential politicians and Stoics. Seneca was the best-known in both categories, as a prolific writer of stoic philosophy and Nero's chief minister. Of more importance for its continued resonances into the Flavian period was the prosecution, condemnation and death in AD 66 of Thrasea Paetus and Barea Soranus (Tac. *Ann.* 16.21 and 23–34). Though it seems unlikely that either man actually had a philosophical objection to monarchy (stoicism did not, and perhaps the most famous Roman stoic was the emperor Marcus Aurelius – and see *'Meditations'* 1.14), their stoic beliefs probably encouraged them to take a more principled stance than most of the senate. Paetus' son-in-law, Helvidius Priscus was also condemned to exile and returned after the death of Nero. Under Vespasian he attacked Paetus' prosecutor, but also seems to have turned Paetus' 'quietism' into a determination to speak up against aspects of Vespasian's principate. He was initially exiled (certainly by 75) and subsequently put to death (the dates are unclear). Helvidius' son was consul under Domitian, but executed in AD 93. Thus the opposition might be said to be as much based around a circle of family and friends (a 'hereditary feud' – Syme, *Tacitus* 557) as around a philosophy. But the circle also overlaps and is confused (e.g. by Dio) with wider philosophical disquiet about the principate, shown by the 'Cynic' philosophers, who challenged and questioned everything. Their leader was probably Demetrius (whose conversation with the dying Paetus forms the last extant sentence of Tacitus' *Annals*) and who was exiled by Vespasian.

P1a   Seneca on the unpopularity of Stoic philosophers
It seems to me a mistake to think that those who whole-heartedly devote themselves to philosophy are contumacious and deliberately awkward, holding in contempt magistrates, kings, and those who see to the running of the state.

[Seneca, *Letters to Lucilius* 73.1]

Seneca wrote this towards the end of his life while in 'retirement' from public life under Nero. Though the letter argues that philosophers should be grateful to the king who ensures their quiet comfort, the opening here suggests that philosophers were disliked for their assumed superiority. Dio of Prusa also gives plenty of contemporary evidence for the unpopularity of philosophers, e.g. *Oration* 32.9, attacking would-be Cynics for giving philosophy a bad name, or 72.2 suggesting that in a city (not named, but probably Rome) wearing a beard was enough to make one obviously a philosopher and thus a target of abuse.

P1b   Quintilian's criticism of those opting out of oratory

Others of laziness and arrogance suddenly knit their brows and let their beards grow. As if they had come to despise the precepts of public speaking they took their seats in the schools of philosophers so that, disapproving in public, but in private dissolute, they might seize the moral high ground by despising everyone else. This is because philosophy can be feigned but eloquence cannot.

[Quintilian, *The Orator's Education* 12.3.12]

For a similar attack on the personal morality of those who pretend to be philosophers, see *preface* 15. Quintilian acknowledges the need for an orator to consider right and wrong, but is clearly deeply suspicious of those choosing philosophy above public life. He may very well have had the likes of Thrasea Paetus and Helvidius in mind.

P1c   Family Tree of Thrasea Paetus

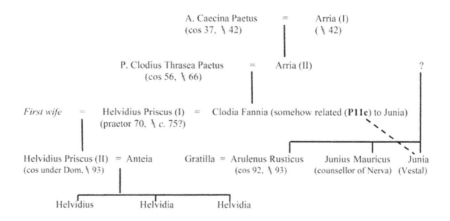

P1d   An admiring view of Helvidius Priscus

[5] Since this is the second time[217] we have mentioned a man who will feature quite often in our history,[218] a few words are called for about his life, his interests and what happened to him. Helvidius Priscus came from the town of Cluviae and his father had led the line as chief centurion. As a young man he devoted his notable talents to higher scholarship, not, like many, to clothe a life of idleness under a pretentious name, but to be better able to withstand the vicissitudes of public office. He followed those teachers of philosophy who hold that virtuous conduct is the only good; that wrong-doing is shameful; that power, noble birth and other things outside what one can control should be counted as neither good nor wrong.[219] While still a quaestor he was chosen by Thrasea Paetus as his son-in-law, and from his father-in-law's character he learnt freedom (*libertas*) above all.[220] As a citizen, senator, husband, son-in-law, friend he

---

[217] Helvidius had been previously mentioned at *Hist.* 2.91, opposing the emperor Vitellius.

[218] Of course all references after AD 70 are lost.

[219] This is Tacitus' definition of Stoic philosophy.

[220] *Libertas* is a difficult concept, as Wirszubski, in still the definitive book on the subject explains, 'Libertas means either personal or civic rights, or republicanism, or both'. Here it means that H. 'asserted his freedom of opinion and championed the rights and dignity of the senate'. (Wirszubski, *Libertas*, p.125 and 147).

was just in all his duties in life, uncorrupted by wealth, resolute in righteousness, dauntless in the face of fear.[221]

[6] There were people who thought he was too keen to seek fame, since even philosophers rid themselves, last of all, of desire for glory. Driven to exile by the downfall of his father-in-law, he returned in the principate of Galba to attack in court Marcellus Eprius, the prosecutor of Thrasea. This act of retaliation, either great or just, completely split the senate – if Marcellus fell, a whole line of defendants would be laid low. At first the case was fiercely contested, as shown by the outstanding speeches of each side. But presently, since Galba seemed unenthusiastic and many senators raised objections, Priscus dropped the case. What people said about this varied, like men's characters: some praised his moderation, others thought he lacked resolve. But on the very day on which the senate was deciding on Vespasian's powers, it had been decided to send a delegation to the emperor. This led to a bitter dispute between Helvidius and Eprius, since Priscus demanded that existing magistrates should be chosen individually, Marcellus that they should be chosen by lot, as proposed by the consul designate.

[Tacitus, *Histories* 4.5–6]

Tacitus *Dialogus* 5.5–7 gives this dispute as an example of the power of oratory – Eprius Marcellus being able to defend himself against Helvidius and a hostile senate.

P1e   Helvidius claims Vespasian was a friend of Thrasea Paetus

Helvidius said that … the good of the state required, as indeed did respect for Vespasian, that those going to meet him, to accustom his ears to speeches in his honour, should be the most irreproachable the senate could provide. Vespasian had been friends with Thrasea, Soranus, and Sentius: it might not be expedient to punish their prosecutors, but they must not be put on display.

[Tacitus, *Histories* 4.7]

This forms part of Helvidius' argument from the previous passage. Q. Marcius Barea Soranus, cos 52, was prosecuted and condemned with Thrasea Paetus in AD 66 (Tac. *Ann.* 16.21, 23–34). It is not certain which 'Sentius' is meant here. This is the only evidence for Vespasian's friendship with the two most prominent members of the 'Stoic opposition' to Nero.

P1f   A warning to Helvidius

Marcellus replied … In short it was all very well for Helvidius to liken his loyalty and bravery to that of men like Cato or Brutus: he, Marcellus, was just one member of the senate who had all been compelled to serve. Furthermore he would advise Priscus not to seek to climb higher than the emperor, nor lecture Vespasian, who was no longer young, had won a triumph, and was the father of grown-up sons. The worst emperors liked absolute power, but even the best wanted a limit to freedom (*libertas*).

[Tacitus, *Histories* 4.8]

This is part of Eprius Marcellus' answer, and one must surely suspect, from Tacitus' introduction to Helvidius (above, **P1a**), that it was very much a warning that went unheeded.

---

221 The last sentence of chapter 5 is described by Chilver, *Commentary on Histories IV and V,* p.28, compare p.7 as 'a sentence more laudatory than of any character in *Histories* or *Annals*'

P1g   Parties to celebrate the birthdays of the tyrannicides
Wine such as Thrasea and Helvidius would drink at parties
On the birthdays of Brutus and Cassius.

[Juvenal, *Satire* 5.36–37]

Written celebration of Brutus and Cassius had caused Cremutius Cordus' prosecution and death in AD 25 (Tac. *Ann.* 4.34–5). Juvenal's reference to vintage wine shows the fame and reputation of Thrasea and Helvidius around AD 120. But later commentators tried to explain... (**P1h**).

P1h   Ancient Juvenal commentary, explaining Helvidius
Thrasea and Helvidius: after the condemnation (according to Probus) of his father-in-law, Thrasea Paetus, Helvidius was banned from Italy and allowed to go to Apollonia. But after Nero was killed, he was restored by Galba and conducted himself just as if in a free state. He, however, was so industrious that when, under Nero, he was administrating Achaia as a quaestor, certain communities which he had not approached, shouted 'it suits us too'. He afterwards offended Vespasian by his enthusiasm for liberty as he thought **as was wished by his uncle Claudius** that the ancient type of liberty could be brought back. Under this charge he was put on trial and unexpectedly acquitted.

[Valla, *Scholia on Juvenal Satires* lines 5.36]

As not infrequently with ancient commentaries, this entry appears to combine useful information and drivel. Claudius was not his uncle (the text may be corrupt), and an acquittal of Helvidius is hard to fit with other sources. Probus did, however, provide an explanation of Thrasea which entirely fits with Tacitus' account.

P1i   Helvidius Priscus as a troublemaker
It was becoming perfectly obvious that Vespasian heartily disliked Helvidius Priscus, not so much for his shortcomings or even for those of his friends that he had insulted, but because the man was a troublemaker. He made himself popular with the mob, constantly denouncing monarchy and praising democracy. He cultivated a following and formed a clique, on the ridiculous proposition that it was the task of philosophy to hurl abuse at those in power, to stir up popular feeling, to overturn the rule of law, and to promote revolution. [12.3] As the son-in-law of Thrasea Paetus, he had taken it into his head to cast himself in the same mould. But in this he fell far short of the mark. Thrasea had lived under Nero and disapproved of him utterly. But he had never said or done anything to denigrate him beyond merely refusing to take part in his activities. Helvidius, by contrast, disliked Vespasian and would not keep away from him, in private or in public. His actions were potentially lethal for him; and by constantly making trouble, he was bound to pay for it in the end.

[*On Virtues and Vices*, Valesius' Excerpts 273 = Dio 66.12.2–3]

Helvidius doubtless praised *libertas* – 'freedom' which potentially encompassed freedom of speech as well as political freedom. Helvidius Priscus offended as praetor in AD 70, was exiled by 75 and later executed. Suet. also takes Vespasian's side in reporting on Helvidius (*Vesp.* 15). Tacitus' account is lost, except for the very early stages, but his summary of his character at *Hist.* 4.5 is highly, perhaps uniquely, generous (see **P1d**).

P1j   Helvidius refuses to toe the line

[19] Helvidius Priscus also saw this and acted accordingly. When Vespasian summoned him to tell him not to attend the senate, he replied, "It is within your rights not to allow me to be a senator, but as long as I am, I must attend." [20] "In that case, go in, but keep silent." "Don't call on me to give an opinion, and I'll keep silent." "But I must ask for opinions." "And I must say what I think is right." "But if you speak, I shall have you killed." [21] "When did I tell you that I am immortal? You do your job and I'll do mine. Yours is to kill, mine is to die fearlessly: yours to banish, mine to leave without regret.

[Epictetus, *Discourses*, 1.2.19–21]

Epictetus was an important Stoic philosopher and teacher. A slave of Nero's freedman Epaphroditus he taught in Rome until Domitian expelled the philosophers in AD 89 (**P11e**), then in Nicopolis (near Actium). His oral teachings were published by his pupil Arrian the historian.

P1k   Mucianus' attack on philosophers

Mucianus made a great number of improbable statements to Vespasian against the Stoics. He maintained that they were full of empty boasts, and that if any of them allowed his beard to grow long or raised his eyebrows to give himself an air of superiority, wore his cloak off-the-shoulder, or went about in bare feet, he would immediately develop pretensions to wisdom, courage, and goodness. They would become thoroughly arrogant, even if the simplest alphabet left them floundering. They would look down their noses at everyone, calling noblemen 'spoilt brats', and lower class people 'dimwits', anyone good looking a 'sex-maniac', and their opposites 'morons', rich men 'greedy capitalists', and poor men 'slave-material'.

[Petrus Patricius, *Sayings* – 'Vatican Excerpts 106 = Dio 66.13.1a]

As Murison, *Commentary* on 13.1a eloquently puts it, the only problem with this lengthy and splendid diatribe against the Stoics is that it has nothing to do with Stoicism. Mucianus, as reported by Dio, has completely confused Stoics and Cynics (see also note 61).

P1m   Helvidius twice exiled

Only Fannia's mind and spirit remain strong, as is most worthy of her husband Helvidius and her father Thrasea. ... Twice she followed her husband into exile, and the third time she was banished herself on his account.

[Pliny the Younger, *Letters* 7.19.3–4]

Helvidius was first exiled by Nero at the time of Thrasea's death, then by Vespasian. For the context of this information, see **P11c**.

P1n   Vespasian ignores 'philosophical opposition'

[4] Is it any surprise that he behaved like this with his friends when he even ignored the insinuations of attorneys and the insults of philosophers?

[*Epitome de Caesaribus* 9.4]

The *Epitome* has just related his witty retort to Mucianus (see **U3**). It is likely that some reference to 'philosophical' opposition to Vespasian (e.g. from Helvidius) existed in the source for the *Epitome*.

P2   Conspiracy of Caecina Alienus, *c.* AD 78
'Endless conspiracies' against Vespasian are mentioned by Suetonius (*Vesp.* 25), but only this one is named
by any source. Suet. *Titus* 6 records Caecina being killed in melodramatic circumstances by Titus as does
Dio (**C16b**) who links Eprius Marcellus to the conspiracy. The epitome provides details but these are hard
to fit to a period near the death of Vespasian. For Caecina, cos 69, see Tac. *Hist.* 2.56, 2.92, 2.100–1.

P2a   Caecina killed
Amongst these victims was Caecina, a former consul, who had been present at a
dinner, and had only just left the dining-room when Titus ordered that he be murdered
on the suspicion of his wife, Berenice whom he had raped.

[*Epitome de Caesaribus* 10.4]

P3   False Neros
The circumstances of Nero's final flight and hasty funeral (Suet. *Nero* 48–50), combined with a certain
degree of popularity seem to have led to rumours of his survival, and of people pretending to be him.
Tacitus reports one such example in AD 69 (*Hist.* 2.8–9) and promises to tell other such stories at the
appropriate place in his narrative, now lost. One such was under Titus, while Suetonius (*Nero* 57.2)
mentions a 'sighting' in AD 88, while Dio of Prusa attests to other 'sightings'.

P3a   The 'False Nero'
[19.3b] Titus' reign also saw the appearance of the False Nero, a native of Asia Minor
by the name of Terentius Maximus. He closely resembled Nero in both appearance
and voice even to the extent of accompanying himself on the lyre. He acquired a
modest following in Asia, but as he advanced towards the Euphrates he built up a
much more significant army of supporters. [19.3c] In the end he fled to the Parthian
chieftain, Artabanus, who had a grudge against Titus. He made Terentius welcome
and planned to reinstate him in Rome.

[Zonaras, *Summary of Dio*, 11.18 = Dio 66.19.3b–c]

The same story is told in John of Antioch, a seventh-century chronicler, thought to have used Dio. He adds
that the identity was soon discovered.

P3b   Nero still alive?
Even now this matter (Nero's death) is not clear. For as far as everyone else (outside
the imperial court) was concerned, there was nothing to prevent him ruling for ever:
even now everybody wishes he were still alive. The great majority actually think he
is, although in one sense he has died not just once but a number of times, along with
those who were quite certain he was alive!

[Dio of Prusa (Dio Chrysostom), *Orations* 21.10]

P4   Prophecy to Titus of his death, *c.* AD 81
"And how shall I die?" asked Titus. "The same way Odysseus is said to have died,
with death coming to him from the sea." Damis interprets this in the following way:
Titus guarded himself against the sting of a *trugon,* by which Odysseus is said to have
been struck, but having held power for two years after his father he was killed by a
sea hare. This fish produces a terrible poison, and is the most deadly thing on land or
sea. Nero added this hare to dishes he made for his most deadly enemies; Domitian

for his own brother, not because he resented sharing power with his brother but with someone gentle and good.

[Philostratos, *Life of Apollonius of Tyana* 6.32.1–2]

Aur. Vict. 10.5 claims murder while Dio 66.26.2 (**C26**) mentions *rumours* of murder.

P5   Purges in the early 80s
In AD 82, Flavius Sabinus (see **J14**) was executed. He may have been Dio of Prusa's patron (**P5a**), but neither that account nor the trivial reason given by Suet. *Dom.* 10.4 provide any evidence of any conspiracy or whether it involved others. Jerome mentions a purge in AD 83 which should be connected with a mention in Dio/Xiphilinus (67.3.3.1 = **D3**) of murder or exile of many senators, and probably with a similar statement in Byzantine excerpts below.

P5a   Dio of Prusa exiled and his patron killed, *c.* AD 82
I once had the misfortune to be exiled because of my reported friendship with a man of importance who had previously been very close to those in prosperity and power. He was killed for the very reasons which made most if not all men think of him as fortunate, namely his familiarity and family relationship with those men. This was the charge against me – that I was friend and adviser to this man: for it is way of tyrants, just as Scythians bury cup-bearers, cooks and concubines together with their kings, to add many others to those they put to death, and for no reason. When this happened, I began to consider whether this exile was really such a terrible misfortune …

[Dio of Prusa (Dio Chrysostom) *Oration* 13.1–2]

In speech 7.66, Dio of Prusa also says that he 'knew the homes of satraps and kings' (evoking the Persian empire which once included his home town (now NW Turkey) but meaning governors and emperors).

P5b   Jerome, *Chronicle* AD 83
Domitian sends very many senators into exile.

[Jerome, *Chronicle*, 2099 years after Abraham = AD 83]

P5c   'Persuaded to suicide'
He removed many of them to other locations and then had them murdered. A significant number were also 'persuaded' by one means or another to commit suicide, so that it would appear that they had died voluntarily rather than by compulsion.

[*On Virtues and Vices*, Valesius' Excerpts 277 = Dio 67.3.4.2]

P6   A conspiracy recorded by the Arval Brothers, 22 September, AD 87 (= A87j)
This event cannot be firmly linked to any known conspiracy though Jones, *Domitian* 43–44 suggests a link to the fall of Arrecinus Clemens (see **J20**) around this time.

P7   Execution of proconsul of Asia, *c.* AD 88
It was now the year for Agricola to draw lots to be proconsul of Africa or Asia. Civica's recent execution was an obvious warning to Agricola and precedent for Domitian.

[Tacitus, *Agricola* 42.1]

C. Vettulenus Civica Cerialis, was cos c. 76, legate of Moesia AD 82 (*ILS* 1995 – diploma), and was executed while governor (proconsul) of Asia (Suet. *Dom.* 10.2 and *ILS* 1374 = **U45**). The proconsulship of Africa or Asia, the most important public provinces, seems to have been awarded to the most senior ex-consul 12 to 15 years after his consulship: in Agricola's case this would be between AD 89 and 92.

P8   Antonius Saturninus revolt, AD 89

This revolt can be securely dated by the Arval records (**A89c, d, f, g**), but much else is unclear, despite the narrative of Dio (Xiphilinus: **D11**). L. Antonius Saturninus had been enlisted into the senate by Vespasian, suffect consul *c.* 82 and sent to govern the four legions of Upper Germany by 87/88. The revolt started at the winter quarters of the legions at Moguntiacum (Mainz, Germany) on 1 Jan. 89 when legionaries would take an oath of loyalty to the emperor, and involved legions XIV and XXI. On 12 Jan, the arvals met to make vows for Domitian's victory and safe return (**A89c**). News of Saturninus' defeat reached Rome on 24 Jan (**A89f** and Plut. *Aem. Paul.* 25.4): A. Bucius Lappius Maximus (cos 86), the commander of the Lower German armies had marched from their quarters at Cologne, defeating Saturninus, with help from the governor of Raetia, Norbanus (the *Epitome* (**P8e**) combines the names). Domitian probably continued to Germany after hearing the news to conduct reprisals against officers in Saturninus' legions and on German tribes thought to have been involved (Suet. *Dom.* 6.2), hence allowing the episode to be portrayed as a 'German War'. Lappius received a second consulship, his legions the title '*pia fidelis Domitiana*' 'Domitian's own, loyal and trusty'. Various reforms to prevent similar uprisings followed (Suet. *Dom.* 7.3). Despite the clear narrative and suggestions of a wider conspiracy (burnt papers and wider purge in Dio) Saturninus seems an unlikely possible emperor and Syme (*RP* 3.1070ff) may be right to see an element of chance, with Saturninus not fully in control of his troops, egged on by junior supporters and events spiralling out of control. This would fit with the very quick crushing of the revolt.

P8a   Antonius Saturninus' head displayed in Rome

In fact, there is no way of knowing the total number of executions Domitian was responsible for, but he seems to have had such a guilty conscience about the whole matter that he allowed no record of their deaths to be retained, and forbade their names to be kept on any kind of official record. Nor did he submit any sort of report to the senate about those who had been eliminated, though he did send their heads, including that of Antonius, back to Rome for public display in the Forum.

[On Virtues and Vices, Valesius' Excerpts 283 = Dio 67.11.3]

P8b   Saturninus defeated by Lappius

[9] Incensed by Domitian's savagery and especially aggrieved by being insulted in words and called a prostitute, Antonius who was in charge of Upper Germany, made a grab for power. [10] When he had been overthrown in battle by Norbanus Lappius, Domitian, now far more loathsome, began to attack all of mankind, even his own family, like a wild animal.

[Epitome de Caesaribus 11.9–10]

The epitome has garbled the names of those who defeated Saturninus, see introduction to **P8** above.

P8c   A notorious pervert

When Antonius Saturninus, notorious and loathsome, was enrolled into the senate by Vespasian, though Vespasian was prudent, he did something quite ridiculous: pandering to his vice, he invested him with high office – a reward that was unprofitable but also brought honour. Antonius lived a notorious and loathsome life, and was not entrusted with any power over imperial finances.

[Aelian, History fragment 112 (ed. Hercher)]

P8d   News of Saturninus' defeat reaches Rome

[3] When Antonius revolted from Domitian and a great war was anticipated from Germany, Rome was in confusion; but suddenly and unprompted, the people generated

news of a victory, and the story raced through Rome that Antonius had been killed and his army defeated and utterly annihilated. Confidence in the story became so conspicuous and overpowering that many magistrates carried out sacrifices. [4] But when search was made for the man who first reported it, there was none, but the story, tracked from one man to another, escaped and, as if sinking into the gaping sea, finally disappeared in the countless throng, with no clear source. So the rumour quickly vanished from the city, but when Domitian was marching out in force for war, and was already en route, message and letters announcing victory met him. And the day of the success and of the report was one and the same, though the places were two thousand, five hundred miles apart. Everyone of our generation knows these facts.

[Plutarch, *Life of Aemilius Paullus* 25.3–4]

Plutarch is prompted to tell this story from his own day by a similar supernatural rumour from the career of the second-century BC politician and general (censor 164 BC). The story perhaps derived from the very great speed at which events unfolded.

P8e   Martial mocks another usurping Antony
While you were proud to bear Antonius' name,
And that of Saturninus did declaim;
Arms in Germany against Caesar you bore;
As Antony in Egypt did before.
What fate attends that name did you not fear?   5
Of his disgrace at Actium never hear?
Or did the Rhine promise success to thee
Though Nile to him denied the victory?
That Antony, who by Rome's swords did fall,
Compared to you, true Caesar we should call.   10
[Martial *Epigram* 4.11, (publ. December 89) trans. H. Killigrew, 1689, slightly adapted]

Martial plays on Saturninus sharing a name with Mark Antony, opponent of Augustus.

P8f   Martial's praise for Norbanus' role
Norbanus, when your pious loyalty to Caesar
Our Lord, stood firm against the sacrilegious madness,
I was at leisure, safe in the Peirian shade,
Well-known as one who cultivated your friendship.
The Raetian in the realms of Vindelicia, told you   5
About me; Northern lands did recognise my name.
How often it was that, not denying your old friend
You said out loud "Mine he is, that poet, mine!"
All my work which formerly, for twice three years
A reader used to give, the author now gives you.   10
[Martial, *Epigram* 9.84 (published December 94)]

Martial's poem celebrates Norbanus' return to Rome after six years of service in areas north of Rome, probably to take up the post of praetorian prefect he held at Domitian's death (Dio 67.15.2 = **D15**).

P8g   Epitaph to Lappius' wife, Rome
To Aelia, wife of [L]appius Maximus, twice consul, who finished off the German war.
[Rome: MW 60 = ILS 1006 = EDCS–17800498]

P9   Mettius family fall, early 90s
The family came from Arles in Gaul and rose with M. Mettius Modestus, equestrian procurator of Syria under Claudius. His elder son of the same name was possibly cos 82, his younger son, M. Mettius Rufus was prefect of Egypt (Suet. *Dom.* 4, **M30**). Mettius Pomposianus, assumed to be a relative, was consul under Vespasian, but executed by Domitian (Suet. *Dom.* 10.3, Dio 67.12.2–3) because horoscopes predicted his rule (Suet. *Vesp.* 14 and below). His relatives are somehow involved in his fall, with Mettius Modestus exiled (**P9b**) and the prefect of Egypt's name found erased on several papyri and probably on **M31**.

P9a   Mettius Pomposianus and Vespasian
[14] When friends warned him to take care of Mettius Pomposianus, who was destined to rule, according to widespread gossip, he made him consul, joking about it with the following quip, "As long as he is mindful of this great debt he owes me."
[Epitome de Caesaribus 9.14]

P9b   Mettius Modestus in exile
We were relying for part of our case on an opinion by Mettius Modestus, an excellent man. At the time he was in exile, banished by Domitian.
[Y. Pliny, Letters 1.5.5]

For the context of this letter, see note on **P11d**, below.

P10   Domitian accuses Nerva, Orfitus, Rufus
Nerva seemed suited to imperial power, which he held after Domitian, and with good sense; and the same was thought about Orfitus and Rufus. Domitian declared that these men were plotting against him, and the latter two were confined on islands, while Nerva was ordered to live at Tarentum.
[Philostratos, Life of Apollonius of Tyana 7.8.1]

Salvidienus Orfitus is mentioned by Suetonius (*Dom.* 10.2) as one of three former consuls executed by Domitian on charge of conspiracy. He was Servius Cornelius Salvidienus Orfitus, son of the consul ordinarius of AD 51, and father of the consul of AD 110. Rufus could possibly be Verginius Rufus, see **B69**; or Minicius Rufus, cos ord 88; neither of them is otherwise thought to have faced persecution by Domitian, and nor is Nerva; but the story may well reflect efforts by them, or their supporters, to distance themselves from the previous regime (compare **T33–T38**). Orfitus' execution cannot be dated.

P11   Persecution of 'Stoic Opposition' in AD 93
Late in 93, a group of senators and stoic philosophers connected to the family of Helvidius Priscus (I) were prosecuted in the senate on treason charges, the substance of which is obscure, but was said by their supporters to have related to public praise for Helvidius Priscus (I). Helvidius Priscus (II), Herennius Senecio and Junius Arulenus Rusticus were all condemned and executed, while their wives and Junius Mauricus were exiled.

P11a   Censorship of literature and philosophy
[2.1] We have read that it was a capital offence when Thrasea Paetus was praised by Arulenus Rusticus, and Priscus Helvidius by Herennius Senecio, that not only the authors themselves but their books were savaged; and that the task was delegated to the three officials in charge of capital punishment of burning masterpieces of most distinguished genius in the assembly and the forum. [2.2] Doubtless they thought that, in that fire, the voice of the Roman people and the liberty of the senate and the accumulated knowledge of the human race would be abolished; that with professors of philosophy also being expelled and with all fine arts being driven to exile, integrity would nowhere survive.

[Tacitus, *Agricola*, 2.1–2]

Near the start of the biography of his father-in-law, Tacitus sets the scene for the period in which Agricola's career should have culminated: at the same time he is suggesting that he is writing a similar work in praise of a recently deceased close family connection, a virtuous man and public figure who also suffered at the hands of a tyrant.

P11b   The Senate's condemnation of Helvidius and others
[44.5] For given that he was not to be allowed to survive until the light of this most blessed age, and to see Trajan as emperor which he often predicted in our hearing in omens and prayer, it came as a significant consolation that he avoided that final period in which Domitian no longer allowed any interval or breathing space but destroyed the state as if by one, continuous assault. [45.1] Agricola did not see the senate house besieged and the senators blocked in by armed men; nor the murder of so many former consuls in one massacre; nor the exile or banishment of so many noble ladies. Only one success had yet been attributed to Carus Mettius, and the opinions of Messalinus were being screamed only within the Alban fortress, and Massa Baebius was still on trial. But before long our hands led Helvidius into prison; the expressions of Mauricus and Rusticus condemned us; we were drenched in the innocent blood of Senecio. [45.2] Even Nero looked away when he ordered crimes and did not watch them, whereas an especial part of the miseries under Domitian was to watch and to be observed when our sighs were noted down and when his savage and purple face (which saved him from blushing for shame) was enough to mark out all those who had turned pale.

[Tacitus, *Agricola*, 44.5–45.2]

Baebius Massa had supported Vespasian in the civil wars. Early in 93, Y. Pliny and Herennius Senecio successfully prosecuted him for extortion in his recent governorship of Baetica (*Letters* 7.33). Mauricus and Rusticus are the brothers Junius Arulenus Rusticus and Junius Mauricus, the former executed, the latter exiled.

P11c   Fannia
[1] The illness of Fannia worries me a great deal. She contracted this illness while taking care of Junia, one of the Vestal virgins, at first voluntarily, Junia being a relative, and then on the authority of the *pontifices*. [2] For these virgins, when they are forced to move from the Temple of Vesta because of the seriousness of the illness, are always entrusted to the care and custody of married women. While performing this duty diligently, Fannia caught this dangerous illness. [3] She has a constant fever; her cough grows worse; she is very thin, and constantly exhausted. Only her mind and spirit remain strong, as is most worthy of her husband Helvidius and her father Thrasea. Everything else is failing and this affects me and makes me not only afraid

but also sorrowful. [4] For I am sad that so excellent a woman is being snatched from the gaze of the city, and doubt whether her like will ever be seen again. She has such purity, such integrity, such great dignity and loyal steadfastness! Twice she followed her husband into exile, and the third time she was banished herself on his account. [5] For Senecio, when on trial for writing books on the life of Helvidius, said in his defence that he had been asked by Fannia. Mettius Carus, in threatening manner, asked her whether she had asked him, and she replied, "I did." He asked whether she gave him his memoirs for that purpose. She replied "I did." He then asked whether her mother knew about it. Her reply was "She did not." Finally, she said nothing which showed any fear of danger. [6] Instead, she kept and preserved those very books, which were destroyed by decree of the senate because of the pressures and fear of those times, even when her property was confiscated. So she took into exile the books which had caused her to be exiled.

[Pliny the Younger, *Letters* 7.19.1–6]

The letter was addressed to Neratius Priscus who cannot be firmly identified. Other letters in book 7 seem to date from around AD 107. For Fannia and Junia see **P1c**: this letter provides the evidence for their relationship and thus for the connection between the Junius brothers, Arulenus Rusticus and Mauricus and the Helvidius family. The rest of the letter continues the praise of Fannia and her mother Arria.

P11d   Regulus' attacks on the Stoics
Did you see anyone more afraid and abject than Marcus Regulus now that Domitian is dead? Under Domitian the crimes he committed were no less than under Nero, but they were better hidden. He began to fear that I was angry with him and he was not mistaken: I was angry. [2] He had assisted in the ruin of Arulenus Rusticus; he had rejoiced at his death, to such an extent that he recited in public and later published a book attacking Rusticus and calling him 'the Stoics' ape'; he even added 'branded with the mark of Vitellius'. You recognise the eloquence of Regulus. [3] He was so unrestrained in tearing Herennius Senecio to pieces that Mettius Carus said to him, "What concern have you with my dead men? Have I ever attacked your Crassus or Camerinus?" – these men Regulus had accused during Nero's reign. [4] Regulus believed that I was very annoyed because of this, and so he did not invite me to his recital.

[Pliny the Younger, *Letters* 1.5.1–4]

This letter was written to Voconius Romanus, a regular correspondent, and dates to the start of AD 97, since section 10 refers to Mauricus about to return from exile. Y. Pliny here attacks Regulus for his part in the prosecution of his friend Arulenus Rusticus (see **B92**) whose family he helped after Rusticus' death (*Letters* 1.14, 2.18) Mettius Carus was a notorious informer (**P11b, c, T33**): the point of his comment was that Regulus appeared to be poaching his victim Senecio.

P11e   Philosophers including Epictetus expelled under Domitian
Nor was it only in those more primitive times, as yet unpolished by Greek learning, that the philosophers were driven from the city of Rome, but even in the reign of Domitian, they were thrown out of the city and banned from Italy. That was the time when the philosopher Epictetus left Rome for Nicopolis because of that decree of the senate.

[Aulus Gellius, *Nights in Attica* 15.11.3–5]

Aulus Gellius has just quoted directly senatorial decrees of 161 and 92 BC, expelling philosophers from Rome.

P11f   Pliny the Younger helps an exiled philosopher, Artemidorus

The nature of our friend Artemidorus is so entirely generous that he exaggerates the kindnesses of his friends. So, even though what he says is true, his praise of me is above what I deserve. [2] In fact, when philosophers were banished from the city, I was with him in his suburban villa, and the visit was all the more noteworthy and (this is the point) more dangerous to me, because I was praetor at that time. In addition, he needed quite a large amount of money in order to pay off some debts brought about for the most honourable reasons. I myself borrowed the sum and gave it to him without interest, when certain powerful and rich friends were afraid to act. [3] I did this even though seven of my friends had been executed or banished; Senecio, Rusticus, and Helvidius were killed; Mauricus, Gratilla, Arria, and Fannia exiled. It was as if I had been burnt by so many thunderbolts falling round me, and I guessed, from certain obvious signs, that the same end was threatening me. [4] I believe, however, that I did not deserve such exaggerated glory as he proclaimed for me, but that I simply avoided disgracing myself. [5] For I loved and admired his father-in-law, Gaius Musonius, as far as the difference in our ages allowed; as for Artemidorus himself, during the time when I served as military tribune in Syria, I was a close friend of his, and the first proof I gave of having any natural ability at all was that I seemed to realise that he was either a true wise man, or the very nearest thing to a wise man.

[Pliny the Younger, *Letters* 3.11]

Julius Genitor, a teacher of rhetoric, was a recent acquaintance of Y. Pliny (*Letter* 3.3) who could be regaled with this tale of his derring-do. Artemidorus is only known from this letter, though his father Musonius Rufus was a very famous Stoic philosopher and teacher (**C13.2** and note). Clearly after the persecution of Helvidius (II) and friends, and the order expelling the philosophers, Artemidorus turned to Y. Pliny for money to leave Italy.

P11g   Pliny the Younger attacks an opponent of Helvidius

Your care and eagerness in reading the published speeches I wrote on the vindication of Helvidius have made you all the more earnest in demanding that I write to you about what was not in them and matters surrounding the subject, and finally the entire sequence of events at which you were not present because of your age. [2] When Domitian had been killed, I decided after some thought that a great and noble opportunity presented itself of pursuing the guilty, avenging those who suffered, and improving my own standing. But among the many crimes of so many people, none appeared to me more atrocious than that a senator, of praetorian rank, and a judge, should, in the senate itself, violently attack a fellow senator, a former consul, who was then on trial. [3] In addition to this I had a friendship with Helvidius, as far as possible with a man who, through fear of the times, tried to hide his great name and his equally great qualities, in retirement. I was friends also with Arria and Fannia, the latter being Helvidius' step-mother, the former the mother of his step-mother. But I was urged on not so much by private obligations as by what was right and just for the state, by my indignation at the unworthy action, and by the thought of setting an example. [4] In the first days of our restored liberty each man had, for himself, sought out his own enemies (as long as they were of a lesser rank or power), in the confusion and disorder, and destroyed them. I thought it would be more honest and more effective not to oppress the monstrous criminal with the general ill-will of those times, but to crush him with the appropriate charge, at a time when the initial fury began to die down, and anger, growing less day by day, turned to justice. Although

I was then especially sad at the recent loss of my wife, I sent to Anteia, – she had been married to Helvidius – and asked her to come to me, because my recent mourning for my loss kept me from leaving home. [5] When she arrived, I said to her, "I have decided that your husband should not be allowed to go unavenged. Tell this to Arria and Fannia" (who had returned from exile); "consider both of you whether you would want to join with me in the prosecution. I do not need a partner, but I do not promote my own glory so jealously as to begrudge you a part in this action." Anteia took this message to them and they agreed without delay.

[Pliny the Younger, *Letters* 9.13.1–5]

This letter was written to Ummidius Quadratus, a young advocate (see 6.11, 7.24), enabling Y. Pliny to explain events of 93 and 97. Pliny had published a speech vindicating Helvidius (II), also mentioned at 7.30. The target of Pliny's attack was Publicius Certus (named in section 13 – Pliny deliberately delays naming him in the letter as in the debate). The rest of this letter is equally revealing of the atmosphere in the senate in Nerva's principate. Pliny also mentions his speech on Helvidius at 7.30.

P12   Saying of Domitian on suspicion
What will people say about Domitian? He was physically strong. The pleasures of listening to drums or musical instruments which undermine courage, he shunned; but he derived enjoyment from the pain of others and the cries they made. Mistrust, he said, was what keep cities safe from tyrants and tyrants safe from everyone. Night, he thought, should stop a ruler's works and start his killings. Therefore the senate was mutilated, losing its most distinguished members, and philosophy was so terrified, that throwing aside what it stood for, some of its proponents ran away to the Celts in the west or the Libyan or Scythian deserts, while others were induced to speeches encouraging his crimes.

[Philostratos, *Life of Apollonius of Tyana* 7.4.1]

P13   Acilius Glabrio, AD 95
Ordinary consul of 91, see **B91**. His condemnation is foreshadowed by Dio 67.12.1, and described at 67.14.3 (providing the date), also by Suet. *Dom.* 10.2 (for allegedly plotting revolution) and Juv. *Sat.* 4.94–101 (**G1**.94). But no details are given by the sources who prefer the sensational aspect of Glabrio fighting wild animals (lions or bears).

P13a   Fronto sets Marcus Aurelius a composition exercise
[5.37] I slept late. I sent you a topic; it is on a serious subject: a consul of the Roman people took off his senator's toga and put on a gauntlet. Then, with Romans watching, he shot a lion in the company of young men at Minerva's festival. He was called to account by the censors. Set out and expand on the case. Farewell, sweetest Lord. Greet my Lady.

[5.38 – reply] When was this and was it at Rome? Do you say this was done at the Alban villa under Domitian? At any rate in this topic it will be a longer task to make this event believable than outrageous. The hypothesis seems incredible to me and certainly not full of gold-dust, like I had wanted. Write back at once about the time.

[Fronto, *Correspondence with Marcus Caesar* 5.37 and 5.38]

Fronto (*c.* 95 – *c.* 166) was tutor of Marcus Aurelius (emperor 161–180). They kept up an extremely regular and intimate correspondence. Here Fronto sets a composition exercise based on Acilius Glabrio.

P14   Domitian condemns Epaphroditus for helping Nero commit suicide,
         AD 95
Have we forgotten in our troubles that Nero has only just been avenged? I suppose he
who avenged Nero's death would have allowed Nero's life and reputation to be picked
apart, or that he would not have interpreted what was said about Nero as aimed at him,
since it was said about emperors who were absolutely comparable.

[Pliny the Younger, *Panegyric to Trajan* 53.4]

Y. Pliny is being sarcastic here. Suetonius, *Domitian* 14.4 and Dio (67.14.4) explain Epaphroditus'
condemnation, 27 years after the event, as intended to suggest that any act encompassing the death of the
emperor would be punished. Domitian had exiled Epaphroditus a few years before (Dio).

P15   An emperor's lot is not a happy one
For you yourself know what your grandfather Hadrian said: it is a wretched thing to
be an emperor since only when emperors are killed are attempts to seize the throne
believed. I have preferred to attribute the remark to him rather than Domitian who is
said to have made it first, since even the good sayings of tyrants do not get as much
credit as they deserve.

[*HA*, Avidius Cassius 2]

The *Historiae Augustae* claims this is a letter of Marcus Aurelius to Lucius Verus. But given that Marcus
Aurelius apparently predicts but dismisses a rebellion by Avidius which later occurred, it is highly suspect,
like most of the documents 'quoted' by the *Historiae Augustae*. Whatever its authenticity as a letter, it
shows awareness of the quotation from Domitian, given in different words by Suetonius, *Domitian* 21 (its
possible source).

P16   Domitian's assassination, AD 96
Various accounts survive of Domitian's assassination. The most coherent is Suet. *Dom.* 16–17; Dio/
Xiphilinus provides quite a long account 67.14.5–18.1 (**D14–D18**); briefer accounts are in Eutropius 7.23
(**T2**); Aur. Vict. 11.11–12, in addition to the passages below. For a modern synthesis, Jones, *Domitian*
193–6.

P16a   Official calendar at Ostia
18 Sept: Domitian k[illed]
         On the same day, M. Cocceius N[erva was] named emperor.
19 Sept: a decree of the senate was made […]

[MW 65 = *Inscr. It.* 13.1.194–5 = EDCS–20200012*]

Part of the *Fasti Ostienses*, the official record at Ostia listing magistrates and significant events at Rome
and Ostia.

P16b   Domitian's assassination
[11] Therefore in fear of his cruelty and their own conscience, many formed a
conspiracy led by Parthenius, master of the bedchamber, and Stephanus; and later,
Clodianus, who thought he would be punished for deceit in embezzling money. Even
Domitia, wife of the tyrant, was admitted to the plan, fearing torture by the emperor
because of her love for the actor Paris. [12] Domitian was stabbed to death by many
wounds after his forty-fifth year of life. [13] But the senate decreed that his funeral
should be carried out in the manner of a gladiator and that his name should be erased.

[*Epitome de Caesaribus* 11.11–13]

P16c   Visionary account of Domitian's end

[25] The gods were now pushing Domitian from his presidency of mankind. He had just had Clemens killed, an ex-consul, to whom he had married his own sister, and had given an order about two or three days after the murder that she should join her husband. Then Stephanus, a freedman of hers, who had been marked out by a sign from Zeus, taking to heart the death of that man, or of all those killed, set in motion a plot against the tyrant worthy of the most freedom-loving Athenians. Hiding a sword under his left forearm and holding his hand in a sling as if it were broken, he approached Domitian as he was leaving the courtroom. "I need you to hear me in private, my king, about something of importance." The tyrant thought this information should not be ignored so Stephanus led him to the men's quarters where the royal suite was, and said, "He is not dead as you suppose, the man who hates you most, Clemens; I know where he is and that he is organising himself to attack you."

Domitian gave a great shout at what he had heard and while he was off guard, Stephanus attacked him, drawing the sword hidden in his arm, stabbed him in the thigh which did not immediately prove fatal but did, later on. Domitian was physically strong and about forty-five years of age, and though wounded, he wrestled with Stephanus, throwing him to the ground and lying on top of him, gouging at his eyes and pounding at his face with the base of a golden cup, standing there for religious use. He called on Athene for help. So his bodyguard, realising that he was being attacked, came in all together and killed the tyrant when he was losing consciousness.

[26] This happened in Rome, but was seen by Apollonius in Ephesus. He was talking by the trees in the colonnade at about noon, when events in the palace were taking place. At first he lowered his voice, as if afraid, then spoke in a voice lacking its usual force, like people do when they are looking at something else while speaking. Next he fell silent like one forgetting his lines. He stared hard at the ground, then took three or four strides forward, shouting "Strike the tyrant! Strike!" not as if he was taking an image of reality from a mirror, but seeing the actual thing and seeming to be part of the action.

[Philostratos, *Life of Apollonius of Tyana* 8.25–26]

P16d   Domitian's death

[49] Yet within those very walls which seemed to him to guard his safety he enclosed treachery, plots and the god of vengeance for his crimes. Retribution removed and broke through his guards, and burst in through narrow and barred passageways as easily as through open doors and welcoming entrances. Far off, then, was his divinity, far off those secret rooms and cruel retreats to which he was driven by his fear, his arrogance, his hatred of the human race. [2] How much safer, how much more secure is that same house now that its master is safeguarded by love not cruelty, and by citizens crowding round him, not by isolation and barred doors.

[Pliny the Younger, *Panegyric to Trajan* 49.1–2]

This passage continues **J10h** but offers no factual details of the assassination.

SECTION Q
POPULAR ENTERTAINMENT

The filthy plebs haunting the circus and theatres ...

[Tacitus, *Histories* 1.4.3]

Introduction: Despite Tacitus' scathing statement above, the Flavian emperors' most famous legacy to Rome and the world, the Flavian Amphitheatre, better known as the Colosseum to its 4 million visitors each year, shows their appreciation of the importance of popular entertainment. For the building itself, which also combined visual condemnation of the previous dynasty and promotion of the new dynasty's military triumph, see **K12–K19**. We should remember that building work on the amphitheatre, finally dedicated in 80, will have occupied the great majority of Vespasian's reign while the 100 days of games held then (Dio 66.25.1–5) represents one eighth of Titus' total reign. For the dedication we have a whole book of Martial, *On the Shows*, 36 poems in all, totalling over 200 lines.

Behaviour at the games was a regular index for Suetonius of an emperor's quality: Vespasian showed old-fashioned values by staging traditional drama at the rededication of the Theatre of Marcellus (presumably tragedy or 'old comedy' rather than mime). He also claimed Augustus as his authority for the amphitheatre (*Vesp.* 19.1). Titus was a model in this respect, giving the people the shows they, not he, wanted, while maintaining his dignity (Suet. *Titus* 8.2). In contrast Domitian put himself firmly amongst the worst emperors by showing off himself (*Dom.* 19) and being far too partisan in his support for Thracian gladiators (*Dom.* 10.1, compare *Titus* 8.2). Domitian showed more interest in chariot-racing, even introducing two news teams to the traditional four (Suet. *Dom.* 7, Dio 67.4.4). This cannot have been at all popular even in respect of their names, golds and purples: their introduction must have resulted in drivers and horses being transferred from existing teams and a statistical reduction in the likelihood of a fan seeing his team win. He also introduced significant new games of Greek sport and culture, with the quadrennial Capitoline Games in Rome, for which he built the Stadium (**K50–K51**) and the annual 'Panathenaic' festival at his Alban villa (*Dom.* 4.4).

Sources in this chapter are arranged by theme: **Q1–Q9** gladiatorial shows; **Q10–Q11** theatrical shows; **Q12–Q14** circus racing; **Q16–Q19** Capitoline Games; **Q20–Q21** Alban Festival.

Q1   Gladiatorial games for the well-being of the imperial family, Pompeii
For the well-being of the [emperor Vespasian] Caesar Augustus and of his children, [and on account of the] dedication of the altar, [the gladiatorial troupe] of Gnaeus [All]eius Nigidius Maius, high priest of Caesar Augustus, will fight at Pompeii, without delay, on 4 July. There will be a hunt and awnings.

[*CIL* 4.1180 = Cooley² D28 = EDCS–16300473]

This notice was painted in red lettering, outside the main entrance of the Gladiatorial Barracks, on the external wall of the Large Theatre at Pompeii, announcing games to be held for the imperial family. It is just possible that the emperor was Claudius, but much more likely from mention of children and the preservation of the painted notice, to be Vespasian.

Q2   Dated gladiatorial token, Rome AD 74
Maximus, (slave) of Valerius, watched(?) on 13 January, when T. Caesar, son of Augustus, for the 3rd time and Aelianus, for the 2nd, were consuls.

[MW 529 = *ILS* 5161i]

Several other so-called *tesserae gladiatoriae* (gladiatorial tokens – small, oblong tokens in bone or wood), e.g. *ILS* 5161a–e, have the word 'spectavit' – 'he watched'. This inscription has only 'SP' which could be short for this or for '*spectaculis*' 'at the games'.

Q3   Titus and elephant, *denarius* AD 80 (Rome)

Obv: Head of Titus, laureate, right.
           IMP TITVS CAES VESPASIAN AVG P M (Emperor Titus Caesar Vespasian
           Augustus, *pontifex maximus*)
Rev: Elephant, cuirassed, standing left.
           TR P IX IMP XV COS VIII P P (Tribunician power for the 9th time, hailed
           imperator 15 times, consul 8 times, father of the fatherland)

[*RIC* 2.1 Titus 115 = *BMCRE²* 44, p.231 = BM no. R.10955]

Q4   An elephant worships Caesar, AD 80
           The elephant, just now so frightening to a bull,
           Now, Caesar, worships you, as pious supplicant.
           He does not do this by command, or ringmaster's
           Instructions. No, believe me, he too knows our god.

[Martial, *On the Shows* 20]

Elephants were well-known as performing circus tricks in this period (Plutarch, *Moralia* 968c; Pliny *NH* 8.6)

Q5   Rhinoceros at the Games, AD 80
           Paraded round your whole arena, Caesar, giving
           Combats greater than was thought: rhinoceros!
           How terribly its anger burned in headlong charge!
           How massive was that beast which made a bull a plaything!

[Martial, *On the Shows* 11]

Martial, *On the Shows* 26 also describes (presumably the same) rhino being goaded into taking on various
wild animals, including a lion, while *Epigram* 14.53) also refers to this same event.

Q6   Domitian and rhinoceros, *quadrans* AD 84/5 (Rome)

Obv: Rhinoceros standing left.
No legend.
Rev: Legend, S C (By decree of the senate)
IMP DOMIT AVG GERM (Emperor Domitian Augustus Germanicus)

[*RIC* 2.1 Domitian 250 = *BMCRE*² 499, p.411 = BM no. R11460]

Maximum circulation for the showing of the rhinoceros, (perhaps the same one as above) was ensured by the issue of this image on the lowest-value coin, the *quadrans*. For the show, see Coleman, *Martial,* pages liv-lvi, and Buttrey, 'Domitian, the Rhinoceros, and the Date of Martial's *Liber de Spectaculis*' in *The Journal of Roman Studies,* 97 (2007) – also on the elephant above.

Q7   Bravery of Lucius Scaevola re-enacted in Flavian Amphitheatre, AD 93

The play now being performed in Caesar's arena
Was the height of valour in the days of Brutus.
You see the hand that grasps the flames, that revels in its
Punishment and bravely rules in astonished fire!
The man himself is there to watch and loves the noble   5
Death of his right hand that's fed by all the rite.
Had not the punishment been snatched away, against
His will, his left, still more determined, set itself
To enter the tired fires. I'm loath to know what came
Before such glory: enough to know just what I saw.   10

[Martial, *Epigram* 8.30 (published January 94)]

According to Livy's history of Rome (2.12–13), a young nobleman, Gaius Mucius had attempted to end the siege of Rome in 508 BC by assassinating the Etruscan leader, Lars Porsenna. Captured and threatened with being burnt alive, he had thrust his right hand in fire to show how little he cared for this threat, earning release and the name 'Scaevola' = 'Leftie'. Martial's *On the Shows* attests various mythological stories being re-enacted in the Flavian amphitheatre, such as Pasiphae (6), Prometheus (9), Daedalus (10), Orpheus (24–25), either as a means to execute condemned criminals or with some possibility of escape, as presumably here – the criminal escapes execution if he burns his own hand. See Coleman, 'Fatal Charades: Roman Executions Staged as Mythological Enactments' *The Journal of Roman Studies* 80 (1990) 44–73.

Q8   Better, at least, than third-rate poetry, AD 94
Not the least impressive way in which your shows,
Surpass those staged by leaders prior to you, o Caesar,
(For which our eyes confess great thanks, our ears yet more)
Is that while watching them, hack poets do not bore us.

[Martial, *Epigram* 9.83 (published December 94)]

Here Martial light-heartedly undercuts praise of the emperor's games by saying the chief benefit is in stopping recitals by third-rate poets. 'It was, within certain limits, possible to pull the emperor's leg.' (Henriksen, Commentary, 327).

Q9   Dangers of gladiatorial shows under Domitian
[3] Now the spectators could show their enthusiasm with freedom, their support with confidence! No one faced a charge of impiety because they hated a particular gladiator; none of the spectators became the spectacle to satisfy the lust for torture on the executioner's hook or in the flames. [4] He was insane and utterly unaware of his true position who used to collect charges of treason in the arena and thought himself insulted and criticised if we did not revere his gladiators, interpreting any criticism of them as aimed at him and ruining his divine and godlike status, since he thought he was equivalent to the gods, but the gladiators equivalent to him.

[Pliny the Younger, *Panegyric to Trajan* 33.3–4]

Suetonius (*Dom.* 10.1) tells of the fate of a spectator who suggested that a Thracian gladiator had only lost because Domitian was biased against Thracians.

Q10   Actor Latinus
Sweet glory of the stage, and icon of the games,
Latinus, your applause and darling, I am he,
Who could have made stern Cato come as spectator
And loosened up strict Curius and Fabricius.
But my life has taken nothing from the stage,   5
I'm known as 'actor' only for the sake of art:
For I could not be favoured by my lord, without
Good morals – deep into our hearts that God can see.
So call me laurel-crowned Apollo's parasite, as long as
Rome knows that I am servant of her Jupiter.   10

[Martial, *Epigram* 9.28 (published December 94)]

C. Fabricius Luscinus , M'. Curius Dentatus, and M. Porcius Cato, were all famously austere politicians and censors in 275, 272, 184 BC. Actors on the other hand were generally notorious for immorality. Guilds of 'Apollo's parasites' are known from inscriptions.

Q11   Actor Paris

> Traveller, whoever you are who treads the
> Flaminian Way, don't ignore this fine marble:
> The darling of Rome and the wit of the Nile,
> Man of art, grace, playfulness and naughtiness,
> Glory and grief of the Roman theatre,   5
> Together with every Venus and Cupid
> Lie buried in this tomb along with Paris.
>
> [Martial, *Epigram* 11.13 (published December 96)]

For Paris, alleged lover of Domitia, killed by Domitian, see Suetonius, *Domitian* 3.1, 10.1 and Dio 67.3.1 (**D3**). Martial's poem commemorated this popular actor as soon as it was safe to do so.

Q12   Martial's epitaph to Scorpus

> I am that Scorpus, glory of the noisy Circus,
> Favourite, and briefly darling of all Rome.
> The jealous fates snatched me away aged twenty-seven:
> Counting my victories, they thought I must be old.
>
> [Martial, *Epigram* 10.53 (published December 95)]

Martial also mentions Scorpus as famous and wealthy in epigrams 4.67 and 5.25. In 10.48, 'Scorpus and the Greens' are mentioned as a safe, non-political topic for conversation at a dinner party. 10.50 is another elegy on his early death.

Q13   Imperial freedman's tombstone, with Scorpus and chariot team

To the divine shades of T. Flavius Abascantus, imperial freedman in charge of trials. Flavia Hesperis made this for her well-deserving husband: in grief for him I have had nothing but death. Scorpus with Ingenuus, Admetus, Passerinus, Atmetus.

[MW 207 = *ILS* 1679 = EDCS–18500275*]

Tombstone, Rome. At the top is a relief of a man reclining with cupids on either side. The inscription below occupies about half the remaining space. In the bottom third is a relief of a charioteer with four horses: he holds a crown and palm of victory. The names of the charioteer and each of his four horses appear above the figures, in very small letters right at the bottom of the inscription. Abascantus was presumably a fan of Scorpus (and not the same freedman as **S10**).

Q14   A 'Purple' charioteer

To the Spirits of the Departed. Epaphroditus, driver of the red team, won 178 times, and for the purples willingly won 8 times. Beia Felicula made this for her own well-deserving husband.

[MW 517 = *CIL* 6.10062 = EDCS–19400144]

Suetonius *Domitian* 7 and Dio 67.4.4 mention Domitian's introduction of 'golds' and 'purples' to the traditional four colours of chariot teams. The teams were not popular (hence, perhaps 'willingly won') and were disbanded after Domitian's death.

Q15   For Domitian's birthday, AD 89

Come, gentle day of Caesar, holier than the dawn
On which Mount Ida knowingly gave birth to Jove.
Last long, and come in greater number than Nestor's age,
And shine, I beg, with no less favour than you do today.
May he honour Pallas many times in Alban gold,   5
May many oak-leaves pass through his almighty hands;
May he celebrate the jubilee returned at last,
And the sacred rites of Romulus held at Tarentum.
Much, we ask, o gods, but it is owed to earth:
What prayers, indeed, would not be right for such a god?   10

[Martial, *Epigram* 4.1 (published December 89)]

For Capitoline and Alban Games see below, for Centennial Games, see **L17–L21**; for all three, see Suet. *Dom.* 4.3–4. Epigram 9.39 celebrates the wife of a friend of Martial having the same birthday as Domitian (24 October).

Q16   Capitoline Games inaugurated, 12 January AD 86

However the same 'great year' began to be observed more carefully through the Capitoline Games: the first of these games was instituted by Domitian on the twelfth day of his consulship and that of Servius Cornelius Dolabella [AD 86]. Therefore the games, which is celebrated this year, is the thirty-ninth.

[Censorinus, *On the Birthday* 18.15]

Censorinus preserves much information from earlier sources about time and its divisions. He has mentioned the ancient tradition of holding a 'lustrum' (ceremony of purification) every four years to mark the end of the census (**H53** – that of Vespasian and Titus). He describes the year of the census as a 'great year'. 12 January 86 as the date of the first games fits with the 39th being celebrated in the year Censorinus dedicated his work (AD 238).

Q17   Collinus wins the poetry prize at the first Capitoline festival in AD 86

You who have the right to touch Tarpeian oak
And deserved to crown your head with freshest leaves,
If you are wise, Collinus, all your days enjoy,
Remembering always that this one might be your last.

[Martial, *Epigram* 4.54.1–4 (published December 89)]

From the date of the poem, Collinus must have been the first winner of the Capitoline prize for Latin poetry in AD 86. In the remaining six lines of the poem, Martial offers further advice on the theme, '*carpe diem*'. The Tarpeian Rock formed part of the Capitoline Hill. Winners of the Capitoline festival were awarded a crown of oak-leaves.

Q18   Olympic victor at *pankration* also wins at Capitoline Games, AD 86
T. Flavius Artemidorus, son of Artemidorus, of the tribe Quirina, from Adana and
Antioch-on-Daphne, having won the competition of the Great Capitoline Games, held
for the first time, in the men's *pankration*, twice at the Olympics, twice at the Pythian
Games, twice at the Nemean Games, at the Actian Games, the Naples *pankration*;
(and a long list of victories in youth and boys' pankration all round the Greek East).

[MW 473 = *IGRR* 1.445 = *SEG* 14.605]

Antioch-on-Daphne or Antioch-on-the-Orontes, was a major city in the far NE corner of the Mediterranean
(modern border between Turkey and Syria). The area attracted considerable Flavian building (see **M17–
M21**). *Pankration* was an ancient, popular and brutal combat sport with few rules.

Q19   An eleven-year old poet at the Capitoline Games, AD 94
To the Spirits of the Departed: Quintus Sulpicius Maximus, son of Quintus, of the
Claudian tribe, from Rome, lived 11 years, 5 months, 12 days. In the third cycle of
the games he competed against 52 Greek poets and his talent converted the applause
won by his tender years to admiration, and he departed with honour. Impromptu
verses were set him, so that his parents would not be thought to have been unduly
influenced by their affection. Quintus Sulpicius Eugramus and Licinia Januaria, his
unfortunate parents, set this up in memory of their devoted son, for themselves and
their descendants.

[MW 64 = *ILS* 5177 = EDCS–24100482*]

This ostentatious funerary monument at Rome is centred round a life-size sculpture of a boy, dressed
in a toga, carrying a scroll. To left and right is a Greek hexameter poem, over thirty lines long, entitled
"Impromptu poem of Quintus Sulpicius Maximus: what words would Zeus have used when chiding Helios
for giving his chariot to Phaethon?" The Latin inscription is underneath. The Capitoline Games were
established in AD 86, and the third games in 94.

Q20   Statius' victory at the Alban Games, AD 90
        The day you gave me blessed feasts and sacred place
        Around your table, so much light upon me shone
        As many years before, when under Alban hills of Troy   65
        I sang of German and of Dacian wars as well,
        And your own hand did place on me Minerva's wreath of gold.

[Statius, *Silvae* 4.2.63–67 (published 95)]

These lines form the ending of a poem thanking Domitian for an invitation to dine in the recently completed
dining room of his palace and describing its magnificence (see **T5** and **K45**). Despite his description of it
as 'many years before', the topic of Statius' poem was Domitian's campaigns of 89, so the festival was that
of 90 or less likely 91. Statius also mentions his victory at the Alban festival at 3.5.28–30, and 5.3.227–9.

Q21   Carus wins at the Alban festival, AD 94
You had the luck to turn fair with the virgin's gold
Tell me, Carus, where you keep Minerva's prize.
"Do you see our master's features, shining in marble?
My crown, all of its own accord, came to his hair."
Pious oak may envy Alban olive-wreath   5
Which did first encircle your victorious head.

[Martial, *Epigram* 9.23 (published December 94)]

Domitian celebrated the Quinquatrus festival of Minerva (Pallas Athene) in his Alban villa each year (19–22 March: Suet. *Dom.* 4.4; Dio 67.1.2); Statius was victorious in 90 (e.g. *Silvae* 4.2.63–67 = **Q20**). For Acilius Glabrio fighting at the Alban Games, see **P13**.

Q22   Domitian's support for Delphi and the Pythian Games, AD 90
The god. To Good Fortune. The city of Delphi decided to inscribe the letters [sent] to them concerning the Pythian Games on a [stone] *stele* in the most prominent [place of the temple].

Emperor Caesar ~~Domitian~~ Augustus Germanicus, chief priest, holding tribunician power for the 9th time, hailed *imperator* 21 times, consul 15 times, censor for life, father of the fatherland, greets the magistrates of the city. It is naturally right and pious to preserve the day fixed for the Pythian Games in accordance with the Amphictyonic laws, with no part of the ancient traditions assailed: so that this should happen in accordance with my purpose, I have written to the proconsul [*(name lost)*…]. Your ambassadors were Epineikos, son of Eudoros; Rusticus, son of Eudamos [… you] judge the ambassadors deserve [… *(the rest lost)*]

Separate letters (MW 463d, 463e) from the proconsul (whose name is also lost on both letters) to the Delphians and to the Amphictyons follow, in which he reiterates that Domitian (described as our lord and most manifest emperor) wishes the games to be held in accordance with tradition.

[*SIG³* 821 = MW 463b]

The Pythian games, held at Delphi in honour of Apollo every four years were only just behind the Olympic Games in importance. As Domitian's Capitoline Games (first held in AD 86) were given equal status to Pythian or Olympic Games, Domitian is presumably intending to reassure Delphi about the importance of their games.

Q23   Complaints at Roman 'entertainment' spreading to Athens
Apollonius corrected another failing at Athens where the people filled the theatre under the Acropolis, intent on butchering human beings. Enthusiasm for this was greater there than it is in Corinth today. Adulterers, rent-boys, burglars, muggers, kidnappers, and people of that sort were being bought for large sums and brought on. They were armed and told to fight each other. Apollonius attacked this too, and when the Athenians

summoned him to an assembly refused to enter a place that was impure and full of gore. This was in a letter, which added that he was "surprised the goddess is not already leaving the Acropolis, now that you pour out blood of that kind for her benefit".

[Philostratos, *Life of Apollonius of Tyana* 4.22]

Gladiatorial and wild beast shows spread in the first and second centuries, primarily in connection with celebration of the imperial cult, to the disgust of some.

SECTION R

LEARNING, LITERATURE, ARTS AND CULTURE

... feigning an enthusiasm for literature and a love of poetry to hide
his real character ...

[Tacitus, *Histories* 4.86 on Domitian]

Aurelius Victor, passing judgement on the Julio-Claudians suggests that emperors need good character but also culture and literature. His first comment on Vespasian is that he had both. (*On Caesars* 8–9). Suetonius comments on the Flavians' culture *Vesp.* 18, 23; *Titus* 3, *Dom.* 2.2, 4.4, 18.2, 20. Notwithstanding Tacitus' cynicism on the one hand or the invocation of the Flavians as the new muses on the other, it is quite clear that the arts continued to flourish under the Flavians, at least in part through their own interest and encouragement. So after sources relating to works by the Flavians and their closest advisers (**R1–R9**) this section gives information, mostly by contemporaries, on Flavian writers of prose (Quintilian and the Elder Pliny, **R10–R19**) and poetry (Statius, Silius, Martial, **R20–R27**). Next some of the Younger Pliny's reflections on writing Flavian history (**R28–R31**) are followed by various other sources on culture and learning in the Flavian period (**R32–R37**).

R1   Vespasian's memoirs

[342] I am not the only one who says this: the same thing is written in the memoirs of the Emperor Vespasian, and how at Ptolemais the inhabitants of the Decapolis shouted to Vespasian to ask that you should be punished as the man responsible. ... [358] But perhaps you will say that you have written an accurate account of the things inflicted on Jerusalem. How can that be, when you had no part in that war, and have not even read Caesar's commentaries. That can be clearly demonstrated, since you have written the opposite of Caesar's commentaries.

[Josephus, *'My Life'* 342 and 358]

Josephus is criticising his enemy, Justus of Tiberias, but giving evidence for Vespasian's memoirs. The passages are cited as Vespasian, T1 and F1 in Cornell (ed.), *The Fragments of the Roman Historians* (Oxford 2013).

R2   Titus as an author

[5] There has never shone in anyone else the dictatorial force of eloquence or the tribunician power of wit. How greatly the praises of your father sound in your mouth! How greatly the fame of your brother! How great you are as a poet! What fertility of intellect in thinking up a way of imitating your brother!

[Pliny, *Natural History*, Preface 5]

R3   Titus' poem on a comet

The most recent appearance of this type of comet was recorded in a famous poem by Titus Imperator Caesar in his fifth consulship (AD 76).

[Pliny, *Natural History* 2.89]

For Titus' literary skills see **J8d** and **T1**.

R4 **Valerius Flaccus invokes Vespasian to help his epic poem**
And you too, greatly famed for opening up the deep 7
After the Caledonian ocean had borne your ship,
(For all that it rejected men of Trojan birth)
Raise me above the people and the cloud-bound earth, 10
Holy father, and help me as I sing the famous lay
Of men of old. Your son shall tell – how well he may –
Of Judah's fall, his brother black with Jewish mire,
Attacking every watch-tower armed with fire.
Shrines to your race he shall ordain and cult divine 15
To you, his father, as you from the heavens shine.
The Dog-Star shall no more guide ships of Palestine
Nor Helice the Greeks ones, if you light the dark;
And fleets of Greece, Sidon and Nile embark
With you as guide. Now kindly watch my enterprise 20
So that my voice through towns of Latium may rise.
[Valerius Flaccus, *Voyage of the Argo*, 1.7–21]

Flaccus' epic can only be dated by a reference to the eruption of Vesuvius, and to Quintilian's mention (**R5**) of his death as 'recent' which is also how he describes Caesius Bassus' death in the eruption of Vesuvius (**R20**).

7: *And you too*: Flaccus had first invoked Apollo; next Vespasian. His praise for Vespasian's share in Claudius' conquest of Britain going beyond the Ocean is partly traditional, but also appropriate in an epic about the voyage of the Argonauts.

8: *Caledonian*: exaggeration as regards Vespasian, since Agricola was campaigning in Caledonia (Scotland) in the 90s (Tac. *Agr.* 25–27; compare Silius Italicus, *Punic Wars* 598 = **H62**)

9: *rejected ... Trojan birth*: Flaccus mentions 'Phrygian Julii' alluding to Aeneas as ancestor of Julius Caesar. Ocean 'rejected' potential attempts by Julius Caesar, Augustus and Gaius (Caligula) permanently to conquer Britannia (e.g. Dio 53.22.5, 53.25.2; Suet. *Cal.* 46).

12: *your son*: Domitian. For flattery of his poetry, see Silius, **H62**.618–9; Pliny **R2**; Quintilian **R5**; Martial **R6**

13: *his brother*: Titus. Josephus' account certainly portrays Titus as fighting in the front line.

15: *Shrines*: a reference to the Temple of the Flavian family, see **K54–K56**.

16: *from the heavens shine*: Vespasian's deification. Following the main precedent of Julius Caesar's deification being linked to the appearance of the comet at his assassination (e.g. Pliny, *NH* 2.94), deification was linked to stars (compare **J12a** – Domitian's baby son on coin), and symbolism such as a radiate crown (**J13a**). The flattery has point in the epic context since ancient world navigation relied heavily on steering by the stars.

17, 19: *Palestine, Sidon*: the Phoenicians who came from these places were famous sea-farers.

R5 **Quintilian on Domitian's poetry**
[90] We have recently suffered a great loss in the death of Valerius Flaccus. Saleius Bassus had a striking poetic talent which did not mature into old age. …
(Quintilian then praises Rabirius and Pedo (contemporaries of Ovid) and Lucan.)
[91] We name these because responsibility for the whole world has deflected Germanicus Augustus from the literary pursuits he had begun: the gods thought that being the greatest of poets was not enough for him. Yet what could have been more sublime, more learned, in short more outstanding in every category, than those works of his which he

withdrew from public life to write as a young man, giving supreme power to others? Who could sing of wars better than he who wages them as he does? Whom would the patron goddesses of literature heed more than him? To whom would Minerva, his patron deity more readily reveal her skills? [92] Future ages will speak of this at greater length; at present this glory of his is blunted by the brightness of his other virtues. Nonetheless, Caesar, since I am a devotee of the cult of literature, you will put up with my not passing this by in silence, but bearing witness that, to quote Virgil,

"The ivy creeps between your victorious laurel." [*Eclogue* 8.13]

[Quintilian, *The Orator's Education* 10.1.91–2]

Nothing survives of Domitian's verse, even in quotation. Quintilian had evoked Domitian as an appropriate 'muse' to inspire his own writing, see **J18b**.

R6   Domitian as poet
Cultured worshipper of Palatine Minerva,
Who at close hand enjoys the genius of our god,
Since you have the right to know our lord's concerns,
However small, and secrets of our leader's heart.
May there be room somewhere for my small books, Sextus,   5
Where Pedo, Marsus and Catullus will be found.
Place majestic Virgil's greatest work beside
The heavenly epic of the Capitoline War.

[Martial, *Epigram* 5.5 (published December 90)]

Sextus (unidentifiable from just this first name) was probably in charge of the library associated with the Temple of Apollo on the Palatine. Only fragments of Albinovanus Pedo (Tiberian) and Domitius Marsus (Augustan) survive. The love and other poems of Catullus (contemporary of Julius Caesar) are still famous. Martial asks for a place among these epigrammatists, whom he cited as models in his preface to Book 1. Domitian's poem on the fighting on the Capitol in December 69 is sycophantically described as equal to Virgil's *Aeneid.*

R7   Mucianus' editions of *Records* and *Letters*
I don't know whether you have laid hands on those old documents which are still found in the libraries of antiquarians, and which are just now being compiled by Mucianus. So far, I think, eleven books of *Records* and three of *Letters* have been collected and published.

[Tacitus, *Dialogue* 37.2 (dramatic date, AD 75)]

R8   Mucianus as source for Pliny's *NH*
Mucianus who was three times consul, wrote that recently when he was governing Lycia, he read, in a certain temple, a letter of Sarpedon, written on paper at Troy.

[Pliny, *Natural History* 13.88]

C. Licinius Mucianus is frequently mentioned as a source for Pliny. His work clearly included material that we would regard as geography (e.g. the source of the Euphrates, 5.83) and natural history (e.g. elephants 8.6). In the extract above and several others, Mucianus does not (despite Pliny's comments below) appear to have been the most critical of authors.

R9   Mucianus dead before publication of Pliny's *Natural History*
I shall speak of countries [sc. that produce oysters] but in the words of another, someone who was the greatest expert in this field in our generation: here then is what Mucianus wrote: ...

[Pliny, *Natural History* 32.62]

R10   A brief life of Pliny the Elder
Plinius Secundus from New Comum ably carried out his equestrian military career and performed a series of the highest administrative offices with the greatest integrity. Despite this he paid such attention to the liberal arts that no one without a job could easily have written more. Thus he included all the wars which had ever been waged with the Germans in 20 volumes and completed a *Natural History* in 37 books. He died in a disaster in Campania; for when in command of the fleet at Misenum, during the eruption of Vesuvius, he claimed that the reasons ought to be investigated at closer hand in a warship, and was unable to return in the face of adverse winds. He was overcome by the force of the dust and ashes, or, as some think, he was killed by his slave, whom he had asked to hasten his death when he was being overcome by the heat.

[Suetonius, *On Distinguished Men* – Pliny the Elder]

Pliny the Younger gave a full list of his uncle's works at *Letters* 3.5.1–6 (= LACTOR 19, R14), and, of course of his death (*Letters* 6.16 = Cooley[2] C10).

R11   Quintilian on Elder Pliny
I am surprised at the opinion of Pliny, a man of learning and in this book, anyway, almost too scholarly, that Cicero wore his toga long to cover his varicose veins, since this style of clothing also appears in statues of people after Cicero's time.

[Quintilian, *The Orator's Education* 11.3.143]

The Elder Pliny's opinion probably came in his book on oratory, the *Studiosus*. Also interesting is Quintilian's implication that some of Pliny's other works were not especially scholarly. Elsewhere (12.10.11) he describes Pliny's especial quality as being 'elegance'.

R12   Pliny dedicates his *Natural History* to Titus, AD 77
Plinius Secundus to his dear Vespasian, greetings.
My books on Natural History, a new work for the Muses of your Roman People, which I have given birth to most recently, I have decided to dedicate to you, in a rather presumptuous letter, most approachable commander – let this title, a fully justified one, be yours, while the title of 'greatest' grows old with your father.

[Pliny, *Natural History*, Preface 1]

R13   Pliny on his own *History*
[20] We have written about your father, your brother and you yourself in a proper work, a history of our own day, a continuation of Aufidius Bassus. Where is this work, you will ask. It is already finished and kept safely; and anyway I had decided to entrust it to my heir, so that my lifetime should not be judged to have made any concession to ambition.

[Pliny, *Natural History*, Preface 20]

The Elder Pliny's history probably ended in AD 71, with the Jewish Triumph and closing of the Gates of Janus to symbolise peace. It was in 31 'books' (Pliny the Younger, *Letters* 3.5.6).

R14   Pliny the Younger on his uncle's writing

[7] Are you amazed how a busy man completed such a lot of books, many of them very scholarly? You will be more amazed to learn that for some time he practised at the bar, that he died at the age of fifty-five, and that in between his time was filled and engaged with holding important posts and friendship with the emperors. [8] But he had a fierce intellect, unbelievable diligence, and kept very long hours. From the festival of Vulcan he began to work by lamplight, not for any religious observance, but to study from the middle of the night, in winter at the seventh hour, the eighth at the very latest, often the sixth (*i.e. between midnight and 2 a.m.*). He did indeed fall asleep very easily, sometimes even falling asleep and waking up while studying. [9] Before dawn, he used to go to the Emperor Vespasian – for he also used his nights to work – then he would go to his appointed duties. When he returned home, he used what remained of the time for his studies. [10] After lunch (during the day he ate lightly and simply, in the old-fashioned way) he would often lie in the sun in the summer when not busy while a book was read aloud, taking notes and making excerpts. He made excerpts on everything he read, and used to say that no book was so bad as not to contain something useful. [11] After sunning himself he usually took a cold bath, ate a little and had a short sleep. Before long he began, as it were, a new day's work, until dinner time. During dinner a book was read and notes taken, and rapidly too. [12] I can remember one of his friends making a reader go back and repeat a word he had mispronounced; my uncle then said, "You surely understood him?", and when his friend admitted as much, "Why did you make him go back? Your interruption has cost us more than ten lines." That was how he begrudged time. [13] In the summer he used to leave the table while it was still light, in the winter during the first hour of night as if compelled by some law.

[14] This was in the midst of his duties and the bustle of Rome. When away from the city only his time in the baths was lost from study (when I say baths I mean in the water, since while the strigil was being used and while being dried, he would listen to a reading or dictate notes). [15] While travelling, as if released from other tasks, he would be free only for study: at his side was a short-hand writer with book and writing-tablets, his hands protected in winter by long sleeves so that not even the harshness of the weather could remove any study time. For the same reason he was carried in a sedan-chair at Rome. [16] I recall being told off by him because I would walk: "You could have not wasted those hours"; for he regarded any time wasted which was not spent studying. [17] By this attitude he completed all those volumes and left me one hundred and sixty notebooks of selected passages in the tiniest writing and using both sides of the paper, so that one should multiply this number. He used to tell the story that he could, while procurator in Spain, have sold his notebooks to Larcius Licinus for four hundred thousand sesterces, even though there were fewer then. [18] It may well seem to you, when you reflect on it, that he could not have held any positions or have been 'friend of the emperor', given how much he read and

wrote; or then again when you hear of how he devoted himself to studying, that he did not read or write enough. Yet what was there that those official duties did not hamper, or his determination not manage to overcome?

[Pliny the Younger, *Letters* 3.5.7–18]

Baebius Macer (consul 103, city prefect 117) had written to Y. Pliny asking about his uncle's literary output. Y. Pliny replied with a list of his works (LACTOR 19, R14) which is annoyingly devoid of any details about his most important work, his history. He then explains how his uncle did everything he could to maximise the time available for his writing.

R15   Jerome's *Chronicle* on Quintilian

[AD 68] Galba brought Marcus Fabius Quinctilianus to Rome.
[AD 88] Quinctilianus, a Calaguritan from Spain, who first established a public school at Rome and received a salary from the treasury, was famous.

[Jerome, *Chronicle*, Years 2084 and 2104 after Abraham = AD 68 and 88]

Marcus Fabius Quin(c)tilianus was born *c.* AD 35 in Spain. His father was a noted orator, and Quintilian was certainly educated at Rome. Jerome's *Chronicle* shows particular interest in prose writers.

R16   Vespasian establishes 'regius chairs'

After this Vespasian established in Rome teachers of Latin and Greek culture, who drew their salaries from the public purse.

[Zonaras, *Summary of Dio*, 11.17 = Dio 66.12.1a]

The establishment, at a salary of 100,000 sesterces is mentioned by Suet. *Vesp.* 18. Quintilian was probably the first such 'regius professor'. See Philostratos, *Lives of the Sophists* 2.8.580, 10.589, 33.627.

R17   Martial on Quintilian

Quintilian, greatest guide of wayward youth,
Quintilian, glory of the Roman toga,

[Martial, *Epigram* 2.90.1–2 (published 85)]

This is the only mention in Martial of his great contemporary and compatriot. In the poem Martial suggests that Quintilian has given him advice about following a public career, but Martial politely rejects this advice, preferring that of '*carpe diem*'.

R18   Quintilian's consular decorations

Quintilian, having obtained consular decorations through Clemens seemed to have the dignity of the title rather than the insignia of power.

[Ausonius 10.7.31]

See **J16** and **J18b** for Flavius Clemens and Quintilian's tutorship of that man's sons.

R19   Quintilian's praise for contemporary orators

People who write in the future about orators will have much that they can fairly praise in those who are currently in their prime. For there are today great talents which grace the forum.

[Quintilian, *The Orator's Education* 10.1.122]

Quintilian's practice of not naming contemporary writers means that we cannot know whom he means, though Pliny the Younger and Tacitus are obvious possibilities (both in their late thirties at time of publication)

R20   Quintilian's assessment of Flavian lyric poets
[96] Of lyric poets, Horace is virtually the only one worth reading. ... If you wish to add anyone, it will be Caesius Bassus, whom we recently had with us; but talents of living writers far exceed his.

[Quintilian, The Orator's Education 10.1.96]

Caesius Bassus was addressed by Persius' sixth satire. Scholia say that he died in the eruption of Vesuvius. Quintilian does not name living writers (except Domitian!): the lyric poet he most likely refers to here is Statius.

R21   Statius and poets reduced to script-writers
People rush to his delightful voice and the poem of his beloved
Thebaid, and Statius makes Rome happy when he names a day.
He inspires their captive hearts with such delight,
Is heard by the common folk with such passion. But though   85
He brings the house down with his poetry, he goes
Hungry if he can't sell Paris his 'Virgin Agave'.
He it is who distributes military honours to many
And for six-months' service puts a ring round poets' fingers.
What aristocrats can't bestow, the actor will.   90
Are you anxious about the great halls of the aristocrats?
Pelopea makes men prefects, Philomela tribunes.

[Juvenal, Satire 7.82–92]

'Names a day' Juvenal means a day for Statius publicly to recite his poem, but also plays on the idea of Statius being in love with his own poem. Paris (**Q11**) was a famous pantomime actor (or stage name used by different actors) alleged to have had an affair with Domitia (Suet. *Dom.* 3, Dio 67.3.1). He might have acted a role such as Agave (who in mythology killed her son, Pentheus, during a frenzy inspired by Dionysus). Pelopea, Philomela: i.e. actors like Paris who play these roles of mythological women both sexually abused by male relations.

R22   Praise of Silius Italicus
You who read the works immortal Silius wrote
His poems worthy of Latin gown that will never die
Do you think the bard loved only Bacchic wreathes
That crown the Muses' heads far in their mountain homes?
He did not touch the sacred rites of epic Virgil   5
Before he'd matched the works of mighty Cicero:
The solemn spear of the Centumviral Court admires
The man, and many grateful clients still sing his praises.
And once he had as consul ruled that glorious year
Held sacred by a world that claimed its liberty,   10
He gave to Phoebus and the Muses the years he'd earned
And dwells on Helicon instead of his own forum.

[Martial, Epigram 7.63 (published December 92)]

Martial (4.14) praises Silius Italicus' epic poem on the Punic Wars while asking him to read his lighter poetry. At 6.64.10 he claims Silius as a reader of his epigrams. The Cemtumviral Court (named after the

100 men who potentially formed the jury, and symbolised by a spear in the ground) was where famous legal cases usually took place. Silius had been consul in 68, the year of Nero's fall. Silius took over and preserved Virgil's estates and tomb (Martial 11.48, 11.50).

R23   **Martial asks Parthenius to ensure favourable reception for his poems**

If it be not too much trouble and concern,
Muses, ask this of your friend Parthenius,
"May a late and happy old age end some day
While Augustus is still safe; may good fortune
Still be yours, and jealousy be on your side.   5
And may Burrus soon take after his father.
Do please allow this timid, slender volume
Within the inner sanctum of the palace:
You know the times when Jupiter is serene,
When he shines with his own placid expression   10
And so is likely to refuse no requests.
[Martial, Epigram 5.6.1–11 (published December 90)]

Parthenius was Domitian's chamberlain, party to his assassination (**P16b**). Martial celebrates the fourth birthday of his son (4.45); thanks Parthenius for the gift of a new toga (8.28); dedicates book 11 to him (11.1). From 12.11 it seems that Parthenius too wrote poetry. On Martial's own poems, see also 3.69, 4.49, 7.81, 8.3, 8.55.

R24   **Martial's fifth book**

This is the fifth book of my verse,
And no one has by them fared worse.
Some have, in fact, won greater fame,
By being coupled to my name.
This brings me little or no pay,
But joy at saying what I may.
[Martial, Epigram 5.15, (published December 90) translated Gary Wills, 2008]

R25   **Martial aims to provoke**

All Rome is mad about my book:
It's praised, they hum the lines, shops stock it,
It peeps from every hand and pocket.
There's a man reading it! Just look –
He blushes, turn pale, reels, yawns, curses.
That's what I'm after. Bravo, verses!
[Martial, Epigram 6.60 (published December 91) translated by James Michie, 1972]

R26   A place for poetry
While people with petitions crowd around, Augustus,
We offer books of little poems to our master.
We know that you as god have time alike for Muses
And affairs of state, and that these garlands please you.
Support your bards, Augustus; we are your sweet glory,   5
What used to interest and delight you previously.
Oak-leaves suit you well, and so does Phoebus' laurel:
But let a civic ivy crown be yours from us.

[Martial, *Epigram* 8.82 (published January 94)]

Martial alludes (lines 6–7) to the emperor's civic crown of oak awarded to Augustus for saving citizen lives by
ending civil war, as well as to his triumph and love of poetry. Ivy was sacred to Bacchus and therefore poets.

R27   Pliny the Younger on the death of Martial
To Cornelius Priscus.
I hear that Valerius Martial has died, and I have taken this badly. He was a gifted
writer, intelligent, and subtle, and in his writings he had a great deal of wit and
satirical bite with no less integrity and honesty. [2] When he left Rome I gave him his
travelling expenses, in return for the friendship we had and in return for the verses he
had composed about me. [3] It was the custom in the past to reward those who had
written in praise of individuals or cities with offices or money. Nowadays this custom,
as with other splendid and excellent ones, was among the first to cease. For after we
stop doing things that ought to be praised, we think it is foolish to be praised. [4] Do
you ask what the verses are for which I was grateful? I would refer you to the book
itself, except that I know certain ones by heart, and if you like these, you may look up
the others in the book. [5] He addresses the Muse and instructs her to seek my house
on the Esquiline and approach it with great respect:
            But do be careful you don't knock drunkenly
            On the eloquent door at the wrong moment:
            He gives all his daytime to strict Minerva,
            Working for the ears of the Hundred Judges,   15
            On something people in ages still to come
            Can compare to the writings of Cicero.
            You're safer going late, when the lamps are lit:
            That hour belongs to you, when Bacchus runs riot,
            When the rose is in command and hair is wet: 20
            Then let even unbending Catos read me.
[6] Was I right to say farewell then in the most friendly way to a poet who wrote this
poem about me, and now to grieve as a most dear friend over his death? For he gave
me the greatest gift he could, and would have given me more if he had been able. And
yet what greater gift can be given to a man than glory and praise and immortality?
Yet what Martial wrote will not be immortal. Well, maybe not immortal; however, he
wrote them as though they would be. Farewell.

[Pliny the Younger, *Letters* 3.21, quoting Martial, *Epigrams* 10.20.11–21]

Priscus was probably the governor of Asia *c.* 120/1, consul *c.* 103. Martial retired to Spain shortly after
Nerva adopted Trajan (10.104) and published book 12 there, probably at the end of 101. Other datable

letters of Y. Pliny in book 3 are from the three years after his consulship in late 100. This letter is the only contemporary mention of Martial, whose only epigram on Y. Pliny is 10.20. For the 100 judges (line 15) see note on **R22**. Marcus Porcius Cato (line 21), was the dominant politician and intellectual of the first half of the second century BC, censor 183 BC, and a watchword for strict moral standards.

R28   Pliny the Younger's introduction to his published letters

You have frequently urged me to collect together and publish any of the more carefully composed letters which I have written. I have collected them but not in chronological order – for I was not composing a history – but as each came to hand. It only remains that you do not regret giving the advice and I do not regret taking it. For I shall get to work recovering any letters previously neglected and not suppress any I may write after this.

[Pliny the Younger, *Letters* 1.1]

Y. Pliny's brief explanation of his methodology raises as many questions as it answers, and the literary side of his letters (rather than their historical or social side) is currently a popular area for study. Despite Pliny's statement here, it is generally accepted that his letters are in roughly chronological order, but carefully arranged so that each book contains a variety of types of letter.

R29   The dangers of writing history

But you should now at least consider what particular period of history I might deal. Ancient history already written about by others? The research has been done, but putting it together would be a chore. A modern period not so far dealt with? Little thanks and chance of serious offence. [13] For, besides the fact that with such great vices among men there is much more to blame than to praise, then if you praise, it will be said to be too little and if you blame, it will be said to be too much, though you may have been most fulsome in the former and restrained the latter.

[Pliny the Younger, *Letters* 5.8.12–13]

In this two-page letter, written *c.* 105–6 to judge from other datable letters in the book, Y. Pliny responds to the suggestion of a former imperial secretary, Titinius Capito that he should write history.

R30   Pressure not to publish a contemporary history

I have frequently had a sense of the greatness of the power, the worth, the excellence and the inspiration of history at other times but especially most recently. A certain author had recited a work of genuine truthfulness, and had saved part of it for another day. [2] Yet the friends of a certain person begged and pleaded with him not to recite the rest. So great is the shame of some at the thought of hearing about their actions, men who have no shame when they act but blush to hear about it. The author in fact agreed to what they asked – his belief in his honesty allowed him to do so; the book, however, remains, and will remain, like the action. It will always be read, the more so because it was not read straightaway. For men always have a desire to find out about what is kept back. Farewell.

[Pliny the Younger, *Letters* 9.27]

The work might most obviously be Tacitus' *Histories*, but given Y. Pliny's deliberate silence, we cannot be sure. Datable letters in book 9 seem mostly to be from 106–8 which would fit with the date of the *Histories*.

R31   Pliny the Younger eager for a place in Tacitus' *Histories*

I prophesy (and am not mistaken in prophesying) that your histories will be immortal. For this reason (I confess openly) I am all the more eager to be included. [2] If it is usual for us to take care to have our faces portrayed by the best artists, surely we ought to desire that our actions may be praised by an author like yourself? [3] Therefore I am explaining this matter to you, although it cannot have escaped your attention, as it is in the public records. Even so I am describing it to you so that you may all the more believe that it would be pleasing to me if you enhance my action, the importance of which was increased by the danger it involved, with the evidence of your genius. ...

(For the substance of Pliny's claim to fame, the prosecution of Baebius Massa, see M53).

[10] However significant it may be, you will make this better known, more illustrious and even greater; although I do not require you to overstep the limits of the facts as they stand. For history ought not to deviate from the truth, and the truth is all that honourable actions need. Farewell.

[Pliny the Younger, *Letters* 7.33.1–3 and 10]

Letters in book 7 seem to date to AD 107. The date of the events described by Y. Pliny is August 93 – fixed by it coinciding with Agricola's death (see **P11b**) suggesting that Tacitus was nearing the end of his *Histories* at this time. Y. Pliny assumes Tacitus will use the public records.

R32   Great statues in Titus' palace

[34.55] Polyclitus made ... a statue of two naked boys playing dice, called *Astragalizontes* [Greek for dice-players]. This is now in Emperor Titus' atrium, and is considered by most people to be most perfect work of art there is. ... [36.37] *Laocoon*, in the palace of Emperor Titus, is a greater work of art than any painting or statue.

[Pliny, *Natural History* 34.55 and 36.37]

Laocoon, now one of the prize exhibits in the Vatican Museum, was rediscovered in the remains of Nero's Golden House in 1506, and made a great impression on both Raphael and Michelangelo. It is clear then, and supported by the archaeology, that while the lake and gardens were restored to public use, along with some sculpture, the new imperial family continued to use Nero's huge palace.

R33   Domitian's interest in libraries

[4] He restored libraries which had burnt down by seeking volumes from all over the empire, especially Alexandria.

[*Epitome de Caesaribus* 11.4]

R34   Epaphroditus, bibliophile freedman of Mettius Modestus

Epaphroditus of Chaeroneia, fostered and educated by Archias of Alexandria, was bought by Modestus, the prefect of Egypt, and taught his son Petelius in Rome. He was prominent under Nero and up to the reign of Nerva, in the same period as Ptolemy, son of Hephaestion, and many others well known in cultural life. He was a persistent buyer of books and collected thirty thousand volumes, serious and recondite, too. In physical appearance he was massive and dark, like an elephant. He lived in the Phaenianokoria district, as it is called, having bought two houses there. When he was in his seventy-fifth year he died, falling ill with dropsy. He left a fair number of written compositions.

[Suidas, *Lexicon*, 'Epaphroditus' (ed. A. Adler, vol. 2, Leipzig, 1931)]

R35 Decrees on teachers and doctors by Vespasian (AD 74) and Domitian (AD 93/4)

{Greek} [Emperor Caesar Vespasian Augustus, chief priest, holding tribunician power for the 7th time, hailed *imperator* 14 times, father of the fatherland, consul 5 times, designated for the 6th time, censor, says "Since … *(account of merits of teachers and doctors)* …] I order that neither is billeting to be imposed [on them], nor are they to be asked for tax contributions in any way. [But if any of those] under my leadership [shall dare] to outrage or demand security from [or take to court] any of the physicians or teachers or physiotherapists, those guilty of the outrage are to pay to Capitoline Jupiter [10,000 drachmas]. Whoever does not have this amount, let him be sold up and let the official [in charge of these matters consecrate to the god] without delay whatever fine [he has imposed]. Likewise if they [find him in hiding], let them take him to court whenever they choose, and [let them not be hindered] by anybody. It is [to be permitted] to them also [to hold assemblies] in whatever precincts and temples and [shrines] wherever they choose, as on sacred ground with the right of asylum. [Whoever does them any violence] is liable to answer to the Roman people on a charge of [impiety towards] the Imperial House. I, Emperor [Caesar Vespasian], signed this and ordered that [it be displayed on] a whitened board. Published in the sixth year on the [?] day of the month [Lous, on the Capitol] six days before first of January.

{Latin} Emperor Caesar Domitian, holding tribunician power for the 13th time, hailed imperator 22 times, censor for life, father of the fatherland, when A. Licinius Mucianus and Gavius Priscus were consuls: [the greed of doctors and] teachers I have decided needs the most severe repression. Their skill, which ought [to be passed on to] select [young men of free birth], is being sold in a most outrageous manner to a number of [personal] slaves who have been sent to acquire [the training, not for cultural reasons] but for greater cash profit. [Whoever therefore shall make] a profit [from the training of slaves, he is to have] taken [from him the tax immunity which was granted by my deified father], just as [if he were practising an art in a city that is not his own].

[MW 458 = EDCS–15700103]

Decrees from Pergamum (NW Turkey) with Domitian's in Latin under an earlier decree in Greek by Vespasian. Vespasian had established chairs of rhetoric at Rome and supported teachers and doctors throughout the Empire, though not philosophers, perhaps because they had been hostile to him for returning Greece once more to Roman rule from the freedom Nero had granted it (Suetonius, *Vespasian* 17–18, **M2** and see **R36**).

R36 Vespasian praises Apollonius as a model philosopher

The Emperor Vespasian greets the philosopher Apollonius: if all wished to be philosophers of your kind, Apollonius, philosophy would be well off, as would poverty; philosophy being uncorruptible and poverty voluntary. Farewell." Let that be your father's speech in my defence, defining the incorruptibility of my philosophy and the voluntary nature of my poverty. This was probably because he remembered events in Egypt, when Euphrates and many would-be philosophers approached him, openly asking for money, while I was the only one who did not approach him for money, but tried to push them away as being unhealthy.

[Philostratos, *Life of Apollonius of Tyana* 8.6.11 = *Letter* 77f]

R37   Banishment of philosophers

What prestige you give to teachers of rhetoric! What great value you place on
professors of philosophy! Under you, scholarship has recovered its lifeblood and its
home! The barbarity of a previous age had punished it with exile since an emperor
expert in every vice had banished skills hostile to vice, not just because he hated it but
because of the respect in which others held it.

[Pliny the Younger, *Panegyric to Trajan* 47.1]

Philosophers were often thought unconducive to Rome's peace. They also become associated with potential
opposition to monarchy. Philosophers were expelled by Vespasian (Dio 66.12–13) around AD 71–2.

SECTION S

SOCIETY IN ROME

Slaves corrupted against their masters, freedmen against their patrons;
and men without a single enemy ruined by their friends.

[Tacitus, *Histories* 1.2.3]

Introduction: this volume does not aim to provide a social history of Rome under the Flavians (for such, see Shelton, *As the Romans Did* (2nd ed. OUP 1998)). This section, however, collects some sources on Roman society with personal or political relevance to the Flavian family. The poetry of Martial, our very best literary source on society in the imperial period, is prominent. This section deals with slaves and freedmen; patrons and clients; and moral legislation.

S1   Funerary inscription of a young slave, 'darling of Domitia', Rome

To the Shades. To Chrysantes Barbarus, darling of Domitia Augusta, his mother Thymele made this for her most dutiful son who lived 4 years, 8 months.

[MW 226 = *AE* 1955, 25]

S2   Funerary inscription to a mule-driver, Rome

To the Shades of Successus, mule-driver, house-slave of Caesar. He lived 36 years, 7 months, 5 days. Antigonus, slave of Domitia Augusta, recorder, made this for his most worthy brother.

[MW 216 = *AE* 1988, 16]

S3   Funerary plaque for a slave architect of Domitian, Rome

To the Shades: To Tychicus Crispillianus, slave of emperor Domitian, architect. Ti. Claudius Primus gave an ossuary jar.

[MW 218 = *ILS* 7733a = EDCS–18700010*]

S4   Funerary inscription of a slave tax-collector, Rome

To the gods and to the divine spirit of Rhodo, slave of Domitia Augusta, collector of tax on inherited money and property. He lived around 24 years. Rhodinus made this for his excellent and most loyal twin brother.

[MW 204 = *ILS* 1523 = EDCS–18200454]

S5   Funerary inscription of a freedman procurator of inheritance, Rome

To Lemnus, imperial freedman, procurator of patrimony and inheritance and to Domitia Phyllis: L. Domitius Lemnus, their son.

[MW 201a = *ILS* 1489 = EDCS–18200523]

S6   … and of his wife, at Volterra

Of Domitia Phyllis, wife of C. Domitius Lemnus, procurator of Germanicus Caesar.

[MW 201b = *ILS* 1490 = EDCS–22000103]

S7   Eutactus, freedman procurator of Asia, AD 80

To Emperor Titus Caesar Vespasian Augustus, son of Divus Vespasian, *pontifex maximus*, holding tribunician power for the 9th time, hailed *imperator* 15 times, consul 8 times, father of the fatherland: Eutactus, freedman, procurator of the provinces of Asia and Lycia dedicated (this) in accordance with the will of Claudius Symmachus.

[MW 199 = EDCS–00400005]

This inscription from Ephesus is repeated in Greek. Eutactus is also known from MW 206 'To Eutactus, imperial freedman, procurator, state-attendant as conferred by Divus Vespasian: Clemens his son, (made this) for his excellent father.'

THE FATHER OF CLAUDIUS ETRUSCUS: S8–S9

Much is known about this important and long-serving freedman, but not his name! Martial wrote to celebrate his return home from exile (**S8**) and shortly afterwards an elegy for his death (7.40), as did Statius in a much longer poem, celebrating his whole career from Tiberius to Domitian (**S9**).

S8   The return from exile of the father of Claudius Etruscus

His father's luck owes much to Etruscus' concern,
But both owe quite as much to you, our greatest leader.
For you called back the thunderbolts your hand did send,
I wish that this too was the way with Jupiter's fires.
If the great Thunderer's nature were the same as yours,   5
Augustus, rarely would his hand use one whole bolt.
Etruscus witnesses both sides of your great gift,
Permitted to accompany his father and bring him home.

[Martial, *Epigram* 6.83 (published December 91)]

S9   Statius' consolation to Claudius Etruscus on his father's death

'The filial piety of my dear Claudius Etruscus deserved some consolation from my writing as he mourned his old father with unfeigned tears – rarest of things, nowadays.' Statius, *Silvae* 3, introduction. The poem itself begins with condolence, before recalling the dead man's career from Tiberius to Nero (lines 60–84 = LACTOR 19, S32a).

S9a   As 'minister of finance' under Vespasian

Then from on high upon your loyal house there shone a glorious light.   85
At full tilt, and at its loftiest, Fortune arrived. Now to one man was given
In trust the management of sacred treasures, riches from all nations
Harvested, the gross domestic product of the whole wide world.
All that Iberia spews from its golden mines; everything that shines
Among the high mountains of Dalmatia; all that from Africa is swept   90
Up in her harvests; all that the sweltering Nile produces from threshing floors;
All that the plunging divers of the eastern seas can gather; offspring too
Of Spartan Galaesus' carefully nurtured herds; transparent snow (rock crystals),
African timber, India's glory, tusks of ivory. All that the wild North Wind,
All that the raging East and cloud-filled South winds bring – all to one minister 95
Are now entrusted, all are obedient to his sole command. Swifter it were
To count the winter's raindrops or the summer's woodland leaves. But he,

Sagacious and sleepless, swiftly calculates the needed sums for every exercise
Of Roman arms in every clime, for distributing to the poor, for temples, how much
The lofty aqueducts demand, what sea-defences, the land's own battlements,   100
How much the far-flung reaches of our Roman roads, how much the gold
That gleams in the fretted ceilings of our emperor's home, the cost
Of gold which, melted in the fire, must take the shape of gods' own faces,
And how much jingle as coinage, stamped in the fires of Italy's Mint.
No wonder was it that you never learned to rest;   105
Pleasure remained an exile from your thoughts; fasting was feasting;
Never were cares beguiled by deep draughts of undiluted wine;
Dear to your heart were marriage bonds, and dear a mind
Bound in fidelity to the marriage bed, to marriage celebration,
And the joy of fathering servants faithful to your lord.   110

[Statius, *Silvae* 3.3.85–110 (published 93/4)]

Line 86: Fortune arrived: Possibly at Vespasian's accession, he became *a rationibus* (in charge of financial accounts) or effectively chancellor of the exchequer. Lines 86–96 give an interesting, if poetic, view of the empire's resources. Lines 98–104 give an even more interesting, and possibly representative view of the main expenses of empire: the army; the dole; maintenance of buildings, especially temples, aqueducts, harbours, roads, imperial luxury, statues of gods; the mint.

S9b   Marriage to Tettia Etrusca, sister of a consul

Who does not know Etrusca's fame, her noble birth, her beauty *sans pareil*?
Myself I never saw her face to face with my own eyes, but yet
Her portrait matched her beauty's reputation, beauty beyond compare,
While in their looks her children showed a matching loveliness.
Hers was no common parentage. Her brother held the *fasces* and the chair   115
Of highest curule office; then with loyalty he led Italy's armies
And her entrusted standards, when their first madness drove
Wild Dacians to war, and doomed their whole people to a mighty triumph.
What if the father's bloodline lacked nobility? The mother made it good.
Her house rejoiced in such a marriage bond, which saw the sunlight rise   120
Upon its once darkened fortunes. The children soon came, those pledges true
Of married love, and fecund Lucina, goddess of childbirth, came
To bless their bearing twice, and with gentle hand to ease the pains of labour.

[Statius, *Silvae* 3.3.111–123 (published 93/4)]

Etrusca's brother was most probably L. Tettius Julianus, consul 83, and general under Domitian. See **B83** for further details of his career. Line 118: Dacians: their king, Decebalus, defeated Roman armies in 85 and 86, but was then defeated at Tapae (SW Transylvania) and Domitian made peace, recognising Decebalus as a client/friendly king (see **N39**). Statius goes on to lament Etrusca's early death (lines 124–137, not included).

S9c   Further honours granted by Vespasian

Vespasian, the god, who now with his nod controls the arches of the heavens,
And has already shared his own offspring with the earth and stars, rejoiced
To grant him a share of honour in his Idumaean triumph, and adjudged   140
Him worthy, and did not refuse the right, to join the victory procession.
His humble parentage proved no impediment. For that same emperor
Down from the people's humble seats escorted him to equestrian benches,
Altered his rank, and from his finger stripped the freedman's ignoble iron ring,
And made him level with the lofty rank of his own sons.   145

[Statius, *Silvae* 3.3.138–145 (published 93/4)]

Line 140: Idumaean: a region of Palestine, but frequently poetic for Jewish. Lines 143–5: Vespasian seems
to have made play of the fact that both his father and mother were from equestrian families, and that he was
happy with this status (Suet. *Vesp.* 2 and 12). Lines 146–153 (omitted) praise the prosperity of Etruscus'
father for 80 years.

S9d   Exiled and then recalled by Domitian

What thanks or pious vows can these young men repay, devoted to you,
Greatest leader, as they are, for the rebirth of their father?   155
Perhaps old age, slowed by decay and worn out by his duties made
Some mistake. Perhaps Fortune, kind for so long, decided to withdraw.
At any rate, the old man was dumbfounded at the coming lightning-bolt,
And terrified, but it was enough for you merely to warn him
With your thunder and a passing squall, though over the bristling seas   160
The partner in his work was leaving the countryside of Italy
Far behind. *He* to the gentle shores of Campania's coast
And the citadels founded by Diomedes, was ordered to withdraw,
And was a visitor, and not an exile. Nor did you long delay,
Germanicus, in once more opening the threshold of Romulus.   165
You cherish him in his grief, you set right his fallen household gods.
No surprise, most mild-tempered leader, since this is the selfsame
Clemency which grants generous terms to the beaten Chatti,
Which returns their mountain homeland to the Dacians
Which recently, after tough wars, did not think the Marcomanni   170
Or nomadic Sarmatians worthy of a Latin triumph.

[Statius, *Silvae* 3.3.154–171 (published 93/4)]

Statius dares not risk offence by explaining the reason for banishment. The metaphor of lightning bolt
as sign of imperial anger and banishment goes right back to Ovid's exile by Augustus. Lines 160–4: it
seems that some unknown partner was banished abroad, while Claudius Etruscus' father was removed to
Campania and then to Arpi in Apulia founded in myth as Argyripa by Diomedes (Virgil, *Aeneid* 11.243–
250). The last 44 lines of the poem (omitted) lament the father's death so soon after being recalled, but
promise pious rites from his son.

S10 T. Flavius Abascantus, freedman secretary

"Priscilla loved my wife ... and besides I always try my humble best to do a favour to every side of the Sacred House, since whoever honestly worships the gods also loves their priests." (Statius, *Letter to Abascantus*) the letter introduces a poem of consolation to Abascantus on the death of his wife, Priscilla, and the great majority of the 262 lines deal with Priscilla's virtues, her death and Abascantus' loss. Statius' description (222–241, **K56**) of the location and interior of the tomb Abascantus built for his wife allows for plausible identification with substantial remains of a tomb just outside the Appian Gate and by the River Anio. But Statius also describes Abascantus' job as *ab epistulis,* in charge of the emperor's correspondence, a very important post, later held by Suetonius. Abascantus may have been the last freedman to hold this post before it became the preserve of equestrians.

> He saw a virtuous young man, quietly studious, 76
> Utterly loyal, his mind prepared for every challenge,
> By nature watchful, his spirit cautious, fit to meet
> Changes great as they unfold. He saw, who knows all
> His men, and goes around approving all his servants. 80
> No wonder: east and west he sees, what the South and
> Wintry North Wind do; he checks the plans and even
> Purposes of war and peace. On shoulders strong
> He puts a massive burden, a load almost too great,
> (No other task so multifaceted in all 85
> The sacred house) to send commands of Romulus
> The leader all across the world, and handle forces
> And levers of power: to know of triumphs in the North;
> Wandering Euphrates; banks of two-named Danube;
> Standards of the Rhine; how far the ends of earth, 90
> And Thule, resounding with roaring rip-tide yield to Rome;
> For every spear comes lifting joyful laurel leaves,
> No lance is marked with the feather bringing news that's bad.
> And when our Lord assigns the swords of loyal command,
> It's *he* who says who ought to rule each century 95
> As equestrian sent to legions; who commands a cohort;
> Who merits higher rank as senatorial tribune;
> And who deserves to give command to cavalry troops.
> A thousand possibilities must *he* predict –
> If the Nile's in flood, or Libya damp with rainy winds: 100

[Statius, *Silvae* 5.1.76–100 (published posthumously, *c.* 96)]

Statius goes on to suggest that enumerating all Abascantus' duties would be a task only possible for various messengers of the gods, including those reporting on Domitian's triumphs, before returning to Priscilla's qualities.) Line 89: The Danube was known in Latin as Hister or Danuvius. Line 91: 'Thule' is the usual poetic way to describe the furthest parts of Britain (compare **H62**.597 and note).

CLIENTS: S11–S14

Martial provides some of our best evidence for the crucial building-block of Roman society, the patron-client relationship. All Romans will have been a patron or a client. Many will have been both – Martial complains about consuls claiming money as clients (10.10) and also about the trials of being a client (10.56, 10.74, 10.82). Clients would visit their patrons first thing in the morning, formally dressed in a toga (1.108, **S11**, 5.22) to pay their respects (**S15**). Patrons would provide a handout (*sportula*) to clients, who would be expected to form part of their patron's retinue in public (**S12**, 3.46); support him in public life, in politics or the law-courts; and maybe fill the odd empty space at a dinner-party. Patrons would also represent their clients in court cases (2.32). The handout (*sportula*) had traditionally been a gift of food or invitation to dinner, but it had become a standard amount of money – 25 *asses* (**S15**). Domitian briefly insisted that the handout should revert to the old-fashioned meal (**S13**, **S14**, 3.30, 3.60 and Suet. *Dom.* 7). This proved unpopular and was rescinded (as shown clearly by **S15**).

S11   **Decianus too often not at home**

May I fall ill if, Decianus, I don't wish
To be with you all day and all night too. And yet
The distance we're apart is two whole miles. Or four,
That is, when I go there and back. You're often not
At home; and when you are, they say you're not; or that   5
You have time only for yourself or your law-suits.
To see you, I do not mind walking two whole miles;
I do mind walking four whole miles *not* to see you.

[Martial, *Epigrams* 2.5 (published 85)]

S12   **A client of a client**

I want a dinner invite, I'm ashamed to say.
Maximus, you want one too. We're equal then.
I come to greet you early. You are said already
To have gone to do the same elsewhere. We're equal then.
I walk before a pompous king, escorting you   5
Myself. You escort someone else. We're equal then.
It's bad enough to be a slave. I won't be vice-slave.
A man who's king, my friend, ought not to have a king.

[Martial, *Epigrams* 2.18 (published 85)]

S13   **Domitian banning dole**

Farewell now our pathetic six sesterces,
That is handed out to a tired-out escort,
Which the soaking bath attendant used to split.
What do you think of that, all my starving friends?
The handouts of our proud kings have gone away.   5
No more tricks: they must give us a salary.

[Martial, *Epigrams* 3.7 (published Autumn 86)]

S14 **No dole, so back to Spain**
Starving Tuccius headed for Rome
All the way from Spain.
Met, at the Mulvian bridge by news of the dole,
He headed home again

[Martial, *Epigrams* 3.14 (published Autumn 86)]

S15 **Martial loses the 'dole' for not calling his patron 'master'**
This morning by mistake I greeted you by name,
Caecilianus, and did not call you 'my master'.
D'you want to know how much my freedom cost me?
It took away from me the sum of six sesterces.

[Martial, *Epigram* 6.88 (published December 91)]

THE RIGHT OF (THREE) CHILDREN – *IUS LIBERORUM*: S16–S19

Augustan marriage legislation had established certain privileges for men and women with three or more children in an effort to increase the population, especially within the upper classes (see **U33a** and **S8**). But the privileges also came to be granted by emperors as an honour (**U50**): Martial asked for the honour (**S16**), and was granted it, though it seems from **S17** that it needed to be renewed by emperors.

S16 **Martial receives the 'right of three children'**
He 'father of three children' me has made,
And all my Muse's labours richly paid,
Who only could: you, wife, I shall not retain,
Lest I my master's bounty render vain.

[Martial *Epigram* 2.92, (publ. 85), tr. Henry Killigrew, 1689, slightly adapted]

S17 **Martial envied**
He bursts with jealousy because both Caesars granted
Me the right of children, bursts with jealousy.

[Martial, *Epigram* 9.97.5–6 (published December 94)]

S18 **British matron, mother of three Roman children**
Though Claudia Redhead's born of Britons dyed with woad
How well she has at heart the ways of the Latin race!
Italian matrons could well think she's Roman, such her
Graceful figure, Greeks too claim her as their own.
She's given children to her virtuous husband, and hopes,   5
Though young, to see those children married, gods be willing.
And may it please the gods that she rejoice always
In her one husband and rejoice in children three.

[Martial, *Epigrams* 11.53 (published December 96)]

EQUESTRIAN STATUS: S19–S24

While many of Martial's poems show him conscious of his status as a client, others show his pride in his equestrian status. It is not quite clear how he arrived at this – whether as honorary tribune or having the census qualification of 400,000 sesterces (not implausible – see Sullivan, *Martial*, section 1.6 on Martial's 'poverty'). In fact, despite **S23** it is not clear that possessing a fortune of 400,000 was sufficient condition to be of equestrian status, see *OCD* under 'equites'. Domitian followed Augustus in reinforcing a law reserving for equestrians the first fourteen rows of seating at the theatre (Suet. *Aug.* 44) and disapproving of inappropriate clothes. Several Martial poems on this theme in book 5 (8 (= **S21**), 14, 23, 25, 27, 35, 37, 38 (= **S22**), 41), and their absence from other books is good evidence that the regulations were a 'hot topic' in AD 90. For equestrians prominent in governing the empire see **U41–U51**.

S19   **Martial as tribune**
Both the Caesars have praised me and rewarded me,   5
Given me the right of father of three children.
I'm read by many lips; Fame's granted me a name
Known in many towns, before I'm dust and ashes.
And there's more: Rome has seen my tribunate,
At the theatre *I* may sit where *you* are not allowed.   10
[Martial *Epigram* 3.95.5–10 (published Autumn 86)]

S20   **Poor but equestrian**
I am, and always have been, poor, Callistratus,
Equestrian too, and not unknown, nor badly thought-of.
[Martial *Epigram* 5.13.1–2 (published December 90)]

S21   **Domitian and theatre regulations**
The edict of our Lord and God regulating
More clearly the rows of seats and restoring
Those reserved for equestrians, was being
Praised in the theatre just the other day
By Phasis, red-faced in his purple toga,   5
By Phasis, who boasted, arrogantly proud,
"Finally we can sit more comfortably,
Now equestrian dignity has been restored;
We are not squashed or polluted by the crowd"
While he was saying this sort of thing and more,   10
Slouching back in his seat, an usher ordered
That purple and arrogant cloak to get up.
[Martial *Epigram* 5.8 (published December 90)]

S22 **Equestrian census qualification**
The census ranks Calliodorus an equestrian,
As the whole world knows, but he has a brother.
To say 'Split four hundred thousand' halves a fig.
Do you believe two men can sit on the same horse?
Why do you need to have a brother, a wretched Pollux? 5
Without this Pollux of yours, you would be a Castor.
Because the brothers *is* all one, *does* they both sit?
Get up, Calliodorus, your grammar is all wrong!
Or copy Leda's children – since you can't sit with
Your brother, Calliodorus, take turns to sit down. 10

[Martial, *Epigram* 5.38 (published December 90)]

Other evidence for the census qualification comes from 4.67 and 5.25. Castor and Pollux, the 'heavenly twins', sons of Leda, in fact had to live alternately in heaven and earth (Martial 1.36)

S23 **Pliny the Younger gives money to a friend to make him equestrian**
Pliny to his friend Romatius Firmus,
You are my fellow townsman, we went to school together, and were friends from an early age; your father was good friends with both my mother and my uncle, and even with me, as far as the difference in our ages allowed. These are great and overwhelming reasons why I ought to try to advance your career and status. [2] The fact of your being a councillor in our town indicates that you have an income of a hundred thousand sesterces. Therefore, I offer you three hundred thousand sesterces to make up the equestrian qualification, so that we may enjoy seeing you not only as a town councillor, but as a Roman equestrian. [3] The length of our friendship is sufficient to ensure that you will remember this favour; I do not even advise you (as I might have advised you, if I did not know that you would do it of your own accord) to enjoy the status given by me as modestly as possible as it was given by me. [4] One ought to guard an honour more carefully, in a case where one is taking care of a gift given by a friend. Farewell.

[Pliny the Younger, *Letters* 1.19]

S24 **Vespasian makes up a property qualification**
Divus Augustus Vespasian, when he had discovered that a particular young man, who was well born, but unsuited to military life, had been led, by shortage of family resources, to attain a fairly high rank, he made up his census requirement and gave him an honourable discharge.

[Frontinus, *On Stratagems* 4.6.4]

This story comes in a section entitled 'On good will and moderation'. Presumably the young man had tried to restore his equestrian status by taking a position as military tribune.

MORAL LEGISLATION: S25–S32

Suetonius provides quite a lengthy list of moral reforms undertaken by Domitian (Suet. *Dom.* 8). These probably started with his censorship in April 85, including banning of libellous writings (**S25**). Many of Martial's poems are obscene – only books 5 and 8, dedicated to Domitian (**S26**), are free of obscenity which may reflect Domitian's ongoing concerns. He certainly legislated on sexual matters, again following Augustus' lead, and facing the charge of hypocrisy (Suet. *Dom.* 8.3 and 3.1, **J10i**). Castration was banned, perhaps from 86/7 (Suet, *Dom.* 7.1, Dio 67.2.3, Statius, *Silvae,* 4.3.13–15, various Martial epigrams, from 2.60). Several of these sources (Suetonius, Statius, Philostratos) mention this together with an edict against vine-growing (**S29**) more plausibly interpreted as reaction to shortage of agricultural land, and later overturned (Suet. *Dom.* 14). Martial (**S32**) provides the main evidence of an edict banning prostitution of boys, (perhaps alluded to at Statius, *Silvae* 3.4.76–7). For Earinus, Domitian's eunuch, see **J23**.

S25   **A plea for Domitian's tolerance as censor**
            If you should ever stumble on my book,
            Briefly put off your world-compelling look,
            Remember, rulers have let insults fly
            At triumphs, to defeat the evil eye.
            You fancy risqué mimes upon the stage –
            So let a lowly author stain his page.
            A censor can relax, wink just one eye:
            My poetry is filthy – but not I.
                                        [Martial, *Epigram* 1.4 (published *c.* 86), translated Gary Wills, 2008)]

S26   **Martial's fifth book, 'clean' and fit for Domitian and Minerva to read**
            Married women, boys, unmarried girls,
            My pages are dedicated to you all.
            You, however, who are much too enamoured
            Of salacious naughtiness and naked jokes,
            You should read my four mischievous little books: 5
            This, fifth book, jokes with our master
            For Germanicus to read unblushingly
            In the presence of the Athenian maid.
                                        [Martial, *Epigram* 5.2 (published December 90)]

S27   **Julian law on adultery revived**
            It's thirty days or less from when the Julian law,
            Faustinus, was revived for all the people, and when
            Chastity was bidden enter in our homes.
            Already Telesilla's marrying her tenth man.
            Adultery by law – that's what she does, not marriage:
            I'm less offended by an honest prostitute.
                                        [Martial, *Epigram* 6.7 (published 91)]

S28   Male castration outlawed
It was a game to mock the sacred marriage torch,
Castrating helpless males a game. You outlaw both,
Germanicus, thus helping future generations,
Bidding them be born in safety. While you reign
None shall now be eunuch or adulterer:
Before, for shame, eunuchs were adulterers.

[Martial, *Epigram* 6.2 (published December 91)]

S29   Domitian's edicts on vines and castration
King Domitian at about the same time made laws prohibiting making eunuchs and
planting vineyards, and to have vineyards already planted cut down.

[Philostratos, *Life of Apollonius of Tyana* 6.42]

S30   Embassy on Domitian's decree on vines
The embassies to the Emperor of which Scopelian was a member were numerous; a
degree of good fortune used to accompany him on his embassies, but the most successful
was on behalf of the vines, when he was sent, not only on behalf of the people of Smyrna,
as on most of his embassies, but for the whole of Asia at once. I shall reveal the purpose
of the embassy: the emperor's view was that Asia should not have any vines, because
he thought that men become seditious under the influence of drink; the existing vines
were to be uprooted and others not to be planted any more. What was needed was a joint
embassy and a man who was going to use his charm on their behalf like another Orpheus
or Thamyris. Accordingly they all chose Scopelian, and he was more than successful on
the mission, so much so that he came back in possession not only of permission to plant,
but with actual penalties to be imposed on those who were failing to do so.

[Philostratos, *Lives of the Sophists* 520]

S31   Rome's moral rebirth
Most mighty censor, king of kings, to whom
Rome owes so many triumphs yet to come,
So many temples growing and restored,
So many shows, and gods, and cities: Lord,
She yet in debt to you does still remain
That she by you is once made pure again.

[Martial, *Epigram* 6.4, (publ. December 91, tr. Robert Fletcher, 1656, slightly adapted)]

S32   Domitian outlaws boy prostitution, AD 94
As if it were a trivial outrage 'gainst our sex
That males were prostituted for abuse by people,
Pimps had taken hold of cradles, so that a boy
Snatched from mother's breast would wail for filthy pay.
Ungrown bodies suffered unspeakable abuse.   5
Italia's father could not bear such monstrous crimes,
Having only just helped tender youths escape
Perverted lust of men who wished to neuter them.
Before now boys and men both young and old adored
You, Caesar; infants now also do the same.   10

[Martial, *Epigram* 9.7 (published December 94)]

SECTION T

TYRANNY: PANEGYRIC OR INVECTIVE

Neither group, the flatterers or the bitter opponents cared about posterity.

[Tacitus, *Histories* 1.1.1]

At the start of his *Histories* and then his *Annals,* Tacitus lamented the unreliability of contemporary or near-contemporary historians under the principate. The Elder Pliny had arguably found the solution of writing, but not publishing (**R13**), but the problem continued to reach the point where Eutropius in **T1** and **T2** is simply presenting the orthodox views of Titus and Domitian. En route, Pliny the Younger's *Panegyric to Trajan* contains explicit praise, but on the other side of the same coin, equally explicit condemnation of the man he ultimately replaced. So this section contains a few historical facts, and much historical judgement that is worthless in itself, but which is often reflected in the accounts of other ancient sources. *Caveat lector* – let the reader beware!

T1   Titus good …

[21] His son Titus, also known as Vespasian, succeeded him. Titus was a man of all the virtues, such a marvel from his birth that he was known as the darling and delight of the whole human race, a superb speaker, a great war-leader, but a man of complete self-control. He pleaded cases in Latin and composed poems and tragedies in Greek. In the assault on Jerusalem when serving under his father, he shot twelve defenders with twelve arrows. At Rome, such was his common touch in ruling that he punished no one at all, and dismissed those convicted of plotting against him or treated them with the same intimacy as before. His approachability and generosity were so great that when he was criticised by his friend for never saying no to anyone, he replied that no one should leave the emperor disappointed. In addition when, one day at dinner, he recalled that he had shown no one a favour during that day, he said, "Friends, today I have wasted a day". He built the amphitheatre at Rome and had five thousand wild beasts killed during its inauguration. [22] For these reasons he was loved with an unprecedented popularity, but died of disease in the same country estate as his father, two years, eight months and twenty days after becoming emperor, at the age of forty. Such was the level of public grief at his death that everyone grieved as if for a family bereavement. The senate, on receiving news of his death around nightfall, rushed to the senate-house at night, and heaped thanks and praises on him in death to a greater extent than they had when he was alive or present. He was deified.

[Eutropius, *Brief History* 21–22]

T2   … Domitian bad

[23] Domitian immediately came to power as Titus' younger brother, but was more like Nero, Caligula or Tiberius than his own father or brother. Although he was restrained in his first years in power, he very soon progressed to huge faults of lust, fury, cruelty, and greed, and he aroused such hatred as to obliterate the good deeds of his father and brother. The greatest noblemen in the senate he killed. He was the first to insist on being called lord and god. He did not allow any statue of himself to be put up on the Capitol unless made of gold or silver. He killed his own cousins. His arrogance too was disgusting. He conducted four campaigns, one against the Sarmatians, another against the Chatti, and two against the Dacians. He celebrated a double triumph over the Dacians and the Chatti, while he claimed only a laurel crown

for the Sarmatians. But he also suffered many disasters in these wars: in Sarmatia his legion and its general were killed; at the hands of the Dacians, the former consul Oppius Sabinus and the praetorian prefect Cornelius Fuscus were killed together with their large armies. He also conducted many building projects in Rome, including the Capitol, the Forum Transitorium, the Portico of the Divi, the Temples of Isis and Serapis, and the Stadium. Indeed when he had begun to be universally loathed for his crimes, he was killed in the palace by a conspiracy of his own circle in his forty-fifth year, the fifteenth of his reign. His funeral was dishonourable in the extreme, with his body carried out by undertakers and humbly buried.

[Eutropius, *Brief History* 23]

T3   Martial's introduction to his eighth book of Epigrams
To Emperor Domitian Caesar Augustus Germanicus Dacicus, Valerius Martialis sends greetings.

All my little books, master, to which you have given publicity, that is existence, have favours to beg of you: and they will, I think, be read for this reason. But this one, entitled the eighth of my books, enjoys the opportunity to show its loyalty even more frequently. Therefore there was less need to work to refine it, since the subject matter was in place: but we have tried, occasionally to vary it by mixing in some jokes, so that every line does not pile up its praises on your heavenly modesty: we could not have enough of this, but it could more easily tire you. What is more, although epigrams have been written by men of the highest station and the strictest standards which seem to approach a freedom of language found in mime, I myself have not allowed these epigrams to speak as rudely as is usual. Since the greater and better part of the book is bound to the majesty of your holy name, it should be noted that people are not allowed to approach temples except after religious purification. So that possible readers might know that I shall keep to this principle, I have decided to announce it right at the start of this book in a very short epigram:

> Our master's laurelled dwelling you are soon to enter,
> So learn to speak more chastely, book, with modest lips.
> Nude Venus move away; this little book's not yours:
> But come to me, Augustus' Minerva, come.

[Martial, *Epigram* 8, introduction and poem 1 (published January 94)]

T4   All Rome loves Domitian's servants
> Rome used to hate the servants of the leaders, that crowd
> There used to be, the arrogance of the Palatine.
> But now, Augustus, such is the love for your servants,
> Felt by all, that each puts his own household second.
> So gentle are their feelings, so great their respect for us,   5
> So peaceful is their calm, so modest their expressions.
> Of Caesar's servants, (as befits the court of power)
> None has his own manners, each those of his Lord.

[Martial, *Epigram* 9.79 (published December 94)]

T5   Statius' thank you for invitation to dinner at the palace
'Second I have given thanks at having been honoured by an invitation to his most sacred banquets.' (Statius,
Silvae 4 introduction). Statius begins the poem (lines 1–8, not included here) by alluding to banquets
described by Virgil and Homer and asking how he can match their descriptions. For the continuation of the
*poem, describing the palace, see **K47, Q20**.)*

... I seem to recline amidst the stars	
With Jove, and take from Trojan Ganymede's right hand	10
The immortal wine he brings! Dull the years I've passed:	
This day's the start for me, the threshold of my life!	
O ruler of the countries of the conquered world,	
Great parent, hope of men, beloved by gods; can I	15
See you from where I lie, yet facing you across	
The wine and feasts, still be permitted not to rise?	

[Statius, *Silvae* 4.2.8–17 (published 95)]

MONTHS RENAMED: T6–T8
With the benefit of hindsight (and the later example of Caracalla who renamed all twelve months after
himself) Domitian renaming September and October after the months of his succession and birth smacks
of megalomania, even though we take 'July' and 'August' for granted. Suetonius, acknowledged as an
authority on the Roman Calendar by Censorinus (*On Birthdays* 20.2) implies (*Dom.* 13) that the changes
coincided with his taking the name 'Germanicus' which appears on coins from the summer of AD 83. But
the Acts of the Arval Brothers did not use these dates in autumn 87 (**A87h–j**), so a date of AD 94/5, fitting
Martial 9.1.1–4 and Statius 4.1.42, is much more likely to explain the very rare mention of the month (or
its deletion) in inscriptions.

T6   Domitian renamed September and October
The month of September has kept its original name, though Domitian had inflicted it
with the name 'Germanicus' and October with his own name. But when it was decided
to erase his ill-omened name from every bronze or stone inscription, the months too
had the name usurped by the tyrant removed.

[Macrobius, *Saturnalia* 1.12.36–7]

T7   Sycophancy of the senate renaming months of the year
[4] We debated increasing the numbers of gladiators or creating a guild of builders.
And as we might have discussed expanding the boundaries of the empire, we now
discussed huge arches, inscriptions too long for the architraves of temples, or then
again the months when we were calling not just one by the names of the Caesars.

[Pliny the Younger, *Panegyric to Trajan* 54.4]

T8   Month 'Germanicus' used in an inscription, Sentinum in Umbria
To C. Aetrius Naso, son of Gaius, of the Lemonian tribe, equestrian of the 'public
horse' in division five, prefect of the first 'German' cohort, military tribune of Legion
I 'Italian'. He ordered this to be set up in his will and also bequeathed 120 sesterces
for a banquet to be given to the townspeople of Sentinum on the 17th day before the
first of Germanicus *(= 16 August)*.

[MW 343 = *ILS* 6644 = EDCS–23000420*]

DOMINUS ET DEUS: T9–T12

Far more offence seems to have been caused by Domitian's reported insistence that he be addressed as *'dominus et deus'* 'master and god', see Suet. *Dom.* 13.1–2, **J10g**. The first term would be used by a slave to his owner, the latter was the word for a 'proper' god rather than a 'Divus' emperor. In fact, 'dominus' seems to have been a perfectly common form of polite address to a more senior member of family, army, senate (Sherwin-White, Commentary on Pliny the Younger, page 557–8, and see on **T11**). Despite **T10**, no surviving letters or official documents address or refer to Domitian as 'master and god', though as with all emperors from Augustus, Roman poets flatter him by calling him a god, while Greek inscriptions continued to mark no distinction between 'divus' and 'deus' with θεος being used in imperial cult for deified and current emperors.

T9   Dominus et Deus from AD 86
Domitian first orders that he be called 'master and god'

[Jerome, *Chronicle,* year 2102 after Abraham = AD 86]

T10   Dominus et Deus
By now Domitian had already decided that he should be regarded as divine, and was immensely proud of titles such as "Master" and "God," which were used not only in speeches, but even in state documents.

[Zonaras, *Summary of Dio,* 11.19 = Dio 67.4.7]

T11   How to praise an emperor
[2] So let those expressions which were prompted by fear go away and stay away. Let us say nothing that we used to say, since we have to endure nothing that we used to endure. Let us not begin our speech in public with the same words as previously, since we no longer say the same things in private as previously. [3] Times have changed, and this should be obvious in our speeches; even from a formal vote of thanks, it should be clear when, and to whom the thanks were given. Nowhere should we flatter him as a god or as a divinity: for we are not talking of a tyrant but of a citizen, not of a master but of a parent. [4] He is one of us, and he especially excels and is pre-eminent, in regarding himself as one of us, and remembering that he is human even when ruling over humans.

[Pliny the Younger, *Panegyric to Trajan* 2.2–4]

Y. Pliny tries to flatter Trajan here by saying that flattery in public speech is no longer needed as it was previously. He perhaps alludes in [3] to Domitian being flattered in being addressed as 'dominus et deus' – 'master and god'. In fact Pliny addresses Trajan as *'dominus'* in 65 of 71 letters sent from Bithynia (book 10), and in all but one of the others, some more flattering expression is used.

T12   Martial rescinds 'Dominus et Deus'
In vain, pathetic Flattery,
With shameful lips you come to me,
To call him falsely 'Lord and God'.
Away, for you here's no abode;
To Parthia's turbaned Monarchs go;   5
There falling prostrate, basely low,
The gaudy king's proud feet adore;
This is no Lord, but Commander,
Of all the justest Senator,
By whom – from Stygian shades – the plain   10

And rustic truth's brought back again.
You dare not, Rome, this Emperor
To flatter as you did before.

[Martial, *Epigram* 10.72, translated Thomas May 1629, slightly adapted)]

Book 10 was published at the end of 95, the version we have was clearly revised, as explicitly acknowledged at the start of poem 2 – **T13**. Martial had referred to Domitian as *dominus* in, e.g. 5.8 and 10.72.

T13   Revised version of Martial's tenth book
Revision of my book, in too much haste at first,
Has now recalled the work that slipped from out my hands.

[Martial, *Epigram* 10.2.1–2 (revised version, December 97?)]

T14   Patron under a harsh emperor
What Maecenas, equestrian, sprung from ancient kings
Was to Horace, Varius and Virgil supreme,
You, Priscus Terentius, were to me, as garrulous fame
And senile paper shall proclaim to all the world.
What talent and ability I seem to have   5
You make; my right to a life of leisure comes from you.
May god bless your rare heart and your style of life,
Which a Numa or a cheerful Cato might have had.
Now men are allowed, expected, to be kind,
To stand out, raise their clients' humble rank, to give   10
What easy gods have stintingly provided. But under
A harsh princeps, in hard times, you dared be good.

[Martial, *Epigram* 12.4 and 12.6.7–12 (= Shackleton-Bailey 12.3) (published 101)]

T15   Informers under Domitian
[42.1] Both public and imperial treasuries used to be enriched not so much by the Voconian and Julian laws as by treason charges – the one and only criminal charge laid against those innocent of all crime. You completely removed our fear of this. ... [3] You have freed us all from someone in our homes accusing us and by this one ensign of public safety you have removed what I might call a slave war ... [4] gratitude will come from those who remember that other emperor bribing slaves to bring about their masters' deaths and showing the charges that he would punish as if they had already informed.

[Pliny the Younger, *Panegyric to Trajan* 42.1–4]

The law of T. Voconius of 169 BC restricted daughters' rights of inheritance, while Augustus' Julian law on marriage of 19 BC did the same for those unmarried or without children. Both laws enriched the treasury and were deeply unpopular.

T16   Tacitus' introduction
The Mediterranean Sea was full of exiles, rocky islands were stained with slaughter. The savagery was even worse in Rome: high birth, wealth, and public office whether held or resigned, all provided grounds for accusation, while virtuous behaviour without exception led to death. The rewards of informers were as detested as their crimes,

since some received priesthoods or consulships as the spoils of their war, while others gained procuratorships or private influence, doing and changing everything amidst hatred and terror. Slaves were bribed against their masters, freedmen against their patrons; and those who had not a single enemy were ruined by their friends.

[Tacitus, *Histories* 1.2.2–3]

In his *Annals,* Tacitus would describe informers as 'a race of men brought about for the extermination of the public' (4.30.3). Domitian's use of informers is also mentioned by Suetonius, *Dom.* 12, though attributed implausibly to the need to bolster state finances.

T17   Domitianic informers rounded up and punished

[34.1] Whereas, Caesar, what a fine spectacle you restored to us compared to that dreadful one! We saw a column of informers brought in, like robbers or thieves. But they had occupied not deserts or highways but temples and the forum. No will was safe, no position secure. It did not help whether one had children or did not. [2] This evil was increased partly by *(some words lost from text)* ... partly by greed. You turned your eyes on the situation and as you had previously with the camps, you restored peace to the forum. You removed the cancer within us, and with strict care for the future, you made sure that a state based on laws should not seem to be overturned by laws.

[3] Therefore since both your position and generosity made it possible for you to offer the sights we saw, there was offered: first men of great strength and great spirit; then huge wild beasts; then ones amazingly trained; then those treasures, once kept hidden and secret, but now shared for the first time under your reign. But nothing was more welcome, nothing more appropriate for this age, than to be lucky enough to look down on the upturned faces of the informers as they bent back their necks. [4] We recognised them and were delighted as they were led over the blood of the guilty, like victims chosen to atone for the troubles of the people, to slow punishment and very serious vengeance. [5] They were piled onto vessels quickly procured and given up to the storms. Let them go in flight from lands wrecked by their informing, and if waves and storms kept any from the cliffs, let him inhabit the barren shore and bare rocks; let him lead a harsh and troubled life; let him bemoan the fact that he has left behind him the whole human race relieved of anxiety.

[35] It was a memorable sight, a fleet of informers, left to all the winds, forced to spread sails before the storms and to go with the angry waves onto whatever rocks they carried them. It was a joy to watch the vessels scattered as soon as they left port and right at the sea to give thanks to the emperor whose saving clemency had entrusted retribution over men of earth to the gods of the sea. [2] How greatly times had changed could then be especially recognised when the rocks on which many completely innocent men had been nailed now held the most guilty, and when islands (of exile) which had recently been crowded with senators were now crowded with informers. In fact you have crushed them not just for the present time, but permanently, kept as punishment in a thousand snares. [3] They went to steal money from others – let them lose the money they had. They longed to evict men from the family homes – let them be thrown from their own. And where previously they presented an unblushing and brazen face which nothing could wound or puncture, while they laughed off all

disgrace, now let them expect losses to equal their ill-gotten gains, let them know fear more than hope, let them be as afraid as their victims used to be.

[Pliny the Younger, *Panegyric to Trajan* 34.1–35.3]

Of course the senators who *were* informers (pointedly ignored or denied by Y. Pliny in [35.2]) survived and often prospered as shown in the brilliant (and brave) reply to Trajan below. Suetonius shows some distaste for the joy shown by the senate (*Dom.* 23.1).

T18   Informers tend to survive and prosper

Junius Mauricus said (nothing is more resolute or honest than that man) that the games should not be restored to Vienne. He added, "I wish they could be taken away from Rome." [4] You may say that this showed some steadfastness and bravery. Why not? But that is nothing new for Mauricus. He was no less bold before the Emperor Nerva when Nerva was dining with a few friends; Veiento was next to him and was leaning on his shoulder – I have said it all in naming the man. [5] The conversation was about Catullus Messalinus, who, deprived of his sight, increased his savage character with the misfortune of blindness. He had no fear, was never ashamed, and showed no pity, and for that reason Domitian used him all the more often for the destruction of the best men in the State, just like a weapon itself carried along blindly and aimlessly. [6] All together were speaking of this man's wickedness and bloody decisions, when the Emperor himself said: "What do we think would have happened to him if he were alive now?" to which Mauricus replied, "He would be dining with us."

[Pliny the Younger, *Letters* 4.22]

The question brought before Trajan's *consilium* concerned whether local games should be held. It is interesting to find Junius Mauricus, brother of Junius Herennius Senecio, and condemned with him under Domitian, on the council. Veiento and Messalinus were notorious as Domitianic counsellors and informers (Juvenal, *Satire* 4). Mauricus' point, boldly and justly made, was that politicians were more adaptable and the change in regime less absolute than men (like Y. Pliny) made out.

T19   Emperors carried in public

Before you, emperors, out of contempt for us and perhaps through fear of being on a level with us had lost the use of their feet. Therefore the shoulders and necks of slaves bore them above our heads.

[Pliny the Younger, *Panegyric to Trajan* 24.5]

Y. Pliny is praising Trajan for instituting the equivalent of the 'royal walkabout' (first done by Queen Elizabeth II in 1970). Suetonius noted Domitian's preference for being carried in a litter, including on campaign (*Dom.* 19). For Pliny the Elder's regular use of a litter, praised by his nephew, see **R14**.

T20   Adulation of Domitian in games, theatre and senate-house

Is there any place remaining which is ignorant of that pathetic adulation, when praises of the emperor were celebrated in games and showy speeches, were performed in dance and were broken down into every sort of mockery with unmanly wails, rhythms and movements? But the real disgrace was that praise was bestowed simultaneously in the senate house and on the stage, by hack-actor and by consul.

[Pliny the Younger, *Panegyric to Trajan* 54.1]

Domitian actually seems to have shared Y. Pliny's dislike of such shows, expelling a senator for such behaviour (Suet. *Dom.* 8.3), and banishing *pantomimi* (below).

T21 Banishment of *pantomimi*

[46.1] What terror could be strong enough to bring about what has been brought about by respect for you? Someone managed to get the Roman people to put up with the shows of *pantomimi* being taken away, but did not manage to get them to support it. [2] You were asked to do what he had done by force, and so what had been forced on the people became a favour granted to them. Indeed there was universal support both for the demand that your father should restore the *pantomimi* and that you should remove them. [3] Both demands were correct. For it was right to restore what a bad emperor had taken away, and right for the restored *pantomimi* to be removed.

[Pliny the Younger, *Panegyric to Trajan* 46.1–3]

Pantomimi acted the whole of a mythological story, without words, through dance and gestures. Quintilian (11.3.88) provides a contemporary account of their great skill. They were very popular, but like other Roman actors were often associated with immorality (e.g. Suet. *Aug.* 45.4), and in particular, effeminacy. So Y. Pliny ought to (and doubtless did at the time) approve their expulsion by Domitian. But in a wonderful example of Orwellian 'doublethink' he here condemns their expulsion (by a bad emperor), approves their recall, and approves their expulsion (by a good emperor),

T22 Senate frightened into silence

[3] Who previously dared to speak or open his mouth, except those poor people who were first asked? The rest, stunned into silence, endured being forced to give silent agreement, staying in their seats, tortured in mind and in terror of keeping their bodies intact. [4] One man alone used to give his opinion, which all followed and all thought wrong, especially the man whose opinion it had been. So nothing is so despised by everyone as things which take place as if everyone supports them. [5] Perhaps the emperor feigned some respect while actually in the senate house, but once outside, he immediately reverted to being emperor and used to cast off, neglect and despise all his duties as a consul. [6] But Trajan as consul, as if this were his only office, thinks nothing beneath him which is not beneath a consul.

[Pliny the Younger, *Panegyric to Trajan* 76.3–6]

T23 The years of repression under Domitian

[2.3] We have certainly produced a great example of passiveness; just as a former age saw the last word in freedom, so we have seen the last word in servility, since cross-examinations have robbed us of even the exchange of speaking and listening. We would have lost memory itself, alongside speech, if it had been equally possible for us to forget as to be silent.

[3.1] Now at last consciousness returns: right at the first birth of the most blessed age, Nerva Caesar mixed things once incompatible – the principate and liberty, and day by day Nerva Trajan increases the happiness of the times, and public security has not only framed hopes and prayers but has assumed confidence and strength from the prayers themselves. And yet, despite all this, by the nature of human frailty, cures are slower than the ills themselves. So just as our bodies grow slowly but are quickly extinguished, so our talents and enthusiasms are more easily crushed than revived: in fact a sort of sweet inertia comes over us, and inaction is first hated, but eventually loved.

[3.2] Does it matter if, for fifteen years, a large part of our human life-span, most have perished, by the vicissitudes of fates, and all the most prominent, by the emperor's savagery? Or if in the meanwhile a few of us have survived not only the others, but also ourselves, so to speak, though so many years have been taken from the best part of our lives – youths have reached old age, the old have reached almost the limits of the span of life, in silence. [3.3] Nonetheless I shall not regret having composed a record of our former slavery and an eye-witness account of or present fortunes, even in an unpolished and rough style. In the meantime this book is intended to honour Agricola, my father-in-law, and may be praised, or at least excused, as a public expression of filial devotion.

[Tacitus, *Agricola* 2.3–3.2]

In the introduction to his biography of his father-in-law Agricola, Tacitus provides this summary of the senate under Domitian as experienced by both Agricola and himself. The silencing of the senate was in terms of politics and literature (for the preceding passage, see **P11a**).

T24   The senate forgets how to operate

Since you are equally knowledgeable in both civil and political law, including that part of the constitution concerning the senate, I wish especially to hear from you whether or not I recently made a mistake in the senate. Not as regards what happened (for that is too late) but really so that I might know should something similar happen in the future. [2] You will say, "Why ask on a matter which you ought to know about anyway?" The slavery of previous times brought it about that we have forgotten and become ignorant of the laws concerning the senate as it did with all other excellent skills. [3] For who is there who is so patient as to want to learn what he would not be in a position to use? Besides, it is difficult to retain what you learn unless you practise it. So liberty restored finds us ignorant and inexperienced: eager to taste its sweetness we are forced to do certain things before we know what to do. ...

[7] We, when young, were certainly in the army camp; but then courage was suspected, and idleness received rewards; generals had no authority, and soldiers no respect; nowhere was there control, nowhere obedience; everywhere there was unrestrained licence, confusion, and even disorder; finally it was a time to forget rather than remember. [8] In the same way I watched the senate, but a senate frightened and speechless at a time when it was dangerous to speak one's mind, but pitiful to do the opposite. What could be learned from this, or what pleasure was there in learning, when the senate was called either to the greatest triviality or to the most terrible crimes and when they were kept for some ludicrous reason or a sorrowful one, never to make serious decisions, but often to make tragic ones? [9] We watched these same evils, as senators, and even as partners in them, and we put up with them for many years. They dulled and broke and crushed our spirits even into the present time. [10] It is only recently – for all time seems shorter the happier it is – that it was pleasing to have knowledge of our status and pleasing to practise that knowledge. For these reasons I can more justly ask you, in the first place, to pardon my mistake (if indeed there was one), and next, to remedy it by your knowledge: for you have always been concerned to examine the laws of your country, both in its public and private aspects, its ancient and modern, its uncommon and usual applications.

[Pliny the Younger, *Letters* 8.14.1–3, 7–10]

This actually forms only the introduction to the point of procedure on which Y. Pliny wished to consult Titius Aristo, a well-known legal expert. The case was in AD 105. Y. Pliny seems to have been legally wrong about the procedure he got the senate to adopt, though morally right in averting punishment for freedmen of a consul, apparently murdered by his slaves. So his letter both excuses his error in law (here) and vaunts his justice, mercy and persuasiveness (the rest of the letter).

T25   Domitian's envy of military success

[39.1] As was usual for Domitian, he received news of this course of events with a pleased expression but an anxious mind, even though Agricola had not added any boastful claims in his letters. He was conscious that his recent false triumph over Germany had exposed him to mockery, with men having been bought at markets whose clothes and hair had been made to look like that of captured prisoners: and now a real and great victory, involving many thousands of enemy dead and great glory, was to be celebrated. [39.2] It was a source of great fear to him that the names of private individuals should be raised above the emperor: it was no use for public speaking and the glory of civilian skills to have been driven to silence if someone else were to seize military fame. However much other qualities could quite easily be ignored, that of being a good general belonged to the emperor. [39.3] Disturbed by such worries, which indicated his savage thoughts, and taking his fill of his usual seclusion, he decided it was best to store up his hatred for the present, until the momentum of his fame and popularity among the troops should die down: for Agricola was still then in command of Britannia.

[Tacitus, *Agricola* 39.1–3]

Jealousy of successful generals by bad emperors is something of a theme with Tacitus, with Corbulo being feared by Claudius (*Ann.* 11.19–20: " 'Lucky the commanders of former times!' Corbulo remarked") and recalled to be killed by Nero. The events of AD 68/9 must have made emperors wary of over-popular generals. But there is not much to suggest that Domitian acted irrationally or out of jealousy in recalling Agricola in AD 84/5, since 'he had already served for an unprecedented time in Britain and could not in the normal course of events have anticipated another command' (Ogilvie & Richmond, *Commentary*).

T26   Agricola's return and deliberate low profile

[40.1] Therefore an honorary triumph and the honour of a triumphal statue, and anything else was awarded, instead of a triumph; many words in his honour were piled up, Domitian commanded that there should be a senatorial decree and that a suggestion be added that Agricola would be marked down for the province of Syria, which was then vacant because of the death of the ex-consul, Atilius Rufus, and reserved for the most senior figures. [40.2] Many people believed that a freedman was sent from the emperor's innermost circle to take written instructions to Agricola giving him Syria, with instructions to deliver them to him if he were in Britain. The freedman encountered Agricola in the English Channel, and without having spoken to Agricola, returned to Domitian. It is not clear whether this was true or a story based on the character of the emperor. [40.3] Meanwhile Agricola had handed over to his successor a province that was safe and peaceful. To prevent his return being marked by a large and distinguished crowd greeting him, he avoided what was owed to him by his friends by coming to Rome at night, and by night to the Palatine, as he had been instructed. He was welcomed by a brief kiss, and without conversation, and was put together with a crowd of officials. [40.4] Yet to downplay his military reputation, unpopular with civilians, by his other qualities, he took his fill of peaceful existence and leisure: he was modest in dress, easy to talk to, and went about accompanied by only one or two of his friends. The result was that most people, who tend to estimate great men by their outward appearance, having seen him and his life-style, questioned his reputation; only a few understood correctly.

[Tacitus, *Agricola* 40]

T27 Dangers of palace gossip

[41.1] At the time he was daily accused in his absence before Domitian, and, in his absence, acquitted. The cause of danger was no charge or complaint of anyone who had been injured, but an emperor who was hostile to virtue, the reputation of a hero, and – the worst group of enemies – those who praised him.

(At this point Tacitus mentions popular calls for Agricola
to be sent to the Danube in the wake of
defeats there – see N36)

[41.4] It is generally agreed that Domitian's ears were also assailed by such talk, since all the freedmen egged on an emperor inclined to the worse course: the best did so out of love and loyalty to him, the worst out of hatred and spite. So Agricola was being driven by his own qualities and the faults of others alike to that dangerous level of prominence.

[Tacitus, *Agricola* 41]

T28 Revival of the Roman army under Trajan

What an impressive thing it is that when army discipline had declined and died, you have revived it, by banishing the evils of the previous age, laziness, insolence and contempt for authority! It is safe to earn respect and affection, and no general fears being hated by his men, or being loved by them. And so, without having to worry about giving offence or currying favour, they can press on with engineering works, be present at training exercises, take care of weapons, fortification and troops. For this is not an emperor who thinks that preparations made to attack the enemy are actually aimed at himself: that was the tendency of those who were afraid of foreign campaigns even as they made them. So they were happy to see a decline in enthusiasm for military life, to see a slackening both physically and mentally, to see swords become dull and blunt through lack of use. Our generals lived in fear, not of being ambushed by foreign kings, but by their own emperor; not of the swords in the hands of the enemy but of their own men.

[Pliny the Younger, *Panegyric to Trajan* 18.1–3]

Y. Pliny's picture of generals fearful Domitian's jealousy mirrors Tacitus', but not as independent confirmation. Domitian had certainly been popular with the legionaries (Suet. *Dom.* 23.1). Trajan's military leadership was later immortalised in the scenes on Trajan's column.

T29   The emperor as heir

[43.3] On his final day, it was known that changes in the condition of the dying man were reported by messengers already in place, and no one believed that anyone sorry to hear such news would want it brought more quickly. Domitian, however, assumed an appearance of grief in his manner and expression, being now free to hate and better able to conceal joy than fear. [43.4] It is well known that when Agricola's will was read, in which he named Domitian as his heir, alongside his excellent wife and most dutiful daughter, that he was delighted as if this showed Agricola's respect and favourable judgement. Constant adulation had so blinded and corrupted him that he was unaware that a good father would only name a bad emperor as heir.

[Tacitus, *Agricola* 43.3–4]

Though Tacitus, husband of Agricola's heir, complains, it had long been Roman practice to give legacies widely (e.g. to patrons or lawyers). The practice was quickly extended to the emperor (Augustus received 1.4 billion sesterces – Suet. *Aug.* 101.3), and might be thought of as not unlike UK inheritance tax (40% on legacies above £325,000 in 2015). But Nero could confiscate the whole estate of those he felt had left him nothing or an insufficient amount (Suet. *Nero* 32.2 – and compare Tac. *Ann.* 16.11). Domitian refused legacies for several years, but took them to boost his resources (Suet. *Dom.* 9.1 and 12.1).

T30   Wills now safe under Trajan

Our wills are now safeguarded: one man is not everyone's heir, either because he has been named or because he has not been named.

[Pliny the Younger, *Panegyric* 43.1]

DAMNATIO MEMORIAE AND ITS CONSEQUENCES: T31–T38

Suetonius, *Domitian* 23 records the senate gleefully decreeing that Domitian's name should be abolished, in other words that his names, Domitian and the *agnomen* Germanicus, had to be removed from public buildings (see also **K25, T6** and individual examples listed in Index of Themes). As a result deep chisel marks marred many inscribed monuments. In nearly all cases, the removed names were left blank, although the titles were often sufficient to indicate the identity of the individual. This is helpful in understanding the objective of *damnatio memoriae*; its aim was not merely to remove and/or forget a name (as the term *abolutio nominis* may suggest) but to monumentalise a person's dishonour. The removal of names also illustrates the personal in nature of the act; the titles and offices of imperial power (e.g. *imperator*, Caesar, consul) were left untouched.

The official condemnation of an emperor made it vital to careerists to distance themselves from the previous regime as quickly and emphatically as possible. This is brilliantly satirised by Juvenal, *Satire* 10.85–8 (=LACTOR 19, P4j): "Quick, let's make a dash for it. While the corpse is still lying exposed by the river, we'll put the boot hard into Caesar's opponent. But always make sure that we're seen by the slaves in case one should deny that we did it." Juvenal had not seen the fall of Sejanus (AD 23), the ostensible subject, but he *had* seen the fall of Domitian and the behaviour of people like Pliny the Younger (**T33–T34, P11f, P11g**), the advantage now to be gained from claims of previous persecution (**T35–T37**, also **P10**), and the opprobrium poured on those associated with the regime.

T31   Inscription showing *damnatio memoriae*

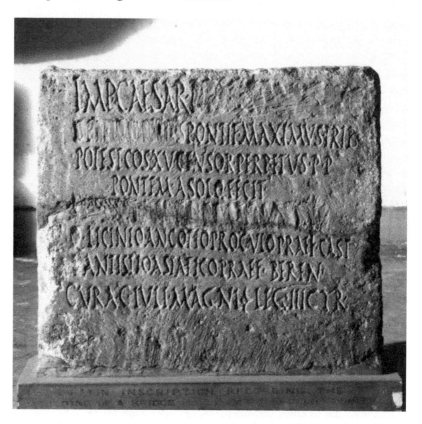

For translation of the text, recording a new bridge at Oift in Egypt, see **M31**. The stone is 58.42 cm high and 71.12 cm wide. BM 1894, 1105.1. As well as Domitian's name in lines 1–2, that of a prefect of Egypt has been removed from line 5 (probably Mettius Rufus, see **P9**).

T32   Domitian's statues melted down

Therefore those few bronze statues of you remain and shall remain as long as the temple itself, while those countless golden ones lie in wrack and ruin, sacrificed to public rejoicing. It was delightful to smash those utterly arrogant faces on the ground, to strike them with swords, to hack at them with axes as if each blow could draw blood and pain. [5] No one, in joy and long-delayed happiness, could hold back from seeing as a form of vengeance the hacked arms and torn-off limbs; then finally those grim and fearsome features cast into and melted down by the fires, so that that object of terror and dread might be changed by the flames into something of use or delight for mankind.

[Pliny the Younger, *Panegyric to Trajan* 52.4–5]

T33 Pliny the Younger's 'narrow escape' from death under Domitian

[12] I have a freedman named Marcus, who is not uneducated. One night, his younger brother was sleeping in the same bed with him. He seemed to see somebody sitting on the bed, who moved a pair of scissors towards his head, and even cut off some hair from the top of his head. When morning came, they found the top of the boy's head was shaved, and the hair was found lying on the floor. [13] A short while later this was confirmed by another similar event. A slave boy of mine was sleeping with several others in their quarters. Two persons dressed in white tunics came in (so he tells the story) through the windows, cut off his hair as he lay in bed, and left the same way they entered. Daylight revealed that this boy too had been shaved, and that his hair was scattered around the room. [14] Nothing remarkable followed, unless that I avoided being put on trial; I would have been, if Domitian (in whose reign these things happened) had lived any longer. For details provided by Carus against me were found in his writing-desk. Therefore it may be guessed, since it is the custom for the accused to let their hair grow, that this cutting of my slaves' hair was a sign that the danger which threatened was removed.

[Pliny the Younger, *Letters* 7.27.12–14]

Y. Pliny is writing to Licinius Sura, Trajan's right-hand man, about ghost stories, and taking the chance to claim to this fellow former protégé of Domitian, and his wider readership that he not been favoured by Domitian (compare stories spread about Nerva (Dio 67.15.5–6 = **D15**, **P10**) and by Y. Pliny about Trajan), but narrowly avoided prosecution by Mettius Carus, a notorious informer (**P11b–d**).

T34 Pliny the Younger claims almost to have fallen victim to Domitian

That destroyer and killer of every honest man had been breathing down the necks of both Tertullus and me through the slaughter of our friends and the thunderbolt hurled near us. For we rejoiced to have the same friends and together mourned their loss.

[Pliny the Younger, *Panegyric to Trajan* 90.5]

For C. Julius Cornutus Tertullus was friend and fellow-consul of Y. Pliny, see *Letters* 5.14 and **U34**.

T35 Trajan almost a victim of Domitian (according to Pliny the Younger)

[1] I pray to you especially, Capitoline Jupiter … [3] The safety of the emperor is the simple, all-embracing prayer of all. And it is no new care we entrust to you. For you took him under your protection previously when you snatched him from the jaws of that most greedy criminal. For when all those of highest position were being shaken, he who was loftier than all could not have stood undamaged without your help. He was overlooked by the worst emperor, but could not be overlooked by the best.

[Pliny the Younger, *Panegyric to Trajan* 94.1 and 3]

T36 Dio of Prusa exiled by Domitian, an 'evil spirit'

[1] My fellow citizens, I wish to give you an account of my time abroad … how I endured being hated, not by one or other of my equals, or peers as they are sometimes called, but by the strongest and most important person, called 'master and god' by all Greeks and foreigners, but in reality an evil spirit. Yet even so I did not flatter him nor deprecate his hatred, but challenged him head on and, by Zeus, I am not only just starting to speak and write about the consequent troubles: no, I have long spoken and written about them, in speeches and writings published everywhere, not driven to do

so by madness or desperation, but trusting in a stronger power and in help from the gods, even though many men scorn this as of no use. [2] But I think that speaking of these things in detail is unnecessary, given that they are well recognised by others and have fitting glory and reputation. But if I were to go through with you my time in exile, people would say I am not lamenting but boasting. When that man died and there was a change of regime, I intended to see the excellent Nerva. But I was prevented by a serious illness and missed the chance completely, losing an emperor who was kind to all, and was in former times well-disposed to me and my friend.

[Dio of Prusa (Dio Chrysostom), *Orations* 45.1–2/28.1–2 (*Perseus Text*)]

T37   Acquittal of Julius Bassus, exiled by Domitian

[1] For the past few days Julius Bassus has speaking in his defence. He is a troubled man and well known for his misfortunes. He was accused during Vespasian's time by two private individuals; the case was referred to the senate, and for a long time he was in suspense, but finally found innocent and acquitted. [2] Because he had been a friend of Domitian, he was afraid of Titus; but was then banished by Domitian; he was recalled by Nerva, appointed by lot to governor Bithynia, and put on trial on his return. He was accused violently but defended no less loyally.

(*Pliny describes his own speech as defence counsel and those of his colleagues and opponents. Bassus was condemned, but allowed to remain a senator.*)

[22] When the court rose, Bassus was welcomed by a great, noisy and joyful crowd of people. What had worked in his favour was bringing to mind again story of his hazardous past, his reputation for having faced dangers, and the effects of old age, trouble and poverty on his tall figure.

[Pliny the Younger, *Letters* 4.9.1–2 and 22]

The trial and Y. Pliny's letter can be securely dated to early AD 103. It is the earliest reference to bad feeling between Domitian and Titus. It is also clear that Pliny could use Bassus' 'persecution' by Domitian to gain sympathy for him within the senate where his trial was held. Bassus was clearly guilty, as Pliny admits (4.9.7, 4.9.17) and his acts as governor were repealed: Pliny omits this, but it emerges from a letter to Trajan (10.56).

T38   Pliny the Younger on the death of Regulus' son

Regulus has lost his son; this is the one misfortune which he did not deserve because I have no idea whether he thinks it was a misfortune. The boy was intelligent and sharp, if untrustworthy, and could have followed the right course if he did not take after his father. [2] Regulus declared him free from his parental control so that he might inherit his mother's property. However, after selling him as property like a slave (for that is how it was commonly described, as in keeping with the character of the man) he tried to win him over by a disgraceful pretence of indulgence, not normal in a parent. Incredible, I know, but consider this was Regulus. [3] He grieves, however, now that he is dead, like a mad man. The boy had a number of ponies, both harnessed and unharnessed for riding; he had larger and smaller dogs, nightingales, parrots and blackbirds – all these Regulus slaughtered around his funeral pyre. [4] That was not grief, but really a display of grief. A remarkable number of people are now calling on him – they all detest and hate him, but, as if they approve and love him, they hurry to crowd around him. To explain what I think briefly: in paying attention to Regulus, they are behaving just like Regulus. [5] He stays in his gardens across the

Tiber, where he has covered a very wide area with enormous porticoes, and filled the bank with statues of himself; for, despite his great meanness he is extravagant, and despite his great notoriety he is boastful and conceited. [6] Therefore, in this, the most unhealthy time of the year, he is annoying the city, and, he thinks it a consolation to annoy everyone. He says he wants to marry, and this again, like everything else, for the wrong reason. [7] It will not be long before you hear that the mourner is married, that the old man is married: for the mourner marriage is too early, for the old man, too late. You might ask where I might get my prediction from; [8] It is not because he declares this openly – for no one lies more than he does – but because it is certain that Regulus will do whatever ought not to be done. Farewell.

[Pliny the Younger, *Letter* 4.2]

An unpleasant letter to have written, let alone published. Regulus had achieved wealth, power and position by prosecutions under Nero (Tac. *Hist.* 4.42, where his prosecutor claims he had gained seven million sesterces). But Y. Pliny's enmity is personal, deriving from Regulus' feud with the Stoics (**P11d**). Pliny accuses Regulus of legacy-hunting (2.20), and mocks him for writing a biography of his son (4.7), but misses him grudgingly after his death (6.2). For Martial's much more favourable view, see **U39**.

T39 Nerva restores liberty, AD 96

To Liberty restored by Emperor Nerva Caesar Augustus, on 18 September, in the 848th year from the founding of the city. The Senate and People of Rome.

[Rome: MW 66 = *ILS* 274 = = EDCS–17300624]

T40 Nerva and Public Liberty, *aureus*, AD 96

Obv: Head of Nerva, laureate, right
        IMP NERVA CAES AVG PM TR P COS II PP (Emperor Nerva Caesar Augsutus, *pontifex maximus,* tribunician power, consul twice, father of the fatherland)
Rev: Liberty, standing, left, holding cap of liberty and sceptre
        LIBERTAS PVBLICA (Public Liberty)
            [*BMCRE* 3, page 3, no 16 = *RIC* 2 (1st ed.) Nerva 7 = BM no. 1867,0101.649]

Coins of Nerva and Public Liberty are known in all denominations and for all three calendar years of Nerva's reign.

T41   The Edict of the Emperor Nerva
'Doubtlessly, there are some matters, citizens of Rome, which the simple happiness of
our times makes clear; nor must a good emperor be expected to make a declaration of
intentions on matters which are sufficiently understood; each one of my citizens does
not need reminding of my pledge and can be sure that, when I gave up my peaceful
retirement for the security of the state, I did so to confer new benefits of my own, and
preserve those granted by emperors before me. [8] However, to avoid any uncertainty
in the public rejoicing, either through the lack of confidence of those who received
benefits or the memory of whoever provided them, I believed it equally necessary and
even pleasing to me to dispel these doubts with my indulgence. [9] I do not want any
man to think that I shall cancel a privilege gained under a previous emperor, either
private or public, so that he may be under an obligation to me for its restoration; let it
all be settled and fixed; nor need any on whom imperial good fortune has looked with
favour, repeat his request to confirm his happiness. Let the citizens allow me the time
to confer new benefits, and let them know finally that they need ask for only those
things which they do not yet have.'

Letter from the same to Tullius Justus

[10] 'Since there is a regulation that all acts begun or completed in previous reigns
should be confirmed, the letters of Domitian must, therefore, remain valid.'

[Pliny the Younger, *Letters* 10.58]

The edict explicitly entitled 'Edict of the Emperor Nerva' is quoted in the correspondence of Y. Pliny as part
of a dispute about Roman citizenship which he refers to the emperor Trajan. This seems to be an extract
from a more general edict. It does not actually say very much, ('feeble and verbose' Syme, *Tacitus* 1; 'turgid'
Sherwin-White, *Pliny Commentary*) but clearly hopes that people would be appeased by privileges confirmed.

T42   Anarchy worse than tyranny
In the midst of the chaos arising from everyone bringing accusations against everyone
else, the consul Fronto is reported to have said that while it is bad to have an emperor
under whom nobody could do anything, it is worse to have one under whom anybody
could do anything. Nerva heard this and ordered that all this should be stopped.

[Dio-Xiphilinus 68.1.3]

The wise consul was Ti. Catius Caesius Fronto.

SECTION U
THE UPPER CLASSES

Some attained priesthoods and consulships as the spoils
of war, others official positions or inside influence.

[Tacitus, *Histories* 1.2.3]

Introduction: Augustus had established clear regulations for senatorial and equestrian orders. Claudius had seen the need to replenish the senate and patriciate (Tac. *Ann.* 11.24–5), a need that became more pressing after the civil wars. Vespasian's censorship replenished the senate from Italian equestrian ranks (see **H52–H55, K98,** and various figures below from **U23** to **U47**), but he remained proud of his equestrian ancestry (Suet. *Vesp.* 2.2). and the Flavian period saw some erosion of the distinction between traditional senatorial and equestrian positions. Titus was praetorian prefect (**H49–H50**); prefects of Egypt are made consuls, **U43**; equestrians begin to replace freedmen in the imperial secretariats. The *consilium principis* increases in importance and semi-official status, and comprises members of both classes. This chapter thus starts with likely or certain members of that body under the Flavians, before listing prominent consuls by year of office, other senators and then important equestrians. The senatorial *cursus* is set out at **U33f**, illustrating the careers of Tacitus and Y. Pliny.

AMICI PRINCIPIS: U1–U11

An *amicus principis*, literally and originally 'friend of the emperor' became effectively a title for the dozen or so members who regularly advised the emperor as part of his *consilium*, 'council' or 'cabinet'. The best description of the *consilium principis* in operation is provided by Juvenal's satire on Domitian, *Satire* 4, given in section G, including brief biographies of the advisers. Some had been in position since Nero's day. Further information on them is found in **U2–5.** For Pliny the Elder as *amicus principis* see **R14**.7

U1   'Friends of the Emperor' demeaning friendship's name

At that time, even in the hearts of private citizens, friendship, that ancient human gift, had faded away and flattery and sycophancy had moved into its place along with a pretence of love that is worse than real hatred. Furthermore in the emperors' palace, only the name of friendship remained, empty of meaning and mocked.

[Pliny the Younger, *Panegyric to Trajan* 85.1]

U2   Vibius Crispus, cos III 83

In our own day, Vibius Crispus, a man of witty and elegant intellect, cleverly defeated this method by saying "I certainly will not say that – what would be the point of saying that again?"

[Quintilian, *The Orator's Education* 5.13.48]

Q. Vibius Crispus (*PIR* V 379, Jones, *Domitian* 57–58) was consul under three different emperors, probably in 61, then 74 and 83. Tacitus described his as 'for his wealth, power, and talent, regarded as famous rather than virtuous' (*Hist.* 2.10), but others (e.g. Quintilian below and Suet. *Dom.* 3.1) were more appreciative of the author of the witticism that 'no one was with Domitian, not even a fly' quoted by several historians (**J10g** with note). Juvenal places him second on Domitian's council (*Sat.* 4.80–92 – **Section G**) with a not unkind description. Quintilian is speaking of the sort of tricks used by barristers – one being to pre-empt one's opponent, e.g. "The prosecutor will say that ..." to which Vibius produced the neat interruption above. Quintilian preserves two other clever sayings of Crispus – 8.5.15, 8.5.17. At 10.1.119 he mentions Vibius Crispus among "famous talents in our lifetime" saying he was "skilful, pleasant and born to please, but better in private cases than in public ones." He also refers to Crispus' wit/pleasantness in a brief list (12.10.11) of the best features of the best speakers.

GAIUS LICINIUS MUCIANUS, COS III 72: U3a–e

Mucianus served under Corbulo in Armenia in AD 58 (**U3a**, Tac. *Ann.* 13.34–41), governed Lycia (**R8, U3b**) before being appointed to Syria, where his four legions and backing for Vespasian were instrumental in putting him on the throne (**U3c**). Sent to march on Rome, he took control of the city for Vespasian (*Hist.* 4.11), gaining consulships in AD 70 and 72 (after a first, under Nero, *c.* 64). He wrote various books (**R7, R8**), dying shortly before the publication of Pliny's *Natural History* in AD 77. Mucianus' name has been found on lead water pipes at Aricia in Latium (MW 259) and also in Rome (*AE* 2010, 140)

U3a   Mucianus with Corbulo in Armenia

The source of the Euphrates is in Caranitis, in the prefecture of Greater Armenia, as is reported by those who have seen it at first hand, Domitius Corbulo placing it at Mount Aga, Licinius Mucianus at the bottom of a mountain he calls Capotes.

[Pliny, *Natural History* 5.83]

U3b   Mucianus honoured as proconsul, Oenoanda in Lycia

Gaius Licinius Mucianus, agent of Nero Claudius Caesar Augustus Germanicus, proconsul: Hermaios Diogenes, natural son of Silleos, honours his benefactor.

[MW 258 = *ILS* 8816]

U3c   Tacitus' character sketch of Mucianus

The East was still quiet. Licinius Mucianus was holding Syria and four legions. He was notorious both in prosperity and adversity. As a young man he had ambitiously sought the friendship of men of note. Before long he had exhausted his fortune and his position was parlous, and even Claudius was thought to be hostile: shut off in a remote part of Asia he was as near to being in exile as later he was to being emperor. [2] He was a mixture of self-indulgence and hard work, courtesy and arrogance, good and bad qualities. When he was idle, he was too fond of enjoying himself; but whenever he went on campaign, his courage was great. You would praise his public life, but bad things were reported about his private life. By various manoeuvrings he was a force to be reckoned with in dealing with subordinates, peers and colleagues, and he found it preferable to bestow rule on another than to hold it himself.

[Tacitus, *Histories* 1.10.1–2]

Tacitus also compares Mucianus and Vespasian at *Hist.* 2.5, and features him prominently throughout the extant *Histories*.

U3d   Mucianus' vices

The fact was that Mucianus longed to be admired by all men, and more than all other men. He used to be infuriated not only by direct insults, however small, but also by anyone's failure to praise him to the skies. As a result he was as extravagant in his praises for those who assisted him in any way, however small, as he was ferociously vindictive towards all those who failed to do so.

[*On Virtues and Vices,* Valesius' Excerpts 272 = Dio 66.2.4]

This character-sketch of Mucianus is not found in Xiphilinus, but in a selection of excerpts 'On Virtues and Vices' in the 'Excerpta Valesiana'. It is certainly by Dio, but does not easily fit at 2.4 where the first modern editor of Dio placed it. Dio also attributed to him an attack on philosophers (**P1k**).

U3e   Vespasian's dig at Mucianus

For example, he nimbly deflected Licinius Mucianus, with whose help he had come
to power, and who was arrogantly confident of what he thought was owed to him, by
saying simply, to someone who was present and a close friend of both of them, "You
know that I'm a man."

[*Epitome de Caesaribus* 9.3]

The Epitome gives this as an example of Vespasian's wit. Suetonius, *Vespasian* 13 reports the same story,
also hinted at by Tacitus, *Histories* 1.10.1 (**U3c**)

T. CLODIUS EPRIUS MARCELLUS, COS II 74: U4a–b

Eprius Marcellus was praetor for one day in 48 (Tac. *Ann.* 12.4) and legate of Lycia, where he was
corruptly acquitted of extortion (Tac. *Ann.* 13.33). His first consulship was around 62. He became notorious
for prosecutions under Nero, especially of Thrasea Paetus in 66 (Tac. *Ann.* 16.22 and 28–9), leading to
unsuccessful attempts by Paetus' son-in-law, Helvidius Priscus to prosecute him after Nero's fall (Tac. *Hist.*
4.6–8, **P1d–e**). Tacitus refers to him at *Histories* 2.95 as Vespasian's chief henchman along with Mucianus,
and he was rewarded with the coveted governorship of Asia for an unusual three-year period (**U4b**), and
a second consulship in 74. His career ended abruptly in 78 when accused of conspiracy against Vespasian
(Dio = **C16b**). As well as the inscription from Cyprus (**U4b**), Marcellus' governorship of Asia is also known
from a statue-base at Dorylaeum in 72 (MW 272) and coins from Sardis (*RPC* 1305) and Cyme (BMC
Aeolis p114, no 99).

U4a   Eprius Marcellus makes his career and fortune through oratory

I would contend that Eprius Marcellus whom I just spoke of and Vibius Crispus (I
prefer to use as examples recent and up to date cases rather than ancient and forgotten
ones) are no less well known in the most remote parts of the world than they are at
Capua or Vercellae, where they are said to have been born. And it's not the former's
two, or the latter's three hundred million sesterces that marks them out, though these
riches themselves could be seen to have been the product of their eloquence, but
rather their very eloquence, whose divine and supernatural force had produced over
the centuries very many examples of men reaching the heights of fortune by dint of
their talents; but these most recent examples are one we can see with our own eyes
rather than knowing by hearsay. The more lowly and humbly born they were, and the
more exceptional the poverty and deprivation that surrounded them at birth, the better
and more striking examples they provide to show the usefulness of oratory: with no
advantages of birth, with no financial resources, neither of them men of character, and
one of them contemptible in physical appearance, they have been now, for many years,
the most powerful figures in the state – holding pride of place in the courts, when
they so wished, and now pride of place in Caesar's friendship. They carry everything
before them and are loved by the emperor with a certain respect, since Vespasian, that
respected old gentleman who sets much store by the truth, knows well that certain
other of his friends rely on what they have received from him and which he could
easily store up and pile on others; but Marcellus and Crispus bring to his friendship
something they have not been given and could not be given by anyone.

[Tacitus, *Dialogue on Oratory,* 8]

U4b   Clodius Marcellus honoured by Cyprus

To T. Clodius Eprius Marcellus, son of Marcus, of the Falerna tribe, twice consul, augur, *curio maximus, sodalis Augustalis,* praetor, proconsul of Asia 3 years running – the province of Cyprus (erected this).

[MW 271 = *ILS* 992 = EDCS–47600057]

The position of *curio maximus* was very prestigious priesthood which Eprius had held since AD 61 (Rüpke, *Fasti Sacerdotum* pages 11 and 192ff.). The dedication was presumably a statue.

U5   L. Tampius Flavianus, cos 45, cos II 76

[L. Tampius F]lavi[anus …] proconsul of the p[rovince …], propraetorian [imperial legate] of Pann[onia, Wa]ter [Commisioner …, …triu]mphal ornament[s …] hostages from tran[s-Danube …] with all the […] to become subject to [tax]ation […] L. Tampius Rufus (erected this).

[MW 274, *ILS* 985 updated by *AE* 2010.67 = EDCS–20800178]

Honoured with a statue at Fundi in Latium, Flavianus was 'a rich old man' (Tac. *Hist.* 2.86), governing Pannonia in 69, where he was unequal to coping with mutinous troops (*Hist.* 3.4, 3.10). His name and province form the last words before the manuscripts of Tacitus' *Histories* fail, but nothing in the existing account suggests why he should have been awarded triumphal ornaments, or even a second consulship in 76 (**B76**) and the prestigious post of Water Commissioner (Frontinus, **K77**).

U6   Ti. Plautius Silvanus Aelianus, cos II 74, city prefect

While legate in Spain he was recalled to hold the city prefecture, and in his prefecture the senate honoured him with triumphal decorations, at the instigation of Emperor Caesar Augustus Vespasian in words from his speech which are written below:

"He governed Moesia so well that the honour of his triumphal decorations should not have been deferred to my time, except that by a delay a more distinguished title fell to his lot as city prefect." Emperor Caesar Augustus Vespasian made him consul for a second time during his tenure as city prefect.

[*ILS* 986 = EDCS–05801598*]

The inscription forms the last part of the epitaph from the imposing family mausoleum at Tibur (Tivoli, near Rome). For the full inscription, including details of Plautius' earlier career, see LACTOR 19, U3.

PLOTIUS PEGASUS: U7a–c

Pegasus was a distinguished lawyer, with two pieces of legislation (Gaius 1.31 and 2.254) known to date from his consulship (unknown date, early in Vespasian's reign). Juvenal gives him rare praise and first place among Domitian's advisers (*Sat.* 4.75–80 = Section G), and an ancient commentator adds interesting personal details, which allow something of his background to be filled in, see **U7c**. Proof of one governship came from discovery of a boundary stone (**U7a**) from Iader in Dalmatia (Zadar, Croatia), where his deputy Petillius Firmus (see **U37**) could have been a relation of Petillius Cerialis. Pegasus was city prefect, probably *c.* 78–84.

U7a   Pegasus, governor of Dalmatia
Gaius Petillius Firm[us], military tribune of Legion IIII, ['Fortunate' and] Flavian, on the authority of Emperor Vespasian, appointed as judge by [L? Plo]tius Pegasus, [propraetorian] l[egate of Emperor] Vespasian [Augustus. He placed boundaries between ...

[*AE* 2001, 1723 = EDCS–09800270]

U7b   Plotius Pegasus, legal expert and city prefect
Proculus was succeeded [as head of the school of law] by Pegasus who was prefect of the city in the times of Vespasian.

[*Digest of Roman Law*, 1.2.2.53]

U7c   Pegasus, 'the book'
Pegasus: he was the son of a naval captain, and got his name from one of his father's warships. His deserved fame from his knowledge of law meant that he was popularly know as 'a book', not a man. He achieved every honour and after governing several provinces took on the role of city prefect.

[Scholia on Juv. 4.77]

U8   Crispinus
When some pleb from the Nile, some Egyptian house-slave,
Crispinus, hitching up his luxury overcoat on his shoulder,
Airs his summer-weight gold ring on his sweating fingers,
... Then it's hard *not* to write satire.

[Juvenal, *Satire* 1.26–8 and 30]

This passage with its famous statement comes as part of Juvenal's 'literary apology' for writing Satire. Crispinus is also a target in *Satire* 4 (**G1**) as sexual pervert, gourmand, and member of the *consilium principis*, probably as praetorian prefect, since he is described as 'head of the equestrian order'. If so this will have heightened typical Roman prejudice against foreigners or freedmen.

U9   Fabricius Veiento, cos II 80
How much do you have to pay Veiento to look at you without saying anything?

[Juvenal, *Satires* 3.184–5]

Fabricius Vei(i)ento held consulships under each of the Flavians, see **B80** and **L36**. As part of Domitian's *consilium* he appears in *Satire* 4 (**G1**) and Statius' *German War* (**G2**). Y. Pliny regards him as one of the worst informers (**T18**). The implication here is that he would take bribes for everything. Juvenal in *Satire* 6.82–113 (part of a famous and very long satire on women) tells the story of Eppia, wife of a senator, who abandoned her husband and children to run off to Egypt with Sergius, a gladiator. Juvenal concludes the account by saying that Sergius was ugly and that once retired he would only be as attractive as Veiento. Either then Veiento was notoriously unattractive, or, much more plausibly and pointedly, he was the husband of Eppia.

C. RUTILIUS GALLICUS, COS II 85: U10a–c

Rutilius Gallicus, cos ?71, cos II 85, is known from an inscription at Ephesus giving his career up to being consul designate, and from a long poem written by Statius to celebrate his recovery from a serious illness shortly after being prefect of the city in AD 89 at the time of Domitian celebrating his Dacian triumph. In AD 92 a *sodalis Augustalis* was co-opted into a vacancy created by his death. For an unconventional analysis of his career, see John Henderson, *A Roman Life: Rutilius Gallicus on Paper and in Stone* (Exeter 1998).

U10a   Inscription of Gallicus' early career, Ephesus

To Gaius Rutilius Gallicus, son of Gaius, of the Stellatine tribe, military tribune of Legion XIII 'Twinned'. Quaestor, curule aedile, legate of Divus Claudius of Legion XV 'Apollo's', praetor, legate of the province of Galatia, *sodalis Augustalis,* consul designate. Marcus Aemilius Pius, son of Marcus, of the Palatine tribe, prefect of cohort I 'Bosporan' and of cohort I 'Spanish', to his legate.

[MW 305 = *ILS* 9499 = EDCS–00400060]

U10b   Statius celebrates Gallicus' recovery from illness

Hurray! You gods exist; the fates can stop their spinning.
Kind Justice guards the good, and reconciled with Jove
Returns to earth, and Gallicus sees months he never
Thought to see. Germanicus, you are most dear
To heaven, as all know well: Fortune blushed to rob you   5
Of so great a helper. ...
The rapid cohorts worshipping our city standards;   9
The laws that rush to you for comfort, worried at
The courts in turmoil; civilised cities everywhere,
Imploring you for justice in long-distant cases;
All now vie in joy, and hills of Rome in turn
Shout out, and let the whispered bad reports fall quiet.
Indeed he stays and long shall stay, restored to life,   15
The gentle wardenship he holds makes Rome feel safe,
So this new age shall make no charge against the fates,
No sin Tarentum's altar, now restored, commit.

[Statius, *Silvae* 1.4.1–6, 9–18]

Statius does not seem to have had any particular relationship with Gallicus, but simply to have written in hope of patronage or other benefit, thus providing an interesting benchmark for flattery of the emperor in other poems. In fact Gallicus had died by the time Statius wrote an introduction to *Silvae* 1 (around AD 91). Gallicus' post as city prefect (line 16) involved command of the four urban cohorts (9) and a special court, which by AD *c.* 200 was judging cases within 100 miles of Rome (12). The 'new age' was that marked by Domitian's celebrations of the *ludi saeculares* in AD 88 traditionally held at a placed named Tarentum (17–18).

U10c   Statius on Gallicus' career

(In the poem Apollo is explaining Gallicus' career to Asclepius)
He offers noble origins to all his forebears   68
Exalts an ancestry not humble but outshone
By future brilliance, pleased to yield to a greater son.   70
Like them he first excelled in court – his speeches brought
Great fame. He served with merit great in countless camps,

Keeping his oath, in east and west, in every land
Where shines the sun. Nor was it granted him to sheathe
His sword or slacken his efforts in times of peace.   75
Galatia boldly dared launch war against him
(Against me too!). For autumns nine, Pamphylia feared him,
Pannonians fierce, Armenians dreaded for their shots
In flight, Araxes too, now subject to a Roman bridge.
Why mention praetorship or two years' rule of mighty   80
Asia, which did wish to keep him three or four?
But greater office called him back – the consulship,
Promised more than once. Why should I sing of Libya's
Marvellous tribute paid, the triumph sent to Rome
From midst of peace, or praise such wealth as he who sent you   85
Never dared expect?   86a
Lake Trasimene, the Alps, and ghosts of Cannae should now   86
All rejoice; the happy ghost of Regulus
Appear as first to note the splendid payment made.
There is no space to tell of Northern armies, nor
Rebellious Rhine, nor captured Veleda's prayers   90
Nor your most recent glory, Gallicus, with Rome placed
In your charge, while Dacians died and you were chosen
To take the reins from such a ruler, as you well deserved.   93

[Statius, *Silvae* 1.4.68–93]

Statius by saying Gallicus gave nobility to his family (lines 68–70) shows that he was the first to reach the consulship. That his forensic oratory helped his rise is shown by 71 and also 23–25 mentioning pleading in the Centumviral court. His military service, known from **U10a** will have been in Pannonia as military tribune and legionary legate. He was legate of Galatia/Pamphylia under Corbulo's general command in the East (hence hyperbolic mention of Armenia and Araxes, lines 78–79). Apollo's sanctuary at Delphi had been attacked by Celts from Galatian in 279 BC (line 77). Two years as proconsul of the prized senatorial province of Asia (lines 80–81) is probably to be explained by early succession after the death of the previous incumbent. Gallicus had conducted the census and established tax-revenues ('tribute') from Libya as legate in 73/4 thus poetically avenging ancient Roman reverses against the Carthaginian empire (lines 86–88). References to Germany (lines 89–90) are confirmed by a diploma of April 78 showing him as legate of Lower Germany (*CIL* 16.23). Gallicus was in charge of the city while Domitian left to campaign in Dacia in AD 89 (lines 91–93). For the poem and his career, see Syme, *RP* 5.514–520 = *Arctos* 1984, 149–56.

M. COCCEIUS NERVA (COS 71, EMPEROR 96–98): U11a–d

Nerva, born *c.* AD 35 was a member of Nero's inner court: both wrote poetry. Nerva was praetor-designate in AD 65 when he was awarded triumphal honours by Nero. These were for unknown services in informing on a conspiracy (Tac. *Ann.* 15.72): 'he had never seen a province or an army' but 'practised that discretion which men called '*quies*' if they approved', (Martial did – **U11c, d**) but sloth or laziness if they did not (Syme, *Tacitus* 1). He continued to serve in Rome as a trusted member of the inner circle (see **U11b** for Y. Pliny being assured that his prosecution of Massa (**M53** and **R31**) had official sanction)

U11a   Portrait bust of M. Cocceius Nerva (John Paul Getty Museum)

U11b   Nerva assures Pliny the Younger that he has official support
Divus Nerva (for he, while still a private citizen, paid attention to any public action
that was right and good) wrote a most serious letter to me, congratulating not only me,
but the age, which had the good fortune to have an example (for that is what he wrote)
so like that of the ancients.

[Pliny the Younger, *Letters* 7.33.9]

For the context of the letter, see **R31** and **M53**.

U11c   Nerva's discretion
        Even if you surpass the Curvius brothers in family loyalty,
        Nerva in discretion (*quies*) … Mauricus in fairness
        Regulus in eloquence …

[Martial, *Epigram* 5.28.3–6 (published December 90)]

U11d   Nerva as a poet, AD 93
        Placid Nerva's eloquent and discreet in equal
        Measure; modesty restrains his force and talent.
        Yet anyone who reads the verse of learned Nero
        Knows Nerva is Tibullus of our present age.

[Martial, *Epigram* 8.70.1–2 and 7–8 (published January 94)]

Tibullus was a younger contemporary of Virgil. In Quintilian's judgement, "Tibullus seems to me the most
refined and elegant writer of elegy." (*The Orator's Education* 10.1.93).

CONSULS (IN ORDER OF THEIR CONSULSHIPS): U12–U34

For consular *fasti* see Section B. For careers of other consuls, see Javolenus Priscus, cos 86 –**M77**; Pomponius Rufus, cos 94, see **H2**.

U12   Calpetanus Rantius Festus, cos 71

To [C.] Calpe[tanus] Rant[ius] Quirinalis [Va]lerius F[estus], son of Publius, of the Pomptine tribe, on the board of four for maintaining roads, [military] tribune of Legion VI 'Victorious', quaestor, [on the board] of six of Roman [equ]estrians, tribune of the people, prae[tor, *sod*]*alis Augustalis*, propraetorian legate of the [Afri]can ar[my], consul, decorated by the empe[ror] with the special spear 4 times, with banners 4 times, with the [4] crowns – rampart, wall, naval, golden; curator of the Tiber banks and river bed, [pri]est, propraetorian Augustan legate of the provin[ce of Pan]nonia and the provin[ce] of Spain. The townspeople to their patron.

[MW 266 = ILS 989 = EDCS–04200620*]

Large stone statue base, found at Tergeste (Trieste, NE Italy). For Calpetanus, see **B71**, **K86**, **M36**.

U13   German campaigns of Pinarius Cornelius, cos 71/2

Gnaeus Pinarius Cornelius [Clemens], son of Lucius, of the Papirian tribe, propraetorian legate of the army which [is in Upper Germany, curator of] sacred [buildings] and public spaces […, honoured] with triumphal decorations [on account of successes] in Germany.

[MW 50 = *ILS* 997 = EDCS–22901843*]

Building inscription from Hispellum (Spello) in Umbria. Pinarius was suffect consul in 71/2 and propraetorian legate in Upper Germany in 74, (**M6**). His successes in Germany may relate to his role in suppressing Civilis' revolt or to campaigns in the triangular area between sources of Rhine and Danube.

U14   Trajan's father, cos 72

[… M. Ulpi]us Traianus, consul, legate of Divus Vespas[ian and of Emperor Titus C]aesar Vespa[sian Augustus, son of Divus Vespasian, of the province of …] and of the province of Syria, proconsul of Asia and of Baetican Spain, on the board of fifteen for the performance of sacrifices, *sodalis Flavialis*, awarded triumphal decorations by decree of the senate […]

[MW 263 = *ILS* 8970 = EDCS–16201823]

Marcus Ulpius Traianus (**B72**), father of the emperor Trajan. The reason for his triumphal decorations is unknown. Besides this building inscription, he is also known from a dedication at Mydna, MW 264.

U15   Lucius Nonius Asprenas, proconsul of Africa, cos 72?

When Emperor Caesar ~~Domitian Augus~~tus, son of Divus Vespasian, ~~was *pontifex maximus*, holding tribunician power for the second time, hailed *imperator* 3/4 times, father of the fatherland, consul, for the 9th time,~~

Lucius Nonius Asprenas, son of Lucius, of the Pomptinan tribe, grandson of Lucius Nonius Asprenas, on the board of seven for sacred feasts, proconsul of the province of Africa for three years, on the board of three for striking gold, silver and bronze coins, (also) on the board of six, a Palatine priest, quaestor of Caesar Augustus, centurion of Roman equestrians, awarded military honours consisting of eight spears, four banners, two wall crowns, two rampart crowns, one gold, praetor for judging cases between citizens and non-citizens, legate with propraetorian powers in charge of the province of Galatia, Paphlagonia, Pamphylia and Pisidia, consul, on the board of seven for sacred feasts, proconsul of the province of Africa, patron of the municipality, dedicated (this), Marcus Cornelius Firmus was his legate with propraetorian powers.

[MW 303 = *IRT* 346* = EDCS–06000342]

Large inscription from Lepcis Magna (Libya) dedicating an unknown building to Domitian. Inscription carved on 17 limestone blocks, total length over 5m. L. Nonius Asprenas, consul in an unknown year under Vespasian, was grandson of L Nonius Asprenas, consul under Augustus; both were proconsul of Africa. He was appointed governor of Galatia etc. by Galba (Tac. *Hist.* 2.9).

U16   Vettulenus Cerialis, cos *c.* 73/4

The people honour of Sextus Vettulenus Cerialis, legate of Emperor Vespasian Caesar Augustus and proconsul.

[*IGRR* 1.863 = MW 280]

Statue base from Bosporus (Crimea). This was a protégé of Vespasian, from the Sabine region (Levick, *Vespasian* p. 53), commander of Legion V 'Macedonian' in Judaea, in 67 and 70. Diplomas show him in charge of armies in Moesia from 75 to 82 (*AE* 2009, 1800; *AE* 2010, 1853; *CIL* 16.28).

U17   Sextus Sentius Caecilianus, cos 75

[Sex. Se]ntius Caecilianus, son of Sextus, on the board of ten for judging law-suits, military tribune of Legion VIII 'Augustan', [quaestor of the province] of Baetica, aedile of the people, praetor, propraetorian legate of the province of [...], curator of the Tiber's banks and river-bed, legate of Legion XV 'Apollo's' and Legion III 'Augustan', propraetorian legate of Both Mauretanias, consul. By decision of his wife [*name lost*] and Atlas his freedman.

[MW 276 = *ILS* 8969 = EDCS–14805225]

Probably a statue base, from Amiternum. See also **M4**, **M5** for Caecilianus in Mauretania.

U18   L. Ceionius, cos ord. 78, great-grandfather of Emperor Antoninus Pius

[To Sextus Appius] Severus, son of Sextus, of the Voltinian tribe, on the board of four for maintaining the roads, military tribune of Legion III 'Gallic', member of the Titian brotherhood, quaestor of [Titus] son of [Em]peror Caesar Augustus. [Appia] Severa, daughter of Sextus and wife of Ceionius Commodus, to her most dutiful father.

[MW 292 = *ILS* 1003 = EDCS–17800499*]

Funerary inscription from Via Cassia, near Rome. L. Ceionius Commodus was cos ord 78, father of cos 106, grandfather of the L. Ceionius Commodus (cos 136) chosen by Hadrian as his successor (with the name L. Aelius Caesar). After his sudden death, his son, Lucius Verus, was adopted by Hadrian's second choice as heir, the emperor Antoninus Pius. For Ceionii see *HA* Aelius 2.8, Verus 1.9. The favour of the Flavians shown by being personal quaestor of Titus and *consul ordinarius* helped the Ceionii family to far higher honours.

U19 Funisulanus Vettonianus, cos 78, governor in the Balkans under Domitian

To L. Funisulanus Vettonianus, son of Lucius, of the Aniensis tribe, military tribune of Legion VI 'Victorious', quaestor of the province of Sicily, tribune of the people, praetor, legate of Legion IV 'Scythian', prefect of the Treasury of Saturn, curator of the Aemilian Road, consul, on the board of seven for sacred feasts, praetorian legate of the province of Dalmatia, likewise of the province of Pannonia, and of Upper Moesia, awarded ~~by the emperor Domitian Augustus Germanicus~~ in the Dacian War four crowns – wall, rampart, naval and golden, four special spears, four banners. By decree of the city council, to its patron.

[MW 307 = *ILS* 1005 = EDCS–26600445*]

Stone statue base from Andautonia in Upper Pannonia (modern Scitarjevo in Croatia). Tacitus, *Annals* 15.7 mentions Funisulanus in command of Legion IV in AD 62. He was consul in 78. Diplomas (*CIL* 16.30 and 16.31) show him in charge of Pannonia in Sept 84 and Sept 85.

U20 P. Calvisius Ruso, cos 79

[P. Calvisius Ruso L. Julius] Frontinus, on the board of three [for striking gold, silver and bronze coins, on the board of six] of Roman equestrians, military tribune [of Legion … … enlis]ted amongst the patricians [by Emperor Divus] Caesar Vespasian Augustus, [quaestor of Augustus, prae]tor, consul, curator of the […] road, [on the board of fifteen] for sacrifices, *sodalis Augustalis*, […] proconsul of Asia, cura[tor of sac]red [buildings] and of [public] places and monuments, propraetorian legate of Emperor Nerva Trajan Augustus Germanicus Dacicus. The colony to its patron.

[MW 286 = *AE* 1987, 937 = EDCS–16000011*]

Double statue base of man and wife, damaged at both ends, found at Pisidian Antioch. Syme, *Roman Papers* 4.397–417 suggests that this man is not the same as P. Calvisius Ruso, suffect consul in 79, but rather a step-brother and nephew of Sex. Julius Frontinus. Syme suggests that his consulship would have been in 84.

GNAEUS JULIUS AGRICOLA: U21a–b

Agricola's career is fully documented in the biography written by his son-in-law, Tacitus (historical commentary by Ogilvie and Richmond, Oxford 1967; literary commentary by Woodman, Cambridge 2014). Dio mentions his proving that Britain was an island (39.50.4 and **C66**). A very fragmentary inscription from St Albans seems to include his name (*AE* 1957, 169) which otherwise appears only on one water-pipe inscription found at Chester (**U21b**). Agricola's legionary command was around AD 60. His career was advanced through support for Vespasian in the civil war (Agr. 7.1–2) with command of legion XX in Britain from March 70, lasting until around his promotion in the census of 73/4 (**U21a**). He returned as governor of Britain (the only Roman known to have served in the same province as military tribune, legionary commander and governor) 77–84 (*Agr.* 18–29) winning a decisive battle at Mons Graupius (*Agr.* 29–38: location still unidentified.). For his return to Rome, see **T25–T27**.

U21a Vespasian promotes Agricola

When he returned from his legionary command, Divus Vespasian enrolled him amongst the patricians. Next he put him in command of the province of Aquitania, one of the most important honours, given its own responsibilities and the promise it offered of the consulship he was destined for.

[Tacitus, *Agricola* 9.1]

U21b Agricola named on water-pipe

When Emperor Vespasian, for the 9th time and Titus Imperator, for the 7th time were consuls, Cn. Julius Agricola, propraetorian legate of Augustus (made this).

[MW 283 = *ILS* 8704a = RIB 2.3, 2434.1 = EDCS–25100850*]

U22 Epitaph of Glitius Gallus, cos ? (before 79)

To P. Glitius Gallus, son of Publius, consul, on the board of three for [...], Palatine priest, quaestor of T. Caesar, praetor, high priest of Augustus, given the special spear through the censorship of Emperor Vespasian Caesar Augustus, father of the fatherland and Titus Imperator Caesar Augustus. A public (burial) space was given by decree of the town councillors.

[MW 260 = *ILS* 999 = EDCS–21000458]

From Falerii in Etruria, 35 miles north of Rome. Glitius' year of consulship is unknown, though presumably prior to Vespasian's death, as he is not referred to as 'Divus'.

U23 The first African consul, Pactumeius, cos 80

[To Q. Aurelius Pactumeius Fronto, son of Publius, of the Quirina tribe, co-opted amongst the praetorians by] Emperor Caesar Vespasian Augustus and Titus Imperator, son of Augustus, priest (*fetialis*), prefect of the military treasury, the first consul from Africa. Pactume[ia (made this as a gift)] to her excellent father.

[MW 298 = *AE* 2007, 106 = EDCS–13002087]

Inscription, probably a statue base, from Cirta, (now Constantine in Algeria), the old capital of Numidia where Julius Caesar had settled a number of Italians, including, it seems, the ancestors of Pactumeius (Birley, *Septimius Severus: The African Emperor,* page 42). A similar inscription (*CIL* 08, 07057 = *AE* 2007, 106) found in the same location shows that his brother Clemens was also enlisted by Vespasian, and guarantees the consul's full name.

THE CURVII BROTHERS: U24–U25

Curvius Lucanus and Curvius Tullus were a famously devoted pair of brothers, whom Martial often mentions as a byword for family love (1.36, 3.20.17, 5.28.3). Y. Pliny wrote a long letter (8.18, around AD 107) describing the testament and legal affairs of Tullus, whom he clearly hated. From this the brothers were born before AD 41, adopted by Domitius Afer, the famous orator, though he had ruined their natural father. The brothers' family, by legal loopholes, acquired the wealth, not only of Afer, but of Lucanus' father-in-law, Curtilius Mancia, apparently owner of great estates in Africa, which perhaps explains why the majority of their career positions related to Africa. Their home town of Fulginae in Umbria, C. Italy (modern Foligno) honoured them during Vespasian's reign with a pair of statues (**U24, U25a**). Lucanus' death is mourned by Martial (**U25b**).

U24 Statue of Curvius Lucanus

To Gnaeus Domitius Afer Titius Marcellus Curvius Lucanus, son of Sextus, of the Voltinian tribe, consul, proconsul of the province of Africa, legate of his brother Tullus in the same province, on the board of seven for sacred feasts, also propraetorian legate of Emperor Caesar Augustus in the province of Africa, in charge of all the auxiliary forces against the Germans, awarded the golden, wall, and rampart crowns by Emperor Vespasian Augustus and Titus Caesar, son of Augustus, the special spear 3 times, banners 3 times, co-opted amongst the patricians, praetor, tribune of the people, quaestor, propraetor of the province of Africa, military [tribune] of Legion V 'The Larks', on the board of four for maintaining the roads. To their excellent patron by decree of the town councillors.

[MW 299 = *ILS* 990 = EDCS–22901152]

U25a   Statue of Curvius Tullus

[To Gnaeus Domitius Afer Titius Marcellus Curvius Tullus, son of Sextus, of the Voltinian tribe, consul, proconsul of the province of Africa], priest (*fetialis*), in charge of all the au[xiliary forces] against the Germans; when he was praetor designate as Caesar's candidate, he was sent by Emperor Vespasian Augustus as propraetorian legate to the army which was in Africa, and in absence was co-opted among those of praetorian rank; he was awarded the golden, wall, and rampart crowns by Emperor Vespasian Augustus and Titus Caesar, son of Augustus, the special spear 3 times, banners 3 times, co-opted amongst the patricians, praetor, tribune of the people, quaestor of Caesar Augustus, military [tribune] of Legion V 'The Larks', on the board of ten for judging law-suits. To their excellent patron by decree of the town councillors.

[MW 300 = *ILS* 991 = EDCS–22901153]

U25b   Martial laments the death of Curvius Lucanus

What you always asked the gods to grant against
Your brother's will, is yours, Lucanus – you
Died first. Tullus envies you; he, though younger,
Wished to go before to Styx's shade.
Elysium's lovely groves are now your place to dwell;   5
For once you wish to be without your brother now.
If it's his turn to come from the shining stars
You tell Castor not to replace Pollux.

[Martial, 9.51 (published December 94)]

The poem forms a counterpart to 1.36 which suggested that each of the Curvii brothers would wish to die in place of his brother if put in the place of Castor and Pollux and having to alternate between life in heaven and in the underworld.

SALVIUS LIBERALIS (COS 85): U26a–c

An inscription (statue base) from Urbs Salvia (in Picenum, E. Italy) gives the career of the local magnate, Salvius Liberalis, anti-hero of the Cambridge Latin Course. Promoted during Vespasian's censorship (73/74), his plain-speaking in court attracted Vespasian's approval (Suet. *Vesp.* 13) and selection as arval (**A78c**). He served as *iuridicus* in Britain in 78–81 (when absent from Arval Records). His consulship was probably in 85, but a further absence from the extant Arval Records for 89–91 suggests that his trial (**U26b**) resulted in exile. He returned to Rome after Domitian's death (Arval Records for the late 90s and **U26c**). For his wife, see **L33**.

U26a   Salvius' career inscription from his home town
To [C. Salv]ius Liberalis [Nonius] Bassus, son of Gaius, of the Velina tribe, consul, proconsul of the province of Macedonia, legate of the Augusti as [*iuridi*]*cus* in Britain, legate of Legion V 'Macedonian', Arval [Brother], co-opted by Divus Vespasian [and Divus Ti]tus to tribunician rank, and [co-opted] by the same into praetorian rank, quinquennial magistrate four times, patron of the colony. This man, having drawn the lot for the [proconsulship] of Asia, excused himself from the office.

[MW 311 = *ILS* 1011 = EDCS–16200615]

U26b   Trial of Salvius Liberalis under Domitian
Two ex-consuls, Pomponius Rufus and Libo Frugi, damaged him [Norbanus Licianus] by giving evidence that he had been one of the accusors at the trial of Salvius Liberalis under Domitian.

[Pliny the Younger, *Letters* 3.9.33]

U26c   Salvius Liberalis as an orator
On the following day Salvius Liberalis spoke on behalf of Marius. Salvius is plain-speaking, clear, fluent, and shrewd: he brought all these qualities into his defence.

[Pliny the Younger, *Letters* 2.11.17]

L. ANTISTIUS RUSTICUS (COS AD 90): U27a–b
Antistius Rusticus was remembered with gratitude by the area of modern Turkey for measures he took against a famine in 93 after a harsh winter there: his decree was inscribed (**M52**) as was a statue base with his career (**U27a**). Martial mentions his death shortly afterwards.

U27a   Dedication from Antioch in Pisidia
To Lucius Antistius Rusticus, son of [Lucius], of the Galerian tribe; consul, propraetorian legate to Emperor Caesar ~~Domitian~~ Augustus ~~Germanicus~~ of the provinces of Cappadocia, Galatia, Pontus, Pisidia, Paphlagonia, Armenia Minor and Lycaonia, prefect of the Treasury of Saturn, proconsul of the province of Further Spain, legate of Divus Vespasian and of Divus Titus and of Emperor Caesar ~~Domitian~~ Augustus ~~Germanicus~~ of Legion VIII 'Augustan', curator of the Aurelian and Cornelian roads; co-opted among the senators of praetorian rank by Divus Vespasian and Divus Titus; awarded military decorations by them, the wall crown, the rampart crown, the golden crown, three banners and three special spears; military tribune of Legion II 'Augustan'; on the board of ten for judging law-suits; patron of the colony: for his diligence in providing for the corn supply.

[MW 464 = EDCS–12700147]

U27b   Death of Antistius Rusticus
Antistius Rusticus has died in Cappadocia's
Hostile shores – land guilty of a dreadful crime!
Nigrina in her bosom brought back home the bones
Of her dear husband, sad the journey was too short;
When she gave the envied tomb the holy urn,
She feels she's being robbed and widowed once again.

[Martial, *Epigram* 9.30 (published December 94)]

U28   C. Caristanius Fronto, cos 90

To C. Caris[ta]nius F[ron]to, son of Gaius, of the Sergian tribe, military tribune, p[refect] of the Bosporan cavalry wing, co-opted into the senate amongst those of rank of tribune, promoted to rank of praetor, propraetorian legate of Pontus & Bithynia, legate of Emperor Divus Vespasian Augustus of Legion IX 'Spanish' in Britian, propraetorian legate of Emperor Divus Titus Caesar Augustus and Emperor Domitian Caesar Augustus of the province of Pamphylia & Lycia, patron of the colony. T. Caristanius Calpurnianus Rufus (erected this) in his honour, on account of his merits.

[MW 315 = *ILS* 9485 = EDCS–16201163]

This dedication (probably of a statue) at Antioch in Pisidia shows the rapid rise of Caristanius Fronto from equestrian rank and command of a cavalry unit under Vespasian (for Bosporan cavalry see **U10a**), by co-option in the census of 73/4. He went on to the consulship in 90.

U29   Publius Baebius Italicus, cos 90

To Publius Baebius Italicus, son of Publius, of the Oufentine tribe, quaestor of Cyprus, tribune of the people, legate of Narbonese Gaul, consul, legate of Legion XIIII 'Twinned, Mars Victorious', honoured in the war against Germany by Augustus with golden crown and wall crown and rampart crown and special spear 3 times, banner [3 times?], legate of empe[ror C]aesar Domitian Augustus Germanicus and proconsul of Lycia & Pamphylia. The people of [Tl]os (erected this) for their [benefa]ctor and founder and holy [justice]giver.

[MW 314 = *ILS* 8818: Greek, Tlos (Lycia)]

The Oufentine tribe was that designated for men from Como or Milan, so Baebius will be another of the Italian elite promoted by Vespasian's census, honoured here with a statue.

U30   Julius Celsus Polemaeanus, cos 92

To Ti. Julius Celsus Polemaeanus, consul, proconsul of Asia, tribune of Legion III 'Cyrene', co-opted with rank of aedile by Divus Vespasian, praetor of the Roman people, legate of the Augusti, Divus Vespasian and Divus Titus, of the provinces of Cappadocia & Galatia, Pontus, Pisidia, Paphlagonia, Armenia Minor, legate of Divus Titus of Legion IIII 'Scythian', proconsul of Pontus & Bithynia, prefect of the military treasury, propraetorian legate of Augustus of the province of Cilicia, on the board of fifteen for sacrifices, curator of sacred buildings and public works of the Roman people. Ti. Julius Aquila Polemaeanus, consul, honoured his father. The heirs of Aquila completed the work.

[MW 316 = *ILS* 8971 = EDCS–05300082]

This is the bilingual dedication of the famous Library of Celsus in Ephesus. The library was funded by Celsus and dedicated as his mausoleum by his son. Celsus was the first consul from the Greek East. His rise was helped by legion III being one of those in Alexandria to have proclaimed Vespasian emperor.

U31   C. Antius A. Julius Quadratus, cos 94, cos II ord 105

C. Antius Aulus Julius Quadratus, son of Aulus, twice consul, proconsul of Asia, on the board of seven for sacred feasts, Arval Brother, propraetorian legate of Pontus & Bithynia, twice legate of Asia, legate of Augustus of the province of Cappadocia, proconsul of Crete & Cyrene, propraetorian legate of Augustus of Lycia & Pamphylia, propraetorian legate of Nerva Caesar Trajan Augustus Germanicus of the province of

Syria. The August Council of the young men honours its benefactor and permanent president of the gymnasium. Those who took care of the carrying out of the decree were Asclepiades the son of Glycon Myrsicus, and Zoilus son of Diomedes, and Theon son of Teleson, the secretaries.

[MW 320 = *IGRR* 4.384]

Another early consul from the Greek East (compare **U29**), honoured in this inscription from his home town of Pergamum (W. Turkey). Arval from mid 70s all the way until 111, when he was president for the third time. Trajan gave him a second, *ordinarius* consulship in 105 and he governed Asia *c.* 109/10.

U32a   Tacitus on his own career under the Flavians

Our senatorial career was started by Vespasian, continued by Titus, considerably advanced by Domitian – I shall not deny this.

[Tacitus, *Histories* 1.1.3]

U32b   Tacitus' epitaph?

To [...]citus Ca[...] board of ten for [judging] law-suits [... quaest]or of Augustus, tribun[e of the people ...]

[*CIL* 6.1574 = *AE* 2000, 160 = EDCS–01000223*]

This very fragmentary inscription from Rome is now thought to be Tacitus' funerary inscription (A. Birley, 'The life and death of Cornelius Tacitus' *Historia* 49 (2000), 230ff). It clearly shows a senatorial career. The identification rests on the rarity of 'cito' (= to [Ta]citus) in Roman names (as can be seen by a search on the electronic epigraphic database). Tacitus is the only known upper class name that would fit. The identification with the author depends on this epitaph not belonging to another 'Tacitus' (and there certainly were such, including a third-century emperor) and on the author having previously unknown additional names (perfectly possible – Dio's full name, for example, is still uncertain). If this is the historian it adds details to his career that could have been guessed anyway – a vigintivirate on the legal board and quaestorship as Caesar's candidate, again very likely given his signal honour of priesthood on the board of fifteen. Other details of Tacitus' career can be put together from his works (**L17**), Y. Pliny's letter explaining that he gave, as consul, the funeral oration for Verginius Rufus in 97, and an inscription mentioning his proconsulship of Asia (*OGIS* 487), datable to 112/3 by Syme, *Tacitus* 664–5. His likely career is set out in **U33f**.

PLINY THE YOUNGER (GAIUS PLINIUS SECUNDUS): U33a–f

We have a better idea of the career of Y. Pliny than of almost anyone else in the Roman world thanks to a combination of his writings and inscriptions. A marble inscription on the baths he had built at Comum listed his full career (**U33d**). It was recorded in the 15th century but later cut up to make a tomb. Another dedication (**U33e**) from the small town of Fecchio near Comum survives from before his governorship which confirms his posts and mentions a further priesthood. The inscriptions show how well his career progressed, throughout Domitian's reign, and give the lie to his claims in **U33c**. His does admit he was quaestor of the emperor (7.16.2, **U33d**) and imply that he did not need to canvass for election (**U33b**), though he does not stress his status as Domitian's candidate.

U33a   Pliny's early career

I have Caelestrius Tiro as a very close friend. We have been associated in both private and public affairs. [2] We were in the army together, and were the emperor's quaestors in the same year. He held the tribunate before me through the rights of fathers of children. However, I caught up in the praetorship when the Emperor granted me a year's remission.

[Pliny the Younger, *Letters* 7.16.1–2]

U33b   More worried about a friend's election

The fact that Sextus Erucus is standing for election makes me anxious and worried. I am afflicted by troubles and suffer, on behalf of my 'second self' fears which I did not experience on my own account.

[Pliny the Younger, *Letters* 2.9.1]

U33c   Pliny the Younger's career under Domitian

You, senators, give your blessing on my task and believe me: If I advanced my career to some extent under that most treacherous emperor, before he made clear his hatred of good men, yet I halted it after he made this hatred clear, when I saw the short-cuts that led to high honour and preferred the longer route; if in evil times I was counted amongst those who were sad and troubled, in good times I now am counted amongst those who are at peace and happy; if, finally, I utterly love the best emperor, so I was utterly hated by the worst.

[Pliny the Younger, *Panegyric to Trajan* 95.2–4]

U33d   Inscription from Comum

Gaius Plinius Caecilius [Secundus], son of Lucius, of the Oufentine voting-tribe, [consul], augur, propraetorian legate of the province of Pon[tus & Bithynia. Sent] with consular power in accordance with [a decree of the senate], by Emperor Caesar Nerva Trajan Augustus Germanicus [Dacicus, father of the fatherland]. Curator of the Tiber bed and of the river-banks a[nd sewers of the city]; prefect of the treasury of Saturn; prefect of the mil[itary] treasury; [praetor; tribune of the people]; quaestor of the emperor; on the board of six Roman equestrians; military tribune of Legion [III] 'Gallic'; [on the board of ten for] judging law-suits.

(The inscription then gives information about moneys left in his will to build, decorate and maintain public baths; to provide for a hundred of his freedmen; for an annual dinner for the townspeople; and about sums given in his lifetime for providing for children of the town and to maintain the library.)

[Smallwood N-H 230 = *ILS* 2927 = EDCS–05100416*]

U33e   Dedication from a neignbouring town

To Gaius Plinius Caecilius Secundus, [son of Lucius], of the Oufentine voting-tribe, consul, augur, curator of the Tiber bed and of the river-banks and sewers of the city; Pr[efect of the tr]easury of Saturn; prefect of the military treasury; [praetor; tribune of the people]; quaestor of the emperor; on the board of six Roman equestrians; military tribune of Legion III 'Gallic'; on the board of ten for judging law-suits, high priest of Divus Titus Augustus. The people of Vercellae.

[*CIL* 5.5667 = EDCS–05100822]

U33f   Table showing senatorial *cursus* and those of Pliny the Younger and Tacitus

Post (age held)*	Tacitus (U32a–b) Born *c.* AD 56	Pliny the Younger (U33a–e) Born AD 61/2
Vigintivir (18+) – (junior magistrate, in Rome)	Board of X for law-suits (a)	Board of X for law-suits (d) *c.* AD 81
Military tribune (18+) (assists commander of a legion)	under Agricola in Britain, *c.* 78?	Legion III in Syria (a, d, *Letter* 1.10.2) *c.* AD 82
Quaestor (25+) (i/c treasury often in provinces)	Q. of Caesar (a)	Quaestor of Caesar (a, d) *c.* AD 90
Aedile/tribube of *plebs* (25+) (in Rome)	Tribune (a)	Tribune, (a, b, d) *c.* AD 92
Priesthoods (any age) show special favour from emperor	*XVvir* for AD 88 (**L17**)	Augur, *c.* 104 (d, *Letter* 4.8); priest of Titus (e), date unknown
Praetor (29+) (legal matters in Rome)	Praetor AD 88 (**L17**)	Praetor (a, b, d) AD 93 (P11f)
Posts in Rome or governing minor provinces	abroad AD 89–93 (*Agr.* 45.5)	Prefect of military treasury (d) 94–6; & of Saturn's treasury (d, 10.8.3), 98–100
Consul (42+) (chief magistrate)	Suffect in AD 97	Suffect consul, Sept. 100 (*Pan.* 60.4–5)
Posts in Rome		Curator of Tiber *c.* 104–6 (d)
Proconsulship (governing major province)	Asia, 112–3	Pontus & Bithynia (Letters 10.17a) *c.* AD 109–111

* age requirements could actually vary with allowances made for patricians (neither Tacitus nor Y. Pliny), for having children, or through the emperor's favour (see **U33a**)

U34   Career of C. Julius Cornutus Tertullus, cos 100

To C. Julius Cornutus Tertullus, son of Publius, of the Horatian tribe, consul, proconsul of the province of Asia, proconsul of the province of Narbonensis, propraetorian legate of Divus Trajan [Parthicus] of the province of Pontus & Bithynia, propraetorian legate of the same of the province of Aquitania, in charge of taking the census, curator of the Aemilian [road], prefect of the Treasury of Saturn, propraetorian legate of the province of Crete & Cyrene, promoted to praetorian rank by Divus Vespasian and Divus Titus during their censorship, aedile of Ceres, urban quaestor. In accordance with his will, C. Julius Plancius Varus Cornutus.

[MW 321 = *ILS* 1024 = EDCS–05800907]

Cornutus Tertullus of Perge in Pamphylia, Y. Pliny's close friend (5.14 etc, and Pan. 90.3–5) and colleague in a suffect consulship in 100. See Syme, *Tacitus*, 82–3.

CO-OPTION AMONGST EX-PRAETORS: U35–U37

Claudius had co-opted men to the lowest levels of the senate. From the start of his reign, Vespasian brought in men with experience of military affairs at the high level of ex-praetor, who could thus be send immediately to provinces (Levick, *Vespasian* 174, and note 12 on 263–4).

U35   Prefect of Archers co-opted as praetor and sent as legate to Asia

To […] tilius Lol[lian]us, military tribune of Legion IIII 'Scythian', by the kindness of Divus Claudius, prefect of the 3rd cohort of archers, co-opted amongst the ex-praetors by Emperor Vespasian Augustus, propraetorian legate of the province of Asia. The Julian Concord Colony of Apamea (erected this) for their patron.

[MW 288 = *CIL* 3.335 = EDCS–26600088]

Apamea is in Bithynia, on the south side of the Sea of Marmara.

U36   Prefect of the Watch co-opted as a praetor, Nimes

To C. Fulvius Lupus Servilianus, son of Gaius, of the Voltinian tribe, co-opted amongst the ex-praetors by Emperor Caesar Augustus Vespas[ian], prefect of the Longinian wing, IIIIvir for the treasury, pontifex, prefect of the Watch. Julia Concessa, daughter of Decimus, (erected this) for her husband.

[MW 289 = *CIL* 12.3166 = EDCS–09201634]

U37   Co-option of highly decorated military tribune of Legion IIII

To [C. Petillius?] Firmus, son of Quintus, of the Pomptinan tribe [on the board of X for judging law-sui]ts, military tribune of Legion IIII [Scyth]ian, legate of Augustus Vespasian, quaestor of Augustus, awarded status of an honorary ex-praetor by the senate, under the authority of Emperors Vespasian and Titus and co-opted (amongst the ex-praetors) [by the same] emperors. Granted the golden crown 3 times, [wall and rampart crowns 3 times, the special spear 3 times, praetor. By decree of the town councillors.

[MW 290 = *ILS* 1000 = EDCS–22000186*]

Though this co-opted praetor's name is missing from this inscription from Arretium in Etruria (Arezzo), he is possibly to be identified with Petillius Firmus, also a military tribune from legion IIII, and under special commission from Vespasian, known from two boundary markers in Dalmatia *AE* 1967, 00355 = *AE* 1983, 00744.

U38   Valerius Asiaticus, cos design 70

To the Shades of D. [Valerius] Asiaticus, consul designate

[MW 257 = *CIL* 6.1528 = EDCS–18000415]

Valerius Asiaticus was governor of Belgica, had apparently supported Vindex against Nero (Tac. *Hist.* 2.94) and joined Vitellius, being betrothed to his daughter (Tac. *Hist.* 1.59), but as consul designate he led senatorial endorsement for Vespasian after Vitellius' death (Tac. *Hist.* 4.4). He must have died very soon after.

U39   Regulus' near accident
This colonnade, collapsed in the mass of dust,
Spread its wreckage along the whole of its length.
What a great disaster it so nearly caused!
For Regulus had only just driven
Under it, and emerged at the other end,   5
When it suddenly gave way under its own
Weight, and having no more fear for its master
Crashed happy that its fall caused no bloodshed.
After the fear of such a great cause of grief
Who could deny that the gods take care of you,   10
Regulus, for whom disaster proved harmless?
                                       [Martial, *Epigram* 1.82 (published 85)]

M. Aquilius Regulus, Y. Pliny's enemy (**T38**), was probably only a praetor, though aristocratic (Tac. *Hist.*
4.42). Several Martial poems are addressed to him (1.11, 1.111, 2.93, 5.10, 5.21, 7.16, 7.31), and he is
mentioned as a critic of literature (5.63) and as a byword for legal expertise (2.74, 4.16, 6.64) and eloquence
(**U11c**). Poem 6.38 wishes prosperity for his 3-year old son, (dead in Y. Pliny, *Letters* 2.4 = **T38**).

U40   Procurator of Lusitania
To L. Baebius Avitus, son of Lucius, of the Galerian tribe, praefect of builders, military
tribune of Legion X 'Twinned', procurator of Emperor Caesar Vespasian Augustus of
the province of Lusitania, co-opted amongst the ex-praetors.
                                       [Rome: MW 291 = *ILS* 1378 = EDCS–17900036]

EQUESTRIANS: U41–U50
For equestrian census qualification, see **S22–S24**. This section deals instead with 'career' equestrians who,
under the Flavians, reached an importance equal to most consuls.

U41   Tiberius Julius Alexander, prefect of Egypt and Praetorian prefect
[…] Tiberius Julius Alexander, who was governor and prae[torian] commander […]
                                       [MW 329b = Papyrus from Hibeh 215]

Tiberius Julius Alexander came from a wealthy Alexandrian Jewish family and was procurator of Judaea, *c.*
46–48, (Jos. *JA* 20.100 = LACTOR 19, **U22**). His brother was Berenice's first husband. After serving under
Corbulo he was made prefect of Egypt by Nero. An edict of his survives, issued after Galba's accession
(MW 328 = Sherk 80). His support was of the greatest importance in Vespasian's accession (**H18, L22,** Tac.
Hist. 2.74.1, 2.79.1), so promotion to praetorian prefect, though only mentioned on this papyrus fragment
from modern El-Hiba on the Nile in Middle Egypt, and difficult to date, is unsurprising.

U42   Prefect of Egypt, commemorated at Assissi
To [C. Tetti]us Africanus, son of Gaius, of the Oufentine tribe, prefect of the guard,
prefect of the corn-supply, prefect of Egypt, most dutiful and most munificent towards
his fatherland and [*(the rest lost)*].
                                       [MW 333 = *CIL* 11.5382 = EDCS–12700050]

U43 Equestrian careers of Julius Ursus and Attius Suburanus, both later consuls

To Sextus Attius Suburanus Aemilianus, son of Lucius, of the Voltinian tribe, prefect of builders, prefect of the Taurian squadron, assistant of Vibius Crispus propraetorian imperial legate in receiving the census in Nearer Spain, assistant of Julius Ursus prefect of the corn-supply, and of the same man when prefect of Egypt as imperial procurator at the Temple of Mercury, imperial procurator of the Cottian Alps and Pedates Tyrii and Cammuntii and Lepontii, procurator of the province of Judaea, procurator of the province of Belgica. The Marii Cethegi, adjutants and most loyal brothers.

[MW 334 = EDCS–15000129*]

This statue base from Heliopolis (Baalbek in Syria) shows various equestrian career progressions. Julius Ursus (see below) progressed from corn–supply to Egypt (**M29** and compare Tettius Africanus above) and then to the equestrian pinnacle, praetorian prefect, while Suburanus held two equestrian posts within the army before a series of posts as assistant, and a series of procuratorships. Most unusually, Julius Ursus, having fallen from imperial favour (Dio 67.3.1), was suddenly appointed consul (Dio 67.4.2), gaining a third consulship in 100. Suburanus followed in his footsteps, being promoted to praetorian prefect by Trajan (Y. Pliny, *Panegyric* 67.8 and Dio 68.16.1.2; same anecdote told by Aurelius Victor, supplying the name) and then consul in 101 and 104.

U44 Papyrus showing equestrian careers of Julius Ursus and Laberius Maximus

[For the sake of your virtue] and loyalty, my dear Maximus, [… wh]ich […] for me, even though you have always received [rewards, yet] I have not been satisfied to have made your honours culminate in rela[tion to the pre]fectship [of Egypt]. Instead, since I had transferred Juliu[s Ursus, who profited from your good wishes,] into the most noble rank [which he had long de]sired, I immediately looked at your most devoted loy[alty and your hard work] and made you a [col]league [in my] coun[cil with Cornelius? F]uscus, with whom I hope you will most delightfully and even most lovingly hold equal collaboration in office. And that the seas may favour your voyage, my dear Maximus, so that as soon as you may […] I do not doubt that you will be most eager to be at my side in Rome. […]

[Berlin Papyrus 8334 = *CPLat* 238]

Though the names are fragmentary, it is agreed that this letter is from Domitian to Laberius Maximus, inviting him to return to Rome to take up the post of praetorian prefect as partner to Fuscus (see **N34–N35**, **N41**), and in succession to Julius Ursus (see above). Laberius is attested as prefect of the corn supply (**A80f**) and procurator of Judaea (**N14**).

U45 Minucius Italus, Prefect of Egypt, honoured at Aquileia

To C. Minucius Italus, son of Gaius, of the Velina tribe, on the board of four for jurisdiction, prefect of Cohort V of Gauls (with cavalry), prefect of Cohort I of Breucians with Roman citizenship (with cavalry), prefect of Cohort II of Varcians (with cavalry), military tribune of Legion VI 'Victorious', prefect of cavalry of Squadron I of elite troops with Roman citizenship, decorated by Divus Vespasian with the golden crown and special spear, procurator of the province of the Hellespont, procurator of the province of Asia, which he was entrusted to govern in the place of the deceased proconsul; procurator of the provinces of Lugdunum and Aquitania, and likewise of Lactora; prefect in charge of the corn-supply; prefect of Egypt, high priest of Divus Claudius, by decree of the council.

[MW 336 = *ILS* 1374 = EDCS–01600153*]

The deceased proconsul honoured at Aquileia, NE Italy, was Civica Cerialis (Tac. *Agr.* 42; Suet. *Dom.* 10.2). Lactora = Lectoure in S. France. On the side of this large statue base is also inscribed a decree of the town council, dated to 105, praising Minucius Italus for using his influence as holder of the highest equestrian offices to win Trajan's favour for his native city.

U46 Adlection to senate declined

His father, Minicius Macrinus, was a leading equestrian, because he did not wish to rise any higher. Though co-opted to the rank of ex-praetor by Divus Vespasian, he was utterly resolute in preferring honest obscurity to high honour or – should I call it ambition?

[Pliny the Younger, *Letters* 1.14.5]

Other recipients of Y. Pliny letters, Terentius Junior (7.25.2) and Maturus Arrianus (3.2.4) are spoken of as preferring to remain equestrians. But Annaeus Mela, brother of Seneca, was described by Tacitus as having gained equal power and quicker wealth from (equestrian) procuratorships (Tac. *Ann.* 16.17)

U47 Co-opted to Equestrian rank?

To M. Valerius Propinquus Grattius Cerialis Edetanus, son of Marcus, of the Galerian tribe; high priest of the province of Nearer Spain, to whom his state granted honours of the community. Co-opted to equestrian rank by Titus Imperator, prefect of builders twice, prefect of Cohort II of Asturians in Germany, tribune of Legion V 'Macedonian' in Moesia, prefect of the Phrygian division, and again prefect of the third Thracian division in Syria. The province of Nearer Spain honoured him.

[MW 342 = *ILS* 2711 = EDCS–05503282]

Valerius Propinquus, honoured by his home town of Tarraco in Spain, should have reached equestrian status automatically on being military tribune, so it is not quite clear what 'co-opted to equestrian rank' means. In fact the phrase was mis-inscribed and actually reads 'co-opted in an equestrian', while 'granted' is the likely intended meaning of a phrase which should translate 'played by his spirit'!

U48 An equestrian given 'freedmen' posts by Vitellius

Sex. Caesius Propertianus, son of Sextus, high priest of Roman Ceres, procurator for the emperor's private fortune and for inheritances and secretary for petitions, military tribune of Legion IV 'Macedonian', prefect of Cohort III 'Spanish', decorated with the special spear and golden crown, quattuorvir with judicial power, quinquennial, *pontifex*, patron of the town.

[MW 338 = *ILS* 1447 = EDCS–22900967*]

Bevagna/Mevagna in Umbria honoured their patron with this statue. Tacitus, *Histories* 1.58 describes Vitellius giving equestrians posts normally held by freedmen, and this man, military tribune of IV 'Macedonian', one of the legions loyal to him and disbanded afterwards, is a case in point. This may have been (Chilver, *Commentary* p.119) because Vitellius did not have many freedmen with him in Germany, but Flavian emperors followed this pattern, moving away from the unpopular imperial freedmen of the Julio-Claudians (see Suet. *Dom.* 7.2).

U49   Titinius Capito as imperial secretary under Domitian, Nerva, Trajan
Cn. Octavius Titinius Capito, prefect of a cohort, military tribune, awarded the special spear and rampart crown, procurator in charge of correspondence and imperial property, and again in charge of correspondence of Divus Nerva, and by his recommendation awarded honorary praetorian status by decree of the senate; in charge of correspondence for a third time to Emperor Nerva Caesar Trajan Augustus Germanicus, prefect of the Watch, made this offering to Vulcan.

[Rome: MW 347 = *ILS* 1448 = EDCS–17300938*]

Titinius Capito receives high praise from Y. Pliny (1.17 and especially 8.12) as a writer and literary patron, with a particular interest in history. He carefully avoids mentioning his career under Domitian, but it is obvious from his use of 'again' and 'for a third time'. By the end of the first century, imperial secretaries were equestrians rather than freedmen. Suetonius represents the culmination of this trend.

**U50   A manumitted freedman given unusual powers in AD 73 and
equestrian status**
Persicus, a manumitted freedman, but with the status of a procurator at the council-chamber of Domitian Caesar, in his second consulship, performed two consular divisions, those concerning roads and lictors. To C. Cornelius Persicus, having the 'public horse', to Cornelia Zosima his mother having the right of four children, by the generosity of Caesar, to his freedmen and freedwomen and their descendants.

[Rome: MW 346 = *ILS* 1910 = EDCS–18100693]

It is not clear what exactly Persicus did in AD 73, as it seems unparalleled, but the point is clearly to stress how well Persicus had done, as with the tautology 'manumitted freedman' (since manumit is the technical term for freeing a slave). 'Public horse' was the highest rank of equestrian, and in the gift of the emperor.

U51   Adoption of children as means to social advance
"You had recently moved a step closer to the expectation of the highest office by adoption into a consular family, and destined to marry the niece of a praetor."

[Quintilian, *The Orator's Education* 6 preface 13]

Quintilian is writing about his son who had recently died aged 10 (*The Orator's Education* 6 preface 10). No reader could doubt the depths of Quintilian's grief or his love for his son. Though a celebrated and wealthy figure, Quintilian will have been of equestrian, not senatorial rank, though he may have been awarded honorary consular rank late in life (Ausonius, *Actio gratiarum* 7.31). So he clearly had his son adopted in the vain hope of furthering his son's prospects in life.

CONCORDANCE

(By document number)

A: LITERARY SOURCES

Aelian
 History fr. 112 (ed. Hercher)   P8c
Ammianus Marcellinus
 16.14–16   K4
Aurelius Victor
 12.2   K40
Ausonius
 10.7.31   R18
Bede
 Ecclesiastical History 1.3   J4c
Censorinus
 On the Birthday 17   L19
 18.15   H53, Q16
Chronicle of 354
 Part 16   H23, K2
Digest of Roman Law
 1.2.2.53   U4b
 36.1.48   M78
Dio (Cassius)
 Book 66 (**Xiphilinus**)   Section C
 Book 67 (**Xiphilinus**)   Section D
 53.17.7   H52
 60.20.3–4   J3a
 66.10.3a   J4i
 66.12.1a   R16
 67.7.2–4   N39
 67.3.5   N51
 68.1.3   T42
Dio of Prusa (Dio Chrysostom)
 Oration 13.1–2   P5a
 Oration 21.10   P3
 Oration 45.1–2   T36
Epictetus
 Discourses 1.2.19–21   P1j
Epitome of the Caesars
 9.1–3   J4g
 9.4   P1n
 9.5–6   J4k
 9.7   J4h
 9.10   K88
 9.14   P9a
 9.15–16   J4f
 9.17–18   J4m
 10.1   J5b
 10.1–3   J8d
 10.4   P2a
 10.5–6   J8e
 10.7   J22b
 10.8–10   J8f
 10.11   J8h
 10.12   K7

 10.12–14   K101
 10.15–16   J8i
 11.1–3   J10c
 11.4   R33
 11.5   J10d
 11.6–8   J10g
 11.9–10   P8b
 11.11–13   P16b
Eusebius
 Church History 3.18.4   J17c
Eutropius
 7.19–20   J4n
 7.21–2   T1
 7.23   T2
Frontinus
 Aqueducts 102.13–17   K77
 Contr. Agr (Lachmann 1.54)   K109
 Stratagems
  1.1.8   N18
  1.3.10   N19
  2.1.17   N4
  2.3.23   N20
  2.11.7   N21
  4.3.14   H32
  4.6.4   S24
Fronto
 Letters 5.37, 5.38   P13a
Gellius
 Nights in Attica
  15.11.3–5   P11e
  16.8.2   K71
Gnomon of the Idios Logos
 18   M27
Herodian
 1.14.3   K72
Historia Augusta
 Avidius Cassius 2   P15
Javolenus
 Letter 11   M78
Jerome
 Chronicle
  2084 = 68   R15
  2090 = 74   M1
  2095 = 79   note 62
  2099 = 83   L10, P5b
  2102 = 86   L61, N31, T9
  2104 = 88   R15
  2107 = 91   L13
Jordanes
 Gothic History
  13.76   N32

9.18	K78	8.25.1	J16a
9.20	K55	8.25–26	P16c
9.23	Q21	*Lives of the Sophists*	
9.28	Q10	520	S30
9.30	U27b	**Pliny the Elder**	
9.31	N59	*Natural History*	
9.51	U25b	preface, 1	R12
9.64	K58	preface, 3	H49
9.65.1–2	L42	preface, 5	R2
9.79	T4	preface, 20	R13
9.83	Q8	2.18–19	L55
9.84	P8f	2.89	R3
9.91	L54	3.30	M32
9.97.5–6	S17	3.66–67	K1
10.2.1–2	T13	5.69	M39
10.20.11–21	R27	5.83	U3a
10.28	K37	6.12	M67
10.53	Q12	6.101	M24
10.72	T12	7.162	H54
11.13	Q11	12.82–84	M25
11.53	S18	12.94	K70
12.4	T14	12.111–3	N9
12.6.7–12	T14	13.88	R8
12.57	K6	19.111–2	M44
14.179	L45	27.3	H39
Shows 1	K17	32.62	R9
Shows 2	K13	34.27	K20
Shows 3	K18	34.45	L6
Shows 4	H57	34.55	R32
Shows 11	Q5	34.84	K66
Shows 20	Q4	34.164	M72
Shows 27	K19	35.74	K67
Orosius		35.102	K67
7.3.7	H42	35.109	K67
7.9.8–9	H43	35.120	K59
7.13.3–4	N37	35.163	H8
7.19.4	H44	36.27	K68
Pausanias		36.37	R32
7.17.3–4	M2	36.58	K69
8.29.3	M20	36.102	K65
Philostratos		**Pliny the Younger**	
Life of Apollonius		*Letters*	
4.22	Q23	1.1	R28
5.29.1–2	H9	1.5.1–4	P11d
5.29.3	H10	1.5.5	P9b
5.31.1	J4d	1.14.5	U46
5.32.2	H11	1.19	S23
5.41	M3	2.9.1	U33b
6.29.1–2	N7	2.11.17	U26c
6.32.1–2	P4	3.5.7–19	R14
6.42	S29	3.5.9	J4e
7.4.1	P12	3.9.33	U26b
7.6	L15	3.11	P11f
7.7	J14b	3.21	R27
7.8.1	P10	4.2	T38
7.24	L49	4.9.1–2	T37
8.6.11	R36	4.11	L14

4.11.6	J15e
4.22	T18
5.8.12–3	R29
7.16.1–2	U33a
7.19.1–6	P11c
7.27.12–14	T33
7.33.1–3	R31
7.33.4–9	M53
7.33.9	U11b
7.33.10	R31
8.14.1–12	T24
9.13.1–5	P11g
9.27	R30
10.58	T41

Panegyric to Trajan

2.2–4	T11
11.1–2	L57
16.3–4	N28
18.1–3	T28
20.3–5	M50
24.5	T19
33.3–4	Q9
34.1–35.3	T17
35.4	H58
42.1–4	T15
43.1	T30
46.1–3	T21
47.1	R37
48.3–5	J10h
49.1–2	P16d
49.6	J10f
49.8	L27
51.1	K3
52.3	K32
52.4–5	T32
53.4	P14
54.1	T20
54.4	T7
76.3–6	T22
82.1–3	J10e
85.1	U1
90.5	T34
94.1–3	T35
95.2–4	U33c

Plutarch

Aemilius Paullus 25.3–4	P8d
Moralia 770d–771c	H34
Numa 10.4–7	L12

Otho

1.2	B3
4.5–6	H14

Publicola 15	K27
Roman Questions 50	L16

Procopius

Vandal War 3.5.8	K31

Quintilian

The Orator's Education

3.7.9	L56
4.pref.2–5	J18b
4.1.19	J22c
5.13.48	U2
6.pref.13	U51
10.1.91–2	R5
10.1.96	R20
10.1.122	R19
11.3.143	R11
12.3.12	P1b

'Regionary Catalogues'

3	K15
8	K62
9	K44, K50, K62

Scholia on Juvenal

4.77	U7c
5.36	P1h

Seneca

Letters to Lucilius 73.1	P1a

Silius Italicus

Punic Wars 3.593–629	H62

Statius

German War, fragment	G2

Silvae

1.1.1–7	K33
1.1.29–40	K34
1.1.91–8	L68
1.4.1–18	U10b
1.4.68–93	U10c
3.3.85–123	S9a–b
3.3.138–145	S9c
3.3.154–171	S9d
3.4.1–81	J24c
4.1	B1
4.2.8–17	T5
4.2.18–31	K47
4.2.63–7	Q20
4.3.1–37	K92
4.3.9–10	K38
5.1.76–100	S10
5.1.239–41	K56

Suetonius

Life of Pliny the Elder	R10

Suidas

Lexicon, 'Epaphroditus'	R34

Tacitus

Agricola

2.1–2	P11a
2.3–3.2	T23
7.2	H19
9.1	U21a
21	M76
39.1–3	T25
40	T26
41.1	T27
41.2–3	N36
41.4	T27

42.1	P7
43.3–4	T29
44.5–45.2	P11b
Annals	
3.55	J4j
11.11.1	L17
Dialogue	
8	U4a
37.2	R7
Germania	
37.4–5	N27
Histories	
1.1	U32a
1.2	T16
1.10.1–2	U3c
1.77.2	B4
2.1	H16
2.2	J8b
2.2	J22a
2.71.2	B5
2.81	M54
3.65	J3c
3.69	J14a
3.74	L50
3.75	J3d
4.5–6	P1d
4.7	P1e
4.8	P1f
4.38	K82
4.52	K82
4.52	J intro
4.68	J20a
5.1	J8c
5.1	M55

Valerius Flaccus
Voyage of the Argo 1.7–21	R4

Voyage around the Red Sea
1 and 19	M26

Zonaras
11.17	H21
11.17	H24
11.17	N8, R16
11.18	J8g, P3a
11.19	N22, N30, N51, T1

CONCORDANCE B: COINS

BMCRE² Vespasian		Syria 1	M53
47	L7	RIC 1² Vitellius	
48	L1	78	H6
168	L23	RIC 2.1 Vespasian	
173	L23	5	H27
290	K83	42	L1
397	H41	67	H47
399	H35	88	H46
425	H25	117	L24
549	H46	121	H45
629	H51	188	H38
722	K28	515	L4
748B	H28	629	H51
773	H38	689	L7
780	L24	775	L23
805	H45	785	L23
810A	H48	886	K28
BMCRE² Titus		963	K83
132	L59	1127	H41
189	K42	1130	H35
190	K16	1166	H48
229	J5c	1321	H28
BMCRE² Domitian		1360	H25
33	L44	RIC 2.1 Titus	
46	N24	89	L32
51	L51	165	K42
60	J11d	184	K16
62	J12a	264	J5c
68	J13a	357	L59
69	J15c	416	H59
237D	K11	RIC 2.1 Domitian	
238	L25	126	L65
239	L26	132	J11c
241	L63	138	L44
242	K30	143	L51
250	J15d	146	J13a
251	K29	147	J15c
284	L65	150	J11d
286A	K10	152	J12a
304	K85	173	N24
326	N25	209	K10
335	N50	285	N52
364	N52	286	K85
418	L47	315	N50
419	L20	351	N25
430	L21	606	L20
453	L43	619	L21
458	L69	651	L47
501	J11c	683	J15d
BMCRE Septimius Severus		710	L43
189	K51	717	L69
BMC		784	K11
Corinth 58	M40	796	K23
Parthia 1	M65	797	K35
Parthia 5	M64	812	L25
Parthia 33	M66	813	L26

814	K63
815	K30
841	K29
960	H60
RIC 2 **Nerva**	
7	N40
RIC 4 **Septimius Severus**	
260	K51
RPC	
1341	M42
2.461	M59

C: INSCRIPTIONS and Papyri

Arangio-Ruiz (1959) 241: Tab. XXIV	L28	10.5382	L67
Bagnall et al., *JRA* 14 (2001) pages 325–333	M29	10.7227	K81
Crawford, ed. *Roman Statutes* I no. 39	H20	10.8024	M11
Feissel, Syria 62 (1985), pages 79–84	M18	11.2999	K90
González and Crawford, *JRS* 76 (1986)	Section F	11.5382	U42
Inscriptions from Philippi, 202	N65	12.3166	U36
Scheid, *Commentarii fratrum arvalium*	Section A	15.548,02	J11h
		16.24	N53

AE

IG

AE		IG	
1902, 40	K103	2².1996	L52
1903, 256	M16	12.1.995	J11g
1945, 85	K106	22.3283b	J10b
1947, 40	J20b		

GRR

		GRR	
1951, 213	M45	1.863	U16
1954, 258	M61	1.903	M63
1956, 265	M45	1.445	Q18
1962, 288	M37	3.444–5	L60
1967, 355	U7a	3.507	M13
1983, 927	M19	4.384	U31
1987, 937	U20	4.715	L66
1991, 1661	N61	4.1152	J11g
1994, 939	M36		

ILS

		ILS	
2000, 160	U32	98c	K76
2001, 1723	U7a	218	K74
2005, 184	P8j	240	H3
2006, 1578	M61	242	H7
2007, 106	U23	244	H20
2010, 67	U5	245	K87
		246	H29

CIL

CIL			
2.14.2, 992	L55	249	K105
3.32	M28	250	K100
3.335	U35	251	K107
3.1358	M31	252	H26
3.6702	M21	252	L8
3.14387	N55	254	M36
4.118	Q1	255	K73
5.889	N57	257	J5a
5.5667	U33e	258	L3
6.94	L31	259	H40
6.814	J6a	261	M34
6.938	K73	263	M14
6.948a	J17a	264	K21
6.1246	K76	264	N10
6.1528	U38	265	K22
6.1574	U32	267	L5
6.10062	Q14	269	M15
6.12037	J21a	274	T39
6.12355	J9a	983	H31
6.19151	K61	984	J3e
6.31210	K73	985	U5
6.40414	J3b	986	U6
6.40854	N18	989	U12
7.1207	M75	990	U24
10.1419	J5a	991	U25a
10.1481	K102	992	U4

995	J7a	6105	M41
997	U13	6487	L75
999	U22	6644	T8
1000	U37	6692	L71
1003	U18	6964	L57
1005	U19	7357	L30
1006	P8j	7733a	S3
1009	L37	8680	K96
1010	L36	8704a	U21b
1011	U26a	8710	M73
1012	L33	8795	M66
1015	M77	8816	U3b
1024	U34	8818	U28
1374	U45	8903	M16
1378	U40	8904	M12
1447	U48	8905	L9
1448	U49	8906	L74
1489	S5	8958	M56
1490	S6	8969	U17
1517	M48	8970	U14
1518	M47	9059	N54
1519	M46	9198	N60
1523	S4	9200	N58
1567	K79	9368	K80
1679	Q13	9485	U28
1834	J18a	9499	U10a
1839	J17b	9518	J11b
1910	U50	9971	U30
1979	M43	*Inscr.It.*	
1981	M33	13.1.62–3	L18
1982	M38	13.1.192–3	H61
2118	N63	13.1.194–5	P16a
2127	N61	**MW**	
2279	N62	1	H20
2711	U47	2–22	Section A
2926	L67	31	H2
2927	U33d	34	H5
3001	L35	40	H31
3191	L39	41	L22
3512	K104	47	N12
3617	L29	49	N60
3813	K99	50	U13
4914	K9	51	N18
5025	L2	51	H56
5161i	Q2	53	K21
5177	Q19	53	N10
5819	K89	54	K102
5831	K91	55	H33
5832	N17	56	H61
5927	K86	58	N61
5942	K108	60	P8j
5955	M4	61	L18
5957	M6	64	Q19
6045	K84	65	P16a
6049	H36	66	T39
6050	H37	76	H3
6092	M35	81	H7

84	H29	244	M61
86	M12	257	U38
87	M36	258	U3b
93	M16	260	U22
97	J3e	263	U14
102	L3	266	U12
103	H40	271	U4
104	M34	274	U5
105	M14	276	U17
107	L66	277	M5
108	K22	280	U16
109	J9a	283	U21b
112	L74	285	J7a
115	L5	286	U20
121	L52	288	U35
122	M15	289	U36
128	L57	290	U37
132	L56	291	U40
138	L58	292	U18
139	L59	298	U23
142	L40	299	U24
145	L29	300	U25a
146	L71	303	U15
147	L75	305	U10a
148	L60	307	U19
149	L60	309	M77
150	L30	311	U26a
151	H26	312	L37
151	L8	314	U29
152	L2	315	U28
154	L35	316	U30
155	L36	317	L41
165	K104	320	U31
171	L39	321	U34
173	L33	329b	U41
192	L48	333	U42
199	S7	334	U43
200	M48	336	U45
201a	S5	337	M11
201b	S6	338	U48
202	M47	339	K108
203	M46	342	U47
204	S4	343	T8
205	K79	344	L70
207	Q13	346	U50
210	J21a	347	U49
216	S2	353	M60
218	S3	355	N55
221	J17b	361	N63
224	J18a	367	N65
225	J11b	368	L38
226	S1	369	M68
227	K96	372	N58
233	M63	374	N64
237	M66	379	N57
239	M56	384	N56
243	M62	387	N62

401	N53
404	N54
408	K74
409	K76
410	K81
411	M31
412	K87
413	K89
414	K90
415	K91
416	N17
425	K28
426	L4
429	J6a
430	K105
431	L31
432	K99
433	K100
436	M23
438	M13
439	M73
440	M74
441	M75
442	K9
443	K86
444	K107
446	M6
447	M7
448	M9
449	M4
458	R35
460	M8
461	M35
462	K110
463	L9
463b	Q22
464	M52
464	U27a
466	M49
468	K84
469	K80
470	K97
473	Q18
480	M38
481	M33
485	M22
486	M41
488	J10b
491	J11g
513	H36
514	H37
517	Q14
520	M43
521	M28
527	M79
529	Q2

Papyri

P. Oxyrhyncus

II 237, col. 8, 27–43	M30
P. Berlin 8334	U44
P. Hibeh 215	U41
P. Fouad 8	L22

RIB

1.258	N56
2.1.2409.4	H74
2.2, 2415.56	M79
2.3.2434.1	U21b

Index of Persons

The following usual and ancient abbreviations for *praenomina* (first names) are used:

A. Aulus
C. Gaius
Cn. Gnaeus
D. Decimus
L. Lucius
M'. Manius

M. Marcus
P. Publius
Q. Quintus
Sex. Sextus
T. Titus
Ti. Tiberius

Other abbreviations:
cos = (suffect) consul
cos ord = consul at the start of the year
mag. = magistrate

pref. = prefect

Ancient authors were inconsistent in how they referred to Romans, who by this period sometimes had as many as six names. So too is modern usage. Well-known figures are referred to by their usual names, others by their family (or only known) names. Emperors appear in CAPITALS with regnal date.

D. Aburius Bassus (cos 85): B85
Q. Accaeus Rufus (cos 90): B90
M'. Acilius Aviola (cos 54): G1.94–5, G2, K76
M'. Acilius Glabrio (cos ord 91): A90h, B91,
    D12, F.'letter', G1.94–6, P13
L. Acilius Strabo (cos 71): B71,
Aelia (wife of Lappius Maximus): P8j
M. Aelius Niger (local mag): M33
L. Aelius Oculatus (cos 73): B73
L. Aelius Plautius Lamia (cos 80): A80f, B80,
    C3, G1.154
L. Aelius Sejanus (cos 31): C14,
C. Aetrius Naso (equestrian): T8
L. Albius Pullaienus Pollio (cos 90): B90
Cn. Alleius Nigidius (priest): Q1
L. Annius Bassus (cos 70): B70, H36
A. Annius Camars (local mag) L29
M. Annius Messalla (cos 83): B83
Anteia (wife of Helvidius Priscus II): P1c, P11g
Antiochus IV (king of Commagene): E1e, M54,
    M55, M57, M59, N1, N58
L. Antistius Asiaticus (Berenice prefect): M31
L. Antistius Rusticus (cos 90): A90d, B90, M52,
    U27a–b,
C. Anstitius Vetus (cos ord 96): B96, D15
C. Antius A. Julius Quadratus (cos 94): B94,
    U31
    Arval A78a–A89j *passim*
L. Antonius Naso (procurator) N55
Antonius Primus (civil war commander): H1
L. Antonius Saturninus (cos 82): B82, D11,
    K110, P8, P8d–h
Apollonius of Tyana (philosopher): D18, H11,
    J4d, J14b, M3, N7, P16a, Q23, R36
Sex. Appius Severus (quaestor): U18

C. Aquilius Proculus (cos 90): B90
M. Aquilius Regulus (senator): P11d, T38,
    U11c, U39
Aristobulus (king of Chalcidice):
Armillatus (lawyer): G1.53
Arrecina Tertulla (Titus' wife): J9a
M. Arrecinus Clemens (cos II 85): B73, B85,
    H37, J9, **J20,**
Arria I (wife of Paetus): P1c
Arria II (wife of Thrasea): P1c, P11f, P11g
P. Arrius Antoninus (cos 69): B4, B69
M. Arrius Flaccus (cos 79): B79, N53
L. Arrius Macer (local mag.) N57
M. Arruntius Aquila (cos 77): B77, M8
C. Arruntius Catellius see L. Pompeius Vopiscus
    and B77note
L. Arruntius Maximus (procurator): M36
Artabanus III (king of Parthia): M70, P3a
Artemidorus (philosopher): P11f
Artemis (priestess): L74
Q. Articuleius Paetus (cos 78): A78e–f, B78
Cn. Arulenus Caelius Sabinus (cos 69): A69p,
    B69, N54
Arulenus Rusticus see Junius
Asconia (priestess): L67
C. Asconius Sardo (local mag.): L67
M. Asinius Atratinus (cos ord 89): B89
L. Asinius Pollio Verrucosus (cos ord 81): A80d,
    A81e, B81
L. Asinius Rufus (praetor): H2
C. Atilius Barbarus (cos 71): B71
M. Atilius Postumus Bradua (cos *ann. inc.*) L40
T. Atilius Rufus (cos *c.* 76) T26
Attica (wife of Didius Gallus): L36
Attius Priscus (artist): K59

M. Junius Rufus (Egypt pref.): N54
Juventius Celsus (jurist): D13

L. Laberius Maximus (praet. pref.): A80f, N14,
    N15, U44
M'. Laberius Maximus (cos 89): B89
C. Laecanius Bassus (cos 70): B70, N36
Laertes (priest): L74
M. Larcius Magnus (cos 82): B82
Larginus Proculus: D16
C. Licinius Mucianus: (cos III 72)
    arval: A70a, B70, B72,
    author: R7–9, U3a
    career: U3b, B70, B72
    character: U3c–e
    & philosophy: C13, P1k
    as V's deputy: C2, C9, E5, H1, H17, H19,
      J20a
M. Lollius Paullinus (cos 94): B94
Sex. Lucilius Bassus (equestrian): H26, N14
Sex. Luc/sianus Proculus (cos 93): B93, D11

L. Maecius Postumus (arval): A69b–A78d
L. Maecius Postumus (cos 98): A86d, A91b
Malchus (king of Arabia): N1
Malichas (king of Nabataea): M26
L. Manlius Patruinus (cos 74): B74, M45
C. Manlius Valens (cos ord 96): B96, D15
MARCUS AURELIUS (AD 161–180): P13a
Marius Celsus (cos 69): B4, B69, M16
C. Marius Marcellus (cos 80): B80
Martial (M. Valerius Martialis), poet): R27,
    S16, S17 (for writings *see* Literary
    Concordance)
Masyus (Semnones chief): N43
Maternus (sophist): D12
L. Mestrius Florus (cos *c.* 75): L73
P. Metilius Nepos (cos 91): B91
Mettius Carus (informer): P11b–d, T33
Mettius Modestus (cos 82): B82?, P9note, R34
Mettius Pompusianus (senator): D12, P9a
M. Mettius Rufus (prefect of Egypt): M30, P9
Minicia Rustica (wife of Junius Calvinus): M28
D. Minicius Faustinus (cos 91): B91
Minicius Macrinus (equestrian): U46
L. Minicius Rufus (cos ord 88): B88, N63, P10?
Mithridates (king of Iberia): M66
L. Mucius Aurelianus (local mag): M38
L. Mucius Novatus (local mag): M38
C. Musonius Rufus (philosopher): C13, P11f

Sex. Neranius Capito (cos 71): B71
L. Neratius Marcellus (cos ord 95): B95
L. Neratius Priscus (cos 87): A87h, B87
NERO (AD 54–68)
    byword for bad emperor: C9, G1.38, H11,
      J8e, K92, P1h

colossus/palace: C14, G.137, K13, K66, L6
consuls: B3, B4
'false Nero': P3a, P3b
frees Greece: M2, M3
    & Vespasian: C11, E1e, E4, H9, J4c
    & Domitian: G1.38, P4, P11b, T2
NERVA (AD 96–98)
    under Flavians: A90a, B71, B90, D15, D16,
      K77, L2, M53, N63, P10, U11a–d
    as emperor: K39, K40, K77, K89, L14,
      L57, R34, T18, T23, T36, T37, T39–
      T42, U49
Nicanor (tribune): E2
Q. Ninnius Hasta (cos 88): B88
L. Nonius Calpurnius Asprenas (cos 72): B72
L. Nonius Calpurnius Asprenas Torquatus (cos
    ord 94): B94, N54, U15
Norbanus (praetorian prefect): D15, P8e, P8i

C. Occeius Niger (local mag.): M41
Sex. Octavius Fronto (cos 86): B86
L. Octavius Memor (cos des 78): M13
C. Octavius Tidius Tossianus Javolenus (cos
    86): B86, M77, M78
C. Octavius Titinius Capito (equestrian): U49
C. Oppius Sabinus (cos 84): B84, N32, T2
M. Otacilius Catulus (cos 88): B88
Otacilius Sagitta (procurator): M8
OTHO (AD 69): A69e–m, B3–5, B69, H1, H4–5,
    H11, N55

Paccius Africanus (cos): M22
Pacorus II (king of Parthia): M71
Palfurius (lawyer): G1.53 with note 182
L. Paquedius Festus (contractor): K104
Paris (actor): D3a, P16b, Q11, R21,
Parthenius (freedman of Dom): D15, D17,
    P16b, R23
L. Pasidienus Firmus (cos 75): B75
Cn. Pedius Cascus (cos 71): B71
Q. Peducaeus Priscinus (cos 93): A89j, B93,
    N54
M. Peducaeus Saenianus (cos 89): B89
L. Pellartius Celer (army doctor): N64
Peponila/Empone (wife of J. Sabinus): C16,
    H34,
Persicus (freedman): U49
Q. Petillius Cerialis Rufus (cos 70): B70, B74,
    C3, H30
C. Petillius Firmus (praetor): U7a, U37
Petronius Secundus (praetorian prefect): D15,
    M28 note
M. Petronius Umbrinus (cos 81): A81k, A87g,
    B81
Phyllis (nurse of Dom): D18, S5?, S6?
Pierus (imperial freedman): J18a
Cn. Pinarius Aemilius Cicatricula (cos 90): B90

character: C18, C19, J8b–f, T1
commander: C4, C5, E1e, H21, H62, M55,
consulships: B70, B72, B74–B77, B79,
  B80, C1, K82
corn-supply: K84
death: C26, J8i, P4,
decrees: C19, F19, F20, F22, F23, FB, F81,
  J8f, M37,
deification: D2, J15c, K73, L41, L56, L57,
  L65, L66, L68, T1, U33e
disasters: C21–C24, K7, K101–K103
Divus Titus (oaths): F25, F26, FG, F59,
  F69, F73, F79,
games: C15, C25, Q3,
gifts: C25, E8, H51
'god': L60, L72
imperator: C20
informers: C19, H58
killer: C16, C17, P2
money: C24, J8g
peace: H40, H43
praetorian prefect: C16, H49, H50
priesthoods: L2, L3
princeps iuventutis: H27
quotations: C19, C26, E5, J8f, N7, T1
religion: L8, L23,
return to Rome: E6a, E6b, N8
road: M13, M14
sacrifices for: A75a, A78a, A79a, A81a,
  A81e
sexual preferences: D2
statue: J8a, M34
Temple of Jerusalem: C6, E1c, E1e, N5, N6
triumph: E6, H43, J4n, K21, K22, N8–N10,
vows for: A75a, A78a, A79a, A81a, A81e,
  L31, L39,
writings of: J8d, R2, R3, T1
  & Berenice: C15, J22a, J22b
  & Domitian: J8h, T37
  & Vespasian: C8, C12, C14, H16, H27–
  H29
TRAJAN (AD 98–117)
  under Domitian: A90h, B91, D12, F97
  letter, M18, M19
  as emperor: J10e, L57, P11b, P16a, T22,
  T23, T28, T30, T35, U33d, U34,
  U49
M. Trebellius Maximus (arval): A72c
M. Trebonius Valens (Berenice prefect): M29
C. Tullius Capito (cos 84): B84, M9
M. Tullius Cerialis (cos 90): B90
Ti. Tutinius Severus (arval): A84a–b, A90a

M. Ulpius Traianus (cos 72): B72, U14
M. Ulpius Traianus (cos 91): *see* Trajan (emperor)
D. Valerius Asiaticus (cos des 70): U38
L. Valerius Catullus Messalinus (cos ord 73):

B73, K76,
Valerius Flaccus (poet): R5,
Valerius Licinianus (praetor): L14
P. Valerius Marinus (cos des 69): A69g, A69j,
  A69m, B5, M44
P. Valerius Marinus (cos 91): B91
L. Valerius Niger (local mag.): L41
P. Valerius Patruinus (cos 82): B82, K110
M. Valerius Propinquus Grattius (equestrian):
  U476
L. Valerius Varus Pollio (local mag.): L41
Q. Valerius Vegetus (cos 91): A91e, B91
Veleda (German priestess): H33, N43, U10c
C. Velius Rufus (equestrian): N58, N59
L. Venuleius Montanus Apronianus (cos 92):
  A80a–c, A84a, A86b, A86d, A87g,
  A89a, A89c–g, A90a, A90f, A91c,
  A91f, B92
Verania Gemina (wife of Piso): H3
Q. Veranius (cos ord 49): H3
L. Veratius Quadratus (arval): A78a–A91b
  passim
L. Verginius Rufus (cos II 69): A69j, B3, B4,
  B69, K76
Vespasia Polla (mother of Vesp): J2
VESPASIAN (AD 69–79)
  accession: C1, E1, E4, H16, H17, H18,
  M54
  'amnesty': C9
  arts: R16, R35
  arval: A80a
  birthday: H36
  building projects: A80c, C15, K12, K21,
  K27, K28, K59, K64–K70, K74,
  K75, K100, M10, M16 M19–M21,
  census: H52–H55, K1, K98, S9c, U21a,
  U22, U23, U26a, U27a, U30, U34,
  U35, U37, U46
  character: C10, H intro, J4g–j, J4n, U4a
  citizenship: M32, M33, M43,
  commander: E1, H62, J4b, J4c, J4n, M17,
  N1, N3, N4, N16
  conspiracies: C16, J4n
  consulships: B70, B71, B72, B74, B75,
  B76, B77, B79, C1, K82
  corn-supply: K82, K83
  criticism of: C8, C10, C11, C12, H34, J4g,
  J4n, P1n
  death: C17, J4m, K2
  decrees: F19, F20, F22, F23, FB, F81, U6
  deification: J13a, K2, K73, L55, L57–L59,
  L61–L64, S9c
  Divus Vespasianus: C17, F25, F26, FG,
  F59, F69, F73, F79, L28,
  fated to rule: C1, C2, C8, E5, H13–H15,
  freedmen of: S9a
  games: C9, C15, Q1

Index of Places

Places are towns or settlements unless otherwise stated, and are followed by the Roman province they were in, in CAPITALS, and the modern country the town is in (as of 1 June, 2015). Provinces are listed with the approximate equivalent in terms of modern countries and are indexed to mention of the province in the texts, not to every town mentioned within the province. Information on the ancient sites relies on R.J.A. Talbert (ed.) *The Barrington Atlas of the Greek and Roman World* (Princeton 2000).

ACHAIA (Greece): J4n, M1, M2, M3, N1, P1h
Actium (Greece): M5 note, P8h, Q18
Adiabeni (tribe in Iraq): E1b
Aeclanum (S. Italy): M60, L71
AFRICA (Tunisia & W. Libya): H2, H62, M22, M44, M77, N58, P7, S9a, U15, U23, U24, U25a,
Alani (tribe around Rostov, Russia): M65
Alban Lake/Mount (nr Rome): C3, C9, D1, D14, G1.60, G1.100, G1.145, K95, K96, K110, L14, P11b, P13, Q15, Q20, Q21, ARABIA: B1, E1b, M25, M26, N1
Alexandria (Egypt): C8, E6a, H17, H18, L22, M44, M47, N1, N54, R33, R34,
ALPES COTTIAE (France/Italy): U42
Amiternum (Sabine territory, C. Italy): U17
Anazarbus (CILICIA, S. Turkey): L41
Ancona (C. Italy): G1.39
Andautonia (PANNONIA): U19
Antioch-on-Orontes (SYRIA = Antayka, Turkey): M17–M21, Q18
Antioch-in-Pisidia (PISIDIA = L64, M52, U20, U27a, U28
Apamea (BITHYNIA, N. Turkey): U35
Apollonia (ACHAIA): P1h
Apsarus (= Adjara in Georgia): M67
Aquae Cutilae (C. Italy): C17, C26
Aquae Flaviae (TARRACONENSIS = Chaves, Portugal): M36
Aquileia (N. Italy): N57, N64, U45
Aquinum (C. Italy): L62
AQUITANIA (SW France): U21a, U34, U44
Arabia (Saudi Arabia): B1, E1b, K18, M25, M26, N1
Arausio (NARBONENSIS = Orange, France): M7
Argentorate (LOWER GERMANY = Strasbourg, France): N17
Aricia (nr Rome): G1.117
ARMENIA MINOR (NE Turkey): J23c, M14, M65, U3a, U10c, U27a, U30
Arsinoite district (the Fayum, Egypt): N53b, N54
ASIA (Turkey): L73, M14, P3a, P7, S7, S30, U3c, U4b, U10c, U14, U20, U26a, U30, U31, U34, U35, U45
Assissi (N. Italy): U41

Assyria (part of Parthia): E1d, K17
Athens (Greece): J10b, K27, L52, M62, Q23

Babylon(ia) (Parthia): B1, E1b, E6d, K17, N5
BAETICA (S. Spain): M15, M53
Baiae (in Campania, Italy): J10e, K92
Baku (Azerbaijan): M68
Banasa (MAURETANIA, Morocco): M5
BELGICA (Belgium): U42
Beneventum (C. Italy = Benevento) C9
Berenice (EGYPT): M24–M30
Berytus (SYRIA = Beirut, Lebanon): M61
BITHYNIA (Turkey): H31, N55, T37, U28, U30, U31, U33d, U34,
Blaundus (ASIA, W. Turkey): L60
Bonna (Germany): N62
Bosporus (= mod Crimea): M63, M64
BRITANNIA (Britain): C20, H30, J3a, J4b, J4c, J4n, M72–M78, S18, T26, U26a
Brundisium (S. ITALY = Brindisi): C9, H21
Byzantium: J4n, M1

Caesarea Maritima (JUDAEA, Israel): H12, M39, N1
Caledonia (Scotland): H62, R4
Calycadnus (river in CILICIA): M13
Campania (region of S. Italy): C21, C24, K7, K92, K101, R10, S9d
Canusium (in Apulia, S. Italy): K106
CAPPADOCIA (C. Turkey): M14, U27a, U27b, U30, U31
Capua (in Campania, Italy): K107, U4a
Carthage (AFRICA, now Tunisia): N61
Celeia (NORICUM = Celje, Slovenia): L70
Celts (tribes of British isles): E1a, P12
Ceutrones (Gallic tribe): M6
Chaeroneia (Greece):R34
Chatti (tribe, area N. of Frankfurt, Germany): D4, G1.146, J10c, N18–N20, N22, N23, N29, S9d, T2,
Chersonesus (in Crimea): U16
Cherusci (German tribe): N29
Chester (BRITANNIA): U12b
China: B1, M25
CILICIA (SE Turkey): K18, M1, M13, M59, U30, J4
Circeii (C. Italy = Monte Circeio): G1.141
Cirta (NUMIDIA = Constantine, Algeria): M9, U23

Index of Themes

actors: D3a, H8, P16b, Q10, Q11, R21, T20, T21
aedile (Rome): U10a, U17, U30, U33f, U34
aedile (local): F19, F26, F27, FG, FJ, F52–F54, F59, F66, F79, F83, F84, F86, F87, L66, M33
amphitheatre: K97, K98 *see also Index of Place: Rome: Flavian Amphitheatre:*
anarchy: E1a, T42
appeal to Caesar: M37
aqueducts: K74–K81, K104, S9a
aqueducts commissioner (*curator aquarum*): K77
arches: H2, K16, K21–K25, K51, K57, K61, K80, M15, M22, N10, T7
army: C3, C5, C14, C25, E1e, E6e, G1.135, H12, H17, H18, H30, H32, H50, M6, M50, **N1–N3**, N14, N34, N35, N37, N38. N41, N51, N58, N61, N64, P8g, T24, T28, U13, U25a, U33a
art: E6d, K66–K69, R32
Arvals: Section A; U26a, U31
astrologers: C9, D12, D15
augur: H3, L1, U4, U33d–f
Augustalis: L35, L36, U4, U10a, U12

baths: C24, C25, F19, H34, J4f, K2, K4, K13, K26, K27, M61, M76, R14, S13, U33d
benefactions: C26, D5, E8, E9, H23, H37, J4g, J11i, K2, K79, L53, L71, M33, N7, N64
bodyguard: C10, D14, J4d, N2e, P16c, P16d
booty: E6f, H12, H32, J8e, K12, M65, N13, N16, N32, N39, T16
boundaries: F29, F82–F84, F91, H20, H42, H56, K9, K86, K106, K107, L58, M4, M6, M8, N18, T7, U7a
'bread and circuses': P4j, Q20
bridges: K90, M13, M19, M31, N35, S14
building works:
    imperial: H24, J10c, **Section K**, L9, M10, M29, T1: see also bridges, roads, canal
    local: J6a, J11i, K80, K81, K97, K98, K104, L41

canals: M18–M21
carpentum: J5c, L69
castration: D2, J23c, S28, S29
cavalry: D8, M59, N1, N2e, N3, N20, N61 note, N63, S10, U28, U45
censors etc: see under Domitian, Titus, Vespasian in Index of Names
Centennial Games: L17–L21

centurions: C20, D10, D13, H29, L38, L70, M26, M31, M59, M68, N2c, N3, N55, N58, N61, N63, N65, P1d, U15
chariot racing: A69s, A69u note, A78e, A80a, A81i, A84a, A87f, A90f, A91c, D5, K6, Q13, Q14,
chastity: L14, S27, T3
Chrisianity: H42, J17c, N6
citizenship: E8, F21–F23, F25, F29, FB, F53, F54, F83, F86, F91, F93, F97, F97 'letter', H26, H45, H51, H53, L20, L35, L72, M18 note, M32, M33, M38, M43, M52, N53, N54, T41, U15, U45
city Prefect: *see* prefect
civil war: E6g, H1, H4, H22, J3d, M2, N27
class: D5, F54, F81, J10g, K110, P1k and see theatre
clemency: C19, E1e, J4g, J8d, J8f, J10c, J22d, J23c, S9d, T17,
clients: L50, R22, S11–S14, T14
clothing: A87f, A90f, B1, C25, D8, E6b, F79, G1.25, H34, H47, J4f, K57, L14, L58, M76, N26, N45, P13a, R11, S21, T33
coinage: C14, K6, S9a
    IIIvir monetalis: U15, U20,
colonies: F79, J4j, K75, K93, K97, L35, L38, M5, M39, M40, M41, M52, M61, N14, U35
concord: A69c, A78b–d, A81o, A86b, A86d, A87b, A89b, A90b, A91b, H47, J11d, K34, L63, U35
consilium principis: Section G, U1–U11, U50
conspiracies: see **Section P**
consulship: B1–B5, C1, C2, C24, D4, D15, H7, H30, K82, M56, P9a, P11b, P13a, R18, T16, U10c, U21a, U23, U43, U51: also see under names of emperors
corn supply: A80f, A87f, A90f, F19, H17, H21, J6a, K14, K82–K85, L20, L32, M52, U27a, U42, U43, U45
councillors: Section F, J10b, J11a, J11e, J11i, J15b, K110, L30, L35, L58, L61, L63, L71, M35, M37, M52, M62, N57, N60, S23, U19, U22, U24, U25a, U31, U37, U45
crowns: *see also* military decorations
    civic crown: H45, H47, R26
    gold/silver: A78e, A81i, A90f, A91c, E6d
    laurel: H41, K57, N7, N46, R26, T2
    of priests: A78e, A81i, A84a, A87f, A90f, A91c
    royal: N39

Flavian Family Tree

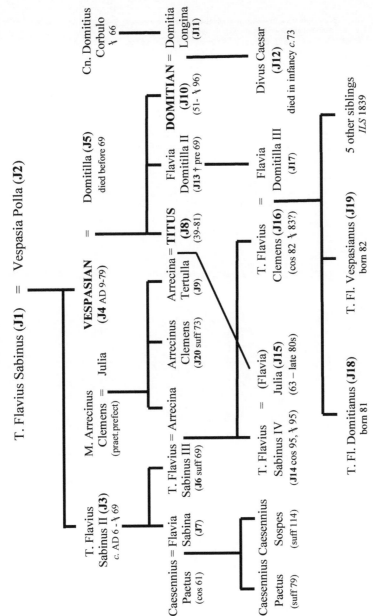

T. Flavius Sabinus (**J1**)   =   Vespasia Polla (**J2**)

T. Flavius Sabinus II (**J3**)
c. AD 6 - † 69

M. Arrecinus Clemens
(praet. prefect)   =   Julia

VESPASIAN (**J4** AD 9-79)   =   Domitilla (**J5**) died before 69 | Cn. Domitius Corbulo † 66

T. Flavius = Flavia Sabina
Paetus (**J7**)
(cos 61)

T. Flavius = Arrecina
Sabinus III
(**J6** suff 69)

Caesennius Caesennius
Sospes
(suff 114)

Caesennius
Paetus
(suff 79)

Arrecinus Clemens
(**J20** suff 73)

Arrecina = **TITUS**
Tertulla (**J8**)
(**J9**)   (39-81)

Flavia Domitilla II
(**J13** † pre 69)

DOMITIAN = Domitia
(**J10**)   Longina
(51- † 96)   (**J11**)

T. Flavius = (Flavia)
Sabinus IV   Julia (**J15**)
(**J14** cos 95, † 95)   (63 – late 80s)

T. Flavius
Clemens (**J16**)
(cos 82 † 83?)   =   Flavia Domitilla III
(**J17**)

Divus Caesar
(**J12**)
died in infancy c.73

T. Fl. Domitianus (**J18**)
born 81

T. Fl. Vespasianus (**J19**)
born 82

5 other siblings
ILS 1839

For EU product safety concerns, contact us at Calle de José Abascal, 56–1°,
28003 Madrid, Spain or eugpsr@cambridge.org.

www.ingramcontent.com/pod-product-compliance
Ingram Content Group UK Ltd.
Pitfield, Milton Keynes, MK11 3LW, UK
UKHW030903150625
459647UK00022B/2829